"One Hell of a Gamble"

KHRUSHCHEV,
CASTRO,
AND
KENNEDY,
1958–1964

"One Hell of a Gamble"

KHRUSHCHEV, CASTRO, AND KENNEDY, 1958–1964

Aleksandr Fursenko and Timothy Naftali

W. W. NORTON & COMPANY

NEW YORK • LONDON

For information about permission to reproduce selections from this book,
write to Permissions, W. W. Norton & Company, Inc.,
500 Fifth Avenue, New York, NY 10110.

The text of this book is composed in Electra
with the display set in Nofret
Desktop composition by Justine Burkat Trubey
Manufacturing by Quebecor Printing, Fairfield, Inc.
Book design by JAM Design

Library of Congress Cataloging-in-Publication Data

Fursenko, A. A.
One hell of a gamble : Khrushchev, Castro, and Kennedy, 1958–1964 / Aleksandr Fursenko
and Timothy Naftali.
    p.   cm.
Includes bibliographical references (p.   ) and index.
ISBN 0-393-04070-4
1. Cuban Missile Crisis, 1962. 2. United States—Foreign relations—Cuba. 3. Cuba—
Foreign relations—United States. 4. United States—Foreign relations—1953–1961.
5. United States—Foreign relations—1961–1963. I. Naftali, Timothy J. II. Title.
E841.F86 1997
973.922—DC21   97-1022
CIP

W. W. Norton & Company, Inc., 500 Fifth Avenue, New York, NY 10110
http://www.wwnorton.com

W. W. Norton & Company Ltd., 10 Coptic Street, London WC1A 1PU

2 3 4 5 6 7 8 9 0

Contents

PART III: THE AFTERMATH

Acknowledgments

This book was made possible by a unique opportunity to study the most secret documents on the most dangerous moment of the Cold War. We wish to express our gratitude to the personnel of the Archive of the President of the Russian Federation (APRF), which contain the Politburo and Presidium records, to the curators of the papers of the Archive of the Foreign Intelligence Service of the Russian Federation (SVR), and the Intelligence Service of the General Staff of the Armed Forces of the Russian Federation (GRU), to the staff at the Russian Center for Storage of Contemporary Documentation (TsKhSD), the Records of the Historical Archival Center of the Ministry of Defense of the Russian Federation, and the Archive of the Ministry of Foreign Affairs of the Russian Federation (AVPRF). In the United States we received assistance from the John F. Kennedy Library, the National Archives, the Sterling Memorial Library at Yale University, the Houghton Library at Harvard University, the Richard M. Nixon Library and Birthplace, Yorba Linda, California, and the National Security Archive in Washington, D.C. In France, we are grateful to the staff at the Archives of the Ministère des Affaires Etrangères and, in the Czech Republic, to the staff of the Czech Foreign Ministry archives.

We enjoyed the sponsorship of many distinguished institutions. We are grateful to the Russian Academy of Sciences and its St. Petersburg Institute of Russian History, to the Kennan Institute for Advanced Russian Studies, Woodrow Wilson International Center for Scholars in Washington, D.C., to the Charles Warren Center for Studies in American History, Harvard University, La Maison des Sciences de l'Homme in Paris, International Security Studies, Yale University, and the University of Hawaii at Manoa.

Many individuals have helped to make this book possible. Professors Ernest R. May, Idus A. Newby, and Arthur M. Schlesinger, Jr., provided valuable counsel and encouragement. We appreciated the assistance of Vitaly Afiani, Maurice Aymard, Charles Bartlett, Tom Blanton, Jim Blight, Paul Boccardi, McGeorge Bundy, Jutta Scherrer, Blair Ruble, Ann Carter-Drier, Sonia Colpart, Richard Helms, Frank Holeman, Susan Hunt, Will Johnson, Paul Kennedy, Brian

Latell, Viktor Pleshkov and Vladimir Noskov, Inna Krupskaia and Antonina Tutova, Rudolph Pikhoia, Aleksandr Korotkov, Luis Rios, Warren Rogers, Sarah Stewart, Vladimir A. Vinogradov, Barbara Vandegrift, James O'S. Wade, Mark Webber, Allen Weinstein, and Theodore Sorensen. In addition, Yuri Kobaladze, Oleg Tsarev, and Vladimir Karpov were very helpful. Very special thanks to Natalia Korsakova, whose invaluable support in archival research and in every-day work made possible the completion of the manuscript. We are grateful to Boris V. Anan'ich, Rafai Sh. Ganelin, Lindon Allin, Cicely Angleton, Barton Aronson, Pamela Auerbach, Esther Coopersmith, Ned Davis, Colby Devitt, Sonja Dumay, Robert Feldman, Joseph Ha, Sam Halpern, Hope M. Harrison, Elaine Hatfield, Frederick Holborn, Merrie and Rick Inderfurth, Zachary Karabell, Jessica Korn, Tom Knock, Anne Mark, Raymond and Gloria Naftali, Philip Nash, Gilad Y. Ohana, Walter Pforzheimer, Richard Rapson, Karen Richardson, Gideon Rose, Brewer Stone, Edward Weismiller, Michael Yaffe, and Fareed Zakaria: friends who abetted one more retelling of the Cuban missile crisis.

We have the late John Costello to thank for introducing us. He initiated our collaboration as part of a major effort to open as many documents on the Cold War as possible in the years following the fall of the Berlin Wall. An untimely death prevented him from completing his own masterwork on Soviet-British relations with Oleg Tsarev. It was John Costello who introduced us to John Hawkins, whose wise counsel subsequently permitted us to navigate the shoals of the publishing world. To him, we are also deeply grateful.

Drake McFeely at Norton encouraged us with his enthusiasm for our topic and his deft use of the editor's pen. Our debt to him is not merely professional. When a personal tragedy intervened, he displayed exceptional compassion.

In the final weeks of the project, Tim's father died suddenly. We remember James D. Naftali as a close adviser and dear friend. Like John Costello, he understood the extraordinary nature of our collaboration and should have been able to see the final result.

The patience and support of our families has kept us going. We thank Aleksandr's wife, Natalia, and sons, Andrei and Sergei Fursenko, and Tim's mother, Marjorie, and his sister, Debbie Naftali.

Finally, this book is dedicated to our teachers. Although from different generations and cultures, they shared a commitment to archival research and the careful reconstruction of the past. In the Stalin period, Boris Aleksandrovitch Romanov kept alive the spirit of independent inquiry by encouraging his students in Leningrad to follow documents wherever they might lead. In the 1980s, in Cambridge, Massachusetts, Ernest R. May challenged a new generation of graduate students to meet the high standard in international history that he had set with his multi-archival study of Woodrow Wilson and the American entry into the First World War.

Responsibility for any mistakes in our re-creation of the international politics of the early 1960s belongs to us alone. But, to the extent that we offer a new and persuasive understanding for this critical period, our work reflects the excellence of the scholarship we were exposed to as students.

Introduction

For a generation of Americans and Russians, there was only one moment in the last half century when a third world war seemed possible. Americans of a certain age recall the flickering and foreshortened image of a handsome John F. Kennedy announcing that Soviet nuclear missiles were in Cuba, the reports of American jets and marines moving toward Florida, and the days of panic buying and uncertainty that ensued. Russians recall harrowing reports from Radio Moscow and the mobilization of the Soviet armed forces. For thirty-five years neither side has known how very close we actually came to a nuclear war in 1962.

On the night of October 22, hours before John Kennedy spoke to the world, the Kremlin indeed seriously considered using nuclear weapons on Americans. The appropriate orders were discussed, and the Soviet leader, Nikita Khrushchev, stayed the night in his office so that he would be able to cable these orders if they were necessary. At the same time 7,000 miles away the young American president, John Kennedy, was being lectured by senior members of the U.S. Congress who wanted him to invade the island of Cuba despite the presence of Soviet troops and nuclear weapons there. "If we go into Cuba," Kennedy cautioned the congressional leadership, "we have to all realize that we have taken the chance that these missiles, which are ready to fire, won't be fired." We "are prepared to take it"; but, the president noted, it would be "one hell of a gamble."

The fall of the Berlin Wall in 1989 has opened a period of reexamination of the recent past not experienced since the intense debates of the 1920s over the causes of the First World War. It was only fifteen years ago that Ronald Reagan found the Cold War so threatening that he launched a crusade against the Soviet Union, and the world seemed to have entered another dangerous phase of a drama that had begun in 1946. Yet a decade later the Soviet Union was no more, communism was in retreat everywhere save China, and many people began to ask, What was the Cold War all about?

Based on unprecedented research across two continents, this is the inside story of the climactic years of the struggle between East and West, when nuclear war became more than a theoretical possibility for reasons that defied prediction. In the early 1960s a most unlikely country, Cuba, was the location and rationale for this challenge to international peace. An object of the American political imagination since the American Revolution, Cuba was described by Thomas Jefferson and John Quincy Adams as inevitably an extension of the United States. Less than a century later, when Spain lost control of its sugar colony, the United States assumed political, military, and economic dominance of the island. By the end of World War II, though Washington had delegated political authority to local Cuban elites, America remained the most powerful foreign presence in the lives of Cubans. These facts are well known. But in the late 1950s the Soviet Union began to take an interest in developments on this island off the coast of Florida, and by 1960 the Cuban issue had come to define the superpower conflict as forcefully as the future of West Berlin or nuclear testing. The reasons why this occurred, so important to the international political landscape of the 1960s and later, need to be told.

This is an international history. No one person or government created the mix of interest, power, and fear that nearly exploded in 1962. The seeds of the Cuban missile crisis lie in the story of the Cuban revolution, Fidel Castro's personality, and his embrace of the Soviet Union. Now Soviet-era KGB records and Nikita Khrushchev's own office files, as well as interviews with key officials, can reveal the process by which Cubans first approached the Soviet Union and then Moscow championed Fidel. It all happened much earlier than Washington suspected and required Khrushchev's personal intervention.

The Cuban-Soviet compact, however, cannot alone account for the sleepless night of October 22, 1962, and those that followed. Thanks to the opening of Soviet files on the Cold War, we are on the verge of learning a lot more about American leaders than we thought possible. The Soviets were compulsive notetakers. The Kremlin viewed the outside world with morbid suspicion. Foreign service bureaucrats, including intelligence officers, knew that they would not get the benefit of the doubt if it was ever discovered that they were too close or too friendly with any foreigners, especially Americans. Consequently Soviet officials reported on all contacts with Americans and the substance of what those Americans said. Allowing for the possibility of bias, Soviet archives constitute a remarkable repository of every American initiative, probe, or gaff associated with the superpower relationship. In the case of John Kennedy, the new information reveals the extent to which he conducted a personal foreign policy toward the Soviet Union in the 1960s. This private policy, which centered on Robert Kennedy and a Soviet military intelligence officer, Georgi N. Bolshakov, shaped the Kremlin's understanding of the U.S. government and stood in stark contrast to John Kennedy's crusade to eliminate Fidel Castro. At best incompatible, the competing urges of the Kennedy

White House alternately encouraged and provoked Khrushchev to realize his objective in America's backyard.

Colorful, impetuous, and ultimately driven by a sense of what was best for themselves and for their people, Castro, Khrushchev, and Kennedy inexorably collided. Castro wanted to lead a revolution throughout Latin America while keeping the Yankee colossus and democrats at bay. Khrushchev sought to equal and surpass the power of the United States in the name of ensuring the longevity of the Soviet Union and its vindication through emulation. And finally, John Kennedy, whose country was feared by Castro and Khrushchev, underestimated his own power and tried to gain quick victories through indirect means but, like the fabled Gulliver, ultimately found himself tied down by myriad concerns. This is a story of unintended consequences, in which as in Flaubert's *Madame Bovary* there are neither heroes nor villains—just human beings, who are flawed, sometimes dangerously so, and whose dramatic risk taking created equally dramatic history.

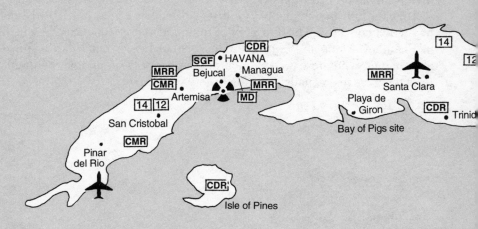

C U B A

CDR

SGF •HAVANA

MRR Bejucal •Managua

CMR   **MRR**

Artemisa   **MD**

14 12

San Cristobal

CMR

Pinar
del Rio

14 12

MRR
    Santa Clara

Playa de
 •Giron   **CDR**

Bay of Pigs site   •Trinid

CDR

Isle of Pines

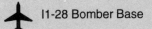

SGF Headquarters, Soviet Group
       of Forces

    I1-28 Bomber Base

    Central Nuclear Depot

MRR Motorized Rifle Regiment
       (Equipped with Luna Rockets)

CDR Coastal Defense (Sopka)
       Rocket Regiment Headquar
       and Launchers

CMR Cruise Missile Regiment (FKR

MD	Missile Division Headquarters
12	R-12 (SS4, MRBM) sites
14	R-14 (SS5, MRBM) sites

THE EMBRACE

"Moscow Is Our Brain and Our Great Leader"

FIDEL CASTRO, **November 1960**

"Where Does Castro Stand regarding Russia?"

Viva Fidel!

"Not since Sandino," the *Nation* exclaimed, "has any Latin American figure so caught the imagination of the world as Fidel Castro."[1] Norman Mailer called him "a modern Cortez." Arriving at Washington's National Airport on April 15, 1959, Castro embarked on a triumphant visit to the United States less than four months after overthrowing the Cuban dictator Fulgencio Batista y Zaldívar. The guest of the American Society of Newspaper Editors, Fidel Castro Ruz felt the time was right to bring his "Operation Truth" to the shores of his country's greatest foreign policy problem.

Ironically in light of what American policy would become, the U.S. government's greatest concern as the visit began was that Castro would be assassinated by a resentful Batistiano during his eleven-day tour. Like Mikhail Gorbachev nearly thirty years later, Fidel Castro gave the U.S. Secret Service fits by plunging into crowds, seeking to absorb every ounce of acclaim. At the National Airport he broke through a ring of security agents on his arrival to greet at least a thousand well-wishers pressing with their banners against the tarmac gates and chanting "Viva Fidel!" Fidel Castro was irrepressibly self-indulgent, and, after two years of running a revolutionary colony in the mountains before his triumphal entry into Havana, he was used to getting his way. Later Cuba would become a Soviet client and protecting Castro's life a concern of the KGB, and it would be the Russians who complained to Castro about taking these personal risks.[2] In April 1959 it was the U.S. government that had to hold its breath.

The enthusiasm of the crowd did not extend to the official U.S. delegation waiting near the plane. Castro's chief greeter at the airport was the assistant secretary of state for inter-American affairs, the seasoned diplomat and former Texas banker Richard Roy Rubottom, Jr., who had "grave doubts concerning the character and motivation" of this famous visitor.[3] With some reluctance Dick Rubottom had recommended to Christian Herter, the acting secretary of state during John Foster Dulles's illness, that special courtesies be accorded this "private visitor" to the United States. Rubottom considered Castro a "dangerous nationalist" and doubted that much could be done to alter his views on the United States.

Since 1957 Rubottom had actively participated in the Eisenhower administration's debates over policy toward Cuba. Described by one historian of the Cuban revolution as "the U.S. official most responsible for defining U.S. Cuba policy," Rubottom at the very least bore responsibility for consistently misreading the phenomenon of Fidel Castro.[4] To his credit, Rubottom had been prescient in taking the position in spring 1958 that Fulgencio Batista was vulnerable. Convinced that Batista had evolved into the worst kind of Latin despot—a leader offensive and corrupt enough to draw the ire of the American people but not powerful enough to stave off disorder in his own country—Rubottom was one of the first high-level foreign policy makers to argue that Batista should go.

Yet, for all his understanding of Batista, Rubottom had been slow to accept that Castro and his rebels would fill the coming vacuum. Castro, both the man himself and the political phenomenon he personified, perplexed the U.S. government. In two short years, after taking a handful of desperadoes into the mountains of southeastern Cuba, this former lawyer and social democrat had become the embodiment of opposition to the Batista regime. Castro's July 26 movement was a coalition of professionals and Cubans of all political persuasions who were tired of decades of authoritarianism and official corruption. Although an umbrella organization, the movement bore the stamp of Castro's larger-than-life personality. The movement took its name from the day in July 1953 when Fidel Castro first emerged on the Cuban scene by leading a band of badly armed men against the Cuban army's Moncada barracks. Twenty-one people died in the attack, and Fidel and his younger brother, Raúl, were imprisoned for two years and then exiled because of it.[5]

Washington knew very little about Castro when he returned to the mountains of Cuba in late 1956 from his exile in Mexico. In the spring of 1957 Washington had sent an official fact-finding mission to the island to learn more about the rebel leader. Led by Lyman B. Kirkpatrick, Jr., a high-ranking officer of the Central Intelligence Agency, the delegation focused its efforts on Santiago de Cuba, the main town of Castro's home province, Oriente, where it was possible to meet people who knew Fidel Castro and could attest to his character and political philosophy.

In general, the Kirkpatrick team gathered encouraging information about Fidel and his family. The Castros, who owned one of the largest sugar plantations in Oriente, were prosperous. Born in 1926, one of seven children of Angel Castro and Lina Ruz Castro, Fidel grew up in a stately house, attended parochial schools, played baseball well, and ultimately graduated in law from the University of Havana. "He was a good Catholic boy," one of Castro's teachers, a cleric, told the delegation. In fact, all of his former teachers agreed that Castro could not be a communist. A Bryn Mawr alumna, Vilma Espín, future wife of Fidel's chief lieutenant and younger brother, Raúl, reinforced the image of the Castros as noncommunist progressives. "We only want," she said, "what you Americans have: clean politics, a clean police system." The American delegation found that the rebels had appealed to a desire in many Cubans, from all classes, who were tired of the Cuban dictatorship. The tour itself had been sponsored by the owner of Bacardi rum as a way of easing American anxieties about the Castros. By the end of the trip, after meeting several lawyers, businessmen, and teachers, members of the delegation joked among themselves, "Doesn't anybody here support Batista?"[6]

Despite information from Cuba that the rebels were stronger and more popular than expected, the Eisenhower administration, especially the State Department, continued to hope in 1957 and 1958 that Batista might be able to save himself through constitutional reform. As for Castro, Washington officials remained cool. In early 1958 the United States demonstrated its preference by selling Batista some of the weapons that he wanted.[7]

The rebel leader had some allies in Washington, where Democrats in Congress and some foreign service officers were arguing for an arms embargo against Batista. But the tide of official opinion turned solidly against Castro when rebels under the command of his brother Raúl began to kidnap Americans in the summer of 1958. Eleven U.S. civilians who worked for a mining company were taken June 26. One day later the rebels grabbed twenty-four U.S. Navy enlisted men, including eleven marines. By June 30 the Cubans were holding nineteen American and Canadian civilians and thirty enlisted men of the U.S. Navy and Marine Corps.[8] The rebels justified the kidnappings by pointing to Washington's continuing support for Batista. The U.S. naval base at Guantánamo, a constant reminder on Cuban soil of the era of Theodore Roosevelt's "big stick" diplomacy, was an especially sore spot for the Fidelistas. The rebels promised to release all of the hostages if Washington stopped the flow of weapons to Batista and vowed not to let the existing regime use the base as a staging ground for counterinsurgency operations.

The hostage incidents of 1958, which ended peacefully in mid-July, after Washington suspended the planned deliveries of military aircraft to Batista, predisposed the most powerful men in Washington to seek an alternative to the rebels. Despite some evidence of a rift between Raúl Castro, who claimed to have ordered the kidnappings, and a seemingly more moderate Fidel, the State Department encouraged the CIA to try to block Fidel Castro's ascension to power.[9] On two occasions the CIA met with potential leaders of a new regime that would include neither Batista nor Fidel Castro. But these efforts came to nothing. Frustrated and resigned to an uncertain relationship with the Cuban leaders, Rubottom admitted in executive session before the Senate Foreign Relations Committee just hours before Batista fled Havana at the stroke of midnight on January 1, 1959, "It has been hard to believe that the Castros alone, that the 26th of July Movement alone could take over. . . ."[10]

Now Fidel Castro was arriving in Washington, D.C., as Cuba's newest strongman. Unlike his predecessors, this strongman had an enthusiastic American public following and apparently widespread support among his island's six million people. Seeing fifteen hundred people wait for two hours to catch a glimpse of Castro, Rubottom may have been wondering how long he would have to deal with this unusual man. It was rainy outside, these people were getting wet, and yet they waited. Perhaps he had misjudged the staying power of the charismatic Cuban leader. Rubottom could be excused for wishing that this be his only mistake in assessing the July 26 movement.

Operation Truth was to be a hectic, six-city tour across the northeastern United States and Canada. There had been widespread sympathy for Castro and the *barbudos*—the bearded ones—in January 1959. But in the three months since the takeover, the bloom was somewhat off the rose for many Americans. Reports of the execution of 521 former Batista officials, following summary war crimes trials, disappointed those who had expected the revolution to take a more moderate course. Reservations about Castro's democratic credentials, at first limited to the conservative Hearst newspapers, could now also be found in the *Atlantic* and the *New Republic* magazines because Castro refused to name a date for elections. Castro saw this visit as an opportunity to reveal the "truth" about revolutionary Cuba. The people were in charge. They wanted justice, which meant bullets through the hearts of the venal and cruel men who had denied them freedom for so long, and they wanted bread, which mattered more to them than the ballot.

Castro did not expect to achieve much with men like Dick Rubottom. He explained to Cuban and American officials alike that he was going to the United States "not to get a change in the sugar quota or to get a government loan but to win the support . . . from American public opinion."[11] Some on board the Cubana airlines flight from Havana were disappointed by their leader's dismissal of any negotiations with U.S. officials to lay the foundations for future economic assistance. But Castro feared American power. Cuba was already economically dependent on the United States. Sugar was Cuba's principal crop, and the country sold between 2.5 and 3 million metric tons of it (50–60 percent of the total production) to the United States every year at a subsidized price. North American subsidiaries employed 10 percent of all Cuban workers, and U.S. interests owned the island's utilities and most of its oil refineries, besides its main sugar plantations. Primarily as a result of U.S. direct investment, Cubans had the second-highest standard of living in Latin America and among the highest literacy rates of any state in the region. However, the success of sugar discouraged the development of other industries and left thousands of Cubans unemployed outside of harvest season. Moreover, in the boom years just after World War II, the emergent Cuban middle class had developed a taste for American-made goods, which became so expensive with the downward slide of sugar prices in the mid-1950s that Cuban currency reserves plummeted as the domestic cost of living skyrocketed.[12]

Despite his privileged background and professional training, Castro lacked any sympathy for the plight of the middle class. His primary objective in the spring of 1959 was to decrease American leverage over Cuban affairs. Not wishing to antagonize Washington, Castro had intentionally brought a group of officials whose ideas on economic reconstruction and trade matched those of the Eisenhower administration. But he had no intention of acting on the economic liberalism of the men on the plane with him.

"Where does Castro stand regarding Russia?" asked America's most famous syndicated columnist, Drew Pearson, on behalf of all official Washington. Pearson's column, "Washington Merry-Go-Round," arrived with coffee on the Cuban delegation's first morning in the United States.[13] The last person to be surprised by the question was Fidel Castro. He knew that in American eyes the acceptability of a Latin American regime depended upon its being perceived as noncommunist. Like all Latin American politicians of his generation, Castro was familiar with the cautionary tale of Guatemala's Jacobo Arbenz and the U.S. role in the overthrow of his regime in 1954. Since 1933, through Franklin Roosevelt's Good Neighbor Policy, the United States had pledged itself to a policy of nonintervention in Latin American countries. This rejection of Theodore Roosevelt's 1904 assertion that the United States could intervene in the domestic affairs of other states in the Western Hemisphere became the basis of all inter-American relations in 1948 with the founding of the Organization of American States (OAS). However, at the 1954 OAS meeting in Caracas, Venezuela, the United States got the organization to accept a loophole in the pledge of nonintervention. According to what was known as the Caracas resolution, the members of the OAS were committed to joint action against any communist beachhead in the hemisphere. It was important for the young Castro regime to do everything necessary to prevent the Caracas resolution from being invoked, because this would give legitimacy to another Guatemalan-style covert operation.

As expected, the communism question dogged Castro throughout his hectic first day in Washington. After exhausting his staff, he slumped into a chair in the Cuban embassy in Dupont Circle to respond to one more attempt to peer inside his political soul. This time a Democratic congressman from Oregon, Charles Porter, was the one asking a variation on the Question: Is it true that the soldiers are learning Marxist doctrine in Havana? Castro had had a long day, and this set him off. "Do you believe that? This is my army. I started it from nothing and I control it. . . . Don't you think I would be the first to be worried if I thought another power was taking it away from me?"[14]

Castro gave the same answer in various forms and at various times during the rest of his trip. "We are against all kinds of dictators. . . . That is why we are against Communism," he told an audience at the National Press

Club.[15] At the United Nations he added that there were "no Communists" in the new Cuban government.[16] And if there was any question about his brother Raúl Castro, who was not officially a member of the government, Fidel categorically denied on NBC's *Meet the Press* that either Raúl or his wife was a communist. He allowed that there might well be some communists in his movement but held that "their influence is nothing."[17]

The most famous test of Castro's connections to Moscow and communism came in Vice President Richard Nixon's small Senate office. Eisenhower had conveniently planned a trip to Georgia's Augusta National, the home course of the Masters golf tournament, for the period of Castro's stay. It was decided that the vice president would greet the revolutionary.[18] Years later Castro recalled the meeting as pleasant. Nixon did as Castro wanted: he let him talk. "I explained the social and economic situation in Cuba, the poverty, the inequality, the hundreds of thousands of unemployed, the landless peasants, the measures that we had to adopt to solve the situation—and Nixon listened, said nothing, and made no remarks."[19]

Crimson Dreams

Fidel Castro spent his last night in the United States at Harvard, as the guest of the university. The Faculty of Arts and Sciences's young, brilliant, and caustic dean, McGeorge Bundy, hosted Castro at a Faculty Club dinner. Though they came from very different backgrounds, the two men could at least exchange war stories. Lieutenant Bundy had waded ashore on Normandy in the Second World War. Castro's combat experiences, of course, were much fresher.

Sometime during the meal, Castro shared a curious confidence. In his six years as the chief academic officer and one of the intellectual leaders of Harvard, Bundy had welcomed many world leaders to the 325-year-old campus. Despite the notoriously strict admissions requirements of the school, it is safe to assume that few of them made a point of telling Bundy that they had actually applied to Harvard and not gotten in. Fidel Castro did.[20]

A decade after being rejected by the Ivy League, Fidel Castro was in the United States to celebrate what he had managed to do with his life instead. Castro included Harvard, in addition to Princeton and Yale, on his swing along the East Coast to make his case before the next generation of the American elite. In New Jersey he had been mobbed. In the afternoon, at the Lawrenceville School, Castro so impressed the schoolboys when he spoke to them in the chapel that they rushed from the back pews to claim the lighted cigar that he carelessly left behind on the lectern.[21] Later at Princeton University, Castro was hoisted onto the shoulders of a group of Finals Club upperclassmen for a quick tour of a quadrangle. Yale apparently treated him more demurely. And as the Yale alumnus McGeorge Bundy checked his watch to be sure that his guest would not be late for the evening's scheduled event, he may well have wondered what Harvard had in store for the popular Cuban.

On an unseasonably warm April night, 8,700 members of the Harvard community gathered outside to greet Fidel. Side by side in a convertible, Castro and the Harvard dean were carried along the stream of people parading to the Dillon Field House. From a speaking platform in front of the building, Bundy used the story of Castro's failed application to introduce the revolutionary idol. Caught up in the exuberance of the event, he declared that Harvard was ready to make amends for its 1948 mistake. It had decided to admit him. How different the world might have been had Fidel Castro accepted a place in the Harvard class of 1963![22]

In Moscow it was twenty degrees colder and early the next morning when Castro started his speech at Harvard. Nikita Khrushchev had just made a decision that would help ensure that the lives of Fidel Castro and McGeorge Bundy, the future national security adviser of a future president, John F. Kennedy, would become deeply entwined. For thirty years neither Bundy nor any other American could have known that in the midst of Castro's successful Operation Truth the Kremlin was planning a covert operation to assist the Cuban army at the explicit request of the Cuban leader's brother Raúl.[23]

As American journalists, officials, and students elicited repeated assurances from Fidel Castro of Cuba's independence from international communism, Raúl Castro was hard at work setting in motion a revolution in the relationship between Moscow and Havana. A secret member of the Cuban communist party—the Partido Socialista Popular (PSP)—the younger Castro had acquired de facto control of the Cuban armed services when his brother became prime minister. In April, Raúl Castro sent Lázaro Peña, a longtime PSP member and former president of the Cuban labor congress, to Moscow to ask for Soviet assistance in consolidating his control of the Cuban army. Raúl Castro said he needed a few men from the group of Spanish communists who had graduated from the Soviet military academy to act as advisers "to help the Cuban army . . . on general matters and for the organization of intelligence work."[24]

Raúl's request found deep wells of support in Moscow. At sixty-five years of age, Nikita Sergeyvich Khrushchev was not much of a revolutionary, but he admired those who could make a revolution. As Joseph Stalin's successor, Khrushchev held two titles. He was both the general secretary of the Communist Party of the Soviet Union and the chairman of the Council of Ministers of the Soviet Union. But it was as general secretary that Khrushchev made the Kremlin's most important decisions. In that post he headed the Presidium of the party's Central Committee, a group of about a dozen of the party's most powerful men, sometimes known collectively in Soviet history as the Politburo. In the forty years since Vladimir Lenin led the Bolsheviks to power in 1917, the Presidium or Politburo had directed Russian political life. Khrushchev joined the Communist Party a year after the October revolution and became a full member of the party's inner circle in the 1940s. The son of Russian peasants living in the Ukraine, Khrushchev proved to be an adept party boss in Moscow. After Stalin's death in 1953, he outmaneuvered all other pretenders to the throne. From 1957 he was in sole command of the party and the government and had the ultimate say on any covert operations.

Khrushchev's Presidium approved Raúl Castro's petition on April 23, 1959, and instructed the International Department of the Central Committee, which handled relations among the various communist parties around the world, the Ministry of Defense, and the KGB to arrange with the leadership of the Spanish Communist Party to send two Spaniards to Cuba who had graduated from Soviet military academies.[25] The Ministry of Finance was also authorized to pay their salaries. A short while later the Presidium sent an additional detachment of fifteen Soviet officers of Spanish origin.[26] The Cuban army had very little money of its own, and the civilian leaders of the Cuban treasury, who were all anticommunists, were not to be told about this Soviet assistance.[27]

A year earlier the Kremlin had been as poorly informed as Washington about Raúl's brother Fidel. For the most part, Stalin had left Latin America to the United States. It was America's backyard, too far away for a man who had never traveled outside his own sphere of influence in Eastern Europe. But under Khrushchev the Soviet Union looked for allies among the young nationalist leaders of what became known as the Third World.

The first serious contact between the Cuban rebels and the Kremlin had been indirect. In December 1958, representatives of a Costa Rican importing company, called Polini San José, approached the Czech embassy in Mexico to discuss "the supply of rifles, mortars and ammunition for the rebel detachments of Fidel Castro." Prague, which since the late 1940s had not made any significant foreign policy decisions without checking first with Moscow, requested guidance on December 17, 1958. Having maintained links with young members of the Cuban communist party since at least the early 1950s, the Czechs wanted to help this shadowy "Costa Rican" group.[28]

Believing that the Soviet Union had an obligation to take risks to support revolutionary movements around the world, the Kremlin on December 27, 1958, approved "the intention of the Czech friends to help the liberation movement in Cuba." As a way of minimizing the risk of disclosure, the Kremlin stipulated precautionary measures. "In no document should it be written," Moscow instructed Prague, "that the weapons delivery was destined for the Cubans." Ever mindful of traps sprung by the CIA, the Presidium wanted the Czechs "to verify painstakingly the seriousness of intent of the company" before going ahead with the deal. And in the spirit of preventive damage control, the Soviets decided that no Soviet-made weapons could be sent. The Czechs were told to restrict assistance to World War II–era German weapons or weapons of Czech design. It was assumed that if Washington found out about the shipment, those kinds of weapons would be easier for President Dwight Eisenhower to swallow.[29]

Contacts between the revolutionaries and Moscow became more direct following the sudden collapse of the Batista regime on New Year's Day 1959. Offering itself as a channel to the new leadership in Havana, the PSP sent a series of emissaries to the Kremlin. In March 1959 a representative of the PSP met with the chief of staff of the Soviet armed forces, Marshal V. Sokolovsky, to discuss future relations between the two armed services.[30] A month later, in addition to what he brought from Raúl Castro, Lázaro Peña conveyed a request from the secretary general of the PSP, Blas Roca, to encourage the Soviets to "develop economic relations with Cuba . . . to buy Cuban sugar and to provide the country with manufacturing and agricultural equipment."[31]

There were limits to what the Kremlin was prepared to do for the Havana revolutionaries in the spring of 1959. Cuban requests for assistance in building a loyal revolutionary army met with Moscow's approval. While the Presidium was favorably discussing the dispatch of advisers to Raúl Castro, Marshal Sokolovsky raised with a PSP representative the possibility of training Cuban pilots and asked about the communists' goals for the army. However, Cuban feelers in behalf of an expansion of economic relations went unsupported by the Soviet Presidium, as did a request for Moscow to unleash its propaganda organs in support of Fidel. The editor of *Pravda* told a PSP visitor from Havana that the Cuban communist party should leave well enough alone. "Things are going well there, and American imperialists might use these *Pravda* articles for future attacks on the democratic structure of Cuba. If matters begin to deteriorate in Cuba, then *Pravda* would provide more information and publish expressions of solidarity."[32]

A lack of confidence in the orientation of the Cuban revolution inspired this caution in Moscow. Despite adherents like Raúl Castro, the communists were far from wielding complete control over the new government. Not one of the high-level PSP emissaries who had come to Moscow since January 1959 even pretended to speak on behalf of Fidel Castro. The Cuban communist leaders all boasted of having "influenced" Castro, but no one dared call him a communist or a Marxist. In fact, what claims they did make contained hidden warnings of Fidel Castro's self-possession and unbridled revolutionary energy. In February, Severro Aguirre had argued that the PSP deserved credit for the triumph of the revolution, because the party had effectively contained some of Castro's wilder urges. "The actions of Fidel Castro, who employed individualistic terror in the beginning of his struggle against tyranny in the mountains," the Cuban communists explained in Moscow, "interfered with the work of the PSP." "We did everything," Aguirre boasted, "such that Fidel Castro would drop these methods." And the implication was that Castro had done so and that subsequently the revolution had picked up steam. Yet this claim naturally left Moscow wondering whether Fidel Castro was indeed capable of the discipline required of a communist.[33]

The central problem for Moscow in 1959, as for Washington, was making sense of Fidel Castro and his revolution. Of the sixteen men who went into the Sierra Maestra in Oriente Province in 1956, four were communists. Yet there was an enduring mistrust between the rank and file of the July 26 movement and the party. The PSP had denounced the 1953 attack on the Moncada barracks as "adventurist" and as "a putschist method peculiar to all bourgeois political factions."[34] After the surviving rebels were thrown in jail and exiled to Mexico, the PSP restored contact with the Castro brothers.[35] But again in 1956 Blas Roca and Lázaro Peña expressed disagreement with Fidel Castro's timetable for grabbing power.

Besides Raúl Castro, Ernesto Guevara was the other highly placed communist in the rebel movement. A trained physician, the Argentine native served as the only doctor among the small group of rebels who sailed to Cuba from Mexico aboard the *Granma* in 1956. Rushing around the sloop looking for medicine, Guevara unsuccessfully tried to calm the churning stomachs of the eighty-two heavily armed rebels on the passage to Oriente Province. Better known by the nickname Che, Guevara despised the PSP for the same reasons he loved Fidel Castro and the other vomit-caked men suffering on the ship. The Cuban communist elite were "talmudists" and bureaucrats, little more than bystanders waiting for history to give them their moment instead of forcing change with revolutionary élan.[36] Grudgingly perhaps, and with Raúl's encouragement, Che joined the Cuban communist party in 1957, when it appeared that some in the PSP leadership were reconsidering their opposition to armed revolution.

Roca, Peña, and Aguirre were very different kinds of communists from Raúl and Che. They had Stalinist views on the proper way for a state to achieve socialism. Even in the Third World, where there were few industrial urban centers, true socialism in their minds required a proletariat, and a proletariat was impossible without an industrial capitalist economy. Che and Raúl belonged instead to a generation shaped by Mao Zedong's victory in China in 1949. By deploying a peasant army as the vanguard of a Chinese communist state, Mao effectively challenged Soviet theories of building socialism. To be successful, a revolution did not need a working class. Maoism, as these theories of armed rebellion became known, seemed more conducive to the conditions of the developing world and to the instincts of men like Che and Raúl.

The old leaders of the PSP put doctrinal matters aside once Raúl Castro's brother garnered mass support from his base in the Sierra Maestra. Although still a long shot, a victory by Fidel's July 26 movement would be the best opportunity ever presented to the PSP to expand its influence in Cuba. Organized in 1919, the party became such a formidable electoral machine that in

1940 a young sergeant named Batista had offered some seats in the cabinet to the general secretary of the PSP, Blas Roca. When Batista came to power a second time, in 1952, he outlawed the communist party, forcing Roca and the other old communists to go into six years of underground work.

Although they would never get over their distrust of Che, the old PSP leaders thought highly of Raúl Castro. Raúl had joined the party years before the revolution, when a student at the University of Havana in the early 1950s. An idealist who rejected his parents' upper-middle-class lifestyle, Raúl came to identify with the workers on his father's plantation. At the University of Havana he read voraciously and acquired a command of the Marxist canon. Raúl Valdés Vivo, who headed the socialist youth group at the university, befriended the young Raúl and recruited him.[37] Fearful of his brother's reaction, Raúl said to Blas Roca that he never told Fidel about his membership in the youth league or, later, in the PSP itself. Fidel, who attended the university a few years before Raúl, had socialized with members of the youth league but refused to join them. He rejected the stifling party discipline and believed that Cuba's injustices could be solved only through action and violence. Knowing Fidel's dislike for the PSP, Raúl was convinced that his suspicious brother would view his membership as a sign of divided loyalties.

It may seem fantastic that Raúl Castro could keep his membership in the Cuban communist party a secret from his mistrustful brother. In the Sierra Maestra, Fidel told an American newsman, "[Raúl] always consults me about all the important questions."[38] Yet when Raúl took a group of American marines hostage in the summer of 1958, Fidel behaved as if his brother had exceeded his instructions. Raúl was capable of independent action. The brothers had a tempestuous relationship. The older Fidel patronized Raúl, describing him to outsiders as "extraordinarily respectful," while admiring him for his intelligence. Raúl was better read and probably more clever than his brother. Physically underdeveloped, he did not project the machismo of Fidel. The importance of such things was that it fed in Raúl a certain insecurity, which was occasionally manifest in acts of cruelty. Raúl was beside Fidel on every rung of the ladder to power. During the revolution he replaced Fidel as chief military officer in Oriente Province when the movement pushed closer to the Cuban capital. After the fall of Batista, Raúl was the first rebel commander to initiate revolutionary tribunals for opponents of the revolution. Fidel asked the July 26 movement to recognize Raúl as his heir apparent, and, after becoming prime minister in February, he brought him to Havana.

Knowledge of Raúl's secret formed the basis of Soviet treatment of both Castros in the months after the revolution.[39] The secret was closely held in Moscow. Mid-level documents from the Foreign Ministry or the Central Committee referred to him only as a "leftist" or a "supporter of the unified left."[40] But when members of Khrushchev's inner cabinet discussed Cuba, they believed they had a special ally in Raúl, who had to be protected from his brother. "[W]e knew that Raul Castro was a good communist," Khrushchev later recalled, "but it appeared that he kept his true convictions hidden from his brother Fidel."[41]

Where's Fidel?

Since Kremlin records do not mention Fidel Castro in connection with the sending of Spanish communists to train the new Cuban army, it remains a matter of speculation as to when Raúl told Fidel of the success of Peña's mission. Could Raúl have kept this a secret, as he did his communist affiliation? As we shall see, the KGB, at least, believed that Fidel did not learn about his brother's communist loyalties until 1962, during something called the Escalante affair, which ripped open the PSP.[42] However, in light of the role that Fidel permitted even overt communists to play in his government as early as May 1959, it seems likely that Raúl was fully authorized to open this channel to Moscow, that Fidel and the commander in chief of the Rebel Army, Camilo Cienfuegos Gorriarán, wanted veterans of the Spanish civil war to train Cuban recruits.

If Mao's achievements in China were the beacon of hope for young Latin American revolutionaries in the 1950s, the CIA's overthrow of Guatemala's Jacobo Arbenz in 1954 was the most powerful cautionary tale of Raúl and Fidel Castro's generation. After his election in 1952, Arbenz moved to implement radical social and political reforms. A Marxist, though not necessarily pro-Moscow, Arbenz included members of the Guatemalan communist party in his inner circle. By 1954 the Eisenhower administration had determined that it could no longer countenance Arbenz as leader of Guatemala. With the support of moderate, Catholic, and conservative interests in the government and the army, Washington undermined Arbenz's hold on power. In June 1954, under pressure from a small band of rebels whose numbers were exaggerated by CIA radio stations, the Guatemalan army collapsed, prompting Arbenz to resign. The essential lesson for the Castros and Che, who was actually in Guatemala at the time of the coup, was that purging and rebuilding the army would have to be a priority in the first months of power. Fidel Castro doubtless knew of the arrival of the Spanish communist military advisers and accepted them as a necessary preventive measure.

There exists the intriguing possibility that Fidel Castro learned of this first high-level contact between the Kremlin and his regime in Boston just before meeting the young Harvard dean McGeorge Bundy on April 25, 1959. Rufo López Fresquet, the Cuban finance minister, who accompanied Fidel to the United States, recalls a long-distance telephone call from Raúl on April 24 or April 25. Whatever Raúl said infuriated Fidel. López Fresquet heard some of the shouting, prompted by Raúl's concern that Fidel was letting "them" seduce him. López Fresquet believed that Raúl Castro had called to advise his brother to tone down his pro-American rhetoric, but in light of new Soviet records the timing of the call may have been linked to the news that on April 23 the Kremlin had decided to provide secret assistance to the revolution. In any case, the incident reflected Raúl's misgivings about his brother's mission to America, at a time when he was hopeful of Soviet sponsorship of the new government.

In Fidel Castro's absence Raúl reinforced the significance of his secret diplomacy by establishing himself as the regime's main critic of the United States. On April 20 he told students at Havana University that "enemies of the Cuban revolution" were in the pay of the United States. He directed attention to comments by Senator George Smathers of Florida, who had proposed an international police force to maintain security in the Caribbean. Raúl decried this as a covert attempt to establish a force to invade Cuba on the slimmest pretext. Knowing the mistrust that many inside Cuba felt for the communists, Raúl combined his anti-American diatribe with an explanation that it was "stylish" to attack him as a communist. He warned the crowd that these calumnies were part of a concerted campaign by those who would do harm to the revolution.[43]

Whereas Raúl Castro excelled at explaining what the revolution was not, Che Guevara spoke confidently to the Cuban people in Fidel Castro's absence of what the revolution could become. When Fidel decided not to return to Havana to lead May Day celebrations, Che stepped into the spotlight. Already responsible for political indoctrination in the army, Che introduced the notion of a militia of part-time soldiers, culled from the peasantry, urban workers, and students, dedicated to fighting for the revolution against all comers. Che also dared praise communists as "revolutionists," while in the same breath he advocated diplomatic relations with the Soviet Union, a topic Fidel had studiously avoided in public.[44]

Although Raúl Castro and Che Guevara spoke of the revolution as if they alone understood it, both men misjudged their power at this moment to shape Cuban events. The elder Castro was not yet ready to establish formal, public ties with the Soviet Union or even the local PSP. When Fidel Castro returned to Cuba from his long trip, which he had ended in Argentina by calling on the United States to create a $30 billion fund for public works in Latin America, the Cuban leader set himself up as a public opponent of the very ideas that his brother and Che had touted only days before. Describing his trip to North and South America as "successful and gratifying," Castro said that he had not expected that in the United States the "people would have responded so enthusiastically and with such comprehension." This is not what Raúl had said. Fidel then gored Che's bull. "There should be no formal militia organized in peacetime," he said. Instead, there should be a "small, well trained, mobile professional army." Castro ended his marathon speech on May 10, stating his hope for good relations with all of the Americas. He vowed to defeat those who hoped to use Cuba as a staging ground for expeditions to overthrow existing governments, and he welcomed official U.S. contributions to Latin American development.[45]

Fidel Castro's actions were contradictory, suggesting complex motives. While attacking Guevara's militia plan, Castro endorsed in May 1959 a land reform system designed by the PSP and assigned well-known Cuban communists to leadership positions in the organization, the National Institute of Agrarian Reform (INRA), created to supervise the reform. The Agrarian Reform Law limited property holdings to 3,333 acres, effectively cutting the size of the country's largest sugar planations and cattle ranches by more than 90 percent. Approximately 2.5 million acres of land came under the regime's control in this manner.[46] At the same time, Castro apparently did nothing to obstruct the political and technical work of the advisers sent by the Spanish communist party to the Cuban army.

Despite these gains Raúl Castro and Che Guevara were furious at Fidel Castro's public vacillations. Fidel had humiliated them in front of the Cuban people and through his speeches had also encouraged the anticommunist left in the July 26 movement. Raúl briefly contemplated splitting the rebel movement to demonstrate to his brother that he needed the communist wing to govern.[47] Che reacted openly and harshly. He threatened Fidel with emigration from Cuba if the militia proposal was not approved.[48] Castro was shaken by the opposition of his closest allies. He was torn between his dependence on them and his own sense of how to hold on to power in Cuba. It is not known whether this was Fidel's idea, but within a few weeks Che was sent on a long "commercial mission" to Europe and Asia. Before leaving, Che married his longtime mistress. Raúl served as his best man, but Fidel did not bother to come.[49]

The threat of a split between Raúl, Che, and Fidel Castro worried the leadership of the PSP, which believed that Moscow's support against U.S. intervention was predicated on communists' remaining in Fidel's inner circle. "We need solidarity now more than ever before," warned Blas Roca on a trip to Moscow in June 1959.[50] Fidel had hurt the revolutionary cause by making some anticommunist statements in the United States and in Cuba. But the cause was not lost. The PSP, he explained, had persuaded Fidel that his anticommunist rhetoric was harmful to the revolution and a change in his speeches was already noticeable. Roca said nothing about the workers' militia; but he tried to assure Moscow that Fidel was still sympathetic to PSP. Roca claimed to enjoy his support and stressed the risks that Castro had already taken in behalf of progressive reform. Hinting at the old adage "The enemy of my enemy is my friend," Roca emphasized that the United States was using the agrarian reform program to pummel the regime.[51] Moscow listened sympathetically but did nothing to increase its minor covert assistance to Havana.

After Fidel Castro left the United States, Assistant Secretary of State Dick Rubottom reflected on the strengths and weaknesses that Castro had shown during his visit. He had said much to allay suspicions that he was pro-Soviet, but despite Castro's direct denials of any brief for communists or communism, Rubottom had his doubts. Why proclaim a desire for independence and then welcome communists into your government, some of whom might be pro-Soviet? Perhaps Castro wanted to avoid seeming too friendly toward the United States, for fear of undermining his nationalist and revolutionary credentials. At the end of the day Rubottom concluded that Castro remained "an enigma."[52]

From Rubottom to Eisenhower no one in the U.S. government knew the steps the Kremlin had taken during Castro's trip to solidify its relations with Raúl Castro and the Cuban army. This information would have helped the administration fend off criticisms that Washington had squandered an opportunity to improve relations with the Cuban leadership. The American left, in particular, believed that Fidel considered himself mistreated in the United States. Had Dwight Eisenhower only put himself out to greet the Cuban prime minister, it was argued, instead of playing golf at Augusta National in Georgia, then Castro might have formed a better image of this country.

Castro's visit did indeed mark a watershed. His public relations campaign across North and South America, however limited in scope, had revealed strains among his key men in Havana. Raúl Castro and Che Guevara were determined to exploit the chaos in Cuba following the rebels' seizure of power to lay down the structures of a Marxist-Leninist state and told Castro that they would resist any opening to Washington. Fidel had a choice to make in the months to come. He was no Marxist ideologue. In fact, simply put, he was the first Fidelista. Castro believed himself to be the embodiment of the Cuban nation and the inheritor of the mantle of Simón Bolívar. His challenge was to find a course of action that guaranteed him continued control over the revolution and the destiny of his people. At the same time, the challenge for Raúl and Che would be to convince this man that the future prospects of his regime and his movement depended on creating a much closer relationship with Moscow and Beijing. As of the summer of 1959 the Kremlin could do little but watch and wait for Fidel Castro to decide his next move.

Our Man in Havana

Mixed Signals

A rumor that Raúl Castro was prepared to overthrow his less doctrinaire brother reached Moscow in the late spring of 1959.[1] While interested in knowing whether this was true, the Kremlin had no way of evaluating any information on this peculiar revolution. Aside from the sporadic accounts of PSP visitors to Moscow, the Soviet government seems not to have had any intelligence assets on the island. A month after the rebel victory, the KGB tried to send an intelligence officer, under the cover of a correspondent for the Soviet state radio, to Havana. But the Cuban Ministry of Foreign Affairs, which was still under the control of the anticommunist wing of the July 26 movement, refused to grant him a visa.[2]

Without any direct communication to the new leaders in Cuba, the Soviets developed a confused picture of the state of affairs on the island. The charismatic Fidel Castro seemed to be in control; but it was unclear what kind of regime he intended to create. Information that Raúl Castro and Che Guevara were secret members of the Cuban communist party suggested that the revolution might take a sharp turn to the left; but as yet Fidel Castro himself had made no effort to show his cards.

One person who could help the Soviets understand the real Fidel Castro, if he would talk, was Che Guevara. Following Castro's refusal in May to establish a popular militia, which for Guevara and Raúl Castro was the symbol of the coming socialist revolution, Che had gone into voluntary exile as Cuba's traveling commercial attaché. Egypt was Che's first port of call. Gamal Abdel Nasser, a hero to the Castros for having struck a blow at European colonialism by nationalizing the Suez Canal in 1956, tried to warn the young Cuban revolutionary not to make the mistake of exchanging one form of dependency for another. Nasser reportedly told Che Guevara that "if one dealt with the imperialists, one would suffer a five per cent loss in one's resources. However, if one dealt with the Communists, one would lose one hundred per cent of his assets."[3] The Egyptian leader, who had learned some hard lessons through personal experience, had reason to wonder whether these eager young Cuban revolutionaries knew how to deal with a superpower with caution and without sacrificing autonomy.

Over the course of the next two months, Che Guevara pointedly stayed away from socialist countries to avoid raising suspicions in Washington. But he had every intention of probing the communist world in search of moral and material benefits for Cuba. In almost every capital on his itinerary, Che spent time with the local Soviet and Eastern bloc representatives, while keeping a low profile. And as he made his rounds, the Kremlin received reports on his comments. In general, Che was telling Soviet officials that Moscow had a new ally in the developing world but that this ally would require assistance different in kind from that given to Egypt or Indonesia, recipients of the largest amount of Soviet aid in the Third World. Cuba had to worry about economic rebuilding and was not interested in military procurement. Alternately stroking and chiding the Soviets, Che expressed Cuba's profound interest in expanding commercial relations with the East, while sharply criticizing the Soviets for their often maladroit handling of Third World regimes. In a July meeting with the Soviet ambassador to Japan, Che invited the Kremlin to start trade negotiations with Cuban representatives in London. "Guevara remarked," the ambassador reported, "that negotiations and contracts must be open."[4] Che also made a point of telling Moscow how important it was that it send someone to these talks who spoke Spanish fluently. Not only was he interested in ensuring Moscow's respect for the Spanish language and Cuban sovereignty; he also shared the rebels' mistrust of the Cuban foreign service. Unlike the veteran staff in the Cuban embassies abroad, the loyal revolutionaries now being sent overseas probably would not know any foreign languages.

Guevara wanted the Kremlin to know that, despite the early setbacks, Fidel's communist allies in the July 26 movement fully intended to build socialism. But their byword had to be "Exercise caution." As Che explained to the Soviet ambassador in Japan, a "rapprochement with socialist countries" had to be "gradual . . . because the enemies of the revolution will try to use every sign to obstruct domestic affairs on the pretext of a communist threat in Cuba." Che had learned his lesson in May. Perhaps speaking to himself as much as to the Kremlin, the thirty-year-old former guerrilla explained that "[o]ne must have endurance, toughness, and consistency to carry out revolutionary policies in Cuba."[5]

Meanwhile, the news from Cuba indicated that Raúl Castro's influence had recovered from the fraternal spat over militia policy and public treatment of the communism question. Over the objections of the noncommunist left in the July 26 movement, Fidel Castro had chosen Osvaldo Dorticós, a lawyer who drafted the agrarian reform legislation, to replace Manuel Urrutia as

Cuba's president in July 1959. A member of the PSP since 1953, Dorticós was Raúl Castro's candidate. Although the position was largely ceremonial, its capture by a party member shored up the faith of PSP leaders that the revolution would ultimately go their way.[6]

Doing the Can-Can

Nikita Khrushchev did not appreciate seeing the actress Shirley MacLaine's white bloomers. Invited by executives at Twentieth Century-Fox to visit the sound studio where the cast members of *Can-Can* were rehearsing in September 1959, Khrushchev noticeably tensed up when the leggy MacLaine and members of the chorus line began twirling their skirts in the air. Disgusted, the Soviet leader told his patrician escort, Henry Cabot Lodge, the U.S. ambassador to the United Nations, that "he could not understand how good and hard working people could indulge in such entertainment." He was coming to the end of an unprecedented ten-day, coast-to-coast tour of the "Main Adversary." Besides the wearying effect of so many new experiences over such a short period of time, the trip was depressing Khrushchev's natural optimism about the triumph of communism. The *Can-Can* episode presented Khrushchev with an opportunity to let off steam about the intimidating vitality and resources of the country he was now visiting for the first time. "[It was] the extreme abundance of wealth in the United States," he told Lodge, "which made the people look for such unusual entertainment."[7]

In a less dramatic and embittered fashion, Khrushchev took Lodge aside at the end of his California stay to reveal his new thinking about the challenges he faced as an opponent of the United States: "[T]he Soviet Union has never denied that the United States had the highest standard of life and the most efficient methods of production in the world, and that was the reason why it had chosen the United States as its partner for competition." Backing away from public claims to the contrary, an uncharacteristically humbled Khrushchev added that he didn't think the Soviet Union could catch up with the United States by 1970; although it might be able to catch up in the total volume of production, it wouldn't be able to catch up as far as per capita production was concerned.[8]

While Khrushchev fretted about growth rates, back in Moscow that third week of September 1959, the Presidium was having its own hard time deciding whether the socialist bloc should challenge the American colossus in the Caribbean. The Cubans were trying to buy weapons from the Polish government, and Warsaw had appealed to Moscow for guidance. Even though Khrushchev and his minister of foreign affairs, Andrei Gromyko, were in the United States, the remainder of the Presidium felt it had to prepare an answer for the Poles, who had brought the issue to the Kremlin's attention.

The Polish ambassador in Moscow had presented the Kremlin with a tangled tale. The Cubans used their legation in Switzerland to quietly purchase supplies from the Polish government. Up to this point the Cubans had restricted their requests to consumer goods. But now they were asking the Polish ambassador in Bern to cable Warsaw for permission to supply weapons. This was the first time the Cubans had looked for military assistance from a communist country since Castro took over. Once again they expected to resort to a covert operation to bring the arms without alerting the United States. The Cubans controlled an Austrian company that could buy weapons from Poland.

The Poles reacted to this in the same manner as the Czechs in December 1958. Like Czechoslovakia, Poland would not consider providing military assistance to Castro without the Kremlin's approval. Accordingly, in mid-September the Polish ambassador in Moscow requested advice from the Soviet government as to whether Poland should supply weapons that had been manufactured under Soviet license.[9]

The Presidium got conflicting advice from the foreign policy bureaucracies of the government and the Communist Party. The Ministry of Foreign Affairs, under Deputy Minister Valerian Zorin's leadership in Gromyko's absence, expressed serious misgivings, fearing that a misstep in a minor relationship with Cuba would harm the "spirit of Camp David." Discussions between Khrushchev and Eisenhower at the presidential retreat symbolized for some in Moscow a new level of civility and mutual understanding between the superpowers. The Committee on Foreign Economic Relations of the Central Committee of the CPSU joined the Ministry of Foreign Affairs in underscoring for the Presidium the possibility that this Cuban request was actually a provocation designed by "adversaries of the lessening of international tensions and the improvement of relations between the Soviet Union and the United States."[10] The memorandum recalled that Che Guevara had not once raised the question of military assistance with any of the Soviet representatives he met in the course of his globetrotting. Finally, the memorandum added disingenuously that it seemed suspicious that an Austrian company and not a Cuban representative would request the weapons.

Khrushchev's successful trip was cause for many in the Kremlin to reconsider taking any chances with Fidel Castro. The issue of the Austrian company's bona fides was a transparent ploy. The Costa Rican firm used by the Cubans in 1958, when the Kremlin approved the sale of Czech weapons, had been just as unknown. But although it called Prague's attention to the possibility of trouble, the Presidium had not ruled out using a private firm. This time there was significant opposition to sending weapons to the Cubans, opposition inspired by concern over the possible consequences for U.S.-Soviet relations if word of the decision to arm Castro ever leaked to Washington. Gromyko's people knew what they were talking about when they warned that "the supply of arms to Cuba will drive the Americans toward active interference in the internal affairs of Latin American affairs and, in the first instance, in the affairs of Cuba."[11]

The Presidium refused to go against the wishes of the Foreign Ministry or the Soviet Communist Party's own Committee of Foreign Trade while Khrushchev was still in the United States. At its meeting of September 23, 1959, the Presidium resolved that it was "inexpedient at the present time to provide weapons to Cuba."[12] Cuba was now a matter of high politics. If Soviet policy toward that country were to change, only Khrushchev could make the decision.

When he returned to Moscow a few days later, the Soviet premier made it clear that he did not share the qualms of the timid Americanists in his foreign policy bureaucracy. The Cuban revolution was too important, and unusual, a phenomenon in world affairs for the Soviets to deny it assistance. Although the subject of Cuba never came up during his talks with President Eisenhower, Khrushchev understood the sensitivity of Americans toward that island. Yet what could the costs be to U.S.-Soviet relations of secretly supplying a few arms to the Cuban army, even if the secret came out? The superpowers had ample reasons to want good relations, the most important of which was to avoid a war over the division of Europe. Tallying up the costs and benefits of a decision was not in Khrushchev's nature, but it is safe to say that, seen from the Kremlin, the international environment in the fall of 1959 was not threatening enough to warrant escaping one's duty to fellow revolutionaries. Khrushchev decided over the opposition of his foreign policy bureaucrats to send Warsaw Pact weapons to Cuba.

If one were to choose the point at which the United States and the Soviet Union started inclining toward their first direct military clash, it was this day in late September 1959. By approving the weapons sale, Khrushchev signaled to the top levels of the Soviet government that he would take risks to pursue Soviet aims in Latin America. Joseph Stalin had left the region to the United States, hoping perhaps to reach the kind of sphere-of-influence agreement with Franklin Roosevelt or Harry Truman that he had with Winston Churchill in 1944. Throughout the first decade of the Cold War, the Soviets had maintained monetary and public support of the communist parties in the region, but at no time had they taken any real risks in America's backyard. As the CIA's station chief in Cuba later recalled, the "Soviets didn't figure" until 1959.[13]

On September 30, 1959, with Khrushchev back at the helm, the Presidium voted to take those risks, giving "approval to the Polish side to provide Cuba with some kinds of rifles, prepared by Polish manufacturers under Soviet licenses."[14] This was how the Soviet government worked in the Khrushchev years. It was not that a consensus developed but that Khrushchev's approach won out. In this case the Foreign Ministry's opposition was overcome, and there emerged an illusory aura of unity around the decision. A representative from the Central Committee at the Presidium meeting argued that the Polish ambassador should be told privately of the decision but that he must be led to believe that no words were spoken against the proposal.

Five years later, when Khrushchev's opponents in the Presidium broke their silence and openly schemed to toss him out of office, this decision was held to be a costly mistake. A fellow member of the Presidium, Dmitri Polyanski, spoke in 1964 for those who understood the futility of Khrushchev's Cuban obsession: "Comrade Khrushchev was pleased to announce that Stalin had not succeeded in penetrating Latin America whereas he had. First, the policy of penetrating Latin America had not been our policy. And second, this meant that our country had to commit itself to providing military supplies an ocean away, 15,000 km."[15] But the superpowers would nearly have to go to war before this would be argued openly in the Kremlin.

Alekseev Arrives

Soviet intelligence, especially the KGB, was slow to adapt to the increasingly complex relations between the Kremlin and the Cubans. In later years, when Khrushchev faced a difficult decision regarding Cuba, he would have at his disposal a summary of key intelligence prepared by the KGB. In September 1959 nothing of the sort was available from his KGB chief, Aleksandr Shelepin—neither precise evidence of hostile U.S. intentions, nor a body of secret intelligence regarding Fidel Castro's true loyalties. Even more embarrassing to the KGB in the fall of 1959 was that it could not explain one of the central questions posed by those nervous about selling arms to the Cubans: why had Cuba's procurement priorities, and by extension its policy toward the Warsaw Pact, shifted since Che's summer trip?

In general, the Soviet leadership knew very little about Castro's Cuba. Ever since Fidel Castro marched triumphantly into Havana in January, the Kremlin had relied on the Cuban PSP for most of its political intelligence on Cuba. Admittedly, some information was also coming from the KGB station, called the *residentura*, in Mexico City and from Czech intelligence, which of all the socialist bloc intelligence services had the most lines into Cuba in 1959. But these intelligence sources were not very good. The Soviets needed to establish contact at the very highest level in Cuba. In February 1959 Soviet intelligence tapped an experienced officer who had already displayed great ingenuity in insinuating himself into the confidence of the political elite of Argentina and Brazil.

Aleksandr Alekseev was born Aleksandr Shitov in Russia's western Komstromskoi Oblast in 1913. He wore thick glasses and had a long, big-boned body that tapered off in a slight stoop. The young Shitov studied French and Spanish at Moscow State University before joining the Soviet intelligence service. In 1941 he adopted the work name of Alekseev to be able to remain in Moscow as a secret intelligence agent in the event the Nazis captured the capital. When Hitler's advance was halted in the suburbs of Moscow, Soviet intelligence sent Alekseev to work at the *residentura* in Teheran, Iran. After two years there, he was posted to Allied-liberated North Africa. Trained to re-

cruit Frenchmen, he followed his agents to France when that country was lib-
erated in 1944 and Moscow was able to reopen its embassy in Paris. Alekseev's
work in France established him as a star in the Soviet intelligence service. He
remained there until 1951, when he was brought back to headquarters. He returned to the field three years later to recruit agents and cultivate pro-Soviet
politicians in Latin America. His base was Buenos Aires, but his activities
spanned the entire continent.[16]

As some in the Kremlin sensed the opportunity for an expansion of Soviet
influence in Latin America, Alekseev was recalled from Argentina in 1958 to
work in the Commission of Cultural Affairs in the Central Committee, where
he could put his expertise and knowledge of Latin American personalities to
work in devising propaganda operations. It was from this position that the
KGB assigned him "the special mission" of going to Havana to establish contact with the top levels of the Cuban leadership.[17] Alekseev had been among
the first to argue that there was something unusual about the Cuban revolution. It did not fit the pattern of the typical Latin American coup. Neither the
military nor the local U.S. representative seemed to have taken control of the
new government. In January 1959 Alekseev asked to be sent to Cuba as a Soviet observer. His superiors in the KGB agreed to do so, but it took over seven
months for the Cubans to grant him a visa.

Raúl Castro and Che Guevara were wary of drawing Washington's attention
to the strength of the radical left in the July 26 movement. This is why the Cubans had used back channels and shell corporations to acquire assistance from
the Eastern bloc in the first months of power. When Raúl requested assistance
from the Kremlin, he wanted Spanish nationals to be sent in part so as to confuse the U.S. government. Consequently, despite the sympathy between the
key leaders of the Cuban revolution and the Soviet Union, there was no rush
to bring Soviets to the island. Alekseev, indeed, would be the first Russian citizen to get a visa to Castro's Cuba.

Alekseev finally arrived in Havana on October 1, 1959. At the airport he was
met by Carlos Rafael Rodríguez, the editor of the communist newspaper, *La
Noticias de Hoy*. Rodríguez was an important figure in the revolution. A symbol of cooperation between the July 26 movement and the communists, he
had gone into the mountains in the summer of 1958 to serve as an adviser to
Fidel Castro. Alekseev, however, was wary of Rodríguez and the leadership of
the PSP, the Cuban communist party. He felt they exaggerated their control
over the Cuban revolution. As expected, Rodríguez wasted no time in bragging about his role in shaping the radical agricultural reforms enacted in the
spring. But even Rodríguez did not describe Fidel Castro as a communist. His
brother and Che were "thoroughly of the left," but Fidel was his own man,
though his sentiments lay with the communists. Alekseev suspected as much.
But was there any truth to the rumor that Raúl had violent thoughts about his
brother in the spring? No evidence—just tension between them. When
Rodríguez tried to introduce Alekseev around to all of the major communist

players, the Soviet resisted. He had worked with many pro-Soviets who were noncommunists and knew that one need not be a communist to assist the USSR. In Moscow what had struck him most about the Cuban revolution was that it was clearly anti-American. This, above all, he recalled, was what Moscow wanted to be sure of. In this early period of Soviet-Castro relations, the communist issue was secondary.[18]

Alekseev spent a lot of time walking around Havana. He was sure that no one knew that a Soviet citizen was on the island, and he hoped to maintain this secret. So like Woody Allen's Zelig, Alekseev appeared everywhere and nowhere at the same time. Castro was in the habit of giving a lot of public speeches. Alekseev attended as many as possible. He sat in cafés and read as many Cuban newspapers as he could find. They all seemed to be strongly anti-Soviet, though many combined that stance with a disdain for American imperialism. "I could not understand," Alekseev later remembered, "what kind of revolution this was, where it was going." Alekseev could figure this out only by meeting Fidel Castro, not Rodríguez or Blas Roca of the PSP. And although Raúl Castro had already worked with Soviet emissaries, Alekseev did not feel the need to go to him either. Careful to build a broad base of support among the revolutionaries, he approached Fidel Castro first through Che Guevara, a true revolutionary whom Moscow understood to be almost as popular with the Cuban people as Fidel was. With the help of a Cuban broadcast journalist, who had visited Moscow with a Cuban press delegation the previous summer, Alekseev got his break and was told Che would see him on October 12.

Che explained to Alekseev that socialism was Cuba's only hope for attaining sovereignty. "There is no other road [to independence] but the construction of a socialist society and friendship with the socialist camp." As he had told Soviet diplomats during his long sojourn in Eurasia, however, Che said that Cuba could defend itself. He admitted that this was his personal opinion. There were other friends of the USSR in the revolutionary leadership, presumably Raúl, who were not so sure.

The meeting almost got off on the wrong foot. Alekseev had bought some packets of Cuban cigarettes to present to the asthmatic Che. Guevara was a smoker; but the Soviet had failed to notice that the brand name of the cigarettes was Texas. "He looked at them . . . began to shiver and looked me in the eye. 'Do you know what this Texas is? It was a republic in the Americas that the North Americans chopped off.' " After this moment of awkwardness, the rest of the meeting went well. "In a word," Alekseev later said of the meeting, "it was the kind of conversation that like-minded individuals have." He "now knew what was what." So did Che. The meeting lasted until five in the morning. Che then arranged to have the Soviet representative meet with Fidel Castro. The doorbell of Alekseev's hotel room rang at 2 A.M. on October 16. A man said, "Señor Alekseev? You asked for a meeting with Comandante Fidel Castro? He will receive you. Are you ready to go to him now?" Alekseev recalled, "I dressed as follows: in a dark suit, a gray tie, in a word as I would for a meeting with a prime minister."

Alekseev realized his sartorial mistake when two bearded men wearing leather jackets and carrying machine guns came into his room to take him to their leader. As he and the phalanx swept out of the hotel room, he was careful to take along the gifts he had brought from Russia—caviar, vodka, and an album of Russian music.

The leather-jacketed men led Alekseev to a government building, whose lights burned alone in the dark Havana night. It was the headquarters of INRA, the National Institute of Agrarian Reform, considered by Cuban communists to be the symbolic heart and "bastion" of the coming socialist revolution.[19] Alekseev was hustled into an elevator and told nothing. Two bearded and well-armed men faced Alekseev when the elevator opened on the eighteenth floor and his security detail spilled out. One was Fidel Castro and the other his assistant, the executive director of INRA, Antonio Núñez Jiménez.

"If Karl Marx could rise from the grave, he would be very glad that I was armed," Castro said, wasting no time in explaining why he had disagreed with the PSP's bureaucrats in the 1950s. The only way to make revolution was to make war. Castro characterized his revolution as a poor people's rebellion that would build a society where men would no longer exploit one another.[20]

Despite these opening words, Castro wanted to keep things light. He looked mischievously at the gifts Alekseev had brought. Admiring the vodka, he called out to his secretary, "Conchita, get some biscuits!" They opened the bottle and clinked glasses. Glancing at the clothes worn by Alekseev, Castro teased him: "Alexandro, how old is your revolution?" When Alekseev reminded him of the date 1917, Castro added, "So, then in forty-two years we will also be as bourgeois." From that moment on, Alekseev never bothered to wear a tie in Cuba.[21]

They tasted the caviar. Castro was pleased with it. "This is so tasty. . . . Jiménez, you know, we must reestablish trade relations with the Soviet Union." The only Soviet product that encountered Fidel's legendary disdain was the Herzegovina Flora cigarettes that Alekseev described as having been Stalin's favorites. Not familiar with the Russian style *papirosi*, which were hollow tubes with a knuckle's length of tobacco at the end, Castro grimaced after a few puffs: "There is too much cardboard and not enough tobacco." Dismissing Alekseev's explanation that by extending the lighted tip, the *papirosi* protected beards from catching fire, Castro shoved a Cuban cigar in his face: "Here, this is what Churchill smoked!" Though he learned to work without a tie, Alekseev never learned to like cigars.[22]

The conversation eventually took a more serious turn. During a discussion of Cuban-Soviet diplomatic relations, which Batista had broken three years before, Castro said that public opinion was still not ready for an exchange of ambassadors between Cuba and the Soviet Union. "You know what Lenin said," Castro interjected, misquoting one of Alekseev's heroes, "in order to bring any kind of idea to life, you have to fling it to the masses." Sounding more like a cynical Madison Avenue type than Lenin, Castro continued, "You suggest a slogan to the masses, and the masses should become possessed of it." He proceeded to give an example: "So now we will spread the slogan 'Friendship with the Soviet Union!' and when the public begins to feel that this is necessary, we will reestablish relations."[23]

Fidel Castro was eager that the Soviet cultural and technological exhibition that Moscow had sent around the world in 1959 come to Cuba. The show had opened in New York earlier in the year and was now about to close in Mexico. Proud of this exhibition, the Kremlin had sent one of the senior members of the Presidium, Anastas Mikoyan, to launch it at each stop along the way. "Why don't you go to Mexico," Castro suggested, "to arrange with Mikoyan that he come to Havana to open this exhibition." Alekseev tried to explain, without success, that the exhibition was supposed to go to Ceylon (now called Sri Lanka) next and could not easily take a detour. Castro was unimpressed: "Are you or are you not revolutionaries?" It was a question that would grow to encompass all of the main tensions in the Soviet-Cuban leadership; but at this point it was merely a taunt to provoke the staid Alekseev to be a little more creative than his training usually allowed.

Alekseev was not reticent about discussing the assistance that Moscow could provide if Fidel asked for it. As an example, Alekseev described the relationship the Soviet Union had developed with Arturo Frondizi, when he was in the opposition in Argentina. "If I become president and if you make me a promise of assistance," the Argentine leader told Alekseev during one of their long conversations, "we could change a lot." When Frondizi moved into the presidential palace in 1958, Alekseev went to Moscow and secured a U.S. $100 million credit for the Argentine leader. Castro respectfully declined to be compared to Frondizi or Nasser: "No, all of that would be difficult. Why be such a burden to you? For Nasser it made sense. First of all, American imperialism was far from him, and you are next door to Egypt. But us? We are so far and hardly can do it. No weapons. We do not ask for any."[24]

Che Guevara had been just what Alekseev hoped he would be. But how to explain Fidel Castro? Here was this revolutionary who still hung crucifixes and pictures of the Virgin Mary on the walls of his office. Even as he was pushing Alekseev to go to Mexico in order to arrange a state visit by Anastas Mikoyan, Castro cried out, "Don't worry, don't worry. All that needs to be done will be done. It is the Madonna who is sending you."

While Castro and Alekseev were about to toast the possibilities of Soviet-Cuban friendship with a Russian feast, it was just another night of Cuban black beans and imported beef for the local representatives of the U.S. intelligence community. The CIA's station in Havana was unaware of Alekseev's activities. The station chief, James Noel, was a veteran of Wild Bill Donovan's Office of Strategic Services (OSS). Having served in the counterintelligence (X-2) branch of OSS in Spain in 1944–45, Noel was well acquainted with the problems of tracking secret agents. X-2, however, had operated with the help of deciphered German intelligence messages. Each time the Abwehr, the intelligence unit of the German Military High Command, radioed that it had moved one of its agents into a new town, X-2 plotted the spy's movement like a pawn in a game of Internet chess. Twenty years later, nothing like those ultra-secret intercepts existed to assist Noel in placing KGB men in their proper squares or even identifying them. Aleksandr Alekseev had arrived in Havana and met with Guevara and Castro without the veteran counterspy Noel's being any the wiser.

The State Department did not feel especially well served by Noel's group. In mid-October the department's intelligence component, the Bureau of Intelligence and Research (INR), sent its own man to find out what was going on in Cuba. Carlos Hall arrived in Havana on October 18 on a "vacation." None of the leaders of the U.S. Chamber of Commerce in Havana or the Cuban business community believed that this State Department official's decision to spend his hard-earned vacation in unstable Cuba was a mere coincidence. Hall was the chief of INR's Latin American division. In the Eisen-hower period the State Department acted as the quarterback for foreign policy; and the new secretary of state, Christian Herter, was not satisfied with the amount of information he was getting on Fidel Castro's intentions. Hall's visit was part of an effort to collect better information.

Hall received a warm greeting from members of the American expatriate and pro-American sectors of Cuban society. Unlike Alekseev, though, he was not able to pierce the secrecy surrounding Fidel. He spent three weeks in Cuba and never turned up evidence that a Soviet official was shuttling from office to office discussing the establishment of commercial and diplomatic relations between Moscow and Havana. Alekseev's secret was safe.

As the fall of 1959 wore on, the meetings with Alekseev, the general development of Castro's authority, and the weakness of the opposition at home or in the United States fed a growing sense of confidence among the left wing in the Cuban revolution. Che, who had cautioned the Soviets in the summer about "a gradual rapprochement" with the East, now recovered the confidence that he and Raúl had in April 1959. After his return from abroad, Che had quickly regained his former position as chief liaison between Fidel Castro and the leadership of the PSP.[25] He was also rewarded with a high-profile job as chief of industrial planning at INRA. "What a shiteater you are!" Guevara yelled at a moderate colleague in the government who suggested that U.S. reactions should shape the pace of social reform. "So, you are one of those who think that we can make a revolution behind the back of the Americans. . . . We must make the revolution in a struggle to the death against imperialism from the first moment."[26]

Che's confidence reflected a subtle change in Fidel Castro's handling of the communist question. The night following his meeting with Alekseev, the so-called Maximum Leader finally revealed to the Cuban people the significant role that his brother Raúl was playing in the Cuban regime. The Cuban cabinet, on his instructions, announced the dissolution of the Ministry of National Defense and its replacement by the Ministry of the Revolutionary Armed Forces. Raúl, who had been the de facto chief of the military wing of Castro's July 26 movement, was named head of the new ministry. Fidel put the Rebel Army, Air Force, Revolutionary Navy, and Revolutionary National Police under Raúl. In September the Cuban leader had abolished the secret police and put all intelligence and security services under his brother. Now Raúl officially had the military under his command as well. There was no longer any question who was second in command, and it was increasingly clear which direction the Cuban revolution intended to take.[27]

Mikoyan and Castro

The reason Castro desired Anastas Mikoyan's visit was that it would put a fine point on these positive developments for the supporters of the socialist way in Cuba. Soon the revolutionary tendencies of Fidel and his closest associates could be expressed publicly as part of an embrace of the Soviet Union.

Mikoyan was Khrushchev's favorite personal emissary. The sixty-five-year-old Armenian, who had fought in the Russian revolution, was the greatest survivor of Soviet history. In the chaos of the 1920s, when the great powers fought for control of his native Caucasus, he built up local communist parties and eluded capture by Mensheviks, White Russians, Germans, Turks, and the British. Then, in the dangerous years of the Great Purges in the 1930s, he joined Stalin's ruling circle and escaped the fate of so many of the old Bolsheviks. Finally, having outlasted Stalin's paranoia, he was left on the Presidium by Khrushchev.

KGB observers of the domestic scene suspected that Khrushchev and Mikoyan never quite trusted each other. Mikoyan's survival during the Stalin years owed much to his ability to speak to Stalin "from Caucasian to Caucasian." In return, Stalin required his trusted lieutenants to dip their pens in the blood of his enemies. The order consigning twenty thousand Polish army officers to death in the Katyn forest in 1940 bears Mikoyan's signature.[28]

Mikoyan, the consummate survivor, was a force to be reckoned with. He and Khrushchev differed at times on the appropriate policy toward the United States. Preferring a more cautious policy, Mikoyan was one of those who would have preferred avoiding risks that might bring the two superpowers closer to war. Although he became a great proponent of the Cuban gambit in the Presidium, Mikoyan consistently looked over his shoulder to gauge the possible reaction of the United States while he was calibrating his support for Castro.

Mikoyan was the first member of the Soviet leadership to receive extensive reports on the situation in Cuba. While presiding over the Soviet exhibition in Mexico City, Mikoyan met with Alekseev in November 1959. Previously,

Alekseev had not sent any messages to Moscow on his first month in Cuba, because the KGB, assuming that he would somehow manage to send anything important through the station in Mexico City, had not provided him with a secure means of communication. Alekseev timed his first trip to Mexico City to be able to provide the Presidium member with a fresh report on the situation in revolutionary Cuba.

Mikoyan was pleased by what Alekseev told him. The KGB officer was accustomed to doing more than providing political intelligence. Despite the often debilitating climate of deference prevailing in Soviet bureaucracies, Alekseev was self-confident enough to offer the Soviet leadership suggestions on how it might interact with its Latin American sympathizers. As he had in his meeting with Castro, Alekseev suggested Argentina as a model for some of the economic assistance that might be sent to Cuba.

Mikoyan subsequently incorporated these suggestions in a report to Moscow that laid out the basis for a new relationship with revolutionary Cuba. First, the Kremlin should sign a sugar deal with Castro that allowed for the purchase of 500,000–600,000 tons of sugar every year for the next five years. He recommended a barter agreement, whereby Moscow purchased a quantity of Cuban sugar equal in value to the amount of Soviet goods sent to Cuba. Second, once it was clear what Soviet equipment the Cubans wanted, they should be offered the same favorable terms available to Frondizi's Argentina. Finally, the Soviet Union should continue to refrain from sending weapons directly to Castro. Anticipating that the Cubans might ask to purchase fifteen Soviet jet fighters via Czechoslovakia to compensate for the recent U.S. decision to prevent Britain from selling jets to Cuba, Mikoyan "suggested that no answer be given at the moment." He wanted Khrushchev to think twice before doing this, and in the meantime it was enough to tell the Cubans that the matter was being studied.[29]

Fidel Castro's difficulties in persuading the British government to let the Cuban government trade Sea Fury aircraft for Hunter jets was just one of many indications that his open endorsement of Raúl in mid-October would have grave costs. Days after the announcement of Raúl's promotion, Comandante Húber Matos, the military chief of Camagüey Province, told Fidel that he would have to resign his position. He could not stay in an army that was coming under communist control. Matos was not a holdover from the Batista years. A man of the political center and the middle class, Matos had flown weapons to Castro from Costa Rica in 1958 before himself joining the rebels in the mountains. In a letter to Castro tinged with regret and enduring respect for the Cuban leader, Matos confessed that resignation was the only honorable course. "I did not want to become an obstacle to revolution."[30]

Castro reacted bitterly. "If anyone has been disloyal, it has been you," he told Matos.[31] Intending to make an example of the principled Matos, Castro had his former ally arrested and sentenced to twenty years in prison. Matos was the second high-level military officer to resign from the Rebel Army over the issue of Raúl Castro's control. The commander of the Cuban Rebel Air Force, Pedro Luis Díaz Lanz had fled to the United States in June 1959, bringing to the U.S. Congress the first inside information on Raúl Castro's recruitment of Spanish communists for political indoctrination of the army.[32] A few days after Matos resigned, Díaz had reappeared as a problem for Fidel. A private aircraft belonging to the Cuban opposition dropped leaflets over Havana bearing Díaz's name. The leaflets excoriated Fidel for belonging to a cabal that planned to deceive the Cuban people and introduce a "system like that in Russia."[33] In the Fidelista maelstrom that followed, Húber Matos caught the full force of Castro's injured pride.

Moscow viewed these events with some anxiety. Opposition to Castro's apparent embrace of the communist wing of the July 26 movement appeared in the Havana press in early November in the form of printed rumors of a possible Mikoyan visit to Cuba.[34] A Soviet source in the Mexican government handed over a copy of the Mexican ambassador to Cuba's dispatch on the press speculation. The ambassador advised the Mexican government that "it was his opinion, and the opinion of several diplomatic observers, that this visit would not bring any positive results."[35] The head of the KGB, Aleksandr Shelepin, forwarded the report to Foreign Minister Andrei Gromyko and stressed that "according to his [the Mexican ambassador's] data, there are opposition groups in the country and because the Cuban government does not exercise enough control, he is afraid for the personal security of Mikoyan."[36]

In addition to expressing concern for Mikoyan's personal safety, Soviet intelligence reports advanced a second argument against going ahead with the visit. The United States might use Mikoyan's trip from Mexico to Cuba as an excuse to increase its pressure on Mexico to break its friendly relations with Cuba. A source close to the president of Mexico, Adolfo López Mateos, reported in mid-November that the president himself had recently complained about Washington's efforts to force on him a new policy toward Cuba. The United States had singled out Mexico for criticism at the most recent meeting of the Organization of American States and was holding López Mateos responsible for the visit to Havana by Mexico's former president Lázaro Cárdenas.[37]

However, it was not until Fidel Castro himself got cold feet that Moscow decided to postpone Mikoyan's visit. On November 28, 1959, the largest crowd to date of the Castro era, over a million people, stood in a cold rain to hear Pope John XXIII speak to the Cuban people over Vatican radio. A torchlight parade and a pontifical mass opened a two-day National Catholic Congress. Clerics and parishioners from every part of the island streamed into Havana for this celebration of Christianity. The U.S. embassy concluded that Cuba's Catholics "certainly marshalled their forces and put on an impressive demonstration of religious devotion."[38] Fidel Castro, whose own piety was vestigial, felt obliged to participate, though this congress represented a challenge to his authority. As he and the archbishop of Havana, Pérez Serantes, acknowledged cheers from the crowd, Castro had to reconsider how best to push the revolution forward.

This display of the power of the Catholic Church momentarily restrained Castro's open drive toward socialism. In a televised address in December, he told the Cuban people, "[O]ur Revolution is in no way against religious sentiment . . . our Revolution aspires to strengthen the noble desires and ideas of men. . . . When Christ's preachings are practiced, it will be possible to say that a revolution is occurring in the world."[39] An element of this new caution was a return to the earlier Cuban policy of delaying a public rapprochement with the communist world.

"It's all bad," Castro confided in Alekseev, whom he had summoned to discuss how the national congress affected his plans.[40] Castro was reminded of the work that still needed to be done to indoctrinate the Cuban laity. With the congress drawing larger crowds to hear priests denounce his movement as a tool of international communism than had ever gathered to hear him, Castro could not very well embrace Anastas Mikoyan. If the Kremlin's representative came now, it would focus attention on Cuba's desire to establish extensive relations with the Soviet Union. "Go back to Mexico and tell Mikoyan," Castro implored Alekseev.

Castro biographers have argued that he felt he had to sell himself to the Soviets.[41] This assertion rests on the assumption that relations between the PSP and Fidel Castro were strained and that Moscow absorbed the prejudices of Blas Roca and Carlos Rodríguez. The opening of KGB and Presidium documents explodes this theory. In the fall of 1959 the Soviets were ready to do more for Castro than Castro felt it prudent to accept, given his domestic struggle for legitimacy.

"What children they are!" Mikoyan screamed at Alekseev when he heard about Castro's misgivings.[42] Even Mikoyan could not understand this level of caution. He did not know enough about the dynamics of Cuban society to respect Castro's concerns. Moreover, it had been a long time since a Bolshevik had to worry about opposition from the Russian Orthodox Church. With his mind unwilling to explore the domestic reasons for Castro's apparent volteface, Mikoyan decided that fear of the United States was the real reason that Castro withdrew his invitation. But Mikoyan did not share this fear. "How could my opening an exhibition bother the enemy?" he asked Alekseev in Mexico City.

Only a few days before the National Catholic Congress forced a postponement, Gromyko had discussed the prospective Mikoyan visit with members of the Presidium. Mikoyan's cabled suggestions for the agenda in Havana seemed sensible to him, and the Soviet foreign minister had recommended that a blanket approval be sent back to Mexico.[43] But there was little Gromyko, Mikoyan, or Khrushchev could do if the mercurial Fidel Castro himself was having second thoughts. Mikoyan would have to return to Moscow and wait—patience being a talent that had served him well in the Stalin period.[44]

La Coubre

Salami Tactics

The year 1960 opened with a series of developments foreshadowing a dramatic breakthrough for the Soviets in Cuba. Che Guevara's military aide Major Emilio Aragonés traveled to Mexico City to report to the Soviet Embassy there, the most important in Latin America, on the steps that the communists around Fidel Castro were planning in order to acquire control of the revolution.[1] Aragonés predicted a purge of the noncommunist wing of the July 26 movement, as personified by the director of the movement (and acting director of the Ministry of Foreign Affairs), Marcelo Fernández, and Comandante Faustino Pérez. Fernández and Pérez had represented the moderate Llano tendency in the Sierra Maestra. It was Pérez who brought Herbert Matthews of the *New York Times* to give foreign legitimacy to the Fidelistas in 1957 when most of the world thought that Castro was dead. The young Aragonés explained that the left within the July 26 movement considered men like Fernández and Pérez impediments to the radicalization of Cuban society and wanted them out.

Explaining that Fidel Castro would be a full participant in the coming socialist revolution, Aragonés told the Soviets to expect in short order the establishment of a new political party, called the Revolutionary Union, which would unite all leftist elements of the revolutionary movement under Castro's leadership. In the meantime, the Cuban leader intended to implement a radical agrarian reform designed to "debourgeoisize" the countryside, nationalize all banks, and pull together industry into "manufacturing-production centers." Just as INRA and "manufacturing-production centers" would be at the heart of the new command economy, so would they provide the basis for a new Cuban political system. Future Cuban parliaments would consist only of representatives of state farms and state industries.[2]

In the course of the month, some of the ambitious predictions of the communist revolutionaries came true with astonishing speed. Jesús Soto, a disciple of Raúl Castro, took control of the Cuban labor movement.[3] The former leader David Salvador was a powerful anticommunist who had outlasted his usefulness. Meanwhile, in the July 26 movement itself, there was a major change of personnel. Fidel Castro removed Marcelo Fernández from the directorship of the movement, and the Soviet embassy in Mexico City described Fernández's replacement as being "closely linked to Friends [Cuban communists]."[4] Fernández was also about to be fired from the Cuban foreign ministry.

Moscow's representatives concluded that Fidel Castro's relationship with the PSP was "improving" and that "his position regarding imperialism [was] becoming stronger every day."[5] Through Carlos Rafael Rodríguez he passed word to the Soviets that if done "very carefully" a dramatic shift in Cuban foreign policy could be carried off. The problem, as Castro saw it, was the general opposition in Cuban society to an alliance with the Soviet Union. But he was prepared to test the waters by formalizing relations with the Czechs. If that went without incident, it would then be Moscow's turn.

Moscow had a right to feel that these encouraging signs were partly the product of two dramatic initiatives taken since Castro's initial postponement of the Mikoyan visit. In mid-December, Moscow had ordered the KGB officer serving as assistant director of the Soviet exhibition in Mexico City to go immediately to Alekseev in Havana with explosive information for the Cuban leader.[6] Having just learned from Polish and Czech sources of a plot against Fidel's government, the Kremlin instructed Alekseev to convey this warning "in a very confidential manner" to Castro.[7] If this incident, which turned out to be a false alarm, was not enough proof for Castro that Khrushchev cared, further evidence came in the form of the Kremlin's decision a month later to approve a covert operation devised in Prague for secretly delivering Czech rifles to Cuba.[8]

By the end of January, Castro announced he was prepared to reinvite Anastas Mikoyan to visit Cuba and bring the Soviet trade and cultural exhibition with him. It seemed the Kremlin's confidence and that of the pro-Soviet lobby in Havana was not misplaced.

Mikoyan Finally in Havana

Since concerns over Mikoyan's personal security had been an issue in the decision to postpone the trip in the first place, the Central Committee ordered the KGB to send one of its men from Mexico to coordinate security with the Cuban security services. Raúl Castro oversaw the Cuban end of the arrangements. He met with the KGB officer from Mexico and introduced him to Ramiro Valdés, whom Raúl had chosen to coordinate all of the arrangements in Cuba. Valdés headed the joint Cuban intelligence and counterintelligence service in the Ministry of the Interior.[9]

The Cubans assigned to Mikoyan a two-story house, which would be guarded around the clock by five people from the personal bodyguard of the Castro brothers. The rest of the Soviet delegation would stay in the Hotel Camadora, which was a five-minute drive from Mikoyan's residence. Mikoyan would have at his disposal two cars and a driver from Cuban intelligence. Valdés would chose all staff serving the Soviet delegation upon the recommendation of the leadership of the Cuban communist party. Finally, Raúl Castro gave his assent for the unimpeded use of the radio on the Soviet plane, to maintain communications with Moscow throughout Mikoyan's stay.[10]

Mikoyan, who had returned to Moscow in late 1959, prepared himself for the trip to Cuba by recalling from Mexico a young KGB officer who had known the Castro brothers longer than anyone else in Soviet intelligence.

"Is it true that you are familiar with the Castro brothers?" Mikoyan asked Nikolai Leonov in his characteristically poor Russian. Mikoyan spoke the language of Pushkin with especially awful diction, making Khrushchev's verbal crudities seem eloquent by contrast.

Yes, of course. I have known Raúl since 1953, before the assault on the Moncada barracks, and Fidel I met in Mexico in 1956, not long before he launched the "Granma" expedition.
Yes, yes . . . and how do you intend to prove that you know them?[11]

The wiry and quick-witted Leonov had met Raúl during a cruise from Genoa to Latin America. Both had been attending a socialist youth conference in Prague. Raúl was on his way home to Cuba; Leonov was en route to a Spanish-language program in Mexico. To this day Leonov avers that he was going to Mexico as an ordinary student. His days in Soviet intelligence, he argues, began only in 1958 when he was recruited into the KGB because of his unusual knowledge of Latin America.[12]

Leonov and Raúl became fast friends in 1953, spending a lot of time together on the ship. Leonov brought along a camera, which Raúl and he used to photograph each other. At the end of his description of his time with Raúl, Leonov mentioned that he had kept the negatives of these schoolboy photographs. Mikoyan ordered the pictures to be produced so that he could see for himself that this KGB upstart was telling the truth. In short order an album of pictures of two skinny teenagers mugging in T-shirts on an Italian freighter landed on the desk of the vice premier of the Union of Soviet Socialist Republics.[13]

Leonov got the job as interpreter to Mikoyan on his trip to what was known in Moscow as the "Island of Freedom." Mikoyan made no bones about hoping to use Leonov to put the Cubans at ease, which he knew to be necessary if relations between the revolution and the Soviet Union were to be broadened.

On the Ilyushin 18 going over, Leonov noticed that Mikoyan had another, less proletarian objective. One could not fly nonstop from Moscow to Havana in 1959. There was much time to read as the plane made stops in Iceland and Canada. Throughout the trip Mikoyan struggled with a two-volume Russian edition of a novel by Ernest Hemingway. Mikoyan intended to alter the history of Soviet activities in Latin America. That was certainly important. But he also harbored a secret desire to meet the Nobel Prize–winning author, whom he knew to be living in Cuba. He could not meet Hemingway without having read at least one of his books.[14]

Fidel Castro personally greeted Mikoyan as he stepped from the reconverted Soviet bomber on February 4, 1960. Surrounding Fidel were representatives of the symbolic government, his ministers, and the real government, the *barbudos*, who in the words of Leonov formed an exalted caste, esteemed in Cuban society for having fought in the Sierra Maestra.

On the eve of Mikoyan's visit, Castro was buoyant. He reminded Alekseev that he disagreed with the Cuban communists who feared an imminent U.S. invasion. He doubted that Eisenhower would risk invading Cuba. "All U.S. attempts to intervene," he boasted, "are condemned to failure."[15] Moreover, he discounted any threat to his regime from domestic opponents. The only threat that mattered for Castro was economic strangulation. Cuba was both weak economically and dependent upon the U.S. economy. He said that U.S. economic sanctions would hurt the Cuban people.

Although Castro admitted that revolutionary Cuba had an Achilles' heel, he wanted the Soviets to know that he would never yield to U.S. imperialism. The KGB reported to the Soviet leadership that Castro suggested that in one or two years the United States could indeed destroy Cuban economy. "But never, even under mortal danger," cabled Alekseev to Moscow, "would Castro make a deal with American imperialism."[16] Castro hoped instead that, if need be, the Soviet Union would bail out his economy.

Thus Castro intended to use Mikoyan's visit to establish an economic safety net for Cuba. Castro told Alekseev at a private dinner on February 3 that what Cuba needed most from the USSR were oil exports and sugar imports. Che Guevara followed up on this discussion a few days later. Inviting Alekseev to his home, Guevara said that the Cuban government had reached the conclusion that it would have to request an enormous credit from Mikoyan during his visit. In November, Alekseev and Castro had bounced around the figure of U.S.$100 million. Now the Cubans were thinking of $500 million as an opening bid. As he always did in discussing nonlethal Soviet assistance, Guevara stressed that the Kremlin could announce this loan publicly. In his mind Soviet actions deterred the United States. "It is very important for Cuba," Guevara told Alekseev, "to feel independent of the U.S. and to demonstrate it."[17]

Mikoyan and Castro negotiated a package of trade credits in Fidel's hunting lodge at Laguna-del-Tesoro shortly before Mikoyan's departure for Moscow on February 13. The discussions went well, because both sides had made up their minds in the fall that Moscow should provide trade and financial assistance to

Cuba and that diplomatic relations should be resumed. Fidel charmed Mikoyan. This was the first time that the old Bolshevik had met a successful revolutionary outside of Russia or China. Within the closest circle of the Soviet delegation, Mikoyan came as close to letting down his hair as it was possible for a Soviet diplomat: "Yes, he is a genuine revolutionary. Completely like us. I felt as though I had returned to my childhood!"[18]

For all of this revolutionary bonding, the Soviets were not quite as generous as Castro had hoped. Mikoyan agreed only to the amount of trade credits that he had intended to offer in December 1959—$100 million—not the $500 million that the Cubans were hoping to receive. However, the Soviets undertook to buy five million tons of sugar over three years. The sugar deal was enough to satisfy the Cubans, although the price would be less than the world price and only 20 percent of it would be payable in convertible currency.[19]

For the United States the Mikoyan visit signified "a long step toward the breaking of the remaining links between the Government of Cuba and the American family of nations."[20] For many in the Eisenhower administration it symbolized the failure of Secretary of State Herter's efforts to tolerate Castro in the hope of either convincing him of American support for liberal reform or providing a pretext for opposition leaders inside and outside Cuba to bring him down.

Admiral Arleigh Burke, the chief of naval operations, was the harshest critic of the State Department's "policy of restraint." The "leather-lunged" Burke, who had a particular interest in Cuba because of the marines' Guantánamo base and the proximity of the strategically vital Panama Canal, spoke for the camp in the administration that already saw Castro as international communism's poster child. Their logic rested on a syllogism: Fidel is to Che Guevara, the notorious Argentine doctor and international soldier of communism who had defended the ill-fated Arbenz regime in Guatemala in 1954, as the moderate Naguib was to the tyrannical Gamal Abdel Nasser.[21] A Havana cartoon of Guevara as puppeteer said it all for Burke and his admirers. Burke also could not forget or excuse the fact that the Castro brothers had kidnapped American sailors and marines, men directly under his command, and held them hostage for nearly a month in 1958. At National Security Council meetings, Assistant Secretary of State Rubottom and Burke were each other's foil: every time Burke brought up rumors of communist influence in the Castro movement, Rubottom would play them down, citing a "lack of evidence."[22]

The Mikoyan visit provided Burke with an opening to begin a pressure campaign for action against Castro. "Cuba appears to be in the process of falling under the domination of International Communism," Burke wrote to the State Department in the weeks following news of Mikoyan's visit and the Soviet-Cuban commercial agreement. The time was right, he believed, to adopt a tougher course: "[P]ositive action to reverse the present trend should be initiated to the end that the communist threat is eliminated and a stable, friendly government established in Cuba." Despite Burke's warnings, President Eisenhower was still far from deciding which course of action to take regarding Cuba.[23]

The Pretext

The Cubans had turned to West Europeans as well as to the Poles and Czechs in search of military supplies in the fall of 1959. For a while it looked as if Great Britain might supply Cuba with high-performance military aircraft. In October, however, Washington made it a point of alliance loyalty that London adhere to a strict arms embargo. Fortunately for Havana, other NATO allies did not see the issue in the same way. Both the French and the Belgians continued to fill Cuban orders for weaponry.

On March 4, 1960, a Belgian arms shipment arrived in the Havana harbor on board the ship *La Coubre*. Contrary to standard procedure, which stipulated that ammunition cargoes be unloaded away from shore, tugs towed the French ship into the harbor, close to office buildings.[24] Ruby Hart Phillips, the *New York Times* correspondent, was coming to the end of a largely unproductive day. "Suddenly a terrible explosion shook the building," she wrote later. "We all rushed to the balcony and saw a huge column of smoke rising near the inner harbor." As the fire jumped across the ammunition containers in the hold, a series of explosions disturbed the normal tranquillity of a lazy Havana afternoon, killing more than one hundred people aboard *La Coubre* and along the shore.[25]

The following day, at the funeral for some of victims of the blast, Fidel Castro delivered a speech in which he compared the sabotage of *La Coubre* to the incident involving the *Maine* that gave rise to the Spanish-American War. Castro's historical sense was not quite as sharp as his political instincts. He said that the United States had staged the *Maine* incident in 1898 as a pretext to enter the war with Spain in order to acquire Cuba as a colony. Castro's point, regardless of its historical accuracy, was that the United States was again looking to provoke a war with Cuba. "We have reason to believe," Castro intoned, "that this was a premeditated attempt to deprive us of the possibility to get weapons." Directing himself to Washington, he proclaimed that the Cuban people would not be intimidated by the threat of intervention and "annihilation under the clouds of nuclear explosions." "Cuba will never be intimidated," he declared; "she will never retreat . . . Patria O Muerte!"

"We saw the face of Fidel," recalled his old friend Carlos Franqui. Sadness and anger contorted Castro's face as he led mourners to the cemetery.[26] Behind that livid grimace, Fidel was coolly revising his tactics. For over a year he had piloted an unwieldy coalition in a leftward direction. Constantly aware of the winds, like a good mariner, he had tried to avoid storms. He believed that U.S. interference was inevitable, like the gales on the Atlantic; and for a while he feared that his grip on the helm was not good enough to ensure that he and the ship would make it through any storm. Certain in the wake of *La Coubre*, that the ordeal could no longer be postponed, Castro prepared to enter the storm. All he needed to know was that he would not be alone. What had seemed to Khrushchev and the KGB as Fidel's "period of vacillation" had come to an end.

The day after the funeral the director of INRA, Antonio Núñez Jiménez, invited Alekseev to lunch at his apartment in Havana. There would be only four at the table. As Alekseev entered, he was greeted by Fidel and Raúl Castro. Fidel wasted little time in getting to the reason for the impromptu lunch. "Under the present circumstances," he explained, "any friendly gesture of the Soviet government toward Cuba our people would accept with gratitude."[27]

Castro could not get *La Coubre* out of his mind. "I am absolutely certain that the United States blew up the ship." While admitting there was "no juridical proof," no smoking gun, he was convinced that the United States, which had been twisting the arms of its allies not to supply him with weapons, sabotaged the ship to send a message. Some time ago, a Colonel Sánchez, the U.S. military attaché in Havana, had been observed telling the Belgians not to go through with the shipment.

"The Americans are deciding on extreme measures," Fidel Castro told Alekseev. The Cuban leader expected the Eisenhower administration to respond swiftly and forcefully to his public accusation of U.S. responsibility for sabotaging *La Coubre*. "The USA will take the following steps," Castro predicted:

1. The implementation of terrorist acts against him or his closest associates.
2. A break in diplomatic relations.
3. The introduction of economic sanctions.
4. An overt attack. In order to justify this, the Americans will arrange an explosion in their consulate or on one of the American steamers or the murder in Havana of American citizens so as to able to blame these acts on the Cubans.

Fidel Castro was mentally prepared to confront the Colossus of the North. He outlined for Alekseev a series of countermeasures that he had in his quiver. The *Coubre* incident had freed him to begin nationalizing all U.S. property, including the sugar enterprises. He would then shut off the fresh-water supply to the U.S. military base at Guantánamo, which depended on a filtration plant thirty miles outside the base, and mobilize the people's militia and the revolutionary army to meet the likely U.S. intervention. Finally, he planned to unleash his security services against all manifestations of the counterrevolution in Cuba. These traitors would be rooted out and get what they deserved. "The struggle will continue until the last drop of blood," the Cuban assured Alekseev.[28]

The day before *La Coubre* blew up, Che Guevara had visited Alekseev to ask whether the Soviet Union might be prepared to "offer assistance in the case of extreme circumstances."[29] At the luncheon, in front of Raúl, Fidel made the same request: "Could [Cuba] count upon the help of the USSR with supplies of goods and weapons in the case of a blockade or [U.S.] intervention?" This was the first time that any of the Cuban leaders had requested direct military assistance from Moscow. For two years the Cubans had wanted Eastern bloc assistance to come covertly so as to deceive the United States regarding the extent of the revolution's anti-Americanism. Now Castro wanted Moscow to consider overt assistance to deter an American intervention.

At this extraordinary lunch he told Alekseev that Cuba had many uninhabited bays that could be used by Soviet ships or submarines. "Write a telegram to Khrushchev," he suggested to Alekseev, "that such a situation is designed to disarm us. Let him give an order to supply small arms and ammunition on submarines. We have here very many caves and all are unoccupied. Thus can all that we need be unloaded." To prevent acts of U.S. sabotage, which he considered "inevitable," Castro recommended that Cuba be allowed to purchase rifles, ammunition and Soviet MiG-17 fighters in Czechoslovakia, transported in the ships of socialist countries.

A "comprehensive rather than a consecutive talker," Castro kept Alekseev at lunch for six hours.[30] Incensed by what he saw as Washington's evil machinations, he talked and talked and talked about the many areas—including, of course, weaponry—where Moscow could help him. Havana lacked economists with experience in building a socialist economy, and he hoped that the USSR could send him some. Most important for Alekseev was that Castro made plain that he now viewed the Soviet Union as a model for Cuba. Castro revealed that he was ready to visit the USSR, though it was too early to select the date. He wanted Khrushchev to know that he would spend fifteen days and that this trip would be combined with a visit to Beijing.

Before the meeting broke up for a late supper, Fidel Castro stressed that, besides himself, only three members of the Cuban leadership—Núñez Jiménez, Raúl, and Che—were to know about the extent of Cuban-Soviet cooperation. Any further discussions about this alliance would be done one-on-one with him or with members of that revolutionary trinity. The rest of Cuba would not yet know about the Soviet-Cuban embrace.

On subsequent days Fidel explained that he was convinced of two things: that socialization of Cuba had to proceed rapidly and that U.S. intervention was inevitable. Although he spoke in terms of a three-year transition to socialism, he did not expect the United States to wait for him to achieve this before attacking.

Fidel Castro's friend Núñez Jiménez would lead the second revolution. INRA, Núñez Jiménez's organization, was to become the government within the government. On March 15 Castro told Alekseev that INRA would accomplish a "step-by-step elimination of property." So as not to stir up too much opposition at one time, this process would have to be gradual. Nevertheless, Castro had firm objectives. INRA would soon control all the press in Cuba. "And in a few years, INRA will be the government." In June, Castro would send Núñez Jiménez on a tour of Eastern bloc capitals to acquire the financial and technical assistance required to build a communist society in Cuba.

The Superpowers React to *La Coubre*

Fidel Castro correctly predicted the way in which each of the superpowers would respond to him in the wake of his denunciation of the Eisenhower administration. The tectonic plates of Cold War geography were now shifting, with Cuba the fault line. The United States and the Soviet Union were preparing to take center stage in the socialist revolution in Cuba.

The explosions had caught the U.S. embassy in Havana off guard. The ambassador, Philip Bonsal, was in Washington receiving instructions, his absence designed to signal the Eisenhower administration's impatience with Fidel Castro. The American chargé d'affaires, Daniel Braddock, did not quite have matters in hand; at least in the weeks following Bonsal's departure, he seemed incapable of producing the comprehensive report on communist influence in Cuba that Washington repeatedly requested. By early March, Braddock had had enough. Ironically, on the day before the French ship blew up, he wrote a letter to the State Department saying that the embassy was ill equipped to mount such an exercise. "Not only does Washington appear to be better staffed to do the job," he wrote, "but it also has experts who are better qualified than any of us here to distinguish between manifestations of Communism and manifestations of nationalism."[31]

Braddock did not know that the Latin American specialists in Washington were just as divided on the question of "Whither Castro?" Furthermore, he, like the rest of the embassy staff, with the likely exception of the CIA chief of station, Jim Noel, was not supposed to know that the insistent requests for information were tied to an impending presidential decision on covert operations against Castro.

The CIA survey, begun in December 1959, had been completed, and an operational plan that flowed from it was ready for Eisenhower's signature. The new Cuban Task Force in the CIA's Directorate of Plans had sent men to Central America to find appropriate locations for camps and airfields where Cubans could be trained in sabotage, radio operations, and spying and then inserted into Cuba.[32]

Castro was prescient. Washington responded to his funeral oration as he had predicted. The Special Group, the high-level committee that oversaw covert operations in the Eisenhower era, met on March 15 to consider the CIA's draft plan for the overthrow of the Castro regime.[33] Since the beginning of the year, the CIA had established the rudiments of a "covert intelligence and action organization" in Cuba that could ultimately work on behalf of an exile group. A few airplanes and a secret airport were already set to resupply the Cuban group. Plans were on the boards to acquire a commercial air fleet for a much larger resupply capability. But what was needed most was an anti-Castro group to carry out the mission. The object of this covert operation was to replace Castro's government with one "more devoted to the true interests of the Cuban people and more acceptable to the US in such a manner as to avoid any appearance of US intervention." The CIA reported that a unified political opposition to Castro could be created within two months. And a paramilitary group could be trained within six to eight months. This group would be ready to rush to Cuba to assist the underground resistance once the counterrevolution started.[34]

"I know of no better plan for dealing with the situation," responded Eisenhower when Allen Dulles outlined the operation to him on March 17. According to Dulles it would take eight months to recruit and train the paramilitary force necessary to bring an exile organization into power. Worried that the Cubans or the Soviets would pick up on this operation, Eisenhower instructed the group, "Everyone must be prepared to swear that he has not heard of it." He wanted U.S. contacts with the Cuban groups kept to minimum, perhaps to as few as two or three Americans. The operation that the KGB and the Cubans had been anticipating since December was now U.S. policy.[35]

At the same time that Castro's public rhetoric forced a change in U.S. policy, Moscow saw Castro's private language as a strategic opening. Alekseev's report on the March 6 lunch reached the Soviet leadership. "I did not write this to Khrushchev," recalled Alekseev, "but it got to him."

The Soviet leadership pounced on Fidel's request for assistance. This was the first time the Cuban leader had himself requested more than economic assistance. The Presidium decided on March 15 that Khrushchev should send his first message to Castro. It would not be in writing: the KGB was told to have Alekseev deliver it orally.

The message began, "You should not have any doubt that our sympathy and fellow-feeling is on the side of the revolutionary government and that we will look upon events in Cuba with optimism."[36]

The Kremlin wanted two big ideas to be conveyed to its newest ally. The first was the general rhetorical embrace of the opening message; the second was more subtle. Moscow now disagreed with Castro's assessment that the United States was likely to attempt to prevent the achievement of socialism in Cuba. The KGB-induced scare of December 1959 had been a bust. Whatever the Poles and Czechs thought they saw was a fantasy. The Kremlin was convinced that the United States was preparing for a general détente with the Soviet Union and would ignore Cuba, if necessary, in order to maintain the momentum of good relations. "In spite of the difficulty and growing tension of the situation," the Kremlin informed Castro, "the USA is today content to restrict itself to measures designed to further the favorable development of international relations, and will under no circumstances cross the line to undertake an open intervention against Cuba."[37]

The upbeat tone of this message to Castro reflected Khrushchev's personal optimism regarding the future of relations with Washington. He had high hopes for the superpower summit that was planned for May 1960 in Paris, at which Eisenhower might meet some of his traditional objections to the allied presence in West Berlin.

To strengthen Castro's trust, in spite of Khrushchev's optimism, the Kremlin decided to give Castro a blank check to buy whatever he needed from the Czechs. "With regard to supplies of weapons," said the letter to Castro, "the Soviet government is prepared to render assistance in the supply and delivery of them from the Czechs . . . and, if necessary, then directly from the Soviet Union." Finally, to put a fine point on this letter, the Kremlin responded to Fidel's expressed interest in coming east by officially inviting him to visit the USSR.[38]

The March 12 message from Khrushchev delighted Fidel Castro. "Could you write down the Spanish translation for me?" Castro asked. The Cuban leader said he wanted to add this document to the collection of vital papers that he kept hidden away in the mountains. Moscow also found an even more personal way to please the Cuban leader. The payment of an honorarium was one of the traditional tools the Kremlin used to stroke foreign communists, leaders of national-liberation movements or "progressive cultural elites." These were paid in compensation for the right to publish articles or speeches by these individuals in the socialist bloc. The Central Committee decided to add Fidel to that list in early 1960; in March, Alekseev informed Castro. Alekseev described him as "visibly moved." Castro remarked when first told about this symbolic payment that though he had had his speeches published in Cuba and in other countries, this "was the first time he had been offered an honorarium."[39] He added with a smile, "If everything I say is published, . . . I will become a millionaire!" Initially the amounts were small; but Castro was at least paid in U.S. dollars. In June he received $385 from Alekseev for a piece published in Moscow.[40]

"You couldn't have chosen a better time," said Castro puckishly at receiving this first payment, "because I just borrowed 10 pesos from Guevara for cigarettes." Che could not help ribbing Castro about this money from Moscow. "The Kremlin is indeed all knowing," Che added in Alekseev's presence; "it knew exactly how to help him." Later Alekseev heard from Núñez Jiménez that Fidel was chronically short of money because "besides a small salary, he has no income at all."[41] Moscow certainly was not all knowing; but it did listen. In 1961 the honoraria got bigger. In February the Central Committee appropriated U.S.$8,000 to compensate Castro for another collection of his speeches.[42]

The bombing in the Havana harbor meant that Fidel Castro could indulge in even more anti-American rhetoric, but as he explained to Alekseev, "the time was not right for an official declaration of the resumption of diplomatic relations." At one point he had tried to hide his caution by blaming the delay in exchanging ambassadors with Moscow "exclusively on a technical reason," because "it required a formal decision of the government." As Alekseev well knew, however, Castro completely controlled his government.

What Castro did not control was Cuban public opinion. He knew that the public roared when he shook his fist at Washington. But he was also well aware of the limits on what he could say to his people about Moscow. Communism was not popular in Cuba. The PSP had barely 17,000 members, and its newspaper was not read by many more people. Despite the public role played by Carlos Rodríguez in its latter stages, the revolution had not brought a change in the relationship between the masses and the Cuban communists. It was the populist themes of the July 26 movement, and Fidel Castro's raw magnetism, that drew public support. Craving a sense of economic and political sovereignty, historically difficult because the powerful United States was nearby, the Cubans would not understand if Castro moved too quickly to establish a special relationship with the world's other superpower. Castro explained to Alekseev that an expansion of relations with the Soviet Union would have to proceed outside of public view until he could convince the Cuban people that it was a matter of national survival. As Alekseev reported to Khrushchev, Castro "wanted to be able to time the establishment of [formal diplomatic] relations with some kind of open hostile act against Cuba by the U.S."

The absence of a Soviet ambassador did not affect the pace of the rapprochement. The Cubans referred to Alekseev as "Coordinator Alekseev" and, though he now ran a KGB station with subordinates, did not treat him with much reserve. Castro confided in him that the current arrangements for communications between the Kremlin and the Cuban revolution were "more effective, since we are able to meet directly, bypassing the Ministry of Foreign Affairs and every rule of protocol." He hoped to keep this form of liaison "into the future."

As a result of the change in Castro's attitude, the Soviet government moved to facilitate arms sales from the Warsaw Pact countries to the Cubans. On March 29 the Presidium informed the Czech government that it looked "favorably upon giving military assistance to the Cuban government." Moscow suggested granting Havana a ten-year credit on favorable terms and offered Prague help in delivering these weapons.

The Czechs had barely begun negotiating the terms of this sale, when information reached the Kremlin that compelled Khrushchev to rethink his program of assistance. A KGB report on Cuban perceptions of the American threat arrived on April 20, and a day later the Kremlin decreed the necessity "to render urgent assistance to the Cuban government."[43] Castro had just submitted a shopping list of weapons, the first the Soviets had ever received directly from the Cubans.[44] The Presidium now said yes to everything that Cuba wanted: "captured German arms, Czech-made weapons and those of Polish design." But the most dramatic sign of a change in Khrushchev's attitude was that at this April meeting the Presidium decided that the Cubans should not have to pay anything for these weapons. In less than a month the Kremlin had become far more generous, though partly with others' funds: the Presidium wanted the Czechs to absorb 15–25 percent of the cost and the Poles 10–20 percent; "then the remaining portion the Soviet government will take upon itself."

Raúl Castro's Visit

In light of the Castro brothers' conviction that the United States would never accept the Soviet-Cuban embrace, Fidel decided to send his brother Raúl to the Kremlin to discuss defense cooperation. In early June, Alekseev reported that Raúl intended to visit Moscow after a stop in Prague to discuss the procurement of Czech weaponry. The Cuban intelligence chief, Ramiro Valdés, would accompany Raúl to Moscow "so that he could stay behind to undergo training and to discuss how to set up and run a security service."[45]

Alekseev assured Moscow that Fidel Castro supported his brother's initiative. Raúl told Alekseev that Fidel had already decided that during Raúl's absence Che Guevara would be appointed to take his place as chief of the Cuban military. Castro's communist advisers, however, were not happy to lose Raúl at this moment. Everyone expected some kind of major attack by the United States; it was merely a matter of when. Even the choice of Che Guevara, another secret member of the PSP, to head the Cuban military while Raúl was away did not alleviate their concerns. Blas Roca and the leaders of the PSP thought Fidel Castro too nonchalant in dealing with the United States. They wanted a contingency plan for the use of the militia and the Cuban army in the event of an attack. Thinking of the fate of Guatemala's president Arbenz, who was toppled by a U.S.-supported coup in 1954, the communists advocated a thoroughgoing purge of the Cuban army and air force, which might welcome an anticommunist intervention. Only Raúl, they believed, could bring this about. "The presence of Raúl Castro in Cuba is necessary," Blas Roca told Alekseev.

Fidel Castro and his closest advisers expected that of all their decisions the purchase of Soviet crude oil would lead to a showdown with the United States. It was May when the U.S. oil companies learned that they would have to refine Soviet crude oil. The Soviets had promised Havana to provide oil that was cheaper than the Venezuelan oil that the U.S. companies in Cuba had been refining for years.

Fidel Castro assumed that the U.S. companies would on their own, or because of pressure from Washington, reject the Cuban demand. Instead of an obstacle, he saw in this an opportunity; or at least, so he told the Soviets. He explained in a private meeting with Alekseev that the conflict with the oil companies would "provide a good pretext for nationalization when they refuse to refine Soviet oil."[46] If Fidel was concerned about the Eisenhower administration's reaction to his decision, he did not betray any sign of it to the Soviet Union's chief intelligence representative in Cuba. "Fidel Castro is very decisively against the oil companies," Alekseev reported, "and is satisfied with present situation, which allows him to present nationalization as an act of self-defense."[47]

The Cubans had correctly anticipated the reaction of ESSO, Texaco, and Shell, the main oil companies with refineries in Cuba, two of which were American. On May 31, representatives of these companies were told by the U.S. treasury secretary, Robert Anderson, that they would be supported by Washington if they refused to refine Soviet crude. "It would be in accordance with this government's policy toward Cuba," Anderson assured them. In return for shutting out Soviet oil, the companies were promised that the U.S. government would discourage other U.S. oil companies from entering the Cuban market and that, if the Cubans reacted by expropriating the companies' Cuban assets, the Eisenhower administration would pressure the Castro regime to provide "adequate, prompt and effective compensation."[48]

As the decision to challenge the oil companies loomed ahead, Castro began to worry that the United States might seek to punish Cuba militarily. In mid-June he sent another letter to Khrushchev, in which he requested additional military assistance. Khrushchev was prepared to do whatever he could to help. "The Cuban republic today leads the anti-imperialist struggle in Latin America," Khrushchev wrote to Castro on June 16. "In this serious struggle, the Cuban people can count on the sympathy and the support of the Soviet people."[49] When Castro's assistant Antonio Núñez Jiménez reached Moscow later that week, he was told that Cuba could count on receiving 100,000 more rifles than Fidel had requested and an unexpected shipment of tanks.

Despite Moscow's reaction, doubts continued to gnaw at Fidel. While Núñez Jiménez was in Moscow, Fidel decided to cancel his brother's trip to the Soviet Union. Alekseev was called in to hear Fidel explain why he did not think Raúl should go:

> Originally, I agreed with the suggestion that Raúl visit USSR and China; but under the influence of our "friends" [codeword for the Cuban communists], and knowing that you would not be offended, we reexamined the decision and decided he would only go to Czechoslovakia, and then he would go to Italy and the United Arab Republic.[50]

Whereas a week before, Castro had seemed prepared to use his brother's visit to symbolize a new phase in his revolution, now he took a more timid line: "At this time, when an intervention is being prepared, Raúl's visit would be seen by our enemies as evidence of a new orientation of Cuba under the military assistance of the USSR."[51]

Curiously, Fidel thought that his "enemies" would accept a trip to Czechoslovakia more readily than one to Moscow. With Alekseev wondering why any socialist country was kept on Raúl's schedule, the elder Castro admitted that a visit to Czechoslovakia at this time was "probably not a good idea" but explained that they did not "know the Czechs as well." Castro had "given his word to the Czech minister of defense" that Raúl would visit the country, and, as he explained to Alekseev, "he did not want to break it."[52]

There was more than just the Czech exception that seemed odd about Fidel's decision. Blas Roca had opposed Raúl's going to Moscow because the trip would take him out of Cuba at a time of real peril. Yet the revised schedule, at least as Fidel described it, with the addition of trips to Italy and Egypt, would keep Raúl out of the country just as long.

Alekseev's cable relaying Castro's decision not to send Raúl to Moscow came at a bad time for Khrushchev and the Soviet leadership. In recent months Sino-Soviet relations, strained since Khrushchev replaced Stalin, had worsened dramatically. On the occasion of the ninetieth anniversary of Lenin's birth, in April, Beijing had charged Khrushchev with "revising, emasculating and betraying" Leninism.[53] Then, in early June, at a meeting of the World Federation of Trade Unions in Beijing, the Chinese had staged a coordinated attack on Khrushchev's leadership of international communism. In addition to the Chinese, the Japanese, Burmese, North Vietnamese, Ceylonese, Zanzibari, Sudanese, Somalian, and Argentine representatives spoke out against Stalin's successor.[54] The root of China's concern could be traced to the Twentieth Party Congress, in 1956, when Khrushchev acknowledged the brutality of Stalinism before an audience of members of the socialist bloc and unveiled a new foreign policy. What angered the Chinese most was the new Khrushchev doctrine of "peaceful coexistence," which asserted that states could enter the socialist camp through peaceful means. But the Chinese believed local wars were inevitable and doubted that communists could come to power by means of political alliances or elections. For the Chinese the Cuban revolution brought the most recent confirmation of their view of violence as a precondition for social reform.

The Chinese maneuver in early June 1960 at the trade union conference, essentially a personal insult to Khrushchev, compelled the Soviets to retaliate. The Kremlin subsequently announced the withdrawal of all Soviet advisers from China. And on June 21, just three days before Shelepin reported to him of Fidel Castro's decision not to send his brother to Moscow, Khrushchev gave a speech at an impromptu meeting of communist leaders in Bucharest that was very critical of the Chinese. The Soviet leader assailed Beijing for having a primitive view of world politics. "One must not only be able to read," he said in reference to Mao, "but must also correctly understand what one has read and apply it to specific conditions of the time in which we live, taking into consideration the situation and the real balance of forces."[55]

With relations at a breaking point with China, Khrushchev was understandably concerned that Moscow might lose the respect and allegiance of its newer allies. The disappointing news that Raúl Castro would not be coming to the Soviet Union gave Khrushchev reason to worry that the Chinese might have gotten to the Cubans as they had a few years earlier to the once friendly Albanians.

When Fidel Castro's erratic behavior worried the Soviets about his basic orientation, the Kremlin opted for a special operation to contact Raúl Castro in Prague. Perhaps Raúl could explain what had happened to Fidel Castro's initial enthusiasm for the Soviet Union. "I was supposed to find a way to establish contact with Raúl Castro," recalls Nikolai Leonov, "without, in any way, turning to our Czechoslovak comrades."[56]

Raúl was enjoying a very public visit to Czechoslovakia. The foreign minister of the People's Republic of Czechoslovakia, Pavol David, greeted him at the airport on June 27. The Czechs took him to Orlik, Karlovy Vary, Pilsin, and Lidice, the town that Hitler's SS had destroyed in retaliation for the assassination of Heinrich Himmler's intelligence chief, Reinhard Heydrich. In Prague, Raúl visited the Chinese, North Korean, and North Vietnamese embassies. However, for reasons still obscure, the KGB opted not to work through the Czech intelligence service to contact the Cuban. There is evidence from a slightly later period that the two services competed for informants in Cuba.[57]

The Czechs housed their Cuban visitor in a closed section of town, making it more difficult for the KGB to arrange an "accidental meeting" between two old friends. Leonov came up with a plan to "run into" Raúl as the Czechs brought him back to his residence for lunch. Because the Prague KGB station could not locate a copy of Raúl's official schedule, Leonov had to wait. He sat on the curb of the road and passed the time by eating cherries from a large bag, eventually building an archipelago of pits across the pavement.

Finally, the small Czech motorcade with the Cuban defense minister drove up. Raúl, who was in the first car, noticed Leonov and told his driver to stop. Getting out of the car, Raúl said, "Nikolai, what are you doing here?"[58] Raúl, who had last seen Leonov in Havana during the Mikoyan visit, invited Leonov into his car. Once they were in private, Leonov removed the mask of surprise and told Raúl that Moscow had ordered him to stage a meeting.

"The Cuban revolution has entered its most critical moment of development," Raúl confided in his old friend. Fidel Castro's June decision to nationalize all of the American oil refineries in Cuba was a red flag to Washington's bull, and Raúl was not optimistic. Already one of the Cubans' predictions of how the United States would respond to the new policies had proved correct. On July 3 the U.S. Congress had slashed the remainder of Cuba's annual sugar quota from 744,000 to 44,000 short tons.[59] Since 1934 Cuba had enjoyed a large annual quota in the U.S. domestic sugar market, for which

American consumers paid more than the world price.[60] Raúl Castro believed that even more drastic action, an open U.S. intervention under the banner of the Organization of American States, was a real danger. If this happened, Cuba could not expect to receive support from any Latin American countries. Although it would be the nationalization of the companies that would push the Americans over the edge, Raúl Castro thought Washington would use as a pretext the supply of weapons to Cuba from the Soviet Union, which he assumed would soon be common knowledge.[61]

Khrushchev's Nuclear Guarantee

Khrushchev now faced his first crisis related to Cuba. The Kremlin did not have any secret information to corroborate Fidel and Raúl Castro's fear that the United States was on the verge of invading Cuba. The closest the KGB came was a report from Che Guevara on June 9, informing Alekseev that a group of counterrevolutionaries who were planning to kill him had been picked up in Havana. These men did not seem to be on the CIA's payroll, and they had nothing to say about U.S. preparations for an invasion.

However, Castro's change of heart about sending his brother to Moscow seemed to indicate a weakening of his trust in Soviet assistance. Could it be that the Cubans were about to side with the Chinese? The Kremlin had reports that even its ally Raúl tended to support the Chinese line on the need to provide weapons to national-liberation movements. Fidel, unlike Raúl, was a revolutionary who was not a communist and, thus, even less likely to follow Moscow's leadership.

With the Cuban picture clouded by a possible ideological challenge from China, Khrushchev was once again reminded that the United States represented a threat to the very existence of the Soviet Union. On June 29 the chief of the KGB personally delivered a very worrisome report to the Soviet leader. On June 16 the KGB in Moscow received a document sent by a NATO liaison officer with the CIA to his own government.

In the CIA it is known that the leadership of the Pentagon is convinced of the need to initiate a war with the Soviet Union "as soon as possible."

According to information available to the Pentagon, the USSR currently does not have enough nuclear missiles to destroy NATO strategic bases. However, in the next little while the Soviet Union will be deploying missiles in sufficient quantity. Right now the USA has the capability to wipe out Soviet missile bases and other military targets with its bomber forces. But over the next little while the defense forces of the Soviet Union will grow even more, and this opportunity will disappear. The existing military parity between the USSR and the USA permits the U.S. to consider prevailing in a war. In the near term the situation will change to the advantage of the Soviet Union.

As a result of these assumptions, the chiefs at the Pentagon are hoping to launch a preventive war against the Soviet Union.[62]

The KGB took this information very seriously. It told Khrushchev and the Central Committee that it was taking "measures to corroborate this report." Only three copies of it were made. Khrushchev received a copy, and Shelepin kept his own copy. The third copy, which went to the files, was destroyed.[63]

The fact that these three challenges landed on Khrushchev's desk at about the same time provides the background to Khrushchev's riskiest initiative yet to help Cuba. Khrushchev sensed the value of making a grand gesture to embrace the Cubans, while at the same time compelling the Americans and the Chinese to respect him. On July 9 before a group of Soviet teachers, Khrushchev for the first time extended Moscow's nuclear umbrella into the Western Hemisphere.

It should be borne in mind that the United States is now not at such an unattainable distance from the Soviet Union as formerly. Figuratively speaking, if need be, Soviet artillerymen can support the Cuban people with their rocket fire should the aggressive forces in the Pentagon dare to start intervention against Cuba. And the Pentagon could be well advised not to forget that, as shown at the latest tests, we have rockets which can land precisely in a preset square target 13,000 kilometers away. This, if you want, is a warning to those who would like to solve international problems by force and not by reason.[64]

With this threat Khrushchev reassured the Cubans and the Chinese that Moscow led the socialist bloc and would do what was necessary to protect its members. At the same time, the Kremlin sent the Americans a warning that they should not exaggerate their sense of strategic superiority.

The Soviet statement did not have any deterrent effect on the United States, which was not planning to invade Cuba anytime soon. On July 7, at a meeting of Eisenhower's National Security Council, a junior member of the group had raised the possibility of a U.S. invasion. Leo A. Hoegh, the director of the Office of Civil and Defense Mobilization, suggested, "[t]he U.S. should charge that the Monroe Doctrine had been violated and should go in and take over." But President Eisenhower was far from ready to use U.S. military force to deal with Castro. The United States, Hoegh continued, would have "to prove a number of things before it could take such action." Eisenhower wanted "American public opinion and Free World public opinion" behind an invasion before flashing the green light. The United States could not use force unless it was clear to the world that the Soviet Union intended to make a military base out of Cuba. His chief Soviet adviser, Charles Bohlen, had assured Eisenhower that the Soviets would not be "so foolish" as to do that. Eisenhower thought that the American people were fickle about the use of force. One had to disentangle expressions of frustration from those of support for action.[65]

Khrushchev's statement, however, had the hoped-for effect in Havana. It delighted the Cuban leadership. Some historians have argued that it somehow embarrassed the Cubans, who either were afraid of admitting their dependence upon the Soviet Union or feared such dependence. In fact, Fidel Castro was apparently so afraid of an imminent U.S. attack that he cabled Raúl in Prague to offer to go to Moscow at once.

A few days after Khrushchev's speech, Raúl Castro informed the Soviets in Prague that he had "received instructions from the Cuban government to go to the USSR and to express Fidel Castro's gratitude for Nikita S. Khrushchev's comments on Cuba." Raúl asked specifically to meet the Soviet leader during his trip. He also asked that the visit have "an official character." He did not want his enemies at home to attack him for having made a secret trip to Moscow. This would undermine his credibility among the revolutionaries and the conservatives in the July 26 movement. Though their usefulness was progressively decreasing, the conservatives could still make trouble. The revolutionaries, on the other hand, were not all of the pro-Moscow persuasion. Some, primarily the followers of Che Guevara, considered Moscow too timid on the question of supporting international revolution.[66]

The next day Raúl sent his assistant, Luis Más Martín, to the Soviet embassy to lay out more conditions for the meeting. Más Martín said that his boss wanted the Kremlin to be prepared to discuss its response in the event that the United States invaded Cuba. Beyond that, Raúl needed to know what additional assistance, apart from the purchase of Cuban sugar, the USSR would provide Havana in the event that Washington tried to cut Cuba off from the international marketplace. Repeating what Fidel Castro had described to Alekseev as his greatest fear, Más Martín warned, "Cuba does not have any raw materials, and in case of blockade, Cuban industry could be paralyzed."[67]

Intelligence cooperation, was the last issue raised by his representative. The Cuban security services were new and weak. Raúl admired the efficiency of the KGB and the bloc services, in general, and wanted the Soviets to send experts in intelligence and counterintelligence to Havana to train the leadership of the Cuban services.[68] Ramiro Valdés, the Cuban security chief, would be accompanying him to Moscow.

The Soviets worked quickly to prepare for Raúl's visit. The KGB resident in Prague cabled his request to visit on July 14. Boris Ponomarev, the head of the secretariat of the Central Committee, prepared a tentative itinerary the next day for approval by Khrushchev. The Soviets would be ready for Raúl to arrive on July 17. In arranging Castro's schedule, Ponomarev took care to keep Raúl's political affiliation a secret. Traditionally, when a foreign communist visited Moscow, he would be met by representatives of the Soviet Communist Party. But, as Ponomarev noted for the Presidium on July 15, "[g]iven that Raúl Castro is a secret member of the PSP and there will be noncommunist members of his delegation, there cannot be any official links acknowledged between him and the Soviet Communist Party." A biographical sketch of Castro prepared for a wider audience in the Central Committee stressed that "many of Raúl Castro's closest associates were members of the PSP" but omitted his own membership.[69]

Ponomarev wanted a chance to explain the Soviet position on China at the beginning of Raúl's stay. "Given that Raúl Castro has shown incorrect views on the Chinese, it is recommended that before he meets Nikita S. Khrushchev, there be a discussion about the Bucharest meeting and that he be shown the June 21 report to the Central Committee."[70] On the day of Raúl Castro's arrival, the Kremlin accepted all of Ponomarev's recommendations. Raúl would be the first Castro brother to meet Khrushchev.

Raúl Castro arrived on July 17 at Moscow's Sheremetyevo Airport and was greeted by Marshal Matvei Zakharov and General Ivanov of the Soviet general staff. He was driven to a KGB guest house in the Lenin hills surrounding Moscow. Over lunch Raúl explained the Cuban leadership's gratitude for Khrushchev's decisive intervention in the U.S.-Cuban dispute. "We believed," said the Cuban defense minister, "that your military assistance would not come in time, before the large U.S. intervention, but after Khrushchev's statement the situation changed. The Americans no longer dared attack us." The Soviet general staff explained to Raúl that he could expect more military assistance from Moscow. Raúl was pleased and asked merely that measures be taken to disguise any tanks that were sent. He feared that Cuba's enemies would exploit the arrival of Soviet tanks as "a pretext for adventurism."[71]

Raúl met Khrushchev the next day. Although it had been planned that Ponomarev of the International Department would give him a touch of reeducation about the proper approach to have toward the People's Republic of China early in the visit, this did not come until after Raúl had met Khrushchev. Raúl may have had a few minutes alone with Khrushchev before the foreign policy leaders of the Soviet Union arrived. Besides Ponomarev and Marshal Zakharov, Khrushchev and Castro were joined by Andrei Gromyko, the Soviet foreign minister, and Skachkov, the minister of foreign trade.[72] The high point of Raúl's visit came when the meetings with Soviet officials produced a joint communiqué that formalized the hoped-for Soviet commitment to Cuban defense: the Soviets promised to use "all means not to consent to an armed United States intervention against the Cuban republic."[73]

AVANPOST

Nikita Khrushchev's threat to use nuclear weapons to protect Cuba from the United States effectively consolidated the gains in Soviet-Cuban relations since La Coubre blew up in the Havana harbor. There was no better symbol of the strength of the relationship than Fidel Castro's decision to let his brother make an open visit to the Kremlin.

The Soviets felt that they had done all they could to ease the development of close relations with the Cubans. They accepted all of the terms requested by Fidel, Raúl, and Che in 1960. Moreover, they surprised the Cubans by coming right out and saying that they did not expect any payment for the weapons purchased. Slyly admitting that "he did not know any price that could be lower," Mikoyan had told Núñez Jiménez in late June that the Cubans would be given outright thirty "topnotch" tanks and 100,000 automatic rifles. That was ten times the number of rifles Castro had requested; and the tanks were an unexpected bonus. Furthermore, in a letter to Alekseev, Mikoyan wanted the Cubans to be reminded that though "a formal price will be attached to whatever weapons they buy . . . they will never have to pay anything." "Any payment, coming to us in such circumstances," wrote Mikoyan, "is purely symbolic."[74]

Castro and Khrushchev had both taken a gamble, and the risk seemed to be paying off for the Soviets in 1960. Cuba was moving into the socialist camp. On July 31, 1960, Alekseev telegraphed that "Fidel Castro expressed deep gratitude to the Soviet government and especially N. S. Khrushchev for the satisfaction of all requests for the supply of military weapons."[75] And so far, despite a few false alarms, the United States seemed prepared to accept this violation of its sphere of influence. To symbolize the start of a new era in Soviet-Cuban relations, the KGB changed the code name for its file on Cuba. Between 1958 and July 1960, it had been "YOUNTSIE"—youngsters. But from August 1960 on, the KGB referred to Cuba as "AVANPOST"—bridgehead. There was now a Soviet ally in the Western Hemisphere.

CHAPTER 4

"Cuba Si, Yankee No!"

The Havana Declaration

In the Plaza Cívica, the setting for generations of Cuban political theater, Fidel Castro staged a grand meeting of the people on September 2, 1960. He called them together to proclaim his desire to take Cuba in a new direction. Watching the event on television, the U.S. ambassador, Philip Bonsal, noted that "the crowd seemed larger and more animated tha[n] at previous mass meetings."[1] Castro began to speak just before 5 P.M., with his speech writer, Carlos Rafael Rodríguez, known in Miami as "the little red billy goat" because of his facial homage to Lenin, standing nearby.[2] Castro described as a "veritable human sea" the throng that greeted his opening words: "We have met to converse today, especially on international matters. Our people know the battle which it is fighting for its survival."[3]

Tonight there was an inner reality, a speech within the speech, which gave an unusual edge to Castro's characteristic sense of the dramatic. The hundreds of thousands of supporters in the crowd—and even the U.S. ambassador tucked safely in his embassy—did not know that Castro had good reason to suspect that Washington planned to make this his last public appearance ever. In a private meeting a few hours before this spectacle, the head of the KGB station in Havana had warned Castro about evidence of a plot to assassinate him at that night's meeting. The information had come, via Moscow, from a reliable source working for the KGB in another country; and the Kremlin wanted Castro to know about it. Cuban intelligence had also picked up similar information. A group of Cubans intended to disable the power station that supplied the flood lights on the Plaza Cívica. At the appointed hour, with the speech scene in total darkness, guerrillas dressed in the uniforms of the workers' revolutionary militia would rush the stage and kill Castro with a volley of hand grenades.[4]

Castro "received this information quietly," Alekseev wrote Moscow on Sep-tember 2, after carrying out instructions to give him this warning privately. Castro's immediate response was to assure the Soviets that his security was ad-equate. Then the Cuban leader gave an eye-opening explanation for his ap-parent lack of concern about such rumors of assassination plots, which was proof either of his disbelief or of a heroic sense of humor. "He believes," Alekseev reported, "that the Americans would not risk such a measure, be-cause his brother Raúl would inherit control of the government and then the Americans would lose whatever they have left in Cuba."[5]

For all of Castro's bravado, he was indeed worried about the United States. In the aftermath of the oil dispute and Khrushchev's July 1960 pledge to wrap Cuba in an atomic security blanket, his relationship with United States as-sumed the form of a two-tiered struggle. On the diplomatic level Washington tried to build a coalition of Latin American states to squeeze Cuba, in the hope that serious economic deprivations and moral pressure from fellow Latin Americans would constrain Castro or, even better, force his removal. And in the nether world of covert action the CIA and its allies in the Cuban emigra-tion worked to destabilize Castro before a Soviet-style police state rendered all effective opposition impossible.

Castro saw evidence of U.S. intentions in the behavior of Secretary of State Christian Herter and the U.S. delegation at the regional foreign ministers' meeting in San José, Costa Rica, in August. Herter had tried to persuade this gathering of Latin American foreign ministers to deplore the intervention of the Soviet Union and China in the Western Hemisphere. At issue for the Americans was the effectiveness of any sanctions against Cuba. Sensitive to generations of criticism of American bullying, the Eisenhower administration sought the support of the entire region in its crusade against Castro, knowing that without it an economic boycott or an overt military operation would probably entail unacceptable risks. In the end, Washington got a watered-down version of what it wanted. The Declaration of San José, which was signed by all of the country delegations except Cuba, decried extra-hemi-spheric intervention without referring to the Soviet Union, China, or even Cuba.[6]

Cuban intelligence had also warned Castro in August that 185 "old Batistianos and simple mercenaries," along with 45 military advisers, many of whom were U.S. citizens, were training at U.S. bases in Guatemala.[7] Guate-malan communists were able to keep a watch over U.S. and Cuban-émigré ac-tivities in the Retalhuleu area of northwest Guatemala. The CIA airfield where Cuban émigrés were trained to fly supply missions was an easy target. Surrounded by trees, it lay between a railroad line and a highway and was only one mile from a town.[8] The Guatemalans passed their observations on to Cuban representatives and later to the KGB station in Mexico.

Indeed, as part of President Eisenhower's March covert-action program, the CIA had opened a training camp for Cuban guerrillas earlier that summer in the mountains along Guatemala's Pacific coast. In June the U.S. government had sponsored the formation of the Frente Revolucionario Democrático (FRD), a Cuban opposition group that would oversee recruitment of émigrés for clandestine activity.[9] The first thirty Cubans arrived in Guatemala a few weeks later. The four-point covert-action program—calling for the creation of a political opposition, mass communications to the Cuban people, covert intelligence and action originating inside Cuba, and the building of an adequate paramilitary force outside Cuba—was still in its infancy. The CIA had not yet begun to drop air supplies to rebels in Cuba or to transmit radio propaganda to Cubans. Yet the level of activity could be detected by Cuban intelligence and was sufficient to worry Havana.

September 2 therefore brought an extraordinary performance by the charismatic Castro, who mounted the dais and unashamedly unveiled the course that Cuba would take in foreign policy. "San Jose," he said referring to the foreign ministers' meeting, "was only a Pyrrhic victory for imperialism."[10] He had asked his friend from the mountains, the editor of the communist newspaper, *Hoy*, Carlos Rodríguez, to draft what became known as the Declaration of Havana. Like Mao Zedong in 1949, who opted to remove any doubt of neutrality with his "Leaning to One Side" declaration, Castro was now ready to endorse the Cuban communist party's line in foreign affairs.

Fidel shook his fist at the United States: "We have nationalized many North American firms, but we have some in reserve. If they continue economic aggression against us, we will continue nationalizing their enterprises."[11] He then embraced Mao's China, a greater provocation for Washington than any other diplomatic gesture: "The United States is saying that Red China is interfering in Latin America. To the contrary, Latin American governments have diplomatic relations with the puppet government on Formosa. We ask the people if they desire to establish diplomatic relations with the Chinese people's republic." The crowd roared its approval.[12]

Calling the crowd the "General Assembly," Fidel shaped the heart of his four-hour speech as an oral referendum on the principles of the next phase of his revolution. He asked his audience to approve a declaration of intention, which he read.

We proclaim before all America:

The Rights of compesino to land
The Rights of workers to fruits of his labor
The Rights of children to education
The Rights to hospitalization
The Right to work
The Right to equality among races
The Right to equality of women
The Rights of intellectuals to carry on their work as they see fit

The Right of states to nationalize monopolies

The Right to sovereignty

The Right to convert military posts into schools

The Right to arm people so that they can defend their rights and destinies

The Right of oppressed countries to struggle for independence

Castro then expressed the revolutionary duty to fight for these rights abroad as well as at home. "We reiterate our faith that Latin America will march forward to free itself of Yankee imperialism in spite of the meetings of domesticated Foreign Ministers." Cuba, he said, hears the voices of the downtrodden in Latin America. "We are here!" Castro shouted. "Cuba will not fail you!"[13] Again the crowd roared its approval: "Cuba Si, Yankee No; Cuba Si, Yankee No!"[14] Che described the hypnotic scene produced when Castro asked the multitude to show its support for the declaration: "more than a million hands raised to the skies, one sixth of the country's total population."[15]

The Cuban communists took the Havana declaration as a major ideological victory. Two days after the event, Rodríguez and the executive secretary of the PSP, Aníbal Escalante, related their achievement to Aleksandr Alekseev. Besides claiming that the central theme of Fidel's four-hour speech had been the brainchild of Rodríguez, they also wanted the KGB resident to know that Fidel was now more open about his willingness to push the socialist revolution forward. In an aside, he had told some members of the PSP that the time had arrived "to begin preparing public opinion for the construction of a socialist state."[16]

Despite the symbolism of the Havana declaration, Soviet representatives in Cuba were increasingly aware of a new division within the Cuban elite that threatened to undermine all of the communists' achievements. Aníbal Escalante, a rising star in the PSP, complained to the KGB and the Soviet embassy that Fidel and even Raúl Castro were finding it hard to marginalize their old guerrilla friends from the Sierra Maestra.[17] Supremely confident of his own charisma, Castro believed that the leftist guerrillas who had followed him into the mountains would also follow him into the communist party. As early as March 1960, Fidel Castro envisioned a smooth transition from the informal July 26 movement to a unified Marxist party. As Escalante explained to the Soviets, there was "some kind of psychological reason for the government's caution and indulgence." Assuming that his real trouble was still the old Batista group living in luxury in Miami, Castro resisted jailing or at least firing those revolutionaries who would never join the communist party. "In fact," Escalante told the Soviets,

the participants in the struggle against Fidel are not those who fled to the USA, or those who sit and hold their tongues, because the Americans are not actively helping them. The organizers of the provocations are those comrades-in-arms of Fidel who fought alongside him in the Sierra Maestra, who fearing the scope of the revolution migrated into the camp of the enemies.[18]

The PSP had an interest in promoting the fact that Fidel's only true allies in 1960 were the communists; nevertheless, the most dangerous counterrevolutionaries in Cuba were in fact those in the noncommunist left who had formed the backbone of the July 26 movement. These were now the supporters of Manuel Ray, Castro's first minister of the interior, student groups at the University of Havana, and Catholic youth groups. The leaders in these groups knew each other well and were already accustomed to working clandestinely because of the first revolution. "So, when the question arises of taking tough steps against these groups," Escalante said caustically, "all kinds of hesitations appear based on the groundless hope that they will come to their senses because the people are united in support of Fidel."[19]

There was only one real nugget of news for Moscow in all of this information. In March and April 1960, after the *Coubre* incident, Fidel Castro had told the Soviet representative privately that there was no alternative to a socialist revolution for Cuba. Then, however, he had talked of biding his time until the Cuban people were ready to accept communism. Now it seemed that Castro was preparing to take some risks to hasten that process. Meanwhile, his new line was breeding an overconfidence in the leadership of the PSP, which was impatient to eliminate the noncommunists who remained in Castro's inner circle.

Soviets Edge Closer

Three weeks after the declaration at the Plaza Cívica, Fidel Castro and Nikita Khrushchev finally met. The incorrigibly late Castro kept the Soviet leader waiting for an hour on the steps of the Soviet consulate in New York. Seemingly unaffected by the wait, Khrushchev rushed to give a bear hug to the man he had sheltered from afar months earlier. Khrushchev was at the start of an unprecedented absence from the Soviet Union, of thirty-five days, twenty-five of which he intended to spend in and around the United Nations Building, ostensibly to welcome the fourteen new African states that were joining the world body for the first time.[20]

After some time listening to Khrushchev make counterrevolutionary jokes from the Lenin era, Castro's entourage asked whether the Soviet leader knew of any jokes about himself. "I can do better than that," he said. "Cubans, form your revolutionary tribunal and sentence Gromyko here. He was the one who recognized Batista." This kind of humor must have brought a smile to Stalin's lips but it left the Cubans cold. They admired Khrushchev's foreign minister for at least being the only Soviet in the delegation who seemed able to handle a cigar.[21]

Amid the attempts at humor Fidel angered some of the members of his delegation. The old revolutionaries in his party felt the steel hand of Ramiro Valdés, who insisted that "security" choose the members of the Cuban press delegation. Carlos Franqui, a revolutionary socialist who hated Stalin and identified Moscow with Stalinism, observed the growing power of the pro-Moscow clique around Fidel and its eagerness to use police methods to establish its authority.[22]

The U.S. State Department, too, noted signs of the ever closer relationship between Castro and Khrushchev. At the UN, Cuba was now the nonbloc country that voted most consistently with the Soviet Union. Moreover, Cuba was the only Third World country that supported Khrushchev's resolution favoring a UN investigation of "U.S. aggressive actions." Meanwhile, Khrushchev used his visit to New York to reaffirm his July 1960 commitment to defend Cuba. The most dramatic instance came during Castro's September 26 address to the General Assembly. Castro denounced the American chief of naval operations, Admiral Arleigh Burke, for having disputed that Khrushchev would act on his pledge of using Soviet nuclear weapons to defend Cuba if the United States reacted to a Cuban seizure of Guantánamo.

> Just see how an estimate is made, an estimate which is dangerous, since he [Burke] intimates that in the case of an attack on us we are to stand alone. This is something that Admiral Burke has not thought up for himself. But suppose for a moment that Admiral Burke is mistaken. Let us imagine that Admiral Burke, although an Admiral, is wrong. If he is wrong, he is playing irresponsibly with the strongest thing in the world.[23]

From his seat with the Soviet delegation, Khrushchev roared, "On Oshibaetsia!" (He is mistaken!), and punched the air with his fist.[24] The Soviets wanted there to be no doubt of their military commitment to Cuba.

The October Invasion Scare

Confident of Soviet protection, the Cuban leadership edged toward revealing its plans for a socialist revolution in Cuba. The Cubans laid plans in early October 1960 for completing the nationalization of key sectors of the economy. On October 12 the Soviets were informed that the Cubans had completed a draft for a new law regarding the "partial nationalization of all foreign and Cuban banks and several American enterprises." "After this order is approved," Alekseev reported, "all main branches of industry will be in the hands of the government."[25]

Two days later the Cuban government announced the expropriation of 382 companies and all Cuban and foreign banks, with the exception of those owned by Canadians. After a sixteen-hour meeting that lasted until four in the morning, Fidel's cabinet adopted a sweeping measure that eliminated all remaining private property in the sugar and textile industries. This measure was not presented as a retort to the Americans. As its rationale for the expropriation, the Cuban government declared that these companies had been "following a policy contrary to the interests of the revolution and the economic development of the country." Only 20 of the 400 firms that came under state control by this act were American owned. The government also enacted an urban reform bill, which effectively turned all tenants into apartment owners, one measure that did not draw upon Soviet experience.[26]

The excitement in Havana at the completion of the next stage of expropriation was mingled with the fear that anticommunist Cubans, with the help of the CIA, were about to launch a campaign of terror. Fidel Castro disagreed with both the Cuban communists and the Cuban security services on how to manage domestic subversion. He wanted to avoid a widespread purge that would undermine the popular appeal of his revolution. He understood that the process of collectivization and rapid industrialization would produce enough ill will and dislocation in the country, without the added unhappiness created by a national witch-hunt. In September he restrained the Cuban Interior Ministry from arresting the "group" that many communists and security officials were convinced was planning to kill the Soviet ambassador, among others.[27]

It is well known because of the congressional investigations of the 1970s that the CIA opened discussions with the Mafia in September 1960 in an effort to arrange a "hit" on Castro. For twenty years there has been speculation as to how much the Soviets and the Cubans knew about the Faustian arrangement struck between the Ivy League elites of the CIA and the Mob. KGB and Kremlin documents confirm that even the reformed Stalinists of Khrushchev's security services never entertained the idea of an alliance between Allen Dulles, Santos Trafficante, and Meyer Lansky. Nevertheless, the Soviets collected information about various plots involving Latin American adventurers.

Moscow was not sure which to be more concerned about—the sudden increase in hostile actions against Fidel since Khrushchev's offer of support in July or the lack of poise shown by Soviet representatives in Cuba in the face of these new challenges. Sergei M. Kudryavtsev, who came to Havana as Soviet ambassador when formal relations were resumed in May, was a snob and a physical coward. At the slightest provocation, he indulged himself in tirades against the Cubans for failing adequately to protect him. And even when he wasn't letting the Cubans know his disdain in the haughtiest ways possible, he grimly wore a bulletproof vest. His bureaucratic competitor, Alekseev of the KGB, wryly observed that the Soviet ambassador behaved toward the Cubans "like one of Batista's generals."[28] Castro and his inner circle and eventually Moscow interpreted Kudryavtsev's demeanor as evidence of a complete lack of empathy for the socialist revolution that the young Fidelistas were attempting to pull off in the Caribbean. Castro could not have made his disgust for the ambassador any clearer than when he instructed him in September 1960 that in the future he wanted the Soviet embassy to coordinate all meetings with the Cuban leadership through Alekseev, ostensibly the cultural attaché at the embassy.

Alas for Moscow, Alekseev too was a captive of his own rigidities. Despite his successful cultivation of Castro, he was partial to the prejudices and opinions of the Cuban communists who did not always agree with Castro. This was odd because Alekseev had a demonstrated gift for cultivating the noncommunist left; yet when push came to shove, he often chose not to believe what these people were telling him. Castro's reaction to the KGB's warning about a possible assassination attempt had surprised him. Alekseev shared with Blas Roca and Rodríguez the sense that Castro was frivolous in his treatment of threats, foreign and domestic. Alekseev looked on approvingly as the leading Cuban communists called for more repression of noncommunists in the July 26 movement.

Alekseev's superiors in Moscow could not have disagreed with him more. They were anxious that Alekseev not alienate Fidel Castro in the manner of the less subtle Kudryavtsev. In September 1960, when Alekseev predicted a reign of violence—"Acts of sabotage and terrorism are being prepared"—Moscow sensed that the KGB representative was losing his composure.[29] What concerned the Lubyanka was not this prediction but the spin that Alekseev was trying to put on it. The KGB had a source in Castro's inner circle code-named OSWALDO, who reported to Alekseev that Castro was failing to take all necessary measures to destroy the assassination group that had targeted Kudryavtsev and Cuban Foreign Minister Raúl Roa, among others. "OSWALDO explained that Fidel Castro has decided not to arrest the members of these groups without concrete evidence." OSWALDO asked Alekseev to persuade the Cuban leadership to "implement repressive measures against enemy elements."[30]

It was understood in Moscow that Alekseev wanted authorization to push Castro to launch a campaign against the enemies of his regime. And Moscow refused to take the bait. The September 2 speech had come off without a hitch. Castro was safe, and there had been no attempts to interfere with his presentation. "In light of the fact that the expected sabotage did not occur, perhaps you should take into consideration that the information you received was specially fabricated by agents."[31] Moscow used this opening to chastise Alekseev for siding with Castro's critics in the Cuban communist party: "we do not consider it reasonable to proceed with arrests without sufficient concrete evidence."[32] The KGB accepted the need to fight terrorism, but Alekseev seemed to be rushing with the communists into a public purge that might be counterproductive at this stage in the revolution. "In a delicate way," Moscow instructed Alekseev, "you could advise the Cubans that in individual cases it is possible to effect the secret detention of certain individuals." A purge, on the other hand, would be too noisy.[33]

The Kremlin could not ignore the concrete evidence that the United States was stepping up its support for the enemies of Castroism. In late September the CIA sponsored its first air drop of supplies (enough to arm one hundred men) to rebels in Oriente Province, the mountainous region in southeast Cuba where the July 26 movement had smoldered for three years before the fateful events of 1959. The operation was botched. The supplies landed seven miles from the reception area, falling into the hands of Castro's revolutionary militia instead of the expectant counterrevolutionary force.[34] Two days earlier a group of twenty-seven Batistianos, relatives and friends of the former wealthy senator Rolando Masferrer, also landed in Oriente Province.[35] This group— intended to stage the first serious "invasion" since Castro's rise to power— came ashore with one large American flag and three pack mules. The State Department characterized this operation as "comic opera"; but the Cubans and the Soviets could not be sure that Allen Dulles was not the mules' theatrical promoter.[36]

And neither could Fidel Castro. The evidence of stepped-up counterrevolutionary activity, and the taint of American involvement, worked on his strategy of restraint like slow drops of water on a stone. Over the course of September 1960, Castro reconsidered his approach to domestic security. In August 1960 a scandal in the Cuban security services had led him to purge the entire security apparatus, including the secret police. The cause was the discovery that a few dissidents in the secret police were using security equipment to tap Raúl Castro's telephone lines and those of some of the leaders of the PSP. The head of this renegade detachment had ordered the destruction of all of the transcripts before his arrest. But some were discovered, including those of telephone conversations between the Castro brothers. Over the opposition of Efigenio Amejeiras, the chief of the secret police, Castro ordered a complete overhaul of the institution.[37]

The purge of the secret police was a small affair in comparison with the scale of a national purge that the members of the PSP and the Soviet representatives in Cuba wanted. By the beginning of October, Castro's resistance to a larger purge was wavering.

Escalante, the executive secretary of the PSP, on October 1 brought the news to the Soviet ambassador that Castro was instituting a neighborhood surveillance system. Every street, neighborhood, and district would have its own government watchers who would inform on unusual behavior and anti-Castro political activity and statements. The police state that the communists believed a prerequisite to achieving their goals was now a real possibility.[38] This was but a first step, and a late one, in the estimation of the leadership of the PSP. Escalante explained to the Soviets that Castro and his inner circle were still having a hard time understanding the nature of the most dangerous opposition to him. "Castro's brother and other members of the leadership understand the danger of counterrevolutionary activity. And it would be wrong to say that Fidel Castro has opposed taking decisive measures to cut off counterrevolutionary activity." Yet it was still the belief of the PSP that the Cuban leaders consistently underestimated what it would take to root out the counterrevolution.

Even more ominous for the Cuban communists that fall were statements by Vice President Richard Nixon and his rival for the presidency, Senator John F. Kennedy of Massachusetts. The same day that Havana radio announced that the Masferrer group had invaded from the United States, Kennedy placed Cuba front and center in the electoral campaign. Kennedy feared he was trailing in the race for the White House, and his advisers suggested that he chip away at Nixon's foreign policy reputation. He tried to turn Nixon's mantra that he "had more foreign policy experience" against the vice president. Kennedy presented the Republican experience in foreign policy as a trail of tears, with Cuba as "the most glaring failure of American foreign policy."

Kennedy preached a form of muscular international liberalism. He recognized that Cuba had needed serious reform in 1959: "At the beginning of 1959, United States companies owned 40 percent of all sugar lands, almost all the cattle ranches, 90 percent of the mines and the mineral concessions, 80 percent of the utilities, practically all the oil industry, and supplied two-thirds of Cuba's imports." The democratic nominee blamed Washington for ignoring the needs of the Cuban people and protecting instead the profit margins of American direct investment: "our actions too often gave the impression that we were more interested in the money we took out of Cuba than we were in seeing Cuba raise its standard of living for its people."

Had Kennedy stopped at this point, Havana might not have started to worry. But after calling Republicans responsible for the tensions in the Caribbean, Kennedy made no bones about his desire to see Castro out of power. "Castro and his gang have betrayed the ideals of the Cuban revolution and the hopes of the Cuban people." If elected, his administration would fight bad reformers with as much intensity as it sponsored good ones. Under his leadership the U.S. government would "assert our support for freedom all over the hemisphere." To remove any doubt that he foresaw armed conflict, Kennedy added that "the struggle with Castro in the next few months will take place not only in the mountains of Cuba, but in the mountains, in the fields and the valleys of all Latin America."[39]

Fidel Castro paid close attention to this shift in the rhetoric of the American campaign. He already had intelligence at his disposal that suggested some kind of American paramilitary training in Central America. This was the season of risk taking for the Cuban leader, who intended to chart a new course for Cuban foreign policy at the same time that he was pushing forward with nationalizations. Castro knew he was especially vulnerable to a U.S. reaction in this period.

By the middle of October, Fidel Castro was convinced that a Yankee force was preparing to leave Guatemala for battle in Cuba. On October 18, a member of the Honduran assembly stated that thirty U.S. transport planes with supplies and former soldiers of the Batista regime had flown to the Guatemalan bases of Puerto Barrios and Retalhuleu. This information dovetailed with Castro's assumption that Eisenhower would make his move before the end of the month to ensure Nixon's victory.[40]

Despite a lack of compelling secret information, Moscow accepted the Cuban argument that an invasion was imminent. The KGB in Paris also picked up some information of a concerted effort by the CIA to recruit Spaniards for operations in Cuba, but Moscow already knew that the United States had stepped up its covert action in and around the Castro regime.[41] The Kremlin used the Soviet newspapers *Pravda* and *Izvestia* to endorse the Cuban charge that the United States was planning to strike from its guerrilla bases in Guatemala. From about October 18 on, banner headlines warned the United States that the Warsaw Pact knew about its intention to harm the Castro regime. On October 22 *Izvestia* ran a photograph of Khrushchev receiving a Cuban flag from a delegation of Cuban journalists alongside reports of "invasion preparations organized by the U.S."[42]

At the United Nations on October 25, both the Cuban and the Soviet representatives denounced U.S. interventionism. Charging the United States with preparing an invasion that might set off a "conflagration of unsuspected proportions," the Cuban government sought international assistance.[43] The Cubans revealed to the General Assembly that the United States was using its own territory and that of some of its Central American allies to train counterrevolutionaries for the planned attack. Besides that general claim, Ambassador Mario García Incháustegui and the Cuban delegation made specific reference to the U.S. aircraft that had violated Cuban airspace on September 29 to drop supplies to the guerrillas and to the abortive landing made by the Masferrer group, which included three U.S. citizens. The Cuban representative predicted that the U.S. initiative would first take the form of a staged attack on the U.S. marine base at Guantánamo Bay, which would serve as a pretext for a U.S. invasion.

Valerian Zorin, the Soviet ambassador to the UN, called on all states to take "urgent measures to prevent military action against Cuba." Behind the scenes the Soviet delegation tried to accelerate UN consideration of Incháustegui's charges. But Costa Rica, Haiti, Panama, and Venezuela joined the United States in tying up Cuban efforts to air their fears of a U.S. intervention.

The United States went on a counteroffensive, as much to save face as to quiet the suspicions of Latin American allies that Moscow and Havana were onto something. The State Department denied all of Castro's charges, and the U.S. representative at the OAS alleged that the Cubans were throwing up a "smokescreen to cover arms procurement and military preparations in Cuba." This was the first time the United States had stated publicly that it knew about Soviet bloc military assistance to Cuba. Besides a public rejection of the Cuban statements, the State Department sent an unfortunate circular to all of its Latin American diplomatic posts, advising U.S. diplomats to decry these "false charges" in discussions with local political figures.[44]

Although it was true that no invasion was planned in the short run, the U.S. State Department knowingly deceived the international community, and its own diplomatic representatives, about the extent and objectives of its covert program against Castro's Cuba. In the Eisenhower administration the State Department oversaw the use of covert action. In October 1960 it was accurate to say that the CIA was nowhere near launching an attack from Guatemala, but the Cubans and the Soviets were right to assume that men were being trained in Guatemala for a future U.S.-sponsored operation against the Castro regime.

The scare was not a "smokescreen." The Cubans and the Soviets believed that an invasion was coming. Fidel and Raúl Castro left Havana to direct defensive measures. On October 25, the day of the debate in the UN General Assembly, they were spotted in Las Villas Province near the Escambray mountains, which were considered the center of rebel activity. Press reports reached Washington that three thousand persons were under arrest as suspected "contacts" for the invaders. Expecting an attack from Guatemala, the Cuban government deployed thousands of militiamen along the southern coast from the western tip of Pinar del Río to Camagüey Province. Meanwhile, the garrison on the Isle of Pines was heavily reinforced, and small craft went out on patrol in the south.[45]

Washington was baffled by the war scare in Cuba. No U.S. policymaker seemed able to detect that the Cubans and the Soviets were caught in an intelligence trap. Understandably, the U.S. ambassador in Moscow, who was not on the "need to know" list for the CIA's Cuban activities, was quick to dismiss the Kremlin's charges. "In view of the forthcoming UN debate," Llewellyn Thompson cabled the State Department, "[it] seems apparent that [the] Soviet psychological plan calls first for build-up of convincing case that invasion threatened in order then to claim credit for forestalling attack, much as Soviets boast of their alleged success in preventing or terminating Western aggression regarding Suez, Lebanon, Syria."[46] What is more interesting in retrospect is that those who did know about the CIA's activities were equally skeptical of the Soviet and Cuban complaints. Washington operated on the basis of two mutually contradictory assumptions as to why the Soviets and the Cubans could not really believe that the exiles in Guatemala were to be employed in an invasion: Soviet bloc intelligence was so good that Soviet and Cuban spies could peer into the decision-making process in Washington; and U.S. security was so effective that the CIA's activities in Guatemala were deniable. Washington did not allow itself to assume that Havana and Moscow had imperfect spy services that delivered enough information to set off alarms—but not enough to know when the aggression would occur.

On October 27 the Cuban military was placed on the highest military alert in anticipation of the start of the U.S.-backed operation. The Guatemalans provided data on the airports and the number of military transports the Cuban counterrevolutionaries and their U.S. advisers were using or planned to use in the attack. Ostensibly bringing dried milk to the peasants of Guatemala, American Globemaster planes were actually carrying weapons and ammunition to staging areas for the Cuban assault. At Guatemalan aerodromes Americans had assembled a fleet of B-26 and Lancaster bombers. By October 26, the Guatemalans reported, forty-seven bombers were being outfitted with 500-pound bombs at an airfield near La Aurora, in the Guatemalan province of Retalhuleu.[47]

Both superpowers maneuvered on October 28 to prevent a clash in the Caribbean. The Pentagon suspended U.S. military exercises in the region. The navy had been conducting amphibious training exercises in the Vieques-Roosevelt Roads area, near Puerto Rico, over the past month. Such exercises were held frequently all year for two to three-week periods, after which marines and sailors aboard the ships would get shore leave. The U.S. Navy hastily announced on October 28 a weekend leave for the marines on four vessels: the men of the assault transports USS *Boxer* and the USS *Rankin* would have some time off in San Juan, Puerto Rico, and those on the landing ships *Lorrain County* and *Spiegel Grove* would be in Kingston, Jamaica. Similarly, 1,450 marines were given an unexpected weekend leave at Guantánamo.

The Kremlin opted to deter a U.S. attack by restating its threat to come to the aid of Castro. Moscow did not have any aircraft carriers, nor do there appear to have been any plans for the airlifting of troops to Cuba. A threat to retaliate with nuclear weapons was the only credible way for the Soviet Union to project a deterrent force into the Caribbean in 1960. Fearful that the United States was contemplating some drastic action, the Soviet news agency TASS on October 28 released a summary of an interview conducted a week earlier between Khrushchev and the prominent Cuban journalist Carlos Franqui, in which Khrushchev expressed his commitment to the Cuban revolution.

Later on October 28 the KGB passed Khrushchev and his top foreign policy advisers—Mikoyan, Suslov, and Gromyko—new evidence of U.S. activities.[48] The Cubans had shared their intelligence from Mexico on Guatemala with Alekseev, who cabled it immediately to Moscow. In light of this new information and other indications that the United States was not taking Khrushchev's warnings seriously, the Kremlin decided to reiterate in even stronger terms his intention to use nuclear weapons, if necessary, to defend Castro. On October 29 TASS released a fuller transcript of the Khrushchev/Franqui interview, which included the Soviet leader's statement that he hoped the United States would not force him to turn a "symbolic" threat to use nuclear weapons to defend Cuba into an actual show of force.

The basis for the alarm was so narrow that some in Moscow wanted to hedge their bets that the U.S. military was about to do something in Cuba. A KGB source in the Argentine capital of Buenos Aires obtained a copy of a secret U.S. State Department circular, which had been sent to all U.S. embassies in Latin America. It indicated Washington's reluctance to do anything provocative. "Disruption of diplomatic relations with Cuba, which is planned by several countries, is not reasonable now because it would free Cuba from different obligations by which she is connected to the rest of the countries in Latin America. It could also bring a strengthening of Soviet-Chinese influence in Cuba."[49]

Only three months before, the KGB's analysts had concluded that it was unlikely the United States would intervene in Cuba in the absence of one of two possible provocations: a Cuban attack on Guantánamo or the establishment of Soviet missiles on Cuba. Some in the KGB, at least, sensed that the circular might represent a relaxation in the U.S. posture. To make sure that Castro knew that not all Soviet information pointed in one direction, Moscow decided to send a copy of this report to the Cuban leadership through Alekseev on October 28.

Castro returned to Havana and met with Alekseev on October 29. He had more information to share with Moscow from his ambassador in Mexico. The Guatemalan communists were now reporting that one thousand Cuban émigrés had been moved to the Caribbean port city of Barrios in preparation for the invasion. Castro said that the Cubans had been told to expect an invasion force of six thousand, which would hit the beaches on October 28. Although this day had come and gone, Castro assured Alekseev that "the reports are reliable."[50] True to this conviction, Castro mobilized the militia in the capital city to repel any attack.

The reports were not reliable. In fact, fewer than five hundred Cubans were in training in Guatemala. The CIA was only just beginning to consider using the trainees as a "shock force" in a single amphibious landing, rather than as a ready reserve for piecemeal infiltrations of Cuban territory. Ironically, this shift in focus was as much in response to the evidence of Cuban knowledge of the camps as it was the inevitable result of the Eisenhower administration's decision in March 1960 to mount a serious covert program to overthrow Castro.

On October 31, as Havana and Moscow awaited a U.S.-led attack on a Cuban beach, the CIA notified its people in Guatemala that headquarters was now ready to plan for the type of invasion that Moscow and the Cubans seemed to be expecting. It would take some time to prepare, the force would have to triple in size to carry off the new mission:

1. Plan [to] employ not over 60 men for inf[iltration] teams. . . .
2. Assault force will consist [of] one or more infantry battalions each having about 600 men. . . .
3. Mission of assault force: to seize and defend lodgement in target by amphibious and airborne assault and establish base for further op[eration]s. Automatic sea and air resupply will be provided.
4. Assault force to receive conventional military training. . . .
6. Possibility of using U.S. Army Special Forces training cadres for assault force being pursued. Will advise. . . .

12. Assault of size now planned cannot be readied before several months. Do not plan strike with less than about 1500 men.[51]

The CIA had a few days earlier sent additional instructors to Retalhuleu to begin the expansion of the paramilitary force. The CIA staff officers had received only "tentative approval" from their superiors at the agency, but in the next month all of the pieces would fall into place.[52] In early November, Richard M. Bissell, Jr., the deputy director for plans, and Allen Dulles okayed the plan. A week later the CIA chiefs unveiled the new concept at a meeting of Eisenhower's Special Group, the covert-action adviser board with representatives from the Departments of State and Defense and the White House.[53]

"Moscow Is Our Brain and Our Great Leader"

When no armada appeared over the horizon, Castro and his inner circle believed that the strategic power of the Soviet Union had deterred a U.S. attack. It was the second such reassurance in only four months. Raúl Castro had expressed his gratitude in Moscow in July for the Soviet declaration that Cuban security constituted a vital interest, to be defended by all means. Similarly, in a speech delivered November 9, Fidel Castro raised the issue of the Soviet nuclear umbrella over Cuba. He paid tribute to its deterrent effect in the most recent crisis with Washington. Castro understood that without such assistance from Moscow, Cuba could not defend itself from an American invasion.

Che Guevara may have gone one step further than the Cuban leader. Guevara had left for Prague, Moscow, and Beijing on October 22 to anchor Cuban demands for assistance in the invasion crisis. On November 7, Che celebrated the anniversary of the Russian revolution as an honored guest atop Lenin and Stalin's mausoleum. As he watched row upon row of shiny missiles pass in front of him, he was thinking of ways to formalize the Soviet nuclear deterrent, to prevent future invasion scares. Sometime during this visit, Che is said to have probed Khrushchev about the possibility of stationing Soviet missiles in Cuba.[54] If Che did raise this matter, it did not produce any Presidium decision in 1960. At this point such a demand was premature and ran counter to Khrushchev's strategy of juggling his Cuban policy with a nonconfrontational international policy. Nevertheless, this was possibly the germ for the decision that would emerge in 1962. And Che, who stated publicly in January 1961 that Khrushchev's "symbolic warning" of rocket retaliation against the United States had stopped the planned American invasion, was certainly one of the fathers of that later, fateful development.

Neither the Eisenhower administration in 1960 nor historians subsequently understood the importance of the Cuban war scare of October 1960 in shaping both Soviet-Cuban relations and the confrontation with the United States. The war scare completed Fidel Castro's journey toward a new role as the leader of a communist revolution. Out of a sense of gratitude toward the Soviet Union for having deterred a U.S. attack for a second time, Castro drew confidence in the choice of Soviet-style socialism for his revolution.

In the early morning of November 8, after attending a reception at the Soviet embassy in celebration of the forty-third anniversary of the Bolshevik revolution, Castro turned up in the editorial offices of the PSP's newspaper, *Hoy.* Castro was in great form. Beginning his soliloquy at 4 A.M., he held an audience of editors, journalists, and typesetters in thrall for five hours. With few interruptions, he laid out the history of Cuban-Soviet relations and his own relationship to communism. This was the first time that Fidel Castro went on record, even among the PSP, to admit that he was a communist. Recognizing the importance of this question, which the Soviets were finding as difficult to answer as the CIA, the KGB placed a copy of this account on Khrushchev's desk.

"I have been a Marxist from my student days and have pulled together all of the fundamental works of Marxism," Castro announced. Having started to read Marxist literature while in high school, he claimed to have "introduced it" to his brother Raúl, whom he now considered "the original revolutionary-Marxist." In his report Alekseev added, "Fidel is convinced that he deserves credit for the formation of Raúl's views."[55]

In the course of the early-morning sermon, the leader of the Cuban revolution explained that he saw "no other path for Cuba but the construction of socialism." And to the evident satisfaction of his audience, Castro assigned a prominent role to the PSP, which he judged "the leading and unswerving force, the only theoretically prepared and organized power." In the new Cuba, he said, communists should occupy "all of the key positions . . . in the government, the cultural apparatus, the army and the state economy." Acknowledging that this could not happen overnight, Castro said that "in the current unsettled period, communists will have to wait for a short while and exert influence through trusted individuals who are already in official positions."[56]

"Moscow is our brain and our great leader, and we must pay attention to its voice," Castro said, abandoning his customary prudence in discussing his feelings for the Soviet Union. This was an unprecedented statement, which some in the audience may have initially doubted. Again and again, however, throughout the five-hour speech, Castro returned to this theme: he was a communist, who revered the Soviet leadership and looked to the Kremlin for guidance in directing his revolution. He even admitted feeling a special communion with the Soviet people. "When I am with Soviet citizens, I feel myself among friends, something I have never experienced before with foreigners." "[J]ust as soon as the threat of external invasion subsides," Castro promised, "I will leave for the Soviet Union to spend three or four months studying the construction of a socialist society."[57]

If Castro had wanted to get a message through to the Kremlin, he succeeded. The report on Castro's speech was widely distributed among the top leaders in Moscow. The routing slip shows that besides Khrushchev, Frol

Kozlov, Aleksei Kosygin, Otto Kuusinen, N. A. Mukhitdinov, Anastas Mikoyan, and Mikhail Suslov each received a copy, as did the chief of the International Department of the Central Committee, Boris Ponomarev.[58] Whatever his other goals, Castro's speech was taken by some Soviets as proof of a transformation in his personal philosophy, which since 1959 had been as much of an enigma for Moscow as for Washington. In a portrait of Castro prepared in advance of his state visit to the Soviet Union in 1963, KGB analysts remarked that the Cuban leader had "avoided a clear presentation of his views" when he first came to power. The Soviets did not see this as an attempt to hide the fact that he was a communist, which his brother had done. Instead, Castro's evasion was a ploy to mask the fact that he "lacked deep political convictions."[59]

Many in official Moscow doubted the sincerity of Castro's autobiographical musings about his communist past. According to evidence on his youth supplied by the Cuban communist party, Moscow could conclude only that Fidel Castro was fantasizing, or was playing the role of supplicant, when he claimed to have been a communist all along. Indeed, the elder Castro had consorted with communists when he was a student at the University of Havana, but Moscow knew that these people considered him a bourgeois revolutionary, a member of the Orthodox Party, and an advocate of the violent overthrow of the Batista regime. The Kremlin was glad to hear that Castro now considered himself a communist, but until mid-1959 this same man, the KGB reported, "took pains to avoid harsh criticisms of the imperialistic policies of the United States and strove not to ally himself with communists." Castro's March 1959 statements that "none of the activity of the July 26 movement has anything in common with communism" and that he was "by no means a communist" still hung in the air in Moscow and inspired much skepticism.[60]

Whatever Fidel Castro's core principles, his speech confirmed for the PSP and its leadership the important role they would play in the coming months. By asserting that the revolution could learn from something or someone other than himself, Castro was indicating in the strongest way possible that he was ready to implement the stream of suggestions from Rodríguez and Roca. He had left military and agrarian reform to the PSP in 1959. Industrial and social reforms were next; and with this speech Castro seemed to be assuring those in the pro-Moscow bloc in the July 26 movement that they would have their way.

Khrushchev's Response

Fidel Castro's early-morning monologue seemed to vindicate the risks that Khrushchev had taken for over a year. President Eisenhower, for whatever reason, had not intervened in Cuba as expected in October. A military action might have helped Richard Nixon, who went down to defeat in the closest election in American political history. Although Castro still avoided a public declaration of his sympathies, to the trained observer there could be no doubt that Cuba had chosen the socialist path. Yet the U.S. intervention had not come.

Castro's survival inspired Khrushchev to take a new tack in his leadership of the international communist movement. At a conference of communist leaders in November, only days after Castro's secret speech in Havana, the Soviets introduced the term "national democracy" to celebrate states like Cuba that were in transition to socialism after a middle-class revolution. This public embrace of the Cuban model was only the first signal of a new role for Castro in Khrushchev's understanding of world politics. For four years before coming right out in the open in spring 1960, the Chinese had subtly criticized Khrushchev for endorsing the doctrine of peaceful coexistence. Now that Cuba was on the verge of becoming the first socialist state ever to develop without having been occupied by the Red Army, Khrushchev decided he had to acknowledge the ideological promise of armed national-liberation movements.

In a speech on January 6, 1961, Khrushchev set an ambitious course for Soviet foreign policy, signaling to the world that he welcomed Fidel Castro as a legitimate member of the Soviet bloc. And in deference to both Castro and Mao Zedong, who considered themselves more revolutionary than the peasant bureaucrat in the Kremlin, Khrushchev added that for the first time the Kremlin viewed national-liberation struggles as "sacred wars" that merited assistance and would probably require violence to succeed. As examples of this kind of war, he offered the struggles in Algeria and Vietnam.[61]

Fidel Castro, who had once looked to the Kremlin like a blank slate, was now transformed into the poster child for a new route to socialism. From January 1961 on, Khrushchev would identify his leadership of the communist world and the prestige of the Soviet Union with the health of Cuba and Castro.[62] Any American attempt now to undermine the Castro regime would entail a grave challenge to Khrushchev's personal authority.

THE CLASH

"It Is One Hell of a Gamble"

JOHN F. KENNEDY, **October 22, 1962**

"This May End in a Big War"

NIKITA S. KHRUSHCHEV, **October 22, 1962**

CHAPTER 5

Bay of Pigs

At forty-three years of age, John Fitzgerald Kennedy was the youngest man ever elected to the presidency. On November 6, 1960, Kennedy had beaten Richard Nixon in a very close election. Now it was January 20, and Kennedy cut a sharp figure next to the septuagenarian Dwight Eisenhower, who bunched up against the cold wind as Kennedy removed his top hat and overcoat to deliver his first and best-known address as president.

"Let the word go forth from this time and place, to friend and foe alike, that the torch has been passed to a new generation of Americans. . . ." On the limousine ride to the Capitol, Kennedy had awkwardly tried to engage General Eisenhower in a discussion of *The Longest Day*, a recently published popular history of the 1944 Normandy landings. Had the former supreme commander of the Allied Expeditionary Force read the book? No. Eisenhower was the man who had taken a gamble on the weather and ordered the troops onto the beaches on June 6.[1] He did not need to read the book.

Having witnessed the war at a much lower level, Kennedy was respectful of the old general's wisdom. In the Pacific campaign Kennedy had demonstrated heroism in saving the crew of his PT boat after a collision with a Japanese destroyer. He and Eisenhower actually met in occupied Germany at the end of the war, but Eisenhower was there to advise Joseph Stalin, Winston Churchill, and Harry Truman at the Potsdam Conference, while John Kennedy was attending as a cub reporter for the Hearst newspapers.

The day before the inauguration Kennedy had gone to the old man for advice, which Eisenhower gave freely. The outgoing president had words of warning for his successor. He believed that Nikita Khrushchev and the communist world were on the offensive. The U.S. economy was growing at a rate of 2 to 3 percent per year, while the CIA and other government agencies estimated that the Soviet economy was growing roughly three times as fast.[2] Moreover, the Soviets seemed to be more effective at getting their message across to the developing world. Eisenhower emphasized the problem of Southeast Asia. "If Laos should fall to the Communists," he said, "then it would be a question of time until South Vietnam, Cambodia, Thailand and Burma would collapse." In a nutshell, this was the domino theory. Cuba was also on Eisenhower's agenda. "We cannot let the present government there go on," he said. Then Kennedy asked, "Should we support guerrilla operations in Cuba?" Eisenhower's response was unequivocal: "To the utmost."[3]

The exigencies of the Cold War dominated the themes of Kennedy's inaugural address. The new generation, despite its energy and optimism, shared the anxieties of the retiring Eisenhower. In the late 1950s the Soviets had scored a series of symbolic triumphs. In 1956 the French and British had embarrassed themselves in colluding with Israel against Egypt, Khrushchev's ally in the Middle East. Hoping to drive Gamal Abdel Nasser from power, the European powers had attacked Egypt on the pretext of protecting international access to the Suez Canal. Although Washington had not been informed of the final plans for the attack, and moved quickly to threaten sanctions against the British if they did not desist, the episode tarnished America's reputation for anticolonialism in the Third World. In 1957 the Soviets startled the West by announcing the successful launch of Sputnik, the first man-made satellite to orbit the earth. And in May 1960, a month before Eisenhower and the French and British leaders were to meet with Khrushchev at Paris, a Soviet SA-2 surface-to-air missile shot down an American U-2 piloted by Francis Gary Powers. The U-2 was a high-altitude reconnaissance plane designed to elude air defenses; but once again Soviet technology proved to be better than the experts had assumed. The downing doomed the Paris summit and complicated U.S. efforts to assess Khrushchev's boast that the Soviet Strategic Rocket Forces had more intercontinental ballistic missiles than the United States.

"Let every nation know, whether it wishes us well or ill, that we shall pay any price, bear any burden, meet any hardship, support any friend, oppose any foe to assure the survival and success of liberty."[4] Kennedy's clarion call to action on this January afternoon was not a mere recitation of the liturgy. Kennedy and the former-junior grade officers around him in the new administration believed that, to ensure its very survival, the United States needed to reinvigorate its leadership of the West. Circulating among them was a copy of Khrushchev's January 6 speech on "sacred wars," which had been broadcast over Moscow radio the previous day. The Soviet leader and his ally in the Caribbean, Fidel Castro, seemed equally prepared to energize their own kind of leadership. "Read, mark, learn and inwardly digest," President Kennedy noted on the Khrushchev speech as he ordered its distribution to his top foreign policy advisers.[5]

The Rush to a Summit

Khrushchev had wanted Kennedy to win because he wanted Nixon to lose.[6] Nixon was a known quantity, a man who sided with what the Kremlin considered the worst elements of the Eisenhower administration. The Soviet leadership did not attempt to conceal its happiness at the change in administrations. In a cable to the new president, Khrushchev suggested the possibility of "radical improvement" in U.S.-Soviet relations. The Kremlin had already symbolically buried the old president by announcing that the U-2 affair of the previous May would be consigned to the past.

But Khrushchev did not know much about Kennedy. Before the election, the Kremlin received little from its principal sources of foreign political information—the KGB and the Soviet foreign ministry—that was not readily available in the U.S. press. In an analysis of the senator just after his nomination by the Democratic Party, the Soviet embassy described Kennedy as "a typical pragmatist" and had a hard time placing him in any particular foreign policy camp.[7] "[O]n relations between the USA and the USSR," Soviet Americanists noted, "Kennedy's position . . . is quite contradictory." Although the candidate chastised the Republicans for failing to come up with imaginative ways to improve U.S.-Soviet relations, Kennedy was interested only in what Moscow considered minor palliatives—arms control, for example, instead of disarmament—and seemed not to reject out of hand the possibility of reversing the tide of socialism in Eastern Europe and China. The embassy warned that because Kennedy believed in a strategic missile gap between the superpowers, he was unlikely to engage in any meaningful negotiations before he had restored the United States's "position of strength," a code word that implied a continuation of the arms race. Both the Soviet ministry and the KGB in their first assessments of Kennedy made a point of noting the strong anticommunism of his father, Joseph P. Kennedy, the former U.S. ambassador to Great Britain, who was friends with the notorious Senator Joseph McCarthy. Although not explicit, the possibility of old Joe's having some nefarious influence over his son was left implied.

Initially the KGB had some expectation of better relations in the wake of Kennedy's election. The Soviet foreign intelligence service chose to place the young Kennedy in the Stevenson wing of the Democratic party.[8] Adlai Stevenson had twice run unsuccessfully for the presidency against Eisenhower and was associated with a less belligerent view of the Soviet Union and a commitment to domestic reform, such as civil rights. Yet Kennedy's tough campaign rhetoric caused a slight shift in the KGB's assessment. Indeed, Kennedy's instincts in foreign policy might be closer to his father's than to Stevenson's. "Now . . . the character of Kennedy's statements," the KGB reported, "is close to that of the Democratic leadership, which lies somewhere between the moderate-liberal faction and the reactionary faction of southern democrats."[9]

Khrushchev opted to test the new leader, to discern his real positions. The immediate goal was to see whether he would be interested in a summit meeting. Gromyko's people at the Foreign Ministry largely dismissed Kennedy as "unlikely to possess the qualities of an outstanding person."[10] Yet Moscow was drawn to the cult of the "new frontiersmen." These were the thousands of talented young men who came to Washington in 1961 to replace the generals of the "I like Ike" army. Moscow had high hopes for the white-shirted leaders of this mini-revolution: Adlai Stevenson, Chester Bowles, G. Mennen Williams, Robert Kennedy, Jerome Wiesner, and Arthur Schlesinger, Jr. These "competent individuals," the KGB explained, were "the authors and advocates of many new ideas and plans in U.S. foreign policy."[11] Perhaps Kennedy, for all his own inconsistencies, would implement their policies.

Less than a week after the election, Averell Harriman, who had been Franklin D. Roosevelt's wartime ambassador to Stalin, was chatting with a group of Soviet diplomats, when one of them, an acquaintance from the days of the Grand Alliance in the Second World War, indicated in a semiofficial way that the Soviet leadership was interested in a "fresh start" in U.S.-Soviet relations. Harriman was not prepared to speak for the president-elect, but he suggested that Moscow could set the tone for an improvement of relations by releasing two American pilots in a Soviet jail after their RB-47 reconnaissance plane strayed into Soviet airspace and was shot down.[12]

Khrushchev viewed the discussion at the Soviet embassy as an opening to be explored. Three days after Harriman had his talk, the Soviet ambassador to the United States, Mikhail Menshikov, delivered a formal message from the Soviet leader to the president-elect. Khrushchev offered Kennedy congratulations on his electoral success and expressed a desire to return U.S.-Soviet relations to the way they had been during the time of Franklin Roosevelt.[13] "I told him," Harriman reported to the president-elect, "that you would want, if possible, to come to an understanding with Mr. Khrushchev for our mutual benefit, but that you would not appease nor make any compromises of principle."[14]

A week later the Kremlin used Menshikov again to let Kennedy know that Khrushchev wanted to arrange high-level negotiations between their representatives as soon as this would be convenient. Harriman suggested caution to Kennedy. Khrushchev, he reported, was displaying a "somewhat overly eager attitude."[15]

Kennedy expected Khrushchev to be interested in a summit. In the final weeks of the campaign, one of the Kennedy camp's biggest fears had been that, because of Khrushchev's evident desire for a meeting, Eisenhower would schedule a snap summit in October, sign a test ban agreement or some other major piece of bilateral diplomacy, and let Vice President Nixon bask in reflected glory. In late September the Kennedy camp sent Chester Bowles, a Connecticut congressman and future Kennedy undersecretary of state, to discourage Eisenhower's secretary of state, Christian Herter, from taking that step.[16] So, nothing that Harriman was telling Jack Kennedy two months later about Khrushchev's eagerness to go to the prom could have been a surprise.

The president-elect chose to slow the tempo of discussions with the Russians until after the inauguration. The election had been very close, and though Kennedy liked to say that "a margin of only one vote would still be a mandate,"[17] he lacked a clear sense of how he intended to improve relations with the Soviets. At the same time, he did not want to discourage Khrushchev. He decided to send a private message of his own through his younger brother Robert F. Kennedy to assure the Soviet leader that his patience would be rewarded. There was no one whom John Kennedy trusted more than his former campaign manager and future attorney general, the thirty-five-year-old Robert Kennedy. The venerable Averell Harriman was a trustworthy democratic warhorse, a reliable fund-raiser, and an adviser to presidents; but Robert was the man to reveal Kennedy's inner thoughts when that was the president-elect's purpose.

On December 1, 1960, at 10:00 A.M., Robert Kennedy welcomed a Mr. B. of the Moscow newspaper *Izvestia* into the office of the transition team.[18] B., as the Kennedys probably guessed, was an undercover KGB officer in the New York *residentura*. His report of the meeting, reproduced below, went straight to Khrushchev. It represented the Kremlin's first inside look at the foreign policy thinking of the president-elect:

To Comrade N. S. Khrushchev:

We are reporting to you that on December 1, 1960, a member of the KGB *residentura* in New York met with the brother and closest adviser of the U.S. President Kennedy—Robert Kennedy. Having stressed that he was not merely expressing his personal opinion but the position of the future president, Robert Kennedy stated the following in the course of the conversation.

President Kennedy will pay a lot of attention to U.S.-Soviet relations. He considers that they could and should improve in the coming years. Kennedy intends to devote special attention to matters of disarmament, to the extent of reaching agreements, in as much as the Soviet Union had already made the serious concessions that had been hoped for in this area. Kennedy believes that a nuclear test ban treaty could be concluded as early as 1961, if both sides take additional steps to bring their positions closer together. In spite of the opposition of some groups in the United States, Kennedy does not intend to resume underground nuclear tests and or to break off the test ban negotiations in Geneva before a definitive exploration of both sides' points of view.

In principle, Kennedy would like to meet with you and hopes that his relations with the Soviet leader will be better than Eisenhower had. However, he will not agree to a summit if he doubts that positive results will ensue. In the first three or four months of his presidency, before he has presented his domestic program to Congress, Kennedy would not be able to participate in a summit.

Kennedy is seriously concerned about the situation in Berlin and will strive to find the means to reach a settlement of the Berlin problem. However, if in the next few months the Soviet Union applies pressure on this question, then Kennedy will certainly defend the position of the West.

Recognizing the importance of the development of Soviet-American trade, Kennedy does not believe, however, that this question is a priority and suggests that it would be easier to resolve this puzzle after the resolution of the more important international problems. Kennedy intends to continue and broaden cultural exchanges between the U.S. and the USSR.

In the course of the discussion, Robert Kennedy recalled that in 1955 he visited the Soviet Union and that he had pleasant memories of this trip. He stated that he would very much like to visit the USSR again; however, he did not have any plans to do so in the near future. From the meeting, the KGB reporter gathered the impression that Robert Kennedy would accept an unofficial invitation to visit the Soviet Union. At the end of the conversation, Robert Kennedy remarked in passing that, in his opinion, the fundamental problem in the next few years would not be U.S.-Soviet relations, but instead Washington's relations with China.[19]

Over the course of this thirty-minute conversation, Robert Kennedy had outlined his brother's tentative design for a modest détente between the superpowers. As the Soviet Foreign Ministry had predicted, there were no revolutionary ideas here. But as the Soviets would discover, John Kennedy intended to push the ideas he did have very energetically. This would not be the last time that Robert Kennedy, on his behalf, appealed directly to Moscow for patience and understanding.

In Moscow, Khrushchev accepted the need for patience. Some other information had come in that reinforced Robert Kennedy's statement that John Kennedy was committed to better relations with Moscow. There was no harm in waiting.[20] Kennedy would be allowed to decide when to start talking about a summit again.

Kennedy and Cuba

Cuba, however, was an immediate priority for John Kennedy. He believed that "time was running out" for the United States in Latin America and that though "the Cold War [would] not be won in Latin America, it [might] very well be lost there."[21] A few days before the inauguration, the United States had broken relations with Cuba. Kennedy had neither endorsed nor condemned Eisenhower's decision, which had been prompted by a Cuban demand that the United States dramatically reduce the size of its delegation in Havana.[22]

On coming to office, Kennedy had a good sense of what he wanted to do in the region. In general, he believed in reform from the top, in what he termed "executive vigor." In Latin America he looked for leaders who could improve living standards without denying civil liberties or courting the far left. He had no doubt about the basic aspirations of the people. "Poverty is not new to

Latin America. . . . The people . . . want better homes, better schools, and better living standards; they want land reform, and tax reform, and an end to corruption which drains off a nation's resources." Land reform was a precondition to the development of healthy Latin American polities. In these states, Kennedy observed, "archaic systems of absentee ownership still keep land in the grip of a few wealthy landowners, while the mass of the people struggle for a subsistence living as tenants."[23]

As for Cuba, Kennedy was not blind to the fact that economic injustice as much as anything else had propelled Castro's July 26 movement to power. "This concentration of land ownership," he argued, "was one of the principal grievances which underlay the Cuban revolution."[24] Consequently John Kennedy respected the magnetic attraction of Fidel Castro's message and believed that in order for the United States to compete in the region it would need a positive program of technical and financial assistance.[25] "The good-neighbor policy is no longer enough," Kennedy argued. Instead, in the course of the campaign he had suggested the Alliance for Progress, which he described as "an alliance of nations with a common interest in freedom and economic advance in a great common effort to develop the resources of the entire hemisphere, strengthen the forces of democracy, and widen the vocational and educational opportunities of every person in all the Americas."[26] Advocating greater U.S. foreign aid and economic assistance to Latin America, Kennedy sought to make the region more economically self-sufficient, by means both of stabilizing commodity prices for single-staple economies and of assisting efforts to facilitate economic diversification.

Kennedy inherited a Cuban policy whose goals were firm but whose means were in flux. Since March 1960 the Eisenhower administration had sought to overthrow the Castro regime through a combination of overt and covert acts. As of January 1961 the United States no longer had diplomatic relations with Cuba and engaged in very little trade with the island. But the source of dispute was the covert side of the ledger because the CIA's four-part program, which Eisenhower had approved following the *La Coubre* incident, was going nowhere.[27] As Castro consolidated his power in the summer and fall of 1960, it became increasingly obvious that the most important element of the program was part four, the creation of an "adequate paramilitary force." Yet the Eisenhower administration never could settle on a definition of what kind of force would be adequate to overthrow Castro. From the arrival of the first CIA instructors in Guatemala, in July 1960, until the end of the year, "adequate" was defined as a 300-man force that would be infiltrated in stages into the Escambray mountains. However, the events in the fall, including the October scare, had forced a reexamination of this approach. In the last weeks of the Eisenhower administration, the CIA was talking about building a 1,500 man guerrilla army in Guatemala.[28]

John Kennedy came to office just as the CIA was refining the second concept for submission to the U.S. military and the White House. CIA Director Allen Dulles had high hopes that the new president would endorse the expanded paramilitary concept. Dulles had been impressed with what he took to be Kennedy's positive response to the description of the March 1960 program at his first detailed briefing on Cuban covert operations, on November 19. At the very first administration meeting on Cuba, chaired by the new secretary of state, Dean Rusk, Dulles was told that "in a day or two" he would know what Kennedy thought of the plan. Yet it was obvious from the assignments that Rusk distributed to the CIA and the Pentagon that the administration intended to continue Eisenhower's policy of using covert means to remove Castro.[29] Rusk asked the Pentagon to see what "support . . . might be provided . . . in the event that conditions [made] support necessary." The analysts at the CIA were to draft an estimate of "the effects of overt U.S. action in Cuba on the rest of the world," while the agency's covert operators were to report on the status of sabotage operations on the island.[30]

Within a few days the CIA and the Pentagon learned that Kennedy did not like the paramilitary program. The CIA outlined plans for a daylight landing near the town of Trinidad by roughly 1,000 trained Cuban exiles. Trinidad, with a population of 18,000, was situated along the coastal plain next to the Escambray mountains. The lesson of the autumn was that Castro's defensive forces were numerous and could be beaten only with a "shock." The CIA hoped that Castro's gradual creeping into the Soviet camp had sown enough popular discontent that a government in exile, which held a beachhead only two hundred miles from Havana, might be able to lead a massive counterrevolution. But the newly inaugurated president doubted the military viability of the beachhead and asked whether the CIA had vetted this program with the Joint Chiefs of Staff.

While the Joint Chiefs were looking at the plan, Kennedy wanted the opinion of his civilian advisers. On February 4 he turned to McGeorge Bundy, his national security adviser and the man who as a dean at Harvard had welcomed Castro two years earlier, to work up a list of options. Bundy assumed that Kennedy doubted the feasibility of the Trinidad plan. He himself had doubts that this was the best way to solve the Castro problem. But to ensure that the president was aware of the range of options for dealing with Castro, he put on top of Kennedy's reading pile a policy memorandum that argued strongly for the plan. The author of the memorandum was the strongest advocate of the paramilitary option in Washington, the deputy director for plans at the CIA, Richard Bissell. Bissell was a rare animal in Washington, a man who had managed to turn everything he touched to gold. In the late 1940s he had earned praise as a Marshall Plan administrator. After a short stint at the Ford Foundation, he was recruited back to government to oversee the development of the U-2, the high-altitude U.S. spy-plane that opened the first significant cracks in the secrecy surrounding the Soviet nuclear arsenal. Kennedy knew Bissell through the Georgetown social circuit, and it was common gossip that Bissell would be his choice to replace the legendary Dulles when he finally stepped down.

Despite his respect for Bissell, Kennedy still preferred the State Department's argument against the Trinidad plan to the case that Bissell made. In mid-February, Kennedy ordered that the operation be suspended pending further review, and on March 11 he set new conditions for this operation. He thought that the Trinidad plan was conceived without much attention to keeping the American hand invisible. In the staff work for the plan, there was ample evidence of the Eisenhower administration's intention to use U.S. military force if necessary. In light of his statements about the importance of Latin American sovereignty and his expressed desire for better relations with Moscow, Kennedy did not want the paramilitary action to be interpreted as a direct U.S. attack on Cuba. He set two new constraints to guide a revision of the plan. The attack had to be "an unspectacular landing at night in an area where there was a minimum likelihood of opposition." And that "[i]f ultimate success would require tactical air support, it should appear to come from a Cuban air base. Therefore, the territory seized should contain a suitable airfield."[31]

Kennedy's political antennae had failed him. He did not know it at the time, but the conditions he set forth sealed the fate of the Cuban paramilitary operation. The only areas that met both conditions were far from the Escambray or any other mountains. In the Trinidad plan, if the beachhead could not be held, then at least the exiles could escape to the nearby mountains and bolster the strength of local anti-Castro rebels. But Kennedy was asking the CIA to put hundreds of men secretly on a beach and leave them there to defend themselves.

Richard Bissell threw a new plan together in four days. Playa Girón, along the Bay of Pigs, was an isolated point on the southern coast of Cuba, where it was assumed an invasion could occur quietly. Unlike the first plan, this one did not require continuous U.S. air support, because it would take the Cuban military a while to reach the site. The president's conditions had been met, but the new plan entailed new risks. The isolated location could work to the plan's disadvantage if the beachhead was not firmly established before Castro's forces counterattacked. Moreover, an isolated struggle might not stir the mass Cuban uprising that many hoped would follow an invasion. Allen Dulles later testified that the CIA "either had to go ahead or we had the alternative of demobilizing these people, and to the world, it would have meant that we were not behind these people who were trying to overthrow Castro."[32] Neither of these reasons had anything to do with the likelihood that this new plan, codenamed Zapata, would work. Nevertheless, Kennedy accepted the advice of his covert specialists and conditionally approved Zapata on March 16, reserving the right to cancel it up to forty-eight hours before the landing.

"A Matter of Defending Soviet Territory"

In the weeks before Kennedy's inauguration, a second Cuban invasion scare, as intense for the Cubans and the Soviets as the false alarm in October, had gripped Cuba.[33] The scare was triggered by a KGB report of an imminent U.S. invasion that arrived in Moscow in late December from a CIA source.[34]

In response to this information and a spate of New Year's bombings in central Havana, Castro gave the U.S. government forty-eight hours to reduce its consulate and embassy staffs to eleven people, including local employees.[35] The demand had surprised Washington, prompting the severing of diplomatic relations on January 4, 1961.

As the Kennedy administration debated its Cuban policy, Havana and Moscow were still suffering from a lack of secret information about the United States's intentions. The Soviets and the Cubans reacted differently to the inadequacies of their spy services. After four months of bad predictions, the KGB initiated a campaign in January 1961 to improve its knowledge of U.S. policy on Cuba.[36] The Cubans, on the other hand, continued to believe the information that had been collected during the two invasion scares. Many in Havana, chiefly Fidel and Raúl Castro, concluded that the Americans did not execute their invasion plans in October 1960 and again in January 1961, because they were deterred by Soviet statements of support for Cuba.

With a new president in the White House, the Cubans could not agree among themselves what to expect from the United States. Castro took a relatively relaxed view of the new administration. He believed that even if Kennedy was as bent on removing him as Eisenhower had been, the Soviet Union's commitment to Cuba would continue to deter U.S. military aggression. Blas Roca and the communist leadership disagreed. They assumed that "Kennedy [had] decided to take action in March."[37] The strategy of the new administration would be to present an invasion of Cuba by a group of counterrevolutionaries as a fait accompli to the rest of Latin America at the upcoming inter-American conference, scheduled to open March 1 in Quito, Ecuador. "The U.S. government," Roca's assistant Aníbal Escalante reported to the Soviet ambassador, "will ask Latin American states to support tighter sanctions on Cuba in light of the 'civil war' taking place there."[38]

The Cuban communists were loath to complain about Fidel Castro, who in recent months had been following their advice especially closely. In October he had adopted the communists' block surveillance scheme after finally purging the secret police and security services of anticommunists. And there was a noticeable change in his ideas about economic policy. "In the past, Fidel Castro did not understand the importance of planning," one Cuban communist leader reported to the Kremlin in the spring of 1961. "Now Castro openly says that the Cuban economy should be planned." The PSP was pleased that Castro had accepted its plan for collectivizing agriculture and was ready to follow advice that the improvement of the country's manufacturing base be a priority in the new plan. Yet the communists worried that Castro was too careless in handling the U.S. threat. In listing the potential support for a counterrevolution in Cuba, Escalante stressed that there were Cubans who would assist any intervention, though the number was manageable. "Fidel Castro is strongly supported by 80 percent of the population. There are no more than 50,000–60,000 counterrevolutionaries in Cuba and only 7,000–8,000 outside the country."[39] However, Escalante and Blas Roca believed that the Cuban government would have to organize itself better to meet even this small challenge. During the war scare of January 1961, it had mobilized 300,000 in the revolutionary militia. Yet there was no plan as to how that militia would be used in the event of an attack.

Raúl Castro agreed with Escalante and Roca that his brother needed a push to devise a contingency plan for defending the country. Fidel had approved sending a military delegation to Moscow in the spring to discuss additional weapons supply. Roca's lieutenant in the leadership of the communist party, Flavio Bravo was sent to represent Castro. Raúl, who may have personally chosen Bravo, spoke to the communist leader before he left for Moscow: "Convey to the Soviet comrades that they should approach the putting together of such a plan as if it were a matter of defending Soviet territory."[40] Raúl and the PSP hoped that with Moscow's help, they could persuade Fidel Castro to take the threat of a U.S. attack more seriously.

Bravo, who received red-carpet treatment when he arrived in March, stressed that "John F. Kennedy [was] taking a more aggressive stance toward Cuba than Eisenhower." He said that, since taking office, Kennedy had "already spoken out five times against Cuba." Fidel Castro believed that Kennedy would be restrained by the fear of sparking a world war, and it was thought that Cuba was not facing an imminent overt U.S. attack. Nevertheless, the Cuban communists worried about what the counterrevolutionaries could achieve with U.S. material and logistical help. Bravo painted for the Soviets a dark picture of the internal situation. Citing a figure of 4,000–5,000 armed anti-Castro rebels roaming the countryside, he told them that the Cubans were "living in a period like your crusade against the kulaks in 1927-30."[41]

Khrushchev's representatives—his heir apparent, Frol Kozlov, and fellow presidium member Mikhail Suslov—assured Raúl Castro's representative of Moscow's continuing support. "[T]he USSR," Kozlov said, "is prepared to give Cuba whatever she needed"; and he promised that he would speak to Kremlin's defense chief, Rodion Malinovsky, about the matter "that very day." But there would be some strings attached. Moscow would be glad to help the PSP and Raúl design a military plan to protect Cuba from a U.S. attack, but both Kozlov and Suslov stressed that "this would be possible only if Soviet specialists were sent to Cuba."[42]

The Summit and the Bay of Pigs

True to his word in December, the new president returned to the matter of a summit soon after his inauguration. Summoning Llewellyn Thompson, Eisenhower's ambassador in Moscow (whom Kennedy would decide to retain), in February, Kennedy canvassed the opinions of the best Sovietologists in the U.S. government on the pluses and minuses of an early summit. The group reinforced Kennedy's instinct to press on with a meeting.[43] Khrushchev first heard about the results of this policy review in March when Thompson carried back to Moscow an invitation to the Soviet leader to meet in a neutral city.

On April 1 Khrushchev told Thompson that he wanted to go ahead with Kennedy's suggestion of a summit meeting in late May, in either Vienna or Stockholm.[44] Kennedy summoned his aides and discussed with them a set of appropriate dates. June 3 and 4 seemed the most convenient because the president had already committed to a state visit to France on June 1.

News that Moscow was interested in a summit crossed paths with final preparations for a covert operation in Cuba. The tight circle of undersecretaries and CIA chiefs allowed into the planning had spent the month of March hashing out a plan for using the Cuban trainees whom the Soviets and Havana had been complaining about since October 1960. The Guatemalan government wanted them out, and the Cuban exile leadership was losing its patience.

The CIA presented Kennedy a fuller version of the Zapata invasion plan on Easter weekend, April 1–3. According to his inner circle, Kennedy decided to go ahead while at the southern White House in Palm Beach and returned to Washington full of determination. "He had made up his mind and told us. He didn't ask us," Bundy later recalled.[45] Kennedy kept a lid on his plan, not even telling his private muse and future biographer Theodore Sorensen what was up for Cuba. Sorensen picked up a "bare hint" at a meeting, but the president's only response was "an earthy expression" to complain that "too many advisors seemed frightened by the prospects of a fight."[46]

The summit likely weighed heavily on how the president dealt with the new phase of the Cuban covert plan. On the night of April 4, just after signing off on the dates for the summit, Kennedy stressed to the team overseeing the Cuban operation that there had to be even less "noise." In his mind, the only way to square this circle, to keep a two-track policy of getting the Soviets out of the Caribbean while bringing them into disarmament discussions, was to mask as much as possible U.S. involvement in ending Castro's revolution.

Alekseev in Brazil

Paradoxically, as John Kennedy and his American national security chiefs were polishing plans for action in Cuba, the Soviets were becoming more relaxed about the security of Fidel Castro's regime. U.S.-Soviet discussions of a superpower summit and the lack of any new confirmatory information in March about Kennedy's intentions strengthened the Kremlin's prejudice against believing that the new administration would make the mistake that Eisenhower and his dark henchman Richard Nixon had flirted with.

With the threat of an invasion apparently receding, Aleksandr Alekseev, the KGB station chief and Fidel Castro's favorite Russian, left Havana for Brazil.

"Brazil was one of those countries with which we needed to establish relations," Alekseev recalls today to explain his strange absence from Cuba in April 1961. He had befriended the new president of Brazil, Jânio Quadros, when Quadros was an opposition political figure. Alekseev had been Quadros's interpreter (Quadros knew Spanish; Alekseev did not speak Portuguese) when the latter visited Moscow and Leningrad in 1959. "I am with the Soviet Union," Quadros explained to the Soviets he met.[47] In 1960 Quadros, who also admired Fidel Castro's revolution, had resumed his acquaintance with Alekseev during a stay in Havana. "Just as soon as I am elected," Quadros said to Alekseev "I give you my word, you will be the first to get a visa," and with Quadros's election it looked as if Brazil was on the verge of opening up to the Soviets. "Everyone in Moscow knew about this invitation," Alekseev remembers with pride.[48]

Soon after Quadros's inauguration on January 31, 1961, the Kremlin moved to exploit Alekseev's unusual access to the new Brazilian president. "I was instructed to return to Moscow," Alekseev recalled later. Moscow wanted him to visit Brazil as soon as possible. Leaving Cuba in early April, Alekseev was confident that Castro had the situation well in hand. "The [invasion] routes were mined," Alekseev explained. As protection against an intervention, the Cuban army had prepared minefields near possible landing sites. Nevertheless, as Alekseev readily admits, neither he nor Moscow expected a major U.S.-backed incursion in April 1961. "I had seen the [U.S.] bombardments. . . . But why did we not believe that it would be such a large invasion, I don't know." Looking darkly through the mists of time, Alekseev can only recall, "We just did not believe it."[49]

The Cubans and Soviets viewed the United States through different glasses that first week of April 1961. What Fidel Castro thought of Alekseev's departure is unknown; but at this time Soviet and Cuban perceptions of the threat from Washington diverged radically. Havana had learned that Khrushchev and Kennedy were edging toward a summit, and Fidel Castro expressed concern to his inner circle that his allies in the Kremlin might sacrifice him on the altar of better U.S.-Soviet relations. Castro said nothing to the Soviets about his concerns, though he might well have informed Alekseev had the latter been in town. Instead, the Cuban communists carried this message confidentially to Ambassador Kudryavtsev on April 7.

Kudryavtsev alerted Moscow that some preventive damage control was required. The Cuban communists did not want Fidel Castro to know that they had conveyed his anxiety to Moscow. Couldn't the Kremlin do or say something to allay Castro's fear? Kudryavtsev asked Moscow on behalf of his informants. "Fidel Castro wants to know whether Comrade Khrushchev raised the issue of Cuba with the U.S. ambassador Thompson."[50]

With Alekseev in Brazil, Kudryavtsev was the principal point of contact between the Cubans and Moscow. The leaders of the PSP were as worried about a U.S. invasion as about Fidel's commitment to Moscow. Despite the silence in Washington, they told the Soviet ambassador on April 8 that the danger of an invasion in support of the newly formed government-in-exile of José Miró Cardona was "very real." The "situation is more dangerous than in October 1960 or in January of this year."[51] The Cuban communists admitted that "the Cuban government does not have at its disposal definite information regarding when and from which points the invasion will take place. But the government considers the invasion inevitable."[52]

The Kremlin responded swiftly, putting Cuba on the agenda for the Presidium meeting scheduled for April 11.[53] Khrushchev and his colleagues discounted the Cuban communists' concerns. Just the day before, the Soviet Foreign Ministry had informed the U.S. embassy of the acceptability of a June summit in Vienna.[54] Moreover, no one had any firm evidence of an American plan to invade. Yet the Soviet leader could not ignore Havana's concerns. Khrushchev did not want bilateral negotiations with the Americans to create suspicions in the socialist camp, especially among the Cubans, who were its newest members. The Chinese had denounced Khrushchev for attempting a high-level exchange with Eisenhower in 1960; and the Kremlin did not want to give the Chinese an excuse to make trouble with the Cubans now.

To reassure Havana, Khrushchev ordered the preparation of a confidential summary for Castro of the portions of his talk with Thompson that concerned Cuba.[55] The Soviets chose a section where Khrushchev had attempted, in a rambling fashion, to reassure Thompson that the Soviet Union did not intend to make a military base out of Cuba. "We disagree with the US conception of Cuba," Khrushchev told Thompson. "The USA for some reason," he added, "believes that it has the right to put military bases along the borders of the USSR." By contrast, however, "[w]e do not . . . have a military base in Cuba, just friendly relations."[56]

The Kremlin's optimism about the situation in Cuba was put to the test only a day later, when the KGB passed on to Khrushchev a very serious report on the Guatemalan situation. The activity in the U.S. training camps in Guatemala was a barometer of Washington's intentions regarding Castro. On April 12, for the first time since the end of February, some serious warning signals came in. The network set up by the Guatemalan communist party, which since October 1960 had been feeding the KGB in Mexico, reported that the CIA had started the final preparations for the invasion of Cuba. The information, which was a few days old, predicted an attack any day. The Soviet government did not know whether Cuban sources had received this information. Thinking it serious enough, the KGB decided to tell Alekseev's stand-in at the *residentura* to pass it along to both the Cuban government and the PSP.

In the past whenever Khrushchev believed that Cuba was threatened, he had never hesitated to make a statement to defend the country or to use *Pravda* to warn the United States that he was watching. This time he and *Pravda* stayed silent. Khrushchev's silence suggests the possibility that he had prepared to abandon Cuba, realizing that if Kennedy indeed wanted to invade

Cuba, he could prevail over Castro without the Soviet Union's being able to do anything. It also suggests, however, that whereas in October and January the Soviets had gone out on a limb and been proven wrong, the Kremlin now had doubts about its information.

Kennedy was probably the reason that Moscow did not take the warnings seriously this time. At a press conference on April 12, the same day that the Guatemalan information arrived, John F. Kennedy assured the world that the United States did not intend to invade the island: "there will not be, under any conditions, any intervention in Cuba by United States armed forces, and this government will do everything it possibly can—and I think it can meet its responsibilities—to make sure that there are no Americans involved in any actions inside."[57]

Curiously, the KGB had even better intelligence about Kennedy's intention, but it passed unnoticed by the Kremlin. Since the debacle of the fall of 1960, the Soviets had developed a source in or around the Cuban exile community in New York. On April 8 the New York station reported,

Manuel Varona, a representative of the Cuban government in exile, is conducting negotiations about an intervention in Cuba that will take place from April 10 to 11. 3,500 mercenaries will participate in the landing. They will defend some part of the island to create territory, which would allow the government in exile to proclaim itself the provisional government. Then the provisional government would appeal to Cuban people and the U.S. government to recognize them and to support them with military forces and to help them in all other respects. Varona asked for transport planes and submarines. In principle the U.S. accepted all his plans, though it did reject his requests for transportation to avoid the accusation that it participated in the invasion. Despite this, Americans promised him to help these groups financially.[58]

The KGB may have informed Khrushchev orally of this information. But unlike the warnings from Kudryavtsev and the information from the KGB station in Mexico, the Varona report did not land on Khrushchev's desk. It certainly would have reinforced Khrushchev's already strong assumption that Kennedy would not risk the summit on this adventure, but the size of the invasion that Varona described was three times the earlier estimate given to Moscow. This might have set off an alarm bell or two.

The timing of Kennedy's declaration played right into the Kremlin's efforts to mollify Castro. With Kennedy's words still ringing in his ears, Castro was informed by the Soviet ambassador of Khrushchev's statements to Thompson. Castro naturally concluded that Khrushchev's initiative of April 1 and Kennedy's more recent speech were linked, that once again Moscow's forthrightness had deterred American aggression.

On the night of April 13, Blas Roca and Fidel Castro discussed Khrushchev's warning to the United States and the effect it might have on Kennedy's plans. Castro announced himself satisfied with the Soviet initiative, and Roca, at least, left assured that Khrushchev's personal intervention would work the same magic it allegedly had worked in 1960.[59]

The Cuban communist leader made the same point the next day, April 14, in a meeting in his apartment with the Soviet ambassador. Roca asked Kudryavtsev to convey to Khrushchev his "genuine and warm gratitude to Khrushchev for his assistance against the aggressive attacks from American imperialism." Roca stressed that Khrushchev's warning "would undoubtedly have a restraining influence upon the Kennedy administration." The Cubans thought that Kennedy's April 12 assurance was the product of Soviet declarations of support. "There are serious concerns in the U.S.," explained Roca, "that Kennedy's aggressive politics toward Cuba will lead to war."[60] Roca also gave credit to the Soviet space program. On April 12 the Soviet cosmonaut Yuri Gagarin became the first man to go into space. Roca felt that this achievement could only inspire more respect and fear from the Americans. It compels Washington, he said, "to stop rattling sabers."

The Kremlin and the Cubans could live with Kennedy's statement that "the basic issue in Cuba . . . is between the Cubans themselves." The socialist bloc was slightly more than halfway through a program of military assistance to Cuba. Cuba had received 125 of 205 tanks expected to be sent. It had already received 167,000 rifles and 7,250 machine guns; but 128 of the Soviet Union's largest howitzers were still in the pipeline. Much of the antiaircraft and anti-tank support was already on the island. The greatest gap was assistance to the fledgling Cuban air force. Not one of the MiG fighters promised by the Soviet government had been sent. If Khrushchev had believed in the U.S. threat in the spring of 1961 as he had in October 1960 or would in September 1962, he might well have hastened these deliveries.

The Attack

The Bay of Pigs, which would end as a military victory for the Soviet bloc, began as a Cuban intelligence surprise. Only hours after Blas Roca informed the Kremlin of his confidence that once again the American eagle and its allies had been restrained, B-26s piloted by Cuban émigrés began strafing Cuban airfields in the morning of April 15.

The Cuban brigade needed air superiority to have any hope of holding a beachhead in Cuba for more than twenty-four or forty-eight hours. A Pentagon inspection team that evaluated the CIA Cuban force in March had warned that "an aircraft armed with 50 caliber machine guns could sink all or most of the invasion force."[61] Reconnaissance missions flown by U-2s on April 8, 11, and 13 picked up that the Cubans had thirty-six combat aircraft, some of which were T-33 jets.[62] In the small Cuban exile air force created by the

CIA, there were no jets.[63] The most powerful plane was the propeller-driven B-26, a World War II stalwart that was no match for the Cold War T-33. In the planning stages of the air component of this proxy war, the CIA assumed that Castro's few T-33s, which were trainers sent to the Batista government by the United States in 1950s, would not be armed.

The night of April 16 Kennedy alerted his advisers that he was suspending a portion of the original plan because of the effects it might have on his country's international reputation. The previous day's air attack had led to an embarrassing debate at the United Nations, where the U.S. ambassador, Adlai Stevenson, had been forced to lie about U.S. involvement. Kennedy decided that he could not risk another air strike before the émigrés had established their beachhead in the morning. This decision doomed the operation. The air strike on April 15 had eliminated only 60 percent of Castro's air force, which was more powerful than had been assumed. Without air superiority the expedition would be a sitting duck the next morning.

Moscow's national security apparatus began to mobilize to assess the situation as soon as the first reports of the B-26 bombing runs reached Moscow on April 15. "We were waiting . . . in general [for something to occur in Cuba]," recalls one member of the hastily established war room in the Lubyanka. Oleg Nechiporenko was a two-year veteran of the KGB when he was pulled in to monitor the events in Cuba. A former student of Spanish at the Soviet Academy of Foreign Languages, Nechiporenko was slated for a position in the KGB's large station in Mexico City. In Moscow, where only a handful of men in any of the ministries described themselves as Latin American experts, his linguistic ability qualified him for helping Aleksandr Shelepin, the KGB chairman, make sense of the evolving situation in Cuba.[64] "We were hearing by international radio [all available] informations, and all the cables which came we immediately gave to the chiefs."

"We put two maps on the wall, one where we plotted the movements as they were described on American radio and the other according to our own information," recalls Nikolai Leonov. Leonov, Raúl Castro's friend and one of the best-known Spanish linguists in official Moscow, was the other man brought into the KGB war room on April 16. Leonov had a deeper knowledge of Cuba than Nechiporenko did, having visited the island. But at that moment what the Soviet leadership needed was less analytical capability than aural comprehension of Spanish.[65]

The first intelligence information from the field on April 17 gave Moscow cause for concern. The Cuban defense forces were taken by surprise. Like Moscow, Castro had no idea where the attack would occur. The Cuban communists reported that about one thousand counterrevolutionaries had landed at Playa Girón and forced the small Cuban garrison stationed there to retreat to the interior. Apparently the brigade's operational objective was the airfield at Cienfuegos, sixty miles east of the landing area.[66] The Castro forces should

have been able to deal with a thousand invaders. But later in the day Blas
Roca came to the KGB station to warn that it seemed that an airborne assault
had occurred at the same time as the landing. These forces landed twenty-five
miles behind the beaches in an area called Covadonga, with the intention of
intercepting Cuban forces sent south through the major railroad junction at
Aguada de Pasajeros. Did this mean that Kennedy had broken his word and
that American special forces were in Cuba? The Cuban communists also reported, without comment, that the U.S.-supported José Miró Cardona was
calling for an uprising.[67]

The good news for the Kremlin was that the Cuban air force was starting to
hit the counterrevolutionaries on the beaches. Moscow had promised MiG
fighters, but these had not arrived in time. Fortunately for the Cubans and the
Kremlin, the Cuban T-33s and Sea Furies were proving effective. By April 18
the Cubans were reporting that the invaders were finding their ability to
broaden the beachhead hampered by a lack of supplies.[68] There was also word
that Fidel Castro had stayed in Havana but was in control of the Cuban military response.

Leonov recalled that U.S. radio broadcasts described the campaign in terms
more pessimistic for the exiles than what Moscow received from the Cubans
or their own people on the island. On April 18 the fight was still going on.
The Cubans reported that it was proceeding on four fronts, and on only one
of these was the U.S.-backed group retreating. Moscow was also informed of
the opening of a new front. Apparently there was a small invasion at the western tip of the island, in the province of Pinar del Río, with which the Cubans
seemed to be dealing effectively.[69] While the situation remained confused in
Cuba, Leonov and Nechiporenko stayed nights in the Lubyanka to follow
events.[70]

Washington learned that the invasion was doomed before Moscow did. By
the evening of April 17, the CIA was reporting to Allen Dulles that the brigade was trapped on the beaches. The president's decision to cancel the second strike had eliminated any chance that Castro's air force would be
grounded before the landings began.[71] This left enough of Castro's planes in
the air to attack the Cuban émigré air force and the U.S.-backed armada. The
T-33s shot down six of the B-26s in the CIA's Cuban air force, and another
two were lost to antiaircraft fire. The most telling blow came from T-33 attacks that sank two ships in the operational convoy, one of which carried the
brigade's ammunition and communications. The beachhead would have been
difficult to hold under any scenario; but the CIA had war-gamed this exercise
assuming that all of the ammunition would make it to shore under U.S. protective air cover.

The next morning Kennedy was told that the operation was teetering on the
brink of collapse. "[T]he situation in Cuba is not a bit good," McGeorge
Bundy warned Kennedy as he headed into a meeting of his Cuban crisis

team.[72] "The Cuban armed forces are stronger," Bundy explained, "the popular response is weaker, and our tactical position is feebler than we had hoped."[73] The disaster in Cuba affected Bundy, formerly a skeptic, who was now recommending to Kennedy that unmarked U.S. Air Force jets be sent into Cuban airspace to destroy Castro's air force, so that the Cuban brigade would have a fighting chance on the beaches.

The briefing was just as dreary as Bundy had warned. The Cuban group had lost the battle on one of the beaches after Castro committed twelve Soviet-made tanks to flush them out. Meanwhile, additional tanks and Castro's remaining planes were pounding the other beachhead. "Nobody knew what to do," the chief of naval operations, Admiral Arleigh Burke, recalled of this moment.[74] Even the CIA's Richard Bissell, who had relentlessly urged covert action on the new administration, was dumbfounded. Everything seemed to have gone wrong. Burke, whose ships were off the coast of Cuba watching the disaster unfold, stayed quiet. Occasionally his self-control did break down and he would interject "Balls!" to remind everyone that he was seething with anger.

Burke caught Kennedy's attention, who was looking for someone with Washington experience and combat savvy to get him out of this mess. Kennedy brought Rusk, McNamara, Dulles, Lemnitzer, and Burke into the Oval Office after the noon meeting. Rusk irritated him by suggesting the United States sit on its hands and let the operation die. Kennedy wanted action and called Burke in for a private meeting a short while later. Could the admiral arrange for the *Essex*, the aircraft carrier off Cuba, to fly a team over the combat area to bring back a report? Burke worked quickly, impressing Kennedy.

The president caucused with his brother. Robert had known about the CIA's plan in January but had not directly participated in any of the meetings that reshaped it. It is likely that the president kept him generally informed; in the first months of the administration, however, Robert Kennedy had to master the levers at the Justice Department and probably appreciated not having the extra responsibility. In a crisis, though, he was the president's chancellor. "Robert Kennedy called me up," Burke said, "and said the President is going to rely upon [me] to advise him on this situation." Burke warned the attorney general that this would involve bypassing his bosses, the chairman of the JCS and the secretary of defense. Robert Kennedy agreed, and twenty-five minutes later the president called to assure a surprised Burke that this is what he intended.[75]

Kennedy came to understand, perhaps with Burke's coaching, that if this mission was to have any chance of succeeding, he would have to risk direct U.S. involvement. "Prepare unmarked Navy planes for possible combat use," read the top-secret telegram from the JCS operation room. Kennedy stood next to Burke as the admiral called the order into the Pentagon. The Kennedy administration was not optimistic that the situation could be turned around. Included in this order was an instruction to prepare for the possible evacuation of the anti-Castro units.[76] Kennedy also had Burke tell the CIA to instruct the Cuban exiles to dissolve into guerrilla-sized groups. "If CEF [Cuban expeditionary force] cannot hold beachhead or fight their way inland," Burke cabled for Kennedy, "it would be desirable for them to become guerrillas and head for known destination and be supplied by air."[77] Kennedy did not understand that this was an impossibility. Not only had the CIA not prepared its Cuban invaders for this eventuality; but the most recent intelligence showed that there were only 850 guerrillas operating within a hundred-mile radius of the beaches and that the Cuban brigade would have to leapfrog Castro's mechanized reinforcements to reach those groups.[78]

Kennedy agonized over sending U.S. pilots into Cuba. Finally, after a meeting that started at midnight and lasted until nearly 3 A.M., April 19, Kennedy okayed a limited operation for later that morning. Six "unmarked" jets were permitted to fly over the beaches "to defend CEF forces from air attack." These planes were not to attack any Cuban targets on the ground or to go looking for a fight. The Cuban émigrés had planned an airdrop for 6:30 A.M., and the U.S. planes were to chase away any of Castro's planes that tried to interfere.[79]

The minor air operation failed later that morning because of a timing error, and soon the White House was forced to accept the hopelessness of the operation. At noon the commander of the special naval task force covering the Cuban operation reported that the CIA's Cubans held a beachhead of one-fourth to one-half of a mile along a single beach to a depth of about a quarter of a mile. The original mission involved creating lodgments on three beaches; but the group had lost its hold on one beach on the first day and never made it to the third beach. Now the remnants of the expeditionary force on the last beach were surrounded and "under artillery fire with tanks and vehicles to both east and west."[80] By 1 P.M., April 19, the JCS concluded that there was nothing left to do but evacuate those Cubans who could be rescued. "God be with you," the Pentagon blessed the commander in chief, Atlantic, Admiral Dennison.[81] Ultimately only 14 of the exiles were rescued, and 1,189 surrendered to Castro's military.

Amid the crumbling of Operation Zapata, Robert Kennedy dictated a letter to steel his brother's resolve. As the final cables were sent out on April 19, the president had gone to the family quarters of the White House to be alone with his wife, Jacqueline. Too excited to sob or rest, Robert spun ideas about a second try. "Our long-range foreign policy objectives in Cuba are tied to survival far more than what is happening in Laos or the Congo or any other place in the world." The attorney general advised his brother not to let the Bay of Pigs disaster stand in the way of eliminating Castro. John Kennedy had opposed using U.S. forces to overthrow Castro. His brother respected this caution, but warned, "The time has come for a showdown for in a year or two years the situation will be vastly worse." Securing the support of most of Latin America was essential to the future success of a military intervention. Robert Kennedy advised his brother to consider covert operations, such as faking a Cuban attack on Guantánamo, to gain hemispheric support. Robert was insistent. With cool prescience, he warned, "If we don't want Russia to set up missile bases in Cuba, we had better decide now what we are willing to do to stop it."[82]

In front of the press a few days later, John Kennedy took personal responsibility. "There's an old saying," Kennedy explained, "that victory has a hundred fathers and defeat is an orphan."[83] The president genuinely believed himself largely at fault. He always understood that the Trinidad plan was better from a military standpoint than the Zapata project, but political considerations had invalidated Trinidad. Kennedy blamed himself, however, for calling off the second air strike. He had not understood how essential air superiority would be to the success of the entire operation. He wished that the CIA and the JCS had stressed this factor in their conversations with him. But he also should have asked. Much of his other criticism—that the guerrilla option was a fantasy he had been led to believe in—was outweighed by the mistakes made in the air war. The Cuban expeditionary force's ability to spark a general uprising or to recruit ordinary Cubans was never tested, because the establishment of a secure beachhead was never possible.[84]

They Were Lucky

After the Bay of Pigs the Cubans propagated a myth about the performance of their security forces in April 1961. In an interview with the Castro biographer Tad Szulc in the 1980s, Castro's longtime interior minister Ramiro Valdés stated that "Cuban intelligence was able to track invasion preparations step by step, from Miami to the training camps in Guatemala."[85] Valdés confirmed a common assumption among Cuba watchers: "We were very seriously infiltrated in the counterrevolutionary bands."[86] Soviet documents show this not to have been true. As Castro would privately lament to Khrushchev as late as May 1963, two years after the Bay of Pigs, the Cubans were actually not very good at infiltrating the Cuban émigré movement abroad. They felt confident they could control those who worked in Cuba, but despite the cliché that everything was "an open secret" in Miami's Little Havana, Castro's men had to admit in 1961 that there was still much that they did not know about the activities of their greatest enemies—Manuel Ray, José Miró Cardona, and Tony Varona.[87]

The Soviets and the Cubans thought they had barely escaped disaster in April 1961. As the fight subsided on the beaches, the Castro brothers requested support from the KGB. The intelligence failure had been harrowing. Though Raúl Castro had initiated widespread intelligence cooperation in the fall of 1960, the KGB had kept the number of its "counselors" in Cuba intelligence low. In light of the Bay of Pigs near-miss, Raúl Castro asked that this number be significantly increased. The Soviets complied very quickly.

With the full agreement of the Castro government, Moscow put the Cuban security services into receivership. On April 25, 1961, less than a week after the CIA brigade had been mopped up on the beaches, the KGB chief, Shelepin, requested authorization to send to Cuba "an additional 8 KGB employees . . . with the necessary technical equipment, costing 171,000 Rubles [roughly U.S.$180,000]" in order "to satisfy the request of Cuban leadership for intelligence cooperation."[88] Meanwhile, the KGB station in Havana suggested that Manuel Piñeiro, the head of the Cuban G-2 (military intelligence), name seven of these new KGB men to head the various departments of Cuban intelligence.[89]

Once back in Cuba, Alekseev assumed control of the negotiations with the heads of the Cuban services to hammer out the role these KGB "counselors" would play. Symbolizing his new stature in the leadership, Aníbal Escalante acted as Castro's representative in these discussions on the new shape that Soviet-Cuban intelligence cooperation would take. Only six months before, Raúl Castro had described a triumvirate of Fidel, himself, and Valdés as the three men who could speak about such delicate matters with Moscow. With Escalante and the Cuban intelligence chiefs, Alekseev negotiated an agreement governing the broadening of intelligence cooperation and the sharing of responsibility for work against the United States and the Cuban emigration. Moscow and Havana anticipated an expansion of the Cuban intelligence community.[90] There were already seventeen Cubans in Soviet intelligence schools, and the Cuban government wished to increase that number by fifty.[91]

Moscow was eager to assist the Cuban secret services, but Alekseev found that he had to rein in the Cuban communists, who sensed an opportunity to act unilaterally in the aftermath of the Bay of Pigs. Blas Roca and Escalante prepared on their own a plan to assassinate the leading members of the counterrevolution. Manuel Ray, the minister of the interior in Castro's first cabinet, was their primary target. Assuming that the Soviets might raise objections, Roca and Escalante even tried to conceal the plan from Alekseev. They were stopped, however, when Alekseev was warned by the deputy minister of the interior. Alekseev sent the two Cubans the message that in Moscow's view "it was probably not the time to take these measures."[92]

The Soviet military acted defensively in light of the Bay of Pigs. Evidently Fidel's success had been due to the overwhelming firepower he was able to bring to bear on the tiny beachhead. His Soviet-made T-34 tanks and the 122-mm Howitzers had pounded the counterrevolutionaries into submission when they themselves ran out of American ammunition. Yet the Red Army felt it had to draft a statement of what it had provided to the Cubans, lest perhaps Fidel rail against Moscow for not providing the MiGs in time to minimize the threat posed by the U.S.-backed invasion. While Alekseev was hammering out the details of the KGB's reform of the Cuban security apparatus, Khrushchev's minister of defense prepared for the Presidium a list of every piece of war matériel that Moscow had provided the Cubans since 1959.*

What were the consequences of the Bay of Pigs? The United States did not understand that the Bay of Pigs attack came at the end of the fourth invasion scare in less than a year. Although the Soviet Union had not completed its shipments of war supplies to Castro, it had sent enough to equip the battle group that reclaimed the beachhead. The advantage of a year's preparation for an attack was nearly neutralized by the inefficiency of the Castro regime and the corrosive effect of three earlier nonevents. In April 1961 the Cubans and the Soviets were convinced that Kennedy would be deterred from providing significant assistance to the counterrevolutionaries. In effect, they were right in that John Kennedy did not authorize the air coverage that the beachhead needed to have any chance at survival. Nevertheless, the invasion of fifteen hundred men was much larger than the Cubans or Khrushchev had expected. After surviving this close call, the Soviets did what the Cuban communists had been advocating for some time—they took a commanding role in the Cuban security services.

The attack permitted Castro to reveal to the Cuban people his desire of a socialist Cuba. Having only hinted to Soviet representatives in the spring of 1960, and privately committed himself to the rank and file of the communist party in November 1960, Fidel told his people and the world of his intention on April 16, 1961. The attack also softened the effect of that announcement on his stature at home. The U.S. action confirmed the enemy image that Castro had employed to push ever more radical solutions to Cuba's problems of development in 1959 and 1960. From April 1961 on, the events at the Bay of Pigs served as the great unifying symbol of a movement. The choice of communism that had been made by Raúl Castro in the early 1950s, by Che in 1957, and by Fidel in late 1959 or early 1960 could now be presented as the only possible response to the crime of the Yankees.

The most tragic consequence of the Bay of Pigs was the ascendancy of Aníbal Escalante and a Cuban security service dominated by the Soviet Union. For over a year Fidel Castro had backed away from initiatives that could have transformed Cuba into a police state. Confronted with an increase

* As of the end of April 1961, Cuba had received from the USSR, Czechoslovakia, and China a huge amount of military technology: 125 tanks (IS-2M and T-34-85), 50 self-propelled Arams SAU-100 guns, 428 field artillery pieces (from 76 mm to 128 mm), 170 57 mm antitank guns, 898 large machine guns (82 mm and 120 mm), 920 antiaircraft guns (37 mm and 12.7 mm), 7,250 smaller machine guns, and 167,000 pistols and rifles, all of which came with ammunition. The Bay of Pigs crisis had occurred before the Soviets could complete their military supply program for Cuba. According to a May 4, 1961, report by Soviet Defense Minister Malinovsky, the Cubans were also scheduled to receive 41 jet fighters and reconnaissance aircraft (MIG-19s and MIG-15s), an additional 80 tanks, 54 57 mm antiaircraft guns and 128 field artillery pieces (including the mammoth 152 mm guns).

in counterrevolutionary activity in the fall of 1960, however, Castro had taken the first important steps. The Bay of Pigs operation accelerated these changes, creating a momentum toward the building of a surveillance state that Fidel Castro had once considered avoidable. Escalante and his Soviet discussion partners, Kudryavtsev and Alekseev, were probably right to assume that a socialist revolution would be met by violent internal opposition; but the Kennedy administration's investment in a big, awkward, and ultimately ineffective operation removed the last major inhibitions holding Castro back from a domestic crackdown.

The Bay of Pigs had brought John Kennedy the worst possible outcome: a coup-proof Cuba in a Caribbean even more unwilling to approve the use of outside force. He now faced a communist state, an eight-minute flight away from Miami. The question that the world asked in the aftermath of this personal debacle was whether the United States could come to terms with a Soviet beachhead in its backyard. Not only the fate of six million Cubans but the very nature of the rivalry between the superpowers rested on the answer to that question.

The Education of a President

A Cruel April

The failure on the shores of Cuba left Kennedy with several awkward decisions. John Kennedy hated to lose. But here it was not simply a matter of a lost love or game of football; at stake was the world's impression of the new leadership in Washington and the administration's own self-image.

"Right now the greatest problem we face is not to have the whole of our foreign policy thrown off balance by what we feel and what we do about Cuba itself," as Walt Whitman Rostow, McGeorge Bundy's deputy and one of the more imaginative members of the National Security Council staff, put it to Kennedy. Rostow suggested returning to the "Grand Strategy" of the administration: "Our central aim has been to bind up the northern half of the Free World more closely and begin to link it constructively with the south." Having seen Robert Kennedy breathing fire around the Oval Office, Rostow worried that the president might try again to remove Castro before repairing the damage to U.S. foreign policy caused by the Bay of Pigs fiasco.[1]

Central to the administration's original strategy was a relaxation of tensions with the Soviet Union. The term "détente" first appeared in 1955 as a way of describing a reprieve in the struggle with Moscow, after Khrushchev met with the leaders of France, Britain, and the United States in Geneva. The "spirit of Geneva" did not survive the 1956 Hungarian revolution and the Suez crisis of the same year. But public hunger for détente, especially in Europe, encouraged another period of hope in 1959 when Khrushchev became the first Soviet leader to agree to cross an ocean on official business. This second détente had also been short-lived, ending with the Gary Powers incident, in May 1960, when the Soviets shot down a U-2 spy plane and subsequently walked out of a great-power summit in Paris. In 1961 the youthful Kennedy administration had wanted to try again.

Kennedy knew that in giving the green light to the planners of the Bay of Pigs operation, he had risked increasing U.S.-Soviet tensions. Just five days before the first U.S. airplane took off from Central America to bomb targets in Cuba, Kennedy and Khrushchev had agreed to a June 3 summit in the Austrian capital, Vienna. Yet, as we have seen, the administration's fervent desire to do something about Castro, the bureaucratic forces pressing for the use of covert action, and Kennedy's and his advisers' stubborn belief that the Soviets would inevitably accept anything that happened to Castro argued for going ahead with the CIA's plan.

In the aftermath of the Bay of Pigs operation, however, the White House perceived its first objective to be restoring Europe's faith in Kennedy, not rekindling the possibilities of a summit. "Kennedy has lost his magic," commented one European leader in summing up the effect of the disaster in Cuba on overseas opinion.[2] In Britain, a country for which Kennedy felt a special affection, the *Financial Times* spoke of the "barely credible ineptness" of the Cuban venture, while William Reese-Mogg at the *Sunday Times* wrote that the Bay of Pigs operation was "one of the really massive blunders . . . perhaps the most obvious White House mistake since President Roosevelt's plan to pack the Supreme Court."[3] At Oxford a group of fourteen American Rhodes Scholars expressed their dismay at the spectacle of this relatively young and intelligent Harvard graduate not living up to his promise:

> We had hoped that under [the] new Administration US foreign policy would reach new levels of honesty and goodwill. We did not expect our Ambassador to [the] UN would have to resort to deception and evasion; that our actions would have to be justified by balancing them against Soviet suppression in Budapest; and that consequently world opinion would turn against them.[4]

The world seemed a much better place for Nikita Khrushchev at the end of April 1961. Each of Kennedy's headaches presented him with a new opportunity. The flight of Yuri Gagarin on April 12, the first man to travel into space, extended the streak of Soviet technological firsts that began with the launch of Sputnik in 1957. Three days after Gagarin safely returned to earth, the Kremlin got another boost when the American effort to overturn Castro ended up a humiliating disaster.

Khrushchev understood that such victories were magnified in the rarefied atmosphere of a political war. The Gagarin flight and the triumph of Castro signaled the virility of the socialist bloc. Had he not predicted such achievements in his January speech to the Soviet people on the next phase of international communist work? "Our epoch," he had asserted, "is the epoch of the triumph of Marxism-Leninism."[5]

Even events in Southeast Asia, an area where the Soviets competed for influence with the increasingly ornery Chinese, were encouraging. In December the

Soviet air force had begun airlifting supplies to the Pathet Lao, a communist guerrilla movement in the hills of Laos. The Pathet Lao looked primarily to the North Vietnamese and the Chinese for assistance, but by establishing a regular airlift and increasing supplies as needed, the Soviets had built up some leverage for themselves. After some setbacks in the first months of 1961, the Pathet Lao had begun to make gains in an effort to take the capital, Vientiane, and the royal seat farther in the interior. When their drive began to slow once more, the Pathet Lao were asked by the Soviets to accept a cease-fire. Though the guerrillas initially refused, determined to demonstrate their independence from Moscow, they did eventually agree to one. Despite the inconsistency of his Laotian allies, Khrushchev had every reason to view events in Laos as confirming his optimistic evaluation of the future for communism in the developing world.

The Soviets Go First

Khrushchev waited for the outcome of the battle at the Bay of Pigs to resume discussion of a summit. On April 18, when the KGB's Spanish-language experts were straining to hear every possible radio report and the situation on the battlefield seemed chaotic, the Presidium authorized a very stern letter to John F. Kennedy criticizing him for sponsoring this attack on Cuban sovereignty. Four days later, with the roundup of the Cuban exiles nearly complete and the U.S. naval task force on its way home, Khrushchev could afford to be magnanimous. He had his foreign minister, Andrei Gromyko, soften a second stern statement, this time a response to a Kennedy justification of the operation, with an oral coda. "Comrade Khrushchev," Gromyko explained to the U.S. embassy, "feels compelled to answer the president by letter, and to express his understanding of the president's announcement; but he hopes that the differences which have arisen recently would be resolved and U.S.-Soviet relations improved, if this be the wish of the U.S. president and the American government."[6]

Moscow waited a week and, having received no word from the White House about the planned Vienna meeting, explicitly asked about the fate of the summit. Gromyko called the U.S. ambassador, Llewellyn Thompson, into his office on May 4.[7] Reading from a prepared paper, Gromyko deplored the "fact that discord [has] occurred of late between our two countries in connection with events regarding Cuba." The Kremlin wanted to know whether Kennedy still intended to meet Khrushchev at Vienna. Was Kennedy's proposal for an exchange of views at the highest level still "valid"? Gromyko asked.

Khrushchev believed that a summit would work to his advantage. In 1960 the Soviets had sacrificed a summit to display their anger over the U-2 incident. This time Khrushchev clearly thought that the value of meeting Kennedy overrode the propaganda gains from blaming the loss of one more chance for peace on American misbehavior.

In looking at Khrushchev's behavior, the State Department's veteran Sovietologist Charles Bohlen emphasized for Kennedy the "duality" of this man's foreign policy. Even as Khrushchev advocated "peaceful coexistence," he armed national-liberation movements and repeatedly threatened nuclear war while bluffing about the size of the Soviet arsenal. Since 1958 Khrushchev had periodically warned the West that if it did not accept his formula for "eradicating the splinter" of West Berlin from the flank of the socialist states, he would see to it that U.S., British, and French soldiers were barred from protecting that city.[8]

As Khrushchev oriented himself and the Soviet leadership to the ways of the new president in Washington, there was less a duality than a conflict of priorities. Despite the successes of April 1961, there were real challenges to Khrushchev's optimistic worldview, stemming from issues central to Soviet power—the U.S.-Soviet military balance and Soviet influence in Central Europe, the crucible of the century's two world wars and possibly of the third, if the Cold War ever got hot.

Since consolidating his hold on the Kremlin, Khrushchev had worked to introduce sweeping changes in the European postwar settlement. Khrushchev had demanded that the other three victorious powers of World War II— France, Great Britain, the United States—join him in signing a peace treaty with both of the Germanies, the three Western occupation zones, which had been fused to form the Federal Republic of Germany, and the Soviet occupation zone, now called the German Democratic Republic. The falling out of the Grand Alliance had prevented this from happening in 1945, and though a peace treaty might have seemed innocuous enough in 1961, its implications were potentially explosive for the West. Hitler's capital had been Berlin, a city in the northeast quadrant of the old Reich. Each of the Allies considered the city a symbol of the defeat of fascism, and despite its being one hundred miles into the Soviet occupation zone, the city was divided in four at the end of the war, with each of the victorious powers controlling a portion. The Soviets never reconciled themselves to this Western island in their sphere of influence. In 1948 Stalin had closed all of the land routes to the city in a brazen attempt to force his former allies to leave Berlin. Washington had responded with the Berlin airlift, which rallied the morale of the Berliners living in the three Western areas and made Berlin into a symbol of freedom and Western resolve. Not wishing to repeat Stalin's mistake, Khrushchev hoped to be able to neutralize the city by means of a diplomatic offensive. In November 1958 he gave the Western powers an ultimatum. If they did not come to some agreement with both Germanies in eleven months, the USSR would unilaterally sign a treaty with East Germany, leaving the East Germans to decide on their own about the future of Western access to the divided city.

Two years later Khrushchev's pressure campaign had not succeeded in moving the Western powers any closer to the Soviet Union's position on Berlin. The only change in Central Europe since 1958 was the condition of East Germany, whose economy was steadily deteriorating because of massive emigration. Some 100,000 East Germans, many of whom were professionals, were leaving the country through West Berlin each year. The situation was so bleak that in January 1961 Khrushchev was forced to promise the leadership of East Germany that he would resolve their difficult situation by the end of the year.[9]

Khrushchev was a gambler. The stakes were Berlin, and he was willing to bet that in a face-to-face meeting he could sway John Kennedy's opinion on Berlin. The Soviet leader believed that his demands were compatible with American interests and that it was due only to weaknesses in Eisenhower's leadership that an agreement had been elusive. In a profile written just before Kennedy's election, the Soviet Foreign Ministry had described him as "a complete pragmatist." Perhaps this pragmatist, Khrushchev hoped, could be persuaded that Berlin had to be the first step toward a détente. But a failure risked more grumbling among members of the leadership over Khrushchev's policy toward the American adversary. Not all of his colleagues in the Presidium agreed with his strategy of détente through negotiations. "Comrade Khrushchev believes that the U.S. and the USSR can eliminate militarism by a stroke of the pen," murmured the newest member of the leadership, Dmitri Polyanski.[10] Khrushchev lobbied his colleagues almost incessantly about the need for U.S.-Soviet treaties, yet in focusing his energies on achieving movement on the matter of Berlin, he was holding such superpower agreements hostage. The risk was that, having talked his way up to the summit, he would return home with nothing.

Kennedy's Gambit

The American who received Gromyko's question about the future of the summit sensed the seriousness of the Soviet leadership. Llewellyn "Tommy" Thompson, gave Kennedy six reasons why he should carefully consider returning to the pre–Bay of Pigs plan for a summit. Thompson, who was on his way to becoming Kennedy's most influential Moscow watcher, believed that the rough edges of Soviet foreign policy could be smoothed. The "prospect of a meeting," he argued in an "eyes only" message to Dean Rusk, would make the Soviets "more reasonable" in discussions on Laos, the nuclear test ban, and general disarmament. He also believed that the onset of better relations with Washington would influence Soviet decisions on how much to allocate to defense spending.[11]

In Washington, Kennedy could not decide whether to go ahead with the summit. The Bay of Pigs created conflicting imperatives in his mind. On the one hand, Kennedy did not want to seem eager to see Khrushchev. This would play into the hands of domestic opponents who had criticized his weak support for the Cuban counterrevolutionaries. Yet Kennedy was even more concerned that if he did not meet Khrushchev face-to-face soon, the Soviet leader might misinterpret the new president's actions as signs of weakness.

Kennedy had decided not to intervene militarily in Cuba and Laos. What did the Kremlin think of a U.S. president who did not intervene? Was his restraint a sign of strength or a sign of weakness to them?

Whenever faced with a close decision, Kennedy's instinct was to buy time. He instructed the State Department to have Thompson assure Gromyko that though the U.S. president had no intention of backing out of a summit, Kennedy was not sure whether everything could be put in place by early June. The White House knew that Khrushchev was about to leave the Kremlin for a two-week tour of Central Asia. Gromyko was to be promised that a decision would be ready before Khrushchev returned on May 20.[12]

While trying to make up his mind, Kennedy studied transcripts of Eisenhower's 1959 meetings with Khrushchev. They revealed two important things about the Soviet leader: he was clever and quick on his feet; and he was stubborn. To Kennedy these conclusions seemed less important than what the transcripts revealed about the seventy-year-old ex-president. Eisenhower had been colorless and his statements stilted. Kennedy respected the older man but thought his time to leave had come in 1956. And the transcripts from 1959 bore this out.[13]

Kennedy would do something different. He intended to lay out his thinking for the Soviet leader in advance of the summit. Kennedy was too impatient a man to be happy with the cumbersome nature of standard diplomatic practice. Too much would then be left to fate or to Khrushchev; and it would all take too long. What was the Soviet leader going to do or say? Kennedy's admiration for Tommy Thompson would grow into an important factor in the conduct of U.S. foreign policy by the time of the Cuban missile crisis. But in April 1961 Kennedy was not close enough to Thompson to use him as a confidential channel to the Soviets. So Kennedy turned to the man who had carried the fledgling administration's first message to Khrushchev in December 1960—his brother Robert.

Sometime in late April 1961, John Kennedy and his brother devised a private strategy to increase the prospects of success in Vienna. Robert had been heard muttering around the White House that the United States was on the verge of being seen as a paper tiger. John Kennedy, too, worried that the Bay of Pigs and the indeterminate outcome in Laos were sending the wrong signals about his resolve to use all means to defend U.S. interests overseas. But the brothers, especially the president, were equally concerned about the costs of a policy of unalloyed belligerence toward the Soviet Union. What could be gained by acting tough, if the end result was a war that few wanted and, in the nuclear age, nobody could control. There were areas where the United States and the Soviet Union could cooperate. If Kennedy could bring the Soviets to accept a significant bilateral agreement or two, on arms control or cooperation in outer space, then perhaps Khrushchev would begin to see continued good relations with Washington as a reason to curb Soviet support for Third World movements. Foreign policy intellectuals like Walt Rostow reinforced Kennedy's belief in the value of stressing the linkage between Soviet activities in the Third World and the strategic competition between the superpowers. "If you want better relations with us, Nikita, then back off in Laos," was the idea.

At one time Kennedy hoped that an agreement on Berlin would provide the basis for better relations with the Kremlin. Kennedy had inherited this difficult puzzle from Eisenhower. The catechism of the New Frontier taught that Eisenhower's people had lacked the intellectual depth to deal creatively with foreign policy. Characteristically, Kennedy assumed that Berlin, like all of the other foreign problems, could have been solved if Dulles and company had not been so dull. Shortly after the inauguration, he asked Harry Truman's secretary of state Dean Acheson to come up with a plan.

In the midst of planning the ill-fated Bay of Pigs operation and while he became convinced of the increasingly pessimistic future for Southeast Asia, Kennedy got the bad news from Acheson. An architect of the Truman Doctrine, Acheson could not lend any reassurance to Kennedy. "There is no 'solution' for the Berlin problem short of the unification of Germany," Acheson advised.[14]

To have any chance of success in Vienna, John Kennedy would have to avoid the Berlin issue and focus Khrushchev's attention instead on an area where a mutually beneficial agreement was possible. The Kennedy brothers let no one into their secret as they came up with a plan to offer Khrushchev directly the chance to sign the first superpower arms control agreement ever.

Since 1958 Washington and the Kremlin had been negotiating a ban on all tests of nuclear devices. To facilitate these talks, in November of that year the Soviet Union had joined the United States and Great Britain in a moratorium on future testing. Traditionally these tests were done in the atmosphere, and there was increasing concern about the effect of the resultant fallout on plants and human beings. In recent years the United States had developed the technique of underground testing, which was much more expensive than atmospheric testing but had the advantage of seemingly not creating any biological hazards.

Dwight Eisenhower had wanted a test ban if a way could be found to verify Soviet compliance. Initially there was optimism among American scientists that even low-level underground tests could be detected. Analyses of the air could detect atmospheric explosions; but it was hard to differentiate underground tests from the approximately one hundred natural seismic events that occurred annually on the territory of the Soviet Union. In 1959 the U.S. scientific community reversed itself, saying that low-level tests, those that produced readings of less than 4.75 on the Richter scale, could not be differentiated from minor earthquakes with any reasonable level of accuracy. Eisenhower, whose greatest concern was the viability of international control of Soviet behavior, subsequently ordered the new position that each side should permit a certain number of on-site inspections to determine whether a seismic reading came from an earthquake or a nuclear test.[15]

Khrushchev had publicly endorsed a test ban even before Eisenhower. In 1956 he had argued that a test ban would be a step toward the eventual normalization of relations between the superpowers. But as U.S. verification requirements increased, Soviet interest began to wane. The 1959 report on the difficulties of differentiating between earthquakes and nuclear events only increased Moscow's reluctance to achieve an agreement. Whereas the U.S. side proposed an annual quota of twenty on-site inspections, each one to follow an unidentified seismic event, the Soviet were thinking in terms of a ceiling of three visits a year. The Soviets suspected that the Americans intended to exploit the seismic issue to spy on Russia. Khrushchev further complicated the negotiation in September 1959 by linking progress on the test ban issue to progress in achieving "general and complete disarmament," a seemingly utopian proposal for the elimination of all armed forces on both sides in phases, the first being the dismantling of strategic rockets. By 1960 the Soviets had added a new twist to their position. So upset were they by the role of the United Nations in the African country of the Congo, where they believed the world body was biased in its dealings with Moscow's ally, the Soviets began to demand not only a small number of inspections but a completely different inspection system. The plan on the table proposed a single administrator who would oversee inspections. Now the Soviets proposed a "troika" with one representative from the communist world, one from either the United States or Great Britain (the two Western nuclear powers), and one from the neutral world. The Soviets refused to believe that a so-called international civil servant could be impartial toward socialist countries.[16]

Despite this evidence of Moscow's recalcitrance, Kennedy selected the achievement of a nuclear test ban as the basis of his strategy for a successful summit. In the Eisenhower administration three different agencies contributed to disarmament policy: the State Department, the Department of Defense, and the CIA. Kennedy wanted to give disarmament a higher profile. He chose John McCloy, one of Henry Stimson's deputies in the War Department during World War II and the president of the Ford Foundation in the 1950s, to head the new Arms Control and Disarmament Agency. The day after the inauguration, McCloy circulated a series of proposals that the U.S. government might want to make in a new round of arms control negotiations. His staff proposed a test ban as the most likely area of agreement and then recommended changes in the Eisenhower administration's positions that could possibly bring this about.

The traditional powers in U.S. security policy, the State and Defense Departments, rejected many of McCloy's positions. But John Kennedy did not. In a private meeting with his brother, he decided to offer some of McCloy's concessions to the Soviets. He would use his brother to try to entice the Soviets with a new position on inspections. McCloy's people suggested a fallback position of ten instead of twenty inspections a year; and there was some talk in the State Department about possibly agreeing to twelve a year.[17] What if

Kennedy could find a way to have the Soviets suggest ten as a compromise, which he could counter with an offer of fifteen, allowing the two sides to settle on twelve? In the end, this horse-trading would produce the first arms control agreement between the superpowers, which the leaders could announce at Vienna.

The Kennedy administration had reason to believe that the Soviets might go along with this bit of theater to reach an agreement. Ambassador Thompson in Moscow reported that the Kremlin was prepared to make real concessions to get a test ban.[18] And since the inauguration Soviet representatives in Washington seemed to be signaling a softness in their position on inspections.[19] A comment in early March by the chief of the TASS bureau may have encouraged John Kennedy, in particular, to think this compromise would be accepted by Khrushchev. On the matter of inspections Mikhail Sagatelyan, the chief of TASS, said "he was sure it would be possible to bargain on this matter and try to find common ground." Sagatelyan then became very specific: "Perhaps the Americans will be able to come down and the Soviets will be able to come up and they will meet in the middle somewhere around twelve or thirteen."[20] And from McGeorge Bundy, Kennedy may have heard that the chief KGB officer in town, Aleksandr Feklisov, was talking about the possibility of compromise on the inspection issue. A few days after Sagatelyan made his test ban comments, Feklisov told an American journalist, whose conversation was later reported to a Kennedy aide, Frederick L. Holborn, that a compromise was "possible."[21]

It was always assumed in Washington that on substantive matters Soviet representatives expressed only official views. Both Sagatelyan and Feklisov had stressed that they were merely expressing their own personal views, and Soviet records indeed show that these men were just fishing for intelligence to send to Moscow. Nevertheless, the Kennedys sensed a flexibility on the Soviet side. They hoped to convey to Moscow that the new administration could be just as imaginative and would be prepared to meet the Kremlin halfway. But to make this offer, to play this game within a game, President Kennedy needed a secret channel to Khrushchev. In late April 1961 Robert Kennedy went looking for one.

Enter Georgi Bolshakov

Georgi Bolshakov joined the GRU, the intelligence service of the Red Army, after two years on active duty as first a Finnish-language interpreter and then a division-level intelligence officer. Returning to Moscow from the northwest front in 1943, he began a seven-year internship in the Soviet Union's main military intelligence schools. Even amid the bloody struggle against Hitler, the GRU maintained a grueling apprenticeship system. After passing his qualifying examinations to become an intelligence officer, Bolshakov was sent on a three-year course at the High Intelligence School of the General Staff.

Following this training, he transferred to the Military-Diplomatic Academy of the Soviet Army, where he stayed until 1950.[22]

Bolshakov, who had acquired impressive English-language skills in the course of his education, was sent to Washington in 1951 on his first foreign assignment. Ostensibly an editor for the TASS news agency, Bolshakov was expected to cultivate sources wherever he could find them. Although competitive agencies, the GRU and the KGB both used TASS to cover their activities. Bolshakov shared the TASS office with a number of KGB officers and even a few real Soviet reporters.

This first assignment lasted four years. In 1955 the GRU recalled Bolshakov and transferred him to the staff of the Soviet minister of defense, Marshal Georgi Zhukov. Bolshakov's personnel file lists his responsibilities in 1955 as "officer for special missions." Bolshakov may well have been Zhukov's intelligence briefer during the tense days of the Hungarian uprising and the Suez crisis of 1956. Zhukov's dismissal in 1957 disrupted Bolshakov's career. The steady rise in authority and proximity to power stopped, and Bolshakov found himself running an office in the department dealing with GRU veterans' affairs.[23]

By the end of the 1950s, Bolshakov's career was back on track. His return from obscurity seems to have been the result of his friendship with the first son-in-law of the Soviet Union, Rada Khrushchev's husband, Aleksei Adzhubei. A proverb captured the common view that Adzhubei had mastered the art of marrying well: "If you don't earn one hundred rubles, it's okay, as long as you marry like Adzhubei." Bolshakov had met Adzhubei while working for Zhukov. The connection brought Bolshakov a second chance at working for the GRU in the United States. It also made plausible Bolshakov's role in Washington as an intermediary between Khrushchev and the new U.S. president, John F. Kennedy.[24]

Bolshakov had met the U.S. journalist Frank Holeman when he was with TASS in the early 1950s. Born in 1922, Bolshakov was roughly the same age as the correspondent for the New York *Daily News.* Holeman had gotten his big break covering Congressman Richard Nixon's actions at the House Un-American Activities Committee hearings on Alger Hiss in 1948. From then on, Holeman was known as one of Washington's best Nixon watchers. After the Checkers issue broke in 1952, involving an alleged secret Nixon campaign fund, the *Daily News* assigned Holeman full-time to Nixon's vice presidential campaign. Holeman stayed with Nixon, riding with the candidate across the country aboard his train. In 1956 he was again assigned to Nixon. In the course of that grueling campaign, Holeman came to know the vice president quite well and, after the election, was one of the few journalists allowed into Nixon's private office on Capitol Hill.

It was a stand that Holeman took as chairman of the board of the National Press Club in the early 1950s that brought him to the attention of Soviet intelligence. In April 1951 the Czech government caused an international uproar by jailing the entire Associated Press bureau in Prague, including its chief, William Nathan Oatis, on charges of espionage. It was the first time in the Cold War that a Western correspondent had been detained anywhere in the bloc. After Oatis "confessed" and was sentenced to ten years in prison, there were calls in Congress to retaliate by throwing all TASS reporters out of the United States. Had Congress pressed ahead with this action, Soviet intelligence would have lost a useful cover, but Moscow would have found other covers for its KGB and GRU representatives. Meanwhile, the National Press Club denounced the Czech action and also considered removing membership privileges from all Soviet journalists. Holeman, who was chairman of its board of governors, disagreed. He wanted the club to stay open to all so that they could "swap lies."[25]

The Soviets approached Holeman after this controversy to ask his assistance in helping the new Soviet press attaché, Aleksandr Zinchuk, to become a member of the National Press Club. After Holeman said he would do it, the Soviet embassy showed its appreciation by hosting a lunch for the U.S. journalist. It was at this affair that Holeman met Georgi Bolshakov. Holeman found Bolshakov engaging, and the two men began to meet infrequently—the Soviet intelligence officer in order to take the pulse of U.S. politics from a veteran observer and Holeman to learn about what lurked behind the façade of official Soviet positions.

Bolshakov liked Holeman. A few months before his death in 1989, Bolshakov wrote, "[O]ur families got to know each other, often paying host to each other."[26] Like the successful small businessman who knows how to mix sales and pleasure at the golf club, Bolshakov was self-confident enough to be able to socialize with his informants. This made him unusual in the Soviet colony in Washington.[27]

The GRU came to view Holeman as a useful informant. When Bolshakov was recalled to Moscow to serve on Marshal Zhukov's staff in 1955, Holeman was passed on to Yuri Gvozdev, ostensibly a cultural attaché, but in fact another member of the GRU station in the embassy. Gvozdev and Holeman continued the tradition of infrequent lunches. At one of them the GRU officer explained to Holeman that the Soviet government felt it needed a way to send private messages to the Eisenhower administration. Holeman approached the vice president about what the Russian had said. Nixon thought that Holeman should continue to meet with Gvozdev. "We want to keep as many lines of communication as possible." Holeman never arranged a meeting between Gvozdev and Nixon but served as a "carrier pigeon" between them.[28]

Nixon's defeat in 1960 did not close off the Holeman-GRU channel. Gvozdev left the United States in the fall of 1959; but the GRU replaced him with Bolshakov, who resumed the meetings with the American journalist. Holeman welcomed a chance to keep his Soviet channel open; and despite the Republican defeat, he hoped to be able to offer it to the New Frontiersmen streaming into Washington. Edwin O. Guthman, Robert Kennedy's press secretary, was one of Holeman's friends in the new administration. Gvozdev had never met Nixon; but Holeman, possibly encouraged by Guthman or the attorney general, had a hunch that Robert Kennedy was the kind of man who might be willing to have a face-to-face meeting with a Soviet intelligence officer.

"Don't you think it would be better to meet directly with Robert Kennedy so that he receives your information at first hand?" Holeman asked Bolshakov on Saturday, April 29, 1961.[29] It was a novel suggestion. To date, no one at the Kremlin or even the GRU had entrusted Bolshakov with any messages for Americans. But wouldn't his bosses be pleased, Holeman added, if he could report on the musings of the president's brother? Bolshakov looked interested but cautioned that he would need the approval of the "embassy" to meet the attorney general.

What Bolshakov needed was permission from his boss, the chief of the GRU station in Washington, D.C. This officer, whose identity is still protected, could not quite believe his ears when he was told that the attorney general of the United States wanted to meet with one of his assistants. "Menshikov [the Soviet ambassador] maybe; but Bolshakov?" asked the GRU chief incredulously. He absolutely forbade Bolshakov's seeing Robert Kennedy. The next day, April 30, 1961, Bolshakov called Holeman to tell him that he could not see Robert Kennedy. These were his instructions, and he was supposed to follow them.[30]

Bolshakov had indeed found the prospect of meeting with Robert Kennedy extremely tempting; after all, he was considered the president's closest confidant. Bolshakov decided to take a risk on May 9 and meet Kennedy without authorization. The day was a national holiday, when all Soviet delegations around the world went on short staff to allow time to celebrate the victory over fascism in 1945. With most of his colleagues out of the office, Bolshakov could move around more easily.

Holeman called to invite him to a very late lunch. It was already 4 P.M., and Bolshakov had long since eaten. When Bolshakov asked why he was calling so late, Holeman responded that he had called around noon but that Bolshakov had been at the typesetters. Holeman suggested they meet at a restaurant in Georgetown.

Bolshakov had barely taken his seat when Holeman said that Robert Kennedy was ready to see him at 8:30 P.M. that night. Holeman planned to take Bolshakov to the entrance of the Justice Department at the corner of Tenth and Constitution. After Holeman told him the news, there was a short pause. Holeman wondered whether Bolshakov was scared. Bolshakov did not admit to any fear. With more than a touch of insincerity, he complained that he was not properly dressed to meet the attorney general—"I am not ready for this meeting." Holeman smiled, "You are always ready, Georgi."

A few hours later Holeman drove Bolshakov to the Justice Department. Government offices along Constitution Avenue were already closed. As planned, Robert Kennedy had taken his private elevator down from his fifth-floor office. He exited past the security guard and waited outside for the Russian. Edward Guthman accompanied him. When Holeman and Bolshakov drew up, the attorney general and his aide were sitting on the granite steps.

"Mr. Attorney General, I would like to present Mr. Georgi Bolshakov." Bolshakov and Kennedy shook hands, and Guthman and Holeman left. As the newspaperman walked away, he caught a glimpse through the soft spring evening of the attorney general of the United States and the Soviet intelligence officer crossing Constitution Avenue to the Mall, the long green space linking the Washington Monument to the Capitol. Holeman's last image was of the two men engrossed in conversation as they turned toward the Museum of Natural History.[31]

Robert Kennedy chose his words carefully. "The American government and the president are concerned," he began, "that the Soviet leadership underestimates the capabilities of the U.S. government and those of the president himself." Recent events in Cuba, Laos, and South Vietnam, Kennedy added, were increasing the danger of Moscow's misunderstanding the administration's resolve. "[I]f this underestimation of U.S. power takes hold," warned the attorney general, "the American government will have to take corrective action, changing the course of its policies."[32]

Robert Kennedy wanted the Soviets to understand that his brother was prepared to depart from the foreign policy of the Eisenhower years, if shown the proper respect. Decrying a decade of "static and feeble" foreign policy, which weighed heavily around the neck of the new administration, Robert Kennedy assured Bolshakov that the president was striving for a "new progressive policy . . . consistent with the national interest." A successful summit could play a helpful role in solidifying this new course.

The background in place, Robert Kennedy made the pitch for a nuclear test ban summit. Although "the president has not lost hope," he explained, "[t]he unfortunate events in Cuba and Laos have somewhat cooled the president's passion for a general resolution of U.S.-Soviet relations." In particular, the president, who had invested "great hopes" in the negotiations in Geneva, did not want to give up on a test ban, despite reports from his secretary of state that an agreement was unlikely. The attorney general told Bolshakov that the administration's public position of twenty annual inspections notwithstanding, his brother would accept half that number, if the Soviets dressed it up as their offer. "The USA could compromise," Robert Kennedy promised, in explaining how U.S. domestic politics constrained his brother, ". . . if this were in response to a Soviet proposal." The U.S. side wanted the details of these agreements to be determined through official diplomatic channels ahead of time so that they would be ready for the two leaders to sign in Vienna. "The president," emphasized Robert Kennedy, "is not interested in a summit where leaders just exchange views." At Vienna the president wanted "agreements on major issues."

A second agreement was also possible. The attorney general mentioned Laos as another area where U.S. and Soviet interests could converge. "The U.S. delegation on Laos in Geneva," he said, "will do its utmost to ensure the existence of a neutral Laos." Laos was a symbol of the Kennedy administration's new approach to the developing world. In general, Robert Kennedy explained, Washington planned to reform U.S. aid programs, even borrowing "good ideas from Soviet aid programs."

Cuba was not completely absent from Robert Kennedy's mind. It came up in the context of his description of his own personal role in redesigning U.S. policy toward the Third World. Latin America, Kennedy offered, was to be his own main area of focus. Kennedy, however, refused to discuss Fidel Castro. "Cuba is a dead issue," was all Robert Kennedy would say.

Robert Kennedy left no doubt that the White House was looking for a back channel to the Kremlin. Asking Bolshakov to consult with his "friends" and to report back on their reaction, the attorney general promised to clarify the president's point of view. Kennedy suggested another meeting, when the initial reactions of both sides were clear, "in an unofficial setting, face-to-face." Afterward Bolshakov left to make his report. The Kremlin was about to get the best look inside the thinking of the Kennedy administration that any spy service could hope for.

Mutual Suspicions

The White House was understandably wary of Georgi Bolshakov at this stage. Despite Frank Holeman's success with Gvozdev in 1959, the American journalist had not provided conclusive evidence that this new Russian had similar high-level contacts. Robert Kennedy had told Bolshakov that the United States was sending positive feelers about the substance of a summit to the Kremlin through Mahomedali Chagla, the Indian ambassador in the United States.

Moscow was equally suspicious of Robert Kennedy in the spring of 1961. The KGB had a sizable file on the president's brother that stretched back to the trip he had made to the Soviet Union in 1955. That visit had produced a wealth of negative stories about the younger Kennedy, with the effect that, in the halls of the Kremlin, he was considered a greater anti-Soviet than his brother.

Supreme Court Associate Justice William O. Douglas had invited the young Kennedy to accompany him to the USSR as a favor to his old friend Joseph Kennedy. Both Douglas and Kennedy had once served as the chairman of the Securities and Exchange Commission. Robert Kennedy was working for Senator Joseph McCarthy at the time and like his boss had a visceral dislike for the Soviets and their system. "He went into the Soviet Union totally prejudiced; Communism was bad; everything was bad," Douglas's wife, Mercedes, recalled.[33] Joseph McCarthy for his own reasons opposed Robert's going; but Kennedy's father was "very anxious" that he travel to Russia with Douglas. Mercedes, who thought that anybody who worked for McCarthy was "pretty terrible," also opposed letting Robert come along. But her husband would have none of it: "Well, anything that Joe [Joseph P. Kennedy] wants I must do."

The KGB shared Mercedes Douglas's opinion of the Robert Kennedy who visited Russia in 1955. Six years later, as the Soviet government tried to put the new Kennedy team into perspective, the younger Kennedy brother was branded as a potential troublemaker because of the 1955 trip. It was, the KGB noted, strong evidence of his "negative opinion of the Soviet Union."[34]

"Kennedy was rude and unduly familiar with the Soviet people that he met," the KGB recorded for the Kremlin. Robert Kennedy "mocked all Soviets," constantly expressed anti-Soviet views, and, the KGB noted sternly and without any sense of irony, had the audacity to tell his Russian interpreter that in the USSR there was "no freedom of speech, that the system did not permit any criticism of the Soviet government, and that Soviet Jews were persecuted." It was the conclusion of the KGB that Robert Kennedy had gone out of his way "to expose only the negative facts in the USSR."[35] "In the course of his visit, he photographed only the very bad things: (crumbling, clay factories, children who were poorly dressed, drunk Soviet officers, old buildings, lines at the market, fights, and the like)."[36]

In short, the KGB thought Robert Kennedy a provocateur. "In meetings with Soviet representatives," it was reported, "Kennedy posed tendentious questions and attempted to discover secret information." In Soviet Central Asia, Kennedy startled the chief of the Kazakh militia by telling him that he "was interested in the techniques of tapping telephone conversations, secret censorship of mail, Soviet intelligence activities abroad, the system of repression, including the means of punishing captured foreign spies." As if this had not been enough for the Kazakh militiaman, and Kennedy's KGB escorts, the American asked how many people were actually in Soviet jails and, of those, how many were in forced labor camps.[37]

Theodore Sorensen met both John and Robert Kennedy in 1953 and later commented that Robert was then "militant, aggressive, intolerant, opinionated, somewhat shallow in his convictions . . . more like his father than his brother."[38] The list of adjectives used by the KGB in its portrait of Kennedy was roughly the same. Furthermore, Soviet intelligence noted for Khrushchev a flaw in his character. "He has a weakness for women," the service reported to the Kremlin. In 1955 the young married man had asked his Intourist guide to send a "woman of loose morals" to his hotel room.[39] Years later, Robert Kennedy acknowledged that he had not been at his best in the USSR. After hearing the "catalogue of horrors" that his friend Theodore Sorensen had used to describe him in his early thirties, Robert wrote, "Teddy old pal — Perhaps we could keep down the number of adjectives and adverbs describing me in 1955 and use a few more in 1967. O.K. — Bob."[40]

Moscow Responds

Bolshakov reported the substance of his conversation to his chief at the embassy, who passed it on to Moscow. Bolshakov's report confused the Soviet government, which had assumed that summit preparations would be handled by Thompson and Gromyko. Kennedy had signaled that he was interested in a summit but wanted to reserve judgment on whether to return to the original schedule. His excuse was that events in Laos or at the negotiating table in Geneva might make it politically impossible for him to meet with Khrushchev. The report from the GRU, despite coming from the despised Robert Kennedy, at the very least confirmed that John Kennedy was serious about resuming preparations for a meeting.

Khrushchev jumped on these signals from Washington that Kennedy wanted to revive the June summit. In a May 12 letter to Kennedy, he wrote that "the international atmosphere has recently become somewhat heated in connection with the well-known events relating to Cuba" and that he thought it a good time for a general exchange of views.[41]

Khrushchev's letter, agreeing to a meeting in Vienna, arrived in Washington via Ambassador Menshikov on May 16. The news was good, but Kennedy had hoped for more. Either Bolshakov was not what Holeman and the attorney general thought he was, or Khrushchev did not consider the American president's approach interesting enough to explore before the summit. In either case, the president felt he had to continue to try to open a dialogue before the summit if there was to be any chance of a major breakthrough. Barely concealing his disappointment at Khrushchev's letter, Kennedy told Menshikov, who delivered it, "[I]f we cannot accomplish anything concrete on a nuclear test ban, it would be doubtful that we could make progress on disarmament."[42] Kennedy did not repeat to the Soviet ambassador the concession that he had already suggested to the Soviets regarding the number of on-site inspections; he left that to Robert's contact. Despite the disappointing letter from Khrushchev and the lack of word from Bolshakov, the White House decided to confirm, in background material to the U.S. media, that a summit was on and to work through the Soviet Foreign Ministry to arrange the details.[43]

Not for the first time, Khrushchev revealed himself as being unlike any politician or statesman John Kennedy had ever met or studied. The Kremlin did not doubt that Bolshakov had met with Robert Kennedy and that the "first brother" had accurately conveyed the president's ideas. However, Kennedy assumed Khrushchev would respond to this serious initiative with one of his own. Evidently this assumption sprang from a view of U.S.-Soviet relations as being, in part, the victim of misunderstandings and bad timing. As a senator, John Kennedy had criticized Eisenhower for approving a U-2 flight just before the scheduled Paris summit. With the Bay of Pigs behind him, John Kennedy did not want anything else to come in the way of a constructive improvement in superpower relations. His minor concessions were designed with that in mind.

But Khrushchev was not interested in altering his established positions to arrive at a common ground with the new U.S. president. After receiving the GRU's report on the first Kennedy-Bolshakov meeting, Khrushchev ordered the Defense Ministry to cooperate with the Foreign Ministry on a suitable response. Lacking specific guidelines from above—in other words, without any protective insurance, lest their suggestions be considered "adventurist"—the ministries produced boilerplate responses.

In the Soviet system all important decisions had to be confirmed by a resolution of the Presidium. The draft of the statement for Bolshakov to use, which was completed by the ministries on May 16, went to the Presidium on May 18. Khrushchev was traveling in Central Asia, but a courier system, and of course the telephone, kept the rest of the Presidium in constant touch with him. In Moscow, Mikhail Suslov, a member of the Presidium, and Foreign Minister Andrei Gromyko, not a member, were primarily responsible for preparing for the upcoming summit.[44]

The Kremlin's response reveals Khrushchev's thinking at the start of a new American administration. Bolshakov's instructions are preserved in both the archives of the GRU and the Presidential Archive, and the authors have been able to compare the two versions. This anodyne rendition of Soviet positions in 1961 should lay to rest the long-held suspicion that Khrushchev used Bolshakov to mislead Kennedy into rushing into a summit in Vienna. The Kremlin's response left little room for optimism.

The Soviet leadership declined to send a message from Khrushchev. Instead, Bolshakov was instructed to tell Robert Kennedy that "since his previous meeting with R. Kennedy, he, Bolshakov, has had a chance to consider and consult with friends the questions raised by Kennedy and would now like to give him his [i.e., Bolshakov's] opinion, with the same candidness, on some of the issues broached by him."[45] This was the gray formulation that Khrushchev wanted.

"Bolshakov's opinions" were of course those of the Soviet Foreign and Defense Ministries. The first point the GRU officer made was that the Soviets attached great importance to the improvement of U.S.-Soviet relations. Despite the ideological differences between these countries, there was no question that in matters of government-to-government relations there were really no insuperable barriers, because the United States and the USSR could conduct their relations in a good-hearted fashion and could decide to resolve existing disagreements through negotiation.

Had the conversation ended there, Robert Kennedy might have wondered whether Moscow was really on the line. But Bolshakov was allowed to say more. He was to add that it was unclear in the USSR what had made Robert Kennedy think that the Soviets underestimated either the new administration or his brother. Moscow, which evidently interpreted "underestimate" to mean "have a negative opinion of," instructed Bolshakov to say, "Kennedy's inauguration was greeted with the hope that our relations could return to what they had been in the time of Franklin Roosevelt." Bolshakov was also to remind Kennedy that Khrushchev had said as much on a number of occasions. More important, Bolshakov was to make explicit the connection between these expectations and the Soviet decision to accept President Kennedy's offer for a summit.

From this point on, Bolshakov gave Robert Kennedy a taste of what Khrushchev would soon tell his brother in person:

> It is impossible to let go by Robert Kennedy's remark that the events in Cuba and in Laos "somewhat diminished the president's drive to normalize relations with the Soviet Union." Of course, it is impossible to deny that the international situation has recently heated up owing to the well-known events in Cuba, and also partly those in Laos, but the Soviet Union bears no responsibility at all for this.[46]

But what of the White House's sweeteners for a successful conference? The Soviet leadership ignored them. Moreover, it twisted Kennedy's request that the Kremlin make the first move and offer concessions into a U.S. demand for unilateral concessions. "The Soviet Union did not seek any kind of advantage, indeed seeks nothing at all other than peaceful coexistence. Such cooperation, of course, does not mean one-sided concessions from the side of the Soviet Union." Khrushchev instructed Bolshakov to aver, "If anyone in the USA has the illusion that the U.S.-Soviet relationship could be built on the damaged interests of the USSR or seeks from the Soviet Union one-sided concessions, then such a policy, of course, will quickly meet failure."

The Soviets welcomed U.S. interest in resolving the three sticking points in the negotiations over a test ban: the number of inspections, the composition of the inspection teams, and the direction over these groups. But Moscow found nothing in what the new president was saying to suggest that an agreement was any closer at hand. Instead, Bolshakov was instructed to remind Robert Kennedy of other obstacles to a test ban agreement. Moscow wanted the executive council that would oversee the treaty itself to have identical representation from each of the three worlds—the West, the Soviet bloc, and the neutral or Third World. The Soviets also wanted a moratorium on underground testing below a certain detectable megatonnage. The Soviet objective, as Bolshakov explained to Kennedy, was to ban all nuclear tests forever.

The only real source of hope was what Bolshakov had to say about Laos. Considering this a problem that Kennedy had inherited from his predecessor, the Soviets welcomed his call for a neutral Laos and suggested that the two leaderships build on "the coincidence of the viewpoints of our governments." The Soviets indicated that an agreement in principle at Vienna to remove Laos from the superpower contest would accelerate the talks in Geneva on

Laos, where the Soviets contended Secretary of State Rusk had been playing the role of spoiler. They added that the successful solution of the Laotian tangle would signal the start of an improvement in the superpower relationship.

But the Kennedys were not to be allowed to think the Soviets were going to give them any other gifts. Following instructions, Bolshakov was to criticize Kennedy's policy toward Berlin. Here, the United States had to understand, there were "serious disagreements" that could undermine all the good that might be achieved in Laos. "We only want, with the cooperation of the United States," said Bolshakov, "to formalize . . . the existing state of affairs." The Soviets hoped that "the ruling circles of the Western powers would show political courage and accept the Soviet position on the German question, accept the necessity of signing a peace treaty with Germany and of deciding the matter of West Berlin." Bolshakov was told to end this with a threat: "Otherwise there will be nothing left for the USSR to do except together with other affected states sign a peace treaty with the GDR, with all the attendant consequences for West Berlin."

Finally, the Soviets raised the issue of Castro and Cuba. Robert Kennedy had expressly told Bolshakov that this was a matter the president did not wish to bring up in Vienna. Nevertheless, the Soviet government wanted to assure itself that the Bay of Pigs would not be repeated. "We don't understand what Robert Kennedy had in mind when he said that Cuba was a dead issue. If by that he meant that the United States will henceforth desist from aggressive actions and from interfering in the internal affairs of Cuba, then, without question, the Soviet Union welcomes this decision." As far as the Kremlin was concerned, only the United States could decide whether there would be peace in the Caribbean.

The Soviets noted that the Cuban government wished to normalize relations with Washington. In light of Robert Kennedy's comments, perhaps there would be a meeting of the minds between the Cubans and the United States. The Soviet regime told Bolshakov,

> Emphasize that the normalization of U.S. relations with the government of Fidel Castro, a sober estimate of the existing situation in Cuba, without a doubt, would only raise the worldwide prestige of the USA and the Kennedy administration, promote the recovery of the international situation, and certainly would create additional opportunities for improving U.S.-Soviet relations.[47]

Bolshakov was not given any leeway. In the Soviet system Moscow sought minute control over not just the themes raised by its representatives but even the exact manner in which they were formulated. Only the leadership could devise variations on positions, let alone establish them. "If R. Kennedy asks other questions, which have not been foreseen in these instructions," the

Kremlin dictated on May 18, "then Comrade Bolshakov, instead of giving a substantive answer, must reserve the right to consider these matters and discuss them with R. Kennedy later."

This disappointing news from Bolshakov reached the president via Robert on May 19 or 20. Despite the blandness and concealed contempt of the Soviet response, the president felt he had to try harder to seek some agreements in Vienna. He decided to ignore this first failure and look instead for additional ways to convince Khrushchev of the possibility of finding common ground. The president pressed his own team to rework his test ban proposal so that common ground might be found. At a meeting of the National Security Council on May 19, he sought a position that would be consistent with U.S. national interests as well as one that would be acceptable to the Soviets. Earlier in the month he had convened his top advisers on the test ban to discuss how to respond to the Soviet demand for a triumvirate. John McCloy, one of the strongest proponents of a test ban treaty in the administration, argued that if the United States wanted an agreement, it would probably have to reconsider its opposition to the troika concept. McCloy cited Khrushchev's talk with the American columnist Walter Lippmann, where the Soviet leader explained how events in the Congo had soured him on the secretary-general of the United Nations, Dag Hammarskjöld. McCloy was sympathetic to these Soviet concerns. He felt that the United States would have objected to the UN in 1945 if the Senate had known how powerful the secretary-general would become.[48]

While reconsidering his negotiating position on the test ban, Kennedy considered another idea for a possible area of agreement with the Soviets. He had asked his science adviser, Jerome Wiesner, to draft a report listing ways in which the Americans and the Soviets could cooperate in space research and exploration. Wiesner brought together a team from the State Department, the National Aeronautics and Space Administration (NASA), and the Department of Defense to discuss how to keep the Cold War out of outer space. Despite the reluctance of the State Department's representative, the group concluded on May 12 that Washington might want to suggest cooperating in or at least coordinating its manned lunar efforts with the Soviets. Initially, Kennedy deemed this an excellent idea. Perhaps this was something else he could offer to Khrushchev.[49]

John Kennedy, by all accounts, just had not thought much about space exploration until the Soviets surprised the world on April 12 by putting the first man into space, Yuri Gagarin. Sometime before the 1960 election, MIT's Charles "Doc" Draper took him and Robert out to dinner at Boston's Locke-Ober. Draper, a pioneer in designing inertial guidance systems for missiles, wanted to excite the brothers' interest in the space program. He later recalled that the Kennedys "could not be convinced that all rockets were not a waste of money, and space navigation even worse."[50] But the Kremlin's success in April 1961 forced Kennedy to pay attention to the role of space exploration in the

Cold War. A month later Alan B. Shepard, an American, became the second man rocketed into space. But despite attempts to equate Shepard's achievement with Yuri Gagarin's, the American space program lagged more than a month behind the Soviet program. Gagarin had orbited the earth, spending two hours in space. Shepard's mission had taken only seventeen minutes and consisted of surviving a launch and then immediately coming back to earth. It would take nine more months for another American, John Glenn, to match Gagarin's achievement.

In early May 1961 a joint committee of representatives from the Defense Department and NASA submitted a report recommending that Kennedy announce that the United States would put a man on the moon by 1967. Flying in the face of most of the scientific and military advice that Kennedy and Eisenhower had received about the feasibility and trade-offs of a program of manned lunar exploration, the report suggested manned flight would be seen as a major coup in the Cold War.

Kennedy was not impressed. Worried about the cost, estimated at more than eight billion dollars, he reserved his options. Moreover, he was concerned about the effect such a challenge to the Soviets might have on his upcoming summit with Khrushchev. "It is no secret that Kennedy would have preferred to cooperate with the Soviets on space exploration," recalls Theodore Sorensen.[51] As of May 17, the day the White House decided to go ahead with the Vienna summit, Kennedy had not decided whether to announce the moon mission. Instead, he instructed Secretary of State Rusk and his brother to suggest joint exploration of space to Khrushchev. Kennedy understood that the psychological realm was the principal battleground of the Cold War. He hesitated using atmospheric nuclear tests to bring the Soviets to heel. Similarly, he did not want to undermine any possibility of success by challenging them to a potentially impractical race to put a man on the moon.

Rusk raised the issue of a joint space program with the Soviet foreign minister on May 20. Gromyko, who was in the United States on a visit to the UN General Assembly, displayed a lack of interest in the secretary of state's proposal. Gromyko warned Rusk not to try to use U.S. priorities to dictate the pace of negotiations: "The Soviet government does not intend to take any step that is directed against its security or would inflict damage on its vital interests."[52]

Again a Kennedy initiative to improve relations left the Kremlin cold. As far as Moscow was concerned, cooperation in space belonged in the category of harmful steps. "The Soviet position," Gromyko explained, "depended above all . . . [on] the position that the United States, together with all Western powers, takes on disarmament." By disarmament, Gromyko said, he meant the "elimination of all military machines, including nuclear, rocket weapons, and also all U.S. military bases on the Soviet border." Rusk explained that Americans considered general and complete disarmament a noble goal but impossible to achieve without a better international environment. Initiatives like the president's—suggesting cooperation in outer space—were a way of laying the foundations for greater trust, the first step in achieving better relations. Gromyko, who was known to Western observers as Mr. Nyet, refused to budge. "Without the implementation of these measures, all cooperation in the field of rocket research and any exchange of information about Soviet rocket technology is inconceivable."[53]

These initial setbacks notwithstanding, the Kennedys decided to send another high-level message with the space proposal and some new thoughts on the test ban to Khrushchev. Time was running short. It was Sunday, and President Kennedy was scheduled to leave Washington at the end of the week. Another meeting between Robert Kennedy and Georgi Bolshakov was therefore arranged for May 21.

"Improving U.S.-Soviet relations is job no. 1 for the U.S. government," began Robert Kennedy at his meeting with Bolshakov. The president wanted his brother to impress on the Soviet representative how hard he was working to create the bases for agreements in Vienna. Robert was to offer the president's additional thoughts on a nuclear test ban and a possible agreement on space cooperation.[54] "My brother is prepared to accept the troika proposal," Kennedy revealed to Bolshakov, "but no veto." Accepting the concept of a troika was merely a symbolic concession. John Kennedy did not much care about the composition of the administrative council for the treaty, so long as the West and the Soviet bloc had the same number of votes and the West was assured of a certain number of on-site inspections per year in order to follow up on suspicious seismic information. A troika would be possible, but unanimity must not be required to trigger an inspection. Perhaps Kennedy thought Khrushchev would accept the form of a troika without the substance of a troika, if it meant getting a deal.

Besides revealing the president's wish that a space agreement be concluded in Vienna, Robert stressed that his brother understood some of Khrushchev's frustration about the situation in Central Europe. He knew why Khrushchev worried about "German revanchism." But Kennedy's policy on Berlin was unchanged. Robert Kennedy assured Bolshakov that his brother was upbeat about the summit. He was informed on everything the Soviet leadership had transmitted through the GRU representative. Kennedy was pleased that Khrushchev wanted to press ahead with neutralizing Laos on the Cold War chessboard. The president's only request was that Cuba not be brought up at Vienna. He just did not want to talk about it.

As of May 23 President Kennedy was downbeat. In fact, he was beginning to worry about this summit. None of the recommendations he had made to the Soviets seemed to be having any effect. It was not only that the summit was less than two weeks away that raised concern, but Kennedy had a major address to give before a joint session of Congress in a few days and he did not know what tone to employ. Should he be conciliatory to the Soviets in advance of Vienna? Originally conceived in mid-April as a boost to flagging European spirits after the Bay of Pigs disaster, the first draft of the speech focused on the Kennedy administration's efforts to strengthen NATO. By mid-May that speech had been supplanted by one stressing the themes of self-sacrifice, challenge, and national survival. Kennedy was thinking of announcing a domestic and foreign crusade to shore up the forces of freedom and democracy. But shouldn't he give the Kremlin a second chance, Kennedy wondered, before giving this speech?

Khrushchev Has His Own Ideas

Khrushchev returned to Moscow on May 20 and decided that he had to send his own personal message to the American president. He was not interested in finding a new channel. Tommy Thompson, whom he had known now for five years, was good enough. Khrushchev's office invited the U.S. ambassador and his wife to sit in the chairman's box at the performance of an American ice skating revue on May 23. Khrushchev was known not to like ice shows. He wanted to talk to Thompson.

Khrushchev and Thompson discussed a wide range of matters, but the Soviet leader intended above all to warn the U.S. government that he did not like Kennedy's agenda for the meeting. Berlin, which Khrushchev termed a "running sore," and not the test ban was what weighed most heavily on his mind. Disarmament, he said, was "impossible as long as the Berlin problem existed." Khrushchev expressed frustration at not being able to convince the West of his loss of patience over the anomalous situation in the heart of Europe. It made no sense, he argued, for there to be an Allied occupation zone in the center of East Germany. West Berlin was an unnecessary reminder of a war that had ended sixteen years before. Moreover, in the Cold War, it was a center of subversion and Allied military power. Once again, as he had been doing periodically since November 1958, Khrushchev warned that if the West refused to grapple with this problem diplomatically, the Soviet Union would sign a separate peace treaty with East Germany and authorize the East Germans to cut Allied access to West Berlin. When Thompson reminded Khrushchev that the West would meet such an eventuality with force, Khrushchev replied enigmatically, "They would not touch our troops in Berlin, but they might have to tighten their belts."

The tone of Khrushchev's message surprised Kennedy. "Tighten their belts"? John Kennedy, who received this cable on the morning of May 24, had no idea what Khrushchev meant. He called his brother at the Department of Justice to ask him to arrange one more meeting with Bolshakov to find out what was going on. "The president has just read the first half of our ambassador's dispatch, and he considers the conversation very harsh," explained Robert Kennedy to Bolshakov in his office a few hours later. "He is especially concerned by the statement on West Berlin, where Khrushchev suggested to the Americans to tighten their belts."[55]

This was the second time in two days that the attorney general had spoken to Bolshakov. He had called the TASS bureau on May 23 to press Bolshakov to do all he could to hurry the Soviet foreign policy process along, so that the White House would have pre-summit responses to the president on cooperating in space and on the troika suggestion. Robert Kennedy told Bolshakov that his brother was losing his patience. He said that the president felt he had to express his disappointment over recent Soviet behavior at a special joint session of Congress the following day. Kennedy said that the Soviets had to understand that his brother would not back down on issues that affected vital U.S. interests. Nevertheless, he cautioned Bolshakov that the language his brother felt he had to use did not indicate any lessening of commitment to a constructive meeting with Khrushchev.

In light of Khrushchev's actions and the disappointing results of working through Bolshakov, John Kennedy was more convinced than ever that the Soviet Union underestimated his willingness to defend U.S. international responsibilities. Kennedy's May 25 speech was quickly redrafted, the language toughened to signal his resolve to Khrushchev, and the entire package given the title "Special Message on Urgent National Needs." Following Khrushchev's rebuff of the offer of cooperation in space on May 20, Kennedy had decided to announce the goal of placing a man on the moon by the end of the decade.

With the summit only days away, President Kennedy's nightmare seemed to be on the verge of realization. He had wanted a successful summit, not another foreign policy failure. Kennedy had been in office only four months and had nothing but the Bay of Pigs and Laos to show for himself in foreign policy. Was Khrushchev planning to use Vienna to lecture Kennedy on Berlin, a problem Kennedy knew could not be solved in a few days, if at all?

Presidium Meeting of May 26

On the eve of Khrushchev's departure for Vienna, the Presidium met to discuss summit strategy. In preparation for this discussion, Andrei Gromyko and the Foreign Ministry had prepared a memorandum on what issues the Soviet side should raise, what points Kennedy would most like to discuss, and possible Soviet responses to them.

The Foreign Ministry concluded that the Soviet Union would want to discuss five different matters with Kennedy: (a) general and complete disarmament; (b) the improvement of the climate of international relations; (c) a German peace treaty, including the question of West Berlin; (d) Laos; and (e) a normalization of U.S.-Soviet relations.[56]

The Foreign Ministry suggested some possible agreements that might arise from the meeting. Khrushchev, it argued, should seek "an agreement of principles that would provide a basis for further negotiations on disarmament." Beyond that, it suggested offering a list of ways the superpowers could reduce international tensions. From an American perspective, it was all old hat.[57]

1. To end war propaganda.
2. A pledge not to be the first to use nuclear weapons in a conflict.
3. The creation of nuclear free zones in various regions of the world.
4. Measures against nuclear proliferation.
5. A NATO-Warsaw Pact nonaggression pact.
6. Full removal of all foreign troops from the Germanys and a moratorium on their reintroduction.
7. Reductions in military forces in Europe, leading to the complete withdrawal of them from areas outside their national territory.
8. Reductions in military budgets.[58]

Given that there was nothing novel in these suggestions, the Soviets anticipated receiving a different wish list from Kennedy. "The Americans could propose steps to create a climate of trust, for example—the cessation of the production of nuclear materials for military purposes, the establishment of controls on ballistic and intercontinental rockets, and measures to prevent a first strike." The Soviets felt the Americans were more interested in controlling the arms race than in ending it altogether.

Bolshakov's meetings with Robert Kennedy had demonstrated the White House's eagerness to achieve a test ban accord. The Soviet Foreign Ministry mentioned U.S. concerns without suggesting any particular response. This silence betrayed the fact that Moscow was not really interested in any compromises on this issue. Similarly, Gromyko's team raised the ill-fated U.S. offer to cooperate in space without proposing any new Soviet response. The Foreign Ministry concluded its proposed instructions with a list of four "other questions" that might be raised but that were not considered priority items. Curiously in this group of four, Cuba was only the third item. Gromyko, at least, saw no advantage in Khrushchev's discussing Castro with Kennedy.[59]

Khrushchev approved the Foreign Ministry's proposals as written. He did not want any new Soviet initiatives or compromises. This was the time to be tough. He was optimistic that if he bullied Kennedy he could achieve movement along the lines he had been pursuing since the late 1950s. He did not greatly respect the young U.S. president. What impressed him was how needy the president seemed to be. Kennedy's efforts to signal the possibility of agreements had backfired—or at least had not reduced Soviet concerns.

Whereas the Presidium accepted the list of instructions, not all of Khrushchev's colleagues agreed with him on how to treat the American president. According to Anatoly Dobrynin, who would later be his country's ambassador to the United States and was then chief of the American department of the Central Committee, Anastas Mikoyan spoke up at the May 26 meeting in favor of a more diplomatic approach: perhaps, he proposed, Kennedy should be dealt with carefully, his offers treated seriously.

Khrushchev would have none of this questioning of his sense of timing. He exploded, displaying that harsh temper and foul language that interpreters worked hard to soften in meetings with foreigners. He rejected the "cautious approach." Kennedy was vulnerable to pressure. If the Soviet Union pushed hard enough, this man would yield—on all of the important issues, like the future of Berlin.[60] Khrushchev's confidence in his strategy did not stem from any special intelligence about Kennedy. However, in the course of preparing to meet him, he did receive information that largely confirmed that the young president was eager to accommodate Soviet concerns within the limits set by basic U.S. interests.

Before the Presidium meeting, Khrushchev received the account of a private meeting between Ambassador Menshikov in Washington and the U.S. permanent representative to the United Nations, Adlai Stevenson. Stevenson had turned the leadership of the Democratic Party over to Kennedy in 1960 but remained highly influential among its liberal wing. On May 18, 1961, Stevenson had invited Menshikov to breakfast. He said that this summit should have happened sooner. "Just between us," Stevenson told the Soviet, "Kennedy has a lot of questionable and even dangerous advisers, to whom he sometimes gives in." Stevenson presented Kennedy as an impressionable man whose views about the Soviets would be changed for the better once he met Khrushchev. Stevenson did not expect any decisions on the great issues to emerge from the summit, but he thought an exchange of views between the leaders of the superpowers useful. Stevenson did say that if there was one area where something substantive might happen, it was in the area of a test ban treaty.[61]

Khrushchev was not surprised to learn that Kennedy had dangerous advisers. He knew that the inheritors of the views of John Foster Dulles lurked throughout Washington. It did not matter which political party was in power. There were influential Americans who believed in what the Soviets called the "position of power" or "peace through strength" approach, which Khrushchev identified with using military threats to deny Soviet rights and even to attempt to roll back Soviet postwar gains. Khrushchev blamed Harry Truman, a Democrat, for magnifying Joseph Stalin's paranoia and ensuring that the Allied partnership collapsed following World War II.

The raw reports that filtered through to Khrushchev reinforced the impression that the Vienna summit presented a great opportunity to both sides. An especially important source of information about the president's objectives came from a group of seventeen distinguished Americans who by coincidence were meeting with their Soviet counterparts in the Crimea in the week before the summit. Under the leadership of Norman Cousins, the editor of the *Saturday Review*, and Philip E. Mosely, of the Council on Foreign Relations, the group included the singer Marian Anderson and Erwin Griswold, of the Harvard Law School.

In a conversation with a Soviet representative on May 24, Norman Cousins warned that Kennedy's advisers were sharply split between those who hoped for an accommodation with Russia and those who thought this impossible.

For that reason, Cousins advised, Vienna could mark a defining moment for the Kennedy presidency. "The course of the negotiations with Khrushchev will determine where Kennedy leans—in the direction of the Pentagon or in the direction of advisers of the type of [Chester] Bowles."

Cousins was explicit about the threat posed by the right wing of the Kennedy team. He had an explanation, congenial to Khrushchev, for the three most important events to affect the superpower relationship in the last year. "[T]he U-2 incident, the defeats in Cuba and Laos have brought the public opinion in the United States to the view that these events were not accidental but premeditative acts of provocation."[62]

Cousins blamed the CIA in particular for working against an improvement of relations. He described CIA analyses and actions as very often the results of the "recommendations of Trotskyite elements, and also of those who having split with the Communist Party of the U.S. now advocate the theory of the inevitability of war." In the last few years, Cousins added, these elements had become more widespread and influential in the CIA, explaining above all the Bay of Pigs mistake. According to Cousins, Kennedy had been inclined to stop the project when he came to office. But when the White House received Khrushchev's truculent letter, it set off Kennedy's right-wing advisers, who used it to say that the Bay of Pigs operation was a test of will in the Cold War struggle. A Kennedy decision to back off Cuba would be perceived as "a manifestation of U.S. weakness in response to Russian pressure."[63]

The KGB had its own informants at the Crimean conference. They corroborated the view of Kennedy as a man caught between warring sets of advisers. One KGB agent reported on a conversation with Robert Bowie, the former chief of the Policy Planning Staff of Dulles's State Department, Paul Doty, a Harvard professor of chemistry, and Shepard Stone, of the Ford Foundation, who discussed the mood in Washington. The three had visited with McGeorge Bundy, Kennedy's national security adviser, and his assistant Walt Rostow before leaving for the Soviet Union. Bundy and Rostow had told them that Kennedy considered the Vienna summit "an opportunity to probe the position of the head of the Soviet regime on fundamental issues." Echoing what Adlai Stevenson had said privately to Ambassador Menshikov, Bowie and the other American experts noted that Kennedy felt it important to hear Khrushchev explain Soviet policy in his own terms. Following the Bay of Pigs disaster, Kennedy "did not trust the conclusions of his own advisers." He wanted to give the Soviets the opportunity to explain what they were up to in Berlin and in Laos and to explore why there had not been further progress on a nuclear test ban. Beyond this, the summit was good domestic politics for Kennedy. In forwarding this report on the group headed by Bowie, the KGB chief, Shelepin, noted for the Foreign Ministry that the U.S. president feared that he had lost the confidence of the American people. The summit was a way to prove "he was capable of establishing personal contact with N. S. Khrushchev."[64]

Would Kennedy be the captive of his hawkish advisers? Khrushchev no doubt wondered as he made his way to Vienna. Everything Khrushchev received, from open as well as confidential sources, supported the view that Kennedy wanted better relations. After all, the U.S. president had used his brother to extend what turned out to be unacceptable concessions, though concessions they were. But what the Soviet leader could not know until he met Kennedy was the extent to which, like Eisenhower, Kennedy was under the thumb of the so-called militarists around him.

Kennedy Prepares

In Washington, John Kennedy tried one final time to establish a personal connection to Khrushchev. The Kennedy brothers spent the last weekend before the summit at Hyannis Port, where the family had gathered to celebrate the president's forty-fourth birthday. Robert Kennedy called Georgi Bolshakov from the Kennedy compound on May 29. "The president would like to know whether he and the Chairman could meet privately, with only their interpreters present." A recent message from the U.S. embassy in Moscow offered a narrow band of hope. Thompson suggested that Khrushchev might be more accommodating if met alone. Khrushchev had actually prefaced his frosty remarks at the ice show by saying that he would be able to speak more freely with the president when the two men would not be in front of assistants.[65] With this in mind, the president authorized his brother to feel out the Soviets on organizing a one-on-one meeting in Vienna, with only interpreters present.

Robert Kennedy stressed the White House's need for a quick reply. The president wanted to hear from Bolshakov before he left for Paris on May 30. Bolshakov cabled this back to Moscow. The GRU officer stressed the Kennedy brothers' sense that their appeals were not being appreciated: "The White House wants to know whether Comrade Khrushchev has received this message."[66] Rumors were swirling in Washington that Vienna was going to be a failure. A good friend and colleague of Kennedy's from the Senate, Mike Mansfield, advised that the president be prepared to walk out of the meetings if they were "degenerating into mere-propaganda exchanges."[67] The rumors mirrored concern among many in the Kennedy inner circle. Kennedy turned to McGeorge Bundy on May 29 to nail down what the pundits were saying about Berlin. There was a spectrum of opinion, Bundy replied, from that of Walter Lippmann and Tommy Thompson on the left of the debate to that of Dean Acheson and Dean Rusk on the right: "You will see that the differences between the Achesonians and Lippmann do not turn on the issue of standing fast to defend our access to Berlin. They turn rather on whether there is any legitimate Soviet interest to which we can give some reassurance."[68]

Like the Kennedys, Khrushchev had also sought familiar surroundings to gather his strength and focus his mind before the summit. He was in Kiev when Bolshakov's dispatch reached the GRU in Moscow. Khrushchev had not seen fit to respond to Kennedy's second batch of questions, and he played the reluctant suitor again. It did not much matter whether he met Kennedy alone or with the entire Central Committee. Khrushchev did not intend to alter his message. But he would agree to some one-on-one meetings when he reached Vienna.

Khrushchev boarded a train in the Ukraine for the journey to Vienna, via Poland and Bratislava, Czechoslovakia. As he crossed the Czech border, Khrushchev flipped through more last-minute reports on his American adversary. In one the KGB chief in Washington cabled that a "trustworthy person close to Robert Kennedy" wanted the Kremlin to know that John Kennedy was still hopeful that the summit would be productive. President Kennedy would also look favorably upon an invitation from Khrushchev to another summit in Moscow. The KGB official assumed that his informant was probably acting under instructions from Robert Kennedy.[69]

Khrushchev had every reason to engage the U.S. president in meaningful negotiations in Vienna. Kennedy had sent more than just feelers to the Soviets. But he had raised the wrong issues. In Khrushchev's eyes, the test ban served American interests more than Soviet interests because the United States enjoyed a qualitative as well as quantitative advantage in nuclear weapons production. In addition, the inspection regime pushed by the Americans would be an affront to Soviet sovereignty. The fear of American espionage was also a reason not to let Americans come too close to the Soviet space program. Kennedy was about to learn a hard lesson in Soviet summitry.

Vienna

Kennedy's fears were realized early on. Khrushchev had come to talk about Berlin and to size up the young leader. The initiatives that John Kennedy had proposed through his brother had no effect on the Soviet leader. In their first day of talks, Khrushchev dismissed them. First, he said that he would not discuss the nuclear test ban in isolation from the larger question of the complete dismantling of the arsenals of the United States and the USSR. And second, he brushed aside discussion of any joint space projects. Like the test ban, Khrushchev argued, such cooperation was also impossible without disarmament.[70]

The first day of the summit found Castro figuratively lurking in the background. Kennedy complained about Khrushchev's new doctrine of support for "sacred wars" and thus provided Khrushchev with an opening to harangue the president on U.S. support for colonial and reactionary regimes. Khrushchev criticized U.S. tendencies to blame the emergence of nationalist movements on outside forces, rather than appreciating the reasons why peoples seek to overthrow their oppressors. The segue to Castro was a natural one. "Castro is not a communist," said Khrushchev, "but you can make him one." Indeed, Khrushchev was betraying a confidence to John Kennedy. Despite all of

Castro's protestations to the contrary, the Kremlin did not think him much of a communist. The Soviet leader knew, of course, that the situation in Cuba was more complicated, that Castro had declared himself to be a communist more than five months before the Bay of Pigs invasion and that, even before this, Moscow had had very influential friends in the Cuban leader's inner circle. Nevertheless, Khrushchev effectively played on the ineptness of U.S. policy toward the Cuban revolution through the disastrous Bay of Pigs. "[W]hen the U.S. put pressure on Fidel Castro and applied sanctions on him," Khrushchev recalled, "we came to his assistance, in the form of trade and technical support. . . . Under the influence of this aid he may turn Communist." Khrushchev said nothing about Soviet bloc military support in 1959.[71]

There would be no serious discussion of the nuclear test ban. Instead, Kennedy learned that Khrushchev would discuss nothing seriously until he had his way on Berlin. Although he did not wish to talk about Berlin, Kennedy had one concession to give. He took Khrushchev aside after lunch and tried to get him to reveal his bottom line in these negotiations. Kennedy hinted that the United States could accept a separate Soviet–East German peace treaty, so long as the West retained the right of access to West Berlin and to leave its troops there. Khrushchev's concession was that the United States could leave troops in West Berlin, so long as the Soviets could have troops there too. The discussion was getting nowhere. Kennedy could not believe that the Soviet leader would so willingly endanger U.S.-Soviet relations to get his way on Berlin. Did he not understand the strength of America's commitment to that occupied city? "If you want war," Khrushchev said, "that is your problem."

At the morning meeting on the second day, Kennedy complained to Khrushchev that the summit was not what he had expected or asked for. The Soviet leader was threatening him over Berlin without giving a thought to ways of reducing tension. Kennedy said he had not come to Vienna "to find out not only that a peace treaty would be signed but also that we would be denied our position in West Berlin and our access to that city." "I came here," he said, "in the hope that relations between our two countries could be improved."[72] Deaf to Kennedy's remonstrations, Khrushchev warned that regardless of Washington's opposition, the Kremlin would sign a peace treaty with East Germany in December. As the day wore on, Kennedy lost any hope of reaching a compromise on this or any other issue, save perhaps on Laotian neutrality, with Khrushchev. As he left the Soviet leader after this first and, as it turned out, last face-to-face meeting, Kennedy remarked, "It will be a cold winter."

The Vienna summit deeply disappointed John Kennedy. He had done everything possible, he thought, to improve the climate between the superpowers. He had gone against most of his advisers in offering a new deal on nuclear tests, he had accepted a draw in Laos, he had admitted that the Soviet Union had reason to fear a rearmed Germany, and he had even hinted at a new status for Berlin. Yet no water could be squeezed from the Russian stone. One of the few men around John Kennedy who understood the depth of his disappointment was his brother. Robert had tried through the gregarious GRU man, Bolshakov, to develop a confidential link to Khrushchev. But for all of the talking, not much had changed as a result of Vienna. Perhaps there was an agreement on Laos; but even this depended on Khrushchev's keeping his word. There was also no reason to expect Soviet caution elsewhere in the Third World. Robert Kennedy later recalled Vienna as a decisive moment in his brother's political education. "Vienna was very revealing: This was the first time the President had ever really come across somebody with whom he couldn't exchange ideas in a meaningful way and feel there was some point to it."[73] As Robert concluded, "it was a shock to him."[74]

Condor and Mongoose

The Train to Zhitomir

A month after the summit at Vienna, Nikita Khrushchev convened an urgent meeting of his nuclear brain trust, what Leonid Brezhnev the Presidium member who routinely handled the nuclear account liked to call "the bomb squad," in the Kremlin's Oval Room. A classical amphitheater, the Oval Room adjoined Khrushchev's private office. It was used whenever a sizable number of outside experts was invited to contribute to a session of the Presidium.

The famed nuclear physicist and future Nobel Prize winner Andrei Sakharov was among those sitting on the risers. "Khrushchev announced his decision at once," Sakharov recalled: "nuclear tests would resume in the fall, because the international situation had deteriorated and because the USSR lagged behind the U.S. in testing." Sakharov had gone to the meeting hoping for "an understanding with Khrushchev and his colleagues." He was concerned because the Kremlin refused to consult with scientists about its policy on testing. Khrushchev had announced a unilateral moratorium in 1957 without giving the scientists and weapons engineers the lead time to plan any last-minute tests. Khrushchev had allowed a few secret underwater tests in the Pacific in 1959, but since 1958 Moscow had generally adhered to a de facto test ban. Scientists were not invited to shape Kremlin decision making and had only a rough idea of the international considerations influencing Khrushchev. So far as a senior scientist like Sakharov knew, in sticking with the moratorium Khrushchev was upholding "some sort of informal agreement." "As usual," Sakharov later recalled, Khrushchev's decision to resume testing "came as a surprise to those most directly affected." The Kurchatov Institute, which directed nuclear research, had not prepared a test schedule for 1961.[1]

"[I]t was perfectly clear that the decision to resume testing was politically motivated," Sakharov noted. The stunned scientists who were seated in a row behind the Presidium were not asked their opinion. The decision was final. Khrushchev made the rounds of the scientists, however, to ask each one to give a ten-minute presentation on their current work. A microcosm of the Soviet system, this meeting had all of the elements of the destructive anti-intellectualism that created such economic and technological hardships for the Soviet people. The politicians had just dictated a research agenda for a bevy of their country's finest scientists, and now they wanted these professionals to throw out their prepared statements and explain how pleased they were with the leadership's decision.

Sakharov squirted lemon into the milk of approval: "I am convinced that a resumption of testing at this time would only favor the USA." Sakharov set himself apart from his colleagues. "Prompted by the success of our Sputniks," Sakharov argued in a note he penned quickly after his speech and had passed down the aisle to Khrushchev, "they could use tests to improve their devices." Sakharov was breaking the rules. After folding the note and sliding it into his pocket, Khrushchev signaled the next speaker to begin. A little later, the speeches over, Khrushchev rose and adjourned the meeting: "On behalf of the Central Committee Presidium, I invite our guests to dine. . . ." Some of the scientists had already lost their appetite.

The note angered Khrushchev, and he was not going to let the dinner end without making sure that everyone knew that what Sakharov and any other doubting Thomases might be thinking was wrong.

Here's a note I've received from Academician Sakharov. Sakharov writes that we don't need tests. But I've got a briefing paper which shows how many tests we've conducted and how many more the Americans have conducted. Can Sakharov really prove that with fewer tests we've gained more valuable information than the Americans? Are they dumber than we are? There's no way I can know all the technical fine points. But the *number* of tests, that's what matters most. . . .

But Sakharov goes further. He's moved beyond science into politics. Here he's poking his nose where it doesn't belong. You can be a good scientist without understanding a thing about politics. Politics is like the old joke about the two Jews traveling on a train. One asks the other: "So, where are you going?" "I'm going to Zhitomir." "What a sly fox," thinks the first Jew. "I know he's really going to Zhitomir, but he told me Zhitomir so I'll think he's going to Zhmerinka."

It was deathly quiet in the Kremlin dining room. Sakharov caught sight of Khrushchev's favorite sparring partner, Anastas Mikoyan, neck folded into his double chin, fighting to hide a grin. Khrushchev continued:

Leave politics to us—we're the specialists. You make your bombs and test them, and we won't interfere with you; we'll help you. But remember, we have to conduct our policies from a position of strength. We don't advertise it, but that's how it is! There can't be any other policy. Our opponents don't understand any other language. Look, we helped elect Kennedy last year. Then we met with him in Vienna, a meeting that could have been a turning point. But what does he say? "Don't ask for too much. Don't put me in a bind. If I make too many concessions, I'll be turned out of office." Quite a guy! He comes to a meeting, but can't perform. What the hell do we need a guy like that for? Why waste time talking to him? Sakharov, don't try to tell us what to do or how to behave. We understand politics. I'd be a jellyfish and not Chairman of the Council of Ministers if I listened to people like Sakharov![2]

In the summer of 1961 the United States and the Soviet Union were entering, in Robert Kennedy's words, "a tougher, harder, meaner period than that which had gone before."[3] The administration had hurt itself in Cuba, and the Kennedys believed that Khrushchev's performance at Vienna was proof that the Soviets had no interest in taking any steps toward a détente. Khrushchev was a bully, and Berlin was his prod. For Khrushchev, though Berlin was the most contested square of the global chessboard, there were still concerns about Cuba.

Assassination Schemes

Less than a month after the Vienna summit, the Kremlin received evidence that Cuba was not a "dead issue" for the CIA. The Cubans and the Soviets felt themselves lucky to have emerged from the Bay of Pigs relatively unscathed. As the sense of relief ebbed, it was displaced by a determination not to let anything like this happen again. In the month following the April invasion, the Cubans arrested twenty thousand people for counterrevolutionary activity.[4]

It is one of the paradoxes of government that better intelligence gathering can increase the sense of insecurity. As the Cuban security service became more professional with KGB help, the Castro regime found it had more reasons to be worried. In Havana, Cuban security officers turned up a cache of eight tons of weapons belonging to the CIA. After diplomatic relations were broken off in January 1961, the CIA had maintained an undercover center in Havana under the direction of a manager of a firm called Izaguirre Orendo. Among the eight tons of captured weapons at the CIA station were two pistols with silencers, which Havana and the KGB concluded were for "the murder of Fidel Castro."[5] The pistols seemed to make some sense of the flawed Bay of Pigs operation. The Kennedy administration had expected Castro to die before he could rally support for destroying the invasion. Quick work by Cuban security, and the even quicker collapse of the émigré beachheads, had forestalled these activities.

Besides the undercover CIA station, in late April the Cubans closed the local offices of the Berlitz language company, described as "the other U.S. intelligence *residentura* [station]," and arrested its director, Drexel Woodrow Wilson or "Gibson." Agents alleged to be working for Wilson were picked up and thrown in jail. In addition, the Cubans believed that they had tracked down the key man, a British subject, in the intelligence net run by MI6, the British foreign intelligence service. "As a result of these arrests," Alekseev boasted, "the fundamental centers and *residenturas* of foreign intelligence and also counterrevolutionary organizations appear to be paralyzed." Among the items found with Wilson or the CIA station were documents written by Manuel Ray's Movement for the Revival of the Revolution (MRR) and "indicating," stated a KGB report to the Kremlin, "that a series of important branches of this organization were defeated, and the majority of their leaders arrested."[6]

Moscow and Havana had no chance to celebrate these security achievements before there were new signs of U.S.-sponsored assassination plans. [7] In June 1961 the GRU acquired copies of documents prepared for the Guatemalan government indicating a new plot to assassinate Castro.[8] The plan, which was approved in Costa Rica by President Miguel Ydígoras of Guatemala, President Rómulo Betancourt of Venezuela, and the former president of Costa Rica José Figueres, involved killing the three top Cuban leaders—Fidel Castro, his brother Raúl, and Che Guevara. The approximate day for the operation was given as June 26, 1961.[9] When this evidence was brought to the attention of Khrushchev and the Presidium on June 24, the Kremlin decided to "inform Fidel Castro about the attempt being prepared on his life and on those of other Cuban leaders."[10]

The Soviets had solid documentary evidence—a memorandum from the head of Guatemalan intelligence to President Ydígorus—outlining the mechanics of Operation Condor, as the plan was code-named. Although Guatemala City provided logistics and may well have inspired the operation, the CIA had a role to play. Condor involved three people specially trained for the attack on Castro: two were former Cuban police lieutenants, Nelson Guteros and Marcelino Balida, who were living in Guatemala, and the third was from Puerto Rico, J. Negrette, who had been recommended to Guatemalan intelligence by the CIA. Negrette was living in Havana under a Mexican passport and reported to the CIA station in Guatemala through the chauffeur of the chief of Cuban military intelligence, Julio Bustamente. In spy jargon, the driver was a CIA "cutout"—who broke the chain of communications for security reasons between the agent and his case officer in Guatemala City. Although the Guatemalans were directing this operation, it was the American CIA that made it possible.[11]

The Soviet intelligence service reported to Khrushchev that the Central American leaders planned Operation Condor because "the counterrevolutionaries came to the firm conviction that only with the physical elimination of Fidel Castro and his colleagues could there be chaos in Cuba and a successful coup." The conspirators chose J. Negrette, who had previously worked for Batista, because he was willing and a decent shot. Negrette was told that because Castro usually wore a bulletproof vest, the Cuban leader should "be shot in the head" at "a regular meeting or during a foreign visit." "In the case of a successful completion of the assassination," the outline of Condor read, "an external attack on Cuba by trained forces was being planned, which this time was being staged on Costa Rican soil."[12] If this invasion succeeded, Guatemala, Nicaragua, Venezuela, El Salvador, and Costa Rica would recognize the new government of Cuba.

Negrette never turned up to kill Castro, and Operation Condor disappeared without a trace. But the Cubans could not relax. In late June they discovered another CIA network. Dr. Avilesa Cautina was on his way to Miami when the Cubans pulled him in for questioning on June 19. At the time of his arrest, Cautina carried plans for the creation of a new anti-Castro organization, the Frente Nacional Cubana, or FNC, which would unify the counterrevolutionary groups operating in Cuba.[13] The CIA envisioned the FNC providing half of an underground movement to support the government in exile of José Miró Cardona. Cautina's point of contact in Havana was a CIA agent whose alias was Caesar. According to Cautina, Caesar belonged to a network named Candela.[14]

The discovery of Candela highlighted the large number of loose ends that the Cubans and their KGB advisers still had to tie. Alfredo Izaguirre de la Riva, whose family presumably owned Izaguirre Orendo, remained at large and might be involved with the as yet unknown Caesar and his Candela team. Besides that of finding Izaguirre, the Cubans faced the challenge of dealing with evidence of fourteen serious counterrevolutionary groups that were still active and might have some connection to Candela as well.[15] Moscow tried to help by canvassing its sources for more information about Candela.

In mid-July the Candela operation became a matter of high politics, when Moscow on its own discovered evidence that Caesar and Candela were part of a U.S.-sponsored plot to kill Fidel Castro in a spectacular operation timed for July 26, the national holiday marking the eighth anniversary of the attack on the Moncada barracks.[16] Moscow's fears were heightened by news that Yuri Gagarin, the world's first cosmonaut, who was expected to be Fidel Castro's guest of honor at a ceremony in Havana, was also on Candela's hit list.

Alekseev and the Cubans discussed how to deal with this new information. Castro's security chief, Ramiro Valdés, directed his deputy Mendoza to take charge of ensuring the protection of Castro and Gagarin. Alekseev trusted Mendoza because he was the Cuban who had blown the whistle to the KGB of Escalante and Roca's hasty plans to kill Manuel Ray just after the Bay of Pigs. Mendoza launched a new series of arrests as soon as the information about the July 26 plot reached him. Alekseev reassured the Central Committee in Moscow that as "a prophylactic measure" the Cubans and the KGB decided "to liquidate the *agentura* [agent network] Candela, all those associated with its direction, and the members of [associated] counterrevolutionary organizations."[17]

The Cuban operation proceeded smoothly. By July 19 the five-man Candela group had been arrested. In addition, Cuban security rounded up about two hundred people from counterrevolutionary groups affiliated with Candela.[18] Interrogations of the captured agents confirmed the plan to kill Castro. But it turned out that the plot was much larger than Moscow had reported. The Candela group had hoped to embroil the Cubans in a shooting war with the United States. On July 26, counterrevolutionaries in Oriente Province were to shell the U.S. naval base at Guantánamo. Washington might then exploit the incident as a pretext to invade the island.

Candela, even more than Condor, served as a warning to the KGB and the Cubans that the domestic situation in Cuba was far from being under control. There was a need for much better intelligence to stay a step ahead of the terrorists. Up to that point the Cubans had made little headway at penetrating the Cuban émigré community in Miami. The KGB suggested a way of exploiting the Candela group to do something about this intelligence gap.[19] The KGB worked with the Cubans to use "Tony," the radio operator in the Candela group, to send false messages to the CIA. Over time the KGB would feed the Americans stories about "new recruits" to the Candela network. It was hoped that if the CIA came to believe these reports, the "new recruits" (actually Cuban security agents) would be invited to Miami for training. The Cubans and the KGB were eager to introduce their agents into the heart of the machine that was working so diligently to kill Castro.

Berlin Days

News of the Condor and Candela operations fit into a pattern of U.S. challenges to Soviet power that by August 1961 led Khrushchev to warn the other leaders of the Warsaw Pact, "War . . . is possible."[20] Cuba as yet was not expected to be the collision point. U.S.-Soviet difficulties in Cuba were symptomatic of what Khrushchev viewed as Washington's unwillingness to respect Soviet interests and prestige. In the summer of 1961 it was Berlin that seemed the most likely arena where conflict might occur. At Vienna, Khrushchev had threatened to sign a separate peace treaty with the East Germans by the end of the year. Circumstances were forcing him to initiate some kind of action to help his German allies. "[I]f the present situation of open borders remains," the East German leader Walter Ulbricht warned the Soviets in July 1961, "collapse is inevitable."[21] Khrushchev preferred a solution that would end West Berlin's status as a rallying point for internal dissatisfaction in East Germany and a military garrison for the West. But the United States had no interest in budging from its traditional defense of West Berlin's security. In late July, as the Kremlin kept one eye on Gagarin's visit to Cuba, this was again brought home to Khrushchev. Kennedy announced on July 25 the preparation of six new combat-ready divisions for European duty. He would triple draft calls and seek congressional approval for an additional $3.2 billion in military spending and for the right to call up the necessary reserves.[22] West Berlin, Kennedy explained, is "the great testing place of Western courage and will."[23]

Indeed, it was Khrushchev who had first baited Kennedy over Berlin, just as it was Kennedy's refusal to accept the status quo in Cuba that was causing palpitations in the Kremlin. But the Soviet leadership held the United States to be in the wrong in both instances, and the alignment of the Kennedy speech and the post–Bay of Pigs provocations in the Caribbean sparked a dangerous response from Moscow. On August 1 Khrushchev approved most of a KGB plan to create "a situation in various areas of the world that would favor [the] dispersion of attention and forces by the United States and their satellites, and would tie them down during the settlement of a German peace treaty and West Berlin."[24]

Among the suggestions for mischief making in colonial Africa, in Western Europe, and among the Kurds in the Middle East, the KGB plan included actions directed at Castro's enemies in Central America. The KGB chief, Aleksandr Shelepin, requested authorization for a plan involving the Cubans and the Revolutionary Front Sandino to spark a mutiny in Nicaragua, an armed uprising in El Salvador, and a rebellion in Guatemala. Despite the ambitious and heated rhetoric of the plans, Soviet involvement would be modest (the KGB requested only U.S.$25,000).[25] The Kremlin probably assumed that Castro's intelligence chiefs would bear the lion's share of the logistical burden of some jointly sponsored operations in Latin America.

Before Soviet intelligence could implement this program, Khrushchev ordered the construction of the Berlin Wall in the week of August 13. This stopgap measure—a barbed-wire fence (and later hideous concrete structure) around all of East Berlin—would reduce to a trickle the flow of East Germans to West Germany. To the Chinese and others who might criticize him for needlessly avoiding a clash with the United States, Khrushchev explained that the wall was not a substitute for a peace treaty with East Germany.[26]

One element of Shelepin's plan that Khrushchev had especially liked involved a campaign to create in Western minds an exaggerated understanding of the size and power of the Soviet nuclear forces. Khrushchev had abetted the development of U.S. fears of Soviet nuclear superiority in the late 1950s with calculated and colorful boasts that Soviet factories could produce missiles like sausages. In fact, Khrushchev knew that production of the first generation of Soviet intercontinental ballistic missiles (ICBMs) had been stopped, after the delivery of fewer than thirty-five of them, because of design flaws. A better rocket, the R-16, was in development, but it would be a matter of years before it could be deployed in sufficient numbers to match the U.S. triad of missiles, bombers, and submarines. The new KGB deception was to persuade NATO that the Soviet Strategic Rocket Forces had increased the number of missile launching pads and that the Soviet navy had submarines with solid-fuel ballistic missiles, like the American Polaris.

However, just as the implementation of the July plan for Latin America was disrupted by Khrushchev's decision to divide Berlin immediately, a U.S. decision compelled Khrushchev to move beyond KGB deception to create the illusion of Soviet strategic prowess. With a standoff at the Berlin Wall between Soviet and American tanks, the Kennedy administration tried to use a speech by Assistant Secretary of Defense Roswell Gilpatric to calm the American public and deter Soviet adventurism. Gilpatric announced to a group of businessmen that despite fears of a "missile gap" the United States had more than enough ICBMs, bombers, and ballistic submarines to deliver a crushing retaliatory blow if the Soviets were to launch a first strike. "This nation has a nuclear retaliatory force of such lethal power," Gilpatric told his audience, "that an enemy move which brought it into play would be an act of self-destruction on his part."[27] Seeing this as a personal affront and concerned that Gilpatric's speech symbolized the increasing power of the hard-liners in the Kennedy administration, Khrushchev opted for an immediate and dramatic response. He ordered the atmospheric test of the largest hydrogen device ever constructed. On October 30 a fifty-megaton bomb dropped 7.5 miles over the Soviet Arctic produced a mushroom cloud estimated as being 50 miles in height.[28]

Castro Also Wants Missiles

As superpower tempers flared over Berlin, Castro feared that Kennedy might seek an easy victory over socialism in Cuba. To try to focus Moscow's attention on the problem of Cuban defense, Castro composed a five-page letter to Khrushchev, dated September 4, that reminded the Kremlin that he had unsuccessfully asked for additional military support in early 1961, before the Bay of Pigs. Now he wanted to return to this problem.

Castro told Khrushchev that he wished to send a high-level Cuban military delegation to negotiate an increase in Soviet assistance.[29] He and Raúl Castro had worked up a list of Soviet weaponry needed for Cuba's defense. The centerpiece of the list was eight divisions of surface-to-air missiles—388 missiles in all.[30] The Soviet antiaircraft program had suffered a series of technological failures until the development of the SA-2 or V-750 Dvina missile. From its deployment in 1957, the SA-2 became "the backbone" of Soviet air defense.[31] In May 1960 the investment paid off when a salvo of V-750 missiles brought down Gary Power's U-2 and gave the SA-2 system an international reputation. Castro was only one among many customers for it.

The Kremlin wasted no time in accepting Castro's request to start negotiations and welcomed the Cubans, who arrived in mid-September.[32] The two Soviet ministries authorized to negotiate with the Cubans, the Ministries of Defense and Foreign Economic Trade, were well disposed to meeting Castro's military requirements. In particular, although the SA-2 was in great demand, the Soviet generals believed they could find the large number that Castro wanted.[33] The two ministries had to do some negotiating of their own to be able to present the Presidium with a set of recommendations. Gosplan, the huge bureaucratic octopus that directed the creation and implementation of the USSR's massive five-year economic plans, would have to sign off on the terms of repayment or credit before the Presidium would consider a new military package for the Cubans.

The Soviet negotiating team and Gosplan worked out a package that minimized the cost to the Cubans of Castro's large request. Castro's list was trimmed by 25 percent—the value of the package was now U.S.$148 million, instead of U.S.$193 million. The Soviet negotiators suggested to Khrushchev that 40 percent of the bill be an outright gift to the Cubans and the rest paid through a ten-year loan with interest or a barter arrangement.[34]

Curiously Khrushchev decided to take his time in acting on Castro's request. As it should have, the arms package first went to the Council of Ministers of the Soviet government for approval.[35] But it did not then go to the Presidium for confirmation. Events in Berlin, where the tensions continued to build despite the erection of the wall in August, may have distracted Khrushchev.

From Havana, Alekseev tried to put gentle pressure on the Kremlin to back Castro's requests. While the negotiations were going on, he sent new evidence—which for the first time came from Little Havana, in Florida—that the Americans were planning a second Bay of Pigs. "The Cubans have received from a reliable person in the July 26 Organization in Miami," he reported, "that according to unconfirmed data, a new intervention in Cuba is being prepared that would take place between September and December 1961." For the benefit of the men in the reports office of the KGB who would decide where to send this report, Alekseev wrote that "in recent months, many reports have either closely or directly supported this information."[36] Alekseev's report arrived a few days after the Council of Ministers met to okay the military assistance plan for Cuba, but it did not move Khrushchev to have the Presidium consider the matter. Instead, the Cuban request would languish for months.[37]

While the Cubans waited for an answer from the Kremlin, they initiated a large-scale program to support armed revolution in Latin America. Since coming to power, Fidel Castro had given financial as well as rhetorical support to members of Latin American leftist and communist groups who wished to emulate his model. In those feverish weeks following his *La Coubre* conversion, Castro vowed "to continue making Cuba the example that can convert the Cordillera of the Andes into the Sierra Maestra of the American continent."[38] Cuban assistance began to increase, and by the second half of 1961 the Cuban government had established a formal structure to create a cohort of revolutionaries of every Latin American nation. Indeed, as early as March 1961, PSP leaders were complaining to Moscow that Che Guevara was making wasteful investments in foreign bandit groups, many of which, like the

Julião peasant league in Brazil and the followers of Juan Perón in Argentina, were not Marxist.[39]

In Castro's mind the rebel training program had defensive as well as offensive implications. "The United States will not be able to hurt us," Castro explained, "if all of Latin America is in flames."[40] But he did not justify this expensive commitment solely in terms of the struggle with Kennedy. He believed in a "revolutionary duty" to the hemisphere. Like Simón Bolívar, the Great Liberator, who championed Venezuelan independence in the early nineteenth century, Castro was determined to inspire and facilitate the overthrow of the old order throughout the region.

The rebel training program, which had brought a few hundred handpicked individuals to Havana by early 1962, foreshadowed a potential rift between the emerging Cuban national security institutions and the Soviet advisers. Despite Khrushchev's call to action in January 1961 and Shelepin's suggestion that summer for possible mischief, Moscow was ambivalent about the merits of Castro's regional offensive. Most of the communist parties in the region opposed armed rebellion as a strategy, preferring strikes and other forms of political action, even (as in the case of the Chilean communists) elections. Consequently, the Cuban Ministry of the Interior, which oversaw the training camps, did not involve the intelligence advisers from the Soviet Union. KGB officials picked up bits and pieces of information, but Moscow was not brought into the planning or funding of the training camps.[41]

In the fall there were other signs of future trouble for the Soviet bloc in Cuba. Just as Castro's request for military assistance stalled in Moscow, the Cubans began to complain about the activity of Soviet and East European intelligence services in their country.[42] The KGB was exempt from this pressure, but when the military intelligence service of the Soviet army, the GRU, sent a group to open a station in October 1961, the Cubans balked, feeling that the Soviet military officers were a little too eager to recruit agents. Alekseev, who ran a small KGB station and relied more on liaison with the main Cuban leaders than on spies, was pleased to exploit Cuban dissatisfaction to undermine a potential rival for information and influence.[43]

"I am not against the GRU," said Alekseev sheepishly to Moscow after the GRU complained of his obstructionism to his superiors, "but [Fidel] Castro has decided that security questions were to be handled through the KGB and not the GRU." Consequently, Alekseev argued, "the question of the creation of a GRU station in Cuba has been insufficiently studied." "Cuban military intelligence," he concluded, "is not ready for this kind of development."[44] But to Alekseev's and Raúl Castro's dismay, the Cuban general staff wanted the GRU to come to Havana. During his visit to Moscow to discuss military assistance, General Sergio del Valle had invited Soviet military intelligence to establish a liaison with Cuban military intelligence, the G-2.[45] Bureaucratic squabbles in Cuba were beginning to mirror those in the Soviet Union.

A Command Operation

For the entire time he was at the August conference of the Inter-American Economic and Social Council in Uruguay, President Kennedy's representative Richard Goodwin was badgered by Brazilian and Argentine diplomats. They wanted him to meet Che Guevara, who was observing the proceedings for Castro. Goodwin resisted, but when the Argentines cornered him at a birthday party for a Brazilian delegate on August 16, he relented. Che was expected at the party and had asked to see Goodwin.[46]

Dressed in green fatigues and sporting his trademark overgrown beard, Che arrived at 2 A.M. "Behind the beard," Goodwin noticed, "his features are quite soft, almost feminine, and his manner is intense." Che, Goodwin, and two Latin American diplomats went to a room to talk. Goodwin sensed that Che had been behind the earlier attempts to set up a meeting. Che relaxed after a short while and spoke "calmly, in a straightforward manner, and with the appearance of detachment and objectivity." He had evidently thought out his comments in advance.

Che called for a truce with the United States. The Cubans were serious about building a socialist state, he explained, and this phase of the revolution was "irreversible." Castro would soon become the secretary-general of an expanded Cuban communist party. Che criticized the United States for harboring unreasonable hopes that this process could be changed. He denied that Castro was a moderate, surrounded by fanatics, who could be coaxed to support the West. And he disputed that the revolution could be overthrown from within. "There is," Che said, "diminishing support for such an effort, and it will never be strong again."

In his speech before the conference on August 16, Che had revealed the story of the foiled attempt to kill Fidel Castro on July 26. The Cubans wanted the world to know the drastic measures that the United States was employing against them. With Goodwin, however, Che was not interested in scoring propaganda points. Instead of raising the story of Candela, Che laid out some ideas he had about the bases for "an interim *modus vivendi*" with the United States. He never expected to reach an "understanding" with the U.S. government; but the level of hostility between the two countries could be reduced and trade relations restored. There were five ways, he believed, in which Cuba could contribute to building a better relationship. First, the Cuban government could offer trade in compensation for expropriated American properties. Second, it might consider not signing any formal political alliances with countries of the Soviet bloc, although Cuban sympathies would continue to go in that direction. Third, Castro might organize free elections, but only after the creation of a one-party state, as in Eastern Europe. Laughing at the absurdity of the idea, Che said that a fourth promise the Cubans would be prepared to make was not to attack the U.S. naval base at Guantánamo. Finally, he mumbled something about future discussions covering Cuban activities in the rest of Latin America.

After Che delivered these ideas, he promised that only Fidel Castro would be told the substance of the conversation. Before leaving Goodwin, who also promised not to publicize the meeting in Washington, Che made a point of thanking the Americans for the Bay of Pigs. It was "a great political victory" that allowed the Castro forces "to consolidate," he said.

Goodwin's conversation with Che revived the White House's interest in Cuba. President Kennedy, who received a report shortly after Goodwin's return, was drawn to his special assistant's interpretation that Che's approach was a sign of growing Cuban concern about their deteriorating economy and a new impatience with Moscow. In early September, Kennedy called for a CIA assessment of the prognosis of the Cuban economy. The president also gave tacit approval to Goodwin's efforts to spur the CIA to take advantage of Che's approach. At a meeting of a mid-level task force on Cuba in September, Goodwin suggested to the CIA that it design new ways of conducting economic warfare against Cuba.[47] Goodwin believed that if a dedicated communist like Che felt the need to approach the United States, it might be possible to use economic pressure to splinter the Castro leadership. "[I]f there is room for any spectrum of viewpoint in Cuba," Goodwin argued optimistically, "there may be other Cuban leaders even more anxious for an accommodation."[48]

Over the course of September and October 1961, while various agencies discussed new covert programs to worsen the Cuban economy, President Kennedy explored ways of getting rid of Fidel Castro. He pushed for "a plan against the contingency that Castro would in some way or other be removed from the Cuban scene." The president was evidently considering assassination as an option because the White House took unusual precautions to restrict knowledge of Kennedy's "personal interest" in the effects of an assassination on Cuban politics. Neither the State Department nor the Cuban experts at CIA were to be told.[49]

There is other evidence that the assassination of Fidel Castro lay on President Kennedy's mind in the fall of 1961. "[W]hat would you think if I ordered Castro to be assassinated?" Kennedy asked a startled reporter from the *New York Times* during an "off the record" talk in November. The Polish-born and Spanish-speaking Tad Szulc was no stranger to the problem of U.S.-Cuban relations. He had filed stories for the *Times* from Cuba during the Bay of Pigs and its aftermath. "I agree with you completely," the president said, when Szulc rejected the idea as self-defeating and morally repugnant. Szulc, who made notes right after the meeting, recorded that Kennedy, who professed to have his own moral qualms about ordering an assassination, complained that he was under "terrific pressure" to give the go-ahead. Kennedy did not identify the source of these pressures, but Szulc thought that Kennedy raised the possibility that it was the CIA.[50]

Robert Kennedy, at least, did not want to have to rely on the CIA to solve America's Castro problem. He had not gotten over his anger at the CIA for the

Bay of Pigs fiasco. He blamed Richard Bissell for having used maps dating from 1895 to convince his brother that the marshy land surrounding the Bay of Pigs was suitable for guerrilla warfare.[51] In October he teamed up with Richard Goodwin to interest the president in a "command operation" to deal with Cuba. The attorney general was enthusiastic about the possibility of sparking an internal revolt in Cuba. Lacking faith in the CIA, which he believed underestimated the odds of overturning Castro from within, Robert Kennedy sought to reduce the agency's control over covert action in Cuba. He offered himself to run an interagency Cuba project that would rely on experts from outside the CIA. In early November he and Goodwin presented their ideas to the president.[52]

Robert Kennedy encouraged his brother to turn to a legendary guerrilla leader for help. Brigadier General Edward Lansdale had earned fame for cultivating the Philippine president Ramon Magsaysay and anchoring Manila's successful offensive in the 1950s against the communist guerrillas, the Hukbalahaps. There had been a special chemistry in the relationship between Magsaysay and Lansdale that produced excellent results. In recent years Lansdale had not been able to top this success. His efforts at a vice-regal relationship with the South Vietnamese president Ngo Dinh Diem had produced only indignation in Saigon in 1961. Despite the slight tarnish on his reputation, Lansdale was a master glad-hander and salesman of tough solutions for tough problems. Descriptions of the Kennedy years abound in macho adjectives: "tough," "virile," "ball-crunching," "hard." To the extent that John and Robert Kennedy gained reassurance from a man's man, Lansdale and the solutions he proffered were extremely satisfying.

By the end of November, the attorney general, Goodwin, and Lansdale had conceived the outline of a program to deal with Castro. In shaping their plan, they discussed Cuba with the president and the secretary of defense, Robert McNamara.[53] The president shared his brother's concern that the United States had to act fast if it was to have any chance to remove Castro. The brothers marveled at the speed with which Cuba was transforming itself into a police state. None of the East European countries occupied by the Soviet army after World War II had become satellites as rapidly. Reports of the block surveillance program and other signs of the increasing power of the Cuban Ministry of the Interior had spread pessimism in Washington, especially in the CIA, that significant resistance in Cuba was possible. But the Kennedys disagreed. What was required was energy and confidence. "We *can* take effective action," said Lansdale in the spirit of this new Kennedy initiative, "if proper management is provided."[54]

Ignoring the CIA's doubts about the likelihood of a popular uprising in Cuba, the president anointed Lansdale chief of operations of the Cuba operation on November 30.[55] A week earlier Kennedy had toyed with the notion of lodging the entire project in the Justice Department, with Lansdale serving as Robert's deputy. He continued to think about the best argument for his Cuban team over Thanksgiving, which he spent at the family compound on Cape Cod. Richard Bissell, who was almost out the door at the CIA, recalls being on the telephone to Hyannis Port two or three times over the Thanksgiving weekend "to reassure [President Kennedy] that the agency was trying to do everything possible to meet Lansdale's request [Lansdale's demand for technical assistance]."[56] When Kennedy returned to the Oval Office, he signed a memorandum that authorized new covert operations to "help the people of Cuba overthrow the Communist regime from within Cuba and institute a new government with which the United States can live in peace."[57] Weighing the potential political risks of associating Lansdale with his brother, Kennedy put Lansdale in the Defense Department and gave him supervisory status over all of the departments sharing a responsibility for covert action against Cuba.

The White House's assertion of control over the Cuban operation dismayed the CIA. "Lansdale was a nut," recalls Samuel Halpern, who first met Lansdale in Asia. Halpern was recruited for the Cuba desk in Richard Bissell's Directorate of Plans in October 1961, when the White House began demanding renewed action against Cuba. Among CIA operatives the famed Lansdale had acquired a reputation for being a fantasist, a lucky amateur who had never had to be tested on the strength of his implausible plans.[58] That such a man could come to enjoy the confidence of presidents and kings tells much about the secret world. Many of his failures were swept under the carpet, and his one success represented for the Kennedys a model that could be applied to other Third World countries.

The long-awaited transition at the top of the CIA occurred during this rush to a new Cuba policy. John Kennedy had first considered his brother to replace Allen Dulles, whose retirement was imminent after the Bay of Pigs disaster. But Robert discouraged this. "I thought it was a bad idea to be head of CIA, because I was a Democrat and his brother." Instead, President Kennedy chose John McCone, who may have been suggested by Senator Henry "Scoop" Jackson, the formidable Democratic warhawk from Washington.[59] McCone was a lifelong Republican who had served as chairman of the Atomic Energy Commission in the Eisenhower period.

Robert Kennedy would later become disenchanted with McCone. "[I] think he liked the President very much," Kennedy recalled for Arthur Schlesinger. "But he liked one person more — and that was John McCone."[60] Nothing else was as certain to alienate Robert Kennedy as showing disloyalty to President Kennedy. Those difficult days, however, still lay ahead. In the early months together, McCone and Robert Kennedy successfully built a personal relationship outside of the office. McCone was a regular visitor to Kennedy's home, Hickory Hill. A personal tragedy early in McCone's term as director of the CIA fostered a close friendship with Robert Kennedy's wife, Ethel. "He liked Ethel very much because, when his wife died, Ethel went over and stayed with him," Robert recalled.[61]

Despite his decision not to accept the directorship of the CIA, Robert Kennedy remained his brother's chief watchdog over U.S. intelligence. In his mind, despite the concern about Berlin, the Congo, and Laos, Cuba would be the arena where the Kennedys would test the CIA's mettle. In June, before McCone had come in, Bobby had complained, "The Cuba matter is being allowed to slide."[62] Cuba would soon become a bone of contention between the Kennedys—Robert, in particular—and the new CIA director. It was where, in their eyes, McCone showed less than complete loyalty.

Disappointment in Havana

Far removed from the Washington stage, in the late fall of 1961 the Cubans were preoccupied with the mysteries of the bureaucracy of the other superpower. Despite the September 20 military assistance agreement, as of December 1961, no new Soviet weapons had reached Cuban shores. Tired of the diplomatic two-step from the Soviet Ministries of Defense and Foreign Trade, Fidel Castro turned to Alekseev for help. On December 17 Castro and the Cuban president, Dorticós, expressed to him their concern over "the expected U.S. aggression against Cuba." He and Dorticós detected an indifference in Moscow's attitude toward their security. Where were the SA-2s and the tanks that had been promised? the Cubans wondered.

Alekseev was sympathetic to the Cubans' impatience. In the roundabout way he always used to prod his superiors, he warned Moscow that the Cubans were very unhappy. He stressed that Castro and Dorticós had said that they had no intention of appealing to Moscow "along official lines," because it was feared that "the results by this approach" could "turn out to be erroneous."[63]

Alekseev knew nothing about Che Guevara's August approach to Richard Goodwin. Although the Kremlin had encouraged the Cubans to normalize their relations with Washington, there is no evidence that Alekseev worked at all to reinforce that message. It was clear to him in December 1961 that the Cubans were frustrated because the only patron they wanted to have, Moscow, was not supplying enough of what they needed.

The Castro brothers sensed correctly that the Kennedy administration was not prepared to leave them be. However, Soviet and Cuban intelligence picked up neither the manic plotting in Washington nor any of the doubts held by some of the key Cuba experts in Washington about the likelihood of ever removing Castro. Nevertheless, in the absence of compelling evidence to the contrary, the Cuban revolutionaries assumed that the president of the United States had a well-oiled, resourceful secret apparatus at his disposal.

Mongoose

"Lansdale wanted a cryptonym," Halpern recalls in telling the story of how Mongoose got its name. The CIA assigned a two-letter designation (a digraph) to every country in the world. The code name for any operation in that country would begin with the digraph. Halpern called Charlotte Gilbert, the woman at the agency whose job it was to sort out codenames. " 'Charlotte, we need a crypt, and I want one that is at least on the other side of the world from Cuba,' said Halpern. 'I want to confuse people for about thirty seconds. No more.' "

Gilbert suggested Thailand, a country closer in spirit to the Asianist Halpern than Cuba. Thailand was "MO" in the CIA's registry. Halpern was expected to chose the code name: "She gave me half a dozen names beginning with MO, and I chose Mongoose." Later Halpern was asked whether his choice had been inspired by Rikki Tikki Tavi, the mongoose in one of Rudyard Kipling's most beloved short stories. Kipling is a favorite among spies. Was Castro not the snake in the grass, the deadly cobra whose venom— revolution—could infect all those in his clutches? Alas, Halpern had never read about Rikki Tikki Tavi. Why did he chose it? "No reason," Halpern says these days with a chuckle.[64]

The first weeks of Operation Mongoose were especially difficult. Lansdale expected the CIA to produce a series of papers on covert action that could be the basis for discussion among the key policymakers. Since the Bay of Pigs the interagency body that reviewed covert-action plans for the president, called unimaginatively the Special Group, had two new members. Now called Special Group (Augmented) to reflect the participation of Attorney General Robert Kennedy and Secretary of the Treasury C. Douglas Dillon, this committee would oversee Lansdale and the CIA's plans. Halpern says that the CIA never used the name Mongoose to discuss the Cuban project, but this designation would become well known among members of the Special Group.

Halpern and Ghosn Zogby, who made up what would be known as Task Force W (the Cuban branch in the Western Hemisphere Division of the CIA's Directorate of Plans), became increasingly apprehensive as they acquainted themselves with the CIA's resources on Cuba.* They went to Bissell with their concerns. "Dick," Halpern said to Bissell, "I have already been on this job a few days, and I know that we have absolutely no assets on the island."[65] Halpern was only exaggerating a little: of the CIA's twenty-eight agents in Cuba, only twelve were in communication with the agency, and those contacts were irregular.[66] And Halpern knew nothing about the joint Soviet/Cuban Candela scheme, so if one of the dozen active agents was "Tony," then some of what little Washington was getting was actually disinformation. "After the Bay of Pigs they [the Cubans] cleaned house," Halpern discovered. "And they did a fine job."[67] To destroy the Castro regime from within, the CIA

---

* Task Force W was one secret organization whose code name carried inner meaning. The "W" signified William Walker, the nineteenth century American adventurer who declared himself the ruler of Nicaragua.

would have to rebuild its intelligence network in Cuba from top to bottom.

Meanwhile, Lansdale was trying to sell the Kennedys and the Special Group (Augmented) on the idea that some kind of action could occur in Cuba before November 1962. The CIA, which did not believe that this target date bore any relation to the capabilities of the U.S. intelligence community at the end of 1961, tried to warn the Kennedys that Lansdale was overselling covert action to them.[68] Halpern, who drafted many of the papers that went to the Special Group, believes that the politically astute Lansdale neutralized these warnings by telling Kennedy what he wanted to hear. Knowing how important the forthcoming congressional elections were to the Kennedys, and how useful a political bogeyman Castro was, Lansdale expected a positive reception for a program set to achieve its primary goal of removing Castro just before the second Tuesday in November. Lansdale, Halpern recalls with reluctant respect, "knew who he was working for."[69]

The White House would make sure the Mongoose team had whatever money it needed. "We are in a combat situation with Cuba," Robert Kennedy told a group from the CIA and the Pentagon in January 1962.[70] A second failure in Cuba was not an option.

Trouble in the Tropics

OPLAN 314

Virginia can be very cold in February. For an old Seadog like Admiral Robert L. Dennison, the commander in chief of U.S. forces in the Atlantic (CINCLANT), there was something refreshing about the nearly frozen, salty air that slaps the back of one's blue tunic. It was February 7, 1962, and a top-secret conference had been planned to discuss the latest phase in the Kennedy administration's struggle with Fidel Castro.

On instructions from the Pentagon, the air, naval, and army components of CINCLANT headquarters had assembled to undertake a rapid revision of the two basic contingency plans for an invasion of Cuba. The White House had instructed the Joint Chiefs of Staff (JCS) to reduce the lead time necessary to initiate the two plans, called Operational Plan (OPLAN) 314-61 and OPLAN 316-61, to four and two days, respectively. Kennedy and his advisers wanted to have a rapid and deadly strike against the Castro regime as a practicable option, in the event that Castro or the counterrevolutionaries provided an acceptable pretext.[1]

The invasion would not be easy. U.S. intelligence estimated that the Cubans had 275,000 men under arms in the regular military, the reserves, and the militia. Besides providing light and heavy weapons to these men, the Soviet Union had, since the Bay of Pigs, helped the Cubans build an air force. U-2 runs across the island, which the president had authorized on a bimonthly basis in January, had already detected forty-five Soviet-made jets.[2]

To meet this challenge CINCLANT was thinking in terms of an attack that involved all of the branches of the armed services. The operation would begin with an assault by two Army Airborne divisions regularly stationed at Fort Campbell, Kentucky, and Fort Bragg, North Carolina, but which would be prepositioned in Florida. Two Marine Corps divisions would follow the paratroopers with an amphibious landing supported by the U.S. Navy. Meanwhile, naval air assets and air force tactical units would provide air cover. After the initial assault, armored support from Fort Benning, Georgia, and Fort Hood, Texas, and infantry units from Georgia, Oklahoma, and Kentucky would arrive by sea and air. Asked to estimate the financial cost, CINCLANT concluded that it would take $6.5 million to mount OPLAN 314, with an additional cost of $153,000 per day.[3] There was no estimate of the cost in terms of lives.

CINCLANT's study formed part of the U.S. government's general review of its policy toward Cuba. A month earlier Robert Kennedy had told the new director of the CIA, John McCone, that Cuba was "the top priority in the U.S. Government—all else is secondary—no time, no money, effort or manpower is to be spared."[4] Since November 1961, when President Kennedy appointed Brigadier General Lansdale to direct a coordinated program against Cuba, the word had gone out at the highest levels that the president had decided "to utilize all resources to unseat Castro."[5] On January 18, after canvassing all relevant agencies in the government, Lansdale reported a plan for "The Cuba Project," or Mongoose, to the president.[6] Evidently pleased with the progress that was being made, Kennedy said to his brother privately, "The final chapter on Cuba [has] not been written."[7] The Kennedy brothers never hid their anger at the national security community, especially the CIA, following the humiliation in April 1961. There were to be no more Bays of Pigs.

Two weeks after CINCLANT discussed ways of facilitating direct U.S. military intervention in Cuba, the JCS directed CINCLANT to formalize these plans, so that they could serve as the bases for new blueprints for possible action in Cuba. The JCS message went to CINCLANT headquarters at Norfolk, Virginia, at thirteen minutes after midnight, on February 22.

It was breakfast time in Moscow, when Norfolk learned that the JCS had made up its mind on how to proceed: "It is desired that . . . Plans Supporting CINCLANT OPLAN 314-61 Be Completed As Expeditiously As Possible."[8]

The Kremlin did not receive a copy of this message. However, Foreign Minister Andrei Gromyko and Defense Minister Rodion Malinovsky had a general idea about what CINCLANT and the JCS were up to. On February 21, one day before CINCLANT received the go-ahead from the JCS, Vladimir Semichastny, the new chairman of the KGB, sent them a special message warning that "military specialists of the USA had revised an operational plan against Cuba, which, according to this information, is supported by President Kennedy."[9]

The KGB report did not mention OPLAN 314 specifically but stated that the activity of the land forces would "be supported by military air assets based in Florida and Texas." The Soviet intelligence source also stated implausibly that Kennedy had predelegated authority to Robert McNamara to launch this attack at will. The KGB reported to the Soviet government, however, that it did not know when McNamara might give the go-ahead: "Concrete data about the start of the operation is as yet unavailable; though there is talk of its being in the next few months."

How did the Soviets know? Was this vague intelligence the product of high-level penetration, or was it merely a coincidence that, on February 22, Soviet and American military leaders were both discussing the likelihood that John F. Kennedy would soon be commanding a second assault on the beaches of Cuba?

The First Son-in-Law

The intelligence regarding U.S. military preparations did not come as any sur-prise to the Kremlin. Nikita Khrushchev and the Presidium were fully expect-ing firm evidence that the Kennedy administration was planning a very serious intervention to overthrow Castro. On December 1, 1961, Castro had publicly declared himself a communist and had vowed to lead Cuba onto the path of socialist construction. Khrushchev and his advisers thought Castro had made a costly error. "We had trouble understanding the timing of this state-ment," Khrushchev later recalled. It had, he argued, "the immediate effect of widening the gap between himself and the people who were against Social-ism, and it narrowed the circle of those he could count on for support against the invasion. . . . [F]rom a tactical standpoint, it didn't make much sense."[10] While on the one hand Castro weakened his hold on Cuba, his declaration made an invasion from the north more likely. As Khrushchev would tell Castro privately in 1963, "[N]o one thought that when you won and opted for the course of building socialism, America would tolerate you. . . ."[11]

The Kremlin therefore was looking for signs in the wake of Castro's public announcement that Kennedy would seek to "strangle," in Khrushchev's color-ful image, the communist child in its cradle. Between Castro's declaration and the beginning of 1962, thirteen governments in Latin America had bro-ken relations with Cuba under U.S. pressure. These efforts to isolate Cuba seemed to confirm Khrushchev's concern. Moscow had no idea that these ini-tiatives constituted the least-secret dimension of the Mongoose campaign; yet the Soviet leadership assumed that something like it was probable.

On February 8, 1962, two weeks before the KGB passed on its sensitive re-port on U.S. military preparations, the Presidium had turned to the question of Cuban defense. It was the first time since September 1961 that the Soviet Union's most powerful men had decided to do something to help Castro de-fend himself. What prompted them was some extremely worrisome intelli-gence from a source even better than any of those reporting to the KGB. Without ever mentioning Mongoose, this source painted the picture of an im-patient American president, who had grown to see little Cuba as a threat to the security of his regime, and whose policy toward Fidel Castro had acquired the characteristics of a personal vendetta. The source for this information was none other than John F. Kennedy himself.

In the first week of February, Khrushchev's son-in-law Aleksei Adzhubei returned home from a lengthy visit to the New World. Adzhubei's crowning achievement was a freewheeling discussion with the American president in Washington. Adzhubei had already reported to the Kremlin on his meeting in a cable sent January 31; but as he explained to his father-in-law upon returning, Kennedy had made an extremely provocative statement about Castro's Cuba, which only Khrushchev himself should see.

Using the Bolshakov-RFK channel, President Kennedy had invited Adzhubei to meet with him. In the course of a conversation that ranged across all of the main points of the U.S.-Soviet confrontation—Laos, Berlin, disarmament—the president raised the issue of Cuba.

"The Cuban question," Kennedy said, "will be decided on Cuba, and not by the involvement of outsiders."

"And what about Punta del Este?" Adzhubei asked, referring to the U.S.-led move to expel Cuba from the Organization of American States.

"The people of the United States were very concerned that Cuba became our enemy. You are worried about having hostile neighbors, and so are we. But, to repeat, the Cuban affair will be decided on Cuba."

"But there remains a threat to Cuba," Adzhubei countered.

"I already told N. S. Khrushchev that I consider the invasion which took place—a mistake; however we cannot fail to follow the development of events on Cuba. You are also not indifferent to events in Finland, for example."

Adzhubei noted that the discussion was "difficult for the president." In a moment of indiscretion, Kennedy revealed that he expected Castro to be an electoral issue in 1964: "If I run for reelection and the Cuban question remains as it is—then Cuba will be the main problem of the campaign, [and] we will have to do something."[12]

If this had been all that Kennedy said, the Kremlin might not have reassessed its support for Cuba in February 1962. However, Kennedy would not just draw a comparison between Soviet anxieties about Finnish developments and his own about Cuba; he took the opportunity of Khrushchev's son-in-law's visit to use even more graphic terms to warn the Soviets to leave him alone in the Caribbean.

In a text that lies in the Politburo archives, which until now was top-secret, Adzhubei filled out the picture of his meeting with John Kennedy. During their exchange on Cuba, Kennedy had slyly compared his problem in Cuba with what Khrushchev had faced in Hungary before he dealt with it forcibly in 1956. Kennedy wanted there to be no doubt in the mind of Adzhubei's father-in-law that the U.S. president intended to defend his sphere of influence in the Caribbean as the Soviets had defended theirs in Eastern Europe with tanks.

This was not lost on Khrushchev. The archives reveal exactly what Adzhubei had concealed from the Soviet ambassador to the United States and was now imparting directly to Khrushchev:

Adzhubei: "You have a right to be interested in events in Cuba. But when we read that the U.S. is gearing up to invade Cuba, we think to ourselves that this is not your right."[13]

Kennedy: "We have no intention of intervening in Cuba."

Adzhubei: "But what about the attacks from Guatemala and some other countries? Have you changed your opinion that the April 1961 invasion was an American mistake?"

According to Adzhubei, this last comment provoked Kennedy to bang his fist on the table.

Kennedy: "At the time I called Allen Dulles into my office and dressed him down. I told him: you should learn from the Russians. When they had difficulties in Hungary, they liquidated the conflict in three days. When they did not like things in Finland, the president of that country goes to visit the Soviet premier in Siberia and all is worked out. But you, Dulles, have never been capable of doing that."

Did President Kennedy say these things, which suggest a deafness to the nuances of power? For Khrushchev, the crackdown in Hungary in 1956 represented an appropriate use of force to protect one's security. He never regretted it; nor would he ever swear off using the military to destroy opposition to his rule. Kennedy's use of this analogy implied that Fidel Castro represented a similar threat to the Kennedy regime and that the White House intended to use all necessary means to destroy him. Did Kennedy assume, by thus equating the Monroe Doctrine to the Soviet sphere of influence in Eastern Europe, that the Soviets would back off? It is also possible that Adzhubei exaggerated, misinterpreted, or misrepresented Kennedy's words. Whatever the case, the Soviet leadership came to believe not only that Kennedy spoke these words but that he was seriously considering a second, even bigger invasion of Cuba, this time involving U.S. troops.

In light of Adzhubei's report, Khrushchev called for an immediate reassessment of Cuban security. The military assistance program for Cuba had been languishing since September 1961. In December a few tanks had arrived at the Cuban port of Mariel; but the Presidium seemed in no hurry to confirm the entire costly program, which included divisions of the much vaunted SA-2 and Sopka conventional missile systems. The news carried by Adzhubei changed all of that. On February 8—four and a half months after the Council of Ministers had forwarded the plan for adoption—the Presidium finally approved the U.S.$133 million military assistance package for Cuba. Kennedy's remarks had moved Cuban security up on the list of Moscow's priorities.

Strategic Threats

Although Khrushchev took Kennedy's threat to Cuba very seriously, he was uncertain in which direction U.S.-Soviet relations would go in 1962. The Kremlin had reasons to assume that in the aftermath of the crisis in Berlin, President Kennedy wanted real progress at the strategic level. In January, John Kennedy used the Bolshakov channel to negotiate reciprocal television appearances and to indicate that his brother wanted to visit the Soviet Union as part of a global junket planned for that spring. The White House had hinted at Kennedy's interest in a second summit, this time in Moscow, and Robert's visit might well have laid the groundwork for it.[14]

In January, Khrushchev raised these probes at a formal meeting of the Presidium. The leadership followed his inclinations to welcome both Robert Kennedy and the White House press secretary, Pierre Salinger. Khrushchev also approved the exchange of television messages.[15]

Adzhubei's report a few weeks later disturbed Khrushchev because of his concern for Castro, but as in 1961, at the time of the Bay of Pigs, the Soviet leader was loath to let Cuba disrupt any possible improvement in the all-important relationship with Washington. So it took something else—reports from Washington of even more dramatic information—to cause him to launch a review of U.S.-Soviet relations at the very moment that he had his Cuba hands checking on Castro's ability to survive a U.S. strike.

On March 2, 1962, Bolshakov and Robert Kennedy met outside the Justice Department, probably at a restaurant selected by Frank Holeman, to discuss the possibility of a second Khrushchev-Kennedy summit.[16] The *Washington Post* that morning had reported that President Kennedy was about to make a speech on nuclear testing. Robert Kennedy began the meeting by assuring Bolshakov that his brother was not happy about resuming these tests. "The president sincerely wants to avoid conducting these nuclear tests and wants an agreement on this issue with Premier Khrushchev, who we trust wants the same."[17]

As the attorney general had done in May 1961, he suggested to Bolshakov a way that the two countries could reach an agreement and thus avert the resumption of American nuclear testing. Since the two superpowers could not agree on a verification regime—the number of on-site inspections, the nationality of the inspectors, etc.—why not start with an agreement that was easily verifiable? Nuclear tests in the open air could not be concealed. With this in mind, Kennedy had told his negotiation team to start talking about an atmospheric test ban, and if the representatives of the two countries could not hammer something out, then he wanted to see Khrushchev again.[18]

The U.S. decision to resume nuclear tests hit the Kremlin in the solar plexus. It reinforced Soviet suspicions that Washington was flexing a muscle that it intended to use in the Caribbean. Furthermore, Khrushchev was not amused by the Kennedys' gimmickry. These secret deals, of which the Kennedys were fond, never confronted the real divisions separating the powers. Khrushchev wanted to catch up to U.S. nuclear power. Then, if there was to be any ban on nuclear testing, it would have to be a comprehensive test ban, which would prevent the Americans from proceeding with underground tests. The Soviets had just performed their first underground test, but these kinds of tests were expensive, and the United States was ahead in the technology required to mount them. Why did this administration believe that he would accept such humiliating deals? To make matters worse, the offer was coming only hours before Kennedy publicly announced his intention to resume testing on April 15 unless a test ban was signed in the interim. Did the Americans think he could accept negotiations that were premised on a threat? As far as Khrushchev was concerned, this was atomic diplomacy—as brazen an attempt to brandish nuclear weapons as Truman's use of atomic bombs to end the war with Japan.

Washington should have been able to anticipate Khrushchev's sensitivity to such threats. But something else happened in the Kremlin in the first two weeks of March that John Kennedy could not have expected. Almost at the very instant that Robert Kennedy was pleading with Kremlin representatives for an arms control agreement, Soviet military intelligence provided Khrushchev with what it considered reliable evidence that the Pentagon had made serious preparations for a nuclear attack on the Soviet Union. According to two reports, received March 9 and March 11, from a well-placed source in the U.S. national security bureaucracy, the huge Soviet nuclear tests in the fall of 1961 had deterred the United States from proceeding with plans to launch a preemptive nuclear strike on the Soviet Union. This source, who was considered reliable and whose reports were passed on to the Soviet leadership, reported that between June 6 and June 12, 1961, the United States had decided to launch a nuclear strike on the USSR in September 1961. It was due only to the Soviet announcement of the new series of atomic tests that the United States reversed its decision. According to the GRU's informant, the tests convinced the United States that the Soviet nuclear arsenal was more powerful than previously assumed.[19]

The GRU's archives do not reveal to whom this report went. However, if it was passed forward, as seems likely, the two GRU reports would have strengthened Khrushchev's tendency to believe that nuclear weapons were the only language that the United States understood. In late June 1960 a similar KGB report on the Pentagon's plans for a nuclear first strike had encouraged Khrushchev to give a public nuclear guarantee to Havana. Now, two years later, Kennedy's maladroit nuclear diplomacy and two frightening reports from the GRU deepened Khrushchev's concerns about Moscow's strategic vulnerability.

Khrushchev showed his displeasure by immediately calling off the exchange of television messages between the two leaders. Gromyko instructed the Soviet embassy in Washington to have Bolshakov tell Kennedy's press secretary, Pierre Salinger, who had been organizing the television appearances from the U.S. end, "Recent events, particularly John F. Kennedy's decision to resume nuclear tests, make it impossible to exchange television messages."[20]

The Soviet leader also decided to toughen his terms for a test ban to make sure Kennedy got the message. It was to be a comprehensive agreement or nothing. In the past he had been prepared to accept two or three inspections as a "political concession" to the ever suspicious West. But now the Soviet position would be no inspections, period. Khrushchev had become increasingly unnerved by the prospect of U.S. experts collecting accurate data on the Soviet nuclear arsenal. Three inspections might convince the Americans that they enjoyed enough of a strategic advantage to warrant taking a chance on a preemptive strike. Khrushchev later recalled his fears: "we couldn't allow the U.S. and its allies to send their inspectors criss-crossing around the Soviet Union. They would have discovered that we were in a relatively weak position, and that realization would have encouraged them to attack us."[21]

Khrushchev had staked his prestige in the Presidium on settling U.S.-Soviet relations through disarmament agreements. More than anything else, Kennedy's decision to resume testing signified the failure of this approach. Khrushchev had no choice but to consider the possibility that he was no longer dealing with an American president who controlled the right wing of his own government. To cover himself, Khrushchev had his son-in-law Adzhubei circulate an expanded version of the notes of his January 30, 1962, meeting with Kennedy, which included the explosive bits that Adzhubei first reported orally to the Kremlin.* Khrushchev sensed that some kind of challenge, possibly in Cuba, was just around the corner.

Mongoose

Despite his keen interest in foreign affairs, in the spring of 1962, John Kennedy had no idea of the dangerous shifts taking place in the Kremlin's understanding of the balance of power. He would have been surprised to learn that Khrushchev was as pessimistic about the Soviet Union's international position as he was about that of the United States. In connection with the Cuba project, Kennedy was constantly being presented with the option of using

---

* This version included not only Kennedy's comments comparing Cuba to Hungary but also his insistence on retaining Allied soldiers in Berlin and his comment that he expected West Germany to acquire nuclear weapons if pressure was not kept on Chancellor Adenauer. In Moscow's eyes all of these were worrisome signs.

U.S. military power against Havana. Each time he considered this option, he worried about the consequences for America's leadership of the free world. He assumed that the United States would prevail in a military contest with the Cubans, though he doubted it would be a rout.[22] But how would his allies in Latin America and Europe react? And how would the Soviets react to his use of U.S. troops? Would Khrushchev seek retribution at a point of American vulnerability, such as Berlin?

The CIA's stubborn refusal to accept Edward Lansdale's roseate predictions of an uprising in Cuba in October 1962 helped keep alive the option of using military force.[23] Chastened by criticisms that Allen Dulles and Richard Bissell had failed to explain the necessity for U.S. military intervention in April 1961, the new leadership at the CIA bluntly informed policymakers in early 1962 that General Lansdale's plan could not work without the eventual involvement of the marines. "Due to the present severity of Communist and police controls inside Cuba," the CIA cautioned in January, "it is not likely that we can make the resistance groups self-sustaining." Therefore, the Kennedys were told, "External support will be essential to their survival." The United States must "be ready," the CIA specified, "with sufficient military assistance to guarantee the success of any uprising."[24]

Kennedy wanted the Cuban problem to be solved without a U.S. invasion. Under the watchful eye of the attorney general, in February the Special Group (Augmented) had ordered an intensification of sabotage and intelligence activity in Cuba. However, because the CIA was not alone in arguing that U.S. military intervention was required to defeat communism in Cuba, Kennedy directed the U.S. military to bring its contingency plans for action in Cuba up to date.[25] In the event that Castro attacked Guantánamo or that an uprising needing U.S. assistance did occur, the president believed, he might be prepared to send in the marines. However, this would be a tough call to make. To lower the risks of sustained international condemnation if he did opt for an invasion later in 1962, Kennedy authorized a revision in the contingency plans to reduce the delay between a presidential order to proceed and the actual start of operations.

Throughout the spring Kennedy played Hamlet on the issue of using military force in Cuba. On the one hand he continued to encourage a study of the option; on the other he refused to say whether and under what circumstances he would ever give the order to proceed. On March 16 at a meeting with John McCone, McGeorge Bundy, military and State Department representatives, and his brother, Kennedy "expressed skepticism that in so far as can now be foreseen, circumstances [would] arise that would justify and make desirable the use of American forces for overt military action."[26]

The president's ambivalence over the correct relationship of the U.S. military to Mongoose weakened the effectiveness of his covert-action program in Cuba. The White House prevented the use of U.S. Air Force assets by the CIA and strictly prohibited CIA case officers from even hinting to Cuban agents that the Pentagon might assist their uprising.[27] In April 1962 the CIA complained that despite the White House's decision to "mount a concentrated operational program" there was no chance that even by August the United States would have orchestrated any sort of central resistance in Cuba. Richard Helms, who had replaced Richard Bissell as the CIA's deputy for operations, advised John McCone, "[I]t will not be possible for us to field, activate, and keep alive large resistance groups." The CIA knew of "no viable long term leadership" in Cuba or within the émigré community in the United States and doubted that one would develop soon. Helms wanted McCone to understand that because of the mismatch between the White House's impatience for the removal of Castro and the political risks that the Kennedys were willing to run, Mongoose would consist of more planning than action for some time to come. Only by August 1962, the CIA experts wrote, "should [we] be able . . . to *begin* to prepare these assets for an organized revolt of substantial proportions."[28]

With Kennedy unwilling to commit himself in advance to support the use of force, in March the U.S. government accepted a two-step covert program for eliminating Castro. In the short term the CIA would concentrate on building up intelligence contacts and organizing sabotage. In July there would be a reexamination of the program to see whether a serious uprising was possible. At that point, in the middle of the summer, President Kennedy would have to decide whether to authorize the CIA to use the Cuban underground to initiate a revolt.[29]

In the course of these springtime discussions, Robert Kennedy prompted the Special Group to think about the Soviet Union as a factor in determining the outcome of Mongoose. "What should we do if the Soviets build a military base there?" he asked.[30] Few people in the group took the question seriously; the possibility was considered "too remote to waste time on."[31] Khrushchev just didn't want to invest that much in Castro. CIA analysts doubted that the Soviet military would even come to Cuba's assistance if the island was attacked by the United States. "Almost certainly," they argued, "the USSR would not resort to general war for the sake of the Castro regime."[32] John Kennedy's Cuba team believed that Mongoose could be designed without regard to Moscow.

Moscow's Cuba Policy Review

In the spring of 1962 Moscow was engaged in its own review of Cuban policy prompted by the fragmentary indications of a hardening of Kennedy's position toward Castro. Rodion Malinovsky and the Soviet Defense Ministry compiled a list of the more than $250 million worth of weapons systems sent to Cuba since the Soviet Union assumed the lion's share of Eastern bloc military assistance to the island in 1960. After completing this task, Malinovsky and Army Chief of Staff Matvei Zakharov prepared a draft resolution for the Presidium on March 8 that would accelerate the delivery of the already promised five

rocket divisions and three technical divisions of the SA-2 system, with 196 surface-to-air missiles.[33]

Like the Defense Ministry, the leadership of the KGB in early March called
for a full-scale review of all intelligence on U.S. actions toward Cuba. Such
reviews were performed by the Analytical Department (Department 16) of the
First Chief Directorate (the foreign intelligence component) of the KGB. In
the 1970s the Analytical Department would be taken over by a group of young
activists who sought to make it an adjunct of Soviet policy-making, but in the
1960s the department was considered a burial ground for operational careers.
The KGB filled the department with agents who had made mistakes in the
field or had otherwise been burned. Although the chief of the department was
usually a career officer, it was sometimes headed by a party hack, and there
was a constant turnover in the staff.[34]

From February 1962 on, the Cuban and the Soviet intelligence had observed a sharp increase in covert and clandestine activity by Cuban exiles.
This is what Kennedy seemed to have meant by his statement to Adzhubei
that "we will have to do something" about Cuba. Most of the guerrilla operations were centered in the provinces of Matanzas and Camagüay. The KGB
concluded that one of the goals of this activity was to "strengthen counterrevolutionary groups to incite an uprising throughout the entire country in the
event of a new intervention."[35]

In late October 1961 Soviet intelligence had concluded that there were
about one hundred counterrevolutionary groups in Cuba, many of whom
were recruited from the intelligentsia, property owners, government officials,
and the local police. Alekseev reported from Havana that the agricultural reform institute, INRA, which had been designed to lead a socialist revolution
in Cuba, and the police were the two groups in Cuban society most affected
by counterrevolutionary activity.[36]

The product of the KGB's March 1962 reassessment of the U.S. threat to
Cuba exemplified the Soviet approach to analysis. The estimate included all
of the secret reports received on the question, yet even though some of the reports suggested the likelihood of an invasion very soon, the paper concluded
that an invasion in the short term was unlikely and that the U.S. government
would attempt to overthrow Castro from within. Nowhere did the analysts acknowledge the contradiction between the data they presented and the conclusions they reached. The KGB was hedging its bets about a U.S. invasion. If
Kennedy did launch an attack, it could point to the paragraphs based on raw
agent data. And if a U.S. invasion did not occur, the concluding paragraph
would show the service's wisdom.

KGB headquarters tended to downplay the concerns of Alekseev and the
Cubans, concluding that the counterrevolution, even with outside assistance,
was likely to fail. The center sent to Alekseev information collected from outside of Cuba that tended to underscore the weakness of the counterrevolution. Somewhere in Europe, probably France, the KGB had acquired a review
of the status of Latin American countries that foresaw a rosy future for Cuba.

In late March the KGB instructed Alekseev to read it and to pass it on to Castro.[37]

Part of the reason for the KGB's skepticism was that its man in Washington doubted that an American military intervention was on the horizon. Aleksandr Feklisov believed that Kennedy would have to be provoked to use military force in Cuba. Before being sent out to the United States to run the KGB's principal station there, Feklisov had overseen the intelligence assessment in 1960 that Eisenhower was unlikely to invade without a Cuban assault on Guantánamo or the creation of a missile base on the island. Two years later he still believed this, despite the change in administration and the experience of the Bay of Pigs. In the middle of March 1962, he reported that Kennedy was not apt to approve an invasion, because a military intervention would undermine the Alliance for Progress, which was Kennedy's preferred weapon for use against the regional appeal of Fidel Castro. Besides being a provocation, an uprising might tempt Kennedy to invade. Kennedy knew about the serious food shortages in Cuba and had called for measures that would further aggravate the situation. But the tone of Feklisov's report suggested that the American president was not overly concerned about Cuba.[38]

When the KGB instructed Feklisov to exploit his sources to determine the current threat to Castro, the KGB station chief turned to the "N ring" that he ran in Washington, D.C., so named because the agents were referred to as "N.1," "N.2," etc. The Russian government continues to protect the names of the members of this ring. There appear to have been at least three people in the ring. Without exception all reported to Feklisov in March 1962 that a U.S. military intervention in Cuba was unlikely.[39]

Feklisov also sought confirmation from a highly regarded source code-named YAR. YAR, whose location was not indicated on the summary prepared for the leadership of the KGB, reported that Kennedy would not risk a military operation before the November congressional elections, because of his concern that it would be used against him by the Republicans. YAR suspected that if the intervention came, it would be launched from Central America.[40]

The Soviet intelligence community's failure to provide compelling evidence that a U.S. attack on Cuba was imminent allowed the policy process to grind to a crawl in Moscow. The Defense Ministry's recommendation to accelerate delivery of the SA-2s was shelved pending a decision by the Presidium. Besides the Kremlin's February 8 decision to approve the September 1961 package of assistance, there was to be no effort either to increase military assistance or even to accelerate delivery of the already promised supplies. Events would have to take a different course for Moscow to pick up the pace.

Castro's Domestic Challenges

For reasons apart from Operation Mongoose, Fidel Castro was in trouble in early 1962. Months before the CIA was able to set anything in motion, the

Castro regime began showing signs of distress. Castro's statement in December 1961 that he was a communist who intended to lead Cuba through a socialist revolution had caused deep divisions in Cuban society. In the estimation of Soviet intelligence, Castro himself was largely to blame for encouraging the Cubans to try to do too much too soon:

> Castro's speech on the socialist character of the Cuban revolution, and the subsequent creation of a united Marxist-Leninist party, proceeded without sufficient preparation of the laboring classes, thus intensifying the class struggle in Cuba and alienating from the revolution a significant portion of the petty bourgeoisie, the intelligentsia, the backward portions of the working class, and the peasantry, and also a series of Castro's revolutionary fighters, who were not ideologically ready for these changes.[41]

A sense of insecurity animated the Bolshevik mind. Despite the acquisition of the instruments of state power, Lenin, Stalin, and their successor Khrushchev conceived of the Communist Party of the Soviet Union as vulnerable. The working class was neither united enough nor pervasive enough to undermine all potential sources of anticommunism, even in a mature socialist state. This self-awareness shaped Moscow's dealings with foreign communists. It was Soviet tradition to encourage foreign communists to lead coalitions of parties until all powerful anticommunists in a society had been neutralized. For instance, in 1948 Stalin had discouraged Mao Zedong from being too hasty in creating a single-party state in China once he defeated Jiang Jieshi's Guomindang.[42] One of Stalin's reasons was that a China that was too openly associated with Moscow would provoke a harsh American reaction. A little more than a decade later, Khrushchev had similar concerns about Fidel Castro.

Moscow was not alone in thinking that Cuba was not ready for a full-throated adoption of communism. Not all of the members of Castro's revolutionary brotherhood—the veterans of the heroic struggle with Fulgencio Batista—were communist, and these men resented Castro's adoption of an ideology that was alien and, to varying degrees, repugnant to them.

The mass of Cubans were not moved either way by the details of communist ideology. The changes that cut into public support of Castro in early 1962 could all be understood by a look at the family dinner table. In January and February there was not enough food in Cuba to meet basic needs. Agricultural production was down, and there were almost no emergency reserves of food in warehouses around the country. Reports sent to the Kremlin emphasized that the Cuban people were suffering because Castro had not gone far enough in socializing agriculture. "Despite an obligation of several years running for peasants to give their crops to the state," lamented Soviet analysts, "they are practically independent." The KGB reported that despite Castro's "nationalization" program, Cuban farmers had actually turned over only 2.5

percent of their crop in 1961.[43] Moreover, because of the weakness of Cuban state controls, "a significant portion of stores and a large number of gangsters are artificially aggravating the deficit in goods." Soviets visitors to Cuba painted a picture of a black market where prices were kept high and products were diverted from true supporters of the revolution.

Ironically it was also some of the good brought by the revolution that could be blamed for the current mess. Since 1959 domestic demand had grown as a function of the improved income distribution in Cuba. Even before this change, Cuba had not been able to produce enough to meet domestic needs, and imports, which were paid for by sugar exports, had filled this gap. But in 1962 the Cubans were also suffering a dramatic foreign exchange shortage and could not import what they needed. The trade embargo imposed by the United States was largely responsible for this. In 1957 Cuba had earned $600 million from its trade with the United States.[44] That figure had been dropping steadily since. The truncation of the Cuban sugar quota in July 1960 had deprived Havana of its greatest source of U.S. dollars. This was followed in October 1960 by the imposition of an embargo on all Cuban goods except medicine, cigars, and some food other than sugar. What little was left of U.S.-Cuban trade disappeared in February 1962, when Kennedy cut Cuba off entirely from the U.S. market, with an exception made for trade in pharmaceuticals.

Castro hated to admit mistakes, yet the domestic crisis was so severe as to wrench a partial mea culpa. With extraordinary frankness he told Alekseev in February 1962 that he accepted one of the main charges of the opposition in Miami: "We are primarily responsible for the current economic difficulties. We have allowed agriculture to drift, and because of a lack of experienced cadres, we really can't mount a distribution system for goods and necessities."[45]

The economic difficulties forced Castro to take drastic steps. First, he reorganized INRA, which was supposed to be the showcase of the new Cuba. Over some objections in his official family, he named his friend Carlos Rafael Rodríguez, who had written the Declaration of Havana, to head the agency. The economic situation was so potentially destabilizing that Castro felt institutional changes alone were not enough. Well aware of the possible loss in popularity that this would entail, Castro nevertheless decided to introduce rationing. Havana faced a Hobson's choice. The Cuban leader understood that the introduction of rationing could deal a telling blow to the prestige of his regime. However, the supply situation was so bad that it made sense to do something dramatic to deny the counterrevolutionaries the most fertile source of recruits. Castro told the Soviets in mid-March that he felt he had to take the risk. "For the foreseeable future, surmounting these economic difficulties," Castro confided to Alekseev in the style of an East European leader, "will be one of the most important tasks of the party and the government."

This economic crisis in Cuba so unsettled Castro that it provoked him to reconsider his own political position. Since mid-1961 he had increasingly stayed out of the day-to-day management of the Cuban government. In the summer he had agreed with Raúl Castro and Che Guevara that what was left of the July 26 movement should be merged with the PSP to form the ORI (Integrated Revolutionary Organizations), a temporary coalition of the revolutionary left and the nucleus of a future Cuban communist party. Uninterested in such things, Castro had left the major administrative decisions involving the new ORI to the executive secretary of the Cuban communist party, Aníbal Escalante.

Escalante was an ambitious man who had dreamed of leading a second socialist revolution in Cuba. The architect of Cuba's repressive neighborhood surveillance system, Escalante had worked closely with Ambassador Sergei Kudryavtsev and Alekseev in applying pressure on Castro to take more energetic steps against the rebels in the Escambray mountains and the remnants of the CIA station in Havana. A communist since the 1930s, Escalante was well liked by Moscow and the communist parties of Latin America. He was a brilliant empire builder who understood the power to be gained by controlling nominations to district and provincial party groups. Since the summer of 1961 he had placed members of the PSP—as opposed to the many fellow travelers in the July 26 movement—in positions of authority. Jealous of his own place in the communist hierarchy, he also froze out potential adversaries. One person he tried to undercut was Blas Roca, the general secretary of the party and a close ally of Raúl Castro.

For nearly a year Fidel Castro paid no attention to Escalante's activities and seemed content to let him run the ORI. Castro respected Escalante and did not oppose rumors that this old communist had actually eclipsed Raúl and Che Guevara as the second-most-powerful man in Cuba. The communists were torn. Those loyal to Blas Roca met in September 1961 to discuss what to do about Escalante's ambitions, but ultimately all agreed that he was advancing the party's overarching goal of supplanting the July 26 movement as the motive force behind Castro, so nothing was done.

All of this would change in March 1962, however.[46] Faced with rising public opposition and knowing that the Cuban people generally blamed the food shortage on the influence of communists in his government, Castro was determined to consolidate his own power. He alone chose Rodríguez to head INRA. As it had been months since Castro had made a decision of that significance without consulting Escalante, this was a signal that he was reasserting his power.

Escalante's ambition in 1962 bordered on recklessness. He complained bitterly to a trusted colleague, who later betrayed his trust, that Castro had named Rodríguez without consulting any member of the PSP. When Castro was told of Escalante's criticism, he saw another opportunity to consolidate his power.

Over the course of the following week, Castro met individually with his closest communist advisers, including Blas Roca, Rodríguez, and Flavio

Bravo, to discuss Escalante. Up to that point the leadership of the PSP had withheld from Castro its misgivings about Escalante. Now Roca and the others freely counseled Castro on how to get rid of this embarrassment.

Castro then launched a two-stage operation to root out Escalante and his cronies. First, he expanded the leadership of the ORI with members of the noncommunist left whom he could trust to follow his word. Then he staged a brutal meeting of the leadership of ORI to make an example of Escalante.

Behind closed doors, Castro railed against Escalante, accusing him of responsibility for divisions in the ORI and the revolutionary movement. Castro said that he was not informed of all of the measures taken to achieve the unification of the party, that Escalante took the most important decisions himself. Castro hoped to earn the sympathy of some of the noncommunists in ORI. He spoke in a way that made Escalante and the other Cuban communists uncomfortable. He did not seem to know—or did not want to know—that Che Guevara and his own brother had been members of the party. Since Castro came to power, at least, Escalante had told Che to reveal his membership to Fidel, fearing that Castro would resent this secret and the sooner he knew it, the better. The transcript of this meeting is unavailable, but what Escalante later told Moscow suggests that Castro extolled the virtues of the July 26 movement while implying that those who belonged to the PSP were something less than loyal to him. Only a year earlier Castro had proclaimed to a group in the offices of *Hoy* that he had been a communist all his adult life; but at this meeting he targeted his anger at the PSP.

In the face of Castro's fury, Escalante refused to accept responsibility. After all, had he not enjoyed Castro's public and private support since the founding of the ORI in 1961? This response infuriated Castro, who abruptly ended the meeting, saying that he was too excited and could "say a lot that was unnecessary." In dismissing the group, Castro turned to Escalante and strongly advised him to think over his position and to come back the next day to discuss it.

Escalante knew that his downfall had potentially dramatic implications for the growth of the communist party in Cuba and potentially tragic consequences for himself. Despite the initial burst of self-defense, Escalante realized that he could not challenge Castro in Cuba. He had no independent base of support. In the communist system, in whichever country, losers in a power struggle were expected to admit their mistakes. Escalante knew the rules. His tone at the next meeting was one of contrition. Escalante went through the motions of apologizing for his great errors. On cue, he engaged in self-criticism and then watched quietly as the ORI removed him from its executive board. A few days later, on March 20, the ORI voted officially to fire Escalante from the post of party secretary. Castro took to the airwaves the following day to denounce "sectarianism" and to present Escalante as the bogeyman, the personification of selfishness in the communist movement.

Shaken by the proceedings, Escalante left Havana for the provinces. He invited Emilio Aragonés and his brother to his home to talk over what he was to do next. Together they devised a strategy for getting Escalante out of the country safely. Aragonés and the younger Escalante would go to Castro privately to request permission for Aníbal Escalante to leave for exile in the Soviet Union. Castro agreed.

A few days later, in disgrace, one of the Soviet Union's best friends in Cuba boarded a flight for Moscow. Soviet-Cuban relations seemed on the verge of a crisis.

CHAPTER 9

The Nuclear Decision

In early April 1962 and a world apart, Nikita Khrushchev and John Kennedy took their next steps toward military confrontation over Cuba. On April 9, 1962, the *New York Times* reported that Kennedy and the shah of Iran would be visiting Norfolk on Saturday to observe the largest Atlantic-Caribbean military exercise ever conducted. Some 40,000 men were boarding eighty-four ships to start Lantphibex-62, an exercise that included two amphibious landings. Kennedy and the shah were scheduled to witness 10,000 men disembark from thirty-four amphibious ships onto Onslow Beach, North Carolina. Away from the klieg lights, an even larger practice invasion was scheduled to take place off Vieques Island, Puerto Rico, which was less than fifty miles from Cuba.[1]

News of Lantphibex reached Moscow as the Presidium was considering ways of reassuring Castro that he remained Moscow's choice in Havana. Since mid-1960, when they took over from the Czechs and the Poles primary responsibility for meeting Cuban military needs, the Soviets had sent over $250 million worth of war matériel: 394 tanks and self-propelled weapons, 888 automatic and antiaircraft guns, 41 military planes, 13 ships, 13 radio locators, 308 radio sets, 3,619 automobiles, tractors, and other technology. The Cubans had received most of this arsenal since the Bay of Pigs invasion.[2]

Soviet assistance also came in the form of training the Cubans to use these weapons. As of March 1962 about 300 Soviet military specialists and translators were on the island. Under its supervision the Soviet armed forces had trained 300 crews for tanks and self-propelled weapons, 130 crews for artillery batteries, 20 crews of defensive artillery batteries, 42 pilots for the MiG-15, and 5 pilots for the fighter MiG-19A. Some of the training had taken place in Eastern Europe. Since 1960, 107 Cuban pilots and 618 sailors had been trained in Soviet military schools; meanwhile, 178 Cuban military specialists—including 62 pilots, 55 tankers, and 61 artillery technicians—had been trained in Czechoslovakia.[3]

The rattling of U.S. sabers in the Caribbean fell on very receptive ears in Havana. The Presidium had held up the last installment of the military package for Castro because of a bottleneck in the Soviet defense industries. There were not enough SA-2 systems, including V-750 missiles, to meet both the promised delivery to the Cubans and an older commitment to Egypt. Up until then the Soviet assistance plan for Cuba rested on the assumption that Castro had two or three years to prepare for the next U.S. attack. There was no point offending the volatile Gamal Abdel Nasser if the security of Castro's regime was not immediately threatened.

But something had happened since February, when the Kremlin had most recently revisited the question of U.S. intentions and Cuban security. Escalante's disgrace represented the greatest challenge to Cuban-Soviet relationship since Castro came to power. Moscow had been playing a risky game. Thinking that Raúl Castro and Che Guevera had kept their membership in the party a secret from Fidel, the Soviets had become accomplices to their deception. During Fidel Castro's consolidation of power and alignment with Moscow, the Kremlin had warned its ambassador, Sergei Kudryavtsev, and the KGB's Alekseev to be wary of energetic communists who tried to push Castro too far, too fast. At stake was not communist control in Cuba. Moscow believed that a shared enemy, the USA, and the influence of Blas Roca, Emilio Aragonés, and, of course, Raúl Castro would keep the mercurial Fidel on the right track. What Khrushchev worried about was the shape that communism would take in Cuba. Would the Castro regime associate itself with the Soviet leader's path of "peaceful coexistence," or would it ally with China, whose leader, Mao Zedong, advocated the violent overthrow of imperialist regimes?

Within days of Escalante's removal, information reached Moscow that confirmed the Kremlin's worst fears. Escalante and Castro had not only challenged each other for power in Cuba; they disagreed over Cuba's strategy abroad. In particular, Escalante had been a staunch supporter of Moscow's line on treating national-liberation movements with caution. He was great friends with communist leaders in countries like Argentina, Brazil, and Chile, who believed in using strikes and elections to gain power peacefully. Escalante's great rival was Che Guevara, whom a number of PSP leaders viewed as more pro-Chinese than pro-Soviet because of his oft-stated belief in the necessity of violence for success in revolution. Guevara and Escalante had bitterly disagreed. Now it seemed that Guevara would have greater influence in shaping Cuban foreign policy.

As Escalante's star waned, KGB consultants in the Cuban Ministry of Internal Affairs began to notice that the Cubans were paying particular attention to the preparation of partisan groups to be sent to Venezuela, Guatemala, the Dominican Republic, Ecuador, Peru, Bolivia, Paraguay, Panama, Honduras, Nicaragua, and other Latin American countries. The officials in charge of these operations were not the same as those who regularly worked with the Russians on security and foreign intelligence matters. The KGB later learned that the Cuban leadership had decided to keep the number of partisans, their training, and even the names of the instructors secret from Moscow. The Cubans wanted to train a large number of guerrillas in a hurry. Each course lasted three to five days. Castro maintained general supervision, but the bulk of the work was done by Cuban intelligence, which recruited suitable candidates from stations in Latin America.

Castro sent a representative to Moscow in March, as he was dispensing with Escalante, to explain the new direction he hoped to take. Ramiro Valdés's visit had been in the works for months. In late 1961 Alekseev had cabled Moscow that Valdés and his party would require extra-warm clothes if they were to visit Moscow in the winter.[4]

Finally in Moscow, and appropriately dressed, Valdés had an uncomfortable proposal to make. The official KGB version leaves no doubt as to what Havana wanted: "In March 1962 during the visit of Minister of Internal Affairs Valdés to the USSR, the Cuban leadership suggested to the Soviet Union that it organize in Cuba a Soviet intelligence center with a view to giving active support to revolutionary movements in the countries of Latin America."[5]

Valdés reported that Castro believed the time was ripe to launch an offensive in Latin America. In February, Castro had announced that it was "the duty of every revolutionary . . . to make the revolution."[6] The Cubans assumed that Soviet intelligence officers, past masters in such work, would render irreplaceable assistance to the Cubans.

It was the timing of this proposal that made it so discomfiting for Moscow. The Kremlin had fragmentary information pointing to Kennedy's interest in another attempt against Castro, this time using the U.S. military. At the very least, Kennedy was looking for a pretext to exploit the superiority of his forces in the region. Wouldn't the discovery of a KGB training camp in Cuba provide an excellent pretext, or lay the basis for the defection of the six hold-out states to the American side in the OAS?

The KGB said no to Valdés. And it did so in such a disingenuous way that Valdés knew that Castro had been snubbed. "We don't help national-liberation movements," Valdés was informed. "The KGB only collects intelligence." Valdés was incredulous.[7]

"I cannot myself imagine that Soviet intelligence concerns itself solely with collecting information," Valdés told the Soviets. "If this is so, then who will help international revolutionary movements?"[8] Valdés could not believe that Moscow left such work up to diplomats. He was weaned on stories of the superiority of Soviet covert operations. Valdés, for example, sincerely believed that the KGB had orchestrated the many abortive rocket launches and other failures at Cape Canaveral.[9]

To underscore Castro's disappointment, Valdés deliberately touched a nerve in Moscow. He compared the Soviets unfavorably with the Chinese. "At a time when the Chinese are striving to put a center of Chinese influence on every continent, the Russians must do this as well."[10]

Alekseev tried to mollify Valdés when the latter returned to Havana. A lack of caution in handling revolutionary movements at this moment, said Alekseev, would encourage U.S. aggression. Valdés's response was defiant: "The [Soviet] explanation that such a center would serve as justification for the United States to accuse the Cubans of exporting revolution does not change the situation, for Cuba is already accused of all sorts of sins having to do with Soviet influence."[11]

These were disturbing signals, but the Presidium did not take notice until Escalante himself arrived in Moscow and delivered an explosive report to the Central Committee on his fall from grace in Havana. After relating the story of his opposition to Castro's handling of the Rodríguez appointment, Escalante provided a surprising explanation. "However, in the final analysis," he said, "the reason for Fidel Castro's outburst of unhappiness was not this." Escalante said that Chinese influence was rising among members of Cuba's revolutionary elite. He told of opposition even within the PSP, to Moscow's line on revolution in the Third World. He explained, perhaps in an effort to secure himself a haven in Moscow, that he repeatedly had to defend Moscow's positions in discussions with some of Castro's advisers.

For the Kremlin, Escalante's blaming of China was the equivalent of crying fire in a theater. But it might not have been believed, had it not been for evidence accumulating at the Lubyanka that Castro was putting limits on intelligence sharing.

When they had to, the wheels turned quickly in Moscow. Escalante's report on his downfall was written April 3. In the next week the KGB produced a report on Castro's new policy in the Third World and an explanation of the Escalante affair for the Central Committee. Concerned that Escalante's presence in Moscow would harm relations with Castro, the Kremlin decided to signal its acceptance of Castro's explanation of Escalante's "sectarianism." On April 11 the Central Committee published a lengthy description of the Escalante affair in *Pravda* that supported all of Castro's assertions, even though the KGB and Escalante had denied them in private conversations the week before. However, the most important development was that on April 12 the Presidium took up the issue of the future of Soviet-Cuban relations in light of these threatening developments.

News of Kennedy's joint appearance with the shah of Iran stirred some hearts in Moscow, where government analysts were accustomed to a daily foreign news digest.[12] In the final analysis, though, in light of the timing of the key Kremlin actions, what probably forced the Kremlin to accelerate the delivery of the September 1961 package to Cuba were the disturbing reports coming from Cuba itself of the deteriorating position of Moscow's key allies in the regime. Although on April 11 Vladimir Semichastny, the chairman of the KGB, assured the Kremlin that there was "no reason to speak of the danger of serious Chinese influence on Fidel Castro," Moscow did not want to take any chances.[13] Both the Soviets and Castro interpreted military supplies as a gauge of the health of their relationship. The Cubans were not happy that their air defense system was languishing in some Soviet factory. With Castro looking for reasons to blame communists for his economic and political difficulties, the time had come to satisfy his appetite for conventional missiles.

On April 12 the Presidium made two important decisions. First, Khrushchev and his colleagues finally confirmed the delivery of four divisions of SA-2 antiaircraft launchers and two technical support divisions, with 180 missiles for them. To sweeten this late delivery, which was smaller than what Castro had been told to expect, the Presidium reversed the Soviet military's earlier decision not to send the technologically advanced Sopka cruise missile system. Castro had asked for three of these shore batteries in September. Now the Presidium decided to send him one. In addition, Castro would get a few things he had not asked for: ten used Il-28 medium bombers and four R-15 cruise missile launchers. Finally, the Soviet leadership decided to send General N. I. Gusev, who was to do a survey of additional Cuban military needs, and a 650-man contingent of Soviet soldiers to protect and train the Cubans in using these advanced weapons systems. In all, Khrushchev had increased the September package by 23 million rubles.[14]

The second major decision was to reroute SA-2s destined for Egypt. Nasser was due to receive these missiles in 1962. The Presidium instructed the appropriate ministries to reverse priorities and earmark the Nasser shipments for Castro.[15]

The Escalante affair and Lantphibex reinforced Khrushchev's general concern about the future of a socialist Cuba. Khrushchev had invested his heart and much political capital in Castro's regime. With the Chinese eager to pounce on the defeat of socialism in the Caribbean and the grumblers on the Presidium ready to excoriate him for adventurism, Khrushchev could ill afford to lose Cuba. However, at this point he did not yet feel compelled to make the defense of Cuba the direct responsibility of the Soviet armed forces. Nor was he yet prepared to send nuclear weapons 7,000 miles to protect Castro.

The Fox and the Hedgehog

Deep within Khrushchev was a certainty about how to acquire and use power. An autodidact, never a formal student of military affairs, Khrushchev believed he understood the bases of international affairs. The events of April 1962 had taken their toll on him. Everywhere he turned, he faced a challenge to his authority as leader of the socialist world. The Americans were no more prepared to deal with him from a position of respect than before. Kennedy's offer to negotiate a test ban treaty had been humiliating. Just as annoying were the fruitless negotiations with Washington over the future status of Berlin. The erecting of the wall had solved the problem of the hemorraghing of the East German population for the moment, but Moscow's belief that its demands were right and that U.S. obstinacy symbolized a lack of respect remained. And then there was Cuba, the symbol of Khrushchev's effort to reconcile Stalinist theories of socialist state development with the realities of the developing world. Both John Kennedy and Fidel Castro represented challenges to that dream. Kennedy by his current and future truculence could drive Castro from power any time he decided to use U.S. troops; and Castro's sense of revolutionary identity might lead him to opt for an alliance with Beijing, or perhaps he would follow the model of Tito's Yugoslavia, which had gone its own way in 1948.

Sometime in April, it is likely, Khrushchev began to consider dramatic approaches to meeting the convergence of these problems. According to Dmitri Volkogonov, Khrushchev approached Rodion Malinovsky with an idea of a nuclear solution to his many problems. Malinovsky had just completed his report on the most recent tests of the Soviet Union's new R-16s (known to NATO as the SS-7s), so-called intercontinental ballistic missiles that could hit the U.S. homeland with a one-megaton warhead launched from Soviet Central Asia. The United States had four times as many of these weapons as the Soviet Union. Whereas the Soviet army enjoyed conventional superiority in the European theater of operations, the United States was far ahead in systems that could deliver a nuclear punch. "Why not throw a hedgehog at Uncle Sam's pants?" Khrushchev asked. Arguing that it would take ten years at least for the Soviets to build enough of these new SS-7s to match U.S. strategic power, Khrushchev suggested that Cuba might make a useful base for Soviet intermediate-range missiles, of which Moscow already had many.[16]

Khrushchev was impulsive and imaginative. The Soviet Union had never stationed ballistic missiles outside of its borders. But Khrushchev had broken rules before. Stalin had never seriously considered making inroads into Latin America. The idea of a missile gambit, which began in Khrushchev's mind as a work of inspiration, even whimsy, stayed with him. But it would be weeks before he convinced himself and others that it might work.

In the meantime, Khrushchev faced very pressing problems in Cuba. The Kremlin's April 12 decisions had not calmed Castro as had been hoped. Alekseev in Havana continued to send disheartening reports to Moscow. A few days after scoffing at the KGB's unwillingness to own up to covert action, Ramiro Valdés returned to the Soviet delegation to tell Alekseev that Castro had decided to go it alone. Soviet support in training guerrillas was preferable, but if the Soviets were unwilling to take a risk, he would not let that stop him.[17]

Castro himself approached the Soviet government through Alekseev to make clear that Valdés spoke for him. The Cuban government was impatient for movement in Latin America. If Moscow did not wish to participate, the Soviets would have to answer to their own consciences as revolutionaries. As far as Castro was concerned, revolution was a categorical imperative: "We are going to help communist parties and other progressive movements across these countries in preparation for the possible partisan struggle. In two or three years in Latin America, an uncontrollable revolutionary storm will arise and communists should be prepared to be at the head of it."[18]

When Alekseev raised the inevitable concern over the American reaction, Castro argued that stirring up revolution would have the opposite effect on Washington. Instead of provoking an invasion, it would stay Kennedy's hand, because the United States would never intervene if Latin America was in upheaval.

The Cuban decision to press ahead with an active campaign of revolution signaled a victory for Che and a setback for Moscow. A KGB source close to Che reported that "in principle" the Cubans accepted the idea of peaceful coexistence. But this agreement "does not mean that we must deny help to national-liberation movements and, above all, to our fraternal Latin Americans." Knowing Moscow's concern, the source added, "In doing this, we are not trying to set off either a local or a world war."[19]

This was cold comfort for Khrushchev. With the Americans redoubling their efforts to convince NATO and the rest of Latin America that John Kennedy's obsession with Castro was rational, Castro insisted on helping Washington make its case. Khrushchev was sympathetic to Castro's goals—within the Presidium he was known as one of the stronger supporters of national liberation movements—but Castro's timing was terrible.

What the Kremlin needed was advice on how to handle Castro, to slow him down at least until the Cuban army was built up to a point that it could deter the United States from making a snap decision to invade.

An Unexpected Invitation

Around April 27 a telegram reached Alekseev: "You must immediately return to Moscow." He wondered, "What is this? What have I done?"[20]

Alekseev could assume that Moscow was concerned about the future of Soviet-Cuban relations. The Escalante affair cut across Soviet interests in the island, and although no fingers had been pointed at Alekseev, Moscow certainly knew from Alekseev's KGB reports that Escalante was one of his high-level informants.

Alekseev used some guile to find out whether the recent crisis was the reason for his being summoned. "How should I prepare myself for the meetings in Moscow," he cabled home. "What issues are to be discussed?"[21]

Alekseev asked himself, "If the Kremlin doesn't like my work, why hasn't Moscow said anything to me about it before?" His superiors had reprimanded him in 1960 for sending warning signals about American and Cuban exile terrorist plots that never seemed to materialize. But this could not explain why Moscow wanted him to come home in 1962. Was Moscow afraid that he had lost the confidence of the Castros in the aftermath of the Escalante affair?

Ironically, with the news from Moscow eating at him, Alekseev had to contend with Fidel Castro's new enthusiasm for May Day. Fidel Castro was eager for Alekseev to be in Cuba for the first May 1 celebration since he had publicly revealed himself as a communist. "Fidel told me that the Cubans wanted to celebrate . . . in the socialist way, with all the trimmings of international socialism." The Cuban government had invited forty-one leftist or communist parties to march in Havana.[22]

Castro's insistence provided incentive and a timely excuse for Alekseev to delay acting on Moscow's unexpected order. "Okay, if you must," KGB headquarters responded to Alekseev's request to stay in Havana. His instructions were modified: "Stay there for the May 1 festivities, then fly out on May 2."[23]

Meanwhile, the KGB resident's little attempt to elicit a rationale for the unexpected invitation came to naught. Moscow replied that Alekseev did not have to prepare himself in any special way. Whatever the reason for this visit—and there had to be one—Moscow would keep it to itself. In Stalin's time a surprise invitation to return to Moscow usually meant imprisonment or quick death. Alekseev did not expect so final a punishment.

The secret awaited Alekseev in Moscow. A department chief of the KGB whispered into his ear: "Do you know why you were brought home?"

"Honestly, I was trembling," Alekseev later remembered.

"Well, they are sizing you up as an ambassador. But keep this to yourself."

The news both relieved and disappointed Alekseev. It could have been worse, of course. That was why he was relieved. But it also could have been better. "I was doing such good work there." With the news that he had not lost the Kremlin's respect, Alekseev's self-confidence returned. He began to argue against the idea. Was he not providing the leadership with the best political intelligence on Cuba? He was getting it from the horse's mouth. Why now undermine this by tying him up with the administrative and diplomatic responsibilities of an embassy?

Khrushchev had ended Stalin's practice of holding business meetings after midnight. Otherwise the pattern of bureaucratic life was little changed. Members of the Presidium set all of the rules. If and when they decided to see you, you jumped. You might be told to expect a call, which might not come through for days. Or you might have no idea that you were expected at a meeting until a call came through an hour or so before the event.

May 7 was Alekseev's first full day in Moscow on this unexpected trip. His schedule for the day had already been set, and he didn't know it: "[Alexander] Panyushkin, the director of the Central Committee's foreign service department, called me that morning. 'Come here quickly, [Frol] Kozlov is waiting for us.'"

It was noon, and Panyushkin made clear that Alekseev was expected to join them for a discussion with Kozlov, a member of the Presidium and Khrushchev's designated successor. Alekseev rushed over to the Kremlin, catching up with the bureaucrats from the Central Committee who were filing into Kozlov's office. Kozlov was nowhere to be found. His assistant explained that he had just left for lunch. The bureaucrats and Alekseev would have to wait.

About an hour later, two of the stars of the Central Committee, the former KGB chief, Aleksandr Shelepin, and a future KGB chief and general secretary, Yuri Andropov, walked into Kozlov's waiting room. Alekseev knew Shelepin, who had headed the KGB at the end of the 1950s. They had become acquainted when Alekseev was posted to France in the mid-1950s. Andropov, Alekseev knew only by reputation.

Shelepin decided to ease his former subordinate's mind. "The decision has already been made, don't make trouble, don't extract a high price, just don't give that impression," said Shelepin. "Of course not," replied Alekseev. He would have no choice.

Alekseev hoped that he could still get out of the assignment: "What is needed there now is an economist, who could do ten times more than I can." A few minutes later a call came through, and Alekseev was told to go to the Kremlin, to see Nikita Khrushchev.

"I went to the corridor outside his office [Khrushchev's] on the second floor," recalled Alekseev. "It was a long corridor, and from Khrushchev's office came this troika: Suslov, Mikoyan, Gromyko. I recognized Suslov and Gromyko from their photographs, and Mikoyan I knew because he had been to Cuba. Seeing me, Mikoyan turned to Gromyko: Andrei Andreevich, so this is our new ambassador to Cuba, Aleksandr Ivanovich Alekseev." This is how decisions were made in the Soviet Union. Gromyko had just learned from a member of the Presidium that the Ministry of Foreign Affairs would have a new representative in Havana.

Alekseev then went in to see Khrushchev alone: "He was interested in Cuba, Fidel, the Cuban government, their preoccupations, what they were doing. And once he asked, I told him how completely taken I was by the Cuban revolution, with Fidel."

Khrushchev dismissed Alekseev's concerns that the Cubans needed a Soviet representative who knew something about economics. "No, I don't want a dyarchy any longer. We recognize one ambassador, and the Cubans recognize another. In terms of economics, we will send you as many advisers as you think you will need."

To make his point, Khrushchev grabbed the phone next to him: "Frol Romanovich [Kozlov], Alekseev is here sitting with me, and he says that he doesn't know anything about economics. Get him twenty advisers in this area. There are enough unemployed people in Moscow to go."

What Khrushchev did not say to Alekseev was as interesting as what he did say. He neither mentioned the idea of putting nuclear weapons on Cuba nor discussed in anything but a general way the problem of U.S. imperialism in the Caribbean. At this point in the evolution of his thinking about Cuba, he was sticking to the position that the military equipment that the Presidium had decided on in April would be enough to tide the Cubans over.

The Kremlin's Cuban policy, to which Alekseev now bore witness, was confused. Khrushchev had intended to send an extensive private message to Fidel

Castro with the Gusev delegation. But the group left May 6, and the letter was still not finished. Alekseev was brought in to assist in completing the project.

The effort was marked by improvisation. Khrushchev sent Alekseev to Kozlov to discuss the details of a rescue package for Castro, which would be outlined in the letter. Kozlov was bristling with ideas. "Tell them," he said to Alekseev, "that we are going to send them an expert on timber, on fish, on metallurgy, on everything." Getting excited, Kozlov said, "And even on sugar-cane!"

A Soviet expert on sugar? This was not something that the Soviets knew better than the Cubans. Kozlov answered Alekseev's quizzical look, "You don't understand, and perhaps this will interest you, but in Uzbekistan we can do this. Let the Cubans try our sugar."

Alekseev thought to himself that Moscow seemed to be preparing a shadow government to send to Cuba. Was this not the quintessentially American approach to a client state in the Caribbean? Up to the mid-1940s a series of American commissions were sent to Haiti, Nicaragua, and, most notoriously, Cuba to assist the governments to pay their debts and achieve financial security.[24]

The Presidium adopted the letter as redrafted on May 11. The Kremlin decided to invite Castro to the USSR. "Unfortunately international conditions did not allow you to visit last year," said the letter, "but we hope that it will be possible for you to undertake this trip this year."[25] One can only wonder why the Kremlin assumed that global conditions in 1962 would be more conducive to a Castro state visit.

Besides the invitation, the May 11 letter laid out a plan for guiding the Cubans through the rough waters ahead:

We, in the Central Committee and the government, have exchanged opinions and looked for ways to render real assistance to your country, to relieve the economic difficulties associated with the arms buildup that you are experiencing at the moment.

Within the limits of our capabilities, the CC and the Soviet government have decided:

1) To excuse all Cuban debt. To place in the course of the next two years free of charge, from the account of the Soviet Union, arms and ammunition for the Cuban army, including missiles and other arms, details about the supply of which will be discussed by our delegation in Havana.

2) Regarding the Cuban request to consider the matter of giving assistance in the provision of irrigation in the Republic of Cuba . . . we have taken the decision to send a group of experts on irrigation and land reclamation. This group will be headed by the candidate member of the Presidium and the first secretary of the Uzbekistan Central Committee, R. Rashidov.[26]

The Soviets were concerned that the Cubans would not be able to pay for the buildup that the current situation required. The Soviets still believed that there was time to prevent a U.S. invasion. The Ministry of Defense came up with a two-year plan to build up the Cuban army and to equip it with the latest in surface-to-air missiles and cruise missiles. All would be conventional weapons, destined to be turned over to the Cubans as soon as possible.

An American Visitor

Pierre Salinger, President Kennedy's press secretary, arrived in Moscow on the same day that the Kremlin sent its letter to Castro. Salinger would meet an unusually volatile Khrushchev. He "was the most mercurial man I had ever met," Salinger later wrote. "His mood would change in an instant from blustery anger to gentle humor."[27] Khrushchev decided he wanted to see Kennedy's aide. Whenever he was about to make a major decision regarding U.S.-Soviet relations, he grabbed the nearest prominent American he could find to send a private message.

When Salinger arrived on May 11, he learned that he was to spend the night at a government dacha twenty miles outside Moscow. Khrushchev appeared just before noon on May 12. After greeting Salinger, he took the thirty-year-old American for a motor boat ride on the Moscow River.

Khrushchev used Salinger to let Washington know that he thought the young president was losing his grip on the U.S. government. At a press conference earlier in the week, Kennedy had quoted Churchill in saying that on the Berlin question he preferred "to jaw, jaw, jaw, rather than war, war, war." Khrushchev told Salinger that he "greatly appreciated" Kennedy's statement but that he doubted Kennedy "would have the courage and guts to carry this through."[28]

Khrushchev spent fourteen hours with Salinger, which he used to present a picture of himself as being both extremely reasonable and annoyed at how the United States treated him. Khrushchev never mentioned Cuba. But he talked about the credibility of his word, and how many times did he have to remind the Americans that a socialist Cuba was a vital interest of his? His plan of attack was once again Berlin, the area where Kennedy felt as vulnerable as Khrushchev did in Cuba. Berlin, he argued, was "the central issue dividing the U.S. and the USSR," and its solution would "bring about a solution to all of our problems." He dismissed progress on any other front, as he had done in Vienna. He portrayed himself as being as disappointed as the American people that the Soviet Union and the United States were still so far from a détente. But he doubted that Kennedy was sincerely interested in making progress toward a test ban accord or general disarmament. Khrushchev was playacting at this point, for he knew that he had never seriously attempted to probe Kennedy's flexibility on any issue other than Berlin, where the U.S.

leader's stance was firm. Since 1961 Khrushchev had stuck to the policy of the big stick to compel the White House to adopt his position on Berlin.

The failure of Khrushchev's policy was painfully evident. The Americans had increased their defense budget and resumed atmospheric testing without any significant decrease in Kennedy's credibility as a world leader. If anything, the young man's stature was enhanced by Khrushchev's brinkmanship. In his discussions with Salinger, Khrushchev let off steam by attacking an interview that Kennedy had given to Stewart Alsop of the *Saturday Evening Post.* By May 1962 this interview had become an embarrassment for Kennedy. Initially, he had been proud of it as a presentation of his "Grand Strategy." A careful reader found that Alsop had given Kennedy a forum to explain why Eisenhower and Dulles had erred in relying too heavily on nuclear weapons. The president expressed his preference for an international system whose security did not rest on the threat of suicide. The Soviets, however, chose not to read the piece in this way. In April, a week or so after the interview appeared, TASS zeroed in on one poorly constructed sentence—"Of course in some circumstances we must be prepared to use nuclear weapons at the start, come what may"—to make the case that Kennedy intended to use nuclear weapons first. However, once returned to its context, the sentence was consistent with a policy of avoiding nuclear war:

> I don't think many people really understand the change. As late as 1954 the balance in air power, in the nuclear weapons, was all on our side. The change began about 1958 or 1959, with the missiles. Now we have got to realize that *both* sides have these annihilating weapons, and that changes the problem. Of course in some circumstances we must be prepared to use the nuclear weapon at the start, come what may—a clear attack on Western Europe, for example. But what is important is that if you use these weapons you have to control their use. What you need is control, flexibility, a choice. . . .[29]

In haranguing Salinger, Khrushchev asserted that Eisenhower and Dulles would never had made such a statement. It was a "very bad statement . . . for which [Kennedy] would have to pay." Khrushchev added over Salinger's explanations that "perhaps [the] Soviet Union would have to reassess its position."

The Nuclear Decision

Khrushchev left for Bulgaria the next day. In Bulgaria he was tortured by the idea that the approach in his May 11 letter to Castro was insufficient: "[O]ne thought kept hammering away at my brain: what will happen if we lose Cuba?"[30]

Khrushchev was merely going through the motions on this trip, fulfilling his fraternal responsibility to kiss, shake hands, and wave. Meanwhile, privately he worried about the effect on Soviet prestige of the collapse of the Kremlin's position in the Caribbean. "It would gravely diminish our stature throughout the world, but especially in Latin America."[31]

The threats to Cuba were coming from two directions. There was always the possibility that the fragmentary evidence of serious U.S. military planning was indicative of Kennedy's determination to invade in 1962. "I'm not saying we had any documentary proof that the Americans were preparing a second invasion," Khrushchev later explained; "we didn't need documentary proof. We knew the class affiliation, the class blindness, of the United States, and that was enough to make us expect the worst."[32] And, even if the United States was not on the verge of invading Cuba, Castro seemed determined to proceed on a course that would deliver a perfect pretext to Kennedy for military action pretty soon.

"Any fool could start a war" was a mantra of sorts for Khrushchev, who had a habit of relying on a set of stock anecdotes, proverbs, and axioms. He needed to find a way, as he put it, "which would answer the American threat but which would also avoid war." At some point in his trip to Bulgaria, he concluded that the logical answer was nuclear missiles.[33]

It was no secret that Khrushchev stood in awe of nuclear weapons. At Vienna he had described them as the new "Gods of War." They were the finest weapons in any arsenal. As his jubilation after Sputnik showed, Khrushchev correlated a country's nuclear capabilities with its vitality and potential. In Bulgaria he was reminded of the intermediate-range nuclear missiles under U.S. command in nearby Turkey. In the late 1950s the Soviets learned through their sources at NATO that the United States had decided to deploy Jupiter missiles on the territory of its European allies.[34] By early 1962 Soviet intelligence was tracking increased U.S. military assistance to Turkey.[35] The trip to Bulgaria may well have given a sense of place and urgency to the intelligence reports Khrushchev had received in the Kremlin. As he struggled with the problem of how to ensure Cuban security, he knew that the United States had already set a precedent by using missiles to defend allies who were geographically vulnerable.

In mid-May, Fidel Castro was also having his doubts that the Soviet Presidium had done enough for him. The Soviet military delegation that arrived in Havana on May 6 had met a tragic end. On his first day in Cuba, General N. I. Gusev, a veteran of the Soviet civil war, died of a heart attack while taking a swim in the Caribbean.[36] When Khrushchev's new proposals for military assistance finally arrived in the May 11 letter, Castro understood that Moscow intended to reduce the economic burden of defending Cuba but did not get the impression that the Kremlin was prepared to provide enough hardware to the Cuban army.

The Cuban leader outlined his concerns to a group of Soviet military representatives on May 18, two days before Khrushchev returned to Moscow from Bulgaria. Castro said that his army needed three Sopka shore batteries, not just one. The Sopka were useful as a means of knocking down U.S. jets supporting a landing; and there were three principal landing spots on the island. "It is difficult to determine," Castro had to admit, "how to defend the shores with existing means." Moreover, Cuba needed not fewer than 10,000 Soviet troops to back up the Cuban army. The May 11 plan allocated only one Soviet motorized regiment, or 2,500 men, to the defense of Cuba. "We would very much like to have these units for each of the three regions where a landing from an offshore naval force is most likely." After outlining what he needed, Castro played coy: "I cannot support the request of our military for an increase in the number of units."[37]

The resident of the GRU, Colonel Meshcheriakov, who had participated in this conversation, commented that Castro had added this little remark, like the negation at the end of a German sentence, "to make clear, energetically, that these means were very much required, but at the same time he would never request them if it meant accepting free supplies." Castro was afraid of losing his independence, or at least a semblance of his independence. "We have the growing impression," Meshcheriakov reported, "that Fidel Castro does not wish to articulate requests for more military assistance in a concrete form. Although he has at the same time tried to inform the Soviet government of what is desired." Castro was winking, the GRU winked, and the Cuban request in the form of this memorandum of conversation was lying on Khrushchev's desk when he returned from Bulgaria.[38]

Khrushchev Proposes

Back in the Kremlin on May 20, Khrushchev discussed his idea of putting missiles in Cuba with Andrei Gromyko, Mikoyan, Malinovsky, Kozlov, and Alekseev, his ambassador-designate to Havana. Gromyko had the sense that Khrushchev was merely consulting them about a decision to which he was already firmly committed.[39] But Khrushchev encountered some resistance to his proposal. "Comrade Alekseev, we have decided or are about to decide to put medium-range missiles with nuclear warheads in Cuba. What will Fidel say about this?"

"He will be scared," Alekseev responded, "and I don't think he will take them." Khrushchev could not understand why. "Because Fidel Castro is trying to build security, the defense of the Cuban revolution," Alekseev explained, "by mobilizing Latin American public opinion." As a way of forcing the withdrawal of the U.S. naval base at Guantánamo Bay, Alekseev reminded Khrushchev, Castro had called for the removal of all foreign bases in the Americas. "The deployment of our missiles means the organization of a Soviet military base on Cuba." For a moment the room was still. Malinovsky, responding for Khrushchev, aggressively broke the silence. "How could your celebrated socialist Cuba not take the missiles?" he yelled. Recalling his service in the mid-1930s as a Soviet adviser in the Spanish civil war, Malinovsky added, "I fought in bourgeois-democratic Spain, and they openly took our weapons, but Cuba, socialist Cuba, which has an even greater need to take them. . . . How could they not!" The Presidium member Kozlov tried to calm Malinovsky. "Rodion Yakovlevich, why are you shouting at him? We asked him a question, he spoke to us, so why the anger?" Kozlov was not happy. "I understood that our military's interest in this proposal was great, but . . ." Khrushchev remained silent throughout the entire exchange. He intended to wait out the storm and get his way.[40]

After the session the group went into another room for lunch. Gromyko came up to Khrushchev with the outline of a letter about the missiles to send to Castro. Khrushchev thought it sounded right, but he didn't want to bother with the details. What mattered was the big picture. "We will help Cuba in every way possible," he said; "our declarations in the United Nations have so far not been enough."

On second thought, Khrushchev believed a letter wasn't the right way to advise the Cubans of the Kremlin's new proposal. Instead, he said to Gromyko, a delegation should go to Cuba to tell Castro in person that "we are ready to take a risk" for the Cuban revolution.[41]

The next day Khrushchev convened a meeting of the Defense Council, an interagency group with representatives from the Presidium, the secretariat of the Central Committee, and the Ministry of Defense, to outline his proposal: "I said I had some thoughts to air on the subject of Cuba." Khrushchev then presented the rationale for such a risky operation. "It would be foolish to expect the inevitable second [U.S.] invasion to be as badly planned as the first." Then he turned to the matter of Soviet prestige—the fact that the United States had refused to respect Soviet needs, to accept Soviet positions. "In addition to protecting Cuba, our missiles would have equalized what the West likes to call 'the balance of power.' The Americans had surrounded our country with military bases and threatened us with nuclear weapons, and now they would learn just what it feels like to have enemy missiles pointing at you. . . ."[42]

According to Colonel General of the Army Semyon P. Ivanov, who then headed the main operational department of the general staff of the soviet armed forces, the Defense Council meeting did not go as smoothly as Khrushchev had hoped. "The debates went on a long time," recalled Ivanov, who added that Mikoyan, in particular, "opposed placing our missiles and troops on Cuba." Ultimately, a majority supported Khrushchev's idea, and the Defense Council decided to instruct the Foreign Ministry, the Defense Ministry, and the Ministry of the Navy "to organize the concealed movement of troops and military technology by ship to Cuba."[43]

After declaring a recess in the meeting, Khrushchev directed Colonel General Ivanov, who was still in the secretariat of the Defense Council, to formu-

Fidel Castro leading the rebels of the July 26 movement in the mountains of the Sierra Maestra before the collapse of the regime of Fulgencio Batista on New Year's Day 1959.

(Lester Cole)

Raúl Castro in early 1959 when he was opening a secret channel to Moscow.

An enthusiastic crowd greets Fidel Castro in the rain at Washington's National Airport as he begins his tour of the United States in April 1959.

Harvard students react to Fidel Castro's speech on April 25, 1959. While Castro toured the campus with Harvard dean McGeorge Bundy, Nikita Khrushchev had just authorized a program to develop communist cadres in the Cuban army.

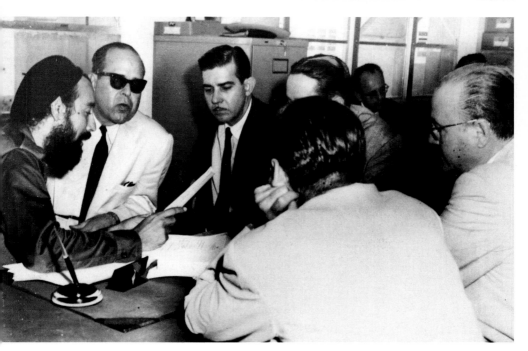

A secret member of the Partido Socialista Popular (Cuban Communist Party) from 1957, Ernesto "Che" Guevara was one of Fidel Castro's closest allies in the Sierra Maestra. Che's threat to abandon the Cuban revolution in 1959 pushed Castro toward Moscow.

The executive director of the National Institute of Agrarian Reform (INRA), Antonio Núñez Jiménez, speaks to a group of businessmen in June 1959, just after the formation of the organization. In March 1960 Fidel Castro told the Soviets that "in a few years, INRA will be the government."

KGB resident (chief of station) Aleksandr Alekseev, who opened a secret channel between Khrushchev and Fidel Castro with Che Guevara's help after reaching Cuba in fall 1959.

Soviet ambassador Sergei Kudryavstev at a photo opportunity in Havana a few months after his arrival in May 1960. Disliked by the Cubans, who considered him haughty and a coward, he was ultimately replaced by his rival, the KGB's Aleksandr Alekseev.

Brandishing a clenched fist, Nikita Khrushchev denounces Gary Powers's U-2 flight at the failed great-power summit in Paris in May 1960. Beside Khrushchev sits the Soviet defense minister, Rodion Malinovsky.

Before a November 1961 ceremony honoring outgoing CIA director Allen Dulles, John F. Kennedy rides with Dulles and the new director, John McCone. The Bay of Pigs fiasco hastened Dulles's retirement from the CIA.

In foreign policy, as in domestic matters, there were "nonsharables" that the Kennedy brothers kept from the rest of the U.S. government. Here the brothers are shown conferring in 1957 when Robert F. Kennedy was counsel of the Senate Committee on Racketeering in Labor and Industry and John was a member of the committee.

Robert F. Kennedy arrives at CIA headquarters in Langley, Virginia, in November 1961 with his wife, Ethel, and the secretary of defense, Robert McNamara. With McNamara's assistance, Kennedy was working to move the center of covert action planning against Fidel Castro outside the CIA.

Frank Holeman, the *Daily News* correspondent who introduced Georgi Bolshakov to Attorney General Robert F. Kennedy in May 1961 and subsequently provided logistical support to the principal secret link between John F. Kennedy and Nikita Khrushchev.

Georgi Bolshakov, the Russian intermediary in back-channel negotiations between John F. Kennedy and Nikita Khrushchev, who met with Robert Kennedy over fifty times in 1961–62.

Khrushchev and Kennedy emerge stony-faced from the Soviet Embassy after their final session at the Vienna summit in June 1961.

In January 1962 John Kennedy's comments to Khrushchev's son-in-law
Aleksei I. Adzhubei about Cuba would inspire a reexamination of Soviet policy
toward Fidel Castro. Here the men are pictured meeting in November 1961.
Seated between Kennedy and Adzhubei are U.S. interpreter Alex Akalovsky
and Georgi Bolshakov.

Nikita Khrushchev and his wife, Nina, attending a Benny Goodman concert in May 1962 with his closest advisers in the Presidium, Frol Kozlov (on Khrushchev's immediate right) and Anastas Mikoyan. A week earlier these men had decided to send nuclear missiles secretly to Cuba.

NATO reconnaissance plane flying over the *Admiral Nachimov* as the Soviet transport cleared the Turkish straits on its way to Cuba in September 1962. On board was the headquarters staff of Major General Igor D. Statsenko, who was preparing to command the R-12 and R-14 missile regiments in Cuba.

Khrushchev's decision to send missiles outside the Soviet Union for the first time forced the Soviet military to improvise. Here a tank is being used to clear boulders from a missile site.

Dressed in fancy civilian clothes as part of the Anadyr cover plan, Major General Igor D. Statsenko is photographed in Cuba in October 1962, where he commanded the Soviet medium-range ballistic missile base.

Soviet military officers in tropical attire overseeing the installation of the missile bases in Cuba, September 1962.

In this hill south of Havana near the town of Bejucal, the Soviets built a special storage facility for their nuclear warheads. Some of the warheads destined for missile units in the central and eastern portion of the island were stored in caves during the crisis.

MRBM FIELD LAUNCH SITE
San Cristobal #1
14 OCTOBER 1962

ERECTOR/LAUNCHER EQUIPMENT

TENT AREAS

8 MISSILE TRAILERS

EQUIPMENT

CONSTRUCTION

The U-2 shot seen around the world.

Kennedy and his crisis management team, the Ex Comm (Executive Committee
of the National Security Council), pictured during the Cuban missile crisis of
October 1962. Kennedy's decision to tape their sessions secretly has left an
extensive audio record of the Ex Comm.

New York Herald Tribune correspondent Warren Rogers (pictured in front of 10 Downing Street in London in 1969), whose barroom comments at the National Press Club on Wednesday night, October 24, 1962, reached the attention of Nikita Khrushchev and altered the course of the Cuban missile crisis.

Johnny Prokov, the longtime bartender in the Tap Room of the National Press Club, who alerted a Soviet intelligence officer to statements he had overheard from Rogers.

KGB Washington chief Aleksandr Feklisov, who reported the information about Rogers to Moscow. During the crisis Feklisov established his own special link to the Kennedy inner circle through ABC news correspondent John Scali.

A group of Soviet officers taking a break in early November from loading Soviet missiles to be shipped back to the Soviet Union. To prevent a return to the dangerous days of October 22–28, Khrushchev ordered that the missiles be removed as rapidly as possible.

Soviet technicians removed the tarpaulin covering the ballistic missiles to give U.S. reconnaissance planes a good look as the R-12s are returned to the Soviet Union in November 1962.

Fidel Castro strolling with Khrushchev at the Soviet leader's dacha on his first visit to the Soviet Union in May 1963. Hoping to repair relations after the missile crisis, Khrushchev had given Castro an open-ended invitation. Walking just behind Khrushchev is Nikolai Leonov, Raúl Castro's friend at the KGB; and striding next to Castro is Soviet ambassador to Cuba and longtime Castro watcher, Aleksandr Alekseev.

Aleksandr Shelepin, chairman of the KGB, 1958–61, who as a member of the Presidium was a leading participant in the overthrow of Khrushchev in October 1964.

Shelepin's replacement as head of the KGB, Vladimir Semichastny, hinted at a coup in the summer of 1964 by warning Soviet ambassador Alekseev that he ought to be discussing Cuban affairs with Leonid Brezhnev.

late a protocol and to obtain the signatures of the participants. All members of the Presidium signed quickly, but there was "a hitch" regarding signatures from the secretaries of the Central Committee, who said that they were "not competent to decide this matter." When Ivanov reported this to Khrushchev, he was surprised but added, "Never mind, now they will sign." Khrushchev quickly arranged a personal meeting with the Central Committee secretaries concerned. In due course they signed the paper, allowing the decision to have been approved "unanimously."[44]

Following the decisions of the May 21 meeting, the Defense Ministry placed a memorandum describing the operation before the Presidium three days later. Although many of the same people were meeting for a second time on the same matter, Soviet practice necessitated that the Presidium of the Central Committee of the Communist Party of the Soviet Union have the last word on Soviet policy. Leonid Brezhnev, Aleksei Kosygin, Frol Kozlov, Anastas Mikoyan, Gennadi Voronov, Dmitri Polyanski, and Otto Kuusinen spoke up at the Presidium meeting. The only known surviving record of the meeting consists of a few notes scrawled on the back of a copy of the resolution. There it is noted that these seven men spoke in favor of the plan.[45] One at least, Polyanski, would later denounce Khrushchev for this adventurism, but at this point the best that can be said for him is that he kept his own counsel.[46]

The Presidium approved the missile proposal wholly and unanimously. Given the need to protect the security of this unusual operation, the Presidium decided to keep the only copy of the plan at the Ministry of Defense.[47] Since there was some concern that Castro would not accept this new offer, the Presidium also took the unusual step of approving the plan without confirming it. "To confirm it when approval from Fidel Castro has been received," it was written in the telegraph language of the concise diary of Presidium actions. Finally, Khrushchev chose the delegation that would present the plan to Fidel Castro. Besides Alekseev, who would be returning as ambassador-designate, and R. Rashidov, whose agricultural mission lent plausible cover to the entire enterprise, the Presidium named Marshal Sergei Biryuzov, who headed the Soviet Strategic Rocket Forces, and Colonel General Ivanov. It was decided to send them as soon as possible. May 28 and May 29 were selected as suitable dates.

Before the Soviet delegation departed for Cuba, its members were invited by Khrushchev to Zhukovka, one of his dachas outside Moscow, where they met with all of the members of the Presidium. It was a Sunday, May 27. The gathering was relaxed. Alekseev later emphasized that "a sense of unanimity reigned" at the affair. There was no evidence of doubt or even rancor at how Khrushchev and Malinovsky had gotten their way.[48] After Khrushchev was removed in 1964, the character of this party was conveniently forgotten.

The party at Khrushchev's home was idyllic. The members of the Presidium sipped tea, ate little tasteless cookies called *sushki*, and quietly discussed Biryuzov and Rashidov's important trip. Once everyone had arrived, Khrushchev stood up and gave a farewell speech to the delegation. "An attack on Cuba is being prepared," he said. "The correlation of forces is unfavorable to us, and the only way to save Cuba is to put missiles there." He revealed that his decision was founded upon an expectation of John Kennedy's reaction. Kennedy is "intelligent" and "would not set off a thermonuclear war if there were our warheads there, just as they put their warheads on missiles in Turkey." The American rockets in Turkey "are aimed at us and scare us." "Our missiles will also be aimed at the United States, even if we do not have as many of them. But if missiles will be deployed near the U.S., they will be even more afraid."[49]

Khrushchev emphasized that the Soviet missiles in Cuba would "not in any case" be used. "Every idiot can start a war, but it is impossible to win this war. . . . Therefore the missiles have one purpose—to scare them, to restrain them so that they have appreciated this business." In a word: "to give them back some of their own medicine." Khrushchev believed it very important that the Soviet scheme not be disclosed before November 6, the day of the congressional elections in the United States. After the election period, he intended to visit the United States to inform Kennedy himself. Faced with this fait accompli, Kennedy would have no alternative to accepting the missiles. Later, between November 25 and 27, Khrushchev intended to visit Cuba, where he would sign a treaty with Castro. "Tell Fidel that there is no other way out." Then the Soviet leader added for effect: "Tell him that we will do all that is necessary to guarantee him—the maintenance of forces, rockets, and equipment." But in the event that Castro did not agree to take these forms of *spetstechnika*, "we will help in other ways."

On Monday, May 28, the delegation left for Havana on a TU-114 transport plane by way of Conakry, Guinea. Thanks to the security measures that were taken, Washington did not detect the purpose of this special mission.

In Agatha Christie's popular mystery *Murder on the Orient Express*, the detective Hercule Poirot encounters a train full of individuals who had motive and opportunity to kill the wealthy American found dead in his luxury compartment. Students of the Cuban missile crisis have suggested a series of plausible explanations for Khrushchev's decision in May 1962 to break with Soviet tradition and station nuclear weapons outside of Eurasia. Some people have claimed that Khrushchev did this to paper over the USSR's strategic inferiority by doubling at a stroke the number of Soviet missiles that could hit the United States. Another explanation, especially popular in the 1980s, was that Khrushchev was genuinely concerned about the likelihood of an American invasion and thought that only a battery of medium- and intermediate-range missiles could deter Kennedy. It has also been suggested that anger at the American decision to station Jupiter missiles in Turkey provoked the impulsive Khrushchev. Finally, there are those who interpreted Khrushchev's decision as an attempt to guarantee the status quo in Cuba and to prevent any attempt by the Chinese to dislodge him from the leadership of international communism. Like the all-star cast in this Christie mystery, all of these factors are responsible for the act. Each played a part in pushing Khrushchev to take the very serious step of May 24.

Yet an answer that ascribes responsibility to everything can also be said to mean nothing. Khrushchev had his reasons. From the moment in December 1961 when Castro unexpectedly proclaimed that Cuba was a socialist country, the Kremlin expected a reaction from Washington. After Kennedy compared Cuba to Hungary in a private talk with Khrushchev's son-in-law, whatever hope there might have been that this administration might tolerate a communist country off American shores evaporated. But a concern for Cuban security alone cannot explain why the Soviets took the risk of sending their most expensive and dangerous weapons seven thousand miles to an island republic. After all, Khrushchev had known all along that Cuba was indefensible and four times in 1960–61 had expected the United States to invade the island.

May 1962 was different from October 1960 or even February 1962, when Khrushchev probably first came to believe that John F. Kennedy was prepared to invade Cuba. Two major problems for the Soviet Union—U.S.-Soviet relations and the future of cooperation with Fidel Castro—collided that month. Kennedy's decision to resume nuclear testing in April 1962 could not have come as a surprise after Moscow's decision to break the moratorium unilaterally in August 1961. But for Khrushchev, who was receiving disturbing signals from the Pentagon, Kennedy's action bespoke a newfound American arrogance. Coupled with the lack of progress in negotiations over Berlin and the evidence of American activity in Southeast Asia, the changes along the strategic plane loomed as a challenge that Khrushchev could not ignore.

Fidel Castro represented the other challenge in May 1962. Aníbal Escalante's misguided effort to marginalize Castro exposed Moscow to a backlash from the Cuban leader. Since Alekseev's arrival in Havana in the fall of 1959, Moscow had followed a two-track policy on the island. While cultivating Fidel Castro, Moscow worked to advance the careers of the influential communists in his entourage. Escalante's disgrace undermined this approach. In its wake several pro-Moscow individuals were removed from the Cuban government, and general cooperation with Moscow on foreign policy and security matters was disrupted. Just as the Caribbean was becoming a more threatening place for Castro, he seemed to be moving away from Moscow.

For these specific reasons, in the late spring of 1962, Khrushchev felt he needed a bold move to remind Washington of Soviet power, to ensure that the Kremlin received the respect it deserved from Washington. At the same time he wanted to demonstrate to Castro personally and dramatically that the Soviet Union would defend his revolution. In Khrushchev's mind—and he made this decision alone—a Soviet nuclear base in Cuba was the only way to manage these two difficult problems at once.

Anadyr

"Tell me Georgi," Robert Kennedy asked carefully, "is there anyone in the Soviet leadership who advocates a decisive clash with the United States?" The attorney general had invited Georgi Bolshakov to spend the first Sunday of June at his family home in Virginia, Hickory Hill.[1] Since Kennedy's return from his world tour at the end of February, the men had met more than a dozen times and were becoming increasingly close. The U.S. attorney general was even talking about going on a summer expedition to the Caucasus with his friend Bolshakov. This unorthodox relationship was not fully endorsed by Nikita Khrushchev, who had made a point in March of writing to President Kennedy that his new ambassador, Anatoly Dobrynin, enjoyed his "complete trust" to encourage the use of regular diplomatic communications.[2] But the personal rapport between the president's brother and the Soviet military intelligence officer was too great for the Kremlin or the White House to wish to close down the Kennedy-Bolshakov back channel.[3]

Although neither of the Kennedys knew what Khrushchev had just decided to do in Cuba, they sensed a hardening of Soviet foreign policy in the late spring of 1962. On both of President Kennedy's barometers of the superpower relationship—arms control and Berlin—the readings were not good. Khrushchev had dismissed the president's efforts at concluding a test ban treaty without any apparent hesitation. And throughout the spring, Soviet representatives were harassing Allied transports at road checkpoints and, in the case of flights to the city, along the air corridors into West Berlin. Concerned by these events, the White House had in late May canvassed the opinions of the chief American experts on the Soviet Union: Charles Bohlen, George Kennan, and Llewellyn Thompson. The request produced an interesting debate between Bohlen and Kennan, both former ambassadors to Moscow, the latter now Kennedy's envoy to Yugoslavia. The experts disagreed over the importance of Khrushchev's personality in understanding Soviet behavior. Stressing the role of Khrushchev's "frustrations," Kennan told the president that the hardening of the Soviet position was "the cumulative effect of the U-2 incident and the Cuban [Bay of Pigs] fiasco." The Soviet leader, according to Kennan, had staked his prestige on achieving a diplomatic breakthrough with the United States, especially with regard to Berlin. Moreover, Kennan sensed that Moscow had come to fear a U.S. nuclear attack.

Bohlen could not explain the apparent shift in Soviet policy, but he challenged Kennan's argument. Khrushchev was too realistic, he believed, not to understand that the chances for agreement on his terms were "pretty slim." Additionally, Bohlen thought Kennan's assertion that the Soviets feared a U.S. attack preposterous. "Surely Khrushchev cannot seriously believe that the United States plans military action against them," Bohlen wrote to the White House.[4]

The U.S. representative in Moscow, Ambassador Llewellyn Thompson, could add little to the discussion, so Robert Kennedy turned to his Russian connection in search of more information for the president. At Hickory Hill, he pushed Bolshakov to explain whether there was a new balance of power in the Kremlin. Like Charles Bohlen, the attorney general doubted that a change of heart by Khrushchev was responsible for the shift in Soviet behavior. Instead, Robert Kennedy was prepared to blame the Soviet military. "Is it really true," he asked Bolshakov, "that in the USSR the most important decisions must be accepted by a majority of votes in the government and that the military do not have a special say in these matters?"[5] Kennedy refused to believe that Khrushchev enjoyed complete control over the Soviet army.

Khrushchev, who received a copy of Bolshakov's report on the meeting, might have dismissed the entire exchange as the product of the younger Kennedy's naïveté. However, in the course of that pleasant Sunday at home, the attorney general said a number of truly astonishing things about civil-military relations in the United States that would worry Moscow. These came when Bolshakov queried him about the Pentagon's role in Washington. Do the advocates of war enjoy any special prerogatives in the American system, he asked. "In the government, no," the president's brother answered, "[b]ut among the generals in the Pentagon . . . there are such people." Bolshakov's question had disarmed Robert Kennedy. "Recently," Kennedy confided in Bolshakov, "the Chiefs [Joint Chiefs of Staff] offered the president a report in which they confirmed that the United States is currently ahead of the Soviet Union in military power and that *in extremis* it would be possible to probe the forces of the Soviet Union." Kennedy did not elaborate on what this "probe" might be. Instead, he reassured the Russian that the president "evaluated the balance of power more realistically" and that he "had decisively rejected any attempt by zealous advocates of a clash between the United States and the Soviet Union to force [him] . . . to accept their point of view."[6]

The Kennedy discussion posed a problem for Khrushchev. Besides revealing that Washington doubted the general secretary's control over the Red

Army, the conversation brought additional evidence that some in the Pentagon were advocating a preemptive war with Moscow. Was not the "probe" referred to by Robert Kennedy a euphemism for the nuclear first strike that a very good GRU agent had warned of in March? Although the report bothered him, Khrushchev did not call a meeting of the Presidium when he first read it.[7] At that moment the Soviet leader's mind was focused on events at home and in Cuba, where the Rashidov mission was still discussing the deployment of nuclear missiles with Fidel Castro. Khrushchev decided to hold off responding to Robert Kennedy's comments, at least until he knew whether the Soviet Union would get its strategic launching pad in Cuba.

An unexpected revolt in the southern city of Novocherkassk had temporarily distracted Khrushchev from international politics. A week after its momentous Cuban missile decision, the Soviet leadership had adopted a measure to raise prices on domestic staples—meat, milk, bread. The May 31 decision inspired minor acts of civil disobedience throughout the country. Men at an electrical plant in Novocherkassk reacted especially strongly to the new prices, refusing to work. The strike grew, and on June 1 Khrushchev ordered the army of the Northern Caucasian Military District and the local militia into the city. Tanks and armored personnel carriers rumbled along paths long used by the region's famous Cossack horsemen; but this time the enemy came not from the east but from within. Khrushchev, the man still remembered in Russia for reuniting hundreds of thousands of Soviet families by freeing the prisoners of Stalin's madness and closing some Siberian penal colonies, was himself not free of Lenin's and Stalin's visceral intolerance of opposition to the Soviet regime. In 1956 and 1959 he had used the Soviet military against domestic demonstrators. The military operation in Novo-cherkassk lasted three days. At least twenty-three Soviet citizens died as soldiers used live ammunition to disperse demonstrators on the street and to dislodge protesters occupying major buildings in the city. The operation was filmed for the Kremlin, but Aleksei Adzhubei found the images so upsetting that he prevented the films from being screened for his father-in-law. Khrushchev did not visit the scene, but he dispatched his deputy Frol Kozlov and Anastas Mikoyan to oversee the operation and to calm Novo-cherkassk's inhabitants.[8]

A response came from Cuba a few days after the small uprising was crushed and, unlike the sad reports from Novocherkassk, gave cause for celebration in the Kremlin. Fidel Castro had approved the missile deployments. Indeed, the Rashidov mission went so smoothly that in retrospect it seemed unreasonable to have assumed otherwise. Arriving to little fanfare on May 29, the Soviet delegation had set about its work quickly. Aleksandr Alekseev took Raúl Castro aside after the delegation came into Havana from the airport to explain that the "Engineer Petrov" in the group was actually the commander of Soviet rocket forces, Marshal Sergei S. Biryuzov, who needed to meet with Fidel Castro without delay.[9] Three hours later the Soviet delegation was shown into Castro's office.

The Cubans demonstrated at the May 29 meeting that they understood that some very significant negotiations lay ahead. "[F]or the first and only time in eight years," Alekseev recalls, "I saw the Cubans writing things down."[10] Raúl Castro sat near the Soviet delegation and transcribed the conversation into a black notebook. Hearing the delegation's presentation, Fidel Castro said that the Cuban government agreed that an armed attack on Cuba by the Americans was likely. But he refused to say whether he agreed with the Kremlin's suggestion for dealing with this problem. Castro's final response would come only after he had discussed the Soviet plan with his inner circle.[11]

The next day Fidel Castro and Raúl met with Che Guevara, Osvaldo Dorticós, and Ramiro Valdés. The Soviets did not receive a report on the nature of their discussion; nonetheless, the end result was that Cuba would welcome Soviet nuclear missiles. At his next meeting with the Kremlin's representatives, Fidel Castro explained that Havana would accept Khrushchev's offer if it could be couched in terms that did not offend Cuban pride. He did not want the Cuban people or the world to believe that the country could not defend itself. Accordingly Castro told Rashidov, Biryuzov, and Alekseev that his regime chose to interpret Khrushchev's magnanimous offer as a gesture to improve the position of the socialist camp in the international arena, not as a desperate ploy to prevent a U.S. attack. So forceful was he in explaining this interpretation of the missile deployment that Castro seemed to be setting a condition before granting final approval.[12]

Castro's quibbling over Khrushchev's motives startled the Soviets, but the delegation soon understood that the Cubans wanted the missiles too much to allow semantics to stand in the way. Whereas Fidel Castro refused to be persuaded that the Kremlin's offer was designed exclusively to promote the defense of the Cuban revolution, he also made it plain that he had no intention of rejecting the missiles over a minor difference of opinion between friends. After a few days of discussion, Castro told the Soviets to expect his brother Raúl to visit Moscow in early July to work out the practical details of an agreement.

Reports of Castro's approval pleased Khrushchev, who was not even concerned by Castro's desire to put on record that international considerations had played a role in the decision to defend Cuba with nuclear missiles. The Soviet leader understood the strategic dimension to the missile offer. Had it not been for the fact that the USSR was militarily inferior to the United States, he believed, Washington would have long ago respected its word and left a Soviet ally like Fidel Castro alone. The missiles would eliminate this strategic imbalance and protect Castro at the same time.

The Presidium met at 11:00 A.M. on June 10 to discuss the results of the mission. Besides the members and candidate members of the Presidium, Khrushchev had assembled his foreign and defense ministers, Gromyko and Malinovsky, Malinovsky's deputies from the general staff (M. V. Zakharov, A. A. Yepishev, S. S. Biryuzov, V. I. Chuikov), and Boris Ponomarev and the other secretaries of the Central Committee.[13] First Rashidov and then Biryuzov rose to report on their experiences in Cuba. They described Castro as grateful and satisfied with the Soviet plan. This is what Khrushchev had wanted. He had faced a concatenation of crises in May, a seemingly restive America, drunk with its own nuclear superiority, and an increasingly restive and insecure Fidel Castro. Now Castro, at least, seemed less of a problem. After the group discussed the "essence" of the problem of Soviet-Cuban relations, Malinovsky read from a memorandum on the missile operation prepared for him by the general staff. The Soviet armed forces recommended sending two kinds of ballistic missiles to Cuba—the R-12, which had a range of 1,050 miles, and the R-14, which could fly twice as far. Both carried nuclear warheads with the firepower of one megaton of TNT. Malinovsky specified that the armed forces would deploy twenty-four of the medium-range R-12s and sixteen of the intermediate-range R-14s, and put half that many of each in reserve.[14] The forty missiles would be taken from units in the Ukraine and European Russia, where they were deployed against European targets. Once installed in Cuba, these missiles would double the number of Soviet nuclear missiles that could reach the U.S. mainland.[15]

The plan outlined by Malinovsky had been formulated quickly. Although the idea of putting nuclear weapons in Cuba may have been discussed by Malinovsky and Khrushchev in April, serious planning at the upper echelons of the Ministry of Defense began only in early May.[16] The plan was to send a Soviet group of forces to Cuba, which would be built around five nuclear missile regiments—three with R-12s and two with R-14s. Besides the missiles, the group was to comprise four motorized regiments, two tank battalions, a MiG-21 fighter wing, forty-two Il-28 light bombers, two cruise missile regiments, some antiaircraft gun batteries, and twelve SA-2 units (with 144 launchers). Each motorized regiment had 2,500 men, and the two battalions would be outfitted with the T-55, the USSR's newest tank.[17] This structure was an innovation for the Soviet military, which had never before included ballistic missiles in an army group.[18]

The medium- and intermediate-range missiles were not the sole nuclear devices in the program outlined by Malinovsky on June 10. The two cruise missile regiments ("frontovye krylatye rakety": FKR) also carried nuclear warheads. The Defense Ministry decided to send eighty of these missiles to defend the Cuban shoreline and the region neighboring the U.S. naval base at Guantánamo. Each of these missiles had a range of about one hundred miles and a nuclear charge equivalent to between 5.6 and 12 kilotons of TNT.[19]

The details of Malinovsky's presentation make it clear that the Soviet military saw the Cuban operation as much an opportunity to project power into the Western Hemisphere as a rescue mission for Fidel Castro. In all, the plan envisaged sending 50,874 military personnel to Cuba. The Soviet navy intended to use Cuba as a base for Soviet as well as for Cuban defense. As part of the new Soviet group in Cuba, the navy decided to build a submarine base in Cuba, complete with facilities for the USSR's new ballistic missile submarines. To defend Castro's shores, the navy intended to send a mini-flotilla: two cruisers, four destroyers (two with missile launchers), and twelve "Komar" ships, each with two conventional R-15 missiles, which had a ten-mile range.[20] To patrol the East Coast of the United States, the navy planned to send a squadron of eleven submarines, including seven that carried nuclear-tipped missiles. Each submarine had three ballistic missiles (R-13s) with a one-megaton warhead. Of all of the weapon systems destined for Cuba, Soviet ballistic missile submarines were more useful as an enhancement of Soviet strategic power than as a deterrent against future U.S. actions against Castro. In terms of nuclear punch, the R-13 missiles that they carried were as powerful as the medium- or intermediate-range missiles.[21]

Following Malinovsky's reading of the memorandum, the Presidium voted unanimously to adopt the plan. With forty missiles staring at Florida, day and night, no general in the Pentagon would again dare consider a nuclear first strike against the Soviet Union or an attack on Cuba.

Khrushchev showed his pleasure at the course of events in a letter to Castro sent two days later: "Rashidov and Petrov's [Biryuzov's] group have returned from Cuba to Moscow. They have reported on all points of their meetings with you. . . . We have discussed their report, and I must tell you frankly that we are satisfied with the results of our comrades' visit with you."[22] Adding that the Soviet leadership believed "that the realization of this agreement will mean a further fortification of the victory of the Cuban revolution and of the greater success of our general affairs," Khrushchev admitted to Castro that it was not only the wish to protect Cuba but also the attempt to improve the strategic position of the USSR that had motivated the Soviet proposal to deploy nuclear missiles on Cuba.[23] Finally, Khrushchev used the letter to ask the Cubans to do what they could to accelerate the program. He expressed his hope for a quick trip to Moscow of a representative who enjoyed Castro's trust in order to work out a draft agreement for the two leaders to sign. In the meantime, so as not to lose more time, Khrushchev had already instituted "definite, practical measures"—in particular, "the imminent secret delivery of a group of our specialists for the implementation of preparatory work." He asked Castro to approve the group's visit to Cuba.[24]

The letter, which was hand-delivered the next day by the chief Soviet military representative in Cuba, Major General A. A. Dementyev, delighted Fidel Castro, who expressed an eagerness to move ahead with preparations. As Dementyev explained to Moscow, an even more enthusiastic response came from the minister of the Revolutionary Army, Raúl Castro. "After reading through the letter," the general reported, "Raúl Castro hugged me and kissed me, expressing joy at the contents of the letter."[25]

With Fidel Castro's acceptance now behind him, Khrushchev could turn to the Kennedys. He convened his colleagues again on June 14 to discuss what to do about Robert Kennedy's two-week-old comments. The Presidium decided that since "Robert Kennedy had asked about the recent worsening of relations," the Soviet government would list the reasons—four in all—for the deterioration in U.S.-Soviet relations.[26] These were typed up—probably after preparation by the Foreign Ministry, which was in charge of handling this particular use of the Bolshakov-Kennedy back channel.[27] And Bolshakov was instructed to deliver them to Kennedy:

The U.S. is responsible [for the worsening of relations] for these reasons:

a) The resumption of atmospheric testing.
b) U.S. military intervention in Southeast Asia.
c) America's NATO policy, especially measures implying the placement of the Bundeswehr [the West German army] on the road to acquiring nuclear weapons.
d) U.S. unwillingness to reach an agreement on West Berlin.[28]

To underscore its displeasure with the Kennedys, the Soviet leadership decided to deny Robert Kennedy a visa to visit the Soviet Union. "Given the aggressive policies followed by the U.S. at home and abroad," Bolshakov was also instructed to tell the attorney general that "his proposal to visit the Caucasus with Bolshakov is impossible."[29] In March, Khrushchev had canceled John F. Kennedy's appearance on Soviet television to send a personal message to the White House about his unhappiness at the resumption of U.S. nuclear testing. This time the Kremlin would penalize Robert Kennedy to make sure the president understood his annoyance at U.S. behavior. Now secure in the knowledge that he had obtained the approval of his government and Cuba to double Soviet capabilities to hit the U.S. mainland with nuclear weapons, Khrushchev may have allowed himself a feeling of confidence that these little diplomatic games would soon become a thing of the past.

A Kick under the Table

The Soviets used deception, or *maskirovka*, to cover nuclear deployments, even those occurring within the Soviet Union. The Soviet army had already successfully secretly deployed tactical, or short-range, nuclear missiles and artillery in East Germany. But the Cuban operation entailed the first attempt to move ballistic missiles outside of the Soviet Union and involved keeping the secret over 7,000 miles and on an island only 90 miles from the U.S. coastline.

The Soviet military knew that it faced an arduous task in trying to keep the secret. For more than three years, Moscow had been paying special attention to the need to hide from U.S. intelligence the level of its support to Castro, and once Soviet military shipments began arriving in 1960, the Red Army shouldered much of the burden of devising how this was to be done. As of late

1961, Soviet military technicians were routinely ordered to wear civilian clothes on the island to confuse American spies.[30] But seventy-foot-long missiles were not as easy to disguise as soldiers.

By the end of May 1962, the Soviet general staff had prepared a cover story for the Cuban operation. The deception planners chose the code name Anadyr for the operation to confuse Soviets and foreigners about the destination of the military equipment. Anadyr was the name of a river at the Pacific tip of Siberia and of a strategic air base in the same area from which Soviet bombers could reach the U.S. mainland. The Anadyr planners promoted the Siberian illusion to conceal the mission. Soldiers, nurses, and engineers called up for the Cuban expedition were to be told only that they were going to a cold region. Those requiring more precise instructions, such as the rocket engineers, could be told they were taking ICBMs to the test site on Novaya Zemlya, an Arctic island. Soviet trains carried carloads of sheepskin coats, felt boots, and Russia's trademark fur hats to loading docks in support of the Arctic cover story.[31]

The plan was impressive; but, as the Soviet military well knew, it had a major flaw. U.S. intelligence regularly flew high-altitude U-2 reconnaissance planes over Cuba, almost guaranteeing that Kennedy would discover the truth before the completion of the operation. The Soviet intelligence community had known about the U-2 flights over Cuba since at least the beginning of the year. In early February 1962, for example, the KGB had reported from Washington that CIA officials had shown the House Appropriations Committee some U-2 pictures of Czech and Polish cargo ships during a closed hearing on Soviet bloc assistance to Cuba.[32] And a little more than a month later, there was another report from Soviet intelligence sources in Washington that the United States was using U-2s to count the number of MiG jet fighters on Cuban airfields.[33] No matter what security precautions the Soviets took, if the CIA continued these flights, then at some point in September or October the missile sites would be visible to American photo interpreters.

An avid consumer of intelligence reports, Khrushchev must also have known in the spring that American U-2s flew regularly over the island. However, at the time he first conceived of sending missiles to Fidel Castro, Khrushchev and his closest advisers seemed to have dismissed the importance of the photographs that the on-board cameras could take. On at least one occasion in May, a high-ranking Soviet military officer had tried and failed to persuade the Kremlin to account for the U-2s in assessing the merits of the Cuban operation. The Soviet Union's chief military representative in Cuba, Major General A. A. Dementyev, raised this issue with Rodion Malinovsky before the Presidium conditionally approved the Anadyr plan. "It will be impossible to hide these missiles from American U-2s," Dementyev warned the Soviet defense minister. The comment provoked an angry response from Malinovsky. According to Alekseev, who was sitting nearby, the defense minister kicked Dementyev under the table to register his disapproval. The defense minister, perhaps like his patron Khrushchev, clung to the thesis that U.S. intelligence would not detect the missiles until it was too late to do anything about them.[34]

By the beginning of July, however, the Soviet leader was himself beginning to worry about when and how the Americans would find out about the Anadyr project. "So it is impossible to move these forces to Cuba secretly," Khrushchev reportedly said at a meeting with eight of his military advisers on July 7, 1962. Khrushchev had just met with Raúl Castro, who was in Moscow to negotiate the mutual defense agreement that would establish the legal structure for the deployment of the Soviet army group in Cuba. It is tempting to ascribe some responsibility for Khrushchev's sudden pessimism about the Anadyr deception to the presence of General Dementyev, who had returned to Moscow with Raúl Castro. In any case, by deciding to intervene personally to shore up the Cuban missile operation, Khrushchev showed that he was fully aware of the cover plan's basic weakness.[35]

Khrushchev ordered that defense against American U-2s become a priority in the operation. The original plan had given priority to erecting the nuclear missiles in Cuba. Khrushchev's suggestion was that the antiaircraft missiles, the fabled SA-2s, go up first so that American spy planes could be shot out of the skies before they detected the early construction of the ballistic missile sites.[36]

The intervention by the general secretary came early enough to reorganize the schedule of the shipments. The eighty-five ships destined to bring the personnel and equipment were spread among six ports from Sevastopol, in the southern Crimea, to Severomorsk, near Murmansk in the north.[37] During the loading phase, to preserve secrecy, none of the ship captains were told where their cargo was to be delivered. Each captain was given a sealed envelope to be placed in his safe, which was to be opened in the presence of the ship's political officer once at sea. The envelopes contained an order to voyage to Cuba. In their instructions the captains were also told to take all possible evasive action in the event of an attempt to board or attack their ship. Should evasive action be impossible, they were to "destroy all documents with state and military secrets," and if it appeared that the foreign group was about to seize the ship and its contents, "the captain and the head of the military echelon [on board] will have to take measures to adequately protect the personnel and to sink the ship."[38] Some of the captains were also told that in the event their ships experienced some mechanical failure on the high seas and needed help, they were to explain to any ship offering assistance that they were exporting automobiles.[39]

Even the newly named commander of the Soviet forces in Cuba had a part to play in the *maskirovka* drama. Looking at the passport prepared for him, General Issa Pliyev exclaimed, "What's this? There must be some kind of mistake." The picture was correct—it was he, all right—but the name was wrong. "I am not named Pavlov," he is said to have declared.[40]

The Presidium's choice of General Pliyev, a.k.a. "Pavlov," on July 7 to lead the Soviet group of forces was controversial. Pliyev was in the artillery, and the obvious candidate was the commander of the rocket army in the Ukraine and Belorussia, Lieutenant General Pavel Borisovich Dankevich, from whose command the missile divisions earmarked for Cuba had been taken.[41] But Khrushchev wanted to discourage any outside speculation about his plans for Cuba, and the choice of someone so obviously identified with the Strategic Rocket Forces as Dankevich would have weakened the cover story for the operation in Cuba. There were other reasons for Khrushchev to choose Pliyev. He was a war hero, known to Khrushchev and friendly with Defense Minister Malinovsky, whose celebrated military career stretched back to the Russian civil war. More recently, as commander of the Northern Caucasian Military District, Pliyev had caught Khrushchev's eye by effectively carrying out the awful duty of putting down the riots in Novocherkassk. Khrushchev felt he could trust this man and exercised his prerogative by putting Pliyev in charge of the Soviet contingent planned for Cuba.[42]

The general staff ordered Pliyev to fly to Cuba on July 10 as the head of a survey expedition. Chairman Khrushchev had just approved the number of nuclear missiles and the size of the accompanying detachments; but the plan had been thrown together in such a rush that no one had chosen the places in Cuba where all of this might be deployed.[43] Accordingly Moscow wanted Pliyev to work fast. His list of fourteen instructions began with the exhortation to report by "ciphered telegram" by July 15 the names of the Cuban ports where the equipment could be off-loaded. The Ministry of the Marine was in a hurry to complete the instructions for Soviet ship captains.[44]

Khrushchev's Efforts to Keep the Secret

As Soviet merchant ships stuffed with soldiers and military equipment began to leave port, the Anadyr operation entered a very vulnerable phase. Between mid-July and late September, when the SA-2s air defense missiles might be operational on Cuba, the movement of a 50,000-man Soviet group of forces across the Atlantic and its deployment in the Caribbean would take place in the open, with little camouflage. In late July, Khrushchev did what little he could to delay the discovery of Anadyr by the White House. For only the second time since Georgi Bolshakov began to meet with Robert Kennedy in 1961, the Kremlin decided to use the channel to propose an initiative.[45] Khrushchev could not get John Kennedy to stop sending U-2s over Cuba; but he might be able to deter him from using reconnaissance planes to photograph the cargoes on the ships making their way to Cuba. Describing U.S. overhead reconnaissance in international waters as "harassment," the Soviet government sent a request through Bolshakov in July 1962 that for the sake of better relations these flights be stopped.[46]

Berlin, and not Cuba, was foremost in President Kennedy's mind in late July when the attorney general relayed the message from Moscow. In less than four months congressional elections would be held in the United States, and Kennedy did not want any surprises from Khrushchev to undermine his reputation for solid stewardship in foreign policy. West Berlin was the place, Kennedy believed, where the Kremlin was most likely to cause trouble. As Press Secretary Pierre Salinger explained to a KGB source that summer, "even a minor retreat of the [U.S.] government from its present position [on West Berlin] would be used by the Republican Party in the election campaign."[47]

John Kennedy missed the significance of Khrushchev's interest in reducing U.S. intelligence collection on Soviet shipping. He thought only about how he could turn the Kremlin's request to his advantage. Deciding to alter the rules of the Bolshakov back channel, the president invited his brother to meet Bolshakov at the White House on July 30 so that he too could participate.[48] Kennedy was prepared to order a halt in U.S. reconnaissance over open waters; but in return he wanted the Soviets to promise to put, in his words, the Berlin issue "on ice."

Initially Khrushchev's ploy seemed to have worked. In early August the Presidium authorized Bolshakov to tell the Kennedys, "N. S. Khrushchev is satisfied with the president's order to curtail U.S. planes' inspections of Soviet ships in open waters." Yet the Soviet leader did not believe that he had to appease Kennedy in Berlin to achieve his aims in Cuba. Berlin still stuck in his craw, and Kennedy's remark about keeping the matter "on ice" suggested that the Soviets were the guilty party in the dispute. Along with the instruction to thank Kennedy for grounding the reconnaissance aircraft, Khrushchev had Bolshakov convey to the White House that he "would like to understand what John F. Kennedy means by 'placing the Berlin question on ice.' "[49]

Arms control was the only dimension of the superpower relationship that Khrushchev was prepared to mention to calm Kennedy's nerves before the missiles were operational in Cuba. In August the Kremlin told Bolshakov to speak to the Kennedys about the test ban issue. This was not straight deception; but it was not straight negotiating either. The Kremlin had no new positions to offer, nor had any indications reached Moscow of a softening in the U.S. position. But Moscow instructed Georgi Bolshakov to tell Robert Kennedy for "John F. Kennedy personally," "[W]e must work harder to achieve a test ban."[50] This might keep the level of suspicion in the White House reduced for a while.

Over the course of the summer, Fidel Castro encountered Khrushchev's caution and could not understand it. In mid-August he sent word to Moscow that he was no longer happy with the draft of the Soviet-Cuban defense pact that his brother had brought home in mid-July. "While the people of Cuba would approve of your [the Soviet] draft, in its present form it could be useful to reactionary propaganda."[51] Nevertheless, Castro was eager to disclose to the world the existence of a defense pact with Moscow and wanted to have Khrushchev sign a new draft before the end of the month. He suggested sending Che Guevara and Emilio Aragonés to Moscow at the end of the month to explain not only why this new draft was better but why Castro believed that the Cuban people were "psychologically prepared" for the mutual defense treaty with the Soviet Union. Khrushchev welcomed Che and Aragonés but poured cold water on Castro's plans to make any defense agreement public. Castro's activism contrasted sharply with Khrushchev's own sense of the situation. Given Kennedy's wish to keep the principal U.S.-Soviet issues "on ice" until the congressional elections and the likelihood that Washington would detect the missiles once they arrived in Cuba, Khrushchev did not want to give him an additional development in Cuba to complain about.[52]

A week after informing the Kremlin that he wanted to revise the Soviet-Cuban defense agreement, Fidel Castro and his brother Raúl ironically gave Khrushchev an additional argument for remaining quiet. Cuban security had intercepted a large number of radio reports from agents near Cuban ports. These reports detailed the movement of Soviet soldiers and matériel throughout the island. Although the Castros promised to take all preventive measures necessary, this information caused concern in Moscow.[53] On August 15 a spy operating in the township of Torriente reported the following to American representatives:

> Russian servicemen are located also in Banya-Honda, San Antonio, San Julian, Isabel Rubio. In Torriente they built three barracks and occupied all buildings formerly used as correctional camps for juvenile offenders. The Russians have ordered all inhabitants within a 2-km radius of Torriente to leave their homes, crops and possessions. More than 100 crates have been delivered to this region for the sake of building a missile base.[54]

Havana and Moscow knew that in terms of its most important nugget, the location of a missile base, this intelligence was wrong. The nearest planned missile site was over three hundred miles from Torriente, and the first missiles were still in Russia. But so far as the Kremlin was concerned, this was irrelevant. What mattered was how Washington would react when it received this information. If the channels monitored by the Cubans were providing this kind of information, what might other, better intelligence sources be telling Kennedy?

Paradoxically, the realization that Washington might very soon detect the missile operation did not produce unmitigated gloom in the Kremlin. Coincidentally the Kremlin detected increased activity at U.S. intermediate-range missile installations in Turkey in midsummer of 1962. The juxtaposition of these activities with the Soviet attempt to create similar bases in Cuba gave some cause for renewed hope that John Kennedy might interpret the R-12s and R-14s as legitimate forms of defense. On July 17 the chairman of the KGB, Vladimir Semichastny, reported to Andrei Gromyko, the foreign minister, that there were seventeen Jupiter intermediate-range missiles in Turkey.[55]

At about the same time Soviet intelligence warned the leadership of the Soviet republic of Georgia and the Red Army that the American missiles along
the Turkish coast were nearly operational.[56] Opting not to use these reports
against the United States in the UN, the Soviet Union held on to them for
later use in an international debate over its missiles in Cuba.

In Soviet eyes the Jupiters legitimated the missiles in Cuba.[57] In the court of
world opinion, there was no difference between U.S. missiles stationed in Turkey and pointed at Moscow and Soviet missiles pointed at Washington, D.C.,
from Cuba. And the Kremlin believed it not out of the question that Kennedy
would feel the same way. "We expected him to swallow the missiles," recalls
Semichastny, "as we accepted the missiles in Turkey."[58]

When Castro's representatives, Emilio Aragonés and Che Guevara, came to
Moscow at the end of August, they discovered a mixture of pessimism and bravado associated with the missile gamble. There was a growing consensus in
the Soviet government that even if the United States learned about the missiles before they were operational, Anadyr would succeed because John
Kennedy would swallow whatever he found in Cuba. Additional information
from confidential sources in the United States had strengthened the image of
an American president who was more concerned with Berlin and the congressional elections and was not about to reopen the debate in his own government over using military forces in Cuba.[59] Even if Kennedy had time to react
to the missiles before they were fully operational, he would not do anything
about them.

Khrushchev's defense minister, Malinovsky, reflected this confidence when
he greeted the Cuban delegation. "You don't have to worry," he told Aragonés
and Guevara; "there will be no big reaction from the U.S. side. And if there is
a problem, we will send the Baltic fleet." In fact, the Soviet navy expected to
move an impressive surface and submarine power into the Caribbean anyway.
Malinovsky was proud of the progress of the maritime operation so far and
could hardly hide his enthusiasm.[60]

Despite the confidence of some others in Moscow, Khrushchev resisted
abandoning the attempt to keep Anadyr a secret. At his meeting with Castro's
representatives on August 30, he argued against publishing the just-renegoti-
ated defense pact. The Kremlin would agree only to a public communiqué
that reaffirmed the Soviet Union's support for Cuban independence.
Khrushchev disagreed with Castro over what it would take to deter a U.S. invasion. Whereas the Cuban leader believed that a defense pact with Moscow
alone would be sufficient, Khrushchev thought Washington understood only
the language of nuclear weapons.[61] But with Khrushchev now expecting the
Anadyr program to be exposed, it seems the Kremlin wished to keep the entire
text a secret for as long as possible, so as not to add to the pressures on
Kennedy to act before the Soviet missiles were operational.

Khrushchev entered a very tense period of waiting. Would the U.S. president tolerate these missiles? After all, this is what Khrushchev had to do with

the missiles in Turkey. It was high time, as Khrushchev often said, that the United States experienced the psychological costs of mutual deterrence. A realist in spite of these hopes, Khrushchev knew that the answer to the question "What will Kennedy do?" was complicated by the nature of the American political system. Kennedy might even understand the logic of accepting the Cuban missiles, but he would almost certainly face determined opposition from "reactionary forces" at the Pentagon and in the Republican Party. Khrushchev found American democracy dismaying, not understanding how the system could function with raucous debates on issues of national security by such "fools," as he called them, in the U.S. Congress. "They should be gotten rid of," he advised one American visitor.[62] Those congressmen and the U.S. military, he feared, were not likely to accept equality of threat, especially in the American hemisphere. Not optimistic about keeping Anadyr a secret for long, Khrushchev had to pin his hopes on Kennedy's demonstrating the strength to control them.

Before the summer ended, Khrushchev made some final efforts to influence how Kennedy responded to the missiles. He instructed Anatoly Dobrynin to tell the White House, "[N]othing will be undertaken before the American Congressional elections that could complicate the international situation or aggravate the tension in the relations between our two countries."[63] And Khrushchev summoned Georgi Bolshakov, who had returned to the USSR in August for his summer vacation. "Do you believe that Kennedy will invade Cuba?" asked Khrushchev. "I told him that Kennedy was under extreme pressure," Bolshakov recalled, "but I felt sure the president would seek a peaceful compromise." Not sure of this himself, Khrushchev instructed Bolshakov to visit Robert Kennedy and explain that the Soviet Union was placing defensive weapons in Cuba.[64]

It had been a hard summer for Khrushchev. His confidence in the possibility of changing the military balance in the Western Hemisphere was replaced with anxiety and caution. Yet he decided not to alter his vacation plans. He intended to enjoy the tail end of August on the Black Sea at a government dacha in Pitsunda, Georgia. Even if his expectation that Kennedy would accept what he saw on the U-2 photographs of Cuba turned out to be a pipe dream, Khrushchev hoped for some warning before the Americans took any drastic action against Cuba.

"Now We Can Swat Your Ass"

John McCone's Crusade

Washington did not expect dozens of Soviet freighters to be speeding toward Cuba with military equipment in August 1962. Neither Moscow nor Havana had said anything lately about U.S. activities; nor had Khrushchev signaled through Bolshakov and or Ambassador Dobrynin any increased impatience with Kennedy's policy toward Castro.[1] However, a stream of reports to Washington that month indicated that Moscow had sent an impressive commercial armada to the New World.

With the help of other NATO navies and intelligence services, and in spite of President Kennedy's promise to the Kremlin to stop spying on Soviet shipping, the U.S. Navy maintained a close watch on these ships from the moment they left Soviet waters. Typical was the surveillance over the Soviet passenger ship *Khabarovsk*. On August 16, it was photographed by a NATO plane rounding the Danish peninsula. Arkady F. Shorokhov, a political commissar on board the ship, recalls that when the plane was spotted, the men tried to create the impression of a spontaneous deck party. They put out tables and invited the female nurses below to come above deck and dance. When the ship later passed the Azores the ruse was repeated, this time for the benefit of a curious U.S. reconnaissance plane.[2]

Photographs of a flotilla of dancing Russians heading for the Caribbean did not spread mirth in the Kennedy administration. August was the month that Edward Lansdale, Robert Kennedy, and the Special Group (Augmented) had set aside for a review of Mongoose. The information about the unusual level of Soviet shipping increased the frustration of those officials who had been working to remove Castro from office since John F. Kennedy's inauguration.

The CIA's frustration was expressed as veiled criticism of the White House's handling of Cuba. John McCone and his assistants did not try to hide their belief that the U.S. government was no closer to overthrowing Castro in August 1962 than it had been in 1961. Since early in the Mongoose process, the leadership of the CIA had warned the White House that it was unrealistic to expect an indigenous uprising to succeed in Cuba in 1962. Three times CIA analysts had concluded that apathy was the dominant characteristic of the Cuban people. Castro enjoyed the fervent support of maybe 20 percent of the population. Most of the rest of the Cuban people were too afraid or too accepting of their lot to oppose the regime. The best the analysts or the covert operators were prepared to promise was civil unrest in 1963. And even this prediction came with the assessment that any likely uprising was doomed to be crushed in a few days.[3]

With new evidence that the Soviets were upping their investment in the island, McCone pressed harder for high-level approval for a more dramatic approach to the Castro problem. In the spring he had bluntly told Robert Kennedy and the rest of the administration's Cuba team that if the president wanted to remove Castro, he would have to use the U.S. military.[4] President Kennedy had not liked that advice and pushed instead to use propaganda, sabotage, and defections to drive a wedge between the communists around Castro and the noncommunist left.[5] McCone never thought that this would be enough; and now that the Soviets seemed to be the ones making the dramatic military commitment to Cuba, he sought to try once more to convince the White House that it would have to take risks to remove Fidel Castro.

McCone's greatest fear was that if the White House did not act, the Soviets might turn Cuba into a ballistic missile facility. As the president's chief adviser on intelligence matters, McCone knew better than anyone else that hard evidence of missiles in Cuba just did not exist in August 1962. He had been after that information for weeks. Yet deductive logic predicted Soviet missiles in Cuba. The Soviets trailed the United States in the arms race, and McCone knew they were having a hard time building the ICBMs required to catch up. If Moscow was worried about lagging behind the United States in nuclear firepower, then Cuba was a tempting place to deploy medium-range missiles to plug the gap temporarily.

McCone was very comfortable in the role of John Kennedy's nuclear Cassandra. Since Russia ended America's monopoly in atomic weaponry in 1949, he had been a highly placed advocate for U.S. strategic superiority. In 1950, as the undersecretary of the air force, he had circulated a memorandum calling for a second Manhattan Project to build the "super," the hydrogen bomb.[6] At the time of the outbreak of the Korean War, McCone belonged to a group of mid-level officials who feared that Truman's devotion to balanced budgets threatened U.S. national security.[7] A lifelong Republican, he benefited from the change in administrations in 1953. Selected by Eisenhower to be chairman of the Atomic Energy Commission (AEC), McCone became the U.S. government's nuclear czar. When the Soviets shot Sputnik into the sky in 1957, McCone warned Eisenhower that U.S. strategic inferiority was a real possibility and passed on to him a copy of the 1950 memorandum to Truman. Liking what he read, Eisenhower asked the AEC chairman to update his recommendations for a second Manhattan Project. McCone responded with a call for centralization of the U.S. military's nuclear development program under the Defense Department.[8] An advocate of more and better nuclear weapons, he was suspicious of arms control. Before leaving office in 1961, he threw up every obstacle he could conceive of to discourage Eisenhower from agreeing to a nuclear test ban treaty with Moscow.[9]

On August 10, 1962, at a Special Group (Augmented) meeting, McCone raised the possibility that the Soviets might be in the process of deploying nuclear missiles to Cuba. General Maxwell Taylor, the chairman of the Joint Chiefs of Staff, later recalled that McCone articulated what a few of Kennedy's advisers had been thinking about Soviet intentions.[10] Not yet forceful in stating this position, McCone issued only a general warning to his colleagues. "Continuing Soviet aid and technical assistance," he asserted, "will present the United States with a more formidable problem in the future than it now confronts or has confronted in the past." McCone wanted only to plant the idea that this "more formidable problem" could be Soviet nuclear-tipped missiles ninety miles off Miami.

General Lansdale had called this meeting of Kennedy's covert-operations advisory group to discuss phase two of the Mongoose program. In light of the intelligence on Soviet shipping, Lansdale also sensed a need to accelerate covert action against Havana. Knowing the preferences of his boss in the White House, however, he had drafted a plan that did not envision using the U.S. Marines to remove Castro. Before the meeting he had circulated a proposal, called "stepped-up Course B," designed to "exert all possible diplomatic, economic, psychological, and other overt pressures to overthrow the Castro Communist regime, without overt employment of U.S. military."[11]

McCone may have been unsure whether the Soviets were indeed putting missiles on Cuba; but he was convinced the U.S. would have to use military force against Cuba before the island became impregnable. Drawing on the West's painful experience of helplessly watching the Hungarian freedom fighters die in 1956, McCone warned that the "stepped-up plan" might lead to an uprising in Cuba that would turn into a "Hungary-type blood bath" if the United States did not intervene.

On the opposite side of the argument from McCone were the secretaries of defense and state, Robert McNamara and Dean Rusk, who raised doubts about the wisdom of any dramatic measures at this time. McNamara worried that an expansion of intelligence assets in Cuba was bound to lead to one or two arrests that would "hurt the U.S. in the eyes of world opinion." Rusk still held out hope that Castro could be managed if he was split off from the old-line communists. The secretary of state, who may have been told of the Kennedys' recent discussions with Georgi Bolshakov, also had an eye on developments in Berlin and worried that the Soviets would pounce on any provocative act in the Caribbean as an excuse to sign a peace treaty with East Germany and shut down the West's access to the former German capital.

Despite the reservations of Rusk and McNamara and the opposition of McCone, the Special Group decided that the CIA should draw up a plan that stressed more economic sabotage and political action.[12] One covert operation that it considered and rejected was the assassination of Fidel Castro. The chief of the CIA's Task Force W (the Cuba Task Force), William King Harvey, later testified before the Church committee in 1975 that McNamara had recommended to the Special Group that it "consider the elimination or assassination of Fidel."[13] McCone and Harvey were appalled that anyone would raise this taboo subject before the Special Group. McCone was morally opposed to assassination. "If I got myself involved in something like this," he told Harvey, "I might end up getting myself excommunicated."[14]

Over the next two weeks McCone collected more information on Soviet military shipments to Cuba. He reported to Kennedy's inner circle that since July the CIA had detected thirty-eight different shipments of Soviet military assistance headed for Cuba, most of which had already been unloaded on the island. The CIA had received sixty reports, most from Opa Locka, their debriefing center south of Miami. At Opa Locka Cuban refugees were interviewed about what they had seen, and this information was cataloged. The picture emerging from these reports was of the arrival of between 4,000 and 6,000 Soviet bloc personnel, the majority of them technicians but with some suspected military personnel. McCone emphasized that there was "no evidence of organized Soviet military units." Cargo was removed from the ships under conditions of maximum security. In some cases trucks had been lowered into the hold of a ship, loaded, and then removed with the payload covered by a tarpaulin. CIA spies were able to report the length of the loads but nothing more.[15]

As this information poured in, McCone again tried to persuade the president to consider seriously using military force against Castro. In an "Eyes Only" memorandum for the president, McCone wrote on August 21 that "more aggressive action is indicated than any heretofore considered." He repudiated the Special Group's strategy: "Modified plan (b) will contribute importantly to our intelligence gathering and will impede Castro's regime's economic progress but will not be sufficient to frustrate the regime's progress in view of the evidences of substantial Soviet technical assistance."[16] Instead, he recommended the preparation of an uprising followed by the "instantaneous commitment of sufficient armed forces to occupy the country, destroy the regime, free the people."[17]

This crusade to change Kennedy's Cuban policy came at a personally awkward time for the sixty-seven-year-old director of the CIA. McCone, who had lost his first wife to cancer within a month of becoming director, was very much in love with Theiline McGee Pigott, a wealthy Seattle widow. McCone and Pigott were due to get married at the end of August, and a honeymoon on the

French Riviera was planned. If he wished to overcome the administration's present tendency to underplay events on Cuba without disappointing his new wife, he would have to make forceful presentations at the highest level in a short period of time.

When Kennedy's top foreign policy advisers gathered in the secretary of state's office on August 21 to reassess the Cuban situation, McCone's words were greeted with little enthusiasm. They raised awkward questions. What could the United States do if the Soviets exploited their Latin satellite as a missile base? Most of the men around the table felt that the United States was too vulnerable to respond. McGeorge Bundy, who spoke for the White House, and Secretary of State Dean Rusk warned that the Soviet would retaliate against a U.S. ally if Washington took drastic action against Cuba.[18] A naval blockade against Cuba might lead to a Berlin crisis like the one in 1948–49, when Stalin closed the land links to West Berlin. Worse still, a U.S. military action against missile bases in Cuba might lead to a copycat response against NATO bases in Turkey and Italy.

Robert Kennedy was the only official to support McCone's call for removing the existing restraints on administration policy. Like McCone, he wanted the president to authorize the use of force against Cuba; but he believed this should come in response to a Cuban attack. Thinking of ways to compel Castro to make the first move against the United States, Kennedy prompted the group to consider "the feasibility of provoking an action against Guantánamo which would permit us to retaliate, or involving a third country in some way."[19] Accordingly, he advocated removing the ban on Mongoose activities directed from Guantánamo. But despite this energetic intervention by the attorney general, McCone's effort produced no change in policy.

On the next day, August 22, McCone met the president in the presence of the chairman of the JCS to try to alter the outcome of the meeting in Rusk's office. Kennedy did not really need to hear McCone's presentation; he had already been told by Bundy or his brother the positions taken at the previous day's meeting. He knew that some of his advisers advocated a stepped-up covert-action program against Castro and that others, especially his brother and McCone, wanted to go even further. Kennedy was not yet ready to make a decision and told McCone that he wanted to reassemble the group, so that he could hear its arguments himself.[20]

Thousands of miles away the Soviets took a step in Berlin that complicated McCone's efforts to force the administration to focus on Cuba. On August 22 the Soviets abolished the post of Soviet commandant in Berlin. It seemed to the U.S. mission in Berlin like "a long step in the direction in which they have been moving for some time."[21] The concern shared by most of Kennedy's advisers was that Khrushchev would choose this moment to act on his four-year-old threat to sign a peace treaty with the East Germans, ending all Soviet rights in East Berlin and calling on NATO to do the same in West Berlin. As the *Economist* editorialized in late August, there was no chess piece more significant to the United States than Berlin.[22] On August 23 Bundy wrote to Ted Sorensen, Kennedy's special counsel, that Berlin was the main problem again: "The Berlin Crisis has warmed up a lot in recent weeks and looks as if it is getting worse."[23] That same day a meeting of the Berlin task force was called to present the president with options and to keep him informed of the latest developments.

August 23 was also the last chance McCone had to change the president's mind before leaving on his honeymoon. Kennedy gathered his closest foreign affairs advisers to discuss McCone's concerns. Less confident than before that McCone was wrong, he wanted to know whether U.S. intelligence would be able to detect Soviet ballistic missiles, if there were any in Cuba. Could the CIA's photoanalysts distinguish between a surface-to-air missile, like the Soviet SA-2, and a surface-to-surface missile that carried a nuclear warhead, he wondered. McCone, who wanted the president to focus on Cuba, gave the most pessimistic answer. He said that the United States could probably not differentiate between an SA-2 and a 350-mile ballistic missile. Seconding this gloomy picture, McNamara added that "portable ground missiles could not be located under any circumstances."[24]

Kennedy crossed a threshold during the course of this discussion. Although he still doubted that Moscow would put nuclear weapons on Cuba, he spoke as if he had made up his mind to use force against those missiles in the event Khrushchev tried. After McCone and McNamara explained the limits on what the United States could know about events in Cuba, Kennedy asked the group to consider the limits on what the country should do to Soviet missile sites on the island. Would an air strike be enough? Was an invasion necessary; or, conversely, could the sites be destroyed by sabotage? On August 23 there seemed to be no doubt in Kennedy's mind that he could never accept Soviet nuclear missiles in Cuba.

Although pleased to see that Kennedy was taking the threat of a Soviet missile base in Cuba seriously, McCone could only be disappointed by the manner in which Kennedy chose to act.[25] Instead of seizing this last opportunity to take Cuba from Castro before the Soviets put missiles there, Kennedy was looking for a way to deter the Soviets from trying to put missiles in Cuba. He raised the possibility of deterring Khrushchev with a presidential statement. In 1950 Truman's secretary of state Dean Acheson had encouraged Stalin to give his okay to the North Koreans to invade the South by stating that the defense of Korea was no longer a vital U.S. interest. A decade later Kennedy hoped that a clear statement of vital U.S. interests in the Caribbean would stop Stalin's successor from concluding that he could act with impunity in Cuba.

After the meeting McCone took Robert Kennedy aside and repeated the main theme of his campaign. He considered the younger Kennedy a hothead but appreciated his support for taking risks in Cuba. McCone hoped that in his own absence Robert Kennedy would keep up the pressure on the White House to deal decisively with Castro. In the course of the just-concluded meeting, McCone had tried to find ways to bolster the president's confidence that the United States could act against Castro without suffering irreparable damage elsewhere in the world. McCone had even suggested that the United States pull its Jupiter missiles out of Turkey so that they would not pose such an inviting target for Soviet vengeance. Forget Berlin and Turkey for the moment, he was saying; Khrushchev's principal challenge would be in the Caribbean. "[I]n my opinion," the frustrated Cold Warrior told the attorney general, "Cuba was the key to all of Latin America, if Cuba succeeds, we can expect all of Latin America to fall."[26]

McCone left for Paris the next day, the review that he had inspired having produced no new policy. With the possible exception of the attorney general, John Kennedy's closest advisers stuck to the view that Khrushchev would have to be a fool—which he manifestly was not—to attempt to put missiles in Cuba. And for the moment the president agreed with them.

Kennedy's Statement

As Khrushchev had feared, intelligence gathered by U-2 aircraft played a decisive role in shaping Kennedy's response to Soviet activities in Cuba. On August 29 a U-2 flying out of Texas found eight SA-2 missile sites that were only a week or two away from being operational. The progress in Cuban defenses since the last U-2 mission, on August 5, was ominous. None of the Soviet Union's most sophisticated air defense units had been detected on the earlier mission; but now the entire western third of the island was completely defended, and fragmentary evidence suggested that the Soviets were installing another sixteen SA-2 sites elsewhere in Cuba. Soon each new U-2 flight over Cuba would risk being shot down.

"[P]ut it back in the box and nail it shut," President Kennedy told McCone's stand-in at the CIA, when he received the readout of the August 29 mission two days later. Kennedy wanted this information to be strictly controlled. "How many people know about it?" he asked the CIA's deputy director, Marshall Carter. Kennedy did not even want the information to be shared with the working analysts at the CIA, for fear of leaks. The honeymooning McCone and McNamara had warned that it would be difficult to differentiate between ballistic missiles and SA-2 air defense missiles on the photographs provided by the U-2s. Kennedy was pleased with the CIA assessment that the August 29 mission had turned up only SA-2s; but there was no guarantee that this interpretation would not change or that something new might not be found on the photographs. The president wanted protection against being blind-sided by a story in the *New York Times* that U.S. intelligence had found conclusive evidence of Soviet missiles on Cuba.[27]

By the end of August, Kennedy was increasingly worried about the political consequences of these developments in and around Cuba. Congressional Republicans had picked up information about the extent of the Soviet arms convoy to Cuba and were using it to criticize the administration's policy toward Castro. On August 31, Kenneth Keating, a liberal Republican senator from New York, charged the administration with willful neglect of events in Cuba. Citing reliable sources, he warned that Moscow had sent twelve hundred soldiers to the island and that there were "ominous reports" of "missile bases" under construction.[28] Keating was not the first Republican to demand an explanation of rumors of a dramatic change in Soviet activities in Cuba, but because of the precision of his charges and his energy in putting them forward, he would become the symbol of public anxiety over events in the Caribbean.[29]

The Kennedy administration was vulnerable to these criticisms, especially regarding its lack of imagination in assessing the Soviet-Cuban relationship. With hard evidence of at least a ring of sophisticated Soviet antiaircraft missiles in Cuba, Kennedy faced the real possibility that one of the key assumptions behind his Castro policy was wrong. Although his brother had warned as early as May 1961 that Moscow might one day put missiles on the island, the president had never expected the Soviet Union to try to establish a military base on Cuba. John Kennedy's opinion reflected the view of the foreign policy experts around him. The U.S. intelligence community repeatedly assured the White House that Moscow did not consider Cuba a vital interest and would neither station a significant force on the island nor send a military force in a conflict to defend Cuba.[30]

A week before the August 29 U-2 mission, the president had mused about making a statement to clarify what the United States would and would not accept in Cuba. Again he asked McGeorge Bundy and Walt Rostow to think about what he should do. A Cuban trawler's unsuccessful attack on an American reconnaissance plane on August 30 added to the sense of urgency at the White House. As Kennedy was requesting diplomatic advice, he also instructed McNamara's deputy Roswell Gilpatric to review the rules of engagement for U.S. aircraft flying near Soviet ships or over Cuba. Unlike Robert Kennedy, who dreamed of a suicidal Castro attack on a U.S. plane or the Guantánamo base, the president did not consider such incidents useful to maintaining control over the rapidly developing situation in the Caribbean.[31]

Not abandoning hope that he could prevent the establishment of a Soviet missile base in Cuba, Kennedy went on the offensive to prove to his critics inside and outside the administration that his "watch and be firm" policy toward Cuba was correct. He decided to go ahead with a public statement that indicated how much Soviet assistance had gone to Cuba and what kinds of assistance the United States would find intolerable. The statement would at once defuse charges that he did not have matters under control and send a wake-up call to Khrushchev so that he did not underestimate U.S. resolve.

After lunch on September 4 Kennedy invited eight leading Democrats from Congress and seven members of the GOP leadership to a special meeting on Cuba. Flanked by Secretary of State Rusk and Secretary of Defense McNamara, he laid out in detail what the CIA and the Pentagon had and had not been able to find on the island. The facts indicated, Kennedy emphasized, that Khrushchev was building up Cuba's defensive capability and nothing more. However annoying to the United States, this operation was not in violation of the Monroe Doctrine. If anything, it symbolized the weakness of the Castro experiment in state socialism.[32]

After apparently satisfying the congressmen, Kennedy had his press secretary, Pierre Salinger, read a presidential statement at a news conference that evening. "Information has reached this Government in the last four days from a variety of sources which established without a doubt that the Soviets have provided the Cuban Government with a number of anti-aircraft defense missiles with a slant range of twenty-five miles which are similar to early models of our Nike [antiaircraft missile system]." The White House assured the American people that the administration had the matter in hand and would "continue to make information available as fast as it [was] obtained and properly verified."[33]

In the context of revealing that the United States knew of the delivery of Soviet-made motor torpedo boats and radar, as well as the arrival of 3,500 Soviet technicians in Cuba, Kennedy's statement defined which kinds of Soviet assistance would be unacceptable. It listed five different changes to the status quo in Cuba that his government would interpret as threats to vital U.S. interests. "The gravest issues would arise," Kennedy warned, if he found evidence of organized Soviet combat troops in Cuba; Soviet military bases on the island; a violation of the 1934 U.S.-Cuban treaty guaranteeing U.S. control over Guantánamo; the presence of offensive ground-to-ground missiles; or any other "significant offensive capability." Kennedy had no idea that very soon the Soviet Union would be in violation of three of these conditions.[34]

The Pitsunda Decision

Kennedy's statement was the sign that Khrushchev had dreaded. It was probably midday on September 5 when Khrushchev, still summering on the Black Sea, received the news. The tough statement seemed to settle the question of which of the two tendencies in American foreign policy was ascendant. The Kremlin could no longer count on the young leader to "swallow" the missile base in Cuba as Khrushchev had done with the Jupiters in Turkey. The assumption that had sustained Khrushchev's confidence in July and August was wrong.

Khrushchev believed he needed a crash program to save Cuba. The U.S. military might be preparing to move against Cuba in the next few days or weeks, and as of September 5 the Soviet Union was in no position to save Castro. According to the schedule of deployments approved in July, the medium-range missiles would not be operational until mid-October, and the intermediate-range missiles would not be ready until even later, at least the end of November. Since abandoning Cuba was not an option that Khrushchev would consider at that time, he reached for a dramatic stopgap measure. He needed weapons small enough to be rushed to Cuba in a matter of days but powerful enough to stop a U.S. amphibious landing. In 1962 only tactical or battlefield nuclear weapons could meet both standards. With this in mind, Khrushchev asked Malinovsky whether tactical nuclear weapons could be flown to Cuba immediately.

The general secretary's request sent the Defense Ministry into a blur of activity. It needed to determine whether there were any Soviet planes that could transport battlefield nuclear weapons. The first Soviet military contingent to go to Cuba had flown via Conakry, Guinea. This would be the route taken by the nuclear warheads if the specifications of the airplanes were acceptable. Then there was the question of how much would be enough to stop a U.S. invasion. If there was any thought of managing the U.S. reaction to a nuclear attack, it did not appear in the staff work prepared for Khrushchev.

Khrushchev also sought more information about John F. Kennedy. By coincidence a member of Kennedy's cabinet was traveling in the Soviet Union at the time. Secretary of the Interior Stewart Udall was nearing the end of a ten-day goodwill tour of Soviet hydroelectric facilities. Udall and his wife, Lee, were frequent dinner companions of Ambassador Anatoly Dobrynin in Washington, and on one of these social evenings Udall let drop an interest in seeing the monster dam at Kuibyshev.[35] Thus Udall became the first member of Kennedy's cabinet to visit the Soviet Union.

With his departure from Russia only days away, Udall did not have any plans to meet the Soviet premier. On September 5 he flew back to Moscow following a tour of the Volga River basin, fully expecting to catch his breath there before returning to the United States the following Monday. But Khrushchev had other plans for him. Udall was told that the Soviet leader wanted to meet him. No sooner had he gotten off the plane from Volgograd than he had to board a commercial flight to Sochi, whence he was driven to Khrushchev's compound at Pitsunda.

Udall had no idea why Khrushchev had summoned him. He did have the distinction of being one of only four members of the FKBW club (For Kennedy before Wisconsin) in the cabinet.[36] But he was not part of the group that decided U.S. foreign policy. John Kennedy drew a solid line between his domestic advisers and his foreign policy advisers, with Robert Kennedy and Treasury Secretary C. Douglas Dillon the lone exceptions to this rule.[37]

Khrushchev's surprise invitation immediately created a foreign policy opportunity for Udall that Washington did not want him to pass up. There is no evidence that the White House had time to prepare him for the meeting, though Udall did get a pep talk from the U.S. embassy in Moscow. As a daily newspaper reader, Udall would have known that at the time the Soviets were emphasizing two press campaigns against the United States. In recent weeks Berlin had returned to the front pages because Moscow was unhappy over a rash of incidents along the demarcation line. And just in the last week the

Kremlin had begun protesting the violation of Soviet airspace over Sakhalin Island, in the Far East, by a stray U-2. In Udall's mind either one of these two issues might have prompted this unusual invitation.

Khrushchev met Udall in front of his retreat but did nothing to ease the American's anxiety. Khrushchev's manner was "gruff"; but the setting, at least, was pleasant. The stone main house, only a few years old, had large windows and three seaside balconies from which to take in the nice view. Khrushchev had conceived the layout of the compound in the late 1950s, after visiting his former rival Georgi M. Malenkov's dacha only a few miles away on the shore road.[38] The center of activity was a glassy pool with a removable roof, which Udall noted as being "swank by any standards," that stretched out along the sea just below the house.[39] Although he did not know how to swim, the general secretary loved to bathe and was happy bobbing around the pool in a rubber inner tube. As Khrushchev guided Udall by the pool to a conference table, the American visitor launched into a mini-presentation that he had prepared on the long trip south. The embassy had advised Udall to "establish [his] personality and convictions," so this awkward diplomat took the initiative and talked.

Khrushchev listened patiently to Udall's labored attempt to find common ground in the similarity between U.S. and Soviet river development policies. After the discussion of hydroelectricity had run its course—and Khrushchev did eventually join in—the Soviet leader turned to the reason for the meeting. The KGB's analyses and his own personal experience of Kennedy at Vienna had convinced Khrushchev that Kennedy was far from being a warmonger. But Kennedy's recent statement on Cuba was very aggressive, and Khrushchev needed to know whether Kennedy had things under control.

"President Kennedy has demonstrated his ability to lead," Udall said in defense of the president. This is not what Khrushchev had meant. Simply put, Khrushchev, who had very little knowledge of the workings of a democracy—other than it was messy, noisy, and bureaucratically incoherent—wanted to know whether domestic political considerations were turning Kennedy into a hawk.[40] What especially interested him was the role the Democratic Party would play in Kennedy's actions in Berlin and Cuba. Khrushchev knew that the Republicans would want to cause trouble for him, but now he wondered whether the Democrats were also looking for votes in the Cold War. "You can always be sure that the Democratic Party will be more liberal—(or to use your terminology, more 'socialistic') and have greater concern for the working people," said Udall, having no idea of what lay behind the Soviet leader's questions.

"As a President he has understanding, but what he lacks is courage," Khrushchev said as he launched into a blistering attack on U.S. policy toward Berlin. The Soviet Union was going to sign a peace treaty with East Germany, regardless. At issue was whether Kennedy had the "courage" to accept the Soviet position short of war. "If we and the President can agree, then there will be great opportunities for cooperation in science, technology, and outer space." But if a solution did not come voluntarily from the White House, Khrushchev swore, "We will put him in a situation where it is necessary to solve it. We will give him a choice—go to war, or sign a peace treaty."[41]

"Do you need Berlin?" Khrushchev said, playing the part of the school yard bully. "Like hell you need it." He had returned to a familiar theme. The USSR was too strong to be pushed around. Its interests deserved recognition, and where its interests were stronger than those of the United States, by the very fact of its power, Moscow should be able to dictate the resolution. "What is Berlin to the United States?" Khrushchev asked a startled and unprepared Udall.[42]

Khrushchev resented the fact that the militarily superior United States had the luxury of throwing the threat of war around whenever it felt diplomatic pressure. With Udall, Khrushchev puffed up Soviet power. "It's been a long time since you could spank us like a little boy—now we can swat your ass." He added, "So let's not talk about force; we're equally strong." Udall had not said anything about force.

After shocking the American, Khrushchev played with him: "Out of respect for your President we won't do anything until November." Then Khrushchev mischievously raised the subject of Cuba, "an area that could really lead to some unexpected consequences." He expressed resentment at the international double standard that caused his efforts to defend Cuba to be criticized when similar efforts by the United States in Japan were accepted as a matter of course. In drawing the analogy with Japan, he even broadly hinted about his future actions in Cuba. "Just recently I was reading that you have placed atomic warheads on Japanese territory, and surely this is not something the Japanese need." A little later on, Khrushchev added, "You have surrounded us with military bases," and then argued that the Soviet Union could never be sure when the hawks in the United States would employ these bases for an attack.

The meeting with Udall revealed the anxieties and much of the rationale that had prompted the Soviet leader to order missiles into Cuba. Between the lines, Khrushchev told the American cabinet secretary that the Soviet Union was tired of the imbalance between the threat experienced by the United States and that lived with from day to day by Moscow. After their discussion he and Udall went for a bob in the Black Sea. A luncheon followed, which was attended by the recently arrived Anastas Mikoyan, the Kremlin's expert on Cuba.

With Mikoyan's arrival, Udall had unknowingly witnessed one of the most important moments of the unfolding Cuban missile drama. It is likely that Mikoyan was the Kremlin official who hand-delivered the military's response to Khrushchev's questions about accelerating the delivery of nuclear warheads to Cuba. The Ministry of Defense produced only the original report for Khrushchev. No copies were made, and the report itself was handwritten by one of the generals, for fear that if typed by a secretary it might leak. The handwritten original was flown down from Moscow to Georgia for Khrushchev's approval. Udall noted Mikoyan's entrance in the late afternoon but recorded no discussion with him for President Kennedy.

After seeing his American guest off, Khrushchev was able to return to the problem of the crash program for Cuba's defense. In its report the Ministry of Defense explained that the short-range Luna missiles, with their nuclear warheads, and the newest nuclear-tipped cruise missiles, the R-11m, could go by plane.[43] Although the operation was feasible, the ministry discouraged rushing the tactical weapons to Cuba by airplane. Either the generals did not share Khrushchev's anxiety or the risk of flying nuclear weapons was too great. In light of these concerns, the Defense Ministry recommended to Khrushchev that one squadron of Il-28 light bombers, with six 8- to 12-kiloton nuclear bombs, be shipped in crates. It also recommended sending an R-11m missile brigade and between two and three divisions of Luna missiles.[44] As for the timing of these reinforcements, the ministry suggested sending the missiles and the bombers in the first half of October. The warheads would go separately on board the ship *Indigirka*, which was already supposed to take forty-five warheads for the medium-range ballistic missiles and would be leaving the Soviet Union on September 15.

Khrushchev had another American guest to see on September 7 before deciding what to do about these recommendations. Udall had helped arrange for the venerable American poet Robert Frost to visit the USSR. Frost's participation at a private dinner thrown by the Udalls for their friends the Dobrynins had sparked discussion of future poet-to-poet cultural exchanges. With the blessing of the U.S. and Soviet governments, it was decided that the eighty-eight-year-old Frost should inaugurate this new program. Unlike Udall, Frost went to Russia expecting to tell Khrushchev to his face "right off, this and that."[45] Frost confided in Udall that he had a special reason for seeing Khrushchev: he had been thinking about the bases for a peaceful rivalry—Frost did not like the term "coexistence"—and wanted to get the Soviet leader's reaction.

Frost was a huge success in Russia, meeting with Soviet literary counterparts and encountering adoring audiences for his poetry, even if in translation. But with only a few days left before his departure, it looked as if Frost would be denied his visit with Khrushchev. But then Kennedy's statement intervened, and, like Udall, Frost was simultaneously invited to Pitsunda and placed on an aircraft headed south.

It is not known when on September 7 Khrushchev sat down and penned his response to the Ministry of Defense's report; but in the course of that day he also found time to visit with the old American poet, who was not feeling up to visiting Khrushchev's celebrated pool. Frost's room had a balcony that overlooked banana and eucalyptus trees and the Black Sea. The window was open and the sun streaking in when Khrushchev arrived, nattily dressed in an olive suit and a beige shirt. Frost sat up, put his shoes on, and dropped his legs over the end of the bed.

Frost hoped to make a wise, grandfatherly intervention in the superpower conflict. He believed that peace would come when the two great powers respected each other and accepted compromise. He pressed Khrushchev to forswear "blackguarding," deception, and propaganda, all of which undermined any dialogue. To humor his sick guest, Khrushchev smiled and agreed. "You have the soul of a Poet," he said, a gentle reminder that his own concerns were real and not ideal. Frost slumped into his bed, exhausted, but exhilarated once Khrushchev had left. "He's a great man; he knows what power is and isn't afraid to take hold of it." Frost's words were prophetic.[46]

When Khrushchev returned to his dacha, he had more than the American sage's words to think about. What could Khrushchev do about his vulnerability in Cuba? None of the options open to him was particularly appealing. He could stop the missile project and face humiliation at home and abroad. Had he not argued for two months in the face of tough opposition for this program? Had he not had to persuade the Cubans that these missiles were in their interests? And now how could he back down? It was too early to reveal the missiles as a fait accompli, because the missile launchers were not ready and none of the missiles had arrived on the island. The other option was to accelerate the program so that it could be revealed sooner.

Until September 7, 1962, the Kremlin had planned to put only one kind of tactical nuclear missiles on Cuba, the coastal batteries of FKR cruise missiles. In general, tactical missiles were designed to fight wars, not to deter aggression; and Khrushchev's original idea was to protect Cuba by transforming the island into a strategic outpost. But now it seemed that the Soviet Union might have to defend Cuba. What the generals gave Khrushchev at his dacha was a list of battlefield nuclear weapons that could be moved into place quickly and yet were powerful enough to complicate any attempt by U.S. marines or paratroopers to establish a beachhead. The bulky FKR missiles, the only other powerful punch the USSR could throw in the Caribbean if the big missiles did not deter Kennedy, were still in transit. Unfortunately there is no way of knowing whether the Soviet premier experienced any angst as he considered the possible consequences of what he was doing. No state had ever used nuclear weapons in battle before. Hiroshima and Nagasaki were part of a strategic bombing campaign at the end of a war. If Kennedy decided to attack Cuba, and Khrushchev gave the green light to his commanders, the Soviet Union would be using nuclear weapons at the start of a war.

What we do know is that Khrushchev was given a couple of options by his military, including that of rejecting the plan, but he chose to put the maximum reliance on nuclear weapons. The document bears his signature where on September 7 he personally authorized the sending of six atomic bombs for the Il-28s and where he asked for Luna missiles. The Defense Ministry had suggested two or three detachments, with eight to twelve missiles. Khrushchev, betraying his concerns and his belief in the value of battlefield nuclear weapons, chose the higher figure. However, he decided not to send a regiment of R-11m cruise missiles.

Khrushchev understood the importance of the decision he had just made and took pains to maintain direct control of these special weapons. A day after he authorized the new shipment, the Ministry of Defense drafted an order permitting the Soviet commander in Cuba, General Issa Pliyev, to employ these battlefield nuclear weapons in the event that communications to Moscow were cut and a U.S.-led invasion had begun. The order required two signatures. Malinovsky's deputy, Marshal Zakharov, signed in his capacity as army chief of staff, but Malinovsky did not. Malinovsky was Khrushchev's man, selected to replace the independent-minded Marshal Georgi Zhukov in 1957. Khrushchev did not want to lose control over the decision to use nuclear weapons. The document was to sit unsigned in the files until events in Cuba warranted a change.

In the days following the presidential statement, the Kennedy administration was also edging toward a military confrontation in the Caribbean. On September 7, at the end of the day when Khrushchev signed off on the tactical weapons, the White House Press Office revealed that Kennedy had requested that 150,000 men in the U.S. Ready Reserve be ordered to active duty for twelve months. In a letter to Vice President Lyndon B. Johnson, Kennedy had submitted a draft of a bill that would expand the U.S. military to face the current international crisis. Also on September 7 the commander in chief of U.S. forces in the Atlantic, Admiral Robert Dennison, recommended to the JCS that for the next five days 113 C-130 transport planes be earmarked for an invasion of Cuba. There were two possible scenarios for an invasion. In the first case—Operational Plan 314—there would be simultaneous airborne and amphibious assaults against western Cuba and a landing at Guantánamo Bay at the eastern end of the island. The other plan, the more likely in this case, was a modified version that would send airborne units to Cuba first, with the amphibious forces coming later. CINCLANT wanted the C-130s in position because they were "invaluable for airborne operations." There was no mention that these paratroopers might be the first U.S. warriors to die in a nuclear blast.[47]

When reported to Khrushchev, the reserve call-up caused him to accelerate preparations for war with the United States. With the tactical nuclear weapons on their way to Cuba, Khrushchev tried in his own way to deter the Americans from taking any precipitate action. He authorized a statement published by TASS on September 11 that reiterated Moscow's ironclad commitment to Castro, and, to put teeth into the statement, he instructed Malinovsky to place the Soviet armed forces on a "limited alert."[48]

With these decisions Khrushchev had reasserted his control over strategy in the Caribbean while simultaneously deepening the Kremlin's nuclear com-

mitment to Fidel Castro. In the week following the decision at Pitsunda, Soviet forces were placed on "the highest state of combat readiness," while
rocket specialists loaded the freighter *Indigirka* with eighteen tactical nuclear
warheads and bombs, besides its planned cargo of forty-five strategic warheads
and thirty-six warheads for the cruise (FKR) missles.[49] Khrushchev restricted
knowledge of the *Indigirka's* movements to his inner circle.*

"We Don't Need Cuba"

Some more ominous news reached Khrushchev at the end of the month. The
September crisis was turning up evidence of widespread dissatisfaction in the
ranks of the Soviet armed forces. The army chief of staff, Zakharov, briefed
the leadership on September 20 that the GRU had reports of soldiers complaining about fighting for Cuba. "There is opposition in the various parts of
the Soviet armed forces to the TASS declaration," Zakharov reported. The opposition stemmed from a pervasive feeling that the situation around Cuba
might lead to war. One soldier was quoted as saying, "We don't need Cuba."[50]

The Defense Ministry smoothed over most of the complication introduced
into Soviet planning by the scare of early September. A few days after
Zakharov's warning of dissension in the ranks, he and Admiral Fokin, the
chief of Soviet naval operations, directed a more hopeful report to the Kremlin on the smooth implementation of the Anadyr plan. Since June 114 shipments had been dispatched to Cuba, with 94 already at their destination.
There were only another 35 to go. All loading was scheduled to be completed
by October 20, with the last shipment to reach Cuba before November 5, the
deadline established because of the impending U.S. election.[51] To improve
the security of the ships in the last phase of the maritime operation, the Defense Ministry distributed 23-millimeter guns to the commercial freighters.[52]

But Kennedy's tough stance on Cuba, especially his decision to call up an
additional 150,000 men, had forced one significant change in the Anadyr
plan. Believing that a noisy naval deployment would inevitably "attract the attention of the Whole World [which] would harm the Soviet Union," the Soviet military suggested canceling the deployment of a squadron of surface
ships, drawn from the Northern, Baltic, and Pacific fleets. Khrushchev agreed
with the recommendation but felt the need for even more caution. Fearing
that a submarine base might be inopportune at that moment, he also canceled
the deployment of a squadron of the Soviet Union's new strategic submarines.
The Hotel-class submarines carried intermediate-range nuclear missiles,
which like the land-based R-12s and R-14s would add significantly to Soviet
strategic strength. However, the submarines would be even more difficult to

---

*At 9:10 A.M. on September 17, 1962, the Ministry of Defense reported to the Presidium
member Frol Kozlov that the *Indigirka* had left for Cuba. Less than an hour later a military
officer also told Khrushchev the news. No other Kremlin leaders were briefed.

hide from U.S. intelligence than the land-based missiles. The U.S. Navy's listening posts, and those controlled by the NATO allies Great Britain and West Germany, would be able to pick up the movement of the submarines once they entered the North Sea. In light of his concern about the American reaction to a fleet of Soviet submarines moving into the North Atlantic, Khrushchev authorized the Soviet navy to send only four diesel-electric Foxtrot submarines. Each submarine carried a payload of twenty-two torpedoes, and it was decided that on all four submarines one of those torpedoes would be nuclear tipped. Scheduled to leave the Kolskii Gulf on October 1, the submarines would reach Cuba in a month.[53]

While Khrushchev acted in anticipation of a U.S. intelligence breakthrough, ironically the Kennedy administration took a step that would complicate its ability to detect the missiles. Uneasy because of the discovery of SA-2 installations in western Cuba, Dean Rusk and McGeorge Bundy believed that the United States would have to pay too high a price if there was a U-2 incident over Cuba in September. Their concerns intensified after a U-2 accidently violated Soviet airspace on August 30 and another, piloted by the Taiwan government, was shot down over the People's Republic of China on September 8. At a meeting on September 10, Rusk argued for a moratorium on flights over areas with known SA-2 sites. Marshall "Pat" Carter, representing McCone, opposed this restriction for the simple reason that the SA-2s might be in Cuba as a protective shield for something important in western Cuba. "Pat, don't you ever let up?" asked Rusk. "How do you expect me to negotiate on Berlin with all these incidents?" A petulant Robert Kennedy had no time for such hand-wringing. "What's the matter, Dean, no guts!" he said. The attorney general disagreed with both Rusk and Bundy. But the advocates of restricting U-2 flights carried the day. So long as the president remained unsure whether Khrushchev would put missiles in Cuba, he was much less willing than his brother to risk an international incident. Accordingly the CIA received instructions to fly its U-2s over international waters, limiting overflights to areas without SA-2s.[54]

As September 1962 ended, Kennedy and Khrushchev were much closer to military action than they had ever wanted to be. Since his inauguration Kennedy had believed he could remove Castro without using the marines. He and his brother had pushed the CIA to use whatever means necessary—including probably assassination—to remove the Castro brothers and Che Guevara from power. This approach had failed, and now Kennedy considered the military contingency plans that his subordinates had been polishing since the failure at the Bay of Pigs in 1961.[55] Similarly, Khrushchev had sought nonviolent means to ensure the security of his ally in the Caribbean. Anadyr was supposed to be a "containment plan," designed to scare the Pentagon into leaving Castro alone. Just as John Kennedy lost confidence in his earlier calculations of what it would take to remove Castro, so Khrushchev began to revise his stake in the events around Cuba. Neither man responded to the increased danger by revising his objectives. Instead, the White House and the Kremlin began to prepare to use military force in Cuba. Unknown to the U.S. government, for the Soviet Union, any recourse to military power in Cuba would likely entail the use of nuclear weapons.

Ex Comm

Khrushchev's decision to speed nuclear weapons to Cuba after Kennedy drew his line in September hastened the completion of the deployment of the R-12 missiles in Cuba by at least two weeks. The R-12s—or SS-4s, as they were designated by the NATO countries—had a range of approximately 1,100 nautical miles and carried a one-megaton warhead. Some 74 feet long, including a 7-foot nose cone, these missiles were mobile in that they were moved to their launch sites by 67-foot trailers. To put the power of the R-12 into perspective, one can note that Hiroshima was flattened by a blast equivalent to 14,000 tons of TNT. A single R-12 represented 1 million tons of TNT, which could be dropped on any point from Dallas, Texas, to Washington, D.C.

Ships with specially configured holds delivered all thirty-six of the R-12s, with an additional six false R-12s to deceive U.S. attack planes, by the end of September. The missiles and equipment were unloaded at three Cuban ports—Bahía Honda, Mariel, on the northern coast, and Casilda, in the south. Not built to negotiate the tight turns of Cuban town streets, the trailers shipped from the Soviet Union to transport the missiles from the three ports left a trail of downed telephone poles and mailboxes when used to move the missiles into the countryside. The R-12s, or medium-range missiles, were to be divided into three regiments, with some held in reserve. Two of the regiments were located west of Havana: the 79th at San Cristóbal and the 181st about 20 miles farther west, north of Los Palacios. The third, the 664th missile regiment, was 400 miles east of Havana, near the town of Calabazar de Sagua. Each missile regiment had two launch sites, and each launch site, in turn, comprised four launchers spread over an area of between 1 and 2.5 miles.[1]

To a generation of Americans, Mariel evokes the images of thousands of Cuban boat people fleeing from Castro's regime in the presidency of Jimmy Carter. In 1962 the port of Mariel was chosen for the deliveries of the nuclear warheads because it was near Bejucal, the place in the mountains south of Havana where the Soviet military had set up its main nuclear depot. While equidistant from the two missile complexes, Bejucal was farther from those launch sites than the equivalent nuclear storage areas in Russia. In Smolensk, for example, the nuclear warheads were housed less than 300 yards from each rocket regiment. However, security conditions associated with this first deployment outside the USSR led the Soviets to house most of the warheads in a reinforced bunker in the mountains.

The first shipment of nuclear warheads, on the Soviet freighter *Indigirka*, reached Mariel on October 4. On board were forty-five one-megaton warheads for the R-12s, twelve 2-kiloton warheads for the Luna tactical weapons, six 12-kiloton bombs for the Il-28 bombers and thirty-six 12-kiloton warheads for the cruise (FKR) missiles. In sum, the ship carried the equivalent of roughly 45,500 kilotons of TNT, over twenty times the explosive power that was dropped by Allied bombers on Germany in all of the Second World War.

Mongoose Again

Although unaware of the *Indigirka*'s cargo, Washington was nevertheless in a high state of anxiety in early October. Frustration over Cuba reached new heights in the White House. Months of discussion about contingencies for dealing with Castro and evidence of mysterious Soviet cargoes going to Cuba had taken their toll on the president. Having devoted more attention to Cuba than to any other country since January 1962, Kennedy not only was no closer to solving the Castro problem but seemed to have lost control over events in the Caribbean.

The president moved on two fronts to improve the situation. He had Robert McNamara alert the armed services on October 2 that they should start preparing for military operations against Cuba. "The President wants no military action within the next three months," McNamara told the JCS, "but he can't be sure as he does not control events." Admiral Robert Dennison, the commander of U.S. forces in the Atlantic (CINCLANT), notified his subordinate commanders to be ready by October 20 to execute an air strike on Cuba, along the lines of contingency plan 312.[2] The aircraft carrier *Independence* was ordered off the coast of northern Florida with an air group, and a Marine Corps air unit was flown to Key West. The president, who followed these military preparations carefully, was concerned that American pilots would have trouble destroying the Soviet-made SA-2s. On October 4 he encouraged McNamara to have the air force build mock-ups of Soviet SA-2 launchers to prepare pilots for their bombing runs.[3] Although he did not want to initiate an invasion, the president also wanted the U.S. armed forces to be prepared for any eventuality in Cuba. Only a few days after Admiral Dennison ordered his command to begin preparing for an air strike, CINCLANT notified his subordinates that they should also be preparing to invade Cuba.[4]

In the first week of October, Kennedy also decided to unleash his intelligence services against Cuba. On the same day that he suggested special training for US pilots who might have to fly missions over Cuba, he had his brother lecture the Special Group on the White House's disappointment with Mongoose and on how much more was expected from this covert-action program. "Nothing was moving forward," complained the attorney general, who yelled at Edward Lansdale for having accomplished so little in the year since his appointment as the White House's operational chief for Cuba.[5]

The White House wanted the intelligence community to accept responsibility for the fact that in 1962 Fidel Castro was still around to accept an offer of Soviet missiles. But John McCone, who had returned from his honeymoon, had a long memory. Considering the attorney general's charges unfair, McCone redirected the blame toward the White House. There was no "forward motion," he explained, because of a "hesitancy" in government circles to approve anything "which would involve attribution to the United States."

Robert Kennedy's yelling left no doubt that the caution McCone decried was a thing of the past. From the beginning, Mongoose had consisted largely of political action and sabotage to weaken Castro while building up domestic dissatisfaction in Cuba. The White House had wanted to "avoid noise," a euphemism for trying to hide the U.S. hand. But now there would be no holds barred. The attorney general made it clear that his brother was ready to take risks—more overflights, larger sabotage actions—to weaken Castro's Cuba before it became so strong that it could not fall.[6]

Robert Kennedy even suggested the administration would approve mining the harbors of Cuba to prevent Soviet ships from unloading their cargo. Twenty years later, when Ronald Reagan's director of the CIA got into hot water for masterminding the mining of Nicaraguan harbors, McCone recalled his opposition to this suggestion from Robert Kennedy:

> I hate to see Bill Casey and the institution to which I am devoted taking a beating in the press over the mining of the harbors in Nicaragua. I see no excuse for what they have done nor do I see any excuse for their failure to inform the Oversight Committees with greater emphasis, which apparently was not the case. I recall my refusal to permit such actions in Cuba when they were proposed by certain "gung ho" operators and this at one point brought me head on with Bobby Kennedy. But I refused to budge and he dropped the issue.[7]

The Special Group did indeed drop serious consideration of mining Havana's harbor at this meeting; but the two-month go-slow policy on U-2 and low-level overflights came to an end. Since late August, President Kennedy, with the firm backing of the State Department, had ordered caution with respect to any risky U-2 flights over known SA-2 sites in Cuba. The overwhelming concern in the White House and at the State Department had been the political fallout from losing a U-2 over Cuba at a time when Kennedy was trying to dampen concerns that something dangerous was happening there. Now the mood was different. The Special Group decided to meet again on October 9 to review plans for "complete sweeps" of the island of Cuba by U-2s, firefly drones, F-101s, or other spy planes on "low level, intermediate level and high level missions."[8] Soviet SA-2s were nearing completion; but the United States had to risk losing a U-2 to determine whether the Soviets were indeed placing missiles on the island.

A day after the tense meeting of the Special Group, Georgi Bolshakov experienced firsthand the administration's anger and frustration over Cuba. Robert Kennedy made time to see him on October 5 because Bolshakov said he had a new message from Khrushchev. Kennedy usually affected a casual, unbuttoned look with his Russian friend; but Bolshakov noticed that today the attorney general's shirt was meticulously buttoned. Nor was there any small talk about Bolshakov's vacation, which months before the men had considered taking together. Kennedy listened and took notes as Bolshakov conveyed a pledge from Khrushchev that the Soviet Union was sending only defensive weapons to Cuba. To be sure he had not missed any nuance, Kennedy asked him to repeat the key phrase in the message. "The weapons that the USSR is sending to Cuba will only be of a defensive character," said Bolshakov. "In a short while," Kennedy explained, "I will have to report this to the president."[9] Bolshakov lived to see the end of the Cold War; but he never got over his bitterness at having been used to deceive the Kennedys. He was in the dark about the Anadyr operation.[10]

Two Campaigns

While the Kennedy administration and the Soviet Union's Washington representatives drifted in a sea of uncertainty and self-doubt, Cuban leaders were flush with newfound confidence. The arrival of the first missiles and warheads delighted Castro's inner circle. At the United Nations on October 8, Cuba's president, Osvaldo Dorticós, ordinarily not noted for his bravura, vowed that Cuba could "become the starting point of a new World War." Cuban officials were bragging that they had the necessary weapons to repel a U.S. attack. "We are, I repeat," stressed Dorticós, "well equipped to defend ourselves, for . . . we can, of course, rely on our unavoidable weapons—weapons we wish we did not need and that we do not want to use."[11] This was coded language, usually employed by great powers to drape a thin veil over their nuclear bombs.

Cuban leaders repeated the same claims at home. In welcoming Dorticós back from New York, Fidel Castro vowed that Cuba was no longer vulnerable to the whims of Washington. "[T]hose times have passed," Castro boasted. "Today," he promised, "they will not be able to do that [invade] with impunity." Hinting at some new retaliatory power, Castro added, "They could begin it [an invasion] but they would not be able to end it."[12] Meanwhile, in a speech opening the University Games in Havana, Raúl Castro warned that though Cuba "cannot foretell the decisions of the feverish minds of our enemies . . . we can, calmly and sincerely, say here that Cuba, its revolution, and its people are invincible. We will repel, crush, and annihilate any attempt to set foot on our country."[13]

Dorticós and the Castros were directing their talk as much to the Cuban people as to Washington. With the deployment of the first medium-range ballistic missiles (MRBMs) in Cuba, the Cuban leadership knew it had to launch a campaign to prepare its citizens to accept this new level of Soviet assistance. Fidel Castro admitted to the Soviet ambassador, Aleksandr Alekseev, that he would play an active role. While Raúl and Dorticós spoke of Cuba's new means to protect itself, Fidel planned to use his own speeches to make sure that the Cubans understood Moscow's key role in strengthening Cuban security.[14]

As the Cubans gloated over their new power, a different campaign drew more of Kennedy's attention in Washington. On October 10 Kenneth Keating alleged on the floor of the Senate that he had evidence that six launch sites for intermediate-range missiles (IRBMs) were under construction in Cuba. Keating had been one of the administration's louder critics in August and September, accusing Kennedy of a lax approach toward Castro while charging that Cuba was likely to become a Soviet missile base. But now the senator claimed to have hard evidence proving that his fears had become reality. Neither the White House nor the CIA, however, had any conclusive evidence of IRBM or MRBM launch sites. The results of all of the U-2 flights up to that point had proven negative.

Keating's charges challenged Kennedy where he was weak. On September 4 the president had promised the American people to maintain a close watch over Cuba. But for a number of reasons this had not been as easy to accomplish as he had hoped. The U-2s had not been used to their maximum advantage over Cuba. Since late August, because of concern over the diplomatic consequences of losing a U-2 to Soviet antiaircraft fire, few photographs of western Cuba had been taken. The problem for Kennedy was not so much that an enemy in the government was leaking to Keating; it was that Keating might turn out to be right and the administration would appear to be incompetent or deceitful. Impatience was building in the White House to accelerate the reconnaissance program over Cuba.

The Shock at San Cristóbal

On October 9, as Castro in Havana was discussing with the Soviet ambassador his campaign to prepare Cubans to accept Soviet missiles, the Kennedy administration geared up for the first direct overflight of Cuba in six weeks. The Committee on Overhead Reconnaissance (COMOR), an interagency group that supervised the use of the U-2, recommended to the Special Group that U-2s photograph the area around San Cristóbal, a town in western Cuba said to be the site of suspicious activity. In the second week of September, a CIA agent in Cuba had reported that Soviet soldiers, accompanied by Peruvians and Colombians, were guarding a fifty-mile swath of territory along the main road from Havana to Pinar del Río, at the western tip of the island. The spy noted the points of the trapezoid roughly formed by the troop deployments: San Cristóbal in the southeast, San Diego de los Baños in the southwest, Consolación del Norte in the northwest, and Las Pozas in the northeast. Convinced that Soviet missiles were being moved into this area, the spy observed that there seemed be some "very secret and important work" on a farm a little southwest of San Diego de los Baños.[15]

This report had initially been viewed with suspicion in Washington. CIA analysts thought it improbable that an area of that size could be cleared.[16] The trapezoid, however, caught the eye of some people in the Defense Intelligence Agency, an organization established in 1961 by McNamara to create order out of the chaos of separate service intelligence agencies. The description of activity in a specific trapezoidal area dovetailed with eyewitness accounts from the same region of large trailer trucks, carrying tarpaulin-covered cargoes, that were knocking off telegraph poles as they negotiated tight corners in village streets.[17] When the White House lifted the restrictions on U-2 flights, COMOR decided that the first flight would fly over San Cristóbal.

With politics no longer a consideration, weather became the prime factor in delaying the U-2 flights over Cuba. The next four days were overcast. Dino Brugioni, who worked at the National Photographic Interpretation Center (NPIC), recalled that "a weather forecast of at least 75 percent of the primary area to be cloud-free was considered requisite for a successful reconnaissance mission."[18] The precondition "cloud-free" meant that there had to be clear visibility from the ground to the U-2's flying ceiling of 70,000 feet for a period lasting from twelve to twenty-four hours before the flight through the completion of the mission. It was hurricane season in the Caribbean, and this was asking a lot.[19]

On October 13 the weather report gave a green light to a U-2 mission scheduled to take off late that night. At 11:30 P.M. a U-2 piloted by Major Richard S. Heyser left Edwards Air Force Base, in California, for western Cuba. If the mission went according to plan, Heyser would be in position to photograph whatever was going on between San Cristóbal and Los Palacios at breakfast time, October 14. Given the time needed to develop and interpret the film from the flight, the policymakers could expect to know something about this mission late on Monday, October 15.

President Kennedy had a full day ahead of him on October 15. A highlight was an 11:00 A.M. meeting with one of the foremost leaders of the struggle for self-determination in the Third World, Ahmed Ben Bella of Algeria. As a senator, Kennedy had made a name for himself in foreign policy by giving a speech in 1957 in support of Algerian independence from France. "Men's lives hang in the balance," Kennedy said, quoting Woodrow Wilson; "men's hopes call upon us to say what we will do. Who shall live up to this trust? Who dares fail to try?"[20] Kennedy thought well of Ben Bella; though in recent years this support for Algeria had become a problem for him because Ben Bella insisted on embracing Fidel Castro. Though no communist, Ben Bella was a revolutionary and cared little whether he helped Marxist or non-Marxist revolutionary movements so long as they overturned what he considered imperialist regimes.

Ben Bella, who later recounted for Castro the story of this trip, used his time at the White House to probe Kennedy about his intentions toward the Caribbean republic. "In three different ways," Ben Bella recalled, "I pressed Kennedy as to whether the U.S. planned to invade Cuba." Kennedy denied any such intention, but he added that he would have no other choice if the Soviets decided to make an offensive base out of Castro's paradise or if—and this he stressed with equal determination—Castro opted to use Cuba as a springboard for the expansion of international communism in the Western Hemisphere. Kennedy surprised Ben Bella by suggesting that a Cuba that respected the status quo, which Ben Bella understood to be contrary to Castro's inclinations as well as his own, would be tolerable. At their meeting the U.S. president spoke of the possibility of reconciliation with Castro if Cuba maintained a "national communist" regime. "Do you mean by this, Mr. Kennedy, a Yugoslavia or Poland?" Ben Bella asked. "Yes," the president nodded.

Twelve hours later McGeorge Bundy, Kennedy's national security adviser, received the results of Heyser's U-2 mission. There appeared to be two 70-foot-long MRBMs at San Cristóbal. Apparently, the Soviets were not going to test Kennedy's willingness to accept a "national communist" neighbor. Bundy did not tell the president that night. He opted to allow him a good night's rest, the last he would have for some time, as it turned out. Bundy felt there was nothing the president could do about the missiles that night anyway, and he would need to be sharp the next morning. Besides Bundy and the leadership of the U.S. intelligence community, Dean Rusk and his team at State, as well as McNamara and the deputy secretary of defense, Roswell Gilpatric, received word of the U-2's discovery before going to bed on October 15.

The First Ex Comm Meeting, October 16, 1962

President Kennedy was reading the Tuesday morning newspapers in bed when McGeorge Bundy told him that a U-2 had spotted two nuclear missiles and six missile transports southwest of Havana. The news made nonsense of Khrushchev's twin promises that nothing would be done to interfere in the congressional elections and that the weapons in Cuba were all of a defensive character. Kennedy called his brother and, using a mild code, suggested that Robert speak to Bundy in his office as soon as he could. Other than Robert Kennedy, no one, not even his messenger that day, Bundy, knew the extent of the efforts Kennedy had made since even before his inauguration to lessen the tensions of the Cold War and to create a businesslike atmosphere in U.S.-Soviet relations. Over forty times the brothers had turned to the Bolshakov back channel to cajole, flatter, and deter Khrushchev. Had he not held up the Pentagon's plans to resume nuclear testing this spring to give the Kremlin one last chance at an agreement that would outlaw all nuclear tests? And what about his efforts to defuse the Berlin situation? What did any of this do for him, except make him vulnerable to Khrushchev's deception?

Kennedy wanted the devastating information from Cuba kept to as small a group as possible. He needed policy advice, but did not want to draw attention with unusual activity at the White House. The first opening on Kennedy's daily schedule for October 16 was 11:45 A.M.; so he instructed Bundy to assemble his foreign policy team from the State Department, the Pentagon, and the CIA as unobtrusively as possible for a meeting in the Cabinet Room at that time.

Kennedy did make room in his schedule to have a private talk with Charles Bohlen. Bohlen, the old Kremlin hand recently named U.S. ambassador to France, was waiting around Washington to leave for Paris. Kennedy had some tentative explanations for Khrushchev's unexpected move and wanted Bohlen's reaction. Kennedy assumed that Khrushchev had to be playing for bigger stakes than just Cuba because of the risks involved. Was the missile gambit a shortcut to nuclear parity with the United States? Or was this some kind of game of chicken to force U.S. concessions in Germany? Bohlen, who saw Kennedy just before the Cuba group meeting at noon, strengthened the president's supposition that Khrushchev had taken this enormous risk in search of grand strategic gains. Bohlen's own special concern was that Khrushchev was probably trying to use Cuba to force American concessions in Europe. Kennedy asked Bohlen to join the group discussions.[21]

We do not know what prompted President Kennedy to tape his most important conversations. For at least a year Kennedy oversaw the business of being president without the aid of listening devices in his office. But in the summer of 1962 he changed his mind—ostensibly to create records for his projected memoirs. Kennedy ordered the installation of a recording system in the Oval Office and the Cabinet Room. Kennedy opted for a manual system that he could activate at will. Switches were placed in the kneehole of his desk and at his place in the Cabinet Room.[22]

The historic nature of the first meeting of the Cuban crisis group, later to be known as the Executive Committee of the National Security Council, or Ex Comm, was evident. Kennedy flipped the switch to capture this initial gathering of the men who would help steer his thinking on what to do now that Khrushchev had put missiles in Cuba. Besides Bohlen, from the State Department came Dean Rusk, Undersecretary of State George Ball, Assistant Secretary of State for Latin America Edwin M. Martin, and Ambassador at Large Llewellyn Thompson. Robert McNamara and his deputies Roswell

Gilpatric and Paul Nitze represented the Defense Department. John McCone, away on an urgent family matter, was replaced by his deputy Marshall "Pat" Carter, and the CIA was also represented by the head of the NPIC, Arthur Lundahl, whose analysts had found the missile sites on the U-2 photographs. General Maxwell Taylor came as chairman of the JCS. Rounding out the group were McGeorge Bundy and the Kennedy speechwriter Theodore Sorensen from the White House, Treasury Secretary C. Douglas Dillon, and Robert Kennedy. Of these men, only Robert Kennedy and the president knew that this meeting was being taped. In the words of Bundy, who learned of the existence of the taping system only a decade later, it was one those "nonsharables" that the brothers kept to themselves. Knowledge of the taping system was held as closely by the Kennedy brothers as the substance of most of Robert's meetings with Bolshakov.

"This is the result of the photography taken Sunday, sir," Arthur Lundahl, who had served as Eisenhower's then Kennedy's principal briefer on photographic intelligence, laid out the bad news for the dozen men seated around the Cabinet Room table.

Kennedy wanted to be sure that the worst-case scenario that McCone and others had been confronting him with since August had turned out to be reality.

"How do you know this is a medium-range ballistic missile?"

"The length, sir," Lundahl explained.

"The what? The length?"

"The length of it. Yes."

"Is this ready to be fired?"

None of the president's advisers could tell him with any confidence whether the missiles were ready to be fired. "Do we have two weeks?" Kennedy asked again, wondering whether there was time to prepare a proper invasion of Cuba before Khrushchev could brandish any of the weapons. Maxwell Taylor could not offer any reassurance: "I don't think we'll ever know, Mr. President, these operational questions because . . . this type of missile . . . can be launched very quickly with a concealed expedience." "[E]ven today," Taylor added, "this, this one . . . area *might* be operational." Bundy then reminded the president that the U-2s had photographed only a small part of the island and that there might be other, similar sites that were operational or nearly operational.

Kennedy himself identified four possible military scenarios to end the crisis. The first was an air strike that wiped out all of the known missile sites; the second was a "general air strike" that included sorties against the Soviet MiG-21 fighter jets and all of the SA-2 sites; the third was an invasion of Cuba, which could take place only after eight days preparation; the fourth was a blockade of the island to prevent, it was hoped, the nuclear warheads and more missiles from reaching Cuba. Kennedy's early preference was a surgical air strike: "We're certainly going to do number one; we're going to take out these . . .

missiles." He repeated himself for effect: "At least we're going to do number one, so it seems to me that we don't have to wait very long. We, we ought to be making *those* preparations."

None of the nonviolent alternatives Kennedy could think of seemed likely to compel Khrushchev to remove the missile threat from Cuba. "I don't see how we could prevent further ones [missiles] from coming in by submarine," he said in reference to a possible blockade. And confronting Khrushchev with an ultimatum, Kennedy thought, could easily backfire. "[O]bviously you can't sort of announce that in four days from now you're going to take them out. They may announce within three days they're going to fire them."

Given that there seemed to be no way around using the U.S. Air Force to get the missiles out of Cuba, Kennedy turned his attention to the problem of locating the missiles quickly enough so that all of them could be knocked out before any became operational.

"How long before we get the information about the rest of the island?"

"Could take weeks, Mr. President."

"Weeks?"

"For complete coverage of a cloud-covered island."

Kennedy wanted pictures taken of the unclouded portion of the island by the next morning. "What about . . . doing that . . . tomorrow plus the clouded part doing low level?" Kennedy was spitting out that he wanted the U.S. Air Force to send reconnaissance planes to scour the rest of the island. The president, of course, got his way. "Then we should be prepared," he emphasized before adjourning this meeting, "almost any day to take those out."

Kennedy was dodging efforts by his advisers to have him concentrate on a nonmilitary exit from this crisis. "You want to be clear, Mr. President," said Bundy, playing the devil's advocate, "whether we have *definitely* decided *against* a political track." McNamara worried that the president's fixation on the air strike option might be the product of wishful thinking. He assumed that nuclear warheads were already present on the island, though invisible to U.S. intelligence. Under those conditions an air strike was folly. Kennedy indeed had doubts about his preference. Preying on his mind was Maxwell Taylor's realistic appraisal of any air strike: "It'll never be a 100 percent, Mr. President, we know." But, at that moment, he saw no other way out.

"Think You Could Do That in One Day?"

Kennedy was still turning the air strike option over in his mind when the Ex Comm met again at 6 P.M. October 16. A more elaborate reading from Heyser's U-2 mission was available, showing three missile sites, with four launchers at each one. Another U-2 had flown over Cuba on October 15, and Kennedy wanted to know when he would have its photographs. "[T]hat was supposed to have covered the whole island, was it?" he asked McCone's deputy Carter. As he had at the first Ex Comm meeting, Taylor weighed in to try to dampen Kennedy's expectations about an air strike. The JCS had met in the interim, and there was no support for an attack restricted to the launch sites and missiles alone.[23] "This is a point target, Mr. President. You're never sure of having, absolutely of getting everything down there." Kennedy had been reluctant to use force before, and the JCS sensed that the missile sites provided an opportunity to cleanse Cuba of all Soviet military hardware. "Our recommendation would be," Taylor explained, "to get complete intelligence, get all the photography we need. . . . Then look at this target system. If it really threatens the United States, then take it right out with one hard crack."

McNamara agreed with the chiefs' desire to slow the president down. But he hoped for a peaceful resolution of the crisis. Describing a blockade as an option that lay "in between the military course we began discussing a moment ago and the political course of action," he championed it as the best of a bad lot of options.

Kennedy was not persuaded. He and McNamara fundamentally disagreed over the significance of the Soviet initiative in Cuba. McNamara tended to downplay the importance of the missiles, because he doubted that there were enough of them to reverse American nuclear superiority. Less concerned with their effect on the nuclear balance, Kennedy believed the missiles posed a strategic threat because of the amount of diplomatic leverage they gave Khrushchev. Gnawing at the president was the sense that if the United States did not act quickly, Khrushchev would have locked in enough nuclear power in Cuba to acquire this leverage and to make an attack on the sites nearly suicidal. "Let's just say that . . . they get these in there and then . . . they get sufficient capacity so we can't . . . with warheads. Then you don't want to knock 'em out . . . there's too much of a gamble. Then they just begin to build up those air bases there and then put more and more. I suppose they really. . . . Then they start getting ready to squeeze us in Berlin. . . ." Summarizing his point of view, Kennedy said, "They've got enough to blow us up now anyway. . . . After all this is a political struggle as much as military."

Robert Kennedy spoke up in support of his brother's opinion that the missiles would be extremely valuable coin. Kennedy wondered whether Castro might not make new threats against Cuba's neighbors, saying, "You move troops down into that part of Venezuela, we're going to fire these missiles." The attorney general was the now strongest advocate for an invasion. He understood his brother's sensitivity toward the political impact of a U.S. reaction that was not considered commensurate to the crime. But Robert Kennedy expected Khrushchev simply to reload if he lost his first group of missiles to an American air strike. Perhaps as a way of showing how a invasion could be made internationally acceptable, Robert Kennedy brought up the quick fix that he had been advocating off and on since the Bay of Pigs disaster: "we should also think of . . . whether there is some *other* way we can get involved in this through . . . Guantanamo Bay, or something, . . . or whether there's some ship that, you know, sink the *Maine* again or something."

Something else was eating away at the Kennedy brothers. Anything less than a decisive blow would send Khrushchev the wrong signal about U.S. resolve. "It seems to me . . . my press statement was so *clear* about how we *wouldn't* do anything under these conditions and under the conditions that we would," said President Kennedy. "He must know that we're going to find out, so it seems to me he just, uh . . .," Kennedy's voice trailed off, but at Vienna in 1961 and now here he had reason to doubt whether Khrushchev respected his authority and his word. "I don't think there's any record of the Soviets ever making this direct a challenge, ever, really."

While the president worried about his own tug-of-war with Khrushchev, Robert Kennedy was nearly overcome by the sense that Castro had once again humiliated the United States. Earlier that afternoon the attorney general had met with McCone's deputy director for plans, Richard Helms, to express the "general dissatisfaction of the President" with the progress of Operation Mongoose. Complaining that in a year there had been "no acts of sabotage," Kennedy vowed that "in view of this lack of progress, he was going to give Mongoose more personal attention." For him this meant holding a Special Group meeting every morning at 9:30 until the end of the crisis.[24] The Kennedys had not completely given up their earlier goal of answering the Soviet challenge in the New World by chasing Castro from office.

By the end of this long day, President Kennedy's position had shifted a little. He was beginning to accept Taylor's and the JCS's view that a small strike might not be enough. "[I]t seems to me we have to go on the assumption that we're going to have the general—number two we called it," Kennedy said over the objections of Bundy, who had just come around to the first presidential preference for a surgical air strike. The date slated for the attack was Saturday, October 20.

McCone Returns

John McCone's personal life had been a roller coaster ride since Kennedy appointed him to the CIA. On the day the U-2 finally flew over San Cristóbal, McCone was hurriedly called to California to pick up the body of his new stepson who had died in an auto race. The CIA director, deputy Pat Carter, therefore had to stand in for McCone at the first Ex Comm meeting, on October 16. Perhaps it was better for all concerned. McCone might have been tempted to whisper, "I told you so," and the Kennedy brothers would have not been at their best in response.

Kennedy found McCone as opinionated as ever at their 9:30 A.M. meeting on October 17, when the CIA director showed up for his first missile crisis briefing. A night's rest had not changed the president's opinion that a swift air strike, possibly including Cuban airfields, would be best. McCone, however, disagreed. For the first time one of Kennedy's associates mentioned Pearl Harbor. "The situation cannot be tolerated," McCone wrote in the memorandum that he carried in to see the president, "However, the United States should not act without warning and thus be forced to live with a 'Pearl Harbor indictment' for the indefinite future." McCone suggested that the U.S. government present an ultimatum to the Soviets vowing swift military action if dismantling of the ballistic missiles did not begin in twenty-four hours. McCone shared the view of the JCS that U.S. security required the removal of all weapons that had a "dual defensive-offensive capability," meaning the Il-28s and even the MiG-21 fighters.[25]

President Kennedy also reviewed the ideas for covert action that the CIA had generated in the hours since his brother upbraided Richard Helms for the general failure of the Mongoose operation. Despite his anger at Khrushchev and Castro, Kennedy refused to approve the mining of Cuban harbors. His brother had pushed for it on October 4; but now that the Soviet Union and the United States were on the brink of war, the president did not want to do anything that might divide Latin American states against him. Kennedy, however, was willing both to take risks and to break international law if necessary to weaken Castro. He approved a grenade attack against the Chinese embassy in Havana. A Cuban recruited by the CIA claimed to have access to the roof overlooking the embassy garden. He also authorized underwater demolition attacks on Soviet bloc shipping and a hit-and-run mortar and gunfire attack on three Soviet surface-to-air missile sites. Any one of these missions could have resulted in the deaths of Russians, Chinese, or other Soviet bloc citizens.[26]

Tropical Calm before the Storm

A few hours before Kennedy received the readout on October 16 from the fateful U-2 mission over San Cristóbal, Khrushchev gathered his foreign and domestic policy team for a routine meeting of the Presidium. Cuba did come up in the meeting, because Frol Kozlov, Khrushchev's heir apparent (and the Presidium member generally deputized to follow the intelligence community), wanted to discuss the KGB's plans for operations in support of the missile deployments. All agreed that the KGB was not quite on target this time.

McCone's counterpart at the KGB, Vladimir Semichastny, had submitted an outline on October 10 of a six-point propaganda operation to coincide with the unveiling of the missiles. Semichastny suggested using the well-known Soviet writer Ilya Ehrenburg and the composer Dmitri Shostakovich to blast the United States for maintaining a "military-economic blockade" of Cuba. He proposed that an open letter be composed in French under Ehrenburg's name that could be given to Parisian intellectuals, such as Jean Paul Sartre, who had been especially sympathetic to Castro's revolution. Meanwhile, Shostakovich would be instructed to back a statement on Soviet radio and to the Western press about U.S. efforts to starve the Cuban people. "The KGB . . . suggests . . . the following measures," Semichastny wrote, "which could create a broad social movement in defense of Cuba and by which to criticize the colonialist and aggressive character of American imperialism."[27]

The operation, which was designed to raise the volume of international condemnation of U.S. policy toward Cuba, made sense to the Kremlin. But the KGB offered overt as well as covert means to achieve this, and the Presidium thought, with the final missile deployments only three weeks away, that it was risky to use Soviet icons like Ehrenburg and Shostakovich, which would draw the attention of the White House and suggest a violation of Khrushchev's pledge not to interfere with the congressional elections. Consequently, the Kremlin turned down all but one of the KGB's six points. The exception was a covert operation involving private approaches to leading West European figures who opposed the blanket extension of the U.S. embargo to European trade with Cuba. The Kremlin agreed that Soviet intelligence should encourage these selected individuals to organize a week-long boycott of U.S. products.[28]

More important to the Presidium on October 16 was Andrei Gromyko's upcoming meeting with John F. Kennedy. Gromyko was in the United States to visit the UN and had arranged a White House visit for October 18. In the eyes of the Kremlin this meeting would say much about the president's mood and might suggest whether there was a chance that Kennedy would accept the changed situation in Cuba. With all of the bulky R-12s already in Cuba, and eight of them operational, it seemed likely that the United States had detected them already. Yet Kennedy had not responded, and perhaps Gromyko would be able to determine whether he had changed his mind about their unacceptability.

The political climate in Havana in mid-October 1962 was even less tense than that in Moscow. The Castro brothers were convinced, as they had been after the war scare of October 1960, that Soviet diplomacy had defused the situation. Raúl Castro conceded to Alekseev in mid-September, following the publication of the TASS statement, that he believed the threat of U.S. intervention had passed. A month later Cuba's best friend in Africa, Ahmed Ben Bella of Algeria, confirmed this rosy interpretation of the shift in U.S. policy. Ben Bella flew to Havana directly from the United States. At dinner on October 17 he gave an expansive report on his recent meeting with Kennedy to Castro and his closest associates. "Kennedy told me," Ben Bella said, "[a]t the present time the U.S. government does not have any plans to intervene militarily in Cuba; however, if it is determined that the USSR is organizing an offensive, rather than a defensive, military base on Cuba, then the U.S. government will revise its plans and won't be able to give any guarantees about its future actions."[29]

Fidel Castro displayed a new swagger in front of Ben Bella. He was eager to discuss support for the national-liberation movements in Latin America. Although sympathetic to Castro's revolutionary spirit, Ben Bella cautioned Cuba that Algeria was in a better position to do its international duty at that time than Cuba. The Algerian leader worried that, even if a U.S. attack was unlikely in 1962, any Cuban misstep would bring the wrath of the house of Kennedy on the island in 1963. "The Cuban leadership," he told Castro, "should demonstrate enormous caution in aiding the Latin American people in their struggle for national liberation, because the United States could use this assistance against Cuba." At the dinner Fidel Castro affected indifference to his guest's advice. Instead of acknowledging the possibility of some trouble from Washington, Castro tried to enlist the Algerian in a political campaign to force the United States from Guantánamo. In the shadow of the missiles in central and western Cuba, Castro seemed to be preparing to pursue ever more ambitious goals.

IRBMs, Too?

While the Cubans congratulated themselves on the spectacular success of Moscow's nuclear gamble, the Kennedy administration was absorbing new indications that the Soviet missile base in Cuba was larger and included a more threatening missile system than earlier suspected. In one of the six U-2 runs over Cuba on October 15, the cameras had caught the telltale signs of preparations for an IRBM launching site. The SS-5, or R-14, had a range nearly twice that of the R-12 and carried the same punch. Whereas the thirty-six R-12s in Cuba were clearly terror weapons directed at U.S. population centers, the R-14s had the range to hit U.S. ICBM bases in the Midwest. In the language of the nuclear priesthood, the Soviets had equipped Cuba with a "counterforce" capability. In laymen's terms this meant that the Soviets seemed to want the ability to knock out the U.S. strategic arsenal in a first strike.

Dean Rusk expressed the sense of the group, when the Ex Comm gathered at 11 A.M. on October 18 to consider the new intelligence from Cuba. "[I]t looks now as if . . . bases are going to pop out like measles all over the world," said the secretary of state. The audacity of Operation Anadyr was becoming clear to the Kennedy administration. Khrushchev had decided—presumably sometime in the spring—to defend Castro with the best weapons in the Soviet arsenal.

Maxwell Taylor altered his advice to Kennedy in light of the new information. "Last evening," he told the group, "it was my personal belief that there were more targets than we knew of, and that it was probable that here would be more targets than we could know of at the start of any one of these strikes. The information of this morning I think simply demonstrates the validity of that conclusion of last evening."[30] Taylor said that he and the rest of the JCS no longer believed that an air strike, even a massive one, would be enough to remove the threat from Cuba. "In other words," he told a concerned President Kennedy, "we consider nothing short of a full invasion, as practical military action."

Not all of the Ex Comm reacted to the news of more missiles in Cuba by suggesting military action. Llewellyn Thompson, who had returned from Moscow in June to become a special adviser on Soviet affairs at the State Department, tried to return the group to a discussion of a naval blockade. Believing it "very highly doubtful the Russians would resist a blockade against military weapons. . . .," Thompson explained that the best hope for a peaceful solution to this crisis was an approach that combined the stern coercion of a blockade with a public demand that Moscow dismantle its missile sites in Cuba. Thompson was no dreamer. He suggested threatening to use force if Khrushchev ignored the U.S. demand. "I think we should be under no illusions that this would probably in the end lead to the same thing," he said with some resignation. "But we would do it under an entirely different posture and background, and much less danger of getting into the big war."

Kennedy considered Thompson's blockade suggestion insufficient to meet the threat in Cuba. "He could go on developing the things he's got there," said the president, referring to the fact that a blockade could do nothing about the missiles that Khrushchev had already deployed on the island. Once again, Kennedy was seconded by the attorney general, who described the blockade as "very slow death." Robert Kennedy envisioned a blockade lasting for months, with "all these people yelling and screaming, examination of Russian ships and shooting down of Russian planes that try to land there. . . ."

President Kennedy still believed he could use force effectively. He overruled concerns—especially those expressed by McNamara—that any use of force implied taking the risk of an inadvertent nuclear war. Kennedy doubted that the Soviets would react to a U.S. military strike by launching their Cuban missiles, "unless they're going to be using them from every place." He assumed that Moscow controlled the missiles and that the danger of a nuclear accident was low. In Kennedy's mind Berlin was his only achilles' heel in this crisis. He assumed that the Soviets' proportional response would be a similar action against West Berlin. Then what would he do? What could he do?

No closer to a personal or even an institutional consensus on what to do about Cuba, Kennedy and Rusk left the Cabinet Room at 5:00 P.M. to meet Andrei Gromyko in the Oval Office.

"The United States Is Not Preparing an Attack Now"

The dour Soviet foreign minister represented the Kremlin's best opportunity to assess Kennedy's mood on the eve of the successful completion of the Anadyr operation. Before coming to the White House, Gromyko had discussed the Kennedy administration with Ambassador Dobrynin and reviewed information collected by the embassy. Dobrynin, who knew nothing about the Cuban missile gamble, assured Gromyko that the United States had shelved whatever previous plans it had to invade Cuba. A shrewd observer of the American scene, the Soviet ambassador had divined that Kennedy was constrained by the expectation that in the event of a U.S. attack on Cuba, the Soviet Union would respond against a U.S. ally somewhere else. "There is no consensus as to how and where this riposte would come," Gromyko later reported to Moscow after hearing Dobrynin's views, "but it would happen—about this there is not doubt."

Entering the Oval Office in the early evening of October 18, Gromyko did not know that he was walking into a trap. He noticed that Kennedy and Rusk were more deliberate than usual. The normally taciturn Rusk was red "like a crab" and seemed to be having an unusually hard time hiding his emotions.[31] But Gromyko did not detect that the president and his secretary of state were keeping a secret from him. "We were not prepared to announce at that time what we were going to do about it [the missiles] ourselves," Rusk later recalled, "we had not completed our staff work and the President had not made his final decision."[32]

Gromyko assumed that the administration's ongoing frustrations with Castro had produced the tension in the room. Even when the president read from a copy of the statement he had issued on September 4, Gromyko did not suspect that Anadyr was a secret no longer. Returning to the embassy that night, Gromyko composed a reassuring message to Khrushchev. Lulled by Kennedy's performance, he informed the Kremlin, "Everything we know about the U.S. position on Cuba permits the conclusion that the situation is in general wholly satisfactory." He believed that the meeting at the White House had confirmed Dobrynin's favorable analysis of the situation.

The Soviets, like the Cubans, were sliding into the mild complacency that had blinded them to U.S. intentions just before the Bay of Pigs operation. Gromyko noted that the public campaign against Cuba was subsiding and that journalists and officials in Washington were now emphasizing Berlin as the principal superpower flash point. "The goal of this change in the work of the American propaganda machine is to deflect public attention from Cuba," Gromyko reported. He was convinced that the invasion lobby was losing steam. He noted that the Gallup organization, whose leadership, he said, was "traditionally sympathetic toward Republicans," had just published a poll indicating a majority against a U.S. invasion. Moreover, the fact that Congress had just recessed until after the November elections meant that "pressure on Kennedy from this extremist group would lessen."

October 19: What Do We Do?

After seeing off the Soviet foreign minister, Kennedy prepared for his last Ex Comm meeting before leaving Washington on a five-day cross-country trip.[33] Although he decided to go ahead with this campaign swing to maintain secrecy, he expected to be back in the White House before the last scheduled event, a big rally in California on October 23. He asked his brother to call him once the Ex Comm had decided on a recommendation, then he would return.[34]

For a moment it seemed that Kennedy might have his recommendation before even leaving Washington. After the initial shock, the discovery of the IRBMs had had a sobering effect on the Ex Comm. Each time Kennedy's war council discussed the costs of an air strike, the option seemed less attractive. While Kennedy and Rusk jousted with the Soviet foreign minister, the Ex Comm continued to meet, and by the time Kennedy returned to the discussions there appeared to be agreement on going ahead with the blockade.

This consensus proved too fragile to survive, especially when it became apparent to some that Kennedy was not yet persuaded that a blockade would get the missiles out of Cuba. "At the beginning," Robert Kennedy recalled, "the meeting seemed to proceed in an orderly and satisfactory way. However, as people talked, as the President raised probing questions, minds and opinions began to change again, and not only on small points."[35] Thursday evening's meeting ended with the members of the group as far away from agreement as they had been before the IRBMs were found.

Before leaving for Chicago the next day, Kennedy invited the Joint Chiefs to discuss their military recommendations to him privately. The Ex Comm would continue to meet in Kennedy's absence, but the president wanted to take the pulse of his military advisers. He found the chiefs impatient and suspicious. Taylor had earlier reported to them that Kennedy was now leaning away from taking military action. It was true that the president had grown far less enamored of the air strike plan, especially in light of each day's new intelligence findings; but he was not yet an advocate of the blockade. Kennedy listened carefully as the chiefs argued for a large surprise air attack, with a few hours' warning for the British and the Germans. The chiefs had not changed their advice at all since October 16, despite the discovery of more missiles. They did support a complete naval blockade, including food and fuel, but only as a complement to the air strike. However, they could not offer Kennedy any guidance as to the utility of an invasion. The chiefs were themselves split over that.[36]

The president's departure gave the Ex Comm one last chance to resolve its deep differences. On Friday morning, October 19, the Ex Comm divided into two groups: Robert Kennedy joined the air strike team, which included Treasury Secretary Dillon, Bundy, McCone, and the former secretary of state Dean Acheson. Favoring a blockade were McNamara, Rusk, Thompson, and George Ball. The groups were responsible for generating by the end of the day position papers that made the strongest case possible for their preference.

Over the course of the next thirty-six hours, Robert Kennedy played a key role in bringing these two groups together. He still considered himself part of the air strike lobby; but he was wavering. The reason was not that he agreed with Thompson and the others who believed a blockade and an ultimatum would compel Khrushchev to back down. It was his growing appreciation of the likely cost of an attack.[37]

Robert Kennedy's views ran the gamut throughout Friday. In the morning's discussions at the State Department, he argued that the United States should "say nothing but simply go ahead and make that attack and then go to the Organization of American States." By the evening he was firmly against striking without warning. "[F]rom here on out," he said, "if we make a surprise attack, we will be accused of another Pearl Harbor." He had not abandoned his preference for military action, and he had some concerns that an air strike would not be successful once the Soviets were warned. But he had changed his mind about resorting to a blockade as a first step.[38]

October 20: The Day of Decision

At 8:12 A.M. on Saturday, October 20, the JCS advised U.S. commanders in chief around the globe that "the state of tension in Cuba could lead to military action." "Are we really going to do anything except talk," General Curtis LeMay of the air force had asked the other chiefs on Thursday. It seemed that this would be the day of decision.[39]

John Kennedy awoke this Saturday in the Blackstone Hotel in Chicago without knowing for sure what he would do about the missiles in Cuba. His advisers—the Ex Comm—had been meeting with and without him since Tuesday and, despite hours of discussion, had not reached a consensus. The president knew that the State Department and his trusted counselor Secretary of Defense McNamara favored the blockade. After speaking to his brother several times on Friday, he also knew that Robert's position was evolving; but Kennedy himself was reluctant to give up on his original desire to knock the missile sites out with an air strike. Kennedy's closest military adviser, General Taylor, informed the rest of the Joint Chiefs that morning that Kennedy "might want to hit them as early as tomorrow morning."[40]

The Pentagon and the State Department assumed that Kennedy would make his decision that afternoon. Taylor assured the generals, who worried about the effect of the "political shenanigans," that he would tell Kennedy that the U.S. Air Force had "every reasonable chance of hitting all those missiles." Taylor was concerned about the effect of a blockade. "If we wait," he said, "they'll have time to hide them."[41]

The president was back at the White House by early afternoon. His brother had called him in the morning to suggest he fly back to Washington. Robert Kennedy was now solidly in the blockade camp. If a vote were taken now, the supporters of an air strike would lose. The brothers had switched their usual roles. John Kennedy was now the one who needed to be convinced of the impracticality of using force against Cuba.

By the end of the day the president would be persuaded. In part this was due to new information from Cuba that he found on his desk. The CIA had prepared an important briefing paper for Saturday afternoon's discussion. Ray Cline, the deputy director for intelligence, drafted a five-page, double-spaced report. The CIA understood that the operational status of the missiles and the possibility of hitherto undiscovered missile sites were the issues closest to the president's heart—and potentially most relevant to his final decision.[42]

"[W]e believe," asserted CIA analysts, "the evidence indicates the probability that eight MRBM missiles can be fired from Cuba today." This was the key statement of the CIA report that greeted President Kennedy when he convened the most decisive meeting of the Ex Comm since the discovery of the first missile sites. Even though it had not yet detected any nuclear warheads, the CIA concluded, "[S]ince the missile systems in question are relatively ineffective without them, we believe warheads either are or will be available." The CIA's estimate that the Soviets probably had effective nuclear missiles in Cuba implied that any military action entailed the possibility of a nuclear launch. Any missile site left standing could well be used by the Soviets in retaliation. Why take that chance now? Why not probe the Soviets to see how they would respond to his firmness?[43]

After a two-hour discussion Kennedy asked the Ex Comm to vote. With the support of Rusk, McNamara, Adlai Stevenson, who had come from New York for the meeting, and the newly converted Robert Kennedy, the blockade group carried the day. On Monday or Tuesday, Kennedy would give a nationally televised address, followed by the imposition of a limited blockade a day later. Kennedy expected that besides McNamara the Pentagon would be against this decision. Turning to Taylor, he said, "I know that you and your colleagues are unhappy with the decision, but I trust that you will support me in this decision." Taylor said that he and the chiefs were "against the decision," but that the U.S. armed services would "back him completely."[44]

So, after five days of discussion, the die was cast. First, Kennedy would inform the American public about the missiles on Cuba, rally support for a blockade, and institute what would be called a "quarantine" to prevent additional offensive weapons systems from reaching Cuba. What came next would be up as much to Khrushchev as to him. As expected there was some grumbling among the generals when word of the decision reached the Pentagon. Disappointed by Kennedy's decision, Earle Wheeler, the army chief of staff, turned to the other military chiefs and said, "I never thought I'd live to see the day when I would want to go to war."[45]

Sunday, October 21, 1962: The British Connection

Although the blockade was about to become the policy of his administration, Kennedy still had misgivings about it. It entailed an enormous political risk if Khrushchev did not back down. Filled with these doubts, Kennedy turned to some of his closest friends to discuss the choices he faced. Besides Robert Kennedy there was another official in Washington with whom President Kennedy felt he could let down his hair to discuss policy matters. David Ormsby-Gore had met the Kennedy family when Joseph P. Kennedy was U.S. ambassador to Great Britain. A solid friendship developed between the families, and John Kennedy's sister Kathleen became godmother to Ormsby-Gore's eldest child. In 1961 the British prime minister, Harold Macmillan, selected Ormsby-Gore to represent London at the court of the newly elected president. "He was almost part of the government," Robert Kennedy later recalled.[46] The president, he added, "[would] rather have his judgment, his ideas, his suggestions and recommendations than even anybody in our own government." John F. Kennedy felt free to try ideas out on his British friend, knowing also that this would strengthen the ties between the two former wartime allies.

The British ambassador sensed from Kennedy's manner this time that the president was being extraordinarily confessional. In his report to London, Ormsby-Gore said of Kennedy's statements, "[I]n some instances they were so frank that I doubt very much whether he would repeat them to any member of his administration except his brother Bobby."[47] Kennedy offered his friend, and the British government, a partial explanation for why he chose the blockade option.[48] Reviewing the course of the Ex Comm deliberations of the previous week, Kennedy said that only two options presented themselves to him: an all-out air strike and the blockade. He noted that an attack on Cuba carried enormous political costs and might provoke Soviet retaliation against Berlin. He said nothing about the military infeasibility of the air strike.

Most interesting were Kennedy's musings about possible ways out of the mess that Khrushchev's decisions had caused. Kennedy said that he hoped for some sort of negotiated settlement, perhaps at a hastily convened summit. In doing so, he returned to the subject of the uselessness of nuclear weapons. "He said with great seriousness," Ormsby-Gore cabled home, "that the existence of nuclear arms made a secure and rational world impossible." In this context Kennedy brought up the subject of U.S. missile bases along the borders of the Soviet Union. He told the Englishman that he saw room for compromise with Khrushchev because these IRBM bases had become "more or less worthless."[49]

Kennedy was floating a trial balloon. If, as he expected, Khrushchev ignored the blockade, he needed to find a political exit. Aware of no military grounds for keeping the Jupiter missiles in Turkey, Kennedy informed Ormsby-Gore that he would have to see "whether political developments would enable him to do a deal on the reciprocal closing of bases."[50] Kennedy knew, and admitted to the British ambassador, that there remained the option of invading Cuba. And the United States "might never have a better opportunity for such action," Kennedy explained. Yet he added that he thought an invasion "not only politically impossible but . . . in any case too dangerous."[51]

Kennedy told another friend that night that he was thinking of some kind of diplomatic solution to end this crisis. Charles Bartlett had known John Kennedy since 1946. The Bartletts, like the Kennedys, were active participants in Palm Beach society. There was even an early Cuba connection in the friendship of the two young bachelors. Both John Kennedy and Charles

Bartlett were friends of two former U.S. ambassadors to Cuba, Earl T. Smith and Arthur Gardner, denizens of Palm Beach's Worth Avenue and Breakers' Row. It was Bartlett who introduced Kennedy to Jackie in 1953. As JFK rose through the ranks of the Democratic Party, Bartlett established himself as a journalist. Eventually becoming a Washington correspondent, Bartlett wrote columns for the *Chattanooga Times*, which were nationally syndicated. Although Bartlett stopped calling him Jack on January 20, 1961, the men remained close, and Kennedy continued to invite the columnist over for intimate family meals at the White House.[52]

Sometime on October 21 Kennedy reviewed for Bartlett the choices that the Soviet move in Cuba had presented to him. As he had for his British friend, Kennedy expressed his preference for a diplomatic solution and admitted that the United States would probably have to sacrifice the Turkish missiles to maintain peace.

The president was not the only Kennedy who was considering what the administration's next move should be. At about the time he was meeting with the British ambassador, his brother called a meeting of his brain trust in the Justice Department to discuss ways out of the crisis. The consensus that emerged over the course of the evening was that "the Turkish missiles would have to be given up in the end, as the price of settlement." The attorney general was opposed to a public offer through the UN, considering it "rather weak and defensive" an opening gambit to make to the Kremlin.[53] But he said nothing about a secret offer. Like his brother, Robert Kennedy was turning over in his mind the advantages of finding a political solution, perhaps using his friend Georgi Bolshakov to deliver the message to Moscow.

As of October 21 the Kremlin was still in the dark about the coming crisis. Some disturbing signals, however, had reached Soviet intelligence. At the "Aquarium," the headquarters of the GRU, four different reports suggested that Kennedy had not ruled out some form of military action in the Caribbean. Noting unusual activity by the air force, the GRU reported on a convoy of military planes that had left for Puerto Rico. It also appeared that the number of bombers on duty in the Strategic Air Command had inexplicably increased. The Soviets detected, too, that the U.S. Navy had increased its presence in the Caribbean under the pretext of participating in an exercise, code-named ORTSAC (Castro spelled backwards). And there seemed to be more American activity to come. The Soviet military picked up that McNamara had ordered senior military officers to remain near the Pentagon to participate in a series of intensive meetings.[54]

This evidence cast doubt on the optimistic report received from Gromyko. The report, which had reached the Kremlin on Sunday, October 20, concluded hopefully; "[A] U.S. military adventure against Cuba is almost beyond belief." The Soviet foreign minister, however, was on his way to East Germany from New York and would not be able to discuss these developments in person for several days. The Anadyr operation was very close to completion, and Kennedy had yet to say anything; but there was the chance that Gromyko had been fooled.

Monday, October 22, 1962: Preparing for the Speech

Kennedy's crisis team met Monday morning to prepare to defend the decision to answer Khrushchev's nuclear initiative with a blockade of Cuba. The morning newspapers were full of speculation. "Capital Crisis Air Hints at Development on Cuba; Kennedy TV Talk Is Likely," blared the headline of the *New York Times*.[55] The night before, Warren Rogers, the Washington correspondent of the *New York Herald Tribune*, had come across the Kennedy administration's top Latin American specialists huddled in conference at a Georgetown bar.[56] Recognizing Rogers, they left. That afternoon's *Tribune* carried the title "Top-Secret Doings in Capital; A Cuba-Berlin Strategy Step?"[57] There was a logic to the speculation. On Sunday night President Kennedy had asked the *New York Times* and the *Washington Post* not to run Cuba stories. Both newspapers had learned through good reporting that the president was on the verge of announcing at least a quarantine.[58] "This town is a sieve," Kennedy had complained earlier in the week. But the two newspapers decided to hold their stories in the interests of national security.[59]

The president had invited the congressional leadership for a confidential briefing that afternoon, and he intended to use the Ex Comm meeting in the morning to rehearse the reasons for his decision. Kennedy would have to explain to Congress why the full military power of the United States would not be used, at least at that moment, against Cuba. "The idea of a quick strike was very tempting," Kennedy said to Bundy, McNamara, Rusk, his brother, the rest of the Ex Comm team, and the tape recorders whirling in the basement, "and I didn't give up on that until yesterday morning." They all knew that on October 16, President Kennedy had wanted to move quickly with an air strike. Kennedy continued his explanation: "It looked like we would have all the difficulties of Pearl Harbor and not have finished the job."

In his short soliloquy on why he would not launch a bolt out of the blue to destroy Khrushchev's strategic hardware in Cuba, Kennedy indicated the role that international norms of behavior played in his decision making. International morality mattered to him, but not as a source of absolute injunctions. Each transgression of the code had a cost, which would have to be factored into the larger calculations before any decision. This is what he meant by "having all the difficulties of Pearl Harbor." Kennedy would have been willing to pay the price of international condemnation, if he could then have dispensed permanently with the Cuba problem.[60] But military considerations had persuaded him to opt for a blockade. He had wanted to unleash the U.S. Air Force without warning, but he feared that "[t]he shock to the [NATO] alliance might have been fatal." Even so, he might still have taken the risk, had he ever been optimistic that the missions would destroy all of the missiles. But U.S. intelligence kept turning up new missile sites, and despite the groove that U.S. reconnaissance planes were making in the airspace over Cuba, Kennedy just did not believe he could take the risk that some remained undetected. It was now up to Khrushchev. If the Soviet leader was not scared by the prospect of war, Kennedy might have to cross the brink first. Then, said Kennedy reluctantly to himself and the Ex Comm, "[t]he job can only be finished by invasion."

Missile Crisis

"This May End in a Big War": Moscow, October 22, 1962

Hours before Americans switched on their radio and television sets to see what their president had to say, Nikita Khrushchev received word that John F. Kennedy was about to make a major public declaration regarding the Soviet threat. Khrushchev's sources did not indicate exactly what John Kennedy would say, but the Soviet leader feared the worst. As Kennedy prepared to receive the congressional leaders at the White House, Khrushchev assembled the members of the Presidium to discuss the likelihood of war.[1]

Pessimism reigned in the Kremlin. The sole agenda item listed for the session was "determining further measures in connection with Cuba and Berlin," a reflection of the bureaucracy's confusion over which Cold War volcano was about to erupt. But Khrushchev and his inner circle were convinced that Kennedy's speech would have something to do with Cuba. Defense Minister Rodion Malinovsky, whose GRU in recent days had been reporting unusual U.S. military activity in the Caribbean, tried to calm Khrushchev and the others. "I don't think they can undertake anything at once," he said. As the trademark limousines of the Soviet elite had rushed to the Kremlin, a feeling of impending doom hung in the air. But Malinovsky, at least, believed that Moscow would have time to prepare an adequate response. "Apparently," he continued, "the radio address is a preelection trick." Nevertheless, the dozen or so men around him were tight-lipped and grim. The news of Kennedy's forthcoming speech had cut through the growing complacency about the Anadyr operation like a knife through butter.

Malinovsky wanted the solemn group to understand that there was no need for panic, the Kremlin would have some time to prepare itself. "If they declare the invasion of Cuba," he explained, "they will need 24 hours more for final preparations." Obviously, the Soviet armed forces expected that the Americans would stage an airborne assault. An amphibious landing, even from Florida, would require more than twenty-four hours to execute. At this point in the crisis, Malinovsky did not want to do too much, too soon.

Khrushchev, though he accepted Malinovsky's assessment of the situation, was in a state of disbelief. "The thing is we were not going to unleash war," he lamented angrily in front of his colleagues. "We just wanted to intimidate them, to deter the anti-Cuban forces." Without specifically blaming himself, Khrushchev acknowledged that mistakes had been made. He mentioned two "difficulties." "We didn't deploy everything that we wanted to," he began, "and we didn't publish the treaty." Khrushchev was now thinking that things might have worked out differently had he gone along with Castro's request to disclose the existence of a Soviet-Cuban defense agreement in late August. He had resisted, fearing that this might elicit a violent reaction from Kennedy. Now Moscow was getting the violent reaction without the treaty.

Khrushchev let the frustration of the moment show. To the men in front of him, most of whom had experienced the Russian civil war and all of whom had endured the Second World War and survived Stalin, Khrushchev bared his soul. "It is tragic," he said. They had come so close to having a deterrent force in Cuba, so close to making this kind of nightmare unimaginable. Now not only was a U.S. invasion of Cuba possible; but so was a nuclear exchange involving the Soviet Union. Nevertheless, Khrushchev was determined to show resolve. "They can attack us," he said, "and we shall respond." Articulating what was on everyone's mind in the hall, he added, "This may end in a big war."

No one in the hall doubted that the United States was contemplating a real war in Cuba. This was not October 1960, January 1961, or even April 1961. This time a U.S. president was going to spill American blood to destroy Fidel Castro. How many times, and in how many ways, had Khrushchev tried to avert this occurrence?

Thinking aloud, Khrushchev started talking about what the United States might do and how the Soviet Union should respond. "There is a possibility they will begin with actions against Cuba." In that case, Khrushchev suggested, the Soviets could announce publicly their obligation to defend the island. On the other hand, Kennedy might choose some form of nonviolent sanction to force removal of the weapons. "They may declare a blockade," offered Khrushchev, "and then do nothing." But he doubted that this was how Kennedy would act. His mind kept returning to what the Soviet Union would have to do if the United States attacked Cuba. As "another possibility . . . in case of attack," said Khrushchev, the Kremlin could declare that "all of the equipment belonged to the Cubans and the Cubans would announce that they will respond." He assured his colleagues that he did not envision letting Castro threaten the use of the medium-range ballistic missiles against a U.S. invasion, but as a way of deterring the United States the Cubans could declare that they would "use the tactical ones."

Khrushchev's musings were not debated. On the assumption that a U.S. invasion was more likely than a blockade, the Presidium worked out a set of instructions for the Soviet commander in Cuba, General Pliyev. The group's first reaction was to take steps to avoid an accidental nuclear exchange. A cable was drafted that ordered Pliyev to "put all of his forces on alert" but not to contemplate using any of the nuclear weapons deployed at his command.[2] The more the Soviet leaders thought about the restrictive language of this cable, however, the less they liked it. If the Americans attacked, Pliyev and the 41,000-man Soviet contingent in Cuba would be outnumbered. The nuclear-tipped Luna and cruise missiles were his only potential salvation. Unwilling to sacrifice the Soviet group, the Presidium tentatively came up with a different set of instructions. Pliyev would be authorized to use the tactical nuclear weapons in the event of a U.S. landing; but without a direct order from Moscow, he was not to fire the 1,100-nautical-mile R-12s.

Soviet military doctrine in October 1962 provided for the use of nuclear weapons on the battlefield. Malinovsky's predecessor as defense minister predicted in 1957, "Atomic weapons will be widely employed as organic weapons in the armies."[3] Articles in Soviet military publications argued that tactical nuclear weapons would make amphibious landings difficult, if not impossible, and would equalize U.S. and Soviet naval power.[4] The nuclear torpedoes carried by the four Foxtrot attack submarines, for example, could knock out an aircraft carrier.

And what would be the U.S. reaction to the first use of nuclear weapons by the Soviet Union? A look at the blast effects of these weapons left little doubt that if Pliyev used his battlefield nuclear weapons there would be enormous pressure on President Kennedy to destroy Cuba, at the very least. Each Luna had a range of 31 miles and a two-kiloton nuclear payload. It was estimated that the plane over Hiroshima had a fourteen-kiloton payload. Although the Luna was much less than one-seventh as powerful as "Fat Boy" (nuclear firepower increases or decreases exponentially, not arithmetically), each one would have a devastating effect on the battlefield. Assuming that the Luna was aimed to detonate in the air, at an optimal height of 600 feet above the ground, just one of these missiles would produce a huge fireball about 31 miles from the launch site. At the epicenter of the blast, there would be 100-mile-an-hour winds and a crater 130 feet in diameter and 130 feet deep. Any tank or armored personnel carrier within 500 yards would be destroyed. Unprotected human beings 1,000 yards from the blast site would probably die immediately as a result of the dramatic increase in air pressure, but those unfortunate enough to survive the explosion and the winds would suffer a painful death by radiation poisoning within two weeks. In addition, fallout would be a long-term problem for areas of Cuba affected by the blast. In the 1950s, to give the ecosystem on Bikini atoll in the Pacific any chance of reviving after using it as a nuclear testing site, the U.S. government had to remove 10 feet of topsoil and replace all of the palm trees.[5]

These figures for nuclear tonnage are hard to grasp without concrete examples of how the missiles could change a battlefield. Had Lunas been available to Field Marshal Erwin Rommel, who defended the Normandy coast of France from an Allied invasion in 1944, the Nazis would probably have been able to obliterate all five D-Day beachheads with no more than ten of these weapons. Moreover, had the Soviets used Lunas in 1961, all of the Cuban émigrés who landed at the two beaches along the Bay of Pigs would have died. Now, in 1962, with the twelve at his disposal the Soviet commander in Cuba could easily destroy any beachhead established by U.S. marines in an invasion of Cuba and obliterate the U.S. base at Guantánamo, at the southeastern tip of the island.

The cruise missiles, the FKR, if used, would not have as dramatic an effect on the battlefield but, as predicted by Soviet military journals, could inflict heavy costs on the U.S. Navy task force participating in an attack. One FKR cruise missile carried enough power, roughly twelve kilotons of TNT, to blow a U.S. aircraft carrier group apart. Of the eighty missiles with nuclear warheads originally ordered to be shipped, the Kremlin had already sent thirty-six to the island.

Concerned that Khrushchev and the Presidium were rushing to the brink of nuclear war prematurely, Malinovsky recommended to the group that it wait until 1 A.M., or 6 P.M. Washington time, to authorize Pliyev to fire the Lunas. Fearful that Washington would somehow learn about this delegation of authority, Malinovsky cautioned that they should not give the Americans "a pretext to use their own nuclear weapons" before this was absolutely necessary.

Persuaded by Malinovsky, the Kremlin decided to send the first set of conservative instructions immediately, barring the use of any nuclear weapons.[6] The second set of instructions—the order prepared in September 1962 but not signed by Malinovsky—would be held pending developments in the Caribbean.

At nearly midnight, Khrushchev and his colleagues began a tense vigil—the worst for Soviet leaders since the initial moments following the news of Hitler's invasion in 1941. In a matter of hours, Kennedy might force them to order a nuclear attack.

Washington, October 22, 6 P.M., EDT (1 A.M., Moscow Time)

While the Soviet minister of defense was transmitting the first set of crisis instructions to Cuba and Khrushchev was preparing for nuclear war, Kennedy welcomed a special congressional delegation—eight senators and seven senior congressmen—to the Cabinet Room at the White House. With less than two hours to go before he would reveal the existence of a nuclear crisis in a speech to the world, Kennedy was looking for bipartisan support.[7]

The president sounded tired as he reviewed the reasons for not using force first. He sensed that the men in front of him wanted a military strike against Castro. Mentally overruling his brother, who had advised him to rely on moral arguments to defend the blockade decision, Kennedy stated flatly why there was not an acceptable military option at this stage in the crisis. The Soviets' mobile MRBM bases "can be set up quite quickly," he explained, and for this reason he was sure there were more on the island than had been detected. Kennedy was no longer persuaded that the Soviets would act prudently to avoid war. They had taken unprecedented risks in sending the missiles to Cuba and had wasted no opportunity to deceive the U.S. government about their intentions. Echoing Kennedy's own thoughts, Rusk said to the congressmen, "It seems clear that the hardline boys have moved into the ascendancy [in the Kremlin]." Prudently, Kennedy assumed that he had to consider the worst possible Soviet reaction to any one of his moves. "If we invade Cuba," he told the congressmen, "there is a chance these weapons will be fired at the United States."[8]

Kennedy's prudence annoyed Senator Richard Russell, the crusty southern chairman of the Armed Services Committee. Russell rejected arguments about giving Khrushchev and America's NATO allies warning. He felt Moscow knew full well that nuclear warheads off the coast of Florida were unacceptable. Moreover, Russell sensed the missile ploy was Khrushchev's way of testing U.S. nerve as part of a coordinated Soviet program to weaken the United States around the world. Russell argued that at some point the United States had to take a risk and fight back—and Cuba was the right place and this was the right time.

Russell's dissent disoriented Kennedy and his defense secretary, Robert McNamara. Both tried to explain that the military option was not ruled out. Kennedy stressed that one of his concerns was not "surfacing preparations for an invasion before now." For some weeks the administration had been considering what it could do before any Cuban crisis, to cut the lead time necessary to stage an invasion. However, since the Atlantic command of the U.S. armed forces could not supply all the men needed for the 90,000-man invasion force, some of the marines would have to come from the West Coast. The administration had started moving these men in the last forty-eight hours, and the president claimed that they would be in a position to act on Cuba in an additional "24 or 48 hours." Indeed, a battalion of marines had left El Toro, California, by air for Guantánamo Bay on the morning of October 21; but Kennedy did not tell the congressmen that the bulk of the Marine Expeditionary Brigade for the projected landings on the east coast of Cuba was still in San Diego and would have to be taken by ship through the Panama Canal, a journey that would take more than a week.[9]

McNamara likewise tried to assure the congressmen, who by their postures and sharp words all seemed to share Russell's misgivings, that the United States was "well prepared for an invasion." The defense secretary revealed that the Pentagon had been revising the operational plans for Cuba since October

1961. As a result, a series of alternate plans had been prepared "in great detail" that "[w]e have reviewed . . . with the President in the last ten months on five different occasions." The invasion of Cuba would require in all 250,000 men, 90,000 of whom would be ground troops. To ensure success and a minimal loss of life, the invasion would have to be preceded by a sustained air campaign of two thousand sorties over a few days. Like the president, McNamara stated that the necessary preparations for an invasion—the movement of army troops by rail across the country and the dispatch of marines from Camp Pendleton on ship—could be accomplished in seven days.

The congressmen wanted to know why the administration had waited so long to act. It was five days since the U-2 intelligence from western Cuba had reached Washington. "One of the reasons why we've been concerned this week," Kennedy explained, "was that we wanted to know all the sites, we wanted to know the firing positions of these missiles."

In light of the deliberations going on simultaneously in the Kremlin, about which the U.S. government knew nothing, President Kennedy's caution was wise. Counterfactual analyses can be a fool's game. Yet Khrushchev's and Malinovsky's decision to hold off on sending final instructions to their commander in Cuba proves that Kennedy was right to assume the worst about the risks involved in invading Cuba. Had he followed the advice of the congressional leadership, instead of his own instincts, Kennedy might well have discovered to his horror on October 23 that he had ordered thousands of American soldiers, marines, and sailors onto the first nuclear battlefield of the Cold War.

Wrapping up the meeting so that he could go to make his speech, Kennedy stressed the principal reason why he had selected the blockade option. "If we go into Cuba, we have to all realize that we have taken the chance that these missiles, which are ready to fire, won't be fired." We "are prepared to take it." But, the president noted, it would be "one hell of a gamble."

Now in its final draft, Kennedy's Cuban speech was ready for delivery at 7:00 P.M., Washington time. Earlier drafts had reflected Kennedy's hesitation over the best way to proceed. On October 18 Theodore Sorensen had written a speech designed to follow a U.S. air attack on Cuba. According to this scenario, the president would have offered an olive branch to Moscow in the form of an invitation to a superpower summit and a pledge to remove eventually U.S. IRBMs from Turkey and Italy. Instead, Kennedy greeted Americans with the news that their government was going to give the Soviets a chance to correct their mistake before initiating more drastic measures:

> This government, as promised, has maintained the closest surveillance of the Soviet military buildup on the island of Cuba. Within the past week, unmistakable evidence has established the fact that a series of offensive missile sites is now in preparation on that imprisoned island. The purpose

of these bases can be none other than to provide a nuclear strike capability against the Western Hemisphere.[10]

The American public had been warned that the president might speak that evening about a foreign policy problem; but his words and the tone in which Kennedy delivered them conveyed a much deeper crisis than anyone had expected. Since the end of the Korean War in 1953, most Americans' experience of the Cold War was a sense of the theoretical possibility of harm—a Soviet bomber gap or a missile gap, or a concern about an education gap after the launch of Sputnik. But in Kennedy's speech what had once been a distant possibility was suddenly very real and very close.

The 1930s taught us a clear lesson: aggressive conduct, if allowed to grow unchecked and unchallenged, ultimately leads to war. . . . Our policy has been one of patience and restraint . . . but now further action is required— and it is underway; and these actions may only be the beginning. We will not prematurely or unnecessarily risk the costs of worldwide nuclear war in which even the fruits of victory would be ashes in our mouth—but neither will we shrink from that risk at any time it must be faced.[11]

Kennedy outlined what that "further action" would be. First, the United States would initiate a "strict quarantine" around Cuba. Contrasting this with the Soviet blockade of Berlin in 1948–49, during which Stalin had tried to prevent all deliveries including food from getting through, Kennedy said that only shipments of "offensive military equipment" would be turned back by U.S. naval forces. Second, he explained that he had ordered "continued and increased close surveillance" of the island. Kennedy warned that if U.S. intelligence found that the Soviets were continuing to work on the missile sites "further action will be justified." And to be sure Moscow understood, he added, "I have directed the Armed Forces to prepare for any eventualities." As a precaution, the families of servicemen were being evacuated from Guantánamo. Kennedy's final dramatic point was that the United States "would regard any nuclear missile launched from Cuba against any nation in the Western Hemisphere as an attack by the Soviet Union on the United States, requiring a full retaliatory response upon the Soviet Union."

Kennedy concluded his speech with an appeal to Khrushchev to "eliminate this clandestine, reckless and provocative threat to world peace and to stable relations between our two nations." "[A]bandon this course of world domination," he pleaded, ". . . move the world back from the abyss of destruction." Not optimistic that Khrushchev would heed this call to remove the missiles, Kennedy tried to prepare Americans for a long crisis. "Many months of sacrifice and self-discipline lie ahead—months in which both our patience and our will will be tested—months in which many threats and denunciations will keep us aware of our dangers." After nearly two decades of armed peace, the United States and the Soviet Union seemed to be in a state of war.

Khrushchev Reacts

The Presidium received its copy of the speech from the U.S. embassy shortly after 1:00 A.M., and the news was better than expected. Khrushchev and Malinovsky did not have to revise the instructions to Pliyev: an American invasion was not imminent. Kennedy had said in his speech that he would approach the United Nations and the Organization of American States to plead his case that the missiles in Cuba were offensive weapons that threatened the security of the Western Hemisphere.

Khrushchev saw no reason to let Kennedy's speech alter his strategy of pushing forward with the completion of the missile sites. The Soviet Union had a right to do in Cuba what the United States had done in Turkey, Italy, and even England, which had U.S. Thor missiles. The Soviet leader was determined to proceed with Anadyr. He had not turned back in September when Kennedy first threatened the use of force against a missile base in Cuba, and he would not now.

As of October 22 thirty ships were plying to Cuba, including the *Aleksandrovsk*, with its cargo of nuclear warheads, and four ships carrying the missiles for the two IRBM regiments. Moreover, four Foxtrot diesel submarines were closing to Cuba with their own complement of nuclear-tipped torpedoes. The Kremlin was especially worried about the *Aleksandrovsk*, which was carrying as many as twenty-four nuclear warheads for the IRBMs and the remaining forty-four warheads for the FKR land-based cruise missiles. Moscow did not want these to fall into enemy hands.

Khrushchev's notetaker at this climatic meeting described the consensus of the group on revisions that would have to be made to the Cuban operation: "The four submarines must continue their cruise and the *Aleksandrovsk* must go to the nearest port." But it was too late for most of the rest of the armada. The Kremlin wanted the four ships carrying the R-14s—the *Almeteevsk*, *Nicolaeev*, *Dubna*, and *Divnogorsk*—to maintain course. However, to reduce the odds of a collision with the U.S. Navy, the Soviet leadership decided that beyond these exceptions any ships that "haven't yet arrived" would have to return to the USSR.[12] The decision to bring the *Aleksandrovsk* and the missile ships to a Cuban port was not merely a recognition of the danger of keeping more than sixty thermonuclear warheads at sea near the U.S. Navy. It also signaled Khrushchev's thinking about the future of Anadyr. Should the Soviet Union continue with its plan of deploying a complete strategic rocket division to Cuba? The Kremlin decided that it had to proceed.

The probability of war now very high, the Presidium approved raising the alert level of the Soviet armed forces and those the other armies of the Warsaw Pact. All leaves were suspended and conscripts due for release from the Strategic Rocket Forces (the arm of the Soviet military that supervised all nuclear missiles), from the country's antiaircraft batteries or from the Soviet submarine fleet, were to remain on duty until further notice. To Marshal Andrei Grechko, the commander of the Warsaw Pact, Malinovsky sent the following message: "Call together the officers of the countries of the Warsaw Pact and order the implementation . . . of measures to raise the military readiness of the military, navy, and air forces of the United Military Force."[13]

Khrushchev had two other important messages to draft: one to Kennedy and one to Fidel Castro. Along with the copy of Kennedy's Cuba speech, the U.S. government had passed a cover letter from the president. Khrushchev opted for a response that was threatening as well as defiant. Decrying the blockade as a violation of international war, the Kremlin tried to scare Kennedy by warning that Soviet ships might not respect the quarantine line. Moscow also held to its earlier assurance that the Soviet arms in Cuba were "intended solely for defensive purposes." As Khrushchev had said before midnight, he felt that the United States entirely misunderstood his motives for placing missiles in Cuba.[14]

Conversely, Castro was to receive a reassuring letter. Khrushchev informed him that Moscow had no intention of backing down. Instead, the Soviet government had taken steps to prepare for any eventuality. He wanted Castro to know that in light of Kennedy's speech Pliyev had received instructions "to be in full readiness" and that Soviet forces at home were also on alert. Khrushchev was not wholly candid with the Cuban leader. He made no mention of the decision to curtail most of the remaining shipments associated with the Anadyr project. Nor did he reveal that the Kremlin had had some warning of Kennedy's speech but had made no effort to warn Havana.[15] He did not want Castro to doubt his commitment to Cuba.

Khrushchev did not go home that night: "I slept on a couch in my office— and I kept my clothes on. I was ready for alarming news to come any moment," he later recalled, "and I wanted to be ready to react immediately."[16]

The Reaction in Soviet Washington

In the hours following Kennedy's quarantine speech, the Soviet embassy in Washington prepared for war. The chief of the KGB *residentura*, Aleksander Feklisov, cabled Moscow that he was destroying "all secret material of operative correspondence that is not necessary." A veteran of the Second World War, Feklisov resolved not to take any chances. He checked the emergency electrical generator that could provide power to the floor with the KGB's offices in the event that the United States shut off all power to the embassy. The KGB traditionally had the most secure communications with Moscow, and it was essential that this link not be severed in this crisis. Feklisov also had someone verify that the KGB's private oxygen supply was in good working order. As Feklisov considered what the future might bring, he refused to dismiss the possibility of a chemical or biological attack against the embassy.

Ambassador Anatoly Dobrynin coordinated the security for the entire embassy and staff with Feklisov. All employees were told that, until further notice, they were not permitted to go to the movies or to shop. Dobrynin's and Feklisov's worries extended beyond the safety of the embassy staff, to the whereabouts of all Soviet citizens in the American capital. A special headache for the embassy was the fact that the Leningrad Symphony Orchestra and the Bolshoi Ballet, two high-profile cultural delegations, happened to be in the United States at the time. The KGB decided to send some of its Washington staff to beef up security for those delegations.[17]

Georgi Bolshakov watched as the local Washington police took up positions around the Soviet embassy. "The Blockade has begun," one of his co-workers in the GRU office commented after looking outside his window.[18] Bolshakov had a right to feel left out of the excitement. Since April 1961 he had been at the center of the U.S.-Soviet relationship. Only a year earlier he and Robert Kennedy were exchanging the messages that prevented the standoff in Berlin from exploding into war. But he had had no contact with the attorney general since their perfunctory meeting on October 5. Worse, what he had been instructed to tell the Americans at that time, that the buildup in Cuba was entirely defensive, directly contradicted what President Kennedy just said was happening in Cuba.

The hoped-for telephone call came the day after Kennedy's speech. It was the journalist Frank Holeman who called to suggest a meeting. Bolshakov had not seen the *Daily News* correspondent for some time; but he knew that Holeman would not want to shoot the breeze and catch up on small talk.

Holeman had grave business to conduct. Someone in the attorney general's office, possibly Robert Kennedy himself, wanted to use Bolshakov to sound out the Kremlin on a possible diplomatic solution to this crisis. Robert Kennedy and his people believed, Holeman explained, that the missiles in Cuba were the Soviet Union's way of responding to U.S. Jupiter missiles in Turkey. "In connection with this [the assumption about Soviet motives]," Bolshakov noted for his superiors, "Robert Kennedy and his circle consider it possible to discuss the following trade: The U.S. would liquidate its missile bases in Turkey and Italy, and the USSR would do the same in Cuba." Indeed, Robert Kennedy had led his staff in a discussion of political solutions to the crisis, including offering to close the Jupiter bases, two days before. But this was not the way the Kennedys usually did business. In May 1961 and April 1962 Robert Kennedy proposed concessions in the name of the president. Was Holeman free-lancing, or did someone who had been at the Justice Department on the night of October 23 decide to float this idea on his own through the journalist? Bolshakov's notes from this unusual meeting end with the cautionary advice that Robert Kennedy allegedly gave Bolshakov through Holeman: "The conditions of such a trade can be discussed only in a time of quiet and not when there is the threat of war."[19]

Apparently Bolshakov received confirmation of Holeman's story from a second journalist with inside information. Whether at the request of President Kennedy or on his own initiative, Charles Bartlett also passed word to Bolshakov in the first, tense hours of the crisis that the White House was thinking about a trade involving the Jupiter missiles.[20]

The Soviet embassy had ample reason to believe that, at the very least, Holeman's and Bartlett's statements reflected official musing about the possible role that the Jupiter missiles might play in averting a catastrophe. The American press was abuzz that morning with potential diplomatic solutions to the missile problem. Summarizing the principal positions of America's most famous foreign policy pundits for Charles de Gaulle on October 23, the French ambassador Hervé Alphand in Washington explained that Max Frankel and James Reston of the *New York Times* were considering some kind of compensation for Russia, possibly involving concessions in Berlin. "However, I have noticed," Alphand wrote, "a different position from Walter Lippmann," who drew attention to the fact that the U.S. intermediate-range nuclear missiles in Turkey were "seriously complicating" Kennedy's position in the crisis.[21] Meanwhile, the Kennedy administration was also canvassing opinion among its allies regarding the consequences of a Cuba-Turkey deal. The State Department sent a telegram to the U.S. delegation at NATO asking what the likely reaction of Turkey would be if the United States withdrew its missiles.[22]

Inexplicably, the GRU station decided to sit on this information from Holeman. At a time so fraught with peril, this was exactly the kind of information that Moscow needed. Moreover, this was unusual behavior on the part of Soviet military intelligence. For a year and a half, the Washington office had immediately reported anything coming to Bolshakov from the president's brother or close Kennedy associates. But nothing went out to the Kremlin from Bolshakov on October 23.

What Is Khrushchev Going to Do?

In his first major decision since the televised address, John Kennedy authorized six low-level reconnaissance flights over Cuba.[23] He had two objectives on October 23. First, he wanted to keep abreast of all military developments on the island in order to know the extent of the threat that the U.S. military might soon have to eliminate. He also had to anticipate Khrushchev's reaction to the crisis. If the Kremlin opted for a hard line, then Khrushchev might order Soviet ships to ignore the blockade. Or, conceivably, he might seek to place equal pressure on West Berlin, NATO's most vulnerable point. Throughout the day, Kennedy and the Ex Comm discussed ways of dealing with either or both of these scenarios. By evening, Kennedy had instructed the Pentagon to prepare a battalion-size probe to go up the German Autobahn to Berlin with two hours' notice if the Soviets and East Germans should attempt to cut West Berlin off from the rest of Europe as they did in 1948.[24]

As the day wore on and the Soviets had not responded, Robert Kennedy turned to the Bolshakov channel. "I sent Charlie Bartlett, who was friendly with him, to see him," recalled Robert Kennedy.[25] At his behest, Bartlett invited Bolshakov to meet at his office in the National Press Club.

Bartlett assured Bolshakov that President Kennedy was also aware of this meeting. "He is very angry about what has happened in Cuba," Bartlett averred. "It reminds him of the Japanese deception before Pearl Harbor." Bartlett described a man whose belief in the possibility of agreements with the Soviets was shaken. Yet "the president does not want to invade Cuba," explained Bartlett; "he only wants to eliminate the medium-range ballistic missile bases, if they are there."[26] He stressed that John Kennedy, who was already thinking in terms of the removal of missiles under international auspices, felt this problem would be better solved through the UN. Kennedy wanted the Soviets to understand that the talks at the UN would proceed more smoothly if in the meantime the Soviets stopped the movement of their convoys to Cuba.

Before the meeting broke up, Bartlett asked whether Bolshakov knew of any way to resolve this crisis. Bolshakov may have offered some suggestion. In his report to Moscow, though, he was careful to write that "the official Soviet statement contains all possible ways of resolving this crisis."[27]

Not satisfied with the results of Bartlett's first meeting, Robert Kennedy asked him to see Bolshakov a second time that same day. He wanted Khrushchev to understand that the United States had excellent evidence of the missile deployments. "I gave Charlie Bartlett a picture of the missiles," Kennedy later recalled.[28] Bolshakov's statements in the morning had been disappointing, reflecting a lack of any creative thinking in Moscow. Perhaps the shock of seeing the U-2 photographs would elicit a response from the Presidium, as these meetings had done so often in the past.

As Bolshakov entered Bartlett's office, he noticed a large easel with sheets of paper that appeared to have been turned over. "On the easel were aerial photographs," he recalled. Bartlett turned them over, and as Bolshakov approached them he could see they were stamped "For the President's Eyes Only."

"So what do you see, Georgi?"

The question burned into Bolshakov. He denied any expertise in rocketry. "I have never seen anything like these photographs," complained Bolshakov, "and cannot understand what is on them." Trying to deflect the intensity of his erstwhile friend, Bolshakov offered that they might just be baseball diamonds. "If you are such a specialist, Charlie, why don't you tell me: are these rockets or not?"[29]

Seized by fear of what the United States might do in response to his government's actions, and perhaps hopeful of reopening a channel to the Kennedys, Bolshakov's boss, the GRU resident in Washington, finally reported to Moscow what Holeman had told Bolshakov on October 23 about Robert Kennedy's interest in a missile swap and Bartlett's earlier comments about the president's own interest in a similar arrangement. Bolshakov had had no choice but to report these hints when he first got them; but his boss exercised his authority to hold on to them until the crisis in the Caribbean grew white hot.[30]

"Bobby Goes to Dobrynin"

Late on the night of October 23, after Holeman's and Bartlett's meetings with Georgi Bolshakov, the president's brother decided to work another special channel. An "agitated" Robert Kennedy was shown in to see Anatoly Dobrynin. The closing of the heavy door to the Soviet ambassador's office unleashed a torrent of emotional language that "abounded in repetition and digression." Kennedy said he came on his own, without any express instructions from the president. But the Soviet ambassador understood that the attorney general was there to begin the process of finding a solution.[31]

"I must tell you," began Robert Kennedy, "that the private relationship between the president and the premier, upon which so much rests, has been severely damaged." He did not try to hide his sense of personal betrayal and the anger in the White House. For nearly two years, he had conducted the president's back-channel diplomacy, and now the Soviets had turned that program into a tool of deception. "You have deceived the president and you have deceived me" was the leitmotif of Kennedy's presentation.[32]

"From the start," continued Kennedy, "the Soviet side—Khrushchev, the Soviet government in its statements and the ambassador in confidential discussions—stressed the defensive character of the weapons being supplied to Cuba." Turning toward Dobrynin, Kennedy protested, "You, for example, particularly told me about the defensive goals behind the supply of Soviet arms, in particular missiles, at the time of our meeting at the beginning of September." Kennedy honed in for the kill. "I understood you as saying that what was involved—at that point and in the future—was purely the sending of missiles of a comparatively short range for the defense of Cuban territory and the approaches to the island and not the sending of missiles that could strike all of the continental United States."

Kennedy stressed that the White House had taken the Soviets at their word. "I told this to the president, who was satisfied with this policy of the Soviet government." Besides this private assurance from Dobrynin, there had been the TASS statement of September 11, affirming that Soviet intentions on the island were purely defensive. Perhaps the most egregious example of deception, Kennedy averred, was a letter from Khrushchev dated September 6, sent to the White House via the presidential aide Theodore Sorensen. "The Soviet promise [in that letter] not to do anything during the congressional election period to disrupt the international situation or to worsen superpower relations," Kennedy recalled, "made a big impression on the president."

When Kennedy began talking about the president's dismay at the evidence contradicting these assurances, the Soviet ambassador asked why the president did not speak up about his concerns at his recent meeting with the Soviet foreign minister "before embarking on such a dangerous path, fraught with the first military confrontation between our countries."

Robert Kennedy defended his brother's decision not to raise the matter with Andrei Gromyko on October 18. "First of all, Gromyko spoke from a text evidently prepared by the Kremlin and did so rigidly that a discussion with him seemed to be pointless." "Secondly," Kennedy continued, "he [Gromyko] reiterated the claim about the defensive character of the Soviet weapons supplied, although the president knew at that time that this was not so and that he was being lied to."

When Dobrynin suggested that the Americans might be wrong about what was going to Cuba, Kennedy blew up. "Why on earth should we turn to a confidential channel, if . . . even the ambassador, who we believe enjoys the full confidence of his own government, does not know that there are already long-range missiles on Cuba that could strike the United States . . . ?"

Kennedy calmed down as Dobrynin explained that he received all the information that Moscow wanted him to have. This was not much solace; but Kennedy seems to have believed that Dobrynin had also been misled by the Kremlin. The Soviet ambassador then reiterated the already well-known Soviet position on the defense of Castro's Cuba.

As he was leaving the ambassador's office, Kennedy stopped in the doorway to ask a final question. "Can you say what instructions were given the captains of the Soviet ships after the president's speech last night and the signing of the quarantine proclamation today?" Dobrynin did not know. He had not been told that the Kremlin had decided early that morning to postpone all but the most important shipments—the warheads and the IRBMs. Instead, he produced an age-old diplomatic reply. "I do know these instructions," he prevaricated, "they must not submit to any illegal demands on the high seas, as these are in violation of the international norms of free passage." Kennedy's parting words were elliptical: "I don't know how all this will end, but we intend to stop your ships."[33]

The *Aleksandrovsk*

In Cuba, Fidel Castro announced a general mobilization of 350,000 solders and militiamen after Kennedy's speech.[34] The Cuban leadership had become quite practiced at this. Alekseev's replacement at the KGB station in Havana noted that Castro did not expect the attack overnight. The mobilization was to run according to a seventy-two-hour schedule. The initial hours of the action had gone smoothly. "No signs of disorder," the Soviet intelligence officer reported confidently. "Generally," he concluded, "the situation is quiet."[35]

By the middle of October 23, Castro no longer seemed rushed, perhaps because of some reassuring reports from Cuban intelligence. In the first hours after Kennedy gave his speech, Cuban sources in the West German and Italian embassies reported that the diplomats feared an immediate U.S. attack. Western diplomats were observed scrambling to get their families out of Havana, if not out of Cuba altogether. But with the dawn of a new day came optimism that Kennedy would give diplomacy time to work. The same Cuban sources that had reported panic in the major European embassies now claimed that high-level diplomats doubted that the United States would attack, at least in the next few days. Reportedly at embassy staff meetings, chiefs of missions and the top political officers were explaining that the missiles had made this a superpower conflict, with the implication that a U.S. attack on Cuba was less likely.[36]

The Soviet colony on the island, however, was in a state of frenzied activity. Pliyev had ordered stepped-up measures to prepare for war. At 2 A.M. Soviet soldiers began digging trenches around the missile installations and manning the antiaircraft batteries. The order was so unexpected that some military commanders were absent from their headquarters. Major N. S. Novikov was the political affairs officer, or commissar, for the MRBM regiment near Santa Clara, in the center of the island. When the order from Pliyev arrived, no regular officers were around and the antiaircraft specialists were asleep. Novikov had to order the troops to dig the trenches and find some energetic soldiers to read the manuals for the antiaircraft guns and sit behind them.[37] The crisis also came before the regiment's nuclear missile bunker was ready. Consequently, the warheads were placed in caves for safekeeping. By sunrise, all necessary precautions having been taken, the situation at Novikov's command, at least for the moment, was under control.

The Soviet frenzy involved more than mounting defensive preparations. Pliyev also maintained the pressure on his command to complete the missile installations and assemble the forty-two Il-28 light bombers, which were still crated, as quickly as possible. And there as the problem of the *Aleksandrovsk*. The ship carrying the nuclear warheads was due at any moment in the port of Mariel. The Soviet had intercepted some U.S. naval traffic describing the tracking of a ship "specially adapted for transporting nuclear warheads." Would the United States allow the ship to dock at Mariel?[38]

Tension mounted throughout the day that the *Aleksandrovsk* might not get through before the blockade went into effect. The ship was behind schedule, and at 4 P.M. on October 23 two U.S. planes flew over Mariel, where it should have already arrived. Concerned for its safety, the Soviet command in Cuba decided to reroute the ship to the port of La Isabela. There were no specially constructed bunkers near that port to store the warheads, but Pliyev decided not to take any risks, since the Americans seemed to have figured out that the nuclear warheads were going to Mariel. Placing them near La Isabela might save them in the event of a U.S. attack. However, since there were no bunkers, Pliyev would have to keep the warheads on board the ship until the crisis subsided.[39]

The *Aleksandrovsk* beat the blockade by a matter of hours. Knowing the level of Moscow's concern about this ship, Ambassador Alekseev rushed a message via KGB channels to announce its arrival. "The ship *Aleksandrovsk*," he cabled to the Kremlin, ". . . adjusted for thermonuclear arms, which was the target of the naval blockade, has just arrived safely in Cuba. It is in the port of La Isabela."[40]

October 24: Running the Blockade

On Wednesday, October 24, Khrushchev awoke to the news that the *Aleksandrovsk* had arrived safely in Cuba. At least now he did not have to worry about the U.S. Navy's commandeering Soviet nuclear warheads on the high seas. Meanwhile, the Foreign Ministry handed him a short letter from Kennedy. In it the American president asked the Soviet leader to "show prudence" and "issue immediately the necessary instructions to your ships to observe the terms of the quarantine."[41] Khrushchev, however, wanted four more of his ships to reach Cuba.

The U.S. naval blockade was just coming into force. Kennedy had waited for approval from the OAS before initiating the blockade. The OAS vote, which came at 3:00 P.M. on October 23, was unanimous. Four hours later in a ceremony at the White House, Kennedy signed a "proclamation of interdiction." At 8 P.M., the proclamation already signed, Secretary of Defense McNamara notified the president that as of 10 A.M., October 24, the U.S. Navy would have all the ships in place for an effective blockade.[42]

The Presidium met to discuss an official response to the U.S. blockade and Kennedy's letter requesting "prudence." Unlike Kennedy, who formalized the Ex Comm on October 23, Khrushchev had not created a special policy team to handle the crisis. Soviet intelligence opened a crisis working group, with representatives from all of the services and the Foreign Ministry, at KGB headquarters in the Lubyanka.[43] But the Soviet foreign policy system remained unchanged. As before, policy discussions occurred in small groups, including Khrushchev and some or all of the foreign policy specialists of the Presidium—Leonid Brezhnev, Frol Kozlov, Aleksei Kosygin, Anastas Mikoyan, and Mikhail Suslov—with staff support and expert advice provided by Malinovsky, Gromyko, and Boris Ponomarev of the Central Committee. Whenever a formal decision was needed, Khrushchev would convene the entire twelve-man Presidium. He decided to threaten the White House with an outbreak of war. In a letter prepared that day, he charged Kennedy with "advancing an ultimatum" and vowed "to reject the arbitrary demands of the

USA." Considering the quarantine "an act of aggression . . . pushing mankind toward the abyss of a world missile-nuclear war," Khrushchev said that "the Soviet government cannot give instructions to the captains of Soviet vessels bound for Cuba to observe the instructions of the American naval forces blockading that island." If the Americans insisted on taking "piratical actions," he continued, "[w]e will then be forced for our part to take the measures which we deem necessary and adequate in order to protect our rights." The text was closely guarded in the Kremlin. Only full members of the Presidium were permitted to see it.[44]

Khrushchev also decided to signal a softer line to Washington. In a long public letter to the philosopher Bertrand Russell, he said he was prepared to meet Kennedy to resolve the crisis. "The question of war and peace is so vital," Khrushchev wrote, "that we should consider useful a top level meeting in order to discuss the problems that have arisen."[45] Khrushchev made the case for a summit a second time that day in a discussion with William E. Knox, the president of Westinghouse International Company of New York, who happened to be in Moscow on business. Knox had not expected to see the leader of the Soviet Union, but Khrushchev was looking for a prominent American to use to send a message and Knox was available. Over the course of a three-hour meeting in the Kremlin, Khrushchev admitted to Knox that he had placed ballistic missiles in Cuba but defended his description of them as defensive. He said that there was no time to argue over definitions. The task at hand was to avoid war, and he offered to meet Kennedy in the United States, Russia, or a neutral site. But "[i]f the United States insists on war," he vowed, "we'll all meet in hell."[46]

At the moment Kennedy signed the quarantine proclamation, all of the MRBMs, complete with warheads, were on the island and nearly operational. Khrushchev could now sit back and hope that the fear of war would force Kennedy to back down.

C H A P T E R   1 4

Climax of the Cold War

Johnny Prokov was a favorite of journalists who frequented the Tap Room in the National Press Club. A Russian émigré from the Baltics, Prokov had worked as a barman since getting a job at the club in 1959. He was famous for disliking the Kremlin. At the slightest opportunity he would describe the trials of his native region, under Soviet occupation since 1940. Years later, as the Soviet Union was collapsing, he regaled patrons with a story about how when Gorbachev was ordering the disarming of all Baltic households, Prokov called up the Soviet embassy on Sixteenth Street to offer his own rifles, if a Soviet diplomat dared to come to Reston, Virginia, to pick them up.[1]

Johnny had other things on his mind as he was preparing to close up the Tap Room at 1 A.M. on Thursday morning, October 25. It was well past last call. Bars in the District of Columbia in 1962 had to stop serving alcohol at midnight. Prokov, however, was not worried about some drunk scribbler asking for one for the road. Since the president's quarantine speech the discussion in the club was of nothing else but the Cuban crisis. Many of the men in the club had already seen action in World War II or Korea; yet there was something especially threatening about this particular crisis. It was potentially more devastating that any previous conflict, and it could happen in a matter of moments. All of the journalists were familiar with John Hersey's crystal-clear evocation of the consequences of nuclear war for one of the two Japanese cities that experienced it in 1945.

Prokov made eye contact with a fellow Russian who entered the Tap Room. Anatoly Gorsky was one of the club's best chess players. Since gaining admission to the National Press Club, the TASS delegation had dominated play in its tournaments. Gorsky was also a KGB officer who reported to Aleksandr Feklisov at the Soviet embassy. It is not known whether Prokov was aware of this, though like most in and around the journalistic community, he probably suspected that Gorsky was not just a TASS correspondent.[2]

Prokov had something to whisper to Gorsky. He was very worried and curiously wanted to unburden himself to a Soviet. While pouring drinks at about 10 P.M., he had overheard a conversation between two celebrated American journalists, Robert Donovan and Warren Rogers, both correspondents of the *New York Herald Tribune*. Apparently, Donovan was supposed to fly south that very night "to cover the operation to capture Cuba, which is expected to start the next day."[3] This was the first solid indication Gorsky had received in the crisis that Kennedy had decided on war, and he rushed back to the embassy that night to make his report.

The KGB's informant had the story half right. Rogers and Donovan had been discussing the invasion; but it was Rogers, not Donovan, who was on the Pentagon's list to go if the invasion happened. Earlier in the day the list was circulated to newsrooms in the city. There was to be one reporter per major newspaper. As far as Rogers knew, eight men had been selected. A journalist who worked for one of the television networks had refused the assignment for an unspecified reason; the rest were keen to go, though well aware of the risks for themselves, and for the country. Donovan, the Washington bureau chief, had selected Rogers for the assignment.[4]

It was a mark of the limitations of Soviet intelligence in this crisis that information from Rogers, who was not especially close to any member of the Kennedy administration—and who was in fact persona non grata around Robert McNamara—would make its way from the alcoholic haze of the National Press Club to the desk of Nikita Sergeyvich Khrushchev.[5]

Though flimsy, this intelligence resonated with something just picked up by the Soviet military. While Prokov was overhearing the two American journalists, the GRU office in the embassy was eavesdropping on an even more ominous signal. The military attachés in the embassy regularly scoured the skies for Pentagon radio signals. The U.S. military routinely transmitted changes to the defense condition (DEFCON) status of Americans forces *en clair*, in an unclassified form.[6] At 10 P.M., Washington time, on Wednesday, the GRU intercepted an order from the Joint Chiefs of Staff to the Strategic Air Command, placing SAC on a nuclear alert.[7] In fifteen years of intercepting U.S. military messages, the Soviet military intelligence service may never have seen anything like this.

In light of these threatening signals, Gorsky and his boss, Feklisov, discussed the urgent need to corroborate Prokov's story. Rogers was known to have irregular contact with one of the political officers in the embassy. This man, a young second secretary whom Rogers remembers today only as "Boris something," was called at home and told to find a way to intercept Rogers before late morning. Boris knew that Rogers usually parked his car in the lot used by many journalists behind the Willard Hotel. The embassy decided to have Boris hang around the lot from the crack of dawn to be sure that Rogers was kept under observation. If the journalist's information was accurate, Moscow would have less than a day to react.

"Right and Reasonable Tactics"

As the Soviet colony in Washington, D.C., scurried before dawn to corroborate the dramatic new information about Kennedy's intentions, it was midday, October 25, in Moscow, and Khrushchev was about to convene the most important meeting of the Presidium since Kennedy made his speech. The Soviet leader had been in constant touch with his colleagues since Monday; but the Presidium went into formal session only when decisions had to be made. Khrushchev was now ready to alter the Soviet approach to this crisis. The tension that pushed Feklisov in Washington to squeeze every last detail out of the journalist Rogers was also weighing heavily upon Khrushchev. He wanted a way out of this crisis.

That morning a disappointing letter had arrived from Washington. In response to the Kremlin's protests of his brinkmanship, Kennedy merely repeated the story of Soviet broken promises and deception. "I ask you to recognize clearly," Kennedy declared to Khrushchev, "that it was not I who issued the first challenge in this case, and that in the light of this record these activities in Cuba required the responses I have announced."[8] The letter said nothing about Khrushchev's efforts on October 24 to interest the United States in a summit to discuss the causes of the current crisis. The tone of the letter made it appear that the White House would accept nothing but a complete Soviet capitulation.

When called to the Kremlin, some Presidium members may have assumed that Khrushchev wanted to discuss an unyielding response to this letter; but Khrushchev had a surprise for them. Referring to what he had just received from Washington, he began the meeting by explaining that he did not want to trade any more "caustic remarks" with Kennedy. Instead, he wanted both to order the four missile transports still on the high seas to turn around and to present the Americans with a plan to defuse the crisis.[9]

Khrushchev was now convinced that the Soviet Union could not keep ballistic missiles in Cuba without going to war, and he wanted the rest of the Presidium to understand that Moscow would have to find another way to protect Fidel Castro. "We must dismantle the missiles to make Cuba into a zone of peace," he advised his colleagues. Trying not to display a sense of urgency, he suggested that before dismantling the R-12s, the Kremlin should "look around" and be sure that Kennedy would not yield. The president had prepared the American people for a long crisis in his blockade speech, and Khrushchev did not expect that a U.S. attack was around the corner. However, he assumed that ultimately a "zone of peace" in the Caribbean could be created only through negotiations. He had in mind offering a deal to Washington and suggested the words "Give us a pledge not to invade Cuba, and we will remove the missiles." In thinking about the form that a diplomatic settlement might take, Khrushchev had also decided that when the time came he would allow the United Nations to inspect the missile sites.

No single piece of information seems to have moved Khrushchev to his new position. The multiple reports on the National Press Club discussion and the change in the status of U.S. forces probably had not yet reached the Kremlin.[10] What intelligence Khrushchev had received reinforced the seriousness of Kennedy's letters; but what impressed him most was a general sense of the military inferiority of the Soviet Union. He could not go to war in the Caribbean with any hope of prevailing. He had tried to achieve some measure of parity with the United States to defend Soviets interests in that region; but clearly he had failed. John Kennedy's actions since Monday showed that he was not deterred by the missiles that the Soviet Union had managed to deliver to Cuba. Khrushchev had witnessed the courage of the Soviet people in staving off defeat at the hands of the Nazis; but a head-to-head struggle in the nuclear era could only bring defeat and devastation to the Soviet Union. These were the cruel, hard facts of life: as inescapable for the leader of the second-most-powerful military alliance in the world as the need for rain was for the peasant farmer.

"These are correct and reasonable tactics," Khrushchev argued. Not only will "this initiative . . . not aggravate the situation," he added, but "[b]y this we will strengthen Cuba." Although it was not all that had been hoped for from the Anadyr operation, a settlement along these lines might at least satisfy Cuba's security needs. Leonid Brezhnev, Aleksei Kosygin, Frol Kozlov, Anastas Mikoyan, Boris Ponomarev, and Mikhail Suslov expressed their support. Meanwhile, the Soviet government's two national security specialists, Andrei Gromyko and Rodion Malinovsky, remained relatively silent. The change in strategy envisioned by Khrushchev was so dramatic that only the leadership of the Communist Party had a right to pass judgment.

After the men voted to approve the plan, Khrushchev had a suggestion to break the tension. "Comrades, let's go to the Bolshoi Theater this evening. Our own people as well as foreign eyes will notice, and perhaps it will calm them down."[11] Kozlov, Brezhnev, and the others followed Khrushchev to Russia's premier opera house. They all needed some distraction. In the next few days, if the Americans kept up the pressure, the Kremlin would be sending John Kennedy an offer to retreat.[12]

Warren Rogers

We were waiting for our cars [in the lot] and the [Russian] said, "What do you think of the situation?"

"I think it is extremely grim."

"Do you think Kennedy means what he says?"

"You're damn right, he does. . . . He will do what he says he will do."[13]

Warren Rogers does not remember having said anything else to his friend Boris in the parking lot behind the Willard Hotel early on Thursday morning, October 25. Rogers then left to start working the telephones at his desk in the Washington bureau of the *New York Herald Tribune*. Boris, however, apparently thought he had heard much more. He hurried back to the Soviet embassy, on Sixteenth Street, only a few blocks from the National Press Club, to report that Rogers had confirmed the barman's story. Aleksandr Feklisov prepared the report for Moscow: "This morning, the other journalist [who had been with Donovan at the National Press Club], the *New York Herald Tribune*'s Rogers, said confidentially that . . . the Kennedy brothers have decided to risk all. The attack on Cuba will start in the next two days."[14]

In the embassy Soviet diplomats were already arranging their own probe of the American journalist that morning. They schemed to set up an impromptu lunch for Rogers with Georgi Kornienko, a first secretary and Dobrynin's chief political adviser, who had already met Rogers on a few occasions.[15]

Rogers had not been at his desk long on Thursday morning when the unexpected telephone call came from the Soviet embassy: "Would you have lunch with Georgi Kornienko?" Rogers didn't really know Kornienko; but he agreed. There might be a story in it.

Kornienko turned the lunch that followed into his own interview with Rogers. Not giving away that he knew about the previous night's discussion in the National Press Club, Kornienko asked the journalist for his opinion of the situation around Cuba. Rogers spoke freely, recounting that he knew "from various governmental sources" that "the Kennedy administration had already taken the principal political decision 'to finish with Castro.' "[16] Moreover, he asserted confidently, the military plan for an attack on Cuba was "prepared to the last detail," the distribution of troops was "completed," and the "attack could begin at any moment." At the same time, he remarked, President Kennedy "attaches very great significance" to making sure that such an action is regarded as "justified," "as much in the eyes of the American people, as in those of a possible majority of the world community." The delay in search of "justification" complicated the Pentagon's military preparations. "Every day of delay," noted Rogers, "makes the implementation of such an attack much more difficult." Nevertheless, he estimated that the probability of military intervention "remains at this point very high."[17]

Soviet representatives in Washington considered the information from Rogers as their best look inside the White House's secret crisis deliberations. Thursday afternoon both the Foreign Ministry and the KGB sent reports on the interview with Rogers to Moscow.[18] One person not impressed by the lunch was Warren Rogers: "We had a good talk. I thought it was deadly serious, and I thought the best thing they could do was to make a face-saving acquiescence to Kennedy's demands. . . . I did most of the talking at the lunch, and he kept asking most of the questions. . . . I don't think he knew very much about what was in Khrushchev's mind."[19] For over thirty years Rogers had no idea of the alarms that this "good talk" set off.

Moscow, Friday, October 26

Vladimir Semichastny slept Thursday night on a bed in a room next to his office in Moscow.[20] Shortly after 8:30 A.M. on Friday, October 26, he was given a copy of Feklisov's report on Kornienko's meeting with Rogers. Twelve hours before, when Feklisov's initial cable on the incident in the journalists' bar first arrived, Semichastny had no idea who Warren Rogers was. Now he seemed to be the KGB's best indicator of Kennedy's intentions.[21]

Semichastny who, at thirty-seven, was the youngest chairman in the history of the KGB, was a newcomer to Soviet intelligence. Less than a year earlier he had been the second secretary of the Central Committee of the Communist Party of Azerbaijian. Khrushchev had picked him to replace Aleksandr Shelepin, who had once been Semichastny's mentor in the communist youth movement. In an effort to dissuade Khrushchev from promoting him to lead the KGB, Semichastny had protested, "I know nothing about this . . . I am not a professional [intelligence officer]." But Khrushchev did not want spy masters at the helm of the KGB: "Our professionals there commit a lot of follies; we need political men, who will be feared a little. . . ." He assured Semichastny that this is what he had expected of Shelepin, who had satisfied Khrushchev at the KGB and was about to be promoted to the Presidium. "You will continue what he started," intoned Khrushchev.[22]

Semichastny's inexperience led him to rely heavily upon the heads of the chief subdivisions of his organization. Despite Khrushchev's initial entreaties, it also put him outside of the inner circle of power in Moscow. Unlike John McCone, Semichastny was rarely invited to brief his boss in person and was not expected to have any foreign policy recommendations of his own.

During the crisis the KGB chief was responsible for coordinating all information received from abroad. His task force oversaw intelligence from the Foreign Ministry, the GRU, and, of course, his KGB. The crisis team met at KGB headquarters, the Lubyanka, in Dzerzhinsky Square, which was named after the head of Lenin's secret service, the Cheka. Semichastny decided which intelligence reports would go into a special grayish blue folder that was placed on Khrushchev's desk every day.[23]

On Friday morning Rogers was the star of Khrushchev's intelligence folder. Khrushchev was usually quite skeptical of intelligence reports, though he read them avidly. Although Khrushchev doubted that John Kennedy would risk a world war; today's batch of intelligence was too unequivocal to ignore. The American journalist's comments strengthened indications from different sources that the U.S. government had lost its patience for a long crisis and was preparing to move against the missile sites very soon. These included disturbing information from the Soviet military. Not only had the Pentagon put U.S. forces on a DEFCON 2 alert condition (DEFCON 5 being peacetime status, and DEFCON 1 meaning war); but the GRU was reporting an order to U.S. hospitals to prepare to receive casualties.[24]

Khrushchev had not wanted to rush into negotiations. He had wanted to "look around," to derive every possible benefit from the missiles before removing them from Cuba. Now that seemed impossible.

The Soviet leader called for a stenographer and began to dictate a letter outlining the proposal he had discussed only the day before with the rest of the Soviet leadership. "You are mistaken if you think that any of our means on Cuba are offensive," he said aloud, thinking of Kennedy. "However, let us not quarrel now. It is apparent that I will not be able to convince you of this."[25]

Khrushchev wanted Kennedy to know that the missiles could be negotiated out of Cuba:

Let us therefore show statesmanlike wisdom. I propose: we, for our part, will declare that our ships, bound for Cuba, will not carry any kind of armaments. You would declare that the United States will not invade Cuba with its forces and will not support any sort of forces which might intend to carry out an invasion of Cuba. Then the necessity for the presence of our military specialists in Cuba would disappear.[26]

To reinforce his point that there was no time to waste, Khrushchev concluded his letter with this thought: "now we and you should not pull on the ends of the rope in which you have tied the knot of war, because the more the two of us pull, the tighter the knot will be tied."[27]

Khrushchev prepared this letter without reconvening the Presidium. It was later speculated in Washington that he sent the October 26 letter on his own, as a kind of cri de coeur for help in fighting back the hard-liners in the Kremlin and the Red Army.[28] However, he often obtained the approval of his colleagues for official letters by distributing them for comment.[29] Before the letter went to Kennedy, Khrushchev's assistants sent copies to all full and candidate members of the Presidium and the secretaries of the Central Committee.[30] Although the October 26 letter would signal to the White House a shift in the Soviet position in the crisis, for the Kremlin it represented a strategy that had already been approved.

At 5 P.M. this first indication of a possible diplomatic end to the crisis was delivered to the U.S. embassy, on Chikovsky Street, a few miles from the Kremlin.[31] In Washington it was 10 A.M., Friday, October 26.

Washington, October 26

At the Soviet embassy in Washington, Feklisov was very worried that Friday morning. In the last twenty-four hours he had sent four cables stressing that the Kennedy administration was on the verge of going to war. Since Gorsky's report on the National Press Club discussion early Thursday, Feklisov had gone to his best sources to test what Rogers had said. One source, code-named GAM, knew the columnist Walter Lippmann personally or worked close to those who knew him. The other agent was a foreign journalist with good sources in the State Department. Both of these agents had reported back in the course of Thursday that the Kennedy administration intended to attack Cuba in the near future, though neither one could provide an exact date or any other details.[32]

In his twenty-year career in Soviet intelligence, Feklisov had managed to avoid any close encounters with war. He had been in the United States during the Second World War. Now it seemed that he would have his first taste of conflict. What would happen to him if the two countries went to war? Would he be treated as a diplomat and detained for eventual trade with the U.S. embassy staff in Moscow? This assumed the war would be contained to the island of Cuba. But what if it escalated? From his work as a case officer for the atomic spy Klaus Fuchs in the late 1940s, Feklisov had a sense of the theoretical power of the hydrogen bomb.

These thoughts raced through his mind, leaving him uneasy. There is reason to believe that what Feklisov had reported to the Kremlin had so unsettled him that he decided to engage in private diplomacy of his own, to turn to a well-connected contact, whom he had code-named MIN.[33] This contact, he believed, might be able to convey a message to the Kennedy administration. Having received no special instructions from Moscow in this crisis, Feklisov assumed that he could meet whomever he wished.

MIN was John Scali, a short, balding, and pugnacious journalist who moderated ABC television's *Issues and Answers*. Over the course of ten months, he and Feklisov had met on an irregular basis. "He came from Boston, and I thought he knew the Kennedys," Feklisov later recalled. "Our talks were interesting, but I mainly wanted to improve my English. That's why we met."[34]

Late Friday morning, while he was munching on a sandwich, Scali received a call at his office at ABC News. It was Feklisov. When the men started meeting in early 1962, the FBI had warned Scali that Feklisov was the KGB resident, the chief of the KGB station, at the Soviet embassy. The first time Scali called the bureau about Feklisov, two FBI agents came over to ABC News to encourage Scali to meet with Feklisov as often as the Russian wanted. The FBI described the KGB man as usually reclusive, and the U.S. government needed to know more about him. "Do I have to continue with this," Scali asked at one point in the discussion. "It's already too late," his FBI handlers responded. From then on, Scali informed the FBI before any meeting with Feklisov. "It saved a lot of problems later," Scali recalled.[35]

This time Feklisov was asking for an urgent meeting. Scali had not heard from him in a while. But with the crisis heating up around Cuba, the journalist understood that this was one meeting he could keep. Scali suggested the Occidental Restaurant, near the Willard Hotel. The lunch was set for 1:30 P.M. "When I arrived, he was already sitting at the table as usual, facing the door. He seemed tired, haggard, and alarmed, in contrast to the usual calm, low-key appearance that he presented."[36]

Feklisov and Scali have left diametrically opposed versions of what subsequently happened. In Feklisov's version of this meeting, Scali is the one who was especially fearful of war. After assuring Feklisov that the United States was planning to launch air strikes and an amphibious landing on Cuba in the next forty-eight hours, Scali asked whether West Berlin would be occupied if the United States attacked Cuba. This sparked a defiant response from Feklisov, who replied that all heaven and earth would fall upon NATO if the United States were to attack Cuba. "At the very least," he said, "the Soviet Union would occupy West Berlin." Feklisov added that, given the size of Soviet conventional forces on the line dividing the Germanys, the situation would be very difficult for the West. And to make matters worse for Washington, he expected the crisis to unify the entire socialist bloc, including China. Perhaps for dramatic effect, Feklisov assured his American interlocutor that the Cubans, and especially Castro, were ready to die like heroes.[37]

"A horrible conflict lies ahead," Scali concluded after hearing what the Soviet response would be to the use of American military force against Cuba. According to Feklisov, Scali fell into such a state of anxiety that he began to muse about possible ways out of the conflict. "Why couldn't Fidel Castro give a speech saying that he was prepared to dismantle and to remove the missile installations if President Kennedy gave a guarantee not to attack Cuba?" Scali asked.[38]

In Scali's version, it was Feklisov who made the offer. The Soviet intelligence officer was distraught, and over the course of their lunch he asked Scali what he "thought" of a three-point plan:

a) The Soviet missiles bases would be dismantled under United Nations supervision.
b) Fidel Castro would promise never to accept offensive weapons of any kind, ever.
c) In return for the above, the United States would pledge not to invade Cuba.[39]

Then Feklisov suggested that Scali run this proposal by his contacts at the State Department and gave him his home telephone number, to be sure he could be reached at any time.[40]

True to their different perceptions of what happened at the lunch, Scali rushed what he thought was a back-channel proposal from Khrushchev to the State Department. Meanwhile, Feklisov returned to the Soviet embassy without any clear sense of what had happened at the lunch. Instead of dispatching an immediate report on his discussions with the American, Feklisov busied himself with other matters for the rest of the afternoon.

Behind the secrecy that the Soviets were finding so hard to pierce, John F. Kennedy had actually not yet decided what to do next. At 10:00 A.M. on Friday, John McCone led off the first Ex Comm meeting of the day with a description of the situation at Soviet military installations around the world. The Red Army was in a defensive crouch. The Soviet armed forces were on full alert, having completed all necessary measures in the three days; but U.S. intelligence had detected "no significant deployments." West Berlin seemed secure for the moment. By contrast, the situation had deteriorated in Cuba, where there had been no letup in activity at the missile sites since Monday. By the end of the day, the two remaining unfinished R-12 launch complexes would become operational, bringing the total number of missiles that were ready to go to twenty-four. In addition, Soviet technicians were working faster than ever to assemble the forty-two Il-28 bombers that had been sent over in crates.[41]

This news was depressing. The blockade was clearly not working, and the Soviets needed to be told that the administration was losing its patience. The Ex Comm faced three options. First, it could strengthen the blockade by extending it to petroleum and oil products. Second, it could increase efforts to reach a negotiated settlement through the UN; or third, it could use force—an air strike followed, if necessary, by an invasion.

The State Department hoped that something would come of the negotiations at the UN. Ambassador Adlai Stevenson, who flew to Washington for the meeting, was working with UN Acting Secretary-General U Thant to obtain a twenty-four- to forty-eight-hour halt in activity at the Soviet missile bases. Dean Rusk suggested to the Ex Comm that Stevenson be given an additional twenty-four hours to see if anything came of the talks before they toughened the blockade.

There was little support around the table for negotiations. Stevenson set off a heated debate by asking whether he could offer the Soviets a lifting of the quarantine in return for stopping their missile buildup on the island. John McCone, McGeorge Bundy, Treasury Secretary C. Douglas Dillon, and even Rusk opposed the idea. They doubted that the Soviets would have any incentive to dismantle their missiles if the blockade was removed prematurely. Stevenson, however, had no illusions that the Soviets would probably want more than a lifting of the blockade to dismantle their missile base. He predicted that Moscow would eventually ask for a U.S. pledge not to invade Cuba and the removal of the Jupiter missiles in Turkey.

Kennedy could see the group beginning to split between the diplomatists and the advocates of a military solution. The hawks were becoming especially vocal. McNamara wanted to launch a limited air strike, using fifty planes, on the six missile sites that were operational and all of the Il-28s. He believed that by limiting the number of Russian and Cuban casualties on the ground, the administration would "avoid [an] unpredictable, excessive, uncontrollable Soviet response." Dillon wanted a broader air strike, though not as large as Maxwell Taylor's preference, a massive aerial operation involving three hundred airplanes that added all of the SA-2 sites, the MiGs, and some Cuban airfields as targets. Finally, the CIA's McCone, who was convinced that only an invasion would solve the Cuban problem, pressed the group to agree that the goal of U.S. actions in this crisis was the removal of Castro.

Listening to Stevenson and to the descriptions of the various military plans, Kennedy spoke up to show that he disagreed with McCone. The primary objective was not to remove Castro but to eliminate the Soviet missile threat. While admitting that it might take an invasion to destroy the sites, Kennedy signaled to his advisers that he did not consider Stevenson wrongheaded either. In Kennedy's mind only two options held any likelihood of success: "We will get the Soviet strategic missiles out of Cuba only by invading Cuba or by trading."

"People who fought off [the] warhawks have won a round," noted one participant at the end of the meeting. The Ex Comm remanded the question of imposing what was called a POL blockade (petroleum, oil, and lubricants) to Sunday's session, and Kennedy agreed to postpone night reconnaissance flights. This was to give the talks at the UN one last chance.

The president and most of his advisers were moving in separate directions. When Kennedy asked, "What do we do if [the UN] negotiations break down?" his close counselor Bundy recommended extending the blockade or launching an air strike. The popularity of this response put Kennedy in the minority. Stevenson, McCloy, Kennedy's arms control czar, and the president were the only members of the Ex Comm who seemed to be seriously considering a negotiated settlement, probably involving a trade of the Jupiter missiles. If the president opted for granting concessions to the Soviets, he would face a hard sell. At McNamara's urging, the Ex Comm decided to return to a serious discussion of an air strike the next morning. Meanwhile, the JCS alerted Admiral Dennison, CINCLANT, to concentrate his attention on preparing for OPLAN 316, the contingency plan involving an air strike followed by an amphibious invasion.[42]

Havana, October 26

General Issa Pliyev, the commander of Soviet forces in Cuba, knew war. As a young man he had fought in the Russian civil war. Twenty years later he had commanded a division in the defense of Moscow when German artillery was close enough to bombard the city. He had seen the tide turn in the bloodiest of ways at Stalingrad. And in the last two years of the Second World War, he had led crucial offensives against Hitler's best armies and then those of the Imperial Japanese Army in Manchuria.

This battle-hardened tank commander was now in the most uncomfortable spot of his celebrated military career. He was stuck on an island, facing a larger, more powerful adversary who could initiate at will a stunning blow from the air and the sea. The odds at Moscow had slightly favored the Nazis. But if the Americans invaded, they would enjoy air superiority and, once a beachhead was secured, a massive advantage over Soviet forces on the ground.

Throughout the day on Friday, October 26, Pliyev received warning signals from Cuban and Czech sources that convinced him that war was near. Expecting a U.S. air strike to occur in the next day or two, he ordered an intensification of deception (*maskirovka*) and, in an intentionally ambiguous phrase, "a dispersal of technology." As the commander of combined Soviet forces that included a nuclear detachment, Pliyev had the authority to arm or disarm his nuclear weapons. As of October 26 all twenty-four launchers were ready. None of the missiles, however, carried a nuclear warhead. The warheads were under guard in storage areas concealed from U.S. reconnaissance. It would take three and a half hours to mate each nuclear warhead to a ballistic missile and to fuel the missile. It is highly likely that by "a dispersal of technology" he meant that the nuclear warheads, normally kept under lock and key in the nuclear storage area at Bejucal and a few caves in the center of the island, were to be moved closer to MRBMs and the tactical weapons.[43]

The Cubans had again turned 180 degrees in their assessment of the threat. Unconcerned on October 20, panicky on October 22, calm on October 25, they now exhibited their earlier anxiety over the imminence of U.S. aggression. On Friday morning Fidel Castro called a meeting of the general staff of the Cuban Revolutionary Army to prepare for hostilities. Cuban intelligence agents working under cover as journalists for *Prensa Latina* had intercepted a U.S. telegram saying that the Kennedy administration had prepared an ultimatum for U Thant, the UN secretary-general, calling for the removal of the "offensive weapons."[44] Persuaded by this information that a U.S. attack would occur in two or three days, Castro ordered the general staff to move all Cuban forces to their command posts and raise their alert status to its highest level. Meanwhile, Raúl Castro left Havana to direct military preparations in Oriente Province, which encompassed the strategic city of Santiago de Cuba and bordered on the U.S. base at Guantánamo. And Che Guevara went west to run operations in Pinar del Río Province.

Convinced that Kennedy had already decided to strike, Fidel Castro saw no reason to worry any longer about provoking Washington. He informed the general staff that, as of the next morning, Cuban antiaircraft guns were authorized to fire on U.S. planes, regardless of their function, if they violated Cuban airspace. In the last twenty-four hours, the United States had stepped up its surveillance of the island. American reconnaissance aircraft were now flying at treetop height, presumably amassing target data for the attack. In preparation for carrying out the order to fire on U.S. planes, Castro dispersed fifty artillery batteries around the island, and commanders were told to remove their safety catches. Expecting a U.S. invasion to follow an air strike on October 29 or October 30, he also ordered that, starting Monday, landmines were to be placed along all mountain passes between Guantánamo and the Cuban cities of Oriente Province.[45]

Pliyev was kept well informed of Castro's actions. Colonel Meshcheriakov of the GRU had attended the meeting with the Cuban general staff. And later in the day, the Cubans asked for a meeting with the Soviet commander at his headquarters southwest of Havana. The Castro regime knew that it would have to convince the Soviets that it was necessary to bloody America's nose. "We cannot tolerate these low-level overflights," Castro himself told Pliyev, "because any day at dawn they're going to destroy all these units." At issue was not simply the need to disrupt U.S. military preparation, but Cuban pride. The Cubans considered it their duty as well as their right to defend Cuban airspace against the "banditry and piratical actions" of the Kennedy administration.[46]

With the exception of the short trip over to Pliyev's headquarters, Castro spent most of Friday at his own command post in Havana. It was there that he hosted his friend Aleksandr Alekseev. From Cuba it seemed that the Kremlin had fallen into a funk. Castro wanted to shake Moscow out of its passivity, and Alekseev, Khrushchev's personal representative in Cuba, was his best line to the Kremlin. With a U.S. attack on the horizon, Castro believed there were steps Moscow could be taking to improve the situation.[47]

"Why do the Soviets insist on denying the existence of the missiles?" Castro asked Alekseev. Together with Osvaldo Dorticós, who attended this meeting with Alekseev, Castro suggested that Moscow make use of the time remaining to criticize the United States for "violating Cuban airspace, and also to attack the U.S. policy of establishing offensive bases on the borders of the USSR." Not simply looking to score propaganda points, the Cubans believed that the Kremlin might still be able to deter a U.S. attack. Castro proposed that Moscow announce that the missiles, and the rest of the weapons denounced by Washington, were under Soviet control. The almost complete lack of word from Washington regarding Soviet forces on the island suggested to the Cubans that the United States was attempting to frame the ultimate attack in the context of U.S.-Cuban antagonism.[48] But this was a superpower crisis, and, in Castro's eyes, Kennedy should not be allowed to get away with ignoring the Soviet Union.

Castro asked Alekseev to inform Moscow immediately of his suggestions. He hoped for some guidance from the Kremlin on coping with the evolving situation before he began to shoot at U.S. planes. So far he had not decided to punish the Americans, for fear of undermining the negotiations at the UN. But he implored Alekseev to make Khrushchev understand that his patience had come to an end.[49]

Washington, October 26, Evening

John Scali's report on his lunch with Aleksandr Feklisov, which reached the State Department late Friday afternoon, provided Roger Hilsman, the director of the State Department's Bureau of Intelligence and Research (INR), with a ray of hope in this crisis. Scali and Hilsman were friends, and it seemed plausible to Hilsman, who believed his friendship with Scali was known to the Soviets, that Moscow had decided to use Scali to open a new channel through the State Department. Hilsman noted the main points of what Scali described as the Soviet proposal and sent a report to Dean Rusk and the White House with the recommendation that it be given a hard look.[50] "We were interested in the Scali-Fomin [Feklisov's alias] contact," Rusk later explained, "because we knew that Fomin was KGB."[51] Rusk considered this to be the first concrete offer from the Soviet leadership for ending the crisis. The messages already exchanged by Khrushchev and Kennedy had only brought about a hardening of each side's position. Rusk could not authorize Scali to accept the Soviet proposal, but he asked the journalist to arrange a second meeting quickly, so that Moscow would know that high-level officials saw promise in the negotiating formula.[52]

Shortly after 7:30 P.M. Scali and Feklisov met at the Statler Hotel, near the Soviet embassy. In a very brief meeting Scali conveyed his message. He was authorized "by the highest authority" to say that there were "real possibilities in this [proposal]" and that "the representatives of the USSR and the United States in New York can work this matter out with U Thant and with each other." Feklisov listened carefully and then repeated the proposal in order to be sure that he understood the White House's offer correctly. Unsure of Scali, he asked repeatedly for confirmation that Scali spoke for the White House. Finally, he added that it was not enough that there be inspection of the dismantling of Soviet missiles; it would be necessary for UN observers to watch the withdrawal of U.S. forces from Florida and the other southern states where troops and jets were massing for a military strike. This last point went beyond Scali's instructions, so the journalist demurred. Then the meeting broke up.

News of the second meeting between Scali and Feklisov percolated through to the Ex Comm just as the State Department began reporting the arrival of a new letter from Khrushchev. Originally delivered to the U.S. embassy in Moscow just before 10 A.M., Washington time, the letter did not start to arrive at the State Department until 6 P.M., eight hours later. Because the letter was long and had to be cabled in sections, it was not until 9 P.M. that the State Department received the portion in which Khrushchev called on Kennedy "to show statesmanlike wisdom" and to offer a guarantee to Cuba in exchange for a Soviet withdrawal of the missiles. As the evening progressed and the contents of Khrushchev's "knot" letter became known to Kennedy and his men, the Scali-Feklisov proposal appeared to confirm a shift in Soviet tactics. As Rusk emphasized years after the crisis,

When you are in contact with KGB, you have to be alert to the question as to whether the KGB is reinforcing the real view of the government in Moscow or whether the KGB is playing a game of some sort. In the Scali-Fomin contacts, it appeared that the KGB was saying in effect what we were implying from the messages we had received from Khrushchev and that a solution could be worked out on the basis of a withdrawal of the missiles from Cuba and a commitment by the United States that we would not invade Cuba militarily.[53]

The Ex Comm met again at 10:00 P.M. to consider the letter and the Feklisov-Scali proposal. The group concluded that an important change had occurred in the Soviet Union's handling of the crisis and that some kind of negotiation might be possible. Robert Kennedy allowed himself "a slight feeling of optimism."[54] "The letter, with all its rhetoric," he believed, "had the beginnings perhaps of some accommodation, some agreement." The president was even happier. The morning meeting had left him with few palatable options. Khrushchev's letter and the curious approach through the American journalist suggested for the first time in this crisis that Khrushchev also wanted to avoid initiating a military action. But the situation remained tense, and Khrushchev's letter was too vague to constitute the basis for a settlement. Cuba still harbored twenty-four ballistic missiles, armed and pointed at the United States. Kennedy was probably concerned that Saturday, October 27, would be the last day he could resist racheting up the pressure on Moscow.

Moscow, October 27, 9:00 A.M. (Havana, 2:00 A.M.)

While members of the Kennedy administration slept on the night of October 26–27, the crisis heated up in Moscow and Havana. Defense Minister Malinovsky awoke Saturday to his most difficult decision since the start of the missile crisis. Just after 9 A.M., Moscow time (2:00 A.M., Washington time), the communications officers in the Soviet Ministry of Defense received the following flash message in code from General Pliyev in Cuba:

> From available intelligence information, the USA has located the arrangement of some of [Major General] Igor Statsenko's installations the [R-12 and R-14 missile regiments], and the leadership of the Strategic Air Command has ordered a full military alert of its strategic aviation military units.
>
> In the opinion of the Cuban friends, the U.S. air strike on our installations in Cuba will occur in the night between October 26 and October 27 or at dawn on October 27.
>
> Fidel Castro has ordered air defense units to fire on U.S. airplanes in the event of an attack on Cuba.
>
> We have taken measures to disperse "techniki" [warheads] in the zone of operations and have intensified *maskirovka*.
>
> We have decided that in the event of a U.S. air attack on our installations, we will employ all available means of air defense.[55]

Pliyev was not requesting permission. But Malinovsky and the Ministry of Defense met immediately to discuss Pliyev's cable. There was no debate. The

U.S. Air Force would have to pay for any assault on Soviet positions in Cuba. It was hoped that the warheads for the R-12s, in addition to the missiles themselves, could be protected. Moscow did not know this for certain; but its use of deception had worked, and the United States had no idea of the location of the warheads.

The Soviet defense minister knew Pliyev very well. Pliyev had served under Malinovsky's command in Hungary and Manchuria. Pliyev's daring had led to a strategic opening for the Soviet forces in Hungary and again, in the last action of the Second World War, in Manchuria. Malinovsky took only thirty-four minutes to consider and approve Pliyev's decision to use force in what could be the first sustained military engagement of the superpowers in the Cold War. At 11:00 A.M. he signed his copy of Pliyev's cable: "I propose to confirm." Then he sent it over to the Kremlin.

While Malinovsky was signing the order in Moscow to permit Pliyev to defend himself in Cuba, an ocean away Fidel Castro came to Alekseev's apartment for an early-morning discussion. Alekseev had been awakened at about 1 A.M., Havana time, by a telephone call from President Dorticós warning him that Fidel Castro was on his way for "an important meeting."[56] Now he and Castro were eating sausages and drinking beer. Generally Castro had a good appetite; but tonight he was eating out of nervousness. He was convinced that U.S. aggression was inevitable sometime in the next three days (he gave odds of 20 to 1 that it would happen). He had received a letter from the Brazilian leader João Goulart that evening, warning him that if the missiles were not dismantled within the next forty-eight hours, they would be destroyed by the United States. Castro had been extremely worried all day, since receiving the intelligence from New York, and the Brazilian warning served to magnify this concern.[57]

Castro decided to write Khrushchev a letter, "to encourage him."[58] He began to dictate and then stopped. Not liking the first draft, he marked it up himself and then dictated something new. Again he was dissatisfied. In all he dictated this letter ten times. Castro had tried to get Moscow to work with him in this crisis. Now he hoped that his words would motivate Khrushchev to act responsibly.

"If . . . the imperialists invade Cuba with the goal of occupying it," Castro wrote, "the danger that that aggressive policy poses for humanity is so great that following that event the Soviet Union must never allow the circumstances in which the imperialists could launch the first nuclear strike against it." Offering his "personal opinion," he stressed that "if they [the Americans] actually carry out the brutal act of invading Cuba . . . that would be the moment to eliminate such danger forever through an act of legitimate defense, however harsh and terrible the solution would be."[59]

"At the beginning I could not understand what he meant by his complicated phrases," Alekseev later reported to Moscow. Castro seemed to be arguing for the use of the Soviet Union's most powerful weapons.[60]

"Do you wish to say that we should be first to launch a nuclear strike on the enemy?" Alekseev finally asked Castro.[61]

"No," answered Castro, "I don't want to say that directly, but under certain circumstances, we must not wait to experience the perfidy of the imperialists, letting them initiate the first strike and deciding that Cuba should be wiped off the face of the earth."[62]

Castro was grimly determined not to allow his revolution to fail. He had taken the Soviet road to consolidate his gains. The missiles had worried him, but Cuba was part of a bigger enterprise, the anti-American bloc of socialist countries. Now that Kennedy was threatening to do what Castro had always assumed the Yankees wanted to do, the Cuban leader did not want Khrushchev to flinch.

Alekseev did not wait for Castro to finish writing his letter to alert Moscow of the tense situation. "Fidel Castro is located with us in the embassy. . . . [H]e is preparing a private communication to N. S. Khrushchev, which we will quickly send to you," Alekseev reported. Castro was still at his apartment; but Alekseev may not have wanted to reveal the informality of the Cuban leader's visit. The Soviet ambassador did, however, want Khrushchev to know the substance of this letter in advance: "Castro believed that an intervention was almost inevitable and would occur in the next 24–72 hours."[63]

Moscow, Saturday, October 27, Noon (4 A.M., EDT)

After spending another difficult night in his Kremlin study, Khrushchev was greeted with the alarming information from Havana. Malinovsky had received Pliyev's report, and it was up to Khrushchev to decide whether to allow the Soviet commander to defend himself against the American air strike expected by all of the experts in Havana. Khrushchev's intelligence folder bulged with information from the United States that substantiated Pliyev's warnings.

One definition of leadership is the capacity to make decisions that run counter to conventional wisdom or current trends. Despite many reasons to do otherwise, Khrushchev chose to ignore the alarming information from Washington and Havana. Then as later, analysts of the Soviet scene assumed that at this crucial moment in his life Khrushchev faced pressure from hardliners in government. In fact, he was a free man in complete control of the Soviet leadership. He signed the order to Pliyev as Malinovsky had recommended. But Khrushchev did not believe John Kennedy was going to use force against the Soviet missiles.

At the Presidium, Khrushchev launched into a monologue to explain his unique view. "Can they attack us now?" he asked. "I think that they won't venture to do his." The experiences of the last few hours had altered Khrushchev's interpretation of Kennedy and the international situation. Originally he had believed that Kennedy did not want to invade Cuba, but he had feared that the young man would not be able to hold off the hawks around him. On Friday, Khrushchev was momentarily convinced that Kennedy had lost control of his administration. But on Saturday, with the dire predictions of a U.S. attack unsubstantiated, Khrushchev returned to his first assessment of Kennedy. "It is necessary to take into consideration," he reminded his colleagues, "that the United States did not attack Cuba." It had been five days since Kennedy's "quarantine" speech, and nothing had happened. Malinovsky had told him that the United States could launch a successful invasion in twenty-four hours. So why hadn't it?

"Kennedy did not make his radio and television address out of courage," said Khrushchev. Now convinced it had been part of a plot to create a pretext for invading Cuba, he added, "They wanted to present us as the guilty ones and then invade Cuba." But by standing firm, Moscow had forced the White House and the Pentagon to reconsider. "To my mind they are not ready to do it now." By showing resolve, Khrushchev explained, Moscow had altered the climate of decision for Kennedy. Consequently, he concluded, "[t]he measures which we have undertaken were right."

Khrushchev warned that though he doubted that Washington would now go ahead with its invasion, "there was no guarantee." The offer he had made on October 26 was not going to be enough to carry them through this. "We cannot liquidate the conflict, if we don't give some satisfaction to the Americans and acknowledge that we have R-12s (MRBMs) there." To put a fine point on his comments, Khrushchev said, "We must not be obstinate."

Aware that he lacked a guarantee of American good behavior, Khrushchev had earlier endorsed Malinovsky's proposal to allow Pliyev to defend himself. But he had not wanted a war. He was not in a position to launch an attack in the Western Hemisphere; nor did he see any advantage in invading Berlin or any other place where he held a local advantage. But the fact that Kennedy had not taken any military action seemed to imply that he was having doubts as well about the utility of U.S. power.

Khrushchev discouraged any grand analysis of Operation Anadyr. "Did we make a mistake or not? It will be possible to determine this later." Instead, he wanted to discuss an idea that he had for dramatically improving the Soviet Union's situation in the crisis. "If we could achieve additionally the liquidation of the bases in Turkey we would win." Turkey had never been a highlight of any previous Presidium discussion in this crisis.[64] However, for a day at least, Khrushchev had been sitting on feelers from the Kennedy camp implying the possibility of exchanging the U.S. missiles in Turkey for the Soviet missiles in Cuba. Now it was the time to act on them. What had not been a determinative issue at all for Khrushchev, the Jupiter missiles in Turkey, now presented the Kremlin with a means of snatching a victory from the jaws of defeat.

The Turkish missiles had long been for Khrushchev a symbol of U.S. nuclear superiority. But if he needed a prod to bring them up as a way of exacting a price from Washington to end the crisis, it may have come in the form of the GRU's October 24 report on Bolshakov's meetings with Bartlett and Holeman, which had reached Moscow midday on October 25. Or it may have taken the form of a column by the prominent American foreign policy pundit Walter Lippmann, advocating a swap to end the crisis. Khrushchev, who followed Lippmann's writings carefully, read the swap column, which was published in American newspapers on October 25, before he headed into the meeting.[65] He did not consider Lippmann a channel to the U.S. government, but he knew that Lippmann was close to the more liberal members of the administration.[66]

Khrushchev had other reasons for believing that the Kennedy administration might respond favorably to this new demand. Since August, Khrushchev had known that NATO was going ahead with the deployment of the Jupiters in Turkey, without much confidence in their deterrent value.[67] Sources at NATO reported to the KGB that Turkey was one of a number of NATO countries that would eventually be receiving U.S. Polaris submarines. Over the course of the next two to three years, the United States intended to train the Turkish navy to run these submarines. The Polaris missiles, however, would always remain under U.S. control. Evidence that NATO was moving to this form of nuclear threat made it even more probable that Washington would approve a trade.

Khrushchev dictated his new letter in the presence of the rest of the Presidium. "It is with great pleasure that I studied your reply to Mr. U Thant," he began. On October 25 Kennedy had sent a message to the acting secretary-general vowing to avoid clashes with any Soviet ships that stayed outside the "interception zone." "This reasonable step on your part," he continued, "persuades me that you are showing solicitude for the preservation of peace, and I note this with satisfaction." After reiterating that the security of Cuba had prompted his putting missiles there, Khrushchev got to the point of this urgent letter:

> We agree to remove those weapons from Cuba which you regard as offensive weapons. We agree to do this and to state this commitment in the United Nations. Your representatives will make a statement to the effect that the United States, on its part, bearing in mind the anxiety and concern of the Soviet state, will evacuate its analogous weapons from Turkey. Let us reach an agreement on what time you and we need to put this into effect.

Khrushchev continued the analogy between Cuba and Turkey. After the missiles are gone from both countries, the Soviet Union will pledge in the Security Council

to respect the integrity of the frontiers and the sovereignty of Turkey, not to intervene in its domestic affairs, not to invade Turkey, not to make available its territory as a place d'armes for such an invasion, and also will restrain those who could think of launching an aggression against Turkey either from Soviet territory or from the territory of the states bordering on Turkey.

Once the USSR does this, Khrushchev argued, "[t]he U.S. government will make the same statement in the Security Council with regard to Cuba."

It appears that Khrushchev stood apart from most of the Presidium in believing that the United States would not attack Cuba. The group decided that additional precautions had to be taken just in case his instincts were wrong. The letter was typed up quickly and mindful of the delay surrounding the previous letter to Washington, the Presidium decided to broadcast the letter on Radio Moscow. On October 22 the Kremlin was prepared to let Pliyev use tactical nuclear weapons to defend himself. A week later the Presidium had no desire to risk a misunderstanding with Pliyev over whether he had this right or not. A terse injunction was prepared and sent at about the same time as the new letter to Kennedy was read over the radio: "You are forbidden to apply nuclear warheads to FKR, Luna, Il-28s without authorization from Moscow."[68]

The Presidium also decided to instruct Pliyev to send the warheads for the as yet undelivered R-14s back to Moscow. They were still on board the Soviet ship *Aleksandrovsk*, in La Isabela harbor.[69] Having reached Cuba just before the blockade went into effect, the *Aleksandrovsk* had seemed the safest place to keep the warheads until a proper nuclear storage area for the R-14s was built. Now the Kremlin's greater concern was that the U.S. Navy would capture or destroy these twenty-four Soviet nuclear warheads in an attack on the Cuban port.

Moscow believed Castro had a role to play in the endgame. There was no time for the Cuban leader to okay the new letter to Kennedy—it would take three to four hours for him to receive and comment on the text. There was the telephone, but this link was not secure. Instead, the Presidium instructed Alekseev to tell Castro as soon as possible that Khrushchev's public letter was designed to "head off whatever the U.S. had planned or was planning." The Kremlin was confident that its maneuver would work. Kennedy, it believed, did not want the world to accuse him of "the worst Hitlerian treachery."

It is almost inconceivable that in response to the steps taken in connection with the initiative to U Thant and especially in answer to our letter of October 27 that the Americans would undertake the adventure of using its military forces in an invasion on Cuba. If the U.S. were to do so, it would be seen by the entire world as the aggressor and an enemy of peace.[70]

Moscow hoped that by persuading Castro of the wisdom of this diplomatic course, he would take steps to reduce the tension in the region. The Kremlin instructed Alekseev to encourage Castro to make a public statement approving the terms of Khrushchev's Turkish proposal. In addition, the Kremlin was hoping the Cubans would provide assurances to Secretary-General U Thant that all work had ceased at Soviet military installations.

For Khrushchev there was now no turning back. He had made his willingness to negotiate public. His actions in the last twenty-four hours served notice to the Cubans, the Americans, and his own colleagues that he lacked confidence in the one deterrent that the Soviet Union had in the Caribbean. All of the MRBMs were fireable, and in less than four hours they could be tipped with nuclear weapons. Why did he not announce that these missiles were ready and that if the United States invaded or launched an air strike, he would feel compelled to use them? After all, he believed that nuclear weapons were the gods of war. He had overridden the caution of the Stalinists around him to put the missiles there in the first place. Why didn't he now use them politically, as he had always intended? In the heat of the crisis, Khrushchev backed away from threatening nuclear war. Time and again between 1956 and 1961, he had threatened nuclear retaliation as a bargaining chip to further his political objectives. But Khrushchev did not have the desire to threaten nuclear war when it might actually lead to one.

Havana, Saturday, October 27, 10 A.M. (5 P.M., Moscow Time)

Saturday, October 27, began badly in Cuba. There was a powerful tropical storm. Soviet and Cuban officers tried to maintain the highest military readiness while worrying that the torrential rains would short-circuit their communications. Not far from the northeastern port of Banes, the headquarters of an antiaircraft unit was huddled in a shack when it received word that an American U-2 had been sighted near Guantánamo. Forbidden to fire without authorization, the commander, Captain N. Antonyets, called Pliyev's headquarters. "The connection, despite the rain, was very clear." Antonyets asked for instructions.[71]

Pliyev was not at his command. His deputy, Lieutenant General Grechko, and the staff chief for military preparedness, Lieutenant General Garbuz, told the air defense commander to wait while they tried to reach Pliyev. The Soviet general had left strict instructions that he alone could authorize the use of force. The phone rang . . . there was no answer. Garbuz had rushed to Pliyev's headquarters at the time of the report that the U-2 had crossed over Guantánamo. There was not a moment to waste before it would leave Cuban airspace. The telephone rang again . . . still no answer. "The decision to terminate this flight was an operational-strategic necessity," Garbuz recalls. He and Grechko discussed their options. If they waited to hear from Pliyev, the plane, flown by Captain Rudolf Anderson, would be out of reach. Nerves were on edge. An American attack was thought to be a matter of hours away. Grechko and Garbuz mistakenly believed that whatever photographs Anderson's plane was taking would facilitate a U.S. air attack later that day or the next.[72]

Captain Antonyets received the order to launch his SA-2 rockets at target 33. At 10:22 A.M. the first shot of the Cuban missile crisis produced its first casualty. The rocket exploded next to the U-2, causing it to plunge to the ground. Anderson died in the crash. When Pliyev reached his command post and was told of Grechko's unilateral decision, he requested a report for the Ministry of Defense. There would be no formal reprimand.[73]

Anderson's plane was destroyed less than one hour after the Ministry of Defense in Moscow began cabling the Kremlin's latest instructions to Pliyev. For all of Khrushchev's efforts to control the use of force in Cuba, he had not been able to prevent the first American casualty. His commanders in Cuba had given a liberal interpretation to his earlier order to defend their positions from a U.S. air attack. The crisis now moved into its most dangerous phase since October 22.

Washington, Saturday, October 27, 10 A.M. (5 P.M., Moscow Time)

The Soviet Union had been the U.S. intelligence community's primary target since early 1946, and yet, as the Kennedy brothers, Bundy, Rusk, and the other key New Frontiersmen were steadying themselves for what many thought would be the most important day of decision since October 21, none of America's intelligence services could tell them what was going on in the Kremlin.

The first order of business, when the Ex Comm gathered at 10 A.M. on Saturday, was supposed to be preparing an answer to Khrushchev's "knot" letter of October 26.[74] But no sooner had the meeting begun than President Kennedy was handed what seemed to be a new letter from the Kremlin, which was being read over Radio Moscow. Unsure of what this was, Kennedy read from the ticker tape: "Premier Khrushchev told President Kennedy yesterday he would withdraw offensive missiles from Cuba if the United States withdrew its rockets from Turkey."[75]

There was a stir in the room, and many of the Ex Comm members began to talk.

"He didn't say that, did he?"

Kennedy, surprised by what seemed to be new terms for ending the crisis, added, "That wasn't in the letter we received, was it?"

Khrushchev's effort to turn a sow's ear into a silk purse caught the Kennedy administration off guard. Kennedy and his advisers had been discussing the possibility of a trade from the moment there was U-2 evidence of Soviet missile emplacements in Cuba. But every scenario considered involved secret, private discussions of the Jupiter missiles. No U.S. leader would want a public deal that might undermine NATO confidence.

At first the administration hoped a mistake had been made. "Will you check and be sure that the letter that's coming in on the ticker is the letter that we were seeing last night," Rusk asked a subordinate. There was no mistake. The president realized he could not duck this offer. "Where are we with our conversations with the Turks about the withdrawal of these . . . ?"

Kennedy was annoyed and confused. So were his advisers. Hadn't the KGB man Feklisov presented an elaboration of the first letter, which clearly stated Khrushchev's terms as a noninvasion pledge in return for the withdrawal of the missiles?

The national security adviser, Bundy, suggested that this second message be ignored. "It's very odd, Mr. President, if he's changed his terms from a long letter to you and an urgent appeal from the Counselor [Feklisov] only last night, set in a purely Cuban context, it seems to me we're well within our— there's nothing wrong with our posture in sticking to that line."

Kennedy did not like Bundy's suggestion. He did not believe he could avoid trading away the Jupiter missiles. "[T]o any man at the United Nations or any other rational man it will look like a very fair trade." Over the objections of most of his advisers, Kennedy outlined the bases for a trade: "I think you're going to find it very difficult to explain why we are going to take hostile military action in Cuba, against these sites—what we've been thinking about—the thing that he's saying is, 'If you'll get yours out of Turkey, we'll get ours out of Cuba.' I think we've got a very tough one here."

Kennedy was alone in his position, and his advisers, particularly Bundy, Sorensen, and the Defense Department's Paul Nitze, wore him down. They convinced him that the cost to NATO of an immediate acceptance of the deal was too high. Instead, he should stall for time, to test Khrushchev again, in the hope that he might settle for the terms laid out in his letter of October 26.

Robert Kennedy agreed with his brother that time was of the essence; but he did not agree that the Jupiters should be traded away. On Friday morning he had said nothing when the president signaled an interest in trading for the Soviet missiles. Now he felt he had to speak up. "I just don't see," he said, "how we can ask the Turks to give up their defense." He felt that the principal threat was to Latin America, and this had to be dealt with first, before any European matters. He offered to work out a response to Khrushchev that dealt with the problem at hand but left open the possibility of future discussions on disarmament in Turkey.

The president had little patience for his brother's plan. He was most concerned that the work on the Soviet bases be halted as soon as possible: "We can't permit ourselves to be impaled on a long negotiating hook while the work goes on at these bases."

One reason why the president found so much opposition to a trade was that many of his advisers were convinced that the two letters were written by different groups in the Soviet government. The second letter, in their view, had to be the product of the Kremlin militarists, who wanted to present Washington with an unacceptable, or at least humiliating, proposal. If Kennedy could find a way to address himself directly to Khrushchev, they believed, the trade might be unnecessary.

Indeed, the Kremlin's actions had puzzled Kennedy. Turning to his favorite Kremlinologist, Llewellyn Thompson, Kennedy asked, "The only thing is, Tommy, why wouldn't they say it privately if they were serious." No one in the room stopped to think that Khrushchev might have changed his mind, that something might have encouraged him to extract a higher price for dismantling his missile bases on Cuba.

The Ex Comm broke off its first session of the day just after noon. A few of the members reconvened at the State Department at 2:30 to continue discussing Khrushchev's two letters and the effect his new demand would have on the Turks. But the main group met again at the White House at 4:00 P.M., to review a draft of Kennedy's response to Khrushchev and to discuss how to handle NATO. There was general agreement that a NATO meeting had to be called in the next few days to explore the implications of the Soviet demand. The Ex Comm, however, could not agree on what should be asked of the Turks.

It was in the midst of a discussion of how to handle the Turks, a little after 4:00 P.M., that the group learned that Rudolf Anderson's U-2 had been shot down.[76]

"U-2 shot down?" asked Robert Kennedy.

"Yes . . . said it was found shot down," responded McNamara.

"This is much of an escalation by them, isn't it?" said the president.

The U-2 had been several hours overdue at McCoy Air Force Base, at Orlando, Florida. A report of a downed U-2 broadcast in the afternoon by Radio Havana solved the mystery. After ascertaining that the pilot was dead, the Ex Comm's concern was whether he had been killed by the Cubans or by the Soviets. Initial reports were that the plane had disappeared near the SA-2 site at Banes. Normally the Soviets and not the Cubans manned all of those sites. Unless a group of Cubans had seized control of the Banes installation, it meant that the Soviets had attacked an American plane without waiting for Kennedy's response to Khrushchev's offers.

"How do we explain the effect?" asked Kennedy. "[T]his Khrushchev message of last night and their decision. . . . How do we—I mean that's a . . ." The president faced a terrible decision. It was established U.S. policy to retaliate against any Cuban SA-2 site that fired on a U-2. For days sixteen U.S. planes had been standing by on thirty-minute alert to destroy any SA-2 site.[77] Should the United States retaliate now? McNamara warned Kennedy that if he wanted the air force to be ready to launch an air strike early in the week, maintaining reconnaissance over the weekend was critical. "We can't very well send a U-2 over there, can we, now?" asked Kennedy. "And have a guy killed again tomorrow." Kennedy decided to wait until morning to decide whether to retaliate.

There were other signs Saturday afternoon that the Soviets and the Cubans were seriously preparing for war. An hour or so before the news of the U-2 reached the Ex Comm, Kennedy learned that some Cuban antiaircraft batteries had fired on U.S. planes doing low-level reconnaissance. None of the planes was shot down, though one was hit. For many in the Ex Comm the flak attack and the loss of a U-2 seemed to imply that Khrushchev was not in complete control of the situation in Moscow. There was already talk in Washington that the second letter, the Turkish swap letter, had to have come from a hard-line faction in the Kremlin. Perhaps Khrushchev was no longer in command?

Following the afternoon session of the Ex Comm, Kennedy's closest foreign policy team gathered to discuss what to do next. Kennedy was ready to sign the new letter to Khrushchev, which essentially ignored Moscow's public demand for a swap, but there was no guarantee that offering a pledge not to invade Cuba would be enough to satisfy the Kremlin. The gaggle of advisers in the room—Rusk, Bundy, Robert Kennedy, and two or three others—agreed that time was running out. With the recent attacks on American planes over Cuba, the White House would very soon have to decide whether to use force in some way.

President Kennedy doubted that the crisis could be solved without mentioning the Jupiters to Khrushchev. As he had so often before, John Kennedy chose his brother to carry out a special task for him. This time Robert would go to the Soviet ambassador to seek a political solution to this fast-deteriorating crisis. Robert was not to lead with the idea of a swap; but the brothers understood that this would probably be the Soviets' price, and John Kennedy was ready to pay it. Dean Rusk participated in shaping Robert Kennedy's instructions. The Kennedys accepted his suggestion that the Soviets be told that the Jupiter missiles could be removed in four to five months. Rusk also stressed that Moscow not be allowed to think of this as a quid pro quo, but Kennedy decided to let his brother draw the fine line between offering a trade to the Soviets and promising them that the Turkish missiles would be dismantled soon.[78]

Rusk played one other part in the evening's drama. The president asked him to get in touch with Andrew Cordier, a professor at Columbia University who had been deputy UN secretary-general. Kennedy wanted Cordier to suggest to U Thant that the UN call on the superpowers to withdraw their missiles from Cuba and Turkey, respectively. In case Robert's mission failed, Kennedy believed, this might present him with another way of resolving the crisis peacefully.[79]

At approximately 7:15 P.M. Robert Kennedy called the Soviet embassy to arrange an appointment with Dobrynin. "I asked him if he would come to the Justice Department at a quarter of eight," Kennedy wrote later.[80] Within half an hour Dobrynin and Robert Kennedy were alone in the latter's office. "I want to lay out the current alarming situation the way the president sees it," Robert Kennedy began.[81] The president, he explained, feared an escalation as a result of the shooting down of the U-2 that day: "there is now strong pressure on the president to give an order to respond with fire if fired upon." He added, "if we start to fire in response—a chain reaction will quickly start that will be very hard to stop." Dobrynin could readily divine what the president's brother meant by "chain reaction."

Kennedy repeated the substance of the new letter to Khrushchev that his brother was about to send. The president considered Khrushchev's order to withdraw the missiles in return for a U.S. commitment not to invade as a "suitable basis for regulating the entire Cuban affair." In the meantime, Robert Kennedy stressed that the cardinal point of the U.S. strategy was to get the Soviets to stop their work on the missile sites.

In exchange for stopping work and disabling the missile sites, the United States would repeal the embargo and, the attorney general promised, "give assurances that there would not be any invasion of Cuba and that other countries of the Western Hemisphere are ready to give the same assurance—the U.S. government is certain of this."

"And what about Turkey?" Dobrynin asked.

Here Robert Kennedy presented the oral coda to John Kennedy's earlier response: "If that is the only obstacle to achieving the regulation I mentioned earlier, then the president doesn't see any insurmountable difficulties in resolving this issue."

As he had done a year earlier with Georgi Bolshakov, the attorney general explained to a Soviet representative what a U.S. president could and could not say publicly. "The greatest difficulty for the president is the public discussion of the issue of Turkey." He told Dobrynin that beside himself and the president only two or three other members of the administration knew about this. He said that the United States would "need four to five months" to remove the missile bases from Turkey. "[I]f such a decision were announced now," he explained, "it would seriously tear apart NATO." Tearing apart NATO had been a Soviet objective since the late 1940s. However, at this moment the offer, despite these conditions, was welcomed.

Kennedy ended his presentation with "a request . . . not an ultimatum." The president wanted a "businesslike, clear answer in principle" through Dobrynin. The White House, Robert Kennedy explained, wanted to bring this alarming moment, with events "developing too quickly," to an end as soon as possible. Kennedy asked specifically that Khrushchev not send one of his trademark rambling letters that tied the interpreters at the State Department in knots and "which might drag these out." He also provided Dobrynin with some direct telephone numbers to the president.

Robert Kennedy returned to the White House in time for Saturday's third Ex Comm session. More than half of the members did not know that the president had authorized this special meeting with the Soviet ambassador.

Even those who knew, however, shared the general sense that a negotiated settlement was at best a fifty-fifty proposition.

Many in the Cabinet Room wanted the United States to respond forcefully if another U-2 was destroyed on Sunday. "Well, I think the point is," argued McNamara, "that if our planes are fired on tomorrow, we ought to fire back." Kennedy had other considerations in mind. "Let me say," he began, "I think we ought to wait till afternoon, to see whether we get any answer . . ." Kennedy did not finish this sentence. He did not say so; but he was obviously thinking in terms of giving Khrushchev time to digest his brother's conversation with Dobrynin.

McNamara also spoke for those who believed an invasion was inevitable, whatever the administration's diplomatic efforts. Turning to Robert Kennedy, McNamara said, "I think the one thing, Bobby, we ought to . . . we need to have two things ready, a government for Cuba, because we're going to need one . . . and secondly, plans for how to respond to the Soviet Union in Europe, because sure as hell they're going to do something there." President Kennedy understood McNamara's concerns. The vulnerability of U.S. allies had constrained Kennedy's actions regarding Cuba throughout this crisis. If the Turkish trade was not enough, the United States would have no choice but to intensify the pressure on Moscow. Then Italy, Berlin, and Turkey might face retribution. Kennedy crossed his fingers that there would be a peaceful way out of this quagmire.[82]

Moscow, Sunday, October 28, 10:45 A.M. (2:45 A.M., EST)*

At 10:45 A.M. on Sunday morning, Malinovsky briefed Khrushchev on what had occurred while he was sleeping.[83] Khrushchev did not leave the Kremlin that night, but it had been decided not to wake him when the report arrived after midnight that an American reconnaissance plane had been shot down over Cuba. Gromyko also had important news to report. Fidel Castro was panicking in Havana. He had written a letter that seemed to advocate the use of strategic nuclear weapons against the United States. Alekseev's summary of the letter had arrived at about 1 A.M. But the news from the Foreign Ministry was not all bad. The Kennedy administration had also sent word via two channels that it was ready to negotiate an end to the crisis along the lines of the Kremlin's October 26 letter. The KGB chief in Washington, Feklisov, had met with an American journalist named Scali, who claimed to have a White House proposal to end the crisis. The Foreign Ministry had considered the proposal barely credible because Scali had never been used before to send private messages to the Kremlin.[84] But this morning a new letter had arrived from Kennedy; it offered essentially the same deal to Khrushchev. Apparently the Americans wanted to ignore the Soviet demand regarding the Jupiter mis-

---

* North Americans had turned their clocks back one hour at 2:00 A.M.

siles and to concentrate instead on providing a pledge not to invade Cuba.[85]

The destruction of the American U-2 worried Khrushchev. It was just the type of incident that the Pentagon would use to force Kennedy's hand. To prevent something like this, he had cautioned Castro the day before not to use his antiaircraft guns. Now one of his own commanders had destroyed a U-2. What was especially infuriating was that this incident came on the heels of what appeared to be an excellent diplomatic proposal from the Kennedys. Khrushchev studied Kennedy's letter and Feklisov's report. The essence of the White House's proposal was contained in the central paragraph of the letter:

1) You would agree to remove these weapons systems from Cuba under appropriate United Nations observation and supervision; and undertake, with suitable safeguards, to halt the further introduction of such weapons systems into Cuba.

2) We, on our part, would agree—upon the establishment of adequate arrangements through the United Nations to ensure the carrying out and continuation of these commitments—(a) to remove promptly the quarantine measures now in effect and (b) to give assurances against an invasion of Cuba. I am confident that other nations of the Western Hemisphere would be prepared to do likewise.[86]

This was not all that Khrushchev had asked for on October 27, but it was consistent with the Presidium's minimum terms for pulling out the missiles. This was an acceptable beginning. Anticipating that a decision would have to be made that day, Khrushchev ordered the entire Presidium, its members and candidate members, and even the relevant secretaries of the Central Committee to meet him at noon at a government dacha in Novo-Ogarevo, a Moscow suburb.

In opening the session, Khrushchev dramatically portrayed the danger facing the Soviet experiment. War was in the air, and under these conditions he needed the Presidium to take a difficult but necessary decision.

There was a time, when we advanced, like in October 1917; but in March 1918 we had to retreat, having signed the Brest-Litovsk agreement with the Germans. Our interests dictated this decision—we had to save Soviet power. Now we found ourselves face to face with the danger of war and of nuclear catastrophe, with the possible result of destroying the human race. In order to save the world, we must retreat. I called you together to consult and debate whether you are in agreement with this kind of decision.[87]

Khrushchev was preparing to ask the Presidium to support him in accepting Kennedy's letter of October 27. It would have been better to have obtained the removal of the Jupiter missiles; but with the situation moving out of control in Cuba it was prudent to accept what Moscow could get. Khrushchev's previous doubts about Washington had returned, and he was no longer convinced that the threat of a U.S. invasion had passed. The Soviet military had picked up a rumor that Kennedy was preparing to deliver a nationally broadcast speech that night.[88]

Before turning to the difficult discussion of acceptable terms for ending the crisis, the Presidium prepared for the possibility that the United States might launch a strike against Cuba that day. It was decided to allow General Pliyev to use force to defend himself. Although it said nothing in its decision about the use of tactical nuclear weapons, the Presidium hinted at the possibility that Pliyev might still receive authorization to use those under his command. "If the attack is provoked," the Presidium decided, "it is ordered to repel it with a responsive blow."[89]

At this point Oleg Troyanovsky, one of Khrushchev's assistants who was also at the dacha, received a telephone call from the Foreign Ministry. A report from Anatoly Dobrynin had just arrived that described an interesting meeting with the president's brother. With an ear cocked to the telephone, Troyanovksy noted down the essentials. Regarding trading the Turkish missiles: he "doesn't see any insurmountable difficulties." Regarding the pace of future negotiations: "[This is] a request . . . not an ultimatum." One part to all of this, however, worried Troyanovsky. Apparently the American president was under severe pressure from the Pentagon to act. Robert Kennedy stressed that the Americans needed an answer from Moscow on Sunday, that very day: "[T]here is very little time to resolve this whole issue. . . . [E]vents are developing too quickly." His notes complete, Troyanovsky entered the hall and interrupted the session: "I . . . began to read my notes on Dobrynin's report. They [Khrushchev and the others] asked me to read the notes again. It goes without saying that the contents of the dispatch increased the nervousness in the hall by some degrees."[90]

There was no time to waste. Khrushchev called a stenographer over and began to dictate in the meeting hall his acceptance of the White House's proposals:

> I have received your message of October 27. I express my satisfaction and thank you for the sense of proportion you have displayed. . . .
>
> In order to eliminate as rapidly as possible the conflict which endangers the cause of peace . . . the Soviet Government, in addition to earlier instructions on the discontinuation of further work on weapons construction sites, has given a new order to dismantle the arms which you described as offensive, and to crate and return them to the Soviet Union."[91]

In addition to the public letter, Khrushchev sent two private messages to Kennedy, which Dobrynin was to convey orally to Robert Kennedy. The first confirmed what Kennedy would soon hear on the radio:

The views which R. Kennedy expressed at the request of the President in the meeting with Dobrynin in the evening of October 27, are known in Moscow. Today the response will be given by radio to the president and this response will be positive. In the main, the issue that agitates the president—namely, the removal of the missile bases from Cuba under international control—does not meet with any objections and will be explicated in detail in the message of N. S. Khrushchev.[92]

The second, a more secret message, explained that the Kremlin expected the White House to keep its promise to withdraw the Turkish missiles. Khrushchev explained that he took Robert Kennedy's statement that "it would take 4–5 months to remove the missile bases from Turkey" and his subsequent request that all discussion of a resolution of the Turkish issue be kept highly confidential to mean that the Kennedy administration had accepted his Turkish demand.

In my letter to you of October 28, which was designed for publication, I did not touch on this matter because of your wish, as conveyed by Robert Kennedy. But all of the offers, which were included in this letter, were given on account of your having agreed to the Turkish issue raised in my letter of October 27 and announced by Robert Kennedy, from your side, in his meeting with the Soviet ambassador that same day.[93]

Though pleased with how well the negotiations were turning out, Khrushchev feared a last-minute surprise. Concerned that some third party—a trigger-happy antiaircraft gunman in Cuba or a disgruntled general in the Pentagon—might undermine a settlement, the Presidium decided, as it had on Saturday, to have the main letter to Kennedy read over Radio Moscow so that it would be received quickly in Washington. Khrushchev instructed Leonid F. Ilichov, one of the Central Committee secretaries, to rush a copy of the letter to Radio Moscow for immediate broadcast. He also wanted the Soviet command in Cuba to exercise better control over the situation on the island. "We think that you were in a hurry to shoot down a U.S. reconnaissance U-2 plane," Khrushchev cabled to Pliyev. Moscow now strictly forbade Pliyev to use the SA-2 missiles and grounded all Soviet jets in Cuba "to avoid a clash with U.S. reconnaissance planes."[94]

Now that a negotiated settlement was within reach, Khrushchev also had to confront the problem of what to do about Castro. From Castro's late-night message he had concluded that the Cuban had lost all sense of proportion and was advocating nuclear suicide. What else could Castro have meant in calling this "the moment to eliminate such danger [of U.S. invasion] forever"? Khrushchev intended to set Castro straight at some later date on why he had been wrong to react the way he did. But the needs of this day required a calming letter that would discourage Castro from doing anything rash to upset the final stages of the negotiations. With the explanation that militarists in Washington would seize upon any opportunity to wreck the diplomatic agreement with Kennedy, Khrushchev asked Castro, in a letter that he hastily dictated along with the rest, to refrain from opening fire against American planes.

At 4:00 P.M.—or 8:00 A.M., EST—an hour before Radio Moscow beamed Khrushchev's letter around the world, Malinovsky ordered Pliyev to begin dismantling the R-12 sites. The nuclear deterrent that Khrushchev had worked so hard to create in the Caribbean, and which had only just now become fully operational, was to be destroyed.

Washington, Sunday Morning, October 28, 9:00 A.M., EST (5 P.M., Moscow Time)

Maxwell Taylor convened an early-morning meeting of the Joint Chiefs on Sunday to discuss the next American move if Khrushchev rejected the proposals contained in the president's October 27 letter. The chiefs, who had not been told about Robert Kennedy's private session with the Soviet ambassador on Saturday evening, felt they had good reason to believe that military action of some sort was inevitable. "Monday will be the last time to attack the missiles before they become fully operational," said Curtis LeMay, who had been ready for days to send his air force into battle. "I want to see the President later today," LeMay insisted. Taylor was about to explain the reconnaissance flights over Cuba that had been prepared that day, when an assistant entered with a ticker tape of uncommon importance.[95] At 9 A.M. Radio Moscow broadcast Khrushchev's acceptance of the Kennedy formula.

Looking over the text of the Kremlin leader's statement, the air force chief was not impressed: "The Soviets may make a charade of withdrawal and keep some weapons in Cuba."[96] The grumbling among the chiefs continued until Defense Secretary McNamara and two of his assistants joined the discussion a short while later. The civilians were satisfied with Khrushchev's statement, arguing that it left the United States "in a much stronger position." LeMay remained unimpressed and again insisted on seeing President Kennedy later that day. Whereas before Khrushchev's statement LeMay had allies, now his fellow chiefs fell silent. It was best to await the latest batch of reconnaissance photographs. They would be the proof of the new pudding.

Meanwhile, the White House was relieved when news of the broadcast from Moscow reached the president. All of the messy contingencies, considered in the expectation that Robert Kennedy's secret mission might fail, could be shelved. Back-channel diplomacy seemed to have succeeded. Robert Kennedy went to see the Soviet ambassador to express the U.S. government's satisfaction. At the Ex Comm meeting that started at 11:10 A.M., Bundy remarked that "everyone knew who were the hawks and who were the doves, but . . . today was the doves' day."[97]

On its own, CIA headquarters ordered a halt to "all action, maritime, and black infiltration." The message was sent to the CIA's Miami station at Opa Locka at 1:30 P.M. Later that afternoon the White House made the same request, and the CIA repeated the halt order at 4:30. Operation Mongoose was frozen.[98]

Havana, Sunday Afternoon, October 28

Not having expected Moscow to back down, Fidel Castro was furious when he heard the news broadcast over Radio Moscow. His missiles were going— and for what? For a verbal promise from his antagonist John Kennedy that he would not invade. Castro called a meeting of his military and political high command at 2:00 P.M. Colonel Meshcheriakov, who represented Soviet military intelligence in Cuba, was preparing to excuse himself from this meeting when Castro ostentatiously said, "I have no secrets from you. I will be saying the same things to Alekseev this evening."[99] With the Soviet representative in attendance, Castro pronounced a valedictory on the Soviet missile project.

"Cuba will not lose anything by the removal of the missiles, because she has already gained so much," Castro stated confidently. The missile crisis had focused international attention on the plight of his country. The fact that the Soviet Union had to go to such great lengths to protect him demonstrated the extent of American imperialism; and Castro hoped that as a result he might receive some international assistance in eliminating the American economic blockade.[100]

Castro's search for a silver lining did not make him any less angry at Moscow. He thought Khrushchev had mishandled the resolution of the crisis. It was not only the substance of Khrushchev's diplomacy that he found annoying; it was the fact that Moscow had cut a deal without any consultation of Havana. If the Soviet objective in deploying the missiles had been to protect his regime, why hadn't the Kremlin bothered to let him in on the negotiations with Kennedy? And Castro could not understand why Khrushchev had apparently given up on getting the Jupiter missiles removed from Turkey. Meshcheriakov knew nothing about the secret Dobrynin-Kennedy discussions, and the Kremlin had decided not to inform Castro. Consequently, Castro argued that Moscow had committed a grave "political mistake" by first publicly demanding the removal of the Jupiters and then dropping the requirement, apparently without any compensation, a day later.

Castro vowed not to make a resolution of the crisis any easier for Khrushchev. "We won't find a better time to demand the liquidation of the American military base at Guantánamo," he told his military. Castro intended to inform Washington that if it wanted to inspect the dismantled Soviet missile sites, the U.S. Navy would have to leave Guantánamo. Kennedy had indicated in his October 27 letter that these inspections were part of the package and that Khrushchev had already indicated his agreement. But Castro intended to exercise a veto over the agreement if Cuban demands were not met.

Alekseev did not see Castro that night. President Dorticós, to whom Alekseev delivered Khrushchev's letter of October 28, explained that Castro was outside of Havana and could not meet the Soviet ambassador. He reiterated Castro's stern appraisal of the Khrushchev-Kennedy agreement. The Cuban people, he said, view the agreement "unfavorably."[101]

Nikita Khrushchev may have averted a war with the United States. But if the removal of the missiles from Cuba alienated Fidel Castro, then the Kremlin's entire strategy in the Caribbean had failed. On October 29 Khrushchev decided to send Anastas Mikoyan to Havana to reassure the Cubans.

Mikoyan's Mission

November 2, 1962, began badly for Anastas Mikoyan. Khrushchev's personal envoy had a plane to catch at New York's Idlewild Airport for Montreal and then Havana. Just as Mikoyan was preparing to leave, the American representative at the United Nations, Ambassador Adlai Stevenson, handed him a list of "offensive weapons" that the United States wanted removed from Cuba as a price for lifting the naval blockade and ending the missile crisis. The Americans were complicating an already tense situation. It was Friday morning, less than a week since the superpowers had begun stepping away from the brink of nuclear war. The Kennedy administration had achieved a Soviet commitment to remove the R-12s and their warheads; now it apparently wanted to remove all of the most important Soviet military technology in Cuba, chiefly the forty-two Il-28 light bombers.

The American list and the demands it implied represented just one of Mikoyan's problems. Known in some Moscow circles as Cuba's man in the Kremlin, Mikoyan was now even unsure of the reception that awaited him in Havana. Moscow's ambassador in Havana, Aleksandr Alekseev, whose dispatches since 1959 had chronicled Castro's embrace of the Soviet Union, was now painting a dark picture for the Kremlin, expressing alarm for the first time at the long-term prospects for Cuban-Soviet relations.[1]

Mikoyan understood the stakes. Fidel Castro had posed as the reluctant suitor when Khrushchev described the nuclear missiles as necessary for the defense of Cuba. Now the Soviets had to explain to Castro, whom Alekseev described as being in a "highly agitated state," why they were prepared to remove these supposedly essential weapons in return for an oral guarantee from Washington not to invade.[2] Moreover, in his haste to demonstrate good will to the international community, Nikita Khrushchev had conceded the need for UN inspectors to visit the dismantled rocket sites in Cuba. No less a friend than Raúl Castro had warned the Kremlin that no Cuban leader could ever accept a settlement involving on-site inspections.

Khrushchev then worsened matters by attempting a curious maneuver to soften the blow in Havana. On October 28, after issuing his call for restraint from Castro, he sent a second message to Havana, in which he encouraged Castro to proclaim his support for the removal of the ballistic missiles.[3] For a generation it was thought that the meetings between Scali and Feklisov had played a role in the Kennedy-Khrushchev negotiations ending the crisis. They did not. But it was never guessed that the Soviets, in a half-baked scheme to convince the Cubans of the wisdom of diplomacy, told Castro about Scali's proposals. The Presidium instructed Alekseev to tell Castro that "in complete trust" the Soviet leaders were sharing a message from a source "we know well," who "circulates with individuals who occupy the very highest levels in the United States." Quoting Scali's suggestion that Castro issue a statement that he was ready to dismantle the missile sites and send them away if President Kennedy gave a guarantee not to invade Cuba, Moscow added, "[T]he proposals presented by this source are wholly acceptable to us." It was a sign of the Kremlin's desperation that Khrushchev could entertain the thought that Castro would assume personal and public responsibility for the removal of the missiles, especially when this proposal originated in the Kennedy White House.

Castro's response was defiance of both superpowers. On October 29 the Cuban newspaper *Revolución* published Castro's five-point program for resolving the crisis in the Caribbean. Feeling abandoned by the Soviet Union at the moment of greatest peril to Cuba, Castro announced that Cuba would seek its own agreement, according to its own needs, and regardless of Moscow's apparent acceptance of Kennedy's noninvasion pledge. The Castro administration would not consider the affair over until the U.S. government accepted five different conditions. It had to end the economic embargo, cease subversive activities against Cuba, prevent "pirate attacks" from offshore bases, stop the violations of Cuban airspace, and withdraw the U.S. Navy from Guantánamo.[4]

Before his plane took off, Mikoyan made a little speech to endorse Castro's five points. He hoped this might begin the process of reconciliation. He would still have his hands full.

Skepticism in Cuba

While welcoming Mikoyan's forthcoming visit, Alekseev was not pleased with the way in which the Kremlin was handling the aftermath of the missile debacle. On October 30 Khrushchev had sent a critical and patronizing letter to Havana that for two very good reasons had ensured that Mikoyan's reception in Havana would be cooler than it needed to be. First, the Kremlin addressed it to Fidel Castro *and the Cuban leadership.* Up to that point all of Khrushchev's letters had been sent to Castro personally. Castro's advisers lost no time in informing Alekseev of his irritation at this faux pas. Second, Khrushchev was freewheeling in his criticism of Castro's conduct during the crisis. "We are not struggling against imperialism," he told Castro, "in order to die."[5] Castro's suggestion, at the height of the crisis, that Moscow launch a first strike against the United States in lieu of giving in to Kennedy's pressure was not even seriously considered by Khrushchev, and the Kremlin wanted the Cuban leader to know that.

> As we learned from our ambassador, some Cubans have the opinion that the Cuban people want a declaration of another nature rather than the declaration of the withdrawal of the missiles. It's possible that this kind of feeling exists among the people. But we, political and government figures, are leaders of a people who don't know everything and can't readily comprehend all that we leaders must deal with. Therefore, we should march at the head of the people and then the people will follow us and respect us.[6]

Shaking his head at this misguided letter, Alekseev offered his bosses some advice on how to treat the volatile Cuban leader. "Knowing how close Castro's emotions are to the surface," he cabled, "I believe that we mustn't hurry and push him or, even more important now, engage him in polemics." After all, he assured Moscow, the problem was not really Castro's communism but his character.[7]

As Alekseev had predicted, Castro showed his anger in a letter that he sent October 31. Citing the "surprising, sudden and practically unconditional decision to withdraw the weapons," Castro criticized Moscow's handling of the missile crisis.[8] News of this retreat, he asserted, brought tears to "[c]ountless eyes of Cuban and Soviet men who were willing to die with supreme dignity."[9] Castro reminded Moscow that he had not been consulted before the Kremlin decided to end the missile operation. He also took issue with Khrushchev's implicit criticism of his call for a Soviet nuclear strike on the United States. "I did not suggest to you," he wrote, ". . . that the USSR should be the aggressor, because that would be more than incorrect, it would be immoral and insane." Having in mind the Soviet Union's failure to act in time to deter Adolf Hitler in 1941, Castro had wanted Khrushchev to be ready to use nuclear weapons if the United States attacked Cuba in 1962. The military position of the socialist camp in the Caribbean was so tenuous that escalation to the nuclear level was unavoidable if Cuba was to be saved.[10]

Even though Castro ended the letter on an upbeat note, pledging that "nothing can destroy the ties of friendship and eternal gratitude we feel toward the USSR," it deepened Alekseev's anxiety. "I take from that," the Soviet ambassador wrote to Moscow, "that one or two years of especially careful work with Castro will be required until he acquires all of the qualities of Marxist-Leninist party spirit."[11] Describing Castro's letter as exhibiting "transitory irritation," he recommended that the Kremlin not respond to it. If Moscow felt the need to respond to Castro, he suggested, with more than a touch of irony, the language to use:

We are pleased that you have been frank with us because it befits Marxism-Leninism. Only under this condition is genuine friendship possible. It is not for us to debate who is right—history will decide. We fully share your assessment of imperialism and will therefore do all that is necessary to obstruct its activities not only through confrontation but by using diplomatic means. In your just struggle you can always rely on us.[12]

Above all, Alekseev saw as integral to shoring up Moscow's jilted ally a statement that emphasized "the virility of the Cuban people and Castro's personal courage and concern for the fate of his people and the work of socialism." As regards Castro's anger at not having participated in the decision to remove the missiles, Alekseev suggested that Khrushchev explain that the events of October were unusual and that the "difficulty of the situation did not allow for the kind of consultation that would be expected under normal circumstances."[13] After reiterating that Moscow had to focus its efforts on Castro the man, Alekseev closed his extraordinary dispatch with the customary Soviet salutation "If I am mistaken, please correct me."[14]

Fidel Castro waited until the last possible moment, when Mikoyan's plane was already in the air, to decide whether to welcome his Soviet guest at the airport. Initially Castro wanted only Moscow's stalwarts, Raúl Castro and Che Guevara, to greet Mikoyan. The Cuban people were not ready to have their leader embrace Mikoyan, and Fidel Castro wanted to signal his personal annoyance at Moscow. But then he received from *Prensa Latina* a copy of a speech that Mikoyan gave before his flight left New York on November 2. Liking the conciliatory tone of the speech and its indication of Soviet support for his five points, Castro made up his mind to lead a delegation of his entire cabinet to meet Mikoyan at the airfield.[15]

The first serious Soviet-Cuban meeting occurred at ten the next morning. "Fidel took me into his private apartment," Mikoyan said in a top secret cable to Moscow. "He met me on the sidewalk in front of the building, where my car stopped, and directed me upstairs." Castro spoke in a "calm, friendly tone," though the content of what he was saying left no doubt he opposed Soviet policy. Mikoyan commented on Castro's courtesy in his first reports of the meetings as if he had expected the revolutionary to misbehave.[16]

Mikoyan understood his mission as calming the Cubans so that they would not complicate the final phase of the crisis. The Kremlin put great stock in obtaining a formal noninvasion pledge from Kennedy, perhaps a treaty lodged with the UN. This would not be possible, however, without some form of inspection on Cuba to convince the Americans that all of the ballistic missiles had been removed. And for that Moscow needed Havana's cooperation.

Mikoyan set out first to persuade the Cubans that, despite the shame of having to remove ballistic missiles under threat of American retaliation, Khrushchev and Cuba had come out the winners in the crisis. Without mentioning the Kennedys' promise to dismantle the U.S. missiles in Turkey, which Khrushchev intended to conceal even from Castro, Mikoyan made the case that Khrushchev's diplomatic achievements in the difficult days of October 27 and October 28 would bring Cuba as much security as the missiles.[17] "We mustn't underestimate the value of the diplomatic means of struggle," Mikoyan noted. "They are very important in periods when there is no war."[18]

Mikoyan was also prepared to admit that this success came in a completely unplanned, traumatic way. "The goal of the installation of Soviet forces and strategic weapons on Cuba," he began, "was solely to shore up your defensive capabilities." He then revealed how matters had gone awry.

This was a containment plan, a plan designed not to be playing with fire in relations with Cuba. If only the strategic weapons would be deployed under conditions of secrecy, and the Americans would not know of their existence in Cuba, then this would be a strong means of containment. We proceeded on the assumption, our military had advised us, that under the palm leaves of Cuba the strategic weapons would be safely hidden from overhead reconnaissance.[19]

Was Mikoyan actually serious, the Cubans must have wondered. But the old Bolshevik betrayed not a smidgen of facetiousness. He admitted that the project began to unravel much sooner than perhaps anyone in Havana had thought. In the middle of September the CIA had learned from the Bundesnachrichtendienst, the West German intelligence service, of the transportation of Soviet strategic missiles to Cuba. Curiously, Mikoyan made no attempt to describe the Presidium's reaction to this news in September or to explain why Cuba had not been warned of these complications. If secrecy had been the key to success, then from mid-September on, Khrushchev knew that the entire operation was doomed. This unsatisfying explanation of an operation gone awry was not likely to increase Cuba's respect for its Soviet protector.

Finally Mikoyan sought to explain why foreign inspections were necessary and acceptable. "What we are speaking of," he told Castro, "is not a broad inspection, but a verification of the sites, known to the Americans due to aerial photography and which have been the locations of the strategic missile launchers." He assured Castro that it "was not a question of any permanent or general inspection" but might involve a one-day visit to the sites by neutral observers and a verification program at Cuban ports that might last, at most, several days. Moscow had offered to permit inspection because otherwise "the Americans would have taken it for our desire to swindle them." However, Mikoyan added, "Cuban issues are [to be] solved by the Cuban leadership only."[20]

Mikoyan's mission had barely begun when a personal tragedy intervened. Nearly two hours into this crucial first meeting with Castro, Mikoyan was handed a cable with the news that his wife had just died in Moscow.[21] In Khrushchev's telegram of condolence, Mikoyan was told that the decision to return for his wife's funeral or to remain in Cuba was a matter left to his own judgment. With this terrible news, the Cubans and Soviets decided to suspend the meeting.

The talks resumed the next day, November 4. Mikoyan did not bother to hide his sadness, but he pressed on professionally. Considered Cuba's biggest advocate in the Presidium, he felt a personal obligation to repair as much of the damage as possible, as soon as possible. He resolved to stay in Cuba and send his son, Sergo, who had accompanied him to Havana, back for the funeral. Mikoyan's lone request was that he be informed "immediately, by all possible means, of the day and hour of the funeral of his wife."[22]

His mind concentrated by his wife's death, Mikoyan threw himself into convincing the Cubans of the validity of Khrushchev's decision to withdraw the missiles. No doubt he tried the patience of the Cubans. His cables to Khrushchev emphasized the length and tediousness of his own presentations: "During the meetings, the Cubans were quiet and they listened attentively, when I in the course of a few hours demonstrated the correctness of our policy, point by point, introducing all possible arguments, trying to dispel all possible doubts."[23] Mikoyan was pleased with himself, telling Moscow that it was his impression that they found him "convincing."[24]

Not really. After listening politely through a series of what must have been excruciating sessions, Castro launched a tirade on November 5. In the midst of a discussion of a Soviet proposition that the UN inspect the ships removing the missiles from Cuba, he explained in no uncertain terms that his tolerance for concession making was at an end.

"I want to tell you, Comrade Mikoyan," explained Castro, "and in this what I say reflects the decision of the Cuban people: we oppose this inspection." Castro said that he did not wish to put Soviet forces in danger and if it came to a threat to the peace of the entire world, he would of course also avoid doing it; however, this was no longer the situation. Now he had to be concerned about the dignity of the Cuban people. "Come what may," he said, "[w]e have the right to defend our dignity."[25]

For a few minutes the room was quiet. It probably seemed longer than this because the silence unsettled the Soviet contingent. "I thought about what my next step should be," Mikoyan recalled for Khrushchev. Convinced that Castro should not be excused this little tantrum, Mikoyan demanded an explanation for the outburst. The issue was not any inspection on Cuban territory but the examination of cargoes on outbound ships from Havana. The only possible affront to Castro, Mikoyan thought, was that these inspections might occur in Cuban waters.[26]

Raúl and a few of the other top Fidelistas passed the word to Mikoyan that they were equally astonished. Even Fidel Castro was embarrassed by this situation, and a recess was called in the talks. Mikoyan concluded that Fidel

Castro had made a mistake: "He did not intend to say it, but it slipped out." In his report to the Kremlin, Mikoyan suggested endorsing Cuba's rejection of foreign inspections. Above all, Moscow had to take into consideration Castro's extraordinary emotional and irrational nature: "What should not be lost sight of is the difficulty of Castro's personality—his sharp pride." Mikoyan criticized Castro's governing style, characterizing some of his comments since coming to power as thoughtless, impressionistic, and the source of later regret. He believed that occasionally Castro had been egged on by the American press, which had played on this egotism by badgering him about Cuba's having lost its independence. "In this regard it is interesting that Castro is always very upset," noted Mikoyan, "whenever he reads reports in the reactionary press that describe him as a puppet of the USSR."[27]

At a dinner to celebrate the forty-fifth anniversary of the Bolshevik revolution, on November 7, the tensions shaping Mikoyan's mission were on display for all to see. Customarily the Soviet embassy invited the Cuban civil and military leadership to a reception and dinner at the Soviet compound. In an attempt to repair the damage caused by the missile crisis, the Soviets went ahead with their party as if nothing were wrong in the Cuban-Soviet relationship. Indeed, the party began in the right spirit, with Raúl Castro going out of his way to act as a peacemaker.

In the days since Fidel Castro had aired his public differences with Moscow, Raúl had tried to placate his Soviet friends. Alekseev's replacement as KGB resident in Havana described him as playing "a positive role" in calming the ageing Cuban warriors. "Raúl Castro alone," the KGB reported to Moscow, ". . . revealed to us his concern over the fact that the irreproachable relations between Cuba and the USSR . . . were now becoming clouded because of the necessity of publicly declaring the existence of some disagreements and disputes on various matters." In confidence, Raúl Castro had told the Soviets that he believed his brother made a mistake in announcing the existence of these disagreements with Moscow.[28]

At the Soviet embassy, Raúl rose to toast Khrushchev's health and his accomplishments in foreign policy. In this toast, which Ambassador Alekseev later described as "practically a political declaration," the Castro who was a committed pro-Moscow communist stated that Cuba would forever be a real friend of the Soviet Union and "never go with the flow." "Unlike Albania or Yugoslavia," Raúl asserted, "Cuba would, in theory and in practice, remain true to the principles of Marxism-Leninism." Emphatically, the younger Castro ended his peroration, "We are and shall forever be Cuban communists."[29]

Raúl Castro's toast was about the only thing that went well that night. General Anatoly Gribkov of the Soviet general staff, who attended the affair, sent a special message to Defense Minister Rodion Malinovsky, which was quickly forwarded to the Presidium. The night had been a disaster. The Soviet military command never bothered to mention Fidel Castro in its toasts, which in the Kabuki theater of intercommunist relations was a major mistake. Worse, it had come to Gribkov's attention that, repeatedly in the course of the meal, the head of Cuban military intelligence, Pedro Luis Rodríguez, had tried to propose a joint toast to Fidel and Stalin at his table. Fortunately the others at the table refused each time to join in, and so the gesture was in vain.

It would be hard to overstate the extent of Khrushchev's anger when he was told what had happened. How could the Cubans dare toast Stalin? This was lèse-majesté of the worst kind. Gribkov knew what the reaction in Moscow would be. So did the rest of the Soviet command in Cuba. Gribkov had asked a deputy chief of Soviet forces, General L. S. Garbuz, to cosign this dispatch, but the latter had refused.[30]

Khrushchev reacted quickly. On November 10 the Kremlin sent detailed instructions directly to Mikoyan. He was ordered to start a personal investigation to determine whether there was any truth to the charge against Pedro Luis Rodríguez. Khrushchev wrote, "We all raised a toast to Fidel Castro. But a toast to Stalin we deplore. It is offensive to us that Pedro Luis, this man, who has been invested with a great deal of trust, this man, who handles intelligence and captures enemies, eulogizes that which we condemn." Khrushchev wanted Mikoyan to put all else aside and interview the members of the Soviet military contingent to be absolutely certain of the accuracy of General Gribkov's report.[31]

A few days later Mikoyan telegraphed that Gribkov had stuck to his story and that he, Mikoyan, would raise this matter in a meeting with Fidel Castro: "I will declare to him that any attempt to toast the health of Stalin could only offend us and even damage the relationship of general trust that has been established between us."[32]

The case eventually disappeared because Soviet military intelligence, which continued to have good relations with Castro's military, came to the rescue of the Cubans. Sitting next to Pedro Luis at the table that night was the chief GRU representative in Cuba, Colonel Meshcheriakov. Meshcheriakov, later the deputy chief of the GRU, cabled Moscow that Pedro Luis had belonged to an underground network before the Cuban revolution. He was a "trusted ally" of three important Cuban communists: Raúl Castro, Chief of the General Staff Sergio del Valle, and President Dorticós. Moreover, Pedro Luis was a regular source of military and political intelligence to the Soviets. It was he who made sure that the GRU received the remains of the ill-fated U-2 flown by Major Rudolf Anderson. "We consider Pedro Luis," the GRU resident explained, "the type of man from whom we can expect to receive important information in the future." He also assured Moscow that this particular Cuban always spoke of Khrushchev and the Soviet leadership in the warmest of terms and "has [r]epeatedly openly expressed himself against the schismatic activities of the leadership of the Albanian and Chinese Communist Parties." Meshcheriakov admitted that Pedro Luis did indeed consider the withdrawal of the missiles "a concession to American imperialism." But he added, in a subtle dig, that the Cuban was not alone in thinking that way.[33]

The November Crisis in Washington

In his September 1962 statement drawing a line between acceptable and unacceptable military assistance to Cuba, John Kennedy had mentioned the Il-28 bomber, which had a range of 750 nautical miles and could carry a 6,500-pound nuclear or conventional payload, as one of the unacceptable offensive weapons system that the Kremlin should not give to Castro. The Il-28 reappeared on the list handed to Mikoyan on November 2.[34]

Moscow had hoped this new demand would go away. Khrushchev answered the president with a formal letter on November 4 that accused him of taking his eyes off the ball by introducing side issues to complicate the missile crisis settlement. "It is hard for us to understand," wrote Khrushchev, "what aim is being pursued by the introduction of that list." He hinted darkly that Kennedy was returning to his earlier policy of using every possible instrument to undermine the Castro regime. "The demand which has been set forth is evidently pursuing . . . some other aims and that—I would wish Mr. President, that you understand me correctly—can lead not to the betterment of our relations but, on the contrary, to their new aggravation." Khrushchev hoped that a few sharp words would be enough to persuade the Americans to retract their new demand.[35]

Khrushchev hoped in vain. U.S. military preparations were continuing apace for an invasion of Cuba. A carrier task force was on its way from the Pacific with the Fifth Marine Expeditionary Brigade (5MEB). Exiting the Panama Canal on November 8, the USS *Okinawa*, which carried the brigade, headed for Vieques, the Puerto Rican port where it would await orders to continue to the beaches of Cuba. Designated Assault Group West in OPLAN 316, the 10,000-man 5MEB was one of two Marine Corps units seconded to the II Marine Expeditionary Force for the invasion. At that moment Assault Group East stood off Mayport, Florida. It spent the second week of November shuttling between northern Florida and South Carolina, as it also awaited a green light from the commander in chief.

The Pentagon did not consider the movements of the II Marine Expeditionary Force an exercise. On November 1 the U.S. military prepared an estimate for the White House of the number of U.S. casualties in an invasion of Cuba. The Joint Chiefs reported that there would be a total of 18,484 casualties (killed, missing, and wounded), 4,462 of which would come the first day.[36]

The Pentagon's November estimate assumed that U.S. forces would encounter neither organized Soviet units nor tactical nuclear weapons in Cuba. On October 25 U.S. intelligence had detected a Soviet contingent with a single Luna launcher in eastern Cuba.[37] Up to this point, although Khrushchev had been able to send 41,902 men, including 10,000 combat troops, and about one hundred tactical nuclear weapons to Cuba before the blockade took effect, U.S. intelligence had not found any of these smaller nuclear devices and had assumed that all Soviets on the island were support personnel for the ballistic missile regiments and associated equipment.[38] One Luna sighting was not definitive evidence of a more disturbing level of Soviet power in Cuba, because those missiles, like the U.S. Honest John, could carry conventional as well as nuclear warheads. But the Atlantic command did caution the White House that "estimates of casualties . . . [if] enemy uses tactical atomic weapons cannot be meaningful." If the Soviets used them against the invasion force on D-day, there would be carnage but "a hit on minor troop concentration" might not be as devastating. Although the Lunas were not considered a reason to reconsider an invasion, the Atlantic command stressed that they had to be taken out in the air strike preceding the invasion.[39]

The possibility that the Soviets might have ground troops equipped with tactical nuclear weapons did not dampen the enthusiasm of most of the Joint Chiefs for an invasion. Curtis LeMay believed that once his pilots had finished with Cuba, the invasion would be a "walk-in."[40] A few days after the casualty estimate was prepared, General Earle Wheeler flew south for a quick visit to the men scheduled to go in the army's first wave. Professing "never [to have] seen more impressive and imaginative training" in his thirty years of military service, Wheeler reported to his fellow chiefs, "[W]e could never be more ready."[41]

At a meeting at the State Department in the first week of November, Kennedy quoted from a poem by a Spanish bullfighter, Domingo Ortega:

Bullfighter critics ranked in rows
Crowd the enormous Plaza full;
But only one man is there who knows
And he's the man who fights the bull.[42]

The Pentagon's drive to get the job done, as well as growing public and congressional frustration over the remaining Il-28 bombers, created severe pressure on Kennedy to do something. On October 28 he had vowed not to get "hung up" on the bomber question.[43] But in recent days Khrushchev had ignored his official requests, and Kennedy worried that he was losing control of this controversy. In thinking through his options, the president concluded that only a private approach to the Kremlin would convince Khrushchev of the seriousness of the Il-28 problem and perhaps set the stage for another round of mutual concessions. He, Kennedy, knew best how to fight this bull.

On November 9 Robert Kennedy invited Georgi Bolshakov, whom he had not seen since the missiles were discovered in Cuba, to come to his home. Believing Bolshakov to have been a passive instrument in the Kremlin's deception plan, the Kennedys had not lost their trust in the Russian.[44] The Kennedy administration decided to renew this secret channel to reach closure on the Il-28 bomber question.

"[T]he President," Robert Kennedy said to Bolshakov, "[needs] to settle the removal of the Il-28 bombers as quickly as possible." Offering this as his "personal opinion," the attorney general suggested two possible approaches to this issue: in the first, the USSR pledged itself to remove the planes "as soon as possible," not naming any particular date; in the second, "the USSR gave an undertaking that these planes would be piloted only by Soviet aviators." Both variants represented a possible shift in the official American position.[45]

Evidently the Kennedys had not secured much support from other members of the Ex Comm before going ahead with this offer. After meeting with Bolshakov, Robert Kennedy changed into a tuxedo to attend a formal dinner and dance at the White House in honor of the World War II hero General James Gavin.[46] At some point early in the dinner, perhaps before President and Mrs. Kennedy appeared in the East Room, Robert Kennedy reported to his brother what had transpired with Khrushchev's representative. In the time since the brothers had first discussed a negotiated settlement, someone in or near the White House had gotten cold feet. Either the president or one of his advisers had changed his mind about the acceptability of leaving the Il-28s in place. In any case, the president told Robert Kennedy to stop hinting at a possible deal that did not include the removal of the bombers.

With his tail between his legs, the attorney general called Bolshakov an hour later to retract his earlier statements. He had merely been giving his "private opinion" about the possibility of leaving the Il-28s in Cuba so long as they were flown only by Soviet pilots. As far as the president was concerned, he explained, a satisfactory resolution of the Cuban problem would require "the rapid removal of the Il-28s from Cuba."[47]

Khrushchev, who received a copy of both of Robert Kennedy's statements, convened a meeting of the Presidium on November 10 to discuss a way out of what appeared to be a new mini-crisis. Although the general tone of the meeting with the president's brother was "courteous," Dobrynin in his dispatch to Moscow had quoted Bolshakov as saying that Robert Kennedy's declaration represented "explicit and persistent pressure on us."[48] Khrushchev wanted to convey to the Americans that his preference was to keep the bombers in Cuba, under Soviet command. "Your brother Robert Kennedy mentioned as one variant of solving the question of Il-28 aircraft that those planes should be piloted by Soviet fliers only—We agree to this."[49] But if that wasn't enough to settle the matter, Khrushchev was prepared to give up more. All that he asked from Kennedy was the kind of deal that the men had reached on removing the Jupiters from Turkey: no timetable, no fanfare, one statesman giving his word to another. Khrushchev would promise to remove the Il-28s when, in Moscow's judgment, "the time was ripe to remove them." He hinted that Cuba would play a large part in determining that timing. "We have our difficulties in this question," he said, in a subtle reference to Mikoyan's troubles in Havana.[50]

The Presidium decided that Fidel Castro should be consulted about these talks. Castro had left no doubt that his resentment at the Kremlin's decision of October 28 was made worse by the fact that he had not been consulted. Khrushchev and his inner circle had no reason to expect Castro to be happy about losing the Il-28s, but at least he would not be able to whine about not having been informed.

Had Mikoyan been in Moscow, he would have participated in the Presidium debate. Because this was not possible, his friend and boss rehearsed for him the debate that had taken place in his absence. In a dispatch sent November 11, Khrushchev posed a hypothetical question: What do we lose and what do we gain if we remove the bombers? And for Mikoyan's benefit, he offered an answer: "We don't lose much at all." "From the military point of view," added Khrushchev, "there is almost nothing lost because, as you know, these planes are obsolete and do not play a role in our armed forces, as we have already shut down their production and are dismantling all armed Il-28s." As for any "moral losses" for Cuba, Moscow well understood that the withdrawal of the Beagles would be met with a negative reaction that would inevitably cause problems for Mikoyan as he attempted to "instill a proper understanding of this matter into the heads of our Cuban friends." Lest Mikoyan think Khrushchev would give him any slack in his dealings with Castro, Moscow injected this condescending aside: "It is inherent in the skill of political actors that, meeting adversity, they display the capability to overcome these difficulties."[51]

The note to Mikoyan bore the characteristics of a letter dictated by Khrushchev. A cool section illustrating cost-benefit analysis dissolved into a lament over the dilemmas faced by an adversary of the United States. Khrushchev did not want Mikoyan, or presumably the Cubans, to think that the Il-28s would be pulled out under threat of another U.S. military intervention. "We don't have to agree to the U.S. demand to remove the bombers," he said in assuring Mikoyan that the Soviet leadership did not believe that a refusal on this demand would bring an invasion from Florida. However, he added, "when you are dealing with madmen nothing is certain." Mikoyan was instructed to study this issue carefully before a final answer was sent to Kennedy.[52]

In a cable to its negotiators in New York, Moscow explained that the withdrawal of the Il-28s should be "its very last position." The Presidium wanted Vasily V. Kuznetsov, a deputy ministry of foreign affairs who was leading the Soviet side in the talks with Adlai Stevenson and John McCloy, to test whether the Americans would accept Robert Kennedy's original proposals to Bolshakov. Under no circumstances was Kuznetsov to agree at this point to withdrawing the Il-28. "It would be wrong for us," the Kremlin explained, "to alter our position so long as we are unsure whether or not the White House endorsed these alternative settlements." Kuznetsov was also told that, given the sensitivity of the Cubans, negotiations with the Americans for the rest of the crisis had to be coordinated with Mikoyan's talks in Havana. "It is our emended position that approval from the Cuban friends, whom you will keep apprised of events, must come before removal of the Il-28s."[53]

The Il-28 Crisis

"Received, Read, Considered," Mikoyan began his response the very next day to Khrushchev's message about the Il-28s. It seemed unavoidable to Mikoyan, as it did to the Presidium, that the USSR would have to withdraw the Il-28s. But Mikoyan anticipated a hard time persuading the Cubans. "Considering the character of our friends and their frame of mind," he said, "this issue will bring them unhappiness and cause pain." Mikoyan expected that consulting alone would not be enough—"again and again it will come down to trying to convince them."[54]

Castro granted Mikoyan a two-hour private conversation on November 12. True to form Mikoyan kicked off this discussion with a drawn-out monologue punctuated by the themes of the significance of Soviet-American negotiations and the necessity of the noninvasion agreement guaranteeing Cuba's security. Mikoyan spoke for so long and used such flowery language that Castro could not endure it any longer and finally interrupted him. "Where are these arguments going? First of all you must tell me: what does the Soviet government want?" Mikoyan cut to the chase and said, "[I]f we will agree to remove the Il-28 bombers from Cuba, then we can wrest a formal agreement from the Americans." After admitting that the Il-28s were not militarily significant, he promised that their removal would be the last concession. "[R]egarding [the removal of] other military means," Mikoyan said, "we will give a complete and firm no to the Americans." He added that the Il-28s posed the only obstacle to getting UN support for a guarantee of the Soviet position in Cuba.[55]

"We very much ask you, Comrade Fidel," continued Mikoyan, "to understand us correctly." He said that he did not want an answer that day: "Consider and discuss this important matter." And perhaps hoping that Raúl Castro and the older communists would help in calming Fidel, Mikoyan suggested that he might want to talk it over with his "comrades."[56]

Not willing to wait, Castro blurted out his reply: "And later won't they put the question to you of on-site inspections?" Castro thought the Soviets completely naive in their strategy. "Whatever position the Soviet Union settles on, regardless of whether you remove the bombers or not," he argued, "the USA will insist on inspection and on the pretext that Cuba will find this unacceptable, the U.S. will maintain its blockade." Mikoyan assured Castro that the Soviet Union would agree only to removing the Il-28s in order to get the Americans to remove the blockade. Castro did not believe the Russian. He returned to the point that Cuba would not under any circumstances accept physical inspection. "Please tell the Soviet government that this decision is final and cannot be reviewed."[57]

The next day, November 13, Mikoyan and Castro returned to the issue, this time in the company of the rest of the Cuban leadership. Castro kicked off the meeting with the statement that neither he nor his comrades-in-arms agreed with either the decision to remove the strategic missiles or the decision to withdraw the bombers. The Soviet Union had presented him with a fait accompli on the strategic missile issue. But there was time to stop the Il-28 giveaway. The Cubans, Fidel explained, did not intend to be unyielding with regard to the Il-28s, so long as certain conditions were met. The naval blockade had to come to an end and U.S. overhead reconnaissance had to cease at the same time that the bombers were pulled out, otherwise Havana would not give its agreement. "I consider this a minimal request," explained Castro, "but it is a firm demand."[58]

On November 12 John Kennedy was wrestling with what to do about the Il-28s. Having received Khrushchev's suggestion of a gentleman's agreement from Robert earlier in the day, he called a meeting of the Ex Comm to discuss the form it should take. Kennedy listened approvingly as Adlai Stevenson and John McCloy, who had flown down from the negotiations with Kuznetsov in New York, suggested that if Khrushchev would promise to remove the planes in thirty days this would be enough of a guarantee to allow the administration to lift the embargo. Dean Rusk opposed the idea of offering Khrushchev a package deal on the bombers. But Kennedy's view prevailed, and by the end of the meeting Robert Kennedy had new marching orders. He was to tell Dobrynin that a Soviet promise to remove the bombers would be enough, if it could happen in one month.[59]

That evening Robert Kennedy conveyed the new proposal to Dobrynin.

N. S. Khrushchev and the president will agree in principle that the Il-28 bombers will be removed according to a definite schedule. Pursuant to such an agreement, and not waiting for the end of the withdrawal of the planes, the U.S. would, as early as the next day, officially lift the quarantine. The American side, understandably, envisions that the agreed-to schedule of withdrawal would be published. However, if the Soviet side has some kind of objection to publishing this schedule, the president would not insist on it. The president would accept the word of N. S. Khrushchev. As regards the schedule, it would be good, if the planes would be removed, let's say, in the course of 30 days.[60]

Robert Kennedy added that the president asked him to give the Soviets his strongest assurance that he would not attack Cuba. He was eager to resolve the final outstanding issues in the crisis.

Castro Wants to Use Force

Mikoyan was worried. The Cubans had not scheduled any meetings with him for Wednesday, November 14. A day of rest was necessary, even in a crisis, but Mikoyan's calendar was also open on Thursday. Sensing that he was being frozen out, Mikoyan at first thought of calling Fidel Castro directly to find out what was wrong. On second thought, he decided to send Alekseev to see President Dorticós. Mikoyan had the idea that a Cuban delegation might come to dinner at the Soviet embassy on Thursday night to pick up were the discussion had left off on Tuesday.[61]

On his mission to Dorticós, Alekseev discovered that the Cubans were angry that the Soviets appeared to be pursuing their own agenda in the talks at the UN. Cuban sources had learned that the draft agreement Kuznetsov had given to Stevenson was different from the one Castro had approved in Havana. Nevertheless, after consulting with Castro, Dorticós agreed that Castro would come to dinner at the embassy at 8:00 P.M. on Thursday.[62]

Fidel Castro was reluctant to see Mikoyan. He saw no point in further discussions so long as the Soviet ignored the security and sovereignty of Cuba. He needed to find a way to shock the superpowers into treating Cuba as an equal participant in resolving the crisis. Since October 16 the United States, with a brief halt during U Thant's visit to Havana on October 30 and 31, had flown several U-2 and low-altitude reconnaissance missions over Cuba. Since ordering the antiaircraft units under his control to open fire on American planes on October 27, Castro had quieted his guns. But in mid-November he was prepared to sting both superpowers.

A few hours before his appointment with Mikoyan, Castro visited an antiaircraft battery outside Havana. Filled with emotion at the sight of several young Cubans who were ready to defend the sovereignty of their country against the much stronger United States, Castro announced that as of Saturday or Sunday he would give the order to open fire again on U.S. warplanes. He was tired of talk. The Soviets still controlled the SA-2 equipment around the island, which meant that American U-2s remained out of reach of Cuban gunners. However, the conventional antiaircraft units under Castro's command could strike planes on low-altitude runs. In recent days Kennedy had stepped up the pace of low-level reconnaissance to monitor the withdrawal of the missiles and the assembly of the Il-28s. Between twenty and thirty planes a day were swooping down over Cuban installations, rattling nerves and splitting ears.[63] Before this visit to the field or just afterward, Castro prepared a note to U Thant in which he protested these "Hitlerite" air tactics and warned that he could not promise that U.S. planes would not be fired upon.[64]

A few minutes before 8 P.M., Castro arrived for dinner at the Soviet embassy. "Fidel was warm, hugged me fraternally, and bore good will," Mikoyan wrote later to Khrushchev.[65] Employing an old diplomatic trick to resume regular contact with Mikoyan, Castro explained to his Soviet guest that he had to suspend his meetings for three days because of a brief bout with sickness. Castro pretended that he wanted nothing more than to reach an agreement with Mikoyan. "Who then beside you and better than you could fulfill this mission? If you can't, then no one can. All of us know this. We have with you an old, strong friendship and trust."[66]

Mikoyan informed Castro of the confidential discussions through Robert Kennedy concerning the Il-28s. He explained that the Americans were prepared to lift the blockade as soon as there was a Soviet promise to remove the Il-28s. Castro expressed satisfaction that the Soviets might obtain the removal of the blockade for the Il-28s, but then he asked whether the Americans were also prepared to stop violating Cuban airspace.[67]

Stressing that his greatest concern was the U.S. spy planes, Castro shocked Mikoyan by telling him about his order to shoot down those planes and about the letter to U Thant. "Why did you not tell me about this letter before sending it to U Thant?" Mikoyan asked. "But we already told you at our last meeting that we would have to warn the United States through U Thant. The missiles are gone. I cannot stand any more of it, and as I said to the antiaircraft technicians today, from Sunday or even Saturday we will open fire on all American military planes" that violate Cuban airspace. Castro added, when Mikoyan objected, that he could not reverse this order.[68]

Mikoyan tried to restrain the Cubans by stressing that the Kennedy administration would never sign an agreement not to invade Cuba if Castro insisted on destroying U.S. planes. Mikoyan's attachment to a pledge from Kennedy brought a derisive response, especially from Che Guevara. "Before October 22 Kennedy and [Lyndon B.] Johnson said that they would not attack Cuba. And this is exactly the same thing they said before the invasion at the Bay of Pigs."[69] When Mikoyan said there was a difference between a public declaration and a guarantee formalized by treaty, Che mocked Soviet power and doubted there was any reason for Kennedy to honor a pledge, even if it was written down. "As the result of Khrushchev's actions in October," Che said, "the imperialists have now decided that in general the Soviet Union will not start a nuclear war in defense of the needs of friendly states."[70] Mikoyan, who was not about to be lured into a discussion of Soviet nuclear strategy, let Guevara's comment drop and tried to focus Cuban minds on the positive aspects of U.S. behavior in the crisis. Mikoyan pointed to the fact that the United States had not "cried victory," and said that Washington was not only unwilling to stick Russia's nose in its failure but "had urged correspondents not to write in this tone." Mikoyan was referring to information that the Czech intelligence service had picked up in Washington. Disingenuously, Mikoyan told Guevara, "[I]f you are right, then the Americans should have made a fuss about their victory, but they did not."[71]

This encounter depressed Mikoyan. "These are good people," he lamented in a letter to Khrushchev, "but of a difficult character, expansive, emotional, nervous, high-strung, quick to explode in anger, and unhealthily apt to concentrate on trivialities." Worse, he added, for Cubans "bitter feelings often overcome reason."[72]

Khrushchev was not depressed when he learned of Castro's new tactics; he was angry. Still shocked by Castro's earlier request for a Soviet nuclear strike, hurt by the Cubans' callous references to Stalin, and now faced with fresh evidence of Castro's recklessness, he breathed fire before his colleagues at a Presidium meeting on November 16. Mikoyan had not yet written to Moscow about the November 15 meeting, but Khrushchev had heard about the letter to U Thant and the warning to American pilots. He excoriated Castro, describing his general position on the missile crisis as "just shouting and unreasonable"; and for the first time in three years he raised serious doubts about the future of Moscow's alliance with him. "It is a lesson to us," Khrushchev warned ominously. From the moment Raúl Castro, Che Guevara, and the older Cuban communists welcomed the Soviet Union into the Caribbean, Moscow had been wary of Comandante Fidel Castro. This self-described communist was undisciplined and too egocentric to think in terms of the welfare of the socialist world. Castro's letter of October 27, challenging Moscow to ignite a nuclear holocaust, revived all of the earlier concerns about him. Now Khrushchev was prepared to pull the plug on Soviet assistance to the Cubans. "Either they will cooperate," he warned, "or we will recall our personnel."[73]

Indeed, so angry were the Soviets on November 16 that the Presidium reversed itself on consulting the Cubans. Khrushchev was no longer prepared to wait for the Cuban leadership to accept a reasonable settlement. The Presidium decided to send an oral message to Kennedy, approving his terms to remove the Il-28s even without Castro's approval.

After the meeting, when Khrushchev had calmed down, one of three men—Gromyko, Kozlov, or Ponomarev—managed to persuade him to give the Cubans one last chance.[74] The Kremlin would wait a few more days to convey its agreement to Kennedy, and in the meantime Mikoyan would offer the Cubans a choice of three inspection plans. The Kremlin suggested either inspection by a delegation from the UN, by representatives from the five Latin American countries that still maintained relations with Castro, or by representatives of ten neutral nations (Ghana, Guinea, Egypt, Austria, Sweden, India, Indonesia, Mexico, and Brazil).

Despite his acceptance of one last initiative, Khrushchev made no attempt in his letter to Mikoyan to hide his anger at Fidel Castro. "We . . . consider that the position of our Cuban friends can never be considered reasonable," Moscow cabled on November 16. "They must show more flexibility. . . . We believed and believe now that we accomplished a great thing for Cuba when we obtained from the president a declaration not to invade Cuba."[75] If Castro refused to budge on the Il-28 and inspections issues, the only leverage left to the Soviets was to threaten to withdraw from Cuba. The Soviets, of course, did not want to lose this extension of the bloc into the Caribbean; but they had other interests, all of which would be jeopardized if some Cuban mistake provoked a shooting war between the superpowers. Mikoyan received stern instructions to make this clear to the Cubans:

> Cuba, which now does not want to confer with us, wants instead to lasso us, hoping that their actions will embroil us in a war with America. We do not intend to move in that direction. . . . If the Cuban comrades do not wish to work with us on this matter and do not want to take steps together with us to resolve this crisis, then, clearly, our presence there is of no utility to our friends. We regret that and also very much regret that so long as our advice is not taken into consideration we will be forced to deny any responsibility for them. Then the Cubans alone will bear the entire responsibility for the situation and for all possible consequences.[76]

"That Would Be a Deal"

U.S. intelligence picked up some evidence of Mikoyan's difficulties in Cuba. And Khrushchev in his letter to Kennedy of November 14 blamed unnamed forces for making it impossible to remove the bombers for another two to three months. However, President Kennedy did not want to wait for Mikoyan to solve the Castro problem. He had his own unreasonable men to keep at bay in his administration. On November 18 he employed two different channels to try to push the Kremlin into accepting a rapid withdrawal of the bombers. At a breakfast at his home in honor of the visiting artists of the Bolshoi Theater on November 18, Robert Kennedy asked Dobrynin whether he expected a response from Moscow. It had been six days since the White House had tendered its offer. Kennedy expressed the hope that the response would be friendly and that at the end of the day all would work out well. He reminded the Soviet ambassador that in less than two days the president would be holding his first press conference in two months, at which he would undoubtedly receive questions about the state of U.S.-Soviet relations in the wake of the missile crisis. It was the hope of the administration, the younger Kennedy made clear, that an answer from Khrushchev would arrive before the press conference.[77] That night Robert Kennedy saw Bolshakov at the theater, where he and his wife attended a performance of Soviet ballet with the famous ballerina Maia Plisetskaya. He rephrased this earlier question in a much harsher form so that it sounded like an ultimatum when he gave it to Bolshakov.

In New York, John McCloy had an even more detailed message for the Soviet negotiator Kuznetsov. The two met informally at the Soviet compound at Glen Cove on November 18. "President Kennedy does not want to postpone his press conference any longer," said McCloy. The White House had already announced that Kennedy would speak to the nation on November 20, the first presidential address since he had appeared on television for two and a half minutes on November 2 to announce that the Soviets were dismantling the missile sites.[78] The answer Kennedy received from the Kremlin on the Il-28s would determine whether he delivered a valediction or a jeremiad. Like Robert Kennedy, McCloy was using a Soviet official to accelerate Moscow's policy process so that the White House received an answer in time. He stressed that Kennedy faced opposition from "extremist groups" and would need a Soviet concession on the bombers to handle these men.

McCloy offered a new concession from Kennedy. Although it would be very difficult for him because of public fears that the Soviets were hiding nuclear missiles in Cuban caves, Kennedy was prepared to rescind his request for on-site inspection if this would permit agreement on all remaining major issues. He rejected Castro's five points but would have Adlai Stevenson at the UN Security Council reaffirm his pledge not to invade Cuba. Similarly, the United States would guarantee the noninvasion of Cuba from other Latin American countries. However, the Soviets would have to accept an oral promise, because Kennedy could not sign a special protocol. Nevertheless, the United States believed that it could verify the removal of the missiles and the Il-28 bombers in the open sea, by photographing the cargoes on the ships returning to the Soviet Union. The White House hoped that the Soviet Union would eventually withdraw the troops that it had sent to protect the missile complexes, though the United States could accept the presence of some Soviet advisers on the island. McCloy stressed that the president was prepared to resolve the on-site inspection problem if the other points made in this conversation were respected. "That would be a deal," McCloy concluded.[79]

In addition to sending out these feelers, the White House prepared for another round of the missile crisis. Concerned that if Soviet intransigence necessitated a tough presidential speech the NATO allies would complain, the White House sent special envoys to meet with the key European leaders. The CIA's Sherman Kent, the chief of the Office of National Estimates, was sent to Paris on November 19 to brief Charles de Gaulle on the situation in Cuba.[80] Kent had no advance warning whatsoever of the trip. He arrived at the new CIA building in Langley, Virginia, and found an order to pull together some overhead photographs of the Soviet removal of the missiles and prepare a briefing on the situation. No one bothered to warn the U.S. embassy in Paris of Kent's mission either. Ambassador Charles Bohlen was surprised to see his old Yale friend. "What the hell is going on?" Bohlen asked Kent. Kent had to admit he did not really know. Then Bohlen passed him a high-priority cable that had arrived from the department that morning. "Well, my boy, you might read this. I thought you had participated in drafting it." The White House had instructed Bohlen to arrange a meeting with de Gaulle to explain that the president was going to give a tough speech, promising new action (probably an extension of the blockade to include petroleum, oil, and lubricants), because the Soviets were not complying with the demand that the Il-28s be pulled out.

Castro Blinks Too Late

While Sherman Kent and the presidential envoys to be sent to Ottawa and London were packing their flight bags, Khrushchev decided that he could wait no longer to hear from Castro. On November 16 the Presidium had authorized him to give an oral promise to the U.S. president. The Kennedy administration's new offer, effectively eliminating the need to press the Cubans for on-site verification, removed the last obstacle so far as Khrushchev was concerned. As he warned Mikoyan, "the Americans have a strategic and geographical advantage over us," and if Washington was nonetheless prepared to offer reasonable proposals, Khrushchev believed the USSR was foolish to delay accepting them.[81] Furthermore, Castro's treatment of Mikoyan and the Cuban leader's stubborn refusal to countermand the order to begin shooting on American planes left Khrushchev no reason to think that the stalling would end soon.[82] After waiting three days for the Cubans to come around, he now authorized the sending of the message to Washington.

"I inform you," wrote Khrushchev to Kennedy, "that we intend to remove them [Il-28s] within a month . . . and may be [*sic*] even sooner since the term for the removal of these planes is not a matter of principle for us."[83] Khrushchev expected that Kennedy would follow through on his promise to remove the quarantine immediately. "Well, I think, this answer of mine gives you not bad material for your statement at your press conference."

Mikoyan in Havana had no idea that the Presidium had already given up on his mission, when he entered Havana's presidential palace at 5:00 P.M. on November 19 (1 A.M., November 20, in Moscow) for a meeting with Castro, Che Guevara, Osvaldo Dorticós, Carlos Rafael Rodríguez, and Emilio Aragonés. Raúl Castro was out of the city.[84]

Fidel Castro had not yet formally given in to Moscow's request that he accept the loss of the Il-28s, but he was moving in that direction. Aware that John Kennedy was planning to give a speech of some kind on Cuba the next day, Castro did not want to be the cause for a second, potentially deadlier phase of the crisis. Castro already feared, as he told Mikoyan, that the American president would assume an arrogant and abusive tone toward Cuba in the press conference, in an attempt "to throw us away like a dirty rag," and that this would seriously affect the morale of the Cuban army and people. Castro had the idea of giving a speech to the Cuban people before the presidential press conference to prevent Kennedy from stirring up a new crisis.[85]

After about two hours, at 7:20 P.M., the Cubans asked Mikoyan and his team to leave so that they could caucus and present the Soviets with some firm decisions in an hour or so. Mikoyan left the palace confident, as he cabled Khrushchev during the break in the meeting, that "all went well." Concerned, however, that he might not have Castro's approval in time for Khrushchev to notify Kennedy that the Il-28s would leave, he suggested that Robert Kennedy be told that "at the present moment arrogant and offensive statements by

American officials and the press and threats regarding Cuba will only complicate the completion of the negotiations between Khrushchev and Kennedy."

When the Cubans did return, Mikoyan learned about a letter the Cuban
leader planned to send to U Thant. This would be Castro's way of informing
the world that Cuba accepted the removal of the Il-28s.[86]

On November 20 Georgi Bolshakov delivered Khrushchev's message to the
president in Washington. It was what the Kennedy administration had hoped
for. "How should we deal with the matter now so that we and you could soon
bring joy to humanity with the news that the crisis over Cuba is completely
liquidated?" Khrushchev asked in his letter. The president decided that it
would be by revising the text of his statement at his evening news conference.
He would report the Soviet Union's concession and lift the blockade. To reassure the Soviets that this was what Kennedy would do, Llewellyn Thompson
called Anatoly Dobrynin from the State Department to inform Khrushchev
that the president had also ordered a reduction in the level of military readiness.[87]

At 6 P.M. John Kennedy announced that the Soviets had agreed to withdraw
their Il-28s within thirty days. In response the United States would lift the
blockade, and the sixty-three ships involved in the operation would return to
their home ports. Admitting that there had not been any progress in negotiations with the Soviets to allow on-site inspections, Kennedy pledged that overhead reconnaissance would continue until there was an agreement. Kennedy
did not tell his audience that for the foreseeable future he had canceled the
low-level flights that had angered Castro so much and would rely on approximately one U-2 run a day. Later the Pentagon joined in the general relaxation
of tension by announcing that the 14,200 air force reservists who had been
called up during the crisis would be released.[88]

Kennedy's actions delighted Moscow. "One more last statement and the
chronicle from me is ended," Khrushchev wrote to Mikoyan, with manifest relief, the day after Washington ended the blockade. "Perhaps this is the ultimate or penultimate message to you," Khrushchev added. ". . . We have the
firm impression that the Americans actively hope to liquidate tension. If they
wanted something else, then they had opportunities to get it. Evidently,
Kennedy himself is not an extremist."[89]

Castro's Revenge

There was more than a hint of celebration in Khrushchev's words. The feeling
was different, however, in Havana. Castro told Mikoyan the day after Kennedy
lifted the blockade, "We must not give up." He continued, "The guarantee in
Kennedy's speech does not suit us. We cannot accept UN observer teams because of this statement. Just because Kennedy removed the blockade doesn't
mean that we have to make new compromises for the sake of our formal obligations in the UN."[90]

There was intense concern in the Cuban leadership that the Soviet defense umbrella was folding up. Havana understood better than Moscow how dedicated to removing Castro the U.S. president and his aides were. Mikoyan had assured the Cubans on November 5 that Moscow would not agree to U.S. demands to remove the Il-28 bombers.[91] Two weeks later Khrushchev let them go. The Cubans knew that Washington wanted all Soviet troops to leave the island. Perhaps Moscow would agree to this as well.

As the Cubans confronted the possibility that most of what Pliyev had under his command might return to Russia, the tactical nuclear weapons that Moscow had rushed to Cuba in September assumed a new importance. The crisis seems to have changed the Cuban leadership's ideas about the role of nuclear weapons in its defense. Initially the Cubans were ambivalent about the placement of Soviet nuclear weapons on their soil. It was one thing to have a nuclear guarantee from Moscow, which Castro had sought in 1960. It was another to have Soviet missiles under the Kremlin's control in your backyard. But the crisis had demonstrated Washington's fear of nuclear devices. If Cuba could keep a few nuclear weapons, there might be some chance that the island could on its own repel a U.S. attack.

To reassure his country's representative at the UN that the Khrushchev-Kennedy deal over the R-12s and R-14s would not compromise Cuban security, the Cuban foreign minister, Raúl Roa, informed the new Cuban representative at the UN, Carlos Lechuga, on November 20, "[W]e still have tactical atomic weapons, which must be kept." Moscow learned about this message through its sources in Havana.[92]

When the Soviets heard that the Cubans were communicating with each other about the remaining tactical weapons, panic set in. If the Americans ever got hold of the Cuban dispatch on the remaining nuclear warheads, the entire Cuban missile crisis settlement would unravel. Only four hours before his brother's press conference on November 20, Robert Kennedy had informed Dobrynin that "according to our reports not all of the warheads had left Cuba." Kennedy was right, but Dobrynin did not know about the tactical weapons and just followed his instructions. Dobrynin denied that any nuclear warheads remained there.[93]

In fact, as of November 20 only the warheads for the R-12s and R-14s had been returned to the USSR; but the tactical warheads and the six atomic bombs remained in Cuba. On October 30 Defense Minister Malinovsky had ordered Pliyev to load all of the MRBM warheads onto the *Aleksandrovsk*, which already carried the nuclear charges for the longer-range R-14 missiles that never arrived. Before dispatching the ship, Pliyev requested guidance on what to do with the remaining hundred nuclear warheads. In response the Soviet Defense Ministry instructed Pliyev to begin training the Cubans to use the Lunas, FKR cruise missiles, and Il-28s. Malinovsky wanted to keep the tactical nuclear weapons on the island. On November 5, the day the *Aleksandrovsk* left port, Malinovsky cabled Pliyev that he should keep all of the tactical charges on the island.[94]

Anastas Mikoyan, who received a copy of Roa's cable from one of Alekseev's sources in the Cuban Foreign Ministry, was the first Soviet leader to react. Mikoyan was convinced that the Cubans were intriguing and had meant for the Soviets to find out about their new position on nuclear weapons. Lacking instructions on this matter from Moscow, he decided to pressure the Cubans to remove the offending sentence from the dispatch. "The Americans are not supposed to know about this [the tactical nuclear weapons]," he told them.[95]

Mikoyan arranged to see Fidel Castro on November 22. "Are the tactical weapons gone or not?" asked Castro. He had heard Kennedy's statement on November 20 that "all nuclear weapons were gone from Cuba," and he wanted to be sure that the American president did not know something he didn't. Mikoyan was on his own in this discussion. Khrushchev had said nothing to him in his messages about the tactical weapons, but from Alekseev and Pliyev he must have learned that the Presidium intended to leave them on the island. However, with this recent display of Cuban recklessness Mikoyan had his doubts about the wisdom of letting the Cubans think they could rely on keeping tactical nuclear weapons. "They remained in Cuba at the present time," he said, "but they would be returned to the Soviet Union and not transferred to the Cubans." Mikoyan explained to the disappointed Castro, "We have a law that prohibits the turning over of any nuclear weapons, including tactical weapons, to another country." He added, however, "Nuclear weapons remained in our hands and would be used in the case of war to defend all socialist lands."[96]

Castro did not want to lose these weapons. "Wouldn't it be impossible," he asked with a double negative, "to keep the atomic weapons in Cuba under Soviet control without turning them over to the Cubans?" Mikoyan curtly responded that it was the second portion of Castro's question that was impossible. "The Americans," he said, "do not know that there are tactical atomic weapons here, and we will take them back not because the U.S. wants us to but of our own volition." Mikoyan left the meeting satisfied that the Cubans were reconciled to losing the last of the Soviet warheads.[97]

Moscow agreed with Mikoyan's handling of the tactical nuclear problem. The resolution of the Il-28 controversy and the lifting of the American blockade seemed to lessen the need for the tactical nuclear weapons on Cuba. Indeed, there is some evidence that on November 20 Malinovsky ordered Pliyev to pack up the tactical missiles.[98] Any lingering uncertainty over whether the Cubans should be allowed to keep any of them, however, was resolved by November 22. After hearing from Mikoyan about the machinations of the Cuban Foreign Ministry, the Kremlin committed itself to removing every last nuclear device from Cuba. "Your thoughts regarding a possible answer to the Cuban leadership are deemed correct," Khrushchev assured Mikoyan. The Kremlin wanted Mikoyan to employ strong measures to prevent the information about Soviet tactical weapons from leaking. The Presidium reiterated the original rules governing the deployment of nuclear weapons in Cuba: "The weapons are ours, they remain in our hands, we have not transferred them to anyone and do not intend to." Finally, the Cubans were to be told, as the Americans were told, that all nuclear weapons had been removed from Cuba. The Kremlin instructed Mikoyan to press the Cuban Foreign Ministry to correct the instruction to Lechuga, which unfortunately he had already received. Moscow wanted Lechuga to be told as soon as possible that the Cubans did not have any nuclear weapons. "All of this is very important," cabled the Kremlin, "because otherwise there would be serious consequences if the Americans were confronted with information not conforming to reality because of the dispatch sent to Lechuga."[99]

The dispute over the future of the nuclear weapons delayed Mikoyan's departure a few days.[100] The Cubans had no choice but to accept the loss of the last nuclear weapons.[101] On November 26 Mikoyan flew to Washington and New York to meet with President Kennedy and UN Secretary-General U Thant. According to Alekseev, Fidel Castro and other Cuban leaders saw him off in a warm ceremony. After Mikoyan's departure Alekseev met with Raúl Castro, who in the name of Fidel said that the Cubans were satisfied with Mikoyan's visit. Raúl added, though, that he was convinced that "the Americans have detected the weak points in our relations and will try to play on them."[102]

Raúl Castro was speaking in anticipation of Mikoyan's meeting with Kennedy, which took place on November 29. Mikoyan opened the White House meeting with a declaration that the "nuclear missiles had been deployed to Cuba not with the goal of attacking the USA but as a means of containment, with a view to strengthening the defensive strength of Cuba and to defend her from a possible attack from without." Kennedy was not pleased with this explanation. "The issue was not whether to inform or not [my] government. Of course, we will not inform you of such things and you are not obliged to inform us." What angered Kennedy was the deliberate deception. "There was no deception," countered Mikoyan. "There is a difference of interpretation over our weapons." Mikoyan added, "One important matter was their mission and the other matter, their character." Kennedy continued by insisting that Khrushchev's denial that there were offensive weapons in Cuba, as well as the TASS statement of September 11 and the simultaneous assurances of Ambassador Dobrynin, was a lie and "a strong insult directed at me personally."[103]

Kennedy explained that the United States was not spoiling for an attack on Cuba. "I stated that we would not attack Cuba but we still consider Castro our adversary." Answering Mikoyan's accusation about American flights over Cuban territory, he said that they were designed purely to inspect the island for violations of the Kennedy-Khrushchev agreement. "It is clear that a large number of the low level flights was hooliganism on the part of the U.S. and the present flights are equally hooliganism, though at a higher altitude." Kennedy said that these rare U-2 flights should not bother Castro. "The USA believes that so long as there aren't adequate means to verify, this must be done in other ways." He added, "I hope to make sure that the American people are not fooled again." At the end of the session, he said, "I hope that Castro will behave himself with restraint and will not provoke us." And yes, the president assured Mikoyan, "I, of course, remember what I wrote to Nikita Khrushchev."[104]

A few days later Mikoyan appeared before the Presidium in Moscow to present an account of the last month of his life. After Mikoyan gave his report, Khrushchev embarked on a postmortem on the crisis. "The line was right," he said, once more justifying his actions. "We saved Cuba." Khrushchev did not mention the Chinese by name, but he launched into an attack on those "who declare that we retreated." "This is nothing but malicious cowardice." This was not pure bluff on the part of Khrushchev. In the course of the week between October 22 and October 27, while he waited for the attack that never came, Khrushchev's confidence in the international position of the Soviet Union grew. "We have gained great power," he said. "Now we are members of the world club." Proof of this, Khrushchev said, was that "[t]hey were themselves afraid during the crisis." He did not show any lack of resolve today. "If we could have resisted longer," he mused, "probably nothing would have happened." Khrushchev now blamed Castro for having forced him to make a deal. "Fidel Castro openly advised us to use nuclear weapons," he said in the Kremlin, "but now he retreats and smears us." Khrushchev was not going to let that man dictate Soviet security policy again. "We must not sign a treaty with him," said Khrushchev. He noted that, in time, the Soviet Union would have to reconsider the nature of its military support to Havana.

The others on the Presidium were somewhat divided as to the lessons of the missile crisis. "The Cuban position appeared to be unreliable," said Aleksei Kosygin, parroting Khrushchev's statements. Yet Malinovsky, the defense minister, took a different tack. He had tried to keep the tactical nuclear warheads on Cuban soil and did not want Castro's misbehavior to spoil the close cooperation between the Soviet and Cuban armed forces. He advocated "conserving our achievements [in the Caribbean]." He advised the Kremlin to "punctually and responsibly fulfill [Soviet] obligations to support Cuba . . . though [the Cubans] are responsible for their own actions." Malinovsky was also a voice of reason regarding the United States and the China. He believed that Kennedy "would keep his word" and discouraged his colleagues from being too critical of the Chinese communists. "Let's not burn our bridges," said Malinovsky—advice that summarized his point of view regarding Washington and Havana, as well as Beijing.[105] Then the Presidium passed a resolution to "commend the work of Comrade Mikoyan."[106]

Despite the self-congratulatory statements of the Presidium sessions after Mikoyan's return, an air of recrimination settled over Moscow. The Presidium set the tone by summarily dismissing the man who had planned Operation Anadyr, Colonel General Semyon Ivanov, a senior member of the Soviet military.[107] The Soviet intelligence community, which had inspired false alarms without ever penetrating the secrets of the Ex Comm, was a second target. At the same time that it relieved Ivanov, the Presidium launched an investigation of the GRU.[108] Semichastny and the KGB escaped as harsh a reprimand for the embarrassments of October; but Aleksandr Feklisov's days in Washington were numbered, for he was soon reassigned. The two key ambassadors in the drama emerged from this scapegoating unscathed: Anatoly Dobrynin had never been in the know about the operation, and Aleksandr Alekseev was simply too valuable to sacrifice in Havana.

The superpowers instructed their representatives at the UN to tidy up the final settlement of the crisis.[109] This last phase dragged on a few more weeks; but by the time Mikoyan left North America all but one of the main issues had practically been resolved. The last remaining issue, the removal of all nuclear weapons from Cuba, the Soviets solved on their own. On Christmas Day 1962 a Soviet ship quietly left Havana with the last of the tactical warheads.[110] Operation Anadyr was over.

THE AFTERMATH

"Plans for the Military 'Penetration' of South America Were Gibberish"

DMITRI POLYANSKI [PRESIDIUM MEMBER], October 1964

CHAPTER 16

To the American University Speech

Kennedy in Palm Beach

The Cuban missile crisis did not reconcile John Kennedy to living forever with Fidel Castro. In a meeting with the Joint Chiefs of Staff in Palm Beach, where the Kennedy family was spending Christmas of 1962, the president reiterated his determination to remove Castro at some point in the future. "[A]lthough we feel that the present Cuban situation is dormant," Kennedy told the chiefs, "we must assume that someday we may have to go into Cuba."[1] He was well aware of the unhappiness in the Pentagon over his handling of the missile crisis and did not want the military to think that he had gone soft on Castro. He assured the chiefs that military action "was a possibility in the next few years whether he was President or not, and that they had to plan for this."[2] As he had done after the Bay of Pigs disaster in the spring of 1961 and again in early 1962, Kennedy conveyed an expectation that if the military could find a way to deliver the decisive blow "as quickly as possible, with a minimum of destruction," he might be prepared to order an invasion of Cuba.[3] As these veterans of the missile crisis well knew, Kennedy had not liked any of the remaining military options when the air strike proved impracticable on October 20 and had opted instead for a diplomatic solution.

John Kennedy was extremely skilled at talking tough when he had to. He gave the JCS the impression that an invasion of Cuba was still very much a live option. He mentioned special forces planning in connection with Cuba and suggested that preparations for post-invasion work in "civil affairs and military government" continue. Finally, he discussed the Cuban brigade, a pet project of his, which involved forming a unit of Cuban exiles in the U.S. Army. Three days later, before forty thousand cheering Cubans in Miami's Orange Bowl, Kennedy left his restrained prepared text and pledged his government's determination to evict the Castro brothers from Havana. After being handed the flag of Brigade 2506, which had come ashore at the Bay of Pigs, he told an appreciative crowd, "I can assure you that this flag will be returned to this brigade in a free Havana."[4]

However, Kennedy's actions betrayed a new caution in handling Castro. Talking invasion was his way of blowing off steam. He understood too well the political limitations that came with the title "Leader of the Free World" to be thinking seriously of violating his pledge to Khrushchev in early 1963.[5] Operation Mongoose had been allowed to die in December 1962. The October 28 freeze on all CIA-sponsored sabotage remained in effect, and since November the Special Group had not authorized any planning for future operations in Cuba. Following the Cuban missile crisis, Edward Lansdale had argued that the operation be "wrapped up," and after some hesitation the president and his brother, who tried to keep Lansdale on the job, agreed that Mongoose had run its course.[6] While Kennedy's opinion of Castro had not changed, he had authorized a ransom payment to Havana for the release of 1,189 Cubans captured during the Bay of Pigs operation. Among those screaming for Castro's head in the Orange Bowl now were members of the Brigade who had recently been reunited with their families in Little Havana at a cost of $53 million in pharmaceuticals and food.[7]

Kennedy's greater foreign policy concern at the dawn of 1963 was building on the strategic opening in U.S.-Soviet relations that the Cuban missile crisis provided. That crisis had been a defining moment for his presidency. Kennedy's public approval rating was consistently high throughout his thousand days in office but, owing to the recession of 1962, had begun to slip below 65 percent just before the missile crisis. The crisis had sent it back up to the mid-70s. Kennedy had reason to believe that the crisis had given him breathing room to return to the foreign policy agenda that had been derailed by the Vienna summit, the Berlin crisis, and, of course, Cuba.

Nikita Khrushchev's actions in the wake of the crisis gave the White House hope that, in social science terms, the Soviet leader had undergone some "nuclear learning" as the result of flirting with thermonuclear war. In his letters at the conclusion of the crisis, Khrushchev had revived the test ban discussion.[8] He returned to his pre-Vienna posture and conceded three annual on-site inspections, which though still unacceptable to Kennedy seemed to indicate some movement in Moscow as a result of the humiliations in the Caribbean. Kennedy briefed the peace activist Norman Cousins on the situation. Cousins, on his way to Moscow in December 1962 as a peace emissary from Pope John XXIII, was asked by Kennedy to press Khrushchev on the test ban question. Kennedy was now prepared to accept eight to ten on-site inspections, even fewer than Robert Kennedy had discussed with Georgi Bolshakov in April 1961.[9] Although Kennedy wrote to President Charles de Gaulle on December 11 that "the moment is not opportune for important Western initiatives on East-West issues," he hoped that the near-disaster over Cuba would provide him with a second chance to effect the limited détente that Khrushchev had rejected in Vienna.[10]

Not content to bask in the afterglow of the crisis, Kennedy feared he would not be able to achieve this détente if the American people discovered how the missile crisis had actually been resolved. To protect his version of events, the president helped his old pal Charles Bartlett, the Washington correspondent for the *Chattanooga Times*, write what would become the first inside account of the Cuban missile crisis.

The day after Khrushchev announced over Radio Moscow that the Soviet Union would withdraw its missiles, Bartlett had asked John Kennedy what he thought of helping him write the story of the Cuban missile crisis.[11] Kennedy approved of the idea but asked to see the article before publication, to "proofread" it. Rumors of a Turkish trade were in the air. The Turkish government was putting pressure on the United States to deny that there had been any connection whatsoever between the removal of the Soviet missiles and future NATO deployments or redeployments. Knowing the sensitivity of the Joint Chiefs, Robert McNamara had assured the Pentagon, "[T]here is no Cuba-Turkey deal at present."[12] Evidently, the White House wanted to dampen any curiosity about the Jupiters. Over lunch with Bartlett, McGeorge Bundy's assistant Michael Forrestal let drop "on background" the presidential version of the connection between Turkey and Cuba. "It was all Adlai's fault," Forrestal argued. Adlai Stevenson had angered the president by suggesting that the United States pull out its missiles in Turkey in an exchange for the Soviet missiles in Cuba. "The president opposed the idea and later prevented Khrushchev from getting it."[13]

Poor Adlai Stevenson, the two-time failed Democratic presidential nominee and now U.S. ambassador to the UN, was being hung out to dry. Kennedy wanted the press to believe that any rumors about the trade had come from Stevenson and his supporters. The myth was designed to remove any doubt that the much tougher JFK, of course, would ever have condoned trading away the security of an ally to resolve the Cuban problem. Since his inauguration Kennedy had tried to differentiate himself from Adlai Stevenson while holding on to the Stevenson wing of the Democratic Party. The real problem was that he shared many of Stevenson's views on foreign policy, especially with regard to the Soviets. But Stevenson was considered an egghead, and therefore a political loser, by many Americans, and some doubted, in particular, that any Stevensonite could deal effectively with the Kremlin. For John F. Kennedy this meant he had to pretend to be tougher than he was.

The White House had authorized Forrestal's "leak." After lunching with Forrestal, Bartlett had a private dinner with the president. He handed over the draft of the article, including the explosive revelation about Stevenson. As Bartlett recalls today, the president "marked it up." Yet Kennedy suggested only one substantive change. He wanted the article to minimize Theodore

Sorensen's role in the crisis to avert any criticisms from the right wing. Sorensen had been a noncombatant in World War II—a conscientious objector. Kennedy told Bartlett that he did not think the American people would understand or respect his decision to have a conscientious objector in the room where there were discussions of war and peace. Otherwise, the president made no significant editorial suggestions. He wanted a little stir over Adlai Stevenson to distract people from asking whether there had been a trade. Kennedy's version of the Cuban missile crisis appeared in the *Saturday Evening Post* in early December.[14]

Georgi Bolshakov was another victim of Kennedy's efforts to shape public understanding of the course of the Cuban missile crisis. The White House, it seems, decided to sacrifice the RFK-Bolshakov channel. Bartlett's article made reference to Khrushchev's use of a Soviet journalist in October to deny the existence of missiles in Cuba. An even more explicit reference to Bolshakov had appeared in a column by Joseph Alsop in early November. Although Bolshakov was not named in Bartlett's article, the authoritativeness of the account confirmed Alsop's earlier claim.

In Soviet eyes Bolshakov's cover was blown. On December 11 Khrushchev wrote to Kennedy to "express . . . disapproval":

> We read now various articles by your columnists and correspondents . . . who as it would seem have no relation to confidential channels set up between us. Judging by the contents of these articles it is clear that their authors are well informed and we get the impression that this is not a result of an accidental leak of the confidential information. . . . This evidently is done for the purpose of informing the public in a one-sided way.[15]

Remarking that "a minimum of personal trust is necessary for leading statesmen of both countries," Khrushchev added that he "considered it useful for us to continue to maintain the possibility of confidential exchanges of opinion." However, he warned that if the intentional leaks continued, "these channels will cease to be of use and may even cause harm."[16]

Despite Khrushchev's continuing commitment to back-channel diplomacy, Bolshakov's career in Washington was over. The GRU had never liked him, considering his personal connection to the Kennedy family and his independent manner of operations dangerous. The Soviet ambassador, Anatoly Dobrynin, also disliked Bolshakov because this gregarious man was an able competitor for Robert Kennedy's attention. Now that Bolshakov had apparently lost the protection of the Kennedys, Moscow was quick to dispense with him.[17]

Bolshakov tried to meet his new predicament with good humor. In front of a large group of American and Russian friends, including a visibly contrite Robert Kennedy, Bolshakov gamely made a joke at his farewell party about his present situation: "You asked us to remove our missiles from Cuba. And we did. You asked us to remove the Il-28s. And we did. Finally, you asked us to remove Georgi Bolshakov. And we did. No more concessions!"

Bolshakov had every right to wonder about his American allies. In response to Khrushchev's criticism of the publicity about Bolshakov, John Kennedy had written in mid-December, "I am sorry to learn that he is returning to Moscow . . . we shall miss him very much."[18] If he was considered so valuable, why had the White House allowed Alsop and Bartlett to destroy his career as superpower intermediary? Perhaps the Kennedys felt they needed a lightning rod to deflect blame for the fact that the missile sites were not detected until mid-October. Dobrynin, like Bolshakov, had carried false information, but he was now the White House's preferred contact with Moscow. Bolshakov had become expendable.

Life would never be the same for the man once nicknamed "iron" by his friends in Soviet intelligence. Bolshakov found bureaucratic exile awaiting him in Moscow. Surrounded by other burned-out intelligence cases from the GRU, he slipped into a new career of vodka, shapely secretaries, and official neglect.

Khrushchev Has Other Concerns

The White House had been right to assume a shift in Khrushchev's thinking. The day after Kennedy's November 20 speech ending the quarantine, Khrushchev used the occasion of a request for military assistance from the communist front in Laos to signal a new spirit in Soviet foreign policy to his colleagues on the Presidium. For over a year the Soviet Union had been secretly airlifting military assistance to the Pathet Lao in violation of Khrushchev's promise to Kennedy at Vienna. On November 21 Khrushchev ordered this to end. He wanted the Soviet ambassador and the Laotians to stop asking for this assistance. "What is most important now is peace." "We will conclude a peace," Khrushchev continued, "without winners or losers." Since 1956 this had been the rhetorical position of the Soviet Union. Now, it seemed, Khrushchev was prepared to act on it. "Tell the Soviet ambassador," he added, "that we have done all we could to help the Pathet Lao." In the wake of the Cuban disaster, the Kremlin believed that its Southeast Asian allies were being too inflexible and reckless. "If they want a war, it will be their own affair."[19]

The change in Khrushchev's thinking was not limited to his willingness to take risks to help ideological allies in faraway places. Khrushchev began to identify his own political future with that of Kennedy. Kennedy's tough negotiating and Castro's impetuosity had contributed to the Soviet decision to remove all nuclear weapons from Cuba in December 1962. The Red Army had hoped to keep some there to destroy any future U.S. attempt at invasion. Now that all nuclear warheads were gone, Cuba was again indefensible by the Soviet armed forces, and Khrushchev had to fall back on a political guarantee from the American president.

Under the new circumstances, Khrushchev saw a need to help the young American hold on to power. He kept his word not to reveal to anyone outside his inner circle that the Kremlin had compelled the United States to remove its Jupiter missiles from Turkey. Although Khrushchev could have used the trade to strengthen his case among the rest of the leaders in the Communist Party that the USSR had not been the loser in October 1962, he did not.

The first major test of Khrushchev's commitment to keep the secret of the Turkish trade came at a meeting of the Central Committee on November 23, 1962, at which the Soviet leader presented his views on the missile crisis. Recalling an earthy Russian expression, Khrushchev put the entire experience in context. "It was not necessary to act like the czarist officer who farted at the ball and then shot himself." "If a government has the misfortune to lose its head in difficult times," he added, "then this could threaten a tragedy for all people."[20]

Khrushchev resolved to defend himself without referring to the one concession that on October 27 the Soviet leader had described as signifying a "win" for him in this mess. In the week preceding the plenum, the Presidium had distributed some of the Kennedy-Khrushchev correspondence among the top members of the Central Committee. Deliberately left out were those letters from October 28 that outlined the Turkey-Cuba trade.[21] In his speech at the session, Khrushchev argued that peace was preserved because "mutual concessions were made to achieve a compromise."[22] John F. Kennedy's promise not to invade Cuba was the only American concession that he mentioned.

At the plenum Khrushchev also concealed his anger at Castro's performance in the crisis, choosing instead to reaffirm Cuba's special significance as a beacon of socialism. Khrushchev was not prepared to abandon Cuba, and it was not in his interest to introduce any doubt in the minds of his audience about the wisdom of ever having depended on the Cuban leader.

Khrushchev reserved his ire for Moscow's socialist competitors in the Third World, the Chinese, who had criticized his performance in regard to Cuba. After explaining that he had sent the missiles to Cuba to deter an American attack, Khrushchev turned on Beijing. "Of course, the least amount of assistance [in 1962] to Cuba came from the Chinese. What did they do at the moment of greatest tension? The workers in the Chinese embassy in Cuba went to a blood donation center and announced, 'We are giving our blood for Cuba.' What demagogic, cheap assistance!" "Cuba didn't need the blood of some men," he roared, "but real military and political assistance so that human blood and flesh should not be spread across the land."

"No one seriously believes," said Khrushchev, "that when we communists see a capitalist we should immediately pull out a knife and slice him up." Like Soviet leaders before him and after, he claimed the legitimacy of his actions from Lenin. "Do you remember that in 1918 Trotsky left Brest-Litovsk, having torn up the signed peace accord with Germany and her allies? But Lenin then sent a delegation led by [Soviet Foreign Minister Georgi] Chicherin, and the Brest peace was signed. Who was right—Lenin or Trotsky?" Khrushchev gave the answer: "Lenin." Khrushchev then explained what this meant for the future of U.S.-Soviet relations: "V. I. Lenin introduced the slogan of peaceful coexistence. And what does it entail? Mutual concession, compromise. Socialism and capitalism—these are antagonistic. . . . We will lead this struggle, as Lenin taught, on the economic and political fronts, not interfering in each other's domestic affairs. We demand that the other side accepts this state of affairs. There is a compromise."[23]

For all his statements to the Central Committee about peaceful coexistence, Khrushchev left no doubt that ideology and military force remained important to the Soviet Union. Moscow was not prepared to accept the status quo in the Third World. Part of Cuba's special significance for the Soviet Union, he argued, was as "a catalyst for revolutionary power in Latin American states." Peaceful coexistence did not imply stagnation either in international communism nor in Soviet defense. Khrushchev assumed that the West would compromise only so long as the Soviet Union remained militarily strong. Getting excited by the end of his presentation, he revised his earlier explanation of how the Cuban missile crisis had ended, this time stressing the role of Soviet power: "The antiaircraft guns shot twice and brought down an American U-2 spy plane. What a shot! And in return we received a pledge not to invade Cuba. Not bad!"[24]

The Cuban crisis had altered Khrushchev's approach to Castro as much as it had his treatment of Kennedy. In the days following Castro's rejection of the missile crisis settlement, the Soviet leader had not known what to do about his ally. He was ready to cut the Cubans off completely on November 16. And on December 3 he roared that under no circumstances would the Soviet Union sign a military agreement with such an irresponsible man.[25]

When Khrushchev's anger subsided in January 1963, he decided to patch up relations with Castro but on slightly different terms. He was now determined to manage the relationship better to lessen the potential for Cuban actions to harm Soviet interests. Following a state visit to East Germany in January 1963, Khrushchev dictated a twenty-seven-page letter to Castro, as his special train retraced the route taken by Hitler's tanks twenty years earlier.[26]

It was important for Khrushchev that Castro not view the missile crisis as a failure. He assigned himself the difficult task of persuading Castro of two concepts that were in conflict. On the one hand, he wanted Fidel Castro to appreciate the cost of war in the nuclear age; yet he did not want the Cubans to lose faith in Moscow's ability and willingness to wage nuclear war to protect the socialist world. In the future he wanted Cuban respect and not Cuban recklessness.

Khrushchev's letter went over familiar ground. Not wanting to stress Soviet strategic weaknesses in May 1962, Khrushchev explained the missile decision

exclusively in terms of Cuba's security needs. The one new element introduced into his narrative was the role played by John Kennedy's discussion
with Aleksei Adzhubei in January 1962. "During meetings with our representatives," wrote Khrushchev, ". . . they often referred to the 1956 events in
Hungary, viewing them as a model of a decisive measure from which to derive
justification for their actions against Cuba's revolution." He continued, "They
said to us, 'You did it in your own interests because Hungary is close to you;
but we also have the right to undertake the same decisive actions against
Cuba, which is close to us.' "

Khrushchev's January 1963 letter received mixed reviews in Cuba. Aleksandr
Alekseev put his ear to the door of a special meeting of the Integrated Revolutionary Organizations (ORI)—the single party produced by the merger of the
Cuban communist party (PSP) and the July 26 movement. The meeting had
been called to discuss Khrushchev's letter. Flavio Bravo, the man who had
served as a personal representative of the PSP to the Kremlin naturally sang
the praises of Khrushchev's initiative. "This letter," he gushed to Alekseev,
"represents the start of the restoration of the genuine fraternal Soviet-Cuban
relationship that existed before the crisis, and it has convinced everyone of the
patience of the Soviet leadership and the height of Soviet principle on the
question of the noninterference in the work of foreign parties."[27] Speaking to
Bravo, however, was the equivalent of preaching to the converted. Yet Ramiro
Valdés, Castro's minister of the interior, and the head of Cuba's guerrilla training camps, also praised Moscow for the letter.[28]

Fidel Castro, however, was not quite as moved. Khrushchev had sweetened
his words with an offer for Castro to visit the USSR. Since November 1960
Castro had signaled his interest in staying a month or so in the Soviet Union
to study how Russia constructed socialism. But insofar as Khrushchev's reitera-
tion of the offer was a subtle way of checking on Castro's political intentions,
it failed.

Castro sent word to the Kremlin that though he would like to visit the
USSR sometime, he needed rest now. He said that he "feared having too
many official meetings." Moreover, and here he did not even try to varnish his
response, Castro said that frankly he "was afraid of Russian hospitality, especially because of his digestive problems."[29] No chicken Kiev and vodka for
him, please.

Indeed, Castro was not healthy. Alekseev had information from Castro's private physicians that, in the wake of the crisis, the Cuban leader was on the verge
of a complete physical and mental collapse.[30] The Soviet decision to negotiate
the withdrawal of the big missiles with Kennedy behind his back had been hard
enough to take; but the later Soviet decision to remove all nuclear weapons, including the stashes of tactical weapons that Castro had assumed Cuba would be
able to keep, had humiliated him. So, when the Cuban cited medical reasons
for not going, Alekseev knew that this was not a case of a diplomatic flu. Yet the

Soviet ambassador also understood how important a Khrushchev-Castro photo opportunity would be for the Kremlin's prestige after the October crisis. In an effort to get Castro to come for a few days, he even suggested that Castro bring his own supplies of water, as if he were a Los Angelino who hoped to avoid Montezuma's revenge in Mexico City. "All will be okay for you," Alekseev said; "during the receptions you could just drink your water."

Nor was Castro's movement politically healthy. The missile crisis had caused deep divisions in the ORI, with some of the revolutionaries prepared to side with China. Unable or unwilling to put these disagreements to a vote, Castro allowed the ORI to describe itself as "neutral" in the Sino-Soviet conflict. Fidel as well as his brother Raúl and the former leadership of the PSP stressed to Moscow that neutrality did not imply neutralism—the path taken by Marshal Joseph Tito's Yugoslavia and increasingly by socialist Romania.[31] Nevertheless, the Kremlin was well aware that Che Guevara believed that the missile crisis had weakened the Soviet Union's leadership of revolutionary movements around the world.[32]

The one heartening statement that Castro made to the Soviets in early February, he wasn't sure he believed. Castro went on record as agreeing with Khrushchev's assessment that as a result of the Caribbean crisis the likelihood of a U.S. invasion in the next one to two years had disappeared. Khrushchev and Castro had expected something from Kennedy before the 1964 election. Now it seemed that so long as Kennedy was reelected, Castro argued, a U.S. invasion was unlikely until 1968 or 1969.

A Mongoose in 1963

Cuba again became a hot political issue for the Kennedy administration in early February 1963. Citing "continuing, absolutely confirmed, and undeniable evidence," Capitol Hill's gadfly on the Cuban issue, Kenneth Keating, claimed that as many as forty Soviet medium-range ballistic missiles were concealed in Cuba. Keating's dire predictions in October had turned out to be accurate, and these new allegations were taken seriously. On February 7 Robert McNamara gave an unprecedented two-hour briefing to the American people, carried live on television, in which he used recent air photographs to puncture fears of hidden Soviet ballistic missiles on the island. Regarding Senator Keating and his charges, McNamara said, "I don't own a hat and I hope he does, because he is going to have to eat it, based on the evidence that we presented today."[33] However, the administration had to admit, indirectly, that its estimates of the number of Soviet forces on Cuba in October had been too low. The latest reconnaissance photographs indicated there were 18,000 Soviet troops on the island, and this was after at least 5,000 had left with the ballistic missiles and the Il-28 bombers.[34]

The political discussion over the Soviet forces in Cuba prompted Kennedy to raise the issue again with the Soviets. In late October and early November, the two leaders had discussed the Soviet troops present on Cuba. The matter had been left with a vague promise from Khrushchev that the technicians associated with the "weapons that you call offensive" would leave with those weapons. This seemed acceptable to the administration until Kennedy realized that his government had underestimated the number of Soviet personnel by a factor of at least two. On February 9, in the midst of media and congressional pressure, Dean Rusk raised the Soviet troop problem with Anatoly Dobrynin. He asked the Soviets to support the Kennedy administration's efforts to satisfy congressional critics, by means of a statement from Moscow that denied any increase in Soviet military personnel and that promised to continue the reduction of existing forces.[35]

As part of his new policy of not allowing Cuba to obstruct better relations with Washington, Khrushchev decided that he would try to remove all of the remaining Soviet troops from Cuba. He could not do so immediately, because Castro's support would be necessary. However, Khrushchev thought that he could at least show the Americans what his intentions were. Within ten days of Rusk's approach, Moscow told Washington that the Kennedy administration could announce to the American press that the Kremlin intended "to withdraw from Cuba by the middle of March several thousand Soviet military personnel."[36]

From sources in and around the State Department, the Soviets picked up hints in the winter of 1963 that Kennedy might resume an aggressive policy toward Cuba. The Soviets learned that Assistant Secretary of State Edwin Martin was on record as saying early in the new year that "Castro would be out by July" because of a new package of measures that the Kennedy administration was set to implement.[37] In mid-February, President Rómulo Betancourt of Venezuela came to Washington on an official visit. The State Department's Venezuela desk officer told a KGB source that Betancourt had joined with the Guatemalans to "urgently demand that the U.S. accept decisive measures against Cuba."[38]

However, the Soviets were convinced that Kennedy was among the least likely in his administration to adopt aggressive measures against Cuba. One KGB source described a White House under siege from congressmen and governors to take action. These hard-liners equated the Castro problem with the state of Kennedy's chances for reelection in 1964. The fault line in the administration debate over a military solution to the Castro problem ran between a pro-intervention group, led by McGeorge Bundy, most of the Pentagon, and a minority in the State Department, and the critics of the military option, most notably Adlai Stevenson, Arthur Schlesinger, Jr., and the chairman of the Joint Chiefs, Maxwell Taylor. The opponents of an invasion explained that it would take at least twenty thousand men and a long time. On the issue of this scheme Kennedy leaned to the side of the opponents of using force.[39]

Nevertheless, as evidence of new U.S. aggressive activity mounted, the Kremlin became increasingly concerned that Kennedy would reverse his policy toward Cuba. The KGB once more produced a digest of its most recent reports on Kennedy's intentions toward Castro. Neither a clearly argued position paper nor an estimate of future U.S. actions, the report provided evidence of a more active Cuban policy by the White House without concluding that another Bay of Pigs was on the way. But this was enough for the Kremlin. A few days after the KGB disseminated five copies of its report to the Foreign Ministry as well as the Central Committee, Andrei Gromyko took the U.S. ambassador, Foy Kohler, to one side and complained that Khrushchev sensed a change in Kennedy's position on Cuba.[40]

Indeed, the Kennedy administration was tightening its policy toward Fidel Castro. With President Kennedy increasingly worried about Cuban subversion in Latin America, especially Venezuela, and as a result of mounting public impatience with the mysterious Soviet presence in the Caribbean, the Special Group (Augmented) took new decisions regarding Cuba in March 1963.[41] On March 15 the group authorized, for the first time since the death of Mongoose in November, a "subtle sabotage program." Through radio propaganda and fictitious letters sent to Cubans, the CIA hoped to encourage a swifter removal of the Soviet contingent.[42] Although the new version of Mongoose authorized by the White House was smaller in scale than the earlier one, the Kennedys were still asking for dramatic results.[43] Once again the CIA felt it necessary to warn policymakers that a massive popular uprising was an "unrealistic" hope.[44] Retrieving its arguments from the debates of the spring of 1962, the CIA reiterated that even if an uprising did occur, it would confront Washington "with the dilemma of U.S. military intervention before the uprising is crushed or by standing helplessly by while a Hungarian-type bloodbath is carried out under our noses."[45] "[T]he only potentially effective course of action," the CIA suggested, "is a pincers strategy of economic strangulation to weaken and undermine the regime in conjunction with an intensive probing effort to identify and establish channels of communication to disaffected and potentially dissident non-Communist elements in the power centers of the regime."[46] John McCone was especially attracted to the idea of having the United States find powerful allies within the Castro government to be able to get rid of Fidel. He asked the CIA to develop a plan for "split[ing] the military establishment from the Castro/Communist regime."[47]

Faced with alternatives that it did not like, the Kennedy administration could not decide how to handle Castro. Despite recommendations from the CIA to resume a major program of sabotage and harassment, the White House chose an unhappy medium, which Desmond Fitzgerald, the new head of the CIA's Cuban Task Force, derided as equivalent to "tying a rock to a wire and throwing it across high tension lines."[48]

Fidel Castro in the USSR

Fidel Castro's moral and physical health had improved enough by March 1963 that he agreed to go to the Soviet Union. Khrushchev was delighted and saw the visit as an opportunity to work with the Cuban leader to eliminate as many potential areas of conflict with the United States in the Caribbean as possible. Andrei Gromyko, Malinovsky, and the army chief of staff, Marshal Biryuzov, prepared arguments for Khrushchev that he could use to turn down a request from Castro to sign a Soviet-Cuban mutual security pact or to join the Warsaw Pact. Castro was known to want an ironclad commitment to the defense of Cuba in the absence of Soviet missiles on Cuba. But Khrushchev's principal advisers on foreign policy matters argued that the United States would use any agreement of this nature as an excuse to further Cuba's international isolation and to stir up opposition to the revolution in Cuba itself. The Kremlin was concerned that Castro would face a formidable domestic opposition if he wasted his energy in fighting with the United States rather than devoting it to clamping down at home.[49]

The Soviet troops in Cuba were another issue that Khrushchev wanted to bring up with Castro, especially in light of his recent statement to the Americans. Khrushchev intended to propose to Castro the eventual removal of all Soviet soldiers from the island. And the third area where Khrushchev hoped for some improvement concerned Cuban participation in regional revolutionary movements. Despite a Cuban reluctance to share information, Soviet intelligence was reasonably well aware of Cuban activities in support of national-liberation movements. Although Moscow did not control Cuba's efforts in this regard, it certainly sympathized with Castro's efforts. Nevertheless, as in the spring of 1962 when the Kremlin tried to dissuade Castro from taking on this revolutionary burden while the CIA was evidently attempting to overthrow him, Khrushchev was concerned about him in the spring of 1963. In preparation for Castro's visit, the KGB supplied the leadership with a study of the relationship between the Castro regime and Latin American revolutionary movements.[50]

The Kremlin's careful preparations extended to the Cuban leader's travel arrangements. After three years of reading dispatches describing various plots to kill Castro, Khrushchev was extremely concerned about his visitor's personal safety. On April 26 Castro left on an unannounced nonstop flight from Havana to the Arctic seaport of Murmansk, instead of Moscow. His itinerary was a state secret, and even the length of time he planned to spend in the Soviet Union was withheld.[51]

Castro would remain over a month in the Soviet Union, visiting settlements and cities ranging from Siberia to Samarkand. He absorbed a lot, but the visit was remarkable in that it gave him and Khrushchev an unprecedented opportunity to get to know each other. Castro had as many questions for Khrushchev as the latter had for him. Over the course of several long meetings, most of them at Khrushchev's dachas at Zavidovo, near Moscow, and at Pitsunda, on the Black Sea, the two men engaged each other in a seminar on the governing of communist societies.

Castro proved his unpredictability, when the leaders met for their first extended session over the May Day weekend, by kicking off the session with a discussion.[52] He was concerned that the Algerian military was preparing to overthrow his friend Ahmed Ben Bella. He was careful not to say so, but Castro wanted the Soviet Union to do something to help Ben Bella. Khrushchev took this in stride, agreeing with Castro's assessment of the situation. But when Castro said he felt the need to visit Algiers to show his support, Khrushchev, who saw adversarial intelligence services around many corners, advised him not to make the trip.

Castro's second idea for a way of helping Ben Bella opened a new chapter in Soviet-Cuban relations and in Soviet activities in Africa. "At present," Castro reported to Khrushchev, "the Ben Bella government is providing energetic assistance to the national-liberation movement in Angola." Castro explained that the Algerians were sending "weapons, money, and medicine" to overthrow the Portuguese colonial government. In addition, Angolan partisan leaders were flying to Algeria for training. The Cubans thought that if Ben Bella was doing this, he deserved all possible assistance. Khrushchev repeated again that going to Algeria was unsafe for Castro; but this time he added that the Soviet Union would supply weapons to Algeria. "Let this be the price," Khrushchev said jokingly, "for your not going to Algeria."[53]

Castro spoke enthusiastically of the potential for revolution in Africa. Khrushchev, by contrast, held out little hope that Africa would soon come alive politically. He felt that Africa had first to undergo a "long evolutionary process" because of the legacy of colonialism. However, he wished to show solidarity with the Cubans.

The men had a marathon session two days later, in which Castro questioned Khrushchev as a student might query a teacher. Castro wanted him to explain the roots of the discord in the socialist camp. First, he was interested in the bases for Sino-Soviet tension. Khrushchev spoke breezily about this, mentioning the problem of nomadic tribes in Central Asia, evidently giving the impression that he did not want to engage the Cuban leader on this matter. His final comment on China was that the sources of the conflict were "unclear" even to him. But Castro continued. "What about the conflict with Albania?" On this Khrushchev was prepared to talk in some detail. "She was a favorite daughter of the socialist camp," Khrushchev explained. "We always wanted to make of Albania the showcase for the Muslim world." But Stalin had scared the Albanians away by promising their country to Marshal Tito of Yugoslavia as part of some future Balkan federation. "Stalin was capable of saying any stupidity in the last years of his life," asserted Khrushchev, "when he was in fact mentally ill."[54]

Later in the day Castro launched into a discussion of the future of the Cuban-Soviet relationship. "It would be useful," he said, "for there to be coordination of Soviet and Cuban foreign policy, especially on cooperation in military matters." This was the opening predicted by Khrushchev's advisers and for which the Soviet leader had prepared a response. Literally moving down the checklist of reasons why Cuba should not join the Warsaw Pact, Khrushchev laid out the arguments that Gromyko and the others had suggested to him the week before.

"Would a military agreement be useful or not to unify the country, to consolidate power, and to weaken the forces of counterrevolution?" Khrushchev asked, pretending to be thinking aloud. "Or, on the other hand, this might significantly weaken the position of Cuba in its relations with the countries of the Western Hemisphere, since American propaganda will strive to convince one and all that Cuba was indeed a Soviet satellite." Before concluding that in the final analysis the decision "was one for the Cubans themselves to make," Khrushchev explained why the agreement was likely to do Cuba more harm than good.

Keeping Castro away from a mutual security agreement was a key element in Khrushchev's strategy of helping Kennedy keep his word in the Caribbean. After Castro raised the possibility of a defense agreement, Khrushchev steered the conversation to the issue of the Soviet brigade that was still in Cuba. Castro did not want the Soviet forces to leave: "The presence of Soviet military personnel in Cuba represents the sole good deterrent against every kind of military adventure." "It is our opinion," continued Castro," that Soviet military personnel located in Cuba, are like the celebrated missiles. So long as they are there, American military circles are convinced that an attack on Cuba would inevitably lead to war with the Soviet Union, which is something that they don't want and fear."

Castro had boxed Khrushchev in with his reference to the missiles. Yet Khrushchev did not want the Cuban leader to think that the Soviet Union was happy to keep its men on the island. After saying that he "agreed" with Castro's analysis, he downplayed the U.S. threat, remarking that "the Soviet forces cannot stay forever, especially since there is evidence of a strong guarantee given confidentially by Kennedy not to invade."

Khrushchev returned to his game plan, which was to convince Castro that too overt a dependence on Moscow would work to his disadvantage. "Many foreign bourgeois politicians and journalists," he noted, "speculate that Soviet forces are in Cuba to support the Castro regime . . . [and] the removal of these forces would undermine the Castro regime." Khrushchev stressed the main theme of his advice: "It is necessary to show that this is not so."

Convinced that Castro underestimated the difficulties of imposing communism from the top, Khrushchev encouraged him to pay more attention to his domestic enemies. In 1960, when Fidel Castro's loyalty was suspect, Moscow had cautioned the Soviet contingent in Cuba not to encourage Aníbal Escalante and the other handwringers in the PSP who were calling for a war on the counterrevolution. But now Khrushchev felt he had to shake the Cuban leader a bit. "On this question," he said, "one must be extremely careful, because determined elements and groups will always look for negative circumstances and will exploit advantageous moments for an antigovernment demonstration." He had in mind his own decisions to use force to crush any anti-Soviet activity: "We, for example, forty years after the October revolution were forced to use force in a series of instances. To be specific, it was so in Tbilisi, it was so in Novocherkassk, it was so in Karaganda and some other areas." This was a seminar on ruthlessness for Castro by one of Lenin's protégés. In 1922 Lenin advised a fellow party member that "if it becomes necessary to use terror to achieve important political goals, then it must be employed energetically and with celerity."[55] In 1963 Khrushchev counseled Castro, "One must always keep in mind that at the very first moment of any antigovernmental activity, one must crush it quickly, decisively, not stopping in the event it is necessary to open fire."[56] Khrushchev believed that the Soviet system was too brittle to permit any domestic détente. "Every hesitation, all of that spinelessness of the intelligentsia," he lectured, as if Castro were an apprentice, "could lead to very ruinous consequences."

Castro rose to the challenge. "My revolution has also not shrunk from serious, decisive measures if dictated by necessity. The proof of this was the shooting of military and political criminals, the arrests of many saboteurs, and intelligence agents of foreign powers." Castro explained that "he was convinced that he had sufficient force to guarantee his control of the country in any situation and to prevent the appearance of any counterrevolutionary activity." With this in mind, he said that Cuba was planning "to set up special tank battalions in the province of Havana."[57]

Three weeks later, after Castro had completed his tour of the Soviet Union, Khrushchev invited him to his beloved swimming pool at Pitsunda, where a year earlier he had entertained the Kennedy administration's Stewart Udall. By all accounts, the Castro visit was going very well. Proof of this was the open-endedness of the Cuban leader's travel plans. Initially scheduled to leave Russia on May 20, he was beginning to seem like the distant relative who came for Christmas dinner and was around to paint eggs at Easter. But the trip was winding down, and with that came the need to decide what military assistance and what kind of security guarantee the Cubans would get.[58]

In the presence of the chiefs of staff of the Soviet army and the Cuban Revolutionary Army, Castro outlined his military needs to Khrushchev. As he had told him at the beginning of May, he intended to create new tank units to use in the streets of Havana. He needed 120 of the Soviet Union's newest tanks, the T-54 and T-55, to form two tank brigades, which would provide battalion-size units to protect Havana and the strategic air base at San Antonio de los Baños. Besides the tanks, Castro asked for additional antiaircraft weaponry, including a new missile that his friends in the Soviet army had alerted him to.

Khrushchev would not accede to all of Castro's wishes, despite a desire to assuage whatever distress the Cubans still felt as a result of the missile crisis. One reason may have been the rising cost of assisting Cuba and the scars Khrushchev himself still bore from the Cuban phase of the crisis. Yet in denying Castro his wish list, Khrushchev pushed a tactical point in encouraging him not to think of tanks as his salvation. "The defense of Cuba," he advised, "will not come only with building up Cuban military power but in effective intelligence activity abroad." Khrushchev was not impressed with Cuban counterintelligence and counterinsurgency. He said that Havana should be trying harder to penetrate Cuban exile communities so as to squelch their invasion plans before they progress very far. Recalling the experience of the Bolsheviks, Khrushchev stressed the importance to Soviet security of actions taken in foreign lands against White Russians and other anti-Bolshevik movements before and, especially, after the Second World War. Khrushchev made no bones about the value of killing one's opponents. "There are times," he counseled, "when the security services should physically eliminate the leaders of the counterrevolution in exile."[59]

Castro responded diplomatically to this bit of advice. Thinking no doubt of the many Cuban intelligence failures since 1959, he admitted that his services had initially concentrated on penetrating counterrevolutionary bands within the country and that until recently they had few successes in Miami or any other nest of counterrevolutionary activity. However, "[i]n recent months," Castro explained, "[we] have been able to take advantage of ships leaving Cuba that brought medicines and other goods in compensation for the release of the Bay of Pigs prisoners." The Cubans trained special agents who were placed on these American ships. Castro did not explain how, but Cuban intelligence prepared these people to join the Cuban community in Miami, where they would insinuate themselves into the leadership while reporting back to Havana.

The details of what military hardware the Cubans would receive were hammered out a couple of days later when the two leaders oversaw a meeting between General del Valle of the Cuban army and Marshal Biryuzov. Khrushchev had asked that "the details of military assistance be left to the generals." But he intervened in this meeting to explain to Castro that Cuba would receive 80 and not 120 tanks; and these would be the World War II era–T-34 workhorse instead of the new generation of tanks. Khrushchev also authorized a reduced level of antiaircraft support.

Despite Soviet parsimony, Castro was not disappointed. Khrushchev gave him something else that he wanted. In the first draft of the Soviet-Cuban communiqué that would have announced Castro's achievements in the Soviet Union to the world, the Soviet Ministry of Foreign Affairs had written nothing about a nuclear guarantee to Cuba. When the Cubans saw this, they complained to Ambassador Alekseev, who was accompanying Castro around the country. Alekseev told Khrushchev that the deputy foreign minister, V. V. Kuznetsov, opposed the nuclear guarantee. "Why that asshole!" Khrushchev replied, saying that of course he would renew the guarantee he had first made in the summer of 1960.[60] True to his word, he instructed Gromyko's professionals to insert the appropriate language into a revised communiqué. This language alone was worth more to Castro than three brigades of tanks.

The Aftermath

A week after Castro's departure, Khrushchev gave to his colleagues on the Presidium a glowing account of the visit: "Evidently, he is a young, thoughtful man, who understands our position correctly," Khrushchev began. Castro seemed to have changed since the difficult days of November.[61] "I told him: 'it was said that we were cowards; but if we were cowards, why then did we deploy missiles on Cuba?' " Khrushchev answered his own question:

> Even fools understand that having put missiles in Cuba, we took a step that could have led to war. Is this cowardice? Nyet. Is this a retreat? Nyet. It is a step forward! Who, besides our party, could have believed that your country Cuba could be saved and could have known how to do it? Who? . . .
>
> I said, 'Now, of course, there are a lot of smart alecks, but I think that no one thought that when you won and opted for the course of building socialism, America would tolerate you and not strangle you. No one believed this; and we thought this was adventurism, that you would not survive. And so that you would survive, we deployed missiles. I said that of course it would have been better not to have had to remove these missiles: even an idiot understands this. It was even our desire; but things do not always work out as one wants. It did not work out. But what is most important is that the goal was justified. We wanted you to live, that a socialist Cuba would develop. . . . You did develop. This was the mission. On the other hand, the Americans wanted to wipe you off the face of the earth. So who suffered defeat? Who did not get what he wanted? We attained our goal; so they lost, we won. . . .'
>
> He said to me a few times: 'Please tell me, isn't it true: we believed that you sent missiles in the interests of the entire socialist bloc, not in the interests of Cuba. . . .'
>
> I said, 'Well, why the hell would we put our missiles 90 km from the USA, 11,000 km from the USSR, when we could more easily get our adversary from our own territory? If you think this way, I am sorry that we did not adequately and in a thoughtful way explain the necessity [of our step] to you.'[62]

During Khrushchev's remarks, a few of his colleagues chimed in with enthusiastic support. "What an enormous accomplishment!" said Kosygin. "This should be known in all countries, especially those countries that are close to the Chinese," exulted Boris Ponomarev, the man responsible for international affairs in the Central Committee.[63]

Much of what Khrushchev said was bluster. But at the end of May he had received from the Kennedy brothers some good news that seemed to reassure him that John Kennedy would not break his word. Robert Kennedy told a Soviet representative in New York that the Cuban missile deal was still in force. Aware that the debate in the newspapers may have raised Soviet suspicions about the administration's policy toward Castro, the attorney general told the Soviet intelligence officer that despite the pressure on his brother, the latter "did not plan any intervention into Cuba now." Kennedy explained there were two reasons for this:

a) Because of the agreement reached as part of the settlement of the Cuban Missile Crisis
b) Because President Kennedy believed that U.S. intelligence overestimated the possibility of opposition to Castro and underestimated the position of the present Cuban government.[64]

John Kennedy soon provided Khrushchev with even better proof that the policy of peaceful coexistence with the United States could be advantageous to the Soviet Union. Awash in public respect after the Cuban missile crisis, Kennedy felt for the first time in his tenure in office that he could openly express his views on the U.S.-Soviet relationship. In June 1963 he instructed Theodore Sorensen to present his vision for the future of the superpower relationship. He would deliver this speech at American University's spring commencement.

McGeorge Bundy told Kennedy intimates that the president believed "the time had come for a major address on peace."[65] Six months had passed since Khrushchev raised the possibility of agreement on a comprehensive test ban in the context of a settlement of the Cuban crisis. Once again the number of inspections was the sticking point. Kennedy had countered Khrushchev's position of two to three annual inspections with a new offer of eight to ten a year, an even smaller number of inspections than what he had authorized Robert Kennedy to suggest before the Vienna meeting in 1961.[66] Weeks turned into months and momentum seemed to be slipping as congressional opposition to a ban increased while little or no additional encouragement came from Moscow. In early May while Khrushchev was hosting Castro, the Kremlin sent a "disappointing" letter to Kennedy. "I'm not hopeful, I'm not hopeful," said the president after reading the letter.[67]

A speech on peace might loosen whatever reserve was holding Khrushchev back. The Cuban missile crisis had brought the two societies to the brink of war, and Kennedy believed that an opportunity had presented itself to return to the hopeful months of 1961 when bilateral agreements, like the test ban, which could lead to a relaxation of tension, were possible.

"[T]he tide of time and events will often bring surprising changes in the relations between nations," Kennedy told the graduating class of 1963 at American University. For the first time since the collapse of the Grand Alliance in 1945, an American president described Soviet sacrifices and praised the Soviet people for their efforts in the Second World War. "No government or social system," he said, "is so evil that its people must be considered as lacking in virtue." Going further, he challenged Americans not to be afraid to extend a hand to Moscow. The expression of peace, the "necessary rational end of rational men," is not the equivalent of unilateral disarmament. "We can seek," he said, "a relaxation of tensions without relaxing our guard." Kennedy asked Americans to have reasonable expectations about the benefits a détente could bring in the early going. "If we cannot end now all our differences," he advised, "at least we can help make the world safe for diversity." In January 1961 he had complained in private to the JCS that the American people expected him to be more belligerent than he thought wise. Now he told the country, "[W]e must reexamine our own attitude—as individuals and as a Nation—for our attitude is as essential as theirs."

At the heart of his speech was the issue that had been the centerpiece of his private diplomacy with Moscow for over two years. Citing it as the first step to peace, Kennedy declared that he would resume negotiations "looking toward early agreement on a comprehensive test ban treaty." Again appealing to the good sense of Americans, he admitted that no treaty could offer absolute security, but this accord would "offer far more security and far fewer risks than an unabated, uncontrolled, unpredictable arms race."[68]

Kennedy's reassuring rhetoric and his willingness to speak openly about desires that he had only hinted at through his brother's back channel, drew an immediate and dramatic response from Khrushchev. In late July, Khrushchev said that he could accept a limited nuclear test ban, proscribing tests in the atmosphere, underwater, and in outer space, areas not requiring on-site inspection for verification purposes. Since Kennedy's election, the Soviet leader had said he wanted a new Roosevelt in the White House. In May 1961 Soviet intelligence had discouraged these hopes. Kennedy's foreign policy was expected to be "flexible"; but it would also be "tough."[69] "On a series of important international issues," KGB analysts reported, "Kennedy's position is as openly aggressive and uncompromising as that of the Eisenhower administration."[70] Nevertheless, contradictory pieces of information continued to filter through, especially those coming from Robert Kennedy himself, suggesting a Kennedy who was very uncomfortable with the Cold War. The American University speech represented for Khrushchev the apotheosis of that side of President Kennedy. In the aftermath of this ground-breaking speech, the Soviet leader welcomed Kennedy's initiative to restart arms control discussions.

A new modus vivendi was emerging between the superpowers that might bring the tension down a notch or two. It was understood that both superpowers would continue the ideological struggle. Khrushchev had just authorized Soviet assistance to Algeria, assuming that this would ultimately help Angola. Kennedy remained intent on defending South Vietnam. But Washington and Moscow committed themselves to finding nonmilitary solutions to their problems. Khrushchev tried to encourage Castro to live without Soviet troops on his island and vowed that they would soon have to leave. For his part Kennedy endorsed a limited program of sabotage in Cuba and rested his hopes for removing Castro on an increasingly less likely revolt or the long wished-for "elimination" of the Cuban leader.

Kennedy's speech had signaled an American policy of tolerating the Soviet Union that seemed much closer to Khrushchev's cherished principle of "peaceful coexistence" than anything the Kremlin had heard before. It was one thing for Robert Kennedy to depict the president as fighting the militarists in Washington, and quite another for the president himself to deliver a public sermon on the necessity of mutual respect.

The Cuban missile crisis may well have opened Khrushchev's eyes to the dangers of an uncontrolled arms race. But it was John Kennedy's courage in June 1963 that drove Khrushchev to give the White House an arms control agreement, which he knew Kennedy personally desired. Khrushchev would not relent on the number of inspections. He continued to believe that the American position was designed by the CIA to open his country to further spying. But at least now he was prepared to agree to an atmospheric test ban, which would not require any inspections and which Kennedy had offered to Moscow as a last-ditch solution in April 1962 when the Pentagon was pressuring him to resume testing.

Thus began a short relaxation of tensions between the superpowers, a so-called détente. In the summer of 1963, besides signing a limited test ban, the two countries established a twenty-four hour communications link, "the hot line," to avert a situation like the one in October 1962, when critical messages took hours to pass from one leader to another. Kennedy again suggested a joint moon shot, which the Soviets again refused. However, in the spirit of improving relations, Moscow accepted for the first time the notion that a disarmament agreement should allow both superpowers to maintain nuclear arsenals for a while. Up to that point the Soviet position had been mutual nuclear disarmament as a first step or nothing.

The Cuban missile crisis had passed into history; but its legacy was that Khrushchev and Kennedy were now willing to take risks for better relations. Khrushchev needed a more predictable relationship with Kennedy; and Kennedy saw an opportunity to move public opinion closer to his understanding of international politics. As ever, Castro loomed in the background as a potential obstacle to these achievements.

Dallas and Moscow

A bullet shattered President Kennedy's skull on November 22, 1963, and the world held its breath. In Moscow and Havana, Nikita Khrushchev and Fidel Castro feared that much more than one man's life had been destroyed that afternoon in Dallas. Within hours of Lee Harvey Oswald's arrest, his attraction to Marxism and his actions in defense of Castro's Cuba became known to the American people. Oswald had a Russian wife, Marina, whom he had married during a three-year stay in the Soviet Union. At first Oswald had renounced his U.S. citizenship; then, in 1962, having tired of the grayness of Soviet life, he brought his wife and their baby daughter to the United States. Appalled at Kennedy's foreign policy generally, Oswald organized his own "Fair Play for Cuba" committee in New Orleans to protest the U.S. containment of Fidel Castro. When news of Oswald's background trickled out to the American public, many assumed that he was a pawn of the Soviet Union. He was not, but in the communist world, which he had ostensibly been trying to assist, Oswald's act seemed sure to return the superpowers to the nether reaches of the Cold War.

News of Kennedy's death shocked and alarmed Khrushchev. He feared that the enemies of the détente that he and Kennedy had been trying to achieve were now successful. At Kennedy's initiative the Americans and the Soviets were preparing a new round of talks on arms control. On September 30, 1963, John Kennedy through his press secretary, Pierre Salinger, had attempted to reestablish a confidential channel to the Soviet leadership. The U.S. side had recommended a Colonel G. V. Karpovich, known to be a KGB officer in the Washington embassy.[1] Khrushchev had approved the use of the KGB as an intermediary to exchange proposals that could not go through regular diplomatic channels. On the evening of November 22, he learned from Foreign Minister Andrei Gromyko that Kennedy was dead. The initiative to use Karpovich, which had seemed to augur a continued thaw in relations, was stillborn and the future of those relations uncertain.

In ways that few Americans understood, Khrushchev needed Kennedy. Exactly a year earlier he had used the fact that Kennedy would likely be president until 1968 to calm critics of the agreement that ended the missile crisis.

Will there be an invasion of Cuba? I am not a prophet and can give neither a prediction nor a promise. It's impossible to vouch for the imperialists; they never seek our advice. One thing that we do know is that for as long as Kennedy is in the White House it will not be easy to renounce the pledge not to invade Cuba. This commitment will bind Kennedy; it will bind the government of the United States. Two years remain before the next presidential elections. Everyone is now saying that Kennedy will be reelected. This means that for the next six years the president of the U.S. will be bound by public pledges not to invade Cuba.[2]

Khrushchev acted quickly to meet the uncertain dangers of a world without Kennedy. He approved placing Soviet forces on alert in case the new American administration chose to provoke the Soviet Union in mistaken retribution for the murder. Although he would have to stay in the Kremlin, Khrushchev thought it necessary to send his lieutenant in foreign matters, Anastas Mikoyan, to Washington for the funeral. Mikoyan's presence at the final rites of the fallen president would symbolize the sincere grief and concern in Moscow. In addition, Mikoyan could size up the new leader of the capitalist bloc.

The KGB produced a report on Lyndon Johnson for Anastas Mikoyan, who would be the first Soviet leader to meet the new president. The KGB was not hopeful in regard to the future of the Kennedy thaw. "On most questions of domestic and foreign affairs," the report began, "Johnson supports conservative and reactionary views." The KGB mentioned his lukewarm support, as Senate majority leader, for civil rights legislation, his vote in favor of the Taft-Hartley Act, and his consistent advocacy of high military spending. All of this was well known about the southern Democratic politician, whom John Kennedy had brought to the ticket in 1960 to win Texas. The only inside information that the KGB had on Johnson came from a source close to Adlai Stevenson in the liberal wing of the Democratic Party. The Americans for Democratic Action had opposed Kennedy's selection of Johnson at the Los Angeles convention in 1960, and not surprisingly the Soviet leadership was now being informed that these liberals saw "no difference between Johnson and Nixon."[3]

The comparison to Nixon was certain to deepen the Kremlin's anxiety in the hours following the assassination. The KGB also made a point of listing instances where Johnson and Kennedy had disagreed on foreign policy. "In the course of the election campaign and in contrast to Kennedy," the report explained, "Johnson expressed his full agreement with the Eisenhower administration's handling of the U-2 affair."[4] The KGB quoted speeches in the Dutch port of Rotterdam and in Beaumont, Texas, where Johnson seemed to be undermining Kennedy's efforts to normalize relations with the Soviet Union by arguing for a "position of strength" that sounded a lot like U.S. strategic superiority. The report stopped short of being a caricature, however, by stressing that Johnson really knew very little about foreign policy. Most of his congressional work concerned domestic affairs, and in three years as vice president he had been "rarely called in by John Kennedy to work over or implement foreign policy." The KGB noted that not once in the four overseas trips that he took for Kennedy was he asked to engage in serious negotiations.[5]

The one source of optimism for the Kremlin came from Soviet intelligence's assessment of the new president's ample skills. Although no specialist on foreign matters, Johnson had twenty-two years of service in Congress under his belt. The Soviets picked up that he was a compromiser. "[In Congress] Johnson's influence," Soviet intelligence informed the Kremlin, "was directed at softening conservatism." In sum, Johnson was "a skillful specialist in the art of compromise and reconciling differing opinions in the Senate." From Moscow's point of view, this might be an asset in future negotiations. "Whereas Kennedy could be very insistent, reluctant to change or depart from his objectives," the analysts explained, "Johnson has shown himself to be more pliant."[6]

This report said nothing about any possible connection between Johnson and the assassination itself. The KGB at first had nothing to report to the Soviet leadership on that question. But at the highest level of Soviet intelligence there were immediate suspicions about the official explanation of the assassination developing in the United States. When the chairman of the KGB, Vladimir Semichastny, heard that Lee Harvey Oswald was under arrest for the murder, he was astonished. "I thought that this man could not possibly be the mastermind of the crime."[7] Semichastny recalled something of the character of Oswald, who had lived in the USSR for three years. Moscow requested the files for the period Oswald was in Minsk. Semichastny's suspicions were, if anything, confirmed by what he read.

Khrushchev was concerned lest the socialist world be held responsible for Kennedy's death. The KGB sent its New York office instructions to spread through its contacts the line that Oswald had lived in the Soviet Union under constant suspicion of being a CIA plant. The Soviet Union regretted his action but was in no way involved in it.[8]

The morning after the assassination, Khrushchev made this point personally to the American ambassador, Foy Kohler. He visited the U.S. embassy to assure Washington that the Kremlin had nothing to do with this reprehensible act. He asked Kohler whether the identity of the assassin was known. The American ambassador said that Oswald was being held as a suspect but that he had to be considered innocent of all charges until found otherwise by a jury. Kohler added that only a madman could have committed such a crime. This provoked Khrushchev to say that the Communist Party of the Soviet Union traditionally abjured terrorist acts. Lenin himself had condemned "nihilist" revolutionary acts against the czar. Kohler got the message and cabled Washington that he was "concerned at political repercussions" of emphasizing the "alleged 'marxism' of Oswald." Kohler suggested that for the good of U.S.-Soviet relations the theme that Oswald was a madman be the point of departure for official statements.[9]

At a meeting of the Presidium in the first days after the tragedy, it was suggested that the Soviet Union move rapidly to insulate Cuba, as much as possible, from the political transition in the United States. Khrushchev decided to send word to Havana that "until Lyndon B. Johnson's course in foreign policy was clear" he would have to postpone his long-awaited visit to Castro. The Presidium worried that the fallen president's enemies in Washington would exploit a Khrushchev visit to reopen debate on what to do about Castro, perhaps forcing the new president to break Kennedy's noninvasion pledge. This was the second time in a little over a year that the Soviet leader had postponed a trip to Cuba. The missile crisis had spoiled Khrushchev's dream of announcing the existence of Soviet nuclear weapons on a November trip to Cuba.[10]

Fidel Castro understood. Like Khrushchev, he was concerned that he would be blamed for the assassination. On November 23, 1963, he asked publicly, "[W]ho benefits from the assassination . . . except the worst reactionaries?" Castro noted that Oswald's act could create a climate of "anti-Soviet, anti-Cuban hysteria . . . highly prejudicial to the interests of peace and of mankind."[11] He also knew very little about Lyndon Johnson and did not wish to test him during the transition.

Another Mission for Mikoyan

Anastas Mikoyan arrived at Andrews Air Force Base late on November 24 and was driven to the Soviet embassy. On the trip over, Mikoyan had much time to reflect on his last meeting with John F. Kennedy. Less than a year before, he and Kennedy had met for over three hours to resolve the outstanding issues of the Cuban missile crisis. Kennedy had been a tough bargainer, especially when Mikoyan pushed for a document that would have outlawed another U.S.-assisted invasion of Cuba. Kennedy would not sign anything that did not include a guarantee that Castro would not interfere in the internal affairs of other Latin American countries. Putting a fine point on his resistance, Kennedy had insisted that any U.S. declaration to forswear the use of military force against Cuba had to be drafted with great care: "This is not to last one month, but for the two years or even six years that I have left as president."[12]

As Mikoyan well knew, the Cuban crisis had ended without any document being signed. The Kremlin, and to a lesser degree the Castro brothers, had relied on Kennedy's keeping his word. Now Kennedy was dead, and the advice that the KGB at least had given Mikoyan about the new power in Washington was not reassuring. An interesting test of Lyndon Johnson would be his approach to Cuba. One of the first things Mikoyan needed to know was whether the promise not to invade Cuba, like the other gentlemen's agreements between Kennedy and Khrushchev, would be kept.

In briefing Johnson for his meeting with Mikoyan, the foreign policy team of the assassinated president assumed that the Soviets would be looking for any signs of deviation from established policy. The team advised Johnson not to create any doubts in Mikoyan's mind as to his commitment to détente, for it was assumed the Soviets would be making important decisions at the December Party Plenum and "uncertainty over your future policies may adversely affect their decision on the question of diversion of resources from military, space and heavy industry to chemical fertilizers." On Cuba, Johnson received the suggestion that he "might reiterate" Kennedy's noninvasion pledge, though the Soviets should understand that Castro's consistent misbehavior was a source of strain in U.S.-Soviet relations.[13]

Johnson had an idea about how to demonstrate his commitment to détente. As vice president, he had chosen the space program as one of his special projects. He genuinely believed that space exploration was an area where the superpowers could cooperate. Kennedy agreed and in September 1963 had proposed, before the General Assembly of the UN, U.S.-Soviet collaboration in outer space. In his first days as president, Johnson instructed McGeorge Bundy to pull together an interdepartmental report on specific space projects where this might be possible. And to make his thinking immediately clear to Khrushchev, Johnson authorized Adlai Stevenson to reaffirm at the UN the U.S. commitment "to explore with the Soviet Union opportunities for working together in the conquest of space, including the sending of men to the moon as representatives of all countries."[14]

A Right-wing Conspiracy?

On November 25, as John F. Kennedy was being laid to rest, Jack Ruby, a nightclub owner with a taste for scandal, shot Lee Harvey Oswald in the basement of the Dallas police headquarters. This event gave free rein to Khrushchev's wildest fears about the larger meaning of the tragedy. "The whole thing is obviously a crude provocation," announced TASS.[15] Khrushchev could not understand why the security around Oswald had been so lax.

Intelligence coming to Khrushchev in the weeks following the assassination seemed to confirm the theory that a right-wing conspiracy had killed Kennedy. On November 25 the Mexican ambassador to Cuba told the members of his embassy's political section about his information that an "extensive conspiracy" had been behind the assassination that would bring "serious political consequences." This report likely came from Cuban intelligence. A source in Mexico City reported that the leader of the Mexican senate had quoted President López Mateos as saying that Kennedy had died at the hands of "extremely right-wing elements that did not like his policies, especially his policy toward Cuba."[16]

These Mexican hunches were bolstered by KGB information from its network in the French government. "The Quai d'Orsay," it was reported to the Kremlin, "has come to the conclusion that Kennedy's assassination was organized by extremely right-wing racist circles, who are dissatisfied with both the domestic and foreign policies of the slain president, especially his intention of improving relations with the Soviet Union." The French permanent representative to the UN, according to Soviet intelligence, believed that the assassination was a "carefully organized act" by a determined group on the far right of American politics.[17]

The most striking information on the assassination came from a member of the Kennedy inner circle. In the first week of December, an emissary from Robert Kennedy flew to Moscow, with news that the Kennedy family believed that the former president had been the victim of a right-wing conspiracy. William Walton had been one of John Kennedy's closest friends. In March 1961 *Life* featured him in an article entitled "The Painting Pal of the President."[18] When John Kennedy narrowed his circle of friends after entering the White House, Walton remained close. A former journalist who had found a new calling as an abstract painter, he assisted Jacqueline in shaping the president's program for the arts. It was Walton who had led the campaign to maintain the architectural unity of Lafayette Park, facing the White House. Walton had last seen Kennedy, radiant and upbeat, on November 19, 1963. Kennedy spoke confidently of his chances for reelection in 1964 and informed his good friend that he intended to be the first U.S. president to visit the Kremlin, as soon as he and Khrushchev reached another arms control agreement. Only three days later, Walton found himself participating in the sad decision over whether Kennedy's casket would be left open in the Rotunda of the Capitol. Walton and Arthur Schlesinger, Jr., suggested to Robert Kennedy that the disfigured president not be the last image of Kennedy glimpsed by the nation. The casket was sealed.[19]

Shortly before his death Kennedy had asked Walton to visit Moscow to meet Soviet artists. He wanted Walton to familiarize himself with the course of Soviet art and the future plans of the artistic community there. The trip had to be delayed because on October 31, 1963, the Soviets had picked up the Yale professor Frederick Barghoorn on a trumped-up charge of espionage. The Barghoorn case was settled quickly, and Walton had a ticket to leave for London and Leningrad on November 22. The shocking news from Dallas delayed his trip a second time. After the assassination Robert Kennedy urged Walton to go. Instead of bringing the greetings of a happy and confident president, Walton traveled east on November 29 in the shadow of the tragedy in Dallas.[20]

In the wake of the assassination, Walton now had a secret mission besides his ostensible visit with Soviet artists. Robert and Jacqueline Kennedy wanted him to meet with Georgi Bolshakov, the man who for twenty months around the time of the Cuba missile crisis had served as the Russian end of a secret link between the White House and the Kremlin. The Kennedys wanted the Russian who they felt best understood John Kennedy to know their personal opinions of the changes in the U.S. government since the assassination. Fearing interference from the Johnson administration, Robert Kennedy instructed Walton to meet Bolshakov before he moved into the U.S. embassy. The new U.S. ambassador, Foy Kohler, was not considered a Kennedy admirer. Walton, Jacqueline Kennedy, and the attorney general had opposed his nomination, and they assumed that Kohler knew this.[21]

Bolshakov and Walton met at the Sovietskaya restaurant. "Dallas was the ideal location for such a crime," Walton told the Soviet intelligence officer. "Perhaps there was only one assassin, but he did not act alone." Bolshakov, who had himself been deeply moved by assassination, listened intently as Walton explained that the Kennedys believed there was a large political conspiracy behind Oswald's rifle.[22] Despite Oswald's connections to the communist world, the Kennedys believed that the president was felled by domestic opponents.

Walton described in some detail the aftermath of the assassination. The crime shocked the Kennedy inner circle and threw all of Washington into confusion. When Bobby Kennedy finally made his way to bed in the early morning of November 23, he spent the next few hours weeping, unable to sleep. In the first twenty-four hours following the assassination, Walton explained with a sense of drama, Kennedy's national security adviser, McGeorge Bundy, had run the entire country because no one else had quite his presence of mind in those trying moments.

More dismaying to Khrushchev, who would have understood Robert Kennedy's natural paralysis from grief, was what Walton told Bolshakov, and therefore the Soviet leadership, about Lyndon Johnson. The Kennedy clan considered the selection of Johnson a dreadful mistake. "He is a clever timeserver," Walton explained, who would be "incapable of realizing Ken-nedy's unfinished plans." Walton relayed his own and Robert Kennedy's fear that Johnson's close ties to big business would bring many more of its representatives into the administration. This was certainly not designed to please Khrushchev. Surprisingly, Walton believed that the one hope for U.S.-Soviet relations was the former automobile executive Robert McNamara, who would probably remain in the cabinet as secretary of defense. Walton described McNamara as "completely sharing the views of President Kennedy on matters of war and peace." For the sake of good relations between Moscow and Washington, Walton assured Bolshakov, it was even more important that McNamara stay put than that Secretary of State Dean Rusk remain.

Walton's purpose was clear in his discussions of Robert Kennedy's political future. He said that Kennedy intended to stay on as attorney general through the end of 1964. He would then run for the governorship of Massachusetts to build up his political capital for an eventual run for the presidency. Walton, and presumably Kennedy, wanted Khrushchev to know that only RFK could implement John Kennedy's vision and that the cooling that might occur in U.S.-Soviet relations because of Johnson would not last forever. He added that he was surprised to hear some Russians say that Bobby was more reactionary in his views on the Soviet Union than his brother. "This is untrue," asserted Walton. "If Robert differed from Jack, it was only in that he is a harder man; but as for his views, Robert agreed completely with his brother and, more important, actively sought to bring John F. Kennedy's ideas to fruition."

Bolshakov was not the only Soviet with whom Walton talked, but their conversation was the most open. Walton bit his tongue and said a kind word about Lyndon Johnson in front of Aleksei Adzhubei and Yuri Zhukov.[23] The latter argued with keen persistence for a summit between the new president and Khrushchev by June of 1964: " 'Who else is there to talk to!' asked Adzhubei. 'Alec Home! [the British prime minister] Ha! The Germans Pfft. Gen. de Gaulle? Nobody can talk to him.' "[24]

The Walton visit was the first of three by prominent Americans that seemed to confirm Khrushchev's fears that Lyndon Johnson would not continue Kennedy's efforts on behalf of détente. A little over a week after Walton lunched with Bolshakov, Kennedy's and now Johnson's special assistant for national security affairs, McGeorge Bundy, had his own long lunch with Anatoly Dobrynin. "On the whole this was the most searching and instructive conversation I have yet had with a Soviet diplomat," Bundy reported to Johnson afterwards.[25] Indeed, over the course of the lunch, the men began to call each other by their first names.

But for Dobrynin the meeting spelled the end of his special channel through Robert Kennedy to the White House, and Bundy did not offer much of a substitute. Bundy told Dobrynin that "he could continue to rely on the Secretary of State, Ambassador Thompson, and myself with the respect to the most private communications." Dobrynin, however, was worried that his preferred link, Robert Kennedy, would not really be a player in this administration. Bundy later wrote to Johnson that he assured the Soviet ambassador that Kennedy would remain a very important member of the team. However, on behalf of Johnson, Bundy tried to steer Dobrynin away from the attorney general, "when the Ambassador asked in the most explicit way where he should go with his most private messages, I told him that I thought his best bet was Ambassador Thompson."[26] Thompson, not a Johnson intimate, was not the intermediary Dobrynin had hoped for.

Three days later the Kremlin learned that the new White House was not really interested in these "most private messages" anyway. On December 21, when the much delayed meeting between Karpovich of the KGB and Salinger finally took place, the White House press secretary had discouraging news for the Soviets. Superpower talks were not on the immediate agenda of the new American regime. Johnson assured Khrushchev through Karpovich that in principle he shared his predecessor's belief in keeping as many lines open to the Kremlin as possible. But at the moment he saw no reason to maintain this confidential channel through the KGB. Johnson was interested in the Soviet reaction to his speech at the UN. Otherwise, he was consumed by the need to reassure Americans that their government was functioning despite the tragedy. Semichastny reported to Khrushchev two days after the meeting that Salinger had said that "at the present time L[yndon] Johnson is devoting serious attention to the preparation of his State of the Union address, which he intends to deliver before Congress on January 8, 1964."[27]

Johnson sent a private message to Khrushchev through Mikoyan just after Kennedy's funeral that was intended to prevent these misunderstandings from arising. "I should like you to know," Johnson wrote, "that I have kept in close touch with the development of relations between the United States and the Soviet Union and that I have been in full accord with the policies of President Kennedy."[28]

The Soviets wanted more proof of Johnson's intention to keep the faith. During the week before Christmas, Moscow received the second official U.S. visitor since the assassination. But though Najeeb Halaby, the administrator of the Federal Aviation Agency, held out hope of a civil air accord, he was too minor an official to carry any special proposals from Johnson. The one feeler that Johnson apparently did send to the Kremlin was crude. The editor of the *Saturday Review*, Norman Cousins, met on two occasions with Soviet representatives at the behest of the new president. Cousins's statements seemed to imply that Johnson feared a Soviet hand behind the tragedy. Cousins told the Soviets, who then reported this to the KGB, that Johnson "had shown great interest in Soviet press reaction to the circumstances of the assassination of the president." Moreover, he explained Johnson's concern that "the USSR would engage in some kind of hasty, unilateral action," such as "harsh criticism of the U.S. in connection with the Kennedy assassination."[29] Khrushchev had paid attention to Cousins before. On the eve of the Vienna summit, Khrushchev had read his statements to a KGB source about the role of the CIA in American society. Cousins had then had harsh words about the "Trotskyite" element that the CIA listened to in writing its assessments of the Soviet Union. These cast the American journalist in the light of an independent-minded critic. But now Cousins was speaking for Lyndon Johnson, of whom the Kremlin was wary, and this time he would not be listened to.

The KGB chose to ignore Johnson's promises to continue the Kennedy approach to foreign policy. The stream of information from the Kennedy circle, along with its own informants, confirmed a dark interpretation of the events in Texas. By the end of December, KGB analysts had concluded that an anti-Soviet coup d'état had occurred.

The assassination of JFK on November 22 of this year in Dallas was organized by a circle of reactionary monopolists in league with pro-fascist groups of the U.S. with the objective of strengthening the reactionary and aggressive aspects of U.S. policy. The aforementioned circle was dissatisfied with the independent features of Kennedy's foreign and domestic policies, in particular, various measures to normalize U.S.-Soviet relations, the broadening of civil rights of the Negro population, and also a significant limitation of the interests of a part of the American bourgeoisie, above all the oil and metallurgical monopolies.[30]

The KGB now had some details as to which members of the American right had been behind the murder. In late November a highly regarded Polish intelligence source, an American businessman who owned a series of companies, informed the Poles that three wealthy Texas oil wildcatters—Sid Richardson, Clint Murchison, and Harold Lafayette Hunt—had organized the plot against President Kennedy. All three were noted sponsors of southern racist and "pro-fascist" organizations.[31] Moreover, a law passed in October 1962 had angered the oil industry by removing the tax provisions that had allowed profits reinvested abroad to be treated differently from repatriated oil profits. The oil lobby expected the situation to worsen in 1963. In talking up tax reform, Kennedy had implied that the oil industry's beloved oil depletion allowance was vulnerable.[32]

The KGB soon received more information that implicated Hunt. In early December, Paul W. Ward, the longtime diplomatic correspondent of the *Baltimore Sun*, told a KGB informant that the Texas oilman Hunt headed the group that decided to have Kennedy killed. According to Ward, Hunt had instructed Jack Ruby in the name of the group to offer Oswald a large amount of money to kill the president. Fearing Oswald's capture, Ruby was to persuade Oswald to hide this contract from his (Oswald's) wife and his mother. Ruby, who was friendly with Oswald, knew that the young man was having money trouble, could not hold a job, and needed assistance to maintain his family. Oswald "was a most appropriate figure for staging the terrorist act against Kennedy because of his past—he implicated the USSR, Cuba, and the Communist Party of the U.S." Consistent with this the conspirators planned to launch an anti-Soviet propaganda blitz following Kennedy's removal from the scene to ensure that Moscow was held responsible. However, Ward added, the conspirators had not known that Oswald was psychologically deranged. Through their sources the conspirators learned that, under interrogation in the Dallas jail, Oswald had said he would tell all at his trial. It was then that Ruby decided to shoot Oswald to shut him up.[33]

Ward was a celebrated journalist who in nearly thirty years as a diplomatic correspondent had a record of shaping as well as covering great events. He won a Pulitzer Prize in 1948 for a series of articles called "Life in the Soviet Union." But it was his work in the twilight of European appeasement before World War II that first earned him notice. Ward interviewed Neville Chamberlain and wrote before the Munich conference that the British leader was "going with a plan and, if the plan works, the result may be worse than war." When Ward's prediction came true that Hitler would swallow the rest of

Czechoslovakia after consuming the Sudetenland as an appetizer, the British *Manchester Guardian* wondered in its pages why MI6 was not as well informed as Paul Ward.[34]

The KGB report to the leadership did not indicate Ward's sources on Hunt. In December 1963, however, Ward was not alone in his suspicions. Harold Lafayette Hunt was a notorious supporter of right-wing causes in Texas. He sponsored a radio show called *Lifeline*, which regularly excoriated Kennedy and his administration. In much the same way that contemporary reactionaries were criticized following the Oklahoma City bombing in 1995 for having incited terrorism through their antigovernment rhetoric, in the days following the assassination of John Kennedy, H. L. Hunt was castigated publicly. the *New Republic* editorialized that Hunt's last radio broadside on Kennedy, broadcast the morning of the assassination, was "[t]he kind of program . . . that the brooding Oswalds of the left- or right-wing listen and sometimes act on."[35]

Ward's report—and by extension the KGB's best estimate on "Who killed JFK?"—probably derived from a discovery made by the FBI in late November that tied the Hunt family to the events in Dallas. In Jack Ruby's notebook, bureau agents found the name "Lamar Hunt," H.L.'s second son from his first marriage. By the time Ward's report reached Moscow, the distinction between Lamar and H. L. Hunt was lost. Indeed, for a while the U.S. government wondered whether the Lamar Hunt connection was significant. On December 17 the FBI interviewed Lamar Hunt about Jack Ruby. Hunt denied ever having known Ruby. In jail Ruby agreed.[36]

The reporting of a seasoned American journalist like Ward was a boon for the disinformation team in the KGB, which was looking for ways to shift world attention away from Oswald's Soviet connections. For the chairman of the KGB, Semichastny, disinformation was a means to "enhance the prestige of the Soviet Union."[37] Under him disinformation became a standard weapon in the KGB's war against the CIA. In December 1963, with the Soviet Union fearful of the rise of the political right in the United States, any evidence could be exploited, however flimsy, that tied American political primitives like H. L. Hunt to the murder of the president.[38]

The KGB likely did not wait for Ward to send this kind of information through its Wurlitzer of disinformation. The CIA reported to Bundy on December 5 that just two days earlier a "known Soviet intelligence officer in New Delhi" had tried to use the communist party of India to send telegrams to President Johnson, Chief Justice Earl Warren, and Robert Kennedy. These telegrams, ostensibly from Indian youth groups, legal personalities, and other important representatives of Indian society, were to call for a full investigation of the Kennedy assassination.[39]

In Khrushchev's mind these intelligence fragments were annealed into a strong belief that a right-wing conspiracy had killed Kennedy. Khrushchev's wife, Nina Petrovna, was also sure that Jacqueline Kennedy was a widow because of an American conspiracy. The Khrushchevs revealed their suspicions to Drew Pearson and his wife, when the latter visited at the end of May 1964. In English, which she spoke quite well, Nina Khrushchev expressed her affection for Jackie Kennedy and her concerns about her welfare. The conversation then turned to the wife of Earl Warren, a mutual friend. When the women began discussing the Warren commission, Khrushchev joined in.[40]

"What really happened?" Khrushchev asked Drew Pearson through his interpreter. Pearson said that the newspapers had gotten it right. Oswald was the lone assassin. Khrushchev refused to accept this. It was impossible for him to imagine that the U.S. security services were so inept as to have allowed a madman to kill the president. No doubt recalling what the KGB had reported, Khrushchev asserted that the Dallas Police Department had been part of a larger conspiracy. None of this surprised the Pearsons. Mrs. Pearson later told the CIA that the Soviet leader's conspiracist mind-set was typical "of every European [she had] ever talked to on this subject." The Pearsons tried to persuade their Soviet guests. "We Americans are peculiar people," Drew Pearson said, as a way to explain away the seemingly fantastic. His efforts were met "with a tolerant smile." The Khrushchevs remained convinced that the official version of the assassination story was false.[41]

Inexplicably, associates of the Kennedy family continued to send information to Moscow that undercut the new president and increased Khrushchev's fears about the shift in U.S. politics. There is no evidence that the KGB acquired any better information about the right-wing plot against Kennedy in early 1964. But a former Kennedy confidant, Charles Bartlett, reported through Soviet intelligence that Johnson was not to be trusted. In the week of January 1964, Bartlett approached a KGB source in New York. What he had to say was taken as such an important indication of the direction of the new government that the KGB sent it via an official channel to the top Soviet leaders: Brezhnev, Mikoyan, Podgorny, Suslov, Ponomarev, Kuznetsov. His essential argument was that "the new president would never equal Kennedy in terms of the consistency and sincerity of his thinking on relations with the USSR." Bartlett continued the litany of criticisms of Johnson by the Kennedys. "Johnson," he said, "is a pragmatic and experienced politician, who would change Kennedy's course with regard to the achievement of agreements with the USSR, if it seemed advantageous to him."[42]

Bartlett's comments bore no relation to the thinking in the Johnson White House. After the State of the Union address, McGeorge Bundy and the National Security Council sought to turn Johnson's attention to U.S.-Soviet relations again. On January 13 Bundy sent Johnson a "personal and preliminary" memorandum on what he termed the "next steps for peace": "The biggest single fact about steps toward peace is that in the last two and a half years we have been doing our best to take all the easy ones, so that what are left are the hard ones."[43]

Bundy, unlike Jack Kennedy's pals Walton and Bartlett, assumed Johnson intended to push farther along the same path to some sort of normalization of relations. In this private way, Bundy explained that the Kennedy administration had really not been able in its thousand days to achieve all that much with the Kremlin. "[E]ven the test ban treaty is a very small matter," he wrote, "since it required only U.S.-Soviet agreement, and did not involve inspection." Nothing requiring the participation of a third power, whether Germany or Cuba, had been achieved.[44]

Bundy laid out for Johnson the extent of the Kennedy effort at détente. The achievements were in unilateral or bilateral steps. Unilaterally, Kennedy had successfully "muzzled the military." This, Bundy added, was "more important than it seems." Moreover, the United States had changed the tone of its propaganda, including maintaining "a high level of courtesy in all Presidential statements."[45] Finally, the United States had single-handedly sought to establish better relations with Yugoslavia and Poland through the extension of most-favored-nation trading status. Bilaterally, beside the test ban, the superpowers had come to an agreement on the sale of wheat, announced reciprocal defense cuts, promised not to station nuclear weapons in space, and agreed in a vague way to cooperate in space.

Bundy proposed a serious attempt to go beyond what Kennedy had been able to achieve. In two months or so he wanted Johnson to give a major speech on "the problem of peace" and urged that it be "more concrete than the Kennedy American University speech."[46] It should include an appeal to the Soviets for assistance with this task. In sum, the speech should be one of "reassessment and recommittal, not one of gimmicks, but it can have a lot of substance."[47]

Bundy wanted to use several channels to underscore this message. He suggested that Johnson ask the old liberal workhorse Averell Harriman to go to Moscow to negotiate an inspected nuclear production cutoff, which Bundy considered a minor achievement but an important beginning. Besides using Harriman, Bundy suggested resuming frequent and intensive use of the Dobrynin channel; instead of the attorney general, though, Johnson's representative would be Dean Rusk. Finally, Bundy thought that the president and the general secretary should continue their private correspondence. "These are tricky," he said about the letters, "because of the danger of publication by the other side, but they do contribute to an atmosphere of efforts for peace."[48]

In November, Johnson had asked Bundy for a report on possible areas of superpower cooperation in outer space, looking for something tangible to offer. By February the interdepartmental foreign policy machinery was back at work, and an answer was ready. The CIA, the Departments of Defense and State, the science adviser, NASA, and the executive secretary of the Space Council proposed an incremental approach that would move along in tandem with the growth in mutual trust. The consensus of the group was that the USSR and the United States should work toward a joint program of unmanned flight projects in support of an eventual manned flight to the moon.

All of the participants in the review understood that this ran counter to the public and congressional belief in a "race to the moon," but the group felt that with proper care Congress and the American people could be persuaded to accept Soviet participation in an eventual moon flight.[49]

Moscow noticed Lyndon Johnson's efforts to continue the Kennedy détente; but the Soviets were skeptical. KGB analysts presented the imminence of the 1964 elections as the most important factor influencing Johnson in the short term. "This will compel the Johnson administration to demonstrate its adherence to Kennedy's foreign policy, because of its popularity with the voters." In addition, the analysts expected that the Johnson regime would have to walk a fine line so as not to supply grounds for Republican charges of "liberalism" or "appeasing" the USSR. The KGB argued that this was the reason for the "hard" character of Johnson's policies in the first weeks following the assassination. From a source in or near the Italian government, the KGB found that the Italian president, Antonio Segni, agreed with this assessment. Segni reportedly said after meeting Johnson in Washington that Italy could expect the same elements of a peace-through-strength policy that had been characteristic of the Eisenhower years.[50]

Consequently, the KGB reported to Khrushchev that the Soviet leadership should not expect Johnson to attempt to resolve any of the many outstanding issues of U.S.-Soviet relations before November 1964. Instead, it was expected that the new president would apply pressure on the Soviet Union to demonstrate his firm resolve. There was no reason, however, to fear that Johnson would provoke a crisis. He would sanction discussions on secondary superpower issues, those not directly affecting the position of the United States's NATO allies.

Soviet intelligence made an exception, however, for Cuba. If Johnson might be willing to push hard anywhere, it was in the U.S.-Cuban tangle. His administration was unhappy over the reluctance of its allies to respect the economic blockade of Castro. The sale of British buses to Havana had angered Johnson. A source close to the Canadian prime minister, Lester B. Pearson, reported to the KGB that Johnson had extracted from him a promise that Canada would not conclude any new contracts to supply Cuba.[51] In May the KGB chief in Washington, Aleksandr Feklisov, wrote that his sources told him that Johnson was more intolerant of Cuba than Kennedy had been. He not only agreed with the economic and political isolation of Cuba but seemed more open to military action.[52]

As 1964 progressed, Khrushchev may have begun to worry that Johnson would revisit the 1962 missile crisis settlement. The Kremlin and Kennedy had reached an understanding about the kinds of concessions each side could make. Khrushchev had to back down from his promise to allow on-site inspection, and Kennedy had demanded, and received, the Kremlin's assurances that the Turkish deal would not be made public. Although Johnson had been part of the Kennedy administration, his lack of foreign policy experience and his apparent differences of opinion with Kennedy suggested he may not have known about those understandings. This did not bode well for the Cuban dimension of U.S.-Soviet relations.

Moscow, October 1964

In the late summer of 1964, Aleksandr Alekseev called his former boss Vladimir Semichastny on the eve of his return to Havana following a short home leave. After exchanging pleasantries, during which Alekseev described a recent discussion about Cuban matters with the vacationing Khrushchev, the KGB chief startled Alekseev.[53]

"And have you discussed Cuba with Comrade Brezhnev?"

"Brezhnev?" Alekseev wondered. Brezhnev was a senior member of the Presidium, who had a reputation for following nuclear matters but not Cuba. Alekseev was confused. He answered Semichastny that he had not talked with every member of the Presidium. "But I have spoken with Comrade Khrushchev," Alekseev countered, hoping to avoid another official call.

"Well, you should talk to Brezhnev."

This was the only warning the old Cuba specialist would get that Khrushchev was about to be overthrown. A group led by the Presidium members Nikolai Podgorny and the former KGB chief Aleksandr Shelepin had schemed to replace the seventy-year-old leader with the much younger Leonid Brezhnev while Khrushchev vacationed at the Black Sea. Semichastny had replaced Shelepin at the KGB, and both men owed their positions in Moscow to Khrushchev's patronage. They nevertheless felt it was time to remove this man.

The coup, when it occurred, was bloodless. First, Khrushchev returned to Moscow without incident from Pitsunda on October 14, 1964. Then he was whisked away to a special plenum of the Central Committee that removed him from all of his positions. In Stalin's time he would have been shot. But Khrushchev himself had changed the rules of party infighting, and murder was no longer acceptable.

The records of that session remain closed. However, notes prepared for one of the speeches made against Khrushchev are available. Dmitri Polyanski drafted a blistering brief for the prosecution. His text sounded the main points of that afternoon's verbal assault on Khrushchev.[54]

When Polyanski got around to Cuba in his lengthy screed, he cited Khrushchev's mishandling of relations with Fidel Castro as the epitome of his general recklessness. "Ask any one of our marshals or generals, and they will tell you that plans for the military 'penetration' of South America were gibberish, fraught with the enormous danger of war." In a world where the Soviet Union was at a strategic disadvantage vis-à-vis the United States, Polyanski argued, Khrushchev's nuclear gamble did not make any sense. "If we agreed to help one of the Latin American states by launching a nulear first strike on the

United States, then not only would they suffer an attack—but we would lose everything."[55]

Polyanski was relentless in vilifying Khrushchev for the Cuban "adventure." "You insisted that we deploy our missiles on Cuba," he recalled. "This provoked the deepest crisis, carried the world to the brink of nuclear war, and even frightened terribly the organizer of this very danger."[56] Rejecting Khrushchev's claims that the Soviet Union had come out ahead, Polyanski spoke instead of humiliation: "Not having any other way out, we had to accept every demand and condition dictated by the U.S., going as far as permitting U.S. airplanes to inspect our ships. At the insistence of the United States, the missiles, and also most of our forces there, had to be withdrawn from Cuba." Who won? According to Polyanski there was no question: "This incident damaged the international prestige of our government, our party, our armed forces, while at the same time helping to raise the authority of the United States."[57]

Polyanski held that Latin America, in general, and Cuba, in particular, had distracted Khrushchev from the core issues of Soviet security. Khrushchev had pushed the Kremlin into Latin America in what his opponent described as a vainglorious attempt to gain influence where Stalin had never dared go. And when Castro arrived on the scene, Khrushchev became the most vocal supporter of Cuba. He pushed for a mutual security pact with Havana and wanted to create a Soviet military presence there. Khrushchev fully expected his Presidium colleagues to scream in protest. But, according to Polyanski, he did not care. "To hell with them, let them scream," Khrushchev seemed to enjoy saying. In his rush to assist nationalist movements in the Third World, Polyanski added, Khrushchev neglected the national interests of the Soviet Union. Lenin, he reminded Khrushchev, said that "we must exhibit stable and peaceful moods, because the imperialists will exploit every possibility to launch a war." Polyanski offered a different view of Soviet priorities. To his mind the United States was Russia's great enemy and as such had to be the focus of its foreign policy. Rounding out his attack on Khrushchevite foreign policy, this prosecutor belittled efforts to achieve paper agreements with Washington, as if these would eliminate the basic differences in outlook and interest.[58]

Khrushchev's colleagues refused to let him forget his Cuban gamble. They rejected the argument he had been so quick to make on October 25, 1962, when he decided to abandon the Anadyr operation in the face of stubborn American opposition. They rejected the notion that a noninvasion pledge from an American president had been worth the time, money, and nervous energy expended in the rush to deploy ballistic missiles in the tropics. Polyanski's attack contained echoes of the Cuban criticism of Mikoyan in November 1962. Of what good is a statesman's word in international politics? The recent assassination of John F. Kennedy had brought home to the entire

Soviet leadership the fragility of agreements founded more on mutual understanding than on mutual interest.

The Cuban question did not unseat Khrushchev; just as it had not killed Kennedy. But the superpower struggle over that island had made each man vulnerable. Over the entire length of his administration, Kennedy invested increasing amounts of political capital into finding an acceptable way to remove Fidel Castro. He established special organizations, funded secret projects, and may well have countenanced an alliance with criminal elements—all with this goal in mind. Although he had failed twice, in April 1961 and in the summer of 1962, Kennedy was still trying when he was killed by a fanatic who hated his Cuban policy. For Khrushchev, Cuba was the physical embodiment of the communist future. Born without the assistance of the Red Army and sustained by nationalism, Cuban communism was a potential model for the many less successful communist parties in the Third World. But Cuba was not a disciplined ally. Unlike the countries of Eastern Europe, Cuba did not wait for Moscow to launch initiatives in foreign policy. On many occasions in the six years that Khrushchev observed Castro closely, Havana opted for the most dangerous course available. Yet Khrushchev, like Kennedy, convinced himself that he could not afford to abandon Cuba.

Finally, out of frustration, ignorance, and fear, both Kennedy and Khrushchev grasped at a magical solution to their Cuba problem; but none was to be found. Kennedy's choice of covert action and Khrushchev's missile gambit proved not only costly failures but catalysts for the single most dangerous moment of the Cold War. Even after the solution of the crisis, Cuba exacted a heavy toll, inspiring the hateful act that claimed John F. Kennedy's life and the political conspiracy that ended Nikita Khrushchev's career.

The Kremlin speeches of October 1964 were the epitaph for Khrushchev's political career, but not for Moscow's Cuban adventure. Soviet relations with Cuba remained strong until the period of glasnost and perestroika in the 1980s. Then the currents of change pulled the two countries in separate directions. Until that time, despite the misgivings of Khrushchev's opponents, the Soviet Union remained committed to Castro. Ultimately, in an ironic twist of fate, socialist Cuba outlived its patron. And as the end of the century approached, Fidel Castro, this man of once indistinct politics, had survived long enough to share with the leaders of China and North Korea the distinction of being the world's last communist ruler.

Notes

ABBREVIATIONS

AGSRF	Historical Archive and Military Memorial Center of the General Staff of the Armed Forces of the Russian Federation
APRF	Archive of the President of the Russian Federation
AVPRF	Archive of the Ministry of Foreign Affairs
CC	Central Committee of the Communist Party of the Soviet Union
CIADCMC	*CIA Documents on the Cuban Missile Crisis 1962*, ed. Mary S. McAuliffe (Washington, D.C., 1992)
CMC/NSA	Cuban Missile Crisis Collection, National Security Archives
CWIHPB	*Cold War International History Project Bulletin*
DOS	Department of State
FRUS	*Foreign Relations of the United States*
GRU	Glavnoe Razvedovatelnoe Upravlenye
JCS	Joint Chiefs of Staff
JFKL	John F. Kennedy Library
LBJ	Lyndon Baines Johnson
MFA	Ministry of Foreign Affairs (USSR)
NA	National Archives, College Park, Md.
NHC	Naval Historical Center, Area Files, Bumpy Road Materials
NSA	National Security Archives, Washington, D.C.
NSC	National Security Council (USA)
NSF	National Security Files
NSK	Nikita S. Khrushchev
NYT	*New York Times*
POF	President's Office Files
RFK	Robert F. Kennedy
RG	Record Group
RockCom	Rockefeller Commission Papers, Gerald R. Ford Library Materials, John F. Kennedy Assasination Materials Project, NA
SDCDF	State Department Central Decimal File

SOVA   Office of Soviet Union Affairs (DOS)
State/FOIA State Department, Freedom of Information Act Room
SVR   Archive of the Russian Foreign Intelligence Service
TsKhSD   Center for Storage of Contemporary Documentation

CHAPTER 1: "WHERE DOES CASTRO STAND REGARDING RUSSIA?"

1. *Nation*, Jan. 17, 1959.
2. Meeting, NSK with Fidel Castro, May 3, 1963, Zavidovo, APRF.
3. Rubottom to Christian Herter, April 15, 1959, *FRUS, 1958–1960*, vol. 6, *Cuba*, p. 468.
4. Thomas G. Paterson, *Contesting Castro: The United States and the Triumph of the Cuban Revolution* (New York, 1994), p. 78.
5. Robert E. Quirk, *Fidel Castro* (New York, 1993), pp. 54–55.
6. Interview with William Caldwell, former CIA station chief in Havana (1954–Aug. 1958), April 22, 1995. The visit with Vilma Espín was sponsored by the owner of Bacardi rum. Caldwell says that this visit occurred in the spring of 1958. His deputy Ignacio Carranza puts the visit in 1957 (interview, April 22, 1995), as does Lyman Kirkpatrick (Kirkpatrick, The Real CIA [New York, 1968], pp. 166, 170, cited in Paterson, Contesting Castro, p. 63). It is likely that the results of this trip persuaded the U.S. intelligence community to conclude, in an April 1957 National Intelligence Estimate, "We do not believe that the Cuban government can fully restore public order or check the emergence of new civilian opposition elements." Cited in Paterson, Contesting Castro, p. 84.
7. Paterson, Contesting Castro, pp. 109–21.
8. Arleigh Burke, chief of naval operations, to JCS, July 10, 1958, FRUS, 1958–1960, 6:140. See the section "Kidnapping of U.S. Citizens by Cuban Rebels, June–July 1958," ibid., pp. 117–57.
9. Ibid.; CIA official J. C. King's comments before Maxwell D. Taylor's Cuban Study Group on the Reasons for the Collapse of the Bay of Pigs Invasion, [n.d., ca. May 1961], in FRUS, 1961–1963, vol. 10, Cuba, collection at State/FOIA; Paterson, Contesting Castro, pp. 206–25.
10. Cited in Paterson, Contesting Castro, p. 252.
11. Nixon memorandum, quoted in Jeffrey J. Safford, "The Nixon-Castro Meeting of 19 April 1959," Diplomatic History 4 (1980): 426–31.
12. Philip W. Bonsal, Cuba, Castro, and the United States (Pittsburgh, 1971), pp. 229–45; CIA, Office of Current Intelligence, "Intelligence Handbook on Cuba," Jan. 1, 1965, NSF, CO:Cuba, vol. 1, box 24, LBJ Library, Austin, Tex. (also NSA); Louis A. Perez, Jr., Cuba and the United States: Ties of Singular Intimacy (Athens, Ga., 1990), pp. 202–63.
13. *Washington Post & Herald Times*, April 17, 1959.
14. Ibid.
15. *NYT*, April 24, 1959.
16. *NYT*, April 23, 1959.
17. *Washington Post & Times Herald*, April 20, 1959.
18. Nixon prepared a summary of his meeting for Senator Mike Mansfield of Montana. It is reproduced in Safford, "Nixon-Castro Meeting," 426–31.

19. James G. Blight, Bruce J. Allyn, and David A. Welch, *Cuba on the Brink: Castro, the Missile Crisis, and the Soviet Collapse* (New York, 1993), p. 178.
20. Van Gosse, *Where the Boys Are: Cuba, Cold War America and the Meaning of a New Left* (London, 1993), p. 116; interview with McGeorge Bundy, Nov. 1994.
21. One of those boys was Professor John J. Stephan, a colleague of one of the authors at the University of Hawaii.
22. Gosse, *Where the Boys Are*, p. 116; Bundy interview; *Harvard Crimson*, April 27, 1959.
23. Ponomarev, Mukhitdinov to CC, April 15, 1959, Folio 3, List 65, File 874, APRF.
24. Ibid.
25. Resolution from Protocol 214, Presidium meeting of April 23, 1959, Folio 3, List 65, File 871, APRF.
26. Ibid.
27. Rufo López Fresquet controlled the Treasury. A few weeks after taking control of Havana, Fidel Castro found he had to approach the new minister of finance to ask for money to buy weapons for the army. The government did not have the revenue for such purchases, but López Fresquet found money for shipments of light rifles from Belgium in a Swiss bank account belonging to the former finance minister. López Fresquet, *My 14 Months with Castro* (Cleveland, 1966), pp. 80–83.
28. Extract from Protocol 198, Presidium meeting of Dec. 27, 1958, Folio 3, List 65, File 871, APRF. Information on the operation is included in a memorandum from Snagkov to the Central Committee, dated Dec. 27, which is in the Presidium file alongside the resolution.
29. Ibid.
30. Report by unnamed PSP representative, "The Traditional and Current Armed Forces of Cuba," with summary of meeting on this topic between the author of the report and Marshal Sokolovsky [undated, from context, roughly March 1, 1959], Folio 5, List 50, File 174, pp. 35–52, Archive of the Secretariat of the CC, TsKhSD.
31. Ponomarev, Mukhitdinov to the CC, April 15, 1959, Folio 3, List 65, File 874, APRF.
32. Letter, Severro Aguirre to CC, March 1, 1959, Folio 5, List 50, File 174, p. 11, TsKhSD.
33. Aleksandr Alekseev, meeting with PSP member Severro Aguirre, Feb. 26, 1959, Folio 5, List 50, File 174, p. 7, TsKhSD.
34. Cited in Tad Szulc, *Fidel: A Critical Portrait* (New York, 1986), p. 290.
35. Ibid., pp. 369–70. From an unpublished interview with Bravo by the Cuban historian Mario Mencia, Szulc learned that Flavio Bravo, a PSP leader, visited Fidel Castro in Mexico in 1956 with Lázaro Peña's assistance.
36. N. Zakharov, deputy chairman of KGB, to CC, O Otnoshenii Kubinskovo Rukovodstva K Natsionalno-osvoboditelnomu Dvizheniu v Latinskoi Amerike" [On the Cuban leadership's relations with the national-liberation movement in Latin America], April 18, 1963, File 88497, vol. 1, pp. 376–89, SVR.
37. Interview with a former member of the GRU with extensive operational experience in Latin America, who asked that his identity be concealed, Feb. 1995.
38. Quirk, *Fidel Castro*, p. 218.
39. Ponomarev to CC, July 15, 1960, Folio 3, List 65, File 893, p. 41, APRF. The

head of the International Department of the CC, whose responsibility it was to manage relations with foreign communist parties, Ponomarev explained the special procedures to be followed during Raúl Castro's visit to preserve the secrecy of his membership in the Cuban communist party (PSP); Aníbal Escalante to CC (Soviet Union), April 3, 1962, Folio 3, List 65, File 903, pp. 39–42, APRF. In this extraordinary report on his expulsion from Castro's inner circle, Escalante describes Fidel Castro's 1962 discovery of Raúl Castro's and Che Guevara's PSP membership; Semichastny to CC, April 25, 1963, "*Spravka* on Fidel Castro," File 88497, vol. 1, pp. 361–75, SVR. This report endorses Escalante's view of how Fidel found out about Raúl's secret.

40. Blatov, an assistant to Khrushchev, to CC, July 18, 1960, *spravka* on Raúl Castro, Folio 5, List 50, File 251, pp. 70–71, TsKhSD.

41. NSK, *Khrushchev Remembers*, trans. and ed. Strobe Talbott (Boston, 1970), p. 489.

42. Semichastny to CC, April 25, 1963, File 88497, p. 372, SVR.

43. Telegram, U.S. embassy in Havana to Washington, April 21, 1959, *FRUS, 1958–1960*, 6:479.

44. Benjamin Stephansky to deputy asst. sec. of state for inter-American affairs, "May Day in Cuba," April 30, 1959, *FRUS, 1958–1960*, 6:498.

45. Bonsal to sec. of state, May 14, 1959, Castro Speech Data Base, Internet, lanic.utexas.edu.

46. Perez, *Cuba*, p. 240.

47. Mexico City [KGB] to Center [Moscow], Jan. 9, 1960, File 78825, pp. 52–54, SVR; Semichastny to CC, April 25, 1963, "*Spravka* on Fidel Castro," File 88497, vol. 1, pp. 361–75, SVR.

48. Information from retired GRU officer; Semichastny to CC, April 25, 1963, "*Spravka* on Fidel Castro," File 88497, vol. 1, pp. 361–75, SVR.

49. Quirk, *Fidel Castro*, pp. 244–45.

50. Blas Roca to CC, June 5, 1959, Folio 6, List 50, File 174, pp. 58–59, TsKhSD.

51. Ibid.

52. Rubottom to Latin American chiefs of mission meeting, Santiago, Chile, May 7, 1959, *FRUS, 1958–1960*, 6:507.

CHAPTER 2: OUR MAN IN HAVANA

1. Interview with Aleksandr Alekseev, Nov. 15, 1995, Moscow.

2. Shelepin to CC, Sept. 15, 1959, Folio 3, List 65, File 891, p. 1, APRF.

3. Allen Dulles reported on this conversation at an NSC meeting on June 25, 1959. While the CIA's informant may have invented this proverb, it does accurately convey Nasser's love/hate approach to the Soviet Union. *FRUS, 1958–1960*, vol. 6, *Cuba*, p. 542.

4. Section from diary of Soviet ambassador to Japan, N. T. Fedorenko, on his visit with Che Guevara, head of Cuban trade mission to Japan, July 21, 1959, Folio 5, List 50, File 174, pp. 87–88, TsKhSD.

5. Ibid.

6. Mexico City to Center, Jan. 9, 1960, File 78825, pp. 52–54, SVR. In this report by an insider on the leading figures of the Cuban government, Dorticós, a former lawyer who drafted the INRA law, was described as "a cultured man who knows

Marxist literature very well." The report continued, "Since 1953 a member of the communist party, gradually moved away from the party but was never expelled." In his memoirs, Carlos Franqui, a Fidelista and leading member of the noncommunist left, describes the selection of Dorticós. Franqui, *Family Portrait with Fidel: A Memoir* (New York, 1984), pp. 42–44. See also Robert E. Quirk, *Fidel Castro* (New York, 1993), pp. 251–52.

7. Memo of conference, "Train Trip from Los Angeles to San Francisco," Sept. 21, 1959, RG 59, Bureau of European Affairs, SOVA, Subject Files, 1957–63, Box 4, NA.

8. Memo, "Conversations in San Francisco," Sept. 21, 1959, RG 59, Bureau of European Affairs, SOVA, Subject Files, 1957–63, Box 4, NA.

9. Kobanov (International Department of the CC) to the CC, Sept. 30, 1959, Folio 3, List 65, File 874, p. 16, APRF.

10. Skatchkov and Zorin, Sept. 23, 1959, Folio 3, List 65, File 874, pp. 19–20, APRF.

11. Ibid.

12. Resolution of the Presidium, Sept. 23, 1959, Folio 3, List 65, File 874, p. 21, APRF.

13. Interview with William B. Caldwell, April 22, 1995. Caldwell was CIA chief of station in Havana, 1954–Aug. 1958.

14. See above, n. 9.

15. Text Prepared by D. S. Polyansky for meeting of Oct. 14, 1964, Register no. 8476, pp. 33–36, APRF.

16. J. Zhukov, A. Shelepin, and A. Orlov to CC, July 20, 1960, Folio 4, List 16, File 869, TsKhSD. This remarkable document comprises a request for cover and a top-secret annex that outlines Shitov/Alekseev's intelligence career.

17. Ibid; Shelepin to CC, Sept. 15, 1959, Folio 3, List 65, File 891, p. 1, APRF.

18. Alekseev interview, Feb. 16, 1994, Moscow. Alekseev was one of those who met with Severro Aguirre when he visited Moscow in Feb.–March 1959.

19. Tad Szulc, *Fidel* (New York, 1986), pp. 493–95.

20. Interview with Alekseev, Feb. 16, 1994.

21. Ibid.

22. Ibid.

23. Ibid.

24. Ibid.

25. Alekseev to Moscow, Oct. 22, 1960, File 86447, vol. 2, pp. 259–60, SVR. Alekseev reported on Guevara's "characteristics" before his expected visit to Moscow.

26. Che to Enrique Oltuski, in Oltuski interview cited by Szulc, *Fidel*, pp. 467–68.

27. Bonsal (U.S. ambassador, Havana) to sec. of state, Oct. 17, 1959, *FRUS, 1958–1960*, 6:627–28.

28. N. S. Leonov, *Lixoleyte* (Moscow, 1994), pp. 49–51.

29. Gromyko to CC, Nov. 23, 1959, Folio 3, List 65, File 871, p. 24, APRF.

30. Quirk, *Fidel Castro*, pp. 264–65.

31. Ibid.

32. Ibid., pp. 248–49.

33. Bonsal to sec. of state, Oct. 22, 1959, *FRUS, 1958–1960*, 6:32.

34. Quirk, *Fidel Castro*, p. 273.

35. Mexico City to Center, Nov. 13, 1959, File 78825, p. 13, SVR.

36. Ibid.

37. Mortin memo to CC, Nov. 14, 1959, "Some Intelligence Data about Mexican Policy toward U.S., USSR, and Some Latin American Countries," File 82761, SVR; Shelepin to Gromyko, Nov. 17, 1959, SVR.
38. See Bonsal's description of the National Catholic Congress, in dispatch, Nov. 30, 1959, *FRUS, 1958–1960,* 6:682–83.
39. Cited in Szulc, *Fidel,* pp. 470–71.
40. Interview with Alekseev, Feb. 16, 1994.
41. Szulc, *Fidel,* p. 506; Quirk, *Fidel Castro,* pp. 290–92. Quirk writes, "Until February 1960, the Soviet Union had paid scant attention to events in Cuba or to Fidel Castro's revolutionary movement."
42. Interview with Alekseev, Feb. 16, 1994.
43. Gromyko to CC, Nov. 23, 1959, APRF, Folio 3, List 65, File 871, APRF.
44. Ibid.

CHAPTER 3: *LA COUBRE*

1. Havana to Center, April 12, 1960, File 78825,p. 227. This reports a Jan. 1960 discussion between Nikolai Leonov of the KGB station and Aragonés in Mexico City. At that time Alekseev did not have direct communications with Moscow. The Aragonés report may have been sent earlier to Moscow by Leonov.
2. Ibid.
3. Alekseev [still lacking his own radio link, Alekseev sent this from the KGB station in Mexico] to Moscow, Jan. 27, 1960, File 86447, vol. 1, SVR. Alekseev had informants in the Cuban labor movement who reported on the communist-leanings of the new chief, Jesús Soto.
4. Ibid.
5. Mexico City to Center, Jan. 9, 1960, File 78825, p. 52–54, SVR.
6. F. Mortin to I. A. Serov, chief, GRU, Dec. 16, 1959, File 82761, p. 107, SVR. The bloc intelligence services had picked up that the United States was training Cuban emigrants to invade Cuba. The Polish service, in particular, received intelligence that there were 3,000 Spanish soldiers training in the Dominican Republic, who would coordinate an attack with military units pre-positioned in Florida.
7. F. Mortin to Mexico City, Dec. 15, 1959, File 86447, vol. 1, SVR.
8. Protocol 260, Meeting of Presidium, Jan. 20, 1960, Folio 3, List 5, File 871, p. 25, APRF.
9. Letter, Shelepin to Mikoyan, Jan. 20, 1960, File 82761, pp. 158–59, SVR.
10. Ibid.
11. N. S. Leonov, *Lixoletye* (Moscow, 1994), p. 51.
12. Interview with N. S. Leonov, Sept. 1994, Moscow.
13. Leonov, *Lixoletye,* p. 52.
14. Ibid.
15. Alekseev [now cabled from Havana], Feb. 7, 1960, File 78825, pp. 108–12, SVR. Alekseev summarized a long meeting with Fidel Castro on Feb. 3.
16. Ibid.
17. Alekseev to Moscow, Feb. 10, 1960, File 78825, p. 113, SVR. A marginal note records that this report was shown to Mikoyan.
18. Ibid., p. 55.

19. NSC Meeting, Feb. 18, 1960, *FRUS, 1958–1960*, vol. 6, *Cuba*, pp. 791–93; memo, Rubottom to acting sec. of state, May 11, 1960, ibid., p. 913.
20. Herter to British Foreign Secretary Selwyn Lloyd, Feb. 21, 1960, *FRUS, 1958–1960*, 6:806.
21. Interview with Samuel Halpern, Nov. 13, 1994.
22. Memo of conference, Undersecretary of State Herter's Office, Dec. 31, 1958, *FRUS, 1958–1960*, 6:323–29.
23. Burke to Undersecretary of State for Political Affairs [Livingston Merchant], *FRUS, 1958–1960*, 6:813–20.
24. Robert E. Quirk, *Fidel Castro* (New York, 1993), pp. 301–3.
25. Ibid.
26. Ibid., p. 301.
27. Alekseev to Moscow, March 8, 1960, File 78825, pp. 164–66, SVR. A copy of this report was passed on to Khrushchev. It appears in Folio 3, List 65, File 871, pp. 42–45, APRF.
28. Ibid.
29. Ibid.
30. This description of Castro's mode of conversation comes from Ambassador Philip Bonsal, who had much less revealing sessions with the Cuban leader. See Bonsal to sec. of state, Sept. 4, 1959, *FRUS, 1958–1960*, 6:595–98.
31. Daniel M. Braddock [Havana] to Philip W. Bonsal [State Department], March 3, 1960, RG 89, Cuba 1960, 350.21, NA.
32. "First Meeting of the Green Study Group," April 23, 1961, CMC/NSA.
33. Wayne G. Jackson, CIA Internal History, "Allen Welsh Dulles as Director of Central Intelligence 26 February 1953–29 November 1961," vol. 3, "Covert Activities," p. 116.
34. March 16, 1960: "A Program of Covert Action against the Castro Regime." White House Office, Office of Staff Sec. International Series, Box 4, Dwight D. Eisenhower Library, Abilene, Kan. We are grateful to Zachary Karabell for providing us with this document.
35. Memo of conference, March 17, 1960, *FRUS, 1958–1960*, 6:861–63.
36. Protocol 270, March 12, 1960; CC to Alekseev, March 12, 1960, Folio 3, List 65, File 871, APRF.
37. Ibid.
38. Ibid.
39. Alekseev to Center, March 7, 1960, Folio 3, List 65, File 871, p. 45, APRF.
40. Alekseev to Center, June 8, 1960, File 78825, p. 299, SVR.
41. Ibid.
42. Archive of the Secretariat of the CC, Folio 4, List 16, File 954, p. 169, TsKhSD.
43. On April 20, 1960, the KGB reported that two days earlier the general staff of the Cuban army had discussed the real threat of aggression against Cuba. The KGB learned that a country, probably the USA, was inordinately interested in the course of negotiations between the USSR, Czechoslovakia, and Cuba regarding military assistance.
44. Some 100 mortar with projectiles, 200 antitank guns of 57-mm caliber, 4,000 light machine guns, 500 antiaircraft machine guns, 100 medium tanks of Czech manufacture, and 10,000 rifles with ammunition.
45. Shelepin to CC, June 8, 1960, Folio 3, List 65, File 893, p. 31, APRF.

46. Letter, Shelepin to CC, June 18, 1960, File 86447, pp. 319–20, SVR.

47. Ibid.

48. Memo, Asst. Sec. of State Rubottom to Sec. of State Herter, June 2, 1960, *FRUS, 1958–1960,* 6:934–35.

49. Protocol, Presidium, June 16, 1960, Folio 3, List 65, File 892, APRF.

50. Shelepin to CC, June 24, 1960, Folio 3, List 65, File 893, pp. 33–34, APRF.

51. Ibid.

52. Ibid.

53. Donald S. Zagoria, *The Sino-Soviet Conflict, 1956–1961* (Princeton, 1962), p. 299.

54. Ibid., p. 323.

55. Ibid., p. 326.

56. Leonov, *Lixoletye,* p. 57.

57. Information on Raúl Castro's trip comes from the archives of the Czech Foreign Ministry, Prague. See Kuba Req 47/2, Krabice 1, Obal 9, r. 1960.

58. Leonov, *Lixoletye,* p. 58.

59. Memo of a discussion, July 6, 1960, doc. 544, *FRUS, 1958–1960,* vol. 6.

60. Quirk, *Fidel Castro,* p. 107.

61. Prague to Center, July 4, 1960, File 86447, vol. 1, SVR.

62. Shelepin to CC, June 29, 1960, File 84124, vol. 12, pp. 237–38, SVR.

63. Ibid.

64. U.S. State Department, "Principal Soviet Public Statements on Defense of Cuba," CMC/NSA.

65. Memo of discussion, 450th meeting of NSC, July 7, 1960, *FRUS, 1958–1960,* 6:980–91.

66. Prague to Center, July 15, 1960, File 86447, vol. 1, SVR.

67. Ibid.

68. Ibid.

69. Ponomarev to CC, July 15, 1960, Folio 3, List 65, File 893, p. 41, APRF. On July 13 the KGB recommended a series of measures to uncover and thwart "American aggressive plans" regarding Cuba. These included a propaganda campaign in support of Cuba and the formation of Cuban defense leagues to demonstrate in various cities. Shelepin to CC, July 13, 1960, File 86447, vol. 1, pp. 392–93, SVR.

70. Ibid.

71. General Ivanov, "Report on Raúl Castro's Visit," July 23, 1960, Folio 3, List 65, File 893, p. 59, APRF.

72. Extract from protocol of Presidium session on July 17, 1960, "On Raúl Castro's Visit to the USSR," Folio 3, List 65, File 893, pp. 37–39, APRF.

73. Tad Szulc, *Fidel* (New York, 1986), p. 539.

74. From Protocol 294 from the Presidium meeting of Aug. 4, 1960, Fol. 3, List 65, File 871, pp. 102–8, APRF.

75. Ibid. In the same telegram Alekseev reported that Czechoslovakia and Cuba had signed an agreement on July 29 for the supply of "special property"—i.e., the provision of 130 million rubles worth of arms to Cuba without any repayment, of which most (114 million worth) would come from the USSR.

Chapter 4: "Cuba Si, Yankee No!"

1. Havana to sec. of state, Sept. 3, 1960, RG 59, SDCDF, 737.000, NA.

2. José M. Gironella, *On China and Cuba*, trans. John F. Byrne (Notre Dame, 1963), p. 128.
3. Havana to sec. of state, Sept. 2, 1960, 7:33 P.M., "General Assembly Cuban People No. 2," RG 59, SDCDF, 737.00, NA.
4. Alekseev to Moscow, Sept. 2, 1960, File 86447, vol. 2, p. 65, SVR.
5. Ibid., pp., 62–64.
6. Richard Welch, *Response to Revolution: The United States and the Cuban Revolution, 1959–1961* (Chapel Hill, 1985), pp. 55–56.
7. Anatoly Dobrynin, MFA to CC, Feb. 23, 1961, Folio 5, Entry 50, File 334, pp. 56–63, CC Secretariat Archive, TsKhSD. In Feb., Dobrynin reported on information collected by the Guatemalans for the Cuban government. From the context it appears that detailed information began to flow in Aug. 1960.
8. "Evaluation of CIA Task Force," March 1961, Washington National Records Center, RG 330, OASD (C) A Files: FRC 71A 2896, Cuba 381 (Sensitive) [to be published in *FRUS, 1961–1963*, vol. 10, *Cuba*].
9. Review of CIA's Cuban project prepared for Taylor Committee, May 1961, NSF, Taylor Papers, Box 12, Memoranda of Meetings, JFKL; Peter Wyden, *Bay of Pigs: The Untold Story* (New York, 1979), pp. 34–38.
10. Havana to sec. of state, Sept. 2, 1960, 9:42 p.m., "General Assembly of Cuban People Number 7," RG 59, SDCDF, 737.00, NA.
11. Ibid.
12. Ibid.
13. Havana to sec. of state, Sept. 2, 1960, 10:16 P.M., RG 59, SDCDF, 737.00, NA.
14. Havana to sec. of state, Sept. 2, 1960, 9:42 P.M., RG 59, SDCDF, 737.00, NA.
15. Che Guevara, "On Growth and Imperialism," Aug. 8, 1961, *Venceremos!*, ed Gerassi (New York, 1968).
16. Alekseev to Moscow, Sept. 4, 1960, File 86447, vol. 2, pp. 67–68, SVR.
17. Alekseev to Moscow, Oct. 1, 1960, File. 86447, vol. 2, SVR. Ambassador Kudryavtsev had reported to Alekseev the substance of his meeting with Escalante.
18. Ibid.
19. Ibid.
20. *NYT*, Oct. 12, 1960.
21. Carlos Franqui, *Family Portrait with Fidel* (New York, 1985), p. 89.
22. Ibid., pp. 86–89.
23. Editorial note, *FRUS, 1958–1960*, vol. 6, *Cuba*, p. 1072.
24. Ibid.
25. Alekseev to Moscow, Oct. 12, 1960, File 86447, vol. 2, p. 220, SVR.
26. *NYT*, Oct. 15, 1960.
27. Alekseev to Moscow, Sept. 2, 1960, File 86447, vol. 2, p. 65, SVR.
28. Interview with Alekseev, Feb. 16, 1994, Moscow.
29. Moscow to Alekseev, Sept. 7, 1960, File 86447, vol. 2, p. 80, SVR. HQ advises Alekseev to be more critical of his information before he predicts a wave of terrorist acts.
30. Alekseev to Moscow, Sept. 2, 1960, File 86447, vol. 2, p. 65, SVR.
31. Moscow to Alekseev, Sept. 7, 1960, File 86447, vol. 2, p. 80, SVR.
32. Ibid.
33. Ibid.

34. Evan Thomas, *The Very Best Men, Four Who Dared: The Early Years of the CIA* (New York, 1995), p. 241.

35. *NYT*, Oct. 7, 1960. Although the Cuban government publicly reported the landing as having occurred on Oct. 5, Cuban security reported that it had occurred on Sept. 26. Havana may have wanted to hide the fact that it took a week to catch all of the men. See "CIA Activity against Cuba," Security Department, Ministry of Internal Affairs, Republic of Cuba, Dec. 12, 1962. This was a roundup of all known and alleged CIA activities against the Castro regime since 1959. The report runs over thirty pages and was handed over to the KGB in June 1963. File 90704, SVR.

36. Some months later the Kennedy administration would bring charges against some of the organizers for violating U.S. neutrality.

37. Shelepin to CC, Aug. 5, 1960, File 86447, vol. 2, p. 17, SVR.

38. Alekseev to Moscow, Oct. 1, 1960, File 86447, vol. 2, SVR. Kudryavtsev reported to Alekseev the substance of his meeting with Escalante.

39. *NYT*, Oct. 7, 1960.

40. Havana to sec. of state, Oct. 16 and 19, 1960, RG 59, SDCDF, 737.00, NA.

41. Paris to Center, Oct. 7, 1960, File 86447, vol. 2, p. 209, SVR.

42. Moscow to State Department, Oct. 25, 1950, RG 59, SDCDF, 1960–63, 320-Cuba-Russia, NA.

43. State Department circular to all U.S. legations, Oct. 28, 1960, RG 59, SDCDF, 611.37, NA.

44. Ibid.

45. *New York Herald Tribune*, Oct. 26, 1960.

46. Thompson to State Department, Oct. 29, 1960, RG 59, SDCDF, 320-Cuba-USSR, NA.

47. Anatoly Dobrynin, MFA to CC, Feb. 23, 1961, Folio 5, Entry 50, File 334, pp. 56–63, CC Secretariat Archive, TsKhSD.

48. Alekseev to Moscow, Oct. 28, 1960, File 86447, vol. 2, p. 284, SVR.

49. Moscow to Alekseev, Oct. 25, 1960, File 86447, vol. 2, p. 273, SVR.

50. Alekseev to Moscow, Oct. 29, 1960, File 86447, vol. 2, p. 285, SVR.

51. XXX to XXX, Oct. 31, 1960, Annex 4, NSF, Box 61A, JFKL, cited in Piero Gleijeses, "Ships in the Night: The CIA, the White House and the Bay of Pigs," *Journal of Latin American Studies* 27 (Feb. 1995): 10. On the basis of his research, Gleijeses determined that Hawkins or Jacob Esterline sent this cable to the field.

52. Ibid.

53. Ibid., pp.10–11.

54. In the 1970s Alekseev wrote an autobiography entitled "Memoirs Not for Publication," for the KGB, which remains confidential. The authors were not permitted to see this document; however, they were informed about some aspects of it. The Che story, apparently, comes from the memoir.

55. Alekseev, Havana, Nov. 19, 1960, File 86447, vol. 2, pp. 315–17, SVR.

56. Ibid.

57. Ibid.

58. Ibid.

59. Semichastny to CC, April 25, 1963, File 88497, pp. 363–64, SVR.

60. Ibid.

61. NSK, Report on Moscow Conference of Representatives of 81 Communist and Workers Parties (Jan. 6, 1961), picked up from the Soviet home radio service, Jan. 19, POF, CO:USSR, Box 126a, JFKL.

62. Donald S. Zagoria, *The Sino-Soviet Conflict, 1956–1961* (Princeton, 1962), pp. 361–62.

CHAPTER 5: BAY OF PIGS

1. Richard Reeves, *President Kennedy: Profile of Power* (New York, 1993) , p. 35.
2. Ibid., p. 37.
3. Ibid., pp. 31–32.
4. Ibid., p. 36.
5. Ibid., pp. 40–41.
6. Thompson to sec. of state, Aug. 31, 1960, RG 59, SDCDF, 611, NA.
7. Gromyko to NSK, Aug. 3, 1960, Folio 5, List 30, File 335, pp. 92–108, TsKhSD, reproduced in *CWIHPB*, no. 4 (Fall 1994): 65–67.
8. Information Department (Department 16) to chief of D Department, May 31, 1961, pp. 96–109, SVR. This is a compendium of information on JFK.
9. Ibid.
10. See above, n. 7.
11. Ibid.
12. Harriman to JFK, Nov. 12, 1960, NSF, Box 176, JFKL.
13. Harriman to JFK, Nov. 15, 1960, NSF, Box 176, JFKL.
14. Ibid.
15. Harriman to JFK, Nov. 21, 1960, NSF, Box 176, JFKL
16. Chester Bowles to Christian Herter, Sept. 22, 1960, Herter Papers, Houghton Library, Harvard University.
17. *"Let the Word Go Forth": The Speeches, Statements, and Writings of John F. Kennedy, 1947 to 1963*, selected by Theodore C. Sorensen (New York, 1991), p. 122.
18. 1960 telephone log, RFK Pre-Administration Political Files, Box 54, JFKL. There is an entry for "Mr. B., Izvestia Daily, coming in" at 10:00 A.M.
19. Shelepin to NSK, Dec. 3, 1960, SVR.
20. See above, n. 8. Walt Rostow, in a conversation with a KGB officer, made similar points as Robert Kennedy, including the statement that President Kennedy was especially committed to a test ban treaty.
21. JFK, campaign speech, Tampa, Fla., Oct. 18, 1960, in *"Let the Word Go Forth,"* 109–17.
22. Telephone conversation, Livingston Merchant and the British ambassador Caccia, Jan. 3, 1961, RG 59, SDCDF, 1960–63, 661.37, NA.
23. See above, n. 21.
24. Ibid.
25. Memo of conference with JFK, Washington, Jan. 25, 1961, 10:15, 1 P.M., NSF, Chester V. Clifton Series, JCS Conferences with the President, vol. 1, JFKL. This comes from a collection prepared for *FRUS, 1961–1963,* vol. 10, *Cuba* (hereafter referred to as *FRUS* collection in the State Department, Freedom of Information Act Room, State/FOIA).
26. See above, no. 21.

27. "A Program of Covert Action against the Castro Regime," March 16, 1960, WHO, Office of the Staff Secretary, International ser., box 4, DDEL, cited in Gleijeses, "Ships in the Night: The CIA, the White House and the Bay of Pigs," *Journal of Latin American Studies* 27 (Feb. 1995): 4–5. The points were the following:
    a. The first requirement is the creation of a responsible, appealing and united Cuban opposition . . . outside of Cuba . . . [to] serve as a magnet for the loyalties of the Cubans. . . .
    b. So that the opposition may be heard and Castro's basis of popular support undermined, it is necessary to develop . . . a long and short wave gray broadcasting facility. . . .
    c. Work is already in progress in the creation of a covert intelligence and action organization within Cuba. . . .
    d. Preparations have already been made for the development of an adequate paramilitary force outside of Cuba.
28. Jan. 3, 1961, 9 A.M., Meeting at White House to Discuss Reaction to Cuba Statement, to appear in *FRUS, 1961–1963*, vol. 10, *Cuba*, currently in State/FOIA. See also the reference to a note by Tracy Barnes in CIA files regarding the possible need for a 1,500-man contingent.
29. CIA memo of conversation, "Conclusion of Dean Rusk's 22 January Meeting on Cuba," Jan. 23, 1961, CIA, Job 85-00664R, Box 3, vol. 4 (6), State/FOIA.
30. Ibid.
31. *Operation ZAPATA: The "Ultrasensitive" Report and Testimony of the Board of Inquiry on the Bay of Pigs* (Frederick, Md., 1984), p. 67.
32. Ibid., p. 110.
33. *NYT*, Jan. 4, 1961.
34. Dec. 24, 1960, File 86447, pt. 2, p. 361, SVR. The information came from the friend of an employee at CIA headquarters in Washington.
35. *NYT*, Jan. 2, 1961.
36. Service dispatch, Jan. 7, 1961, File 86447, pt. 2, p. 421, SVR.
    In connection with the increased threat of intervention against Cuba and the intensification of counterrevolutionary activity within the country, we ask you to request that all corresponding KGB *residentura* take immediate steps to acquire information on the following questions:
    1) U.S. intentions to organize an intervention against Cuba, in particular under the guise of the OAS.
    2) Concrete evidence of U.S. pressure on Latin American countries with a view to organizing collective action against the Cuban government.
    3) Preparations to unify the counterrevolutionary groups outside Cuba and to create a "government in exile." On differences among the various counter-revolutionary groups. On the activity of the Cuban counterrevolution in the USA and in the countries of Latin America. On the links between these groups and U.S. intelligence and with other countries.
    4) On the internal situation in Cuba, on efforts to unite the counterrevolution-ary forces. On the links between these internal forces and the exile organiza-tions.
37. Telegram, Kudryavtsev, Havana, Feb. 24, 1961, Folio 3, List 65, File 871, re: Meeting with Escalante, APRF.
38. Ibid.

39. Ibid.
40. Minutes of meeting of Koslov, Suslov, and Flavio Bravo, March 3, 1961, Folio 3, List 65, File 871, APRF.
41. Ibid.
42. Ibid.
43. Feb. 14, 1961, RG 59, SDCDF, 611.61, NA.
44. Thompson to sec. of state, April 1, 1961, RG 59, SDCDF, 611.61, NA.
45. Christopher Andrew, *For the President's Eyes Only: Secret Intelligence and the American Presidency from Washington to Bush* (New York, 1995), p. 262.
46. Theodore C. Sorensen, *Kennedy* (New York, 1965), p. 295.
47. Interview with Aleksandr Alekseev, Feb. 16, 1994, Moscow.
48. Interview with Aleksandr Alekseev, Nov. 15, 1995, Moscow.
49. Ibid.
50. Kudryavtsev to MFA, April 7, 1961, Folio 3, List 65, File 901, p. 3, APRF.
51. Kudryavtsev to MFA, April 8, 1961, Folio 3, List 65, File 901, pp. 4–7, APRF.
52. Ibid. The Cubans suggested three facts in support of their faith that an invasion had been "well foreshadowed by the present course of the Kennedy regime":
    a) formation in the United States of a Cuban government in exile, with the support of JFK and the State Department.
    b) The publication of the U.S. white paper.
    c) The presence of counterrevolutionary training camps in Nicaragua, in Guatemala, and on Swan Island.
53. Extract from protocol for the Presidium sess. of April 11, 1961, Folio 3, List 65, File 901, p. 8, APRF.
54. Thompson to sec. of state, April 10, 1961, RG 59, SDCDF, 611.61, NA.
55. Ibid.
56. Ibid.
57. Cited in Sorensen, *Kennedy*, p. 298.
58. New York to Center, April 8, 1961, File 88631, vol. 3, p. 154, SVR.
59. Memo on meeting with Blas Roca of April 14, 1961, April 28, 1961, from the notebook of S. M. Kudryavtsev, Folio 5, List 50, File 335, pp. 32–33, Secretariat Archive, TsKhSD.
60. Ibid.
61. General Lyman Lemnitzer, CJCS, to McNamara, March 10, 1961, "Evaluation of the CIA Cuban Volunteer Task Force, March 10, 1961," Washington Records Center, RG 330, OASD (C) A Files: FRC 71 A2896, Cuba 381, State/FOIA.
62. 10:00 A.M. meeting at CIA (n.d.), NSF, Taylor Papers, Box 12, Memoranda of Meetings, JFKL.
63. Ibid. The CIA trained seventeen B-26 crews and five C-46 crews.
64. Interview with Oleg Nechiporenko, Nov. 20, 1995, Moscow.
65. Interview with Nikolai Leonov, Sept. 27, 1994, Moscow.
66. Alekseev to Moscow, April 17, 1961, File 88631, vol. 3, p. 169, SVR.
67. Ibid., p. 170.
68. Alekseev to Moscow, April 18, 1961, File 88631, vol. 3, p. 171, SVR.
69. Ibid. This turned out to be a deception designed by the CIA to divert Cuban attention from the actual invasion in the south. It is not known how many of Castro's forces were diverted; but this maneuver came too late, in any case, to influence the course of the battle in the Zapata marshes.

70. Interview with Nikolai Leonov, Sept. 27, 1994, Moscow.
71. Richard M. Bissell, Jr., *Reflections of a Cold Warrior: From Yalta to the Bay of Pigs* (New Haven, 1996), p. 184.
72. Bundy to JFK, April 18, 1961, POF, CO:Cuba, General, April 1961, to be published in *FRUS,1961–1963*, vol. 10, *Cuba*, State/FOIA.
73. Ibid.
74. Memo of conference, Burke and Naval Commander Chester R. Wilhide, April 18, 1961, NHC, State/FOIA.
75. Ibid. The editorial note in the *FRUS, 1961–1963*, vol. 10, edition of this document mentions that the transcript includes information about the timing of the president's call.
76. Chief of Subsidiary Activities Division (Gray) to CINCLANT (Dennison), April 18, 1961, 2:49 P.M., NSF, CO:Cuba, Subjects, Taylor Report, JFKL, State/FOIA.
77. Burke to Dennison, April 18, 1961, 8:37 P.M., NHC, State/FOIA.
78. "Editorial Note," *FRUS, 1961–1963*, vol. 10, evidence from JCS records, April 19, 1961.
79. JCS to CINCLANT (Dennison), April 19, 1961, 3:37 A.M., NSF, CO:Cuba, Taylor Report, JFKL.
80. Telegram, Clark to Dennison (CINCLANT), April 19, 1961, 12:06 P.M., NHC.
81. JCS to CINCLANT, April 19, 1961, 1:12 P.M., NSC, CO:Cuba, Taylor Report, JFKL.
82. RFK to JFK, April 19, 1961, POF, CO:Cuba, General, April 61, JFKL.
83. Cited in Michael R. Beschloss, *The Crisis Years: Kennedy and Khrushchev* (New York, 1991), p. 130.
84. Burke, memo, "Debrief of Luncheon conversation with the President, 16 May 1961," May 16, 1961, NHC, State/FOIA.
85. Tad Szulc, *Fidel* (New York, 1986), pp. 542–44.
86. Ibid.
87. Meeting, NSK and Fidel Castro, May 5, 1963, Zavidovo, APRF.
88. Letter, Shelepin to CC, April 26, 1961.
89. Havana to Center, April 25, 1961, SVR, File 88631, vol. 3, p. 200.
90. The negotiations ended successfully in early May. Alekseev to Moscow, May 3, 1961, File 88631, vol. 3, p. 205, SVR.
91. Ibid.
92. Cable, Alekseev to Moscow, June 9, 1961.

CHAPTER 6: THE EDUCATION OF A PRESIDENT

1. Rostow to JFK, April 21, 1961, NSF, Subjects: Policy Planning, Box 303, JFKL.
2. A. M. Schlesinger, Jr., to JFK, May 3, 1961, POF, Cuba, Security, 1961, JFKL.
3. London to sec. of state, May 16, 1961, RG 59, 611.37, SDCDF, 1960–63, NA.
4. London to sec. of state, May 17, 1961, RG 59, 611.37, SDCDF, 1960–63, NA.
5. NSK, Report on Moscow Conference of Representatives of 81 Communist and Workers Parties, (Jan. 6, 1961), picked up from the Soviet home radio service, Jan. 19, POF, CO:USSR, Box 126a, JFKL.
6. Gromyko's office diary, notes on oral statement made while delivering the general secretary's response to the Kennedy letter of April 18, April 25, 1961, Folio 3, List

65, File 900, p. 119, APRF.

7. Moscow to sec. of state, May 4, 1961, RG 59, SDCDF, 611.61, NA.

8. Charles Bohlen, "Line of Approach to Khrushchev," June 1, 1961, POF, CO:USSR, Box 126, JFKL.

9. Hope M. Harrison, "Ulbricht and the Concrete 'Rose': New Archival Evidence on the Dynamics of Soviet-East German Relations and the Berlin Crisis, 1958–1961," Working Paper no. 5, CWIHP, Washington, D.C., May 1993.

10. D. S. Polyanski, text for report to plenum of the CC (Oct. 14, 1964), prepared Oct. 13, 1964, Register no. 8476, APRF.

11. Thompson to sec. of state, May 4, 1961, RG 59, SDCDF, 1960–63, 611.61, NA.

12. Sec. of state to Moscow, May 6, 1961, RG 59, SDCDF, 1960–63, 611.61, NA.

13. Sec. of state to president, Feb. 24, 1961, RG 59, SDCDF, 1960–63, 611.61, NA. Kennedy had requested the 1959 memoranda of conversations from Dean Rusk on Feb. 18, 1961.

14. Dean Acheson, "Subject: Berlin," April 3, 1961, NSF, CO:Germany, Box 81, JFKL.

15. Robert Divine, *Blowing on the Wind: The Nuclear Test Ban Debate, 1954–1960* (New York, 1978) pp. 245–61, 281–314.

16. For background see memoranda in NSF: ACDA, Jan. 1961–March 1961, Boxes 255–57, JFKL. See also Divine, *Blowing on the Wind*.

17. John C. Guthrie, "U.S. Position on Nuclear Testing in the Kennedy-Khrushchev Talks," May 25, 1961, RG 59, Bureau of Europe and Africa, Soviet Division, Box 5, NA. The final nuclear testing position paper suggested as a fall-back position, twelve inspections per year. "This position will probably provide some difficulties with Congress," wrote Guthrie.

18. See Thompson's dispatch of Jan. 27 and his memo of Feb. 14, 1961, RG 59, SDCDF, 1960–63, 611.61, NA.

19. London to sec. of state, Jan. 25, 1961, RG 59, SDCDF, 1960–63, NA. Two days later, Thompson cabled from Moscow that he thought a test ban agreement would be the easiest bilateral measure to achieve.

20. Memo of conversation, R. T. Davies with Mikhail Sagatelyan, March 7, 1961, RG 59, SDCDF, 1960–63, 611.61, NA. There is no evidence that this reached the White House, but it was sent to State Department division chiefs and to INR.

21. Frederick L. Holborn to Walt Rostow, March 21, 1961, with enclosed memo from Robert Esterbrook, March 20, 1961, NSF, CO, USSR, 176, JFKL. McGeorge Bundy did not know about the Kennedy brothers' private diplomacy through Bolshakov before Vienna. It was one of the JFK-RFK "nonshareables." Interview with McGeorge Bundy, November 15, 1995, New York City. Theodore Sorensen was also not informed. Interview with Theodore Sorensen, September 19, 1995, New York City.

22. Main Department of the General Staff of the Armed Forces of the Russian Federation (GRU), biography of Georgi Bolshakov.

23. Ibid.

24. Ibid.; interviews conducted with Bolshakov's former colleagues at the GRU, 1995, Moscow.

25. Interview with Frank Holeman, Aug. 6, 1995, Washington, D.C.

26. Georgi Bolshakov, "Goryachaya Linaya" [Hot line], *Novoye Vremya*, no. 4 (1989).

27. A story went around Washington newsrooms of a terrified Soviet diplomat who

always refused social invitations until he was collared by the Washington journalist Nick Gregory. "I know why you won't come. It's because they won't let you." A few days later the Soviet man called back to say he would be at Gregory's house at 6 P.M. that Thursday.

28. Holeman interview. General Matvei Zakharov to NSK, May 26, 1961, Folio 3, List 66, File 311, APRF.
29. *Spravka*, Bolshakov meetings, GRU.
30. GRU information.
31. Holeman interview.
32. "Kratkoye Soderzhanye: Besed G. Bolshakova s R. Kennedi (9 Maya 1961 goda–14 Dekabria 1962 roga)" [Summary: Meeting of G. Bolshakov with R. Kennedy, May 9, 1961–December 14, 1962], GRU.
33. Oral history, Mercedes H. Douglas Einholz, May 14, 1970 [appended to the William Walton oral history of the same date], JFKL.
34. *Spravka* on RFK, Feb. 1, 1962, File 87592, p. 285, SVR.
35. Ibid.
36. Ibid.
37. Ibid.
38. Theodore C. Sorensen, *The Kennedy Legacy* (New York, 1969; reprint, 1993), p. 36.
39. Ibid.
40. Sorensen, *Kennedy Legacy*, p. 36.
41. NSK to JFK, Cabled to Geneva, May 16, 1961, 611.61, RG 59, CFD, 1960–63, NA.
42. Memo of conversation, JFK-Menshikov, May 16, 1961, RG 59, SDCDF, 1960–63, 611.61, NA.
43. *NYT*, May 14, 1961.
44. GRU, entry for May 16, 1961, "Kratkoye Soderzhanye." Protocol of Presidium sess., May 18, 1961, "Regarding the Instructions to Washington in Connection with the Meeting between Comrade Bolshakov and R. Kennedy," Folio 3, List 66, File 311, pp. 10–16, APRF. Suslov's role in organizing the summit is evident from the file.
45. Ibid.
46. Ibid.
47. Ibid.
48. "Record of Meeting on Nuclear Test Ban Issue, 4 May 1961," Declassified Documents, 1994, no. 3069.
49. Jerome B. Wiesner to JFK, May 16, 1961, POF, CO:USSR, Box 126, JFKL.
50. Quoted in Charles Murray and Catherine Bly Cox, *Apollo: The Race to the Moon* (London, 1989), p. 61.
51. Interview with Theodore Sorensen, Sept. 19, 1995.
52. Gromyko to CC, May 20, 1961, Folio 3, List 66, File 311, p. 29, APRF.
53. Ibid.
54. GRU *spravka* on RFK-Bolshakov meetings.
55. GRU, Entry of May 24, 1961, "Kratkoye Soderzhanye."
56. V. V. Kuznetsov (deputy minister of foreign affairs) to CC, May 26, 1961, Folio 3, List 66, File 311, pp. 58–61, APRF.
57. This assessment is based on comparing NSK's negotiating instructions to a

contemporaneous U.S. document, "Soviet positions on various Disarmament Questions," which had been prepared as a briefing paper for JFK, POF:USSR, Box 126, JFKL.

58. See above, n. 56.
59. Ibid.
60. Anatoly Dobrynin, *In Confidence: Moscow's Ambassador to America's Six Cold War Presidents* (New York, 1995), p. 44.
61. Menshikov to MFA, May 18, 1961, Folio 3, List 66, File 311, APRF.
62. Report to NSK, June 1, 1961, Folio 3, List 66, File 311, pp. 77–85, APRF.
63. Ibid.
64. Shelepin to V. V. Kuznetzov, June 2, 1961, File 87592, p. 110, SVR.
65. Moscow to sec. of state, May 24, 1961, (8:33 A.M.), SDCDF, 1960–63, 611.61, NA.
66. GRU, Entry for May 29, 1961, "Kratkoye Soderzhanye."
67. Mansfield to JFK, "Observations on the Forthcoming Talks in Vienna," May 26, 1961, POF, CO:USSR, Box 126, JFKL.
68. Bundy, "Memo to President," May 29, 1961, POF, CO:USSR, Box 126, JFKL.
69. One of the Soviet leaders' aides noted on the report "read by N. Khrushchev, May 30, 1961," Folio 3, List 66, File 311, APRF.
70. "Rough Draft," [lunch, June 3, 1961], DDRS 1994, no. 3355.
71. "(The President and Mr. K. alone.)," draft of 3:00 P.M. meeting, June 3, 1961, Declassified Documents, 1994, no. 3357.
72. Memo of conference, Vienna, June 4, 1961, 10:15 A.M.; *FRUS, 1961–963*, vol. 14, *Berlin Crisis*, p. 91.
73. Edwin O. Guthman and Jeffrey Shulman, eds., *Robert Kennedy: In His Own Words: The Unpublished Recollections of the Kennedy Years* (Toronto, 1988), p. 28.
74. Ibid., p. 29.

CHAPTER 7: CONDOR AND MONGOOSE

1. Andrei Sakharov, *Memoirs*, trans. Richard Lourie (New York, 1990), pp. 205–17.
2. Ibid., 216–17.
3. Edwin O. Guthman and Jeffrey Shulman, eds., *Robert Kennedy: In His Own Words* (Toronto, 1988), p. 278.
4. Shelepin to CC, May 5, 1961, File 84558, pp. 278–79, SVR.
5. Ibid. The Cuban government has published some information about an alleged U.S. agent, Alfredo Izaguirre de la Riva, who may have been involved with "Izaguirre Orendo." See Fabian Escalante, *The Secret War: CIA Covert Operations against Cuba, 1959–62* (New York, 1995), pp. 89–92.
6. Shelepin to the CC, May 4, 1961, File 84558, pp. 278–79, SVR.
7. Protocol, Presidium meeting, June 24, 1961, Folio 3, List 65, File 902, pp. 77–78, APRF. Dmitri Volkogonov also refers to this intelligence information and Khrushchev's reaction in *Sem Vozhdei* [Seven leaders] (Moscow, 1995), p. 425.
8. "Appropriate Soviet organs now have a photocopy of secret memorandum no. 1856 of June 19 to the president of Guatemala Ydígoras and of a secret letter of the general secretary of the anti-Castro powers Gustavo dated June 17 in the name of the leader of this group in Guatemala, Julio Prado García Salas."
9. The point man in the Cuban opposition for the operation was said to be Tony

Varona, who represented the Cuban government in exile in New York.

10. Protocol, Presidium meeting, June 24, 1961, Folio 3, List 65, File 902, pp. 73–75, APRF.

11. Ibid.

12. Ibid.

13. Alekseev to Moscow, June 28, 1961, File 88631, p. 262, SVR.

14. An official Cuban discussion of the Candela case, which Havana refers to as "PATTY-CANDELA," and which is based on some files in the archives of the Cuban state security service, can be found in Escalante, *Secret War*, pp. 92–97.

15. Alekseev to Moscow, July 22, 1961, File 88631, p. 307, SVR.

16. Alekseev to Moscow, July 19, 1961, File 88631, p. 304, SVR. In this dispatch, Alekseev comments on what he has done in response to Shelepin's new information about Candela.

17. Ibid.

18. See above, n. 15.

19. Alekseev to Moscow, July 29, 1961, File 88631, p. 311, SVR.

20. Transcript of conference of the first secretaries of the central committee of communist and workers parties of socialist countries for the exchange of views on questions related to the preparation and conclusion of a German peace treaty, Aug. 3–5, 1961, from the TsKhSD, cited in Vladislav Zubok and Constantine Pleshakov, *Inside the Kremlin's Cold War: From Stalin to Khrushchev* (Cambridge, Mass., 1996), p. 252.

21. Hope M. Harrison, "Ulbricht and the Concrete 'Rose,' " Working Paper no. 5, CWIHP, Washington, D.C., May 1993, p. 47. Professor Harrison cites Yuli Kvitsinsky's book *Vor dem Sturm: Erinnerungen eines Diplomaten* (Berlin, 1993), p. 179.

22. Richard Reeves, *President Kennedy* (New York, 1993), p. 196.

23. JFK, televised address on the Berlin crisis, Washington, D.C., July 25, 1961, in *"Let the Word Go Forth,"* selected by Theodore C. Sorensen (New York, 1991).

24. Shelepin to NSK, July 29, 1961, in st. (Special Dossier of the Secretariat of the CC), 191/75gc, Aug. 1, 1961, Folio 4, List 13, File 81, p. 130, TsKhSD, cited in Zubok and Pleshakov, *Inside the Kremlin's Cold War*, pp. 253–55.

25. Ibid.

26. Zubok and Pleshakov, *Inside the Kremlin's Cold War*, p. 256; Harrison, "Ulbricht and the Concrete 'Rose.' "

27. Cited in Michael R. Beschloss, *The Crisis Years* (New York, 1991), pp. 329–30.

28. Viktor Adamsky and Yuri Smirnov, "Moscow's Biggest Bomb: The 50-Megaton Test of October 1961," *CWIHPB*, no. 4 (1994): 3, 19, cited in Zubok and Pleshakov, *Inside the Kremlin's Cold War*, pp. 257–58.

29. Fidel Castro to NSK, Sept. 4, 1961, Folio 3, List 65, File 872, pp. 146–51, APRF. Castro named Sergio del Valle, the chief of staff of the Cuban army, to head the team. Accompanying del Valle was Flavio Bravo.

30. Matvei Zakharov [Ministry of Defense] and Ivan V. Archipov [Ministry of Foreign Economic Trade] to CC, Sept. 20,1961, Folio 3, List 65, File 872, pp. 136–38, APRF. Besides the SA-2, Castro wanted 282 more antiaircraft guns, with calibers from 37 mm to 100 mm; and 412 more tanks and 100 armored transports. In all, the Soviets figured the bill for this wish list was 174 million rubles, or almost U.S.$193 million.

31. Steven J. Zaloga, *Soviet Air Defence Missiles* (London, 1989), pp. 36–53. Defectors to the United States reported that in trials the SA-2 with its V-750 missiles shot down 80 percent of airborne targets. Though the figure may seem exaggerated, the Soviet government quickly showed its confidence in the new weapons system by reportedly investing roughly 30 billion rubles on the program in 1958.

32. Since this was a military group, it was handled by the Soviet Defense Ministry; but because the group was looking to acquire Soviet exports, the Ministry of Foreign Economic Trade was also involved. Government-to-government negotiations were a slow-moving process in Moscow that comprised three distinct phases. First, there had to be a green light from the leadership of the Central Committee, the Presidium, before any request from a foreign country for negotiations could be accepted. This "green light" was essential but meaningless. Unless Khrushchev himself was involved, the Presidium granted no authority to its representatives. The Presidium's micromanagement extended to designating on the Soviet side the participants in any negotiation.

33. The first Soviet deployment outside the USSR was to East Germany in 1959. After the U-2 incident, requests came in from other Soviet allies for these weapons. By 1961 the Soviets were committed to an expensive deployment of several SA-2 divisions to Warsaw Pact allies, Poland and Czechoslovakia. The Eastern bloc was not alone in wanting the missiles that could shoot down the best the United States had to offer. Nasser's Egypt was eager to be the first non-bloc country to acquire the SA-2.

34. Ibid.

35. See Resolution 18 from Presidium meeting of Feb. 8, 1962, Folio 3, List 65, File 872, pp. 158–59, APRF.

36. Alekseev to Moscow, Sept. 20, 1961, File 88631, vol. 3, p. 457, SVR.

37. Moscow continued to receive worrisome reports from Alekseev. In Nov. he cabled that the Cubans had some evidence that "the U.S. is preparing an attack on Cuba for the end of November–beginning of December" and some other indications that the attack might come in Jan. 1962. The new threat was a U.S.-led operation involving 50,000 men. The Cuban émigrés, it was reported, were afraid to initiate a second assault on the beaches of Cuba without overt U.S. assistance. "Plans for the physical liquidation of Fidel Castro remain in force," Alekseev concluded. Alekseev to Moscow, Nov. 11, 1961, File 86447, vol. 4, p. 96, SVR.

38. Both the CIA and the KGB noted this quotation in their respective analyses of Cuban assistance to Latin American revolutionary movements. CIA, "Cuban Training of Latin American Subversives," March 27, 1963, LBJ Library, CMC/NSA; N. Zakharov to CC, "O Otnoshenii Kubinskovo Rukovodstva K Nationalno-osvoboditelnomu Dvizheniu v Latinskoi Amerike" [On the Cuban leadership's relations with the national-liberation movement in Latin America], April 18, 1963, File 88497, vol. 1, SVR.

39. Minutes of meeting of Koslov, Suslov, and Flavio Bravo, March 3, 1961, Folio 3, List 65, File 871, APRF.

40. Zakharov to CC, see above, n. 38.

41. Ibid.

42. Alekseev to Moscow, Nov. 4, 1961, File 88631, vol. 4, p. 47, SVR. Ramiro Valdés, the head of Cuban security, complained to Alekseev that the GRU was trying to

get information from the Cuban Foreign Ministry. This was not the liaison that the Cubans had hoped for; Alekseev to Moscow, Dec. 8, 1961, File 88631, vol. 4, p. 71, SVR. Alekseev also warned Moscow that the Cubans were losing their patience with the Czechs. Again, the ambitious intelligence officer may have been trying to improve his own field of operations. Alekseev said that Czech intelligence efforts to recruit high-level Cubans were becoming too noticeable. "Czech representatives must be very careful when they hire agents in Cuba," he said. "The Czechs are doing a lot for Cubans; so Cubans are trying to do something in return." Prague should be cautioned, he argued, not to push too hard.

43. Alekseev to Moscow, Dec. 20, 1961, File 86447, vol. 4, p. 87, SVR.

44. Alekseev to Moscow, Oct. 14, 1961, File 88631, vol. 4, p. 25, SVR. Alekseev backpedals in his cable of Oct. 17, 1961, ibid., p. 27.

45. Alekseev to Moscow, Dec. 21, 1961, File 86447, vol. 4, p. 87, SVR.

46. Richard Goodwin, "Conversation with Commandante Ernesto Guevara of Cuba," Aug. 22, 1961, POF, CO:Cuba, Security 1961, Box 115, JFKL.

47. Memo, Sept. 1, 1961, and note on telephone conversation, Sept. 7, 1961, Cuban collection at State/FOIA. This collection will be published in 1997 as *FRUS, 1961–1963*, vol. 10, *Cuba*. In a telephone conversation with George Ball, Goodwin reported on Sept. 7 that President Kennedy had accepted the conclusions reached by the Cuban Task Force at its Sept. 1 meeting.

48. Goodwin, cover letter, Aug. 22, 1961, POF, CO:Cuba, Security 1961, Box 115, JFKL.

49. Thomas Parrott, Oct. 5, 1961, State/FOIA. This document comes from NSF, CO:Cuba, General, June 1961–Dec. 61, JFKL.

50. "Alleged Assassination Plots Involving Foreign Leaders," Select Committee to Study Governmental Operations, U.S. Senate, 94th Cong., Nov. 20, 1975, pp. 138–39.

51. John McCone, meeting with RFK, Nov. 29, 1961, State/FOIA.

52. Goodwin to JFK, Nov. 1, 1961, State/FOIA [source: POF, CO:Cuba, Security, 1961, JFKL].

53. Richard Helms, memo for the director (CIA), Jan. 19, 1962. At a meeting with Helms and McCone, RFK recounted the early history of the Mongoose project. State/FOIA.

54. Lansdale to RFK, Nov. 30, 1961, State/FOIA. Lansdale writes of "your special project" in describing the Cuban operation to the attorney general.

55. JFK to Dean Rusk, Nov. 30, 1961, State/FOIA [source: POF, CO:Cuba, Cuba, Security, 1961]. And see the draft version of this instruction, dated Nov. 22, 1961, ibid.

56. Richard M. Bissell, Jr., *Reflections of a Cold Warrior* (New Haven, 1996), p. 202.

57. Brigadier General Lansdale, "Program Review," Feb. 20, 1962, "NSF Meetings & Memos," Special Group (Augmented) Jan. 1962–June 1962, Box 319, JFK Assassination Collection, NA.

58. Ibid.

59. Guthman and Shulman, eds., *Robert Kennedy*, pp. 253–54.

60. Ibid., p. 14.

61. Ibid.

62. From the RFK papers, cited in David Corn, *Blond Ghosts: Ted Shackley and the*

CIA's Crusades (New York, 1994), p. 70. Corn, in turn, cited Arthur Schlesinger, Jr.'s book on RFK.

63. Alekseev to Moscow, Dec. 17, 1961, File 86447, vol. 4, p. 72, SVR.
64. Interview with Samuel Halpern, Aug. 22, 1995, Washington, D.C.
65. Ibid.
66. John McCone, memo for the record, Dec. 27, 1962, meeting with RFK, State/FOIA [Source: DCI Memoranda for the Record, Nov. 29, 1961–April 5, 1962, Box 2, CIA].
67. Halpern interview.
68. See above, n. 66.
69. Halpern interview.
70. Richard Helms to John McCone, Jan. 19, 1962, State/FOIA.

CHAPTER 8: TROUBLE IN THE TROPICS

1. CINCLANT to All Commands, Feb. 24, 1962, copy in NSF, CO:Cuba, Cuba Cables Feb. 1, 1962–July 11, 1962, JFKL.
2. "Use of U.S. Military Force, Cuba Project," attached to State Department memo dated Feb. 26, 1962, CMC/NSA.
3. See above, n. 1.
4. Donald F. Chamberlain, CIA inspector general, to Walt Elder, June 5, 1975. In this remarkable document, declassified only in Nov. 1995, the CIA's inspector general quoted from a few key documents on Mongoose, including a pencil draft memorandum to McCone, dated Jan. 19, 1962, that recorded that day's conversation with RFK, RockCom.
5. Ibid.
6. "Tasks Assigned to CIA in General Lansdale's Program Review," Jan. 24, 1962, RockCom.
7. Ibid.
8. Ibid.
9. Semichastny to Gromyko and Malinovsky, Feb. 21, 1962, SVR.
10. NSK, *Khrushchev Remembers*, trans. and ed. Strobe Talbott (Boston, 1970), p. 492.
11. Excerpts from meeting between NSK and Fidel Castro, May 5, 1963, Folio 3, List 65, File 874, pp. 59–62, APRF.
12. Smirnovski [Washington] to Moscow, Jan. 31, 1962, Folio 3, List 66, File 315, APRF.
13. Adzhubei, report to CC, March 12, 1962, Folio 3, List 66, File 315, APRF.
14. Presidium resolution, "Regarding Instructions to the Confidential Representative in Soviet Matters in the United States," Jan. 18, 1962, Folio 3, List 66, File 315, APRF.
15. Ibid.
16. There is no mention of the March 2 meeting in RFK's date diary, where he recorded meetings that occurred in his office. However, the files of both the Presidium and Soviet military intelligence confirm that Bolshakov met with RFK on this day.
17. GRU resident to GRU headquarters, March 3, 1962, Folio 3, List 66, File 311, pp. 165–66, APRF.
18. Ibid.

19. *Spravka* [Summary], GRU.

20. Gromyko's instructions to acting Soviet ambassador in Washington [Smirnovski], Folio 3, List 66, File 315, APRF.

21. NSK, *Khrushchev Remembers: The Last Testament*, trans. and ed. Strobe Talbott (Boston, 1974), p. 536.

22. Entries for Nov. 1 and 7, 1962, "Notes Taken from Transcripts of Meetings of the Joint Chiefs of Staff, October–November 1962, Dealing with the Cuban Missile Crisis," CMC/NSA. Fearing a stalemate in Cuba like the one Great Britain encountered during the Boer War, Kennedy discouraged the "mistaken optimism" that "one Yankee could always lick ten Gringos" [*sic*].

23. For Lansdale's prediction, see Lansdale, Program Review: The Cuba Project, February 20, 1962, NSF: Meetings and Memoranda Series, Special Group (Augmented), Jan. 1962–June 1962, Box 319, JFKL.

24. CIA memo to Special Group, "The Cuba Project," Jan. 24, 1962, RockCom.

25. Lansdale to Department of Defense, Jan. 26, 1962. Lansdale asked for "an early determination of the policy on using U.S. force in the Cuba project." This came only two days after the CIA reported to the Special Group its doubts about the effectiveness of a covert plan to incite an effective resistance movement in Cuba. State/FOIA. On Jan. 29, 1962, CINCLANT reported to CINC, Atlantic Fleet, that McNamara wanted the reaction times for 314-61 changed to four days and 316-61 to seven days. CINCLANT wanted the report by Feb. 5; ibid. [source: Office of the Secretary of Defense, Historian's Office, Cable Files, Cuba, Jan.–Aug. 1962]. Lansdale remarked in a memo drafted in May, "The Special Group (Augmented) has assumed that overt U.S. military force will have to be used to end Communist control of Cuba," Lansdale, May 31, 1962, ibid.

26. U. A. Johnson, memo on this meeting, March 16, 1962, State/FOIA.

27. "Notes on Special Group Meeting," March 22, 1962, RockCom. It seems from the agenda for the March 29 meeting (also RockCom) that the option of training Cuban pilots was the one pursued.

28. William K. Harvey through Richard Helms to McCone, "Operation MON-GOOSE—Appraisal of Effectiveness and Results Which Can Be Expected from Implementing the Operational Plan Approved at the Meeting of the Special Group (Augmented) on 16 March 1962," April 10, 1962, RockCom.

29. Special Group Meeting, March 4, 1962, State/FOIA [source: NSF, Meetings and Memoranda Series, Special Group (Augmented), Operation Mongoose, Feb. 1962–April 1962, JFKL].

30. Lansdale, May 31, 1962, State/FOIA.

31. State Department memo, Aug. 10, 1962, State/FOIA. At a time when a Soviet base in Cuba seemed likely, there was a discussion over why Robert Kennedy's question in March had not been thoroughly considered.

32. CIA, Special National Intelligence Estimate, "Probable Reactions to a U.S. Military Intervention in Cuba," April 10, 1962, State/FOIA.

33. Malinovsky and Zakharov to CC, March 8, 1962, Folio 3, List 65, File 872, p. 180, APRF.

34. Interview with Nikolai Leonov, Sept. 1994, Moscow. Leonov led a reform of the Analytical Department of the First Chief Directorate of the KGB in the 1970s.

35. A. Sakharovsky, "O Politikye SshA V Otnoshenii Kuby" [U.S. policy toward Cuba], March 21, 1962, File 88497, vol. 1, pp. 318–35, SVR.

36. Alekseev to Center, Oct. 29, 1961, File 88631, p. 43, SVR.

37. Instructions, Center to Oleg (Alekseev), March 29, 1962, File 88631, pp. 244–45, SVR.

38. Two cables sent the same day, March 15, 1962, suggest both that Feklisov was working fast to help the KGB prepare its review of U.S. policy toward Cuba and the general tone of what Feklisov found. Kallistrat [Feklisov] to KGB, March 15, 1962, File 116, vol. 1 (cables from Washington, D.C., Jan. 1, 1962–Dec. 31, 1962), p. 233; ibid., p. 234, SVR.

39. Ibid., p. 234.

40. Ibid.

41. Semichastny to CC, April 11, 1962, File 88497 (Copies of Special Reports on Cuba, Feb. 15, 1962–May 15, 1963), vol. 1, pp. 61–68, SVR.

42. Andrei Ledovsky, "Mikoyan's Secret Mission to China in January and February 1949," *Far Eastern Affairs*, no. 2 (1995): 72–94.

43. Ibid.

44. See above, n. 35.

45. "O Politikye SshA V Otnoshenii Kuby" [U.S. policy toward Cuba], March 16, 1962, SVR.

46. This account is taken primarily from the KGB's report on the Escalante affair, and Escalante's own statement to Soviet officials after his arrival in Moscow: Semichastny to CC, see above, n. 41; Escalante statement, taken by V. Korionov of the CC, April 3, 1962, Folio 3, List 65, File 903, pp. 39–42, APRF.

CHAPTER 9: THE NUCLEAR DECISION

1. *NYT*, April 10, 1962. James Hershberg was one of the first scholars to note the coverage given to Lantphibex and to inquire about the effect this might have had on Khrushchev.

2. Ibid.

3. Ibid.

4. Alekseev to Moscow, Nov. 21, 1961, File 88631 [Avanpost, Nov. 16, 1961–July 26, 1962], p. 58, SVR.

5. N. Zakharov to CC, "O Otnoshenii Kubinskovo Rukovodstva K Nationalno-osvoboditelnomu Dvizheniu v Latinskoi Amerike" [On the Cuban leadership's relations with the national-liberation movement in Latin America], April 18, 1963, File 88497, vol. 1, SVR.

6. Cited in Philip Brenner, "Thirteen Months," in *The Cuban Missile Crisis Revisited*, ed. James A. Nathan (New York, 1992), p. 192.

7. Semichastny to CC, April 4, 1962, File 88497, vol. 1, SVR.

8. Ibid.

9. Ibid.

10. Ibid.

11. This quotation does not appear in the version of the meeting that the KGB forwarded to the CC on April 4, 1962. However, it does appear in a longer study of the Cuban policy toward the national-liberation movement in Latin America, prepared for the leadership before Castro's first visit to the Soviet Union in April 1963. See Zakharov, cited above, n. 5.

12. Interview with Semichastny, June 10, 1994, Moscow.

13. Semichastny to CC, April 11, 1962, File 88497, vol. 1, SVR.
14. Presidium resolution, April 12, 1962, and draft resolution from the "Osobaya Popka" [Special file], Folio 3, List 65, File 872, pp. 170–74, APRF.
15. Ibid.
16. D. A. Volkogonov, *Sem Vozhdei* [Seven leaders] (Moscow, 1995), p. 420.
17. See above, n. 5.
18. Ibid.
19. Ibid.
20. Interviews with Aleksandr Alekseev, Moscow, Feb. 16, 1994, Nov. 15, 1995, Moscow.
21. Ibid.
22. Ibid.
23. Ibid.
24. Ibid.
25. NSK to Fidel Castro, May 11, 1962, Folio 3, List 65, File 873, p. 24, APRF.
26. Ibid.
27. Pierre Salinger, *With Kennedy* (New York, 1966), p. 235.
28. Moscow to sec. of state, May 13, 1962, RG 59, SDCDF, 1960–63, 611.61, NA.
29. Stewart Alsop, "Kennedy's Grand Strategy," *Saturday Evening Post*, March 31, 1962.
30. NSK, *Khrushchev Remembers*, trans. and ed. Strobe Talbott (Boston, 1970), p. 493.
31. Ibid.
32. NSK, *Khrushchev Remembers: The Last Testament*, trans. and ed. Strobe Talbott (Boston, 1974), p. 511.
33. Ibid.
34. A. Sakharovsky to V.S. Semenov (Ministry of Foreign Affairs), "Some Reports on U.S. Foreign Policy," July 18, 1960, File 88497, vol. 1, SVR.
35. Sofia to Center, April 13, 1962, File 93958, vol. 5 (cables about Turkey, Jan. 2, 1962–Dec. 10, 1962), SVR.
36. Malinovsky to CC, May 7, 1962, Folio 3, List 65, File 873, p. 12, APRF.
37. GRU (Col. Meshcheriakov) to Malinovsky, May 20, 1962, Folio 3, List 65, File 872, pp. 45–47, APRF.
38. Ibid.
39. *Na Krayu Propasti (Karibski Krisis, 1962 Roga)* [On the brink of a precipice (Caribbean crisis, 1962)] (Moscow, 1994), p. 38.
40. Interview with Alekseev, Feb. 16, 1994.
41. Ibid.
42. NSK, *Khrushchev Remembers*, p. 494.
43. Volkogonov, *Sem Vozhdei*, pp. 421–22.
44. Ibid.
45. Extract from protocol 32/1, meeting of the Presidium, May 24, 1962, Folio 3, List 65, File 872, p. 49, APRF. Ivanov's note is located in the AGSRF, Fond 16, Inventory 3753, File 1, Box 3573, Documents on "Anadyr," Aug. 20–Sept. 29, 1962.
46. D. S. Polyanski, text for the report to the Plenum of the CC (Oct. 14, 1964), prepared Oct. 13, 1964, Register no. 8476, APRF.
47. Documents on "Anadyr," cited above, n. 45.

48. Interview with Alekseev, Feb. 16, 1994.
49. Ibid.; interview with Boris Ponomarev, Sept. 1993, Moscow.

CHAPTER 10: ANADYR

1. Dobrynin to MFA, "On the Meeting between Bolshakov and RFK," June 4, 1962, Folio 3, List 66, File 316, pp. 96–97, APRF.
2. NSK to JFK, March 9, 1962, APRF. Khrushchev wrote, "I recommend Dobrynin to you. He enjoys my complete trust and can be used for confidential communications."
3. There is evidence of at least fifty-one discussions between Bolshakov and Kennedy in the period May 1961–Dec. 1962. There are three main sources for this information: RFK's desk diary at the JFKL; RFK's papers (still largely closed) as described by Arthur M. Schlesinger, Jr., in *Robert Kennedy and His Times* (Boston, 1978); and a series of research notes (called *spravkas*) prepared by the GRU, the intelligence service of the General Staff of the Armed Forces of the Russian Federation.
4. Charles E. Bohlen to McGeorge Bundy, May 25, 1962, NSF, CO:USSR, Box 178, JFKL.
5. Dobrynin to MFA, June 4, 1962, Folio 3, List 66, File 313, pp. 96–97, APRF.
6. Ibid.
7. Khrushchev's annoyance at what Kennedy said comes through in the response approved by the Presidium on June 14, 1962. Folio 3, List 66, File 316, pp. 83–94, APRF.
8. Semichastny to CC, June 2, 12, 14, 1962; Ivashutin to CC, June 7, 1962, *Istoricheskii Archiv*, no. 1 (1993): 110–16, 122–34. The leaders of the strike were dealt with harshly. Ultimately more than ninety-three workers were tried and seven shot for "hooliganism."
9. Interview with Aleksandr Alekseev, Feb. 16, 1994, Moscow.
10. Ibid.
11. Ibid.
12. Ibid.
13. This account of the June 10 meeting was noted by General Ivanov and can be found written on the back of a resolution of the Council of Ministers regarding the missiles. See Folio 16, List 3753, File 1, Box 3573, AGSRF.
14. Ibid.
15. Raymond Garthoff estimates that in Oct. 1962 the Soviet Union had between twenty-four and forty-four intercontinental ballistic missiles (ICBMs), and no submarine launched ballistic missiles, SLBMs. Even if, as it seems likely, the Soviets had deployed a few SLBMs at that time, they were not yet regularly patrolling the East Coast of the United States. Thus forty MRBM/IRBM missiles on Cuba would have doubled the number of Soviet missiles that could hit the continental United States. See Garthoff, *Reflections on the Cuban Missile Crisis*, rev. ed. (Washington, D.C., 1989), p. 208, table 1.
16. *Na Krayu Propasti* [On the brink of a precipice] (Moscow, 1994), p. 54; D. A. Volkogonov, *Sem Vozhdei* [Seven leaders] (Moscow, 1995), p. 422. The evidence of May preparations is sketchy. The Russian military historians and Volkogonov were probably persuaded that preparations began in early May by the fact that at

the May 24 Presidium, where the project received its first endorsement, the plan already carried the cover name Anadyr and comprised many of the elements of its final form. Neither the Presidium nor the Ministry of Defense documents consulted by us provided any direct evidence of these preparatory talks.

17. *Na Krayu Propasti*, pp. 54, 73–74.
18. Volkogonov, *Sem Vozhdei*, p. 422.
19. *Na Krayu Propasti*, pp. 58, 73; Volkogonov, *Sem Vozhdei* p. 423.
20. *Na Krayu Propasti*, p.74; Anatoli I. Gribkov and William Y. Smith, *Operation ANADYR: U.S. and Soviet Generals Recount the Cuban Missile Crisis* (Chicago, 1994), pp. 26–29.
21. *Na Krayu Propasti*, p. 58.
22. NSK to Fidel Castro, June 12, 1962, Folio 3, List 65, File 872, pp. 58–59, APRF.
23. Ibid.
24. Ibid.
25. Dementyev to General Ivanov, June 13, 1962, Folio 3, List 65, File 872, APRF, p. 60.
26. Extract of Protocol 36 from Presidium meeting on June 14, 1962, Folio 3, List 66, File 316, pp. 78–82, APRF.
27. The role of the Foreign Ministry is adduced from Gromyko's report to the CC, dated June 12, on the RFK-Bolshakov meeting, which is part of the materials in the Presidium collection for the session of June 14. Folio 3, List 66, File 316, pp. 83–94 (including Dobrynin's report of June 4), APRF.
28. See above, n. 26.
29. Ibid.
30. Alekseev to Moscow, Jan. 21, 1962, File 88631, p. 132, SVR.
31. Malinovsky and Ivanov to deputy minister of defense (the commander of the Forces of the Rear [Interior]), June 15, 1962, Folio 16, Inventory 3753, File 1, Box 3573, AGSRF.
32. Feklisov to Center, Feb. 7, 1962, File 88631, p. 141, SVR.
33. Feklisov to Center, March 28, 1962, File 116, vol. 1 ("Cables from Washington, Jan. 1, 1962–Dec. 31, 1962"), p. 272, SVR.
34. Interview with Alekseev, Feb. 16, 1994.
35. *Na Krayu Propasti*, p. 61.
36. Ibid.
37. Ibid., p. 66.
38. Instruction to the Captain of the Ship and the Head of the Military Echelon, July 4, 1962, Folio 16, Inventory 3753, File 1, Box 3573, documents on "Anadyr," Aug. 20–Sept. 29 1962, AGSRF. This document was approved by Malinovsky and Minister of the Fleet Bakalev.
39. *Na Krayu Propasti*, p. 68. This information came from an interview with A. Kovalenko, who commanded one of the missile regiments in Cuba.
40. Gribkov and Smith, *Operation Anadyr*.
41. Interview with General Leonid Garbuz, Dankevich's deputy for general affairs in May 1962, Moscow, Feb.17, 1994.
42. Ibid.; interview with Yuri Kovalenko, deputy chief of an engineering detachment in Cuba, June 1995, St. Petersburg.
43. *Na Krayu Propasti*, pp. 63–66. The authors of this official history quote directly from the instruction given to Pliyev.

44. Ibid.

45. Khrushchev used this channel to request the withdrawal of U.S. troops from Thailand in May–June 1962. See "Kratkoye Soderzhanye: Besed G. Bolshakova s R. Kennedi (9 Maya 1961 goda–14 Dekabria 1962 roga)" [Summary: Meeting of G. Bolshakov with R. Kennedy, May 9, 1961–December 14, 1962], GRU.

46. Instructions to Soviet ambassador (Dobrynin), [n.d., but in response to RFK-Bolshakov meeting of July 31, 1962], Folio 3, List 66, File 316, pp. 194–95, APRF. Bolshakov and RFK met at least six times in July 1962. The instructions to Dobrynin imply that Bolshakov was used to carry the request for a halt in overhead reconnaissance.

47. Washington to Center, Aug. 20, 1962, File 116, vol. 1, pp. 751–53, SVR.

48. Instructions to Dobrynin (see above, n. 46). JFK's desk diary (JFKL) confirms that he met with Bolshakov and RFK on July 31, 1962.

49. Ibid.

50. Ibid.

51. Alekseev to KGB, Aug. 18, 1962, Folio 3, List 65, File 873, pp. 118–20, APRF. This dispatch was sent to Khrushchev, Kozlov, Ponomarev, and Gromyko. It is interesting that though fully ensconced as Soviet ambassador, Alekseev used the KGB channel to report this information to the Kremlin.

52. Ibid.

53. Deputy KGB Chairman P. Ivashutin to CC, Aug. 23, 1962, Folio 5, List 50, File 1102, pp. 56–57, TsKhSD. A copy was also sent to the deputy minister of defense, Marshal Andrei Grechko. The authors are grateful to George Eliades for finding this document in the files.

54. Skryagin, "Dopolnitelnye Dannye O Kommunisticheskich Voorujennich silach na Kube" [Supplementary information on communist military forces in Cuba], Jan. 11, 1963, File 88497, pt. 1, SVR.

55. Semichastny to Gromyko, July 17, 1962, File 90782, vol. 2 ("Copies of Special Reports from Turkey, July 6, 1962–August 5, 1964"), pp. 14–15, SVR.

56. Mortin (KGB) to I. A. Serov (GRU) and N. A. Inauri (chief, KGB Georgia), [n.d.], File 90782, vol. 2, p. 37, SVR. Given the placement of the report in this file, it is assumed to have been written in Aug. or Sept. In mid-Aug., Officer Agarenkov of the Geographical Department of the First Chief Directorate of the KGB wrote a report entitled "American Activities in Turkey," which discussed the U.S. role in expanding Turkey's strategic power. At the last NATO session, it was reported, the United States pledged to send Polaris submarines, with ballistic missiles, to Turkey. Although under U.S. command, these submarines would be staffed by Turks. The report also mentioned the recent deployment of the Jupiter missiles. Aug. 15, 1962, File 93958, vol. 5 (Jan. 2, 1962–Dec. 10, 1962), pp. 252–56, SVR.

57. Interview with Alekseev, Feb. 16, 1994; interview with Vladimir Semichastny, June 10, 1994.

58. Interview with Semichastny, June 10, 1994.

59. Washington to Center, July 9, 1962, SVR. This was a source with excellent connections to one of Vice President Lyndon Johnson's national security assistants, General William Jackson.

60. James G. Blight, Bruce J. Allyn, and David Welch, *Cuba on the Brink* (New York: 1993), pp. 351–52.

61. As evidence of Castro's thoughts about deterring the United States in the late

summer of 1962, see Alekseev's comments from Havana. Alekseev to MFA, Sept. 7, 1962, trans. in *CWIHPB*, no. 5 (Spring 1995): 63.

62. "Memorandum of Conversation between Secretary of the Interior Udall and Chairman Khrushchev," Sept. 6, 1962, *FRUS, 1961–1963*, vol. 15, *Berlin Crisis, 1962–1963*, pp. 308–10.

63. Theodore C. Sorensen, Memo for the Files, Sept. 6, 1962, Cuba Collection, State/FOIA [source: Sorensen Papers, Classified Subject Files, 1961–64, Cuba, General, 1962, JFKL]. Dobrynin gave this message to Sorensen on Sept. 6.

64. Georgi Bolshakov, "Hot Line" [trans. of title], *Novoye Vremya*, no. 5 (1989).

CHAPTER 11: "NOW WE CAN SWAT YOUR ASS"

1. "Principal Soviet Public Statements on Defense of Cuba: (in chronological order 1960–1962)" [probably State Department], CMC/NSA.

2. Interview with A. F. Shorexov, Jan. 10, 1996.

3. See National Intelligence Estimate, "The Situation and Prospects in Cuba," Nov. 5, 1961; and as revised, March 21, 1962. On April 6, 1962, the Office of National Estimates reviewed this NIE in light of recent events in Cuba and reaffirmed its basic conclusions. State/FOIA, to be published in *FRUS, 1961–1963*, vol. 10, *Cuba*.

4. McCone, record of April 5 Special Group (Augmented) meeting, McCone Files, CIA, State/FOIA, in *FRUS, 1961–1963*, vol. 10.

5. Record of March 16, 1962, meeting, NSF, Meetings and Memoranda Series, Special Group (Augmented), Operation Mongoose, Feb. 1962–April 1962, JFKL.

6. Arthur Krock, *Memoirs: Sixty Years on the Firing Line* (New York, 1968), p. 318.

7. For a discussion of how this group helped effect the militarization of the Cold War, see Ernest R. May, "NSC 68: The Theory and Politics of Strategy," in *American Cold War Strategy: Interpreting NSC 68*, ed. Ernest R. May (New York, 1993), pp. 1–20.

8. Krock, *Memoirs*, pp. 319–20.

9. Ibid., pp. 296–97.

10. Dino A. Brugioni, *Eyeball to Eyeball: The Inside Story of the Cuban Missile Crisis* (New York, 1991), p. 96.

11. Brig. Gen. Lansdale to the Special Group (Augmented), "Stepped Up Course B," Aug. 8, 1962, NSF, MdM, Special Group (C1), Bowles, Box 319, JFKL.

12. Ibid.

13. "Alleged Assassination Plots Involving Foreign Leaders," p. 105.

14. Ibid.

15. McCone, "Memorandum on Cuba," Aug. 20, 1962, doc. 5, CIADCMC.

16. McCone, "Proposed Plan of Action for Cuba," Aug. 21, 1962 [attached to minutes of Aug. 23 meeting with JFK], doc. 9, CIADCMC.

17. Ibid.

18. McCone, memo for the file, "Discussion in Secretary Rusk's Office at 12 o'clock, 21 August 1962," doc. 6, CIADCMC.

19. Ibid.

20. McCone, "Memorandum of the Meeting with the President at 6:00 P.M., on August 22, 1962," doc. 7, CIADCMC.

21. Hulick to DOS, Aug. 23, 1962, *FRUS, 1961–1963*, vol. 15, *Berlin Crisis, 1962–63*, pp. 280–81.

22. Cited in *Newsweek*, Sept. 14, 1962.

23. Bundy to Sorensen, Aug. 23, 1962, *FRUS, 1961–1963*, 15:284–85.

24. McCone, "Memorandum of Meeting with the President," Aug. 23, 1962, doc. 8, CIADCMC.

25. See above, n. 16. McCone suggested a plan for "more aggressive action than any heretofore considered" against Castro. He wanted a three-pronged approach. First, the United States should begin a propaganda campaign "to awaken and alarm all of Latin America" and U.S. allies to the current dangerous situation. Second, immediate action against the island should be taken. Third, this action should be followed up by a U.S. invasion sufficient "to occupy the country, destroy the regime, free the people, and establish in Cuba a peaceful country which will be a member of the community of American states."

26. See above, n. 24.

27. Lyman B. Kirkpatrick, memo for the director, "Action Generated by DCI Cables Concerning Cuban Low-Level Photography and Offensive Weapons," [n.d.], doc. 12, CIADCMC.

28. Keating's Aug. 31, 1962, Senate speech is cited in Mark J. White's, *The Cuban Missile Crisis* (London, 1996), p. 94. In an excellent chapter on Keating's role in the crisis, White provides a persuasive account of Keating's activities, though he was unable to determine the identity of Keating's sources.

29. Ibid., pp. 93–103.

30. Robert Kennedy was virtually ignored by the State and Defense Departments when he made his concerns about a future Soviet missile base in Cuba more widely known in March 1962. See Lansdale Report on Cuban Policy, May 31, 1962; and memo prepared in the Department of State, Aug. 10, 1962.
    With reference to RFK's request on March 22 for contingency planning for the possibility of Soviet missiles in Cuba, the author of the memo explained that nothing was done in response because "it was decided that the possibility was too remote to waste time on." State/FOIA, *FRUS, 1961–1963*, vol. 10.

31. See memo by Carl Kaysen, dated Sept. 1, 1962. A national security staffer, Kaysen describes the president's call to Gilpatric and Gilpatric's subsequent responsibility to "see that we don't do anything this weekend that might lead to another incident." State/FOIA, *FRUS, 1961–1963*, vol. 10.

32. *Newsweek*, Sept. 14, 1962.

33. "President Kennedy's Statement on Soviet Military Shipments to Cuba," Sept. 4, 1962, CMC/NSA.

34. Ibid.

35. Stewart Udall, *The Myths of August: A Personal Exploration of Our Tragic Cold War Affair with the Atom* (New York: 1994), pp. 11–14.

36. Theodore C. Sorensen, *Kennedy* (New York, 1965), p. 253. The others were Arthur Goldberg, Robert Kennedy, and Abe Ribicoff.

37. Arthur M. Schlesinger, Jr., *A Thousand Days: John F. Kennedy in the White House* (New York, 1965), p. 363.

38. Interview with Rada Khrushchev Adzhubei, Jan. 5, 1995, Moscow.

39. Ibid. The account of Udall's visit to Pitsunda comes from his subsequent report, undated, CMC/NSA.

40. Ibid.

41. Ibid.

42. Ibid.
43. Malinovsky to Khrushchev, Sept 6, 1962, photocopy from APRF. For technical reasons, a matter of configuration, only two aircraft in the Soviet air force, the AN-8 and AN-12, were capable of transporting the missiles and the warheads. The workhorse of the Soviet air force, the larger Ilyushin 114 had the necessary range, 8,000 kilometers, but lacked a cargo opening large enough to move the nuclear weapons and the missiles onto the plane intact. The Defense Ministry calculated that the smaller AN-8 and AN-12 could each carry two Lunas and one R-11m. Because these planes were smaller than the Il-114, there would be no room for any additional equipment and personnel to operate the missiles.
44. Ibid. An R-11m brigade comprised three divisions, eighteen missiles, and a support crew of 324. A Luna division would have two missile launchers and 102 people.
45. F. D. Reeve, *Robert Frost in Russia* (New York, 1963), p. 6.
46. Ibid; Khrushchev wrote and dated his decisions regarding the tactical missile plan on the Sept. 6 document, cited in n. 43.
47. Marine Corps Emergency Actions Center, "Summary of Items of Significant Interest," Sept. 7, 1962, CMC/NSA.
48. TASS, Sept. 11, 1962. See Raymond Garthoff, "U.S. Intelligence Assessments in the Cuban Missile Crisis" (unpub. MS), p. 16. The authors are grateful to Ambassador Garthoff for sharing his article.
49. Zakharov to Kozlov, Sept. 16, 1962. A note written by General Ivanov states that Kozlov was told personally at 9:10 A.M. on Sept. 17 and Khrushchev by 10:00 A.M. Code "MO." Documents on "Anadyr," Aug. 20–Sept. 29, 1962, Fond 16, Inventory 3753, File 1, Box 3573, AGSRF.
50. Zakharov to CC, Sept. 20, 1962, Folio 5, List 33, File 164, p. 137, TsKhSD.
51. Zakharov/Fokin, memo to the Presidium, Sept. 25, 1962, photocopy from APRF.
52. M. V. Zakharov, deputy minister of defense to the commander in chief of land and air forces (copy to the head of Operations of the General Staff), Sept. 15, 1962, in documents on "Anadyr," cited above, n. 49.
53. See above, n. 51. Recently, a commander of one of these Foxtrot class submarines in the Cuban missile crisis spoke to the Russian press. Aleksandr Mozgovoi, "Order: In Case of Shooting, Use Nuclear Weapons" [translation of title], *Komsomolskaya Pravda*, June 27, 1995.
54. Memo, Ernest de M. Berkaw, Jr., Feb. 28, 1963. This was based on interviews with participants at the meeting. State/FOIA, *FRUS, 1961–1963*, vol. 10; also memo, "U-2 Overflights of Cuba, 29 August through 14 October 1962," Feb. 27, 1963, doc. 45, *CIACMCD*; Kirkpatrick, memo for the director, "White House Meeting on 10 September 1962 on Cuban Overflights," March 1, 1963, doc. 21, ibid. These documents were presumably prepared in response to the congressional hearings into the Cuban missile crisis in Feb. 1963.
55. At the end of Aug., Robert McNamara asked on the president's behalf to revisit the problem of the number of days' delay the military would need to implement an airborne invasion after a presidential decision.

CHAPTER 12: EX COMM

1. *Na Krayu Propasti* [On the brink of a precipice] (Moscow, 1994), p. 72.

2. McNamara to chairman, JCS [Taylor], Oct. 2, 1962, CMC/NSA; Major John M. Young, *When the Russians Blinked: The U.S. Maritime Response to the Cuban Missile Crisis* (Washington, D.C., 1990), pp. 66–67, 70–71.

3. McNamara to JFK, "Presidential Interest in SA-2 Missile System and Contingency Planning for Cuba," Oct. 4, 1962, Declassified Documents, 1991, no. 3042.

4. Young, *When the Russians Blinked*, pp. 66–67, 70–71.

5. McCone, "Memorandum of MONGOOSE Meeting Held on Thursday, October 4, 1962," doc. 41, *CIADCMC*.

6. Ibid.

7. Letter, John A. McCone to Charles J. V. Murphy, May 4, 1984, courtesy of Dr. Cicely Angleton.

8. See above, n. 5.

9. Georgi Bolshakov, "Hot Line" [trans. of title], *Novoye Vremya*, no. 5 (1989).

10. In his articles Bolshakov says that he met with RFK and a friend of the Kennedy family, Charles Bartlett, in the first week of Oct. In later interviews RFK denied having seen Bolshakov in Oct. 1962, before the missiles were discovered. RFK's date diary has an entry for a meeting with Georgi Bolshakov on Oct. 5.

11. Cited in Dino A. Brugioni, *Eyeball to Eyeball* (New York, 1991), pp. 165–66.

12. Albert H. Haynes [State Department], "Cuban Statements on Soviet Military Aid," NSA.

13. Ibid.

14. Alekseev to MFA, Oct. 9, 1962, Folio 109, List 17, File 21, pp. 58–59, AVPRF.

15. CIA Information Report, Sept. 18, 1962, doc. 37, *CIADCMC*, 1992.

16. Interview with Samuel Halpern, Aug. 22, 1995, Washington, D.C.

17. "Chronology of JCS Decisions concerning the Cuban Crisis," NSA.

18. Brugioni, *Eyeball to Eyeball*, p. 181.

19. Ibid.

20. JFK, "The Challenge of Imperialism: Algeria," July 2, 1957, in "*Let the Word Go Forth*," selected by Theodore C. Sorensen (New York, 1988), pp. 331–37.

21. Brugioni, *Eyeball to Eyeball*, p. 229.

22. In addition to the room microphones, Kennedy set up a system to tape his telephone calls. The first taped call at the JFKL was made in Sept. 1962. It was unintentionally a call made to the president by Jackie—and it has been removed by the family. There is some uncertainty as to when the president had this system installed. The first audio tape in the JFKL's collection is dated July 30, 1962. See the JFK Presidential Recordings Finding Aid, JFKL.

23. "Notes Taken from Transcripts of Meetings of the Joint Chiefs of Staff, October–November 1962, Dealing with the Cuban Missile Crisis" [handwritten notes were made in 1976 and typed in 1993], CMC/NSA.

24. Richard Helms, "MONGOOSE Meeting with the Attorney General," Oct. 16, 1962, RockCom; doc. 49, *CIADCMC*.

25. McCone, "Memorandum for Discussion Today, Oct. 17, 1962," "Subject: Cuba," Oct. 17, 1962, doc. 53, *CIADCMC*; "Brief Discussion with the President—9:30 A.M.—17 October 1962," doc. 55, *CIADCMC*.

26. General Marshall S. Carter, acting director of CIA, "Operation MONGOOSE/Sabotage Proposals," Oct. 16, 1962; Thomas A. Parrott, "Memorandum for the Special Group (Augmented) from General Carter, dated 16 October 1962," Oct. 17, 1962. Both from RockCom.

27. Semichastny to CC, Oct. 10, 1962, APRF.
28. Ibid.; protocol of Presidium meeting, Oct. 16, distributed Oct. 18, APRF.
29. Alekseev to MFA, Oct. 18, 1962, Folio 3, List 65, File 904, pp. 36-41, APRF.
30. "October 18, 1962, 11 A.M., Meeting on the Cuban Missile Crisis," JFK Presidential Recordings, JFKL.
31. Gromyko to the MFA, Oct. 20, 1962, trans. in *CWIHPB*, no. 5 (Spring 1995).
32. Dean Rusk, 3rd Oral History Interview with Dean Rusk, Feb. 19, 1970, JFKL.
33. *Washington Post*, Oct. 23, 1962.
34. RFK, *Thirteen Days: A Memoir of the Cuban Missile Crisis* (New York, 1969), p. 47.
35. Ibid., p. 43. There does not appear to be an audio tape of Thursday evening's meeting in the Oval Office. In Oct. 1996, the JFKL released tape 31.1, consisting ony of a $4^1/_2$ minute monologue by JFK he recorded that evening after meeting Gromyko.
36. Entry for Oct. 19, 1962, "Notes Taken from Transcripts of Meetings of the Joint Chiefs of Staff, October–November 1962, Dealing with the Cuban Missile Crisis," CMC/NSA.
37. Leonard Meeker (State Department), minutes of the Oct. 19, 1962, Executive Committee meeting, 11:00 A.M., doc. 21, in Laurence Chang and Peter Kornbluh, eds., *The Cuban Missile Crisis, 1962: A National Security Archive Documents Reader* (New York, 1992).
38. Entry for Oct. 19, 1962, "Notes Taken from Transcripts of Meetings of the JCS," CMC/NSA. Kennedy was indeed reluctant to abandon the surprise air strike option. Taylor interpreted Kennedy's doubts as indicating a willingness to proceed with an air strike if, at least, the allies could be informed a day in advance. "Would you be willing to accept a 24-hour delay to inform the allies?" Maxwell Taylor asked the chiefs on Kennedy's behalf on Friday afternoon, Oct. 19.
39. Ibid.
40. Entry for Oct. 20, 1962, JCS, "Notes Taken from Transcripts," CMC/NSA.
41. Ibid.
42. Cline, DDI briefing, White House, Oct. 20, 1962, doc. 68, *CIADCMC*.
43. When the air force confirmed the next morning that there were no guarantees that an air strike would take out all of the operational missiles, whatever remaining doubts Kennedy had about leading with a blockade disappeared. Oct. 22, NSC meeting, 3 P.M., JFK Presidential Recordings, JFKL; McNamara, military briefing, "Notes on October 21, 1962, Meeting with the President," doc. 25, in Chang and Kornbluh, eds., *Cuban Missile Crisis*.
44. Entry for Oct. 20, JCS, "Notes Taken from Transcripts," CMC/NSC.
45. "Notes Taken from Transcript of Meetings of the JCS," NSA.
46. Edwin O. Guthman and Jeffrey Shulman, eds., *Robert Kennedy: In His Own Words*, (Toronto, 1988), pp. 29–30.
47. Sir D. Ormsby Gore to Prime Minister Harold Macmillan, Oct. 23, 1962, Public Records Office, Kew, England. The authors are grateful to Professor Philip D. Zelikow for sharing this material.
48. Sir D. Ormsby Gore to Macmillan, Oct. 22, 1962, Public Records Office, Kew, England.
49. See above, n. 47.
50. Ibid.

51. See above, n. 48.
52. Interview with Charles Bartlett, Dec. 5, 1994, Washington, D.C.
53. Barton J. Bernstein, "Reconsidering the Missile Crisis: Dealing with Problems of the American Jupiters in Turkey," in *The Cuban Missile Crisis Revisited*, ed. James A. Nathan (New York 1992), pp.73–74.
54. "Cables Received in Moscow," Oct. 1962, GRU.
55. *NYT*, Oct. 22, 1962.
56. Interview with Warren Rogers, July 12, 1994.
57. *New York Herald Tribune*, Oct. 22, 1962.
58. Pierre Salinger, *With Kennedy* (London, 1967), p. 261.
59. Ibid., p. 253.
60. Oct. 22, 1962, JFK Presidential Recordings, JFKL. RFK wanted historians to remember his brother's restraint as an homage to the chief moral lesson of Pearl Harbor: civilized nations do not attack each other without warning. With the help of his actual words, we can now see that RFK, like his brother and the rest of the Ex Comm, had relied on more complex reasoning to embrace the blockade solution.

CHAPTER 13: MISSILE CRISIS

1. Neither the GRU nor the KGB, including its code and cipher service, claims credit for an intelligence coup on Oct. 22: GRU *spravka*, "Cables Received in Moscow, October 1962," letter from the Signals Intelligence Service of the Russian Federation, and SVR. Evidence of the discussion at the Presidium meeting of Oct. 22, 1962, comes from the APRF. From 1954 until 1965, Vladimir N. Malin, the head of the General Department of the CC, took occasional notes at the sessions of the Presidium. "Kratkie zametki o zasedaniyach Prezidiuma TsK KPSS" [Brief notes on the sessions of the Presidium of the CC of the CPSU], Protocol 60, Oct. 22, 1962, APRF (hereafter cited as Malin notes). The Folio/Entry that covers the Presidium documents from the crisis period does not contain any clues as to what secret intelligence, if any triggered, this meeting.
2. The message was the following: Director (Malinovsky) to Pavlov (Pliyev): "In connection with the tense situation around Cuba, put into effect full military readiness Cuban and Soviet forces. In case of enemy landing on the island of Cuba, take all measures to destroy the enemy by means of the Cuban and Soviet troops, with the exception of the equipment under the command of Statsenko and Beloborodov." Major General Igor D. Statsenko and Colonel Nikolai K. Beloborodov were in charge of the missile regiments and the protection of nuclear warheads, respectively.
3. Marshal Zhukov quoted in H. S. Dinerstein, *War and the Soviet Union: Nuclear Weapons and the Revolution in Soviet Military and Political Thinking* (New York, 1962), p. 220.
4. Ibid., pp. 247–52.
5. The authors are grateful to Dr. Michael Yaffee at the U.S. Arms Control and Disarmament Agency for calculating the blast effects of a two-kiloton and a twelve-kiloton nuclear weapon.
6. The cable was sent to Havana via KGB channels at 2:35 P.M., Moscow time, Oct. 22. Folio 16, Inventory 3753, File 1, Box 3573, AGSRF.

7. "Memorandum of Conference with the President," Oct. 22, 1962, Declassified Documents, 1994, no. 3509; and "John F. Kennedy Presidential Tapes, October 22, 1962," JFKL.

8. "Presidential Tapes, October 22, 1962," JFKL.

9. Major John M. Young, *When the Russians Blinked* (Washington, D.C., 1990), pp. 136–47.

10. "Radio-TV Address of the President to the Nation from the White House," Oct. 22, 1962, doc. 28, in Laurence Chang and Peter Kornbluh, eds., *The Cuban Missile Crisis, 1962* (New York, 1992).

11. Ibid.

12. Malin notes, Protocol 60, Oct. 22, 1962, APRF; regarding the four ships, extract from Protocol 60, Folio 3, List 65, File 904, p. 89, APRF.

13. Extract from Protocol 60, Folio 3, List 65, File 904, p. 91, APRF.

14. NSK to JFK, Oct. 23, 1962, doc. 30, in Chang and Kornbluh, eds., *Cuban Missile Crisis*, p. 156.

15. NSK to Fidel Castro, Oct. 23, 1962, Folio 3, List 65, File 904, p. 77, APRF.

16. NSK, *Khrushchev Remembers*, trans. and ed. Strobe Talbott (Boston, 1970), p. 497. Khrushchev does not give a date for the night he slept in his office. However, in light of the available Kremlin documentation, it is probable that he chose to sleep over on Oct. 22.

17. Feklisov to Center, Oct. 22, 1962, File 116, vol. 1, pp. 987–90, SVR.

18. Georgi Bolshakov, "Hot Line" [trans. of title], *Novoye Vremya*, no. 6 (1989).

19. GRU *spravka*.

20. GRU *spravka*. No confirmation has yet been found in U.S. archives of the Soviet account of Bartlett's or Holeman's statements about the Turkish missiles. In a telephone interview on May 7, 1995, Holeman said, "I am not denying that these things happened. . . . I do not have any recollection one way or the other." Bartlett, however, disputes that he ever mentioned Turkey to Bolshakov. Interview with Bartlett, Dec. 5, 1994, Washington, D.C.

21. Alphand to Paris, Oct. 23, 1962, Archive of the Ministère des Affaires Etrangères, Paris.

22. Barton J. Bernstein, "Reconsidering the Missile Crisis," in *The Cuban Missile Crisis Revisited*, ed. James A. Nathan (New York, 1992), pp. 75–76; Maurice Vaisse, ed., *L'Europe et la crise de Cuba* (Paris, 1993), p. 142.

23. Historical Division, Joint Secretariat, JCS, Dec. 21, 1962, "Chronology of JSC Decisions concerning the Cuban Crisis," CMC/NSA; McCone, "Memorandum of Meeting of Executive Committee of the NSC, 10:00 a.m., October 23, 1962," doc. 82, CIADCMC.

24. Entry for Oct. 24, "[JSC] Notes Taken from Transcripts," CMC/NSA. This entry discusses the Ex Comm meeting of Oct. 23.

25. Ibid.

26. "Kratkoye Soderzhanye: Besed G. Bolshakova s R. Kennedy, 9 Maia 1961 goda–14 Dekabrya 1962 goda" [Short summaries of meetings between G. Bolshakov and R. Kennedy, May 9, 1961–Dec. 14, 1962], GRU.

27. Ibid.

28. Edwin O. Guthman and Jeffrey Shulman, eds., *Robert Kennedy: In His Own Words* (Toronto, 1988), p. 261.

29. See above, n. 18.

30. GRU, entry for Oct. 24, 1962.

31. Dobrynin to Moscow, "On the Meeting with R. Kennedy, October 23," Oct. 24, 1962, AVPRF, p. 121.

32. Ibid.

33. Ibid.

34. Telegram, Alekseev to MFA, Oct. 22, 1962. A translation appears in the *CWIHPB*, no. 5 (Spring 1995): 70.

35. KGB resident to Moscow, Oct. 23, 1962, SVR.

36. Havana to Moscow, Oct. 24, 1962, File 1475 (cables from Havana, Sept. 13, 1962–Dec. 31, 1962), pp. 169–70, SVR. This cable, which was deciphered at KGB HQs at 10:00 A.M., Oct. 25, was sent to Khrushchev, Kozlov, Suslov, Ponomarev, and Gromyko by order of KGB Chairman Semichastny.

37. Interview with N. Novikov, Feb. 15, 1996, St. Petersburg.

38. Alekseev to KGB HQs, Oct. 23, 1963, File 1475, p. 158, SVR. This cable was deciphered in Moscow at 5:10 A.M. local time, Oct. 24.

39. Ibid.

40. Ibid. Grateful though the KGB was to learn that the ship was safely in port, the cable earned Alekseev a stern rebuke. "Prepare a cable for Alekseev," the chief of the KGB's foreign intelligence operations wrote before forwarding the *Aleksandrovsk* cable to Khrushchev, "that he may not write about the location of ships and the character of their cargoes."

41. The Soviet MFA received its copy at 7 A.M. on Oct. 24. See "Kennedy Message of October 23, 1962," *Problems of Communism* 41, special ed. (Spring 1992).

42. White House Press Office, DOD Office of Public Affairs, State Department Bureau of Public Affairs, "Chronology of the Cuban Crisis," Oct. 15–28, 1962, CMC/NSA.

43. Interview with Vladimir Semichastny, June 10, 1994.

44. "Khrushchev Message of October 24, 1962," *Problems of Communism* 41 (Spring 1992). The Soviet Foreign Ministry turned a copy over to the U.S. embassy in Moscow at 11:30 P.M., Moscow time, Oct. 24. Another copy was sent to Bolshakov; "O Konfidentialnom Poslanii T. Khrushcheva N.S. J. Kennedy," resolution of the CC, Oct. 24, 1962, Folio 3, List 65, File 904, p. 148, APRF. After approving the text by vote, the Presidium decided to resuscitate the Bolshakov channel and use the GRU officer to deliver it personally to RFK as a way of underscoring that this was Khrushchev's own message. There is no evidence in RFK's date diary or the Presidium archives that Bolshakov was, in fact, used to deliver the message.

45. Cited in Dino A. Brugioni, *Eyeball to Eyeball* (New York, 1991), p. 405.

46. Ibid., p. 406.

CHAPTER 14: CLIMAX OF THE COLD WAR

1. Interview, Frank Holeman. Aug. 15, 1995. There is a plaque, with biographical details, in Prokov's memory near the bar at the National Press Club. It does not mention Prokov's role in the Cuban misile crisis.

2. Kallistrat (Feklisov) to Center, Oct. 25, 1962, File 116, v. 1, pp. 1026–27, SVR. This file contains the actual cables—not the processed reports, or *spravkas*, disseminated to other government agencies.

3. Ibid.

4. Interview with Warren Rogers, July 12, 1994.

5. Dobrynin to MFA, Oct. 25, 1962, Folio 3, List 65, File 905, pp. 69–70, APRF. This was the copy distributed to NSK.

6. Scott Sagan, *The Limits of Safety: Organizations, Accidents, and Nuclear Weapons* (Princeton, 1993), pp. 68–71.

7. *Spravka*, "Cables Received in Moscow," GRU.

8. "Kennedy Message of October 25, 1962," *Problems of Communism* 41, special ed. (Spring 1992).

9. The quotations in this section come from Malin's notes of the Oct. 25 meeting of the Presidium. Dmitri Volkogonov's version of this meeting, which appears in his book *Sem Vozhdei* [Seven Leaders] (Moscow, 1995), pp. 429–30, differs substantially from our account. Unfortunately General Volkogonov was not permitted to see the transcript of the meeting before his death in 1995 and relied solely upon the brief record left in Folio 3, List 65, File 905, APRF.

10. KGB headquarters deciphered Feklisov's report on what Prokov told Gorsky and on the GRU's interception of the new U.S. military alert at 6:15 P.M., Oct. 25 (and distributed at 7:40 P.M.). Feklisov to Center, Oct. 25, 1962, File 116, vol. 1, pp. 1026–27, SVR. The cable carries a headquarters note dated the next day, Oct. 26, "Report already used along the line of the Embassy. Do not use." The times for the transmissions of the cables from the Foreign Ministry and the GRU are unknown. However, KGB channels were considered the fastest. It is not inconceivable, but unlikely in light of Soviet practice, that the GRU in Washington telephoned the news of the change in the U.S. alert to Moscow.

11. NSK, *Khrushchev Remembers*, trans. and ed. Strobe Talbott (Boston, 1970), p. 497.

12. Malin notes, Protocol 61, Oct. 25, 1962, APRF.

13. Rogers interview, July 12, 1994.

14. Kallistrat [Feklisov] to Moscow, Oct. 25, 1962, File 116, vol. 1, pp. 1026–27, SVR. The paraphrased version of this cable is located in File 90238, pp.48–55, also SVR.

15. G. M. Kornienko, *Kholodnaya Voina: Svidetelstvo Yego Uchastnika* [Cold War: The testimony of a participant] (Moscow, 1994), p. 97.

16. Dobrynin to MFA, Oct. 25, 1962, Folio 3, List 65, File 905, pp. 69–70, APRF. This was the copy distributed to Khrushchev.

17. Ibid.

18. The KGB station in Washington sent a shorter version on Oct. 26. The actual cable from Feklisov is located in File 116, vol. 1, pp. 1032–33; the version as paraphrased for distribution to the Kremlin is in File 90238, vol. 1, p. 48, SVR. The leadership of the KGB decided not to distribute this cable because a copy had also been sent via MFA channels.

19. Rogers interview, July 12, 1994.

20. Interview with Semichastny, June 10, 1995.

21. Kallistrat [Feklisov] to Center, Oct. 24, 1962. The raw cable is in File 88531, vol. 6, pp. 1032–33, SVR. It carries the times of receipt in Moscow and distribution.

22. Interview with Semichastny, June 10, 1994.

23. Sergei Khrushchev, *Nikita Khrushchev: Krisisi i Raketi* [Nikita Khrushchev: Crises and missiles], vol. 2 (Moscow, 1994), pp. 300–301.

24. Ibid.; GRU, "Cables Received in Moscow" [period Oct. 20–27, 1962].

25. "Khrushchev Message of October 26, 1962," *Problems of Communism* 41, special ed. (Spring 1992).

26. Ibid.
27. Ibid.
28. Khrushchev's son, Sergei, speculates that his father dictated this letter at a formal meeting of the Presidium. S. Khrushchev, *Nikita Khrushchev*, 2:301–3. However, in the APRF there is neither a stenographic record of a formal session on Oct. 26, 1962, nor any evidence of an official Presidium protocol from that day. Unlike Khrushchev's letters of Oct. 27 and 28, which were dictated at Presidium meetings, the Oct. 26 letter was distributed without reference to any numbered protocol. Folio 3, List 65, File 905, APRF.
29. Oleg Troyanovsky, "Karibskii Krisis—Vzglyad iz Kremlya" [The Caribbean crisis—The view from the Kremlin], *Myezhdunarodnaya Zhisn*, March–April 1992, p. 174.
30. Oct. 26, 1962, resolution "On Comrade N. S. Khrushchev's response to U.S. President Kennedy's letter," Folio 3, List 65, File 904, p. 26, APRF. NSK's letter, along with the resolution, was sent to the full and candidate members of the Presidium, and the secretaries of the CC.
31 See n. 25.
32. Kallistrat [Feklisov] to Center, Oct. 25, 1962, File 116, vol. 1, p. 1034, SVR. The cable bears the instruction "Given to Semichastny."
33. Kallistrat [Feklisov] to Center, Oct. 26, 1962, File 116, vol. 1, pp. 1062–64, SVR.
34. Interview with Feklisov, Sept. 1994.
35. Interview with John Scali, July 1994.
36. John Scali, ABC Interview, 1964, CMC/NSA.
37. Feklisov to Center, Oct. 26, 1962, File 116, vol. 1, pp. 1062–64, SVR.
38. Ibid.
39. Elie Abel, *The Missile Crisis* (New York, 1966), pp. 177–79. In their first public accounts, both Scali and Hilsman misremembered the details of the proposal. They had Khrushchev giving the pledge to keep Cuba free of offensive weapons, not Fidel Castro. This flawed version of the "Soviet" proposal gained wide currency when Graham T. Allison featured it in his influential *Essence of Decision: Explaining the Cuban Missile Crisis* (Boston, 1971), pp. 260, 263. For Scali's confidential description on Oct. 26, 1962, of what he had just heard from Feklisov, which confirms Abel's account, see "John Scali's notes of first meeting with Soviet embassy counselor and KGB officer Alexandr Fomin, October 26, 1962," doc. 43, in Laurence Change and Peter Kornbluh, eds., *The Cuban Missile Crisis, 1962* (New York, 1992).
40. "John Scali's notes," cited in n. 39.
41. McCone, memo for the file, "Meeting of the NSC Executive Committee, 26 October, 1962, 10:00 A.M.," doc. 96, *CIADCMC*; Guided Missile and Astronautics Intelligence Committee, "Supplement to Joint Evaluation of Soviet Missile Threat in Cuba, 26 October 1962 (Excerpt)," doc. 94, ibid; memo for the director, "Your Briefings of the NSC Executive Committee," Nov. 3, 1962, doc. 109, ibid.; "10:00 A.M., October 26, 1962," Declassified Documents, 1994, no. 3503; "10:00 A.M., October 26, 1962," ibid., no. 3505; Bromley Smith, "Summary Record of NSC Executive Committee Meeting October 26, 1962, 10:00 A.M.," doc. 42, in Chang and Kornbluh, eds., *Cuban Missile Crisis*; entry for Oct. 26, 1962, "Notes Taken from Transcripts of Meetings of the Joint Chiefs of Staff, October–November 1962, Dealing with the Cuban Missile Crisis" [handwritten notes were

made in 1976 and typed in 1993], CNC/NSA.

42. Entry for Oct. 26, 1962, "Notes Taken from Transcripts of Meetings of the Joint Chiefs of Staff, October–November 1962, Dealing with the Cuban Missile Crisis," CMC/NSA.

43. *Na Krayu Propasti* (Moscow, 1994), p. 106.

44. Alekseev to MFA, Oct. 26, 1962, Folio 3, List 65, File 905, pp. 102–3, APRF.

45. *Na Krayu Propasti*, pp. 104–5; Dino A. Brugioni, *Eyeball to Eyeball* (New York, 1991), p. 436.

46. *Na Krayu Propasti*, p. 105. The Castro quotation comes from an interview conducted with the Cuban leader in 1992, in James G. Blight, Bruce J. Allyn, and David Welch, *Cuba on the Brink* (New York, 1993), p. 107.

47. Alekseev to MFA, Oct. 26, 1962, Folio 3, List 65, File 905, pp. 102–3, APRF.

48. Ibid.

49. Ibid.

50. Roger Hilsman, *The Cuban Missile Crisis: The Struggle over Policy* (Westport, Conn., 1996), pp. 121–23.

51. Third Oral History Interview with Dean Rusk, Feb. 19, 1970, JFKL.

52. Roger Hilsman, *To Move a Nation: The Politics of Foreign Policy in the Administration of John F. Kennedy* (Garden City, N.Y., 1967), p. 217–19.

53. See above, n. 50.

54. RFK, *Thirteen Days* (New York, 1969), p. 90.

55. *Na Krayu Propasti*, p. 106. Evidence of Malinovsky's and Khrushchev's reactions to Pliyev's cable comes from two sources: a copy of Malinovsky's morning directive courtesy of Dmitri Volkogonov; and the resulting cable, Director [Malinovsky] to Pavlov [Pliyev], noon, October 27, 1962, Folio 3, List 65, File 905, p. 140, APRF.

56. Alekseev wrote an account of this night for the Soviet leader after Castro complained that his letter had been misinterpreted. Alekseev to MFA, Nov. 2, 1962, Folio 3, List 65, File 907, pp. 144–52, APRF.

57. *Na Krayu Propasti*, p. 108.

58. Blight et al., *Cuba on the Brink*, p. 109.

59. Ibid.

60. Alekseev to MFA, Nov. 2, 1962, Folio 3, List 65, File 907, pp. 144–52, APRF.

61. Ibid.

62. Ibid.

63. Alekseev to MFA, Oct. 27, 1962, Folio 3, List 65, File 905, pp. 7–8, APRF. The telegram was received at 1:10 A.M., Moscow time, Sunday, Oct. 28, 1962.

64. Malin notes, Protocol 62, Oct. 27, 1962, APRF. Anastas Mikoyan confirmed this in conversation with the Cuban leadership in Nov. 1962. "Speaking frankly, we were not thinking about bases in Turkey at all." Mikoyan, memo of conversation, Nov. 4, 1962, trans. in *CWIHPB*, no. 5 (Spring 1995): 98.

65. Anastas Mikoyan told the Cubans in Nov., "[D]uring the discussion of the dangerous situation [on Oct. 27] we received information from the United States of America, including an article by Lippmann, where it was said that the Russians could raise the question of liquidating the USA bases in Turkey." Ibid.

66. At the end of the crisis, Walter Lippmann would himself confirm Soviet assumptions about his interest in this trade. At a meeting with Anatoly Dobrynin, he explained that while not written at the behest of John Kennedy, the Oct. 25

article reflected discussions Lippmann had with figures in the Arms Control and Disarmament Agency, possibly with John McCloy himself. Dobrynin to Moscow, Dec. 1, 1962, MFA, File 22, pp. 72–73. By Oct. 27 Khrushchev also had in his hands a report from yet another KGB source in the U.S. press, a correspondent of the Chicago *Sun and Times* [possibly Carleton Kent]. In a "confidential meeting" with a KGB representative, Kent said that at a closed State Department briefing for U.S. journalists, Dean Rusk had said that the United States was ready to negotiate a settlement of the Cuban missile crisis through the UN. What may have caught Khrushchev's attention was that in response to a question about the Turkish Jupiter missiles, the KGB source reported Rusk as saying, "[W]e do not intend to consider such a deal however negotiations in this direction could be conducted as a part of general negotiations on disarmament." This was a possible opening. Kallistrat to Center, Oct. 25, 1962, File 116, vol. 1, pp. 1039–40, SVR. It was sent to Khrushchev on Oct. 26.

67. Report about American activities in Turkey. Letter, Abarencov, officer in the First Chief Directorate, to KGB Georgia, Aug. 15. 1962, File 90782 (Turkey: July 6, 1962–Aug. 5, 1964), vol. 2, pp. 252–56, SVR.

68. Director [Malinovsky] to Pavlov [Pliyev], Oct. 27, 1962, 16:30, Folio 3, List 65, File 906, p. 2, APRF.

69. Ibid., p. 3.

70. Note from protocol from the Sixty-fourth Meeting of the Presidium of the CC, of Oct. 27, 1962, "Instruction to Alekseev," Folio 3, List 65, File 905, p. 143, APRF.

71. *Na Krayu Propasti*, pp. 111–14.

72. Ibid.

73. Ibid.

74. Papers of JFK, Presidential Papers, POF, Presidential Recordings, Cuban Missile Crisis Meetings, Oct. 27, 1962, JFKL.

75. Ibid.

76. [McCone], notes from 4:00 P.M. NSC Executive Committee meeting, Oct. 27, 1962, doc. 101, *CIADCMC*; Oct. 27, 1962, Presidential Recordings, JFKL.

77. Brugioni, *Eyeball to Eyeball*, p. 463.

78. There remains some controversy over what the president's instructions to his brother were. See Jim Hershberg, "Anatomy of a Controversy: Anatoly F. Dobrynin's Meeting with Robert F. Kennedy, Saturday, October 27, 1962," *CWIHPB*, no. 5 (Spring 1995): 75, 77–80. See also RFK to Sec. of State Dean Rusk, Oct. 30, 1962, POF, CO:Cuba, Box 115, JFKL. This is the draft that presumably RFK sent to his brother of a top-secret memo on the Oct. 27 meeting prepared by him for Rusk. This document provides essentially the same account as that which RFK gave later in *Thirteen Days*: "He then asked me about Khrushchev's other proposal dealing with the removal of the missiles from Turkey. I replied that there could be no *quid pro quo*—no deal of this kind could be made." Hershberg does not refer to this important source in his review of the various accounts of the meeting.

79. Raymond L. Garthoff, *Reflections on the Cuban Missile Crisis*, rev. ed. (Washington, D.C., 1989), pp. 95–96.

80. RFK to Sec. of State Dean Rusk, Oct. 30, 1962, POF, CO:Cuba, Box 115, JFKL.

81. Dobrynin to MFA, Oct. 27, 1962, AVPRF, p. 171.

82. Ibid., item 2.

83. Malinovsky to NSK, Oct. 28, 1962. The document indicates the time. Folio 3, List

65, File 905, p. 151, APRF.

84. Andrei Gromyko to the CC, Oct. 29, 1962, Folio 3, List 65, File 906, p. 67, APRF.

85. Kallistrat [Feklisov] to Moscow, Oct. 26, 1962, (ciphered telegram no. 822 – 31102), File 116, vol. 1, ("Cables from Washington, January 1–December 31, 1962,") SVR. Marked on the actual cable is the story of its tortuous ride through the Soviet bureaucracy. The cable arrived in Moscow on Oct. 27 at 2:20 P.M., it was deciphered at 3:30 P.M., passed on to the secretariat of KGB to be reported to Semichastny at 3:40 P.M. It sat in Semichastny's office for four hours; then the KGB sent it to Gromyko at 7:30 P.M. It was received by the cipher department of the MFA at 8:05 P.M. For evidence that Khrushchev saw this cable on Oct. 28, see instructions to Alekseev, Oct. 28, 1962, extract from protocol 63, Presidium session of Oct. 28, 1962, Folio 3, List 65, File 605, pp. 166–69, APRF.

86. "Kennedy Message of October 27, 1962," *Problems of Communism* 41, special ed. (Spring 1992).

87. Interview with Boris Ponomarev, Sept. 1993.

88. Troyanovsky, "Karibskii Krisis."

89. Malin notes, Protocol 63, Oct. 28, 1962, APRF.

90. Troyanovsky, "Karibskii Krisis," p. 177.

91. "Khrushchev Message of October 28, 1962," *Problems of Communism* 41, special ed. (Spring 1992).

92. "Instructions to Soviet Ambassador in U.S.A.," extract from Protocol 63, Presidium session of Oct. 28, 1962, Folio 3, List 65, File 905, APRF.

93. NSK to JFK, Oct. 28, 1962, Folio 3, List 65, File 905, pp. 164–65, APRF.

94. Malinovsky to Pliyev, Oct. 28, 1962, 4:00 P.M., Folio 3, List 65, File 906, pp. 3–5, APRF.

95. "Notes Taken from Transcripts of Meetings of the Joint Chiefs of Staff, October–November 1962, Dealing with the Cuban Missile Crisis," CMC/NSA.

96. Ibid.

97. Bromley Smith, "Summary Record of NSC Executive Committee Meeting," Oct. 28, 1962, doc. 59, in Chang and Kornbluh, eds., *Cuban Missile Crisis*.

98. William K. Harvey, Chief, Task Force W [Cuban Task Force], chronology of the Matahambre Mine Sabotage Operation, Nov. 14, 1962, RockCom.

99. GRU station to Moscow, Oct. 28, 1962, Folio 3, List 65, File 906, p. 33, APRF.

100. Ibid. As examples of possible agreements in the future, he cited a nuclear nonproliferation treaty, the resolution of the Berlin problem, and a nonaggression pact between NATO and the Warsaw Pact.

101. Alekseev to MFA, Oct. 28, 1962, APRF.

CHAPTER 15: MIKOYAN'S MISSION

1. Alekseev to MFA, Oct. 29, 1962, Folio 3, List 65, File 906, pp. 84–85, APRF.

2. Ibid.

3. Instructions to Alekseev, Oct. 28, 1962, extract from Protocol 63, Presidium session of Oct. 28, 1962, Folio 3, List 65, File 905, pp. 166–69, APRF. Khrushchev sent him a summary of the Feklisov-Scali proposal to demonstrate that the United States appeared to want Castro to announce the removal of the missiles.

4. Philip Brenner, "Thirteen Months: Cuba's Perspectives on the Missile Crisis," in

The Cuban Missile Crisis Revisited, ed. James A. Nathan (New York, 1992), p. 201.

5. NSK to Castro, Oct. 30, 1962, Folio 3, List 65, File 906, pp. 72–73, reprinted in James G. Blight, Bruce J. Allyn, and David A. Welch, *Cuba on the Brink* (New York, 1993), pp. 486–87.

6. NSK to Castro, Oct. 30, 1962, Folio 3, List 65, File 906, p. 71.

7. Ibid.

8. Castro to NSK, Oct. 31, 1962, Folio 3, List 65, File 907, pp. 137–38, reproduced in Blight et al., *Cuba on the Brink*, pp. 489–91.

9. Ibid.

10. Ibid.

11. Alekseev to MFA, Nov. 2, 1962, Folio 3, List 65, File 907, pp. 150–51, APRF.

12. Ibid., p. 151.

13. Ibid.

14. Ibid.

15. Mikoyan to NSK, Nov. 6, 1962, Folio 3, List 65, File 908, pp. 175–76, APRF. Soon after he arrived, Mikoyan telegraphed to Moscow, "Just a few hours before my arrival, the Cuban government had decided that only Guevara and Raúl Castro would participate."

16. Ibid., p. 172.

17. Alekseev to MFA, Nov. 3, 1962, AVPRF.

18. Memo of conversation, Nov. 5, 1962 (afternoon), in *CWIHPB*, no. 5 (Spring 1995).

19. Alekseev to MFA, Nov. 3, 1962, AVPRF.

20. Memo of conversation, Nov. 4, 1962, in *CWIHPB*, no. 5 (Spring 1995).

21. Havana to Center, Nov. 4, 1962, File 1475 (cables from Havana, Sept. 13, 1962–Dec. 31, 1962), p. 218, SVR.

22. Ibid.

23. Mikoyan to NSK, Nov. 6, 1962, Folio 3, List 65, File 908, p. 172, APRF.

24. Ibid.

25. Ibid., p. 184.

26. Ibid., p. 185.

27. Mikoyan to NSK, Nov. 6, 1962, Folio 3, List 65, File 908, p. 187, APRF.

28. KGB resident, Havana, to Moscow, Nov. 5, 1962, Folio 3, List 65, File 908, pp. 106–7, APRF.

29. Alekseev to MFA, Nov. 8, 1962, Folio 3, List 65, File 909, pp. 12–13, APRF.

30. Interview with Leonid S. Garbuz.

31. NSK to Mikoyan, Nov. 10, 1962, extract from Protocol 65, Presidium session of Nov. 10, 1962, Folio 3, List 65, File 909, p. 59, APRF.

32. Mikoyan to NSK, Nov. 14, 1962, Folio 3, List 65, File 911, p. 2, APRF.

33. Meshcheriakov to Mikoyan, Nov. 14, 1962, Folio 3, List 65, File 911, pp. 4–5, APRF.

34. The specifications of the Il-28 bomber are taken from Dino A. Brugioni, *Eyeball to Eyeball* (New York, 1991), p. 173.

35. "Khrushchev Message of November 4, 1962," *Problems of Communism* 41, special ed. (Spring 1992).

36. U.S. Marine Corps summary, Nov. 1, 1962, CMC/NSA.

37. Supplement 7 to Joint Evaluation of Soviet Missile Threat in Cuba, Oct. 27, 1962 (excerpt), doc. 98, *CIADCMC*.

38. Anatoli I. Gribkov and William Y. Smith, *Operation ANADYR* (Chicago, 1994), p. 28.
39. See above, n. 36.
40. Entries for Nov. 7 and 12, 1962, "Notes Taken from Transcripts of Meetings of the Joint Chiefs of Staff, October–November 1962, Dealing with the Cuban Missile Crisis," CMC/NSC.
41. Entry for Nov. 7, 1962, "Notes Taken from Transcripts," CMC/NSC.
42. *Newsweek*, Nov. 12, 1962.
43. Bromley Smith, "Summary Record of NSC Executive Committee Meeting," October 28, 1962," doc. 59, in Laurence Chang and Peter Kornbluh, eds., *The Cuban Missile Crisis, 1962* (New York, 1992).
44. Interview with Edwin O. Guthman, July 14, 1994.
45. Dobrynin to MFA, Nov. 9, 1962, Folio 3, List 65, File 909, pp. 77–78, APRF.
46. RFK desk diary for 1962, JFKL.
47. Ibid., p. 78.
48. Ibid.
49. "Khrushchev Oral Message of November 11, 1962," *Problems of Communism* 41, special ed. (Spring 1992): 82–88. Ironically, NSK can be said to have used the Trollope ploy, a reference to a character in one of Sir Anthony Trollope's novels who receives contradictory answers to one question and decides to accept, or acknowledge, only the one that suits him. RFK had recalled this trope during the missile crisis in response to the Khrushchev letters of Oct. 26 and 27. Three weeks later Khrushchev had decided to do the same thing with regard to RFK's statements about the Il-28s.
50. NSK to Mikoyan, extract from protocol 65, Presidium session of Nov. 10, 1962, Folio 3, List 65, File 909, pp. 44–45, APRF.
51. Ibid., p. 45.
52. Ibid.
53. Instructions to V. Kuznetsov, extract from protocol 65, Presidium session of Nov. 11, 1962, Folio 3, List 65, File 909, pp. 88–93, APRF.
54. Mikoyan to NSK, Nov. 11, 1962, Folio 3, List 65, File 909, p. 107; 110, APRF.
55. Notes on conversations between Mikoyan and Castro, Nov. 12, 1962, Folio 3, List 65, File 909, pp. 121–26, APRF.
56. Ibid., p. 127.
57. Ibid., pp. 129–31.
58. Notes on conversation between Mikoyan and Cuban leaders, Nov. 13, 1962, Folio 3, List 65, File 909, pp. 174–75, APRF.
59. Entry for Nov. 13, 1962, ibid.
60. Dobrynin to MFA, Nov. 12, 1962, Folio 104, List 12, File 28, pp. 71–76, AVPRF.
61. Mikoyan to NSK, Nov. 17, 1962, Folio 3, List 65, File 911, pp. 100–103, APRF.
62. Ibid.
63. Colonel Burris to LBJ, Dec. 4, 1962, "Low-Level Reconnaissance Mission over Cuba," CMC/NSA; Mikoyan to NSK, Nov. 18, 1962, Folio 3, List 65, File 911, pp. 181–83, APRF.
64. *Time*, Nov. 23, 1962; Mikoyan to NSK, Nov. 17, 1962, Folio 3, List 65, File 911, pp. 126–35, APRF. This was the longer of two cables sent by Mikoyan on Nov. 17.
65. Mikoyan to NSK, Nov. 17, 1962, Folio 3, List 65, File 911, pp. 126–35, APRF. This is from the shorter cable of the day.

66. Ibid. This is from the longer cable of that day.
67. Ibid.
68. Ibid.
69. Ibid.
70. Ibid., pp. 102–3, 131.
71. Ibid., p. 132.
72. Ibid. This is from the shorter cable.
73. Malin notes, Nov. 16, 1962, APRF.
74. The authors concluded this on the basis of the contemporaneous notes for the Nov. 16 meeting, which indicate that the group decided to "pass orally to President Kennedy an agreement to remove the IL-28s," and the top-secret instructions that went to Mikoyan the same day. See Presidium resolution, "Regarding Instructions to Mikoyan," Nov. 16, 1962, Folio 3, List 65, File 911, pp. 47–56, APRF. That letter, which was sent to four men (Khrushchev, Kozlov, Ponomarev, and Gromyko), sets out one last diplomatic initiative in Cuba.
75. Ibid., p. 48.
76. Ibid., pp. 51–52.
77. Dobrynin to MFA, Nov. 18, 1962, Folio 3, List 65, File 911, pp. 179–80, APRF.
78. *Washington Post*, Nov. 4, 1962.
79. Kuznetsov to CC, Nov. 18, 1962, Folio 3, List 65, File 911, APRF.
80. Transcript of Kent's memoirs, Sherman Kent Papers, Box 54, Sterling Memorial Library, Yale University.
81. Presidium resolution, "Regarding Instructions to Mikoyan," Nov. 16, 1962, Folio 3, List 65, File 911, pp. 47–56, APRF.
82. Mikoyan to NSK, Nov. 17, 1962, (two cables) and Nov. 18, 1962, Folio 3, List 65, File 911, APRF.
83. "Khrushchev Oral Message of November 19, 1962," *Problems of Communism* 41, special ed. (Spring 1992).
84. Mikoyan to NSK, Nov. 19, 1962, Folio 3, List 65, File 912, pp. 24–26, APRF.
85. Ibid.
86. Castro's letter to UN Secretary General U Thant, Nov. 19, 1962, doc. 75, in Chang and Kornbluh, eds., *Cuban Missile Crisis*.
87. Dobrynin to MFA, Nov. 20, 1962, Folio 3, List 65, File 912, p. 64, APRF.
88. *Time*, Nov. 30, 1962; McGeorge Bundy, "Summary Record of NSC Executive Committee Meeting, November 20, 1962," doc. 77, in Chang and Kornbluh, eds., *Cuban Missile Crisis*; Colonel Burris to LBJ, Dec. 4, 1962, "Low-Level Reconnaissance Mission over Cuba," CMC/NSA.
89. NSK to Mikoyan, Nov. 21, 1962, extract from protocol 68, Presidium session of Nov. 21, 1962, Folio 3, List 65, File 912, pp. 73–75, APRF.
90. Mikoyan to NSK, Nov. 21, 1962, Folio 3, List 65, File 912, p. 106, APRF.
91. Memo of conversation, Nov. 5, 1962, in *CWIHPB*, no. 5 (Spring 1995).
92. Mikoyan to NSK, Nov. 22, 1962, Folio 3, List 65, File 912, p. 91, APRF.
93. Dobrynin to MFA, Nov. 20, 1962, Folio 3, List 65, File 912, p. 62, APRF.
94. General Gribkov's speech at 1994 Moscow Conference, "The Caribbean Crisis in the Archives of the United States, the Russian Federation and the Republic of Cuba." General Gribkov spoke from a summary list of cables exchanged between Malinovsky and Pliyev. These cables are located in the Archives of the Ministry of Defense of the Russian Federation.

95. Mikoyan to NSK, Nov. 22, 1962, Folio 3, List 65, File 912, p. 91, APRF.

96. Ibid., p. 120.

97. Ibid.

98. Malinovsky cable to Pliyev, Nov. 20, 1962, from Gribkov's notes at 1994 Moscow Conference.

99. See Gromyko's notes, Nov. 22, 1962, extract from protocol 68, Presidium session of Nov. 22, 1962, File 3, List 65, File 912, p. 130, APRF.

100. Extract from Protocol 68, Presidium session of Nov. 21, 1962, Folio 3, List 65, File 912, p. 74, APRF.

101. Alekseev to MFA, Nov. 23, 1962, Folio 3, List 65, File 912, pp. 129–30, APRF.

102. Alekseev to MFA, Nov. 26, 1962, Folio 3, List 65, File 912, pp. 190–91, APRF.

103. "Notes on Conversation between Mikoyan and JFK," Nov. 29, 1962, Folio 3, List 65, File 913, pp. 33–35, APRF.

104. Ibid., pp. 42–43.

105. Malin notes, Protocol 71, Dec. 3, 1962, APRF.

106. Extract from Protocol 71, Presidium session of Dec. 3, 1962, Folio 3, List 65, File 913, p. 78, APRF.

107. Malin notes, Protocol 75, Dec. 30, 1962, APRF.

108. Ibid. The Presidium may also have been showing its disapproval over the case of Oleg Penkovsky, a GRU officer recently arrested for spying for the Americans and the British.

109. *Pravda*, Dec. 1, 1962.

110. Pliyev-Malinovsky cables from Gribkov presentation, Moscow Conference 1994.

Chapter 16: To the American University Speech

1. C. V. Clifton, "Memorandum of Conference with the President," Dec. 27, 1962, Palm Beach, NSF:Clifton, Box 345, JFKL.

2. Ibid.

3. Ibid.

4. Richard Reeves, *President Kennedy* (New York, 1993), p. 445.

5. CBS News interview, Dec. 17, 1962, Museum of Television and Radio, New York. In this nationally televised interview, Kennedy spoke of the limitations on the power of the presidency as the greatest lesson he had learned since entering the White House.

6. Richard Helms, memo for the record, Dec. 3, 1962, RockCom.

7. Reeves, *President Kennedy*, p. 445.

8. NSK letters of Oct. 30 and Dec. 10, 1962, in *Problems of Communism* 41, special ed. (Spring 1992).

9. Reeves, *President Kennedy*, p. 456.

10. JFK to Charles de Gaulle, Dec. 11, 1962, Archives of the Ministère des Affaires Etrangères, Paris.

11. Charles Bartlett to JFK, Oct. 29, 1962, POF, Special Corr., Box 28, Bartlett, Charles, JFKL.

12. "Notes Taken from Transcripts of Meetings of the Joint Chiefs of Staff, October–November 1962, Dealing with the Cuban Missile Crisis," NSA.

13. Interview with Charles Bartlett, Dec. 5, 1994, Washington, D.C.

14. Stewart Alsop and Charles Bartlett, "In Times of Crisis," *Saturday Evening Post*,

Dec. 8, 1962.

15. "Khrushchev Oral Communication of December 10, 1962," *Problems of Communism* 41, special ed. (Spring 1992).

16. Ibid.

17. Biographical details of Georgi Bolshakov, GRU.

18. "Kennedy Letter of December 14, 1962," *Problems of Communism* 41, special ed. (Spring 1992).

19. Malin notes, "Regarding Instructions to the Soviet Ambassador in Laos," Protocol 68, Nov. 21, 1962, APRF.

20. Stenographic record of the plenum of Nov. 19–23, 1962, Folio 2, List 2, File 231, pp. 134–36, APRF.

21. Protocol 65, Presidium meeting of Nov. 15, 1962, Folio 3, List 65, File 911 (no page numbers noted), APRF.

22. Ibid.

23. Ibid.

24. Ibid.

25. Malin notes, Protocol 71, Dec. 3, 1962, APRF.

26. NSK to Fidel Castro, Jan. 31, 1963, Folio 3, List 65, File 915, APRF. An identical copy can be found at the NSA.

27. Alekseev to MFA, Feb. 8, 1963, Folio 3, List 65, File 916, pp. 6–11, APRF.

28. N. Zakharov, deputy chairman of KGB, to CC, "Ob Otnoshenii Kubinskoyo Rukovodstva k Natsionalno-osvoboditelnomu Dvizheniu v Latinskoi Amerike" [Report on the Cuban leadership's relations with the national-liberation movement in Latin America], April 17, 1963, File 88497, vol. 1, pp. 376–89, SVR.

29. Alekseev to MFA, Feb. 8, 1963, Folio 3, List 65, File 916, pp. 6–11, APRF.

30. Report by Castro's physicians, Folio 3, List 65, File 916, APRF.

31 N. Zakharov to CC, "O Otnoshenii Kubinskovo Rukovodstva K Natsionalno-osvoboditelnomu Dvizheniu v Latinskoi Amerike" [On the Cuban leadership's relations with the national-liberation movement in Latin America], April 18, 1963, File 88497, vol. 1, SVR.

32. Memo of conversation, Nov. 5, 1962, in *CWIHPB*, no. 5 (Spring 1995).

33. *Newsweek*, Feb. 18, 1963.

34. *Life*, Feb. 22, 1963.

35. Memo of conversation, Feb. 9, 1963, RG 59, Central Foreign Policy Files 1963, Pol. 1, General Policy U.S.-USSR, Background, NA.

36. Llewellyn E. Thompson to Dean Rusk, Feb. 21, 1963, "Visit of Ambassador Anatoly F. Dobrynin, USSR," ibid.

37. New York to Center, Jan. 15, 1963, File 90238, vol. 1, p. 171, SVR.

38. New York to Center, Feb. 21, 1963, File 90238, vol. 1, pp. 202–3, SVR.

39. Ibid.

40. Kohler to sec. of state, March 27, 1963, RG 59, SDDF 611.61, NA.

41. JFK to McCone, Feb. 9, 1963, NSF, CO:Venezuela, Box 192, JFKL.

42. "From the Coordinator of Cuban Affairs to the Special Group," April 2, 1963, RockCom.

43. RFK to the president, March 14, 1962, POF: Departments and Agencies, Justice, Jan. 1963–March 1963, Box 80, JFKL.

44. Deputy director (plans) to DCI, March 19, 1963, RockCom.

45. Ibid.

46. Ibid.
47. Ibid.
48. From notes of PFIAB meeting with DCI [McCone], April 23, 1963, RockCom.
49. Malinovsky, Biryuzov, and Gromyko to the CC, April 29–30, 1963, 3-65-874, Folio 3, List 65, File 874, pp. 84–86, APRF.
50. See above, n. 31.
51. U.S. embassy, Moscow, "WEEKA" no. 18, May 3, 1963, RG 59, Central Foreign Policy Files 1963, Pol. 2-1, NA.
52. Meeting, NSK with Fidel Castro, May 3, 1963, Zavidovo, APRF.
53. Ibid.
54. Notes of meeting, NSK with Fidel Castro, May 5, 1963, Zavidovo, APRF.
55. Quoted in *Izvestia*, 1990, 4, pp. 191–92.
56. See above, n. 54.
57. Ibid.
58. Notes of meeting between NSK and Fidel Castro, Pitsunda, May 29, 1963, APRF.
59. Ibid.
60. Interview with Aleksandr Alekseev, Nov. 15, 1995.
61. Excerpt from stenographic account of the meeting of the Presidium of the CC, June 7, 1963, Folio 3, List 65, File 874, pp. 105–7, APRF.
62. Ibid.
63. Ibid.
64. NY to Center, May 23, 1963, File 90238, p. 265, SVR. The KGB officer described a meeting with RFK on May 20.
65. Arthur M. Schlesinger, Jr., *A Thousand Days* (New York, 1965), p. 821.
66. "Briefing Paper for the President's Press Conference; Subject: Disarmament," Feb. 6, 1963, "Background Materials, I" POF: Press Conferences, Box 58, JFKL.
67. Schlesinger, *Thousand Days*, p. 825.
68. Ibid., p. 824.
69. Head of the Sixteenth Department of the KGB to the head of the D Department of the KGB, May 31, 1961, "Kratkaya spravka o prezidente SshA Johne Kennedy, sostavlennaya s ispolzovanyem nekotoreych razvedyvatelnech danneych" [Short report on U.S. President John Kennedy, based on some intelligence materials], pp. 96–109, SVR.
70. Ibid.

CHAPTER 17: DALLAS AND MOSCOW

1. Semichastny to NSK, Oct. 2, 1963, SVR.
2. NSK, closing statement at the morning session of the plenum of the CC, Nov. 23, 1962. This came after a discussion of his report, "The Economic Development of the USSR and the Party Leadership of the National Economy." Excerpt from the stenographic record of the plenum of Nov. 19–23, 1962.
3. "Prezident SshA Lyndon Johnson (Kratkaya Spravka), November 23, 1963," File 90486, pp. 113–18, SVR.
4. Ibid.
5. Ibid.
6. Ibid.
7. Interview with Vladimir Semichastny, June 10, 1994.

8. Oleg Kalugin, with Fen Montaigne, *The First Directorate: My Thirty-two Years in Intelligence and Espionage against the West* (New York, 1994), p. 58.

9. Kohler, Moscow to DOS, Nov. 23, 1963. JFK Assassination Records, LBJ Library Materials, Box 17, NA.

10. Instructions for the Soviet ambassador to Cuba, Nov. 27, 1963, Folio 3, Index 65, File 842, p. 24, APRF.

11. CIA, current intelligence memo, "Fidel Castro's Speech," Nov. 25, 1963, CMC/ NSA.

12. "Record of Meeting between Comrade A. I. Mikoyan and the President of the United States of America, J. Kennedy, November 29, 1962," Folio 3, List 65, File 913, pp. 33–46, APRF.

13. "President's Meeting with Soviet Deputy Prime Minister Anastas Mikoyan," [n.d.], JFK/LBJ, Box 17, NA.

14. Bundy to Rusk, "Ambassador Stevenson's Speech on Outer Space to the United Nations General Assembly," Nov. 25, 1963, JFK/LBJ, Box 17, NA.

15. Donald M. Wilson (USIA) to William Moyers, "World Reaction to Oswald's Slaying," Nov. 25,1963, JFK/LBJ, Box 17, NA.

16. F. Mortin (head of the KGB's Information Department), "Some Intelligence Information on the Political Objectives and Immediate Consequences of the Assassination of US President J. Kennedy," Dec. 21, 1963, File 90486 (Special Political Reports, Oct. 18, 1963–June 1964), pp. 139–43, SVR.

17. Ibid.

18. *Life*, March 17, 1961.

19. Arthur M. Schlesinger, Jr., *A Thousand Days* (New York, 1965), pp. 615, 670, 676; idem, *Robert Kennedy and His Times* (New York, 1978), p. 658; G. N. Bolshakov, memo of conversation, Bolshakov with William Walton, Dec. 9, 1963, GRU.

20. Memo of conversation, Comrade G. N. Bolshakov and William Walton, Dec. 9, 1963, GRU.

21. Ibid.

22. Interview with Georgi Bolshakov, Jan. 28, 1989. At this interview, Bolshakov described the effect of both Kennedy assassinations on him.

23. Walton, "If Adzhubei made a report to his superiors, it might have run like this," [n.d.], William Walton Private Papers, Box 2, JFKL. Although there is a contradiction between the positions taken by Walton in the GRU report of his meeting with Bolshakov and his own recollection of a meeting with Adzhubei and Zhukov, the authors have concluded that the GRU report is probably reliable. The GRU material on Bolshakov has been corroborated in other cases and some of the details in this document have been corroborated. There are also contextual clues that Walton was not revealing himself to Adzhubei. In a letter, written Jan. 2, 1964, to his old friend the British scientific adviser Sir Solly Zuckerman, Walton wrote, "The main message that I brought back was one that Khrushchev has now made public in his New Year's greetings, i.e. they are extremely anxious for a new round of talks and want a face to face meeting with Johnson in the next six months. Somehow I feel the atmosphere is favorable *strangely enough* [emphasis added], to such a meeting. So who knows, you may be traveling sooner than you think, and I hope it's in this direction." William Walton Private Papers, Box 1, JFKL. Finally, in an oral history made for the JFKL, Walton said that he "detested" Johnson and that Johnson detested him.

24. Walton, "Notes on a Visit to Moscow, December 1963," William Walton Private Papers, Box 2, JFKL.
25. McGeorge Bundy, "Memorandum for the Record, Subject: Lunch with Soviet Ambassador Dobrynin, December 18, 1963," LBJ Library, DDI 1995, 0593.
26. Ibid.
27. Semichastny to NSK, Dec. 28, 1963, SVR.
28. LBJ to NSK, Nov. 26, 1963, JFK Assasination Materials Project, LBJ Library Materials, Box 17, NA.
29. F. Mortin, memorandum to International Department, CC, and the deputy foreign minister, V. V. Kuznetsov, Dec. 21, 1963, File 90486, SVR.
30. See above, n. 16. On Dec. 23 the head of the First Directorate of the KGB, Sakharovski, forwarded a copy of this report to the chief of Department D (Disinformation), I. I. Agayants. On Dec. 23 N. Zakharov, deputy KGB chairman, sent the report to the International Department of the CC and to deputy minister of foreign relations, V. V. Kuznetsov.
31. Ibid.
32. Jim Marrs, *Crossfire: The Plot That Killed Kennedy* (New York, 1989), pp. 276–77.
33. See above, n. 16.
34. Harold A. Williams, *The Baltimore Sun, 1837–1987* (Baltimore, 1987), pp. 332–33.
35. Quoted in Harry Hurt, *Texas Rich: The Hunt Dynasty from the Early Oil Days through the Silver Crash* (New York, 1981), p. 233.
36. Ibid., pp. 234–35.
37. Semichastny interview, June 10, 1995.
38. Semichastny's chief operational deputy, Sakharovski, decided to send the Information Department's survey of intelligence on the assassination to I. I. Agayants, who since 1959 had coordinated all KGB deception.
39. CIA to McGeorge Bundy, Dec. 5, 1963, DDRS, no. 1842, 1995.
40. CIA to J. Lee Rankin, general counsel, President's Commission on the Assassination of President Kennedy [Warren Commission], May 27, 1964, DDRS, no. 1845, 1995.
41. Ibid.
42. *Spravka*, cipher telegram from New York, Jan. 5, 1964, File 90486, SVR.
43. McGeorge Bundy to LBJ, Feb. 29, 1964, JFK Assassination Materials Project, LBJ Library Materials, Box 17, NA.
44. Ibid.
45. Ibid.
46. Ibid.
47. Ibid.
48. Ibid.
49. Ibid.
50. Semichastny to Gromyko, Feb. 11, 1964, File 90486, SVR.
51. Ibid.
52. Washington to Center, May 20, 1964, File 90238, p. 336, SVR.
53. Interview with Aleksandr Alekseev, Nov. 15, 1995.
54. D. S. Polyanski, text for the report to the plenum of the CC (Oct. 14, 1964), prepared Oct. 13, 1964, register no. 8476, APRF; Werner Hahn, "Note: Who Ousted Nikita Sergeyevich," *Problems of Communism* 40, no. 3 (May–June 1991):

109–15. One of the other participants in the plenum recalled his own speech. Aleksandr Shelepin, "Istoria Uchitel Surovyi," *Trud*, March 14, 1991.

55. Polyanski text cited in n. 54.

56. Ibid.

57. Ibid.

58. Ibid.

Select Bibliography

ARCHIVES

Czech Republic:
  Archive of the Ministry of Foreign Affairs, Prague

France:
  Archives of the Ministère des Affaires Etrangères, Paris

Russia (all in Moscow):
  Archive of the President of the Russian Federation (APRF)
  Center for the Storage of Contemporary Documentation (TsKhSD)
  Archive of the Ministry of Foreign Affairs (AVPRF)
  Archive of the Russian Foreign Intelligence Service (SVR)
  Historical Archive and Military Memorial Center of the General Staff of the Armed Forces of the Russian Federation (AGSRF)
  Archive of the Intelligence Service of the General Staff of the Armed Forces of the Russian Federation (GRU)

United States:
  National Security Archives, Washington, D.C.
  Houghton Library, Harvard University
  Sterling Memorial Library, Yale University
  National Archives, College Park, Md.
  John F. Kennedy Library, Boston, Mass.
  Freedom of Information Room, State Department, Washington, D.C.

SECONDARY SOURCES

Allyn, Bruce J., James G. Blight, and David A. Welch, eds. *Back to the Brink: Proceedings of the Moscow Conference on the Cuban Missile Crisis, January 27–28, 1989.* CSIA Occasional Paper no. 9. Latham, Md.: University Press of America, 1992.

Beschloss, Michael R. *The Crisis Years: Kennedy and Khrushchev, 1960–1963.* New York: HarperCollins, 1991.

Blight, James G., Bruce J. Allyn, and David A. Welch. *Cuba on the Brink: Castro, the Missile Crisis and the Soviet Collapse*. New York: Pantheon Books, 1993.

Blight, James G., and David A. Welch. *On the Brink: Americans and Soviets Reexamine the Cuban Missile Crisis*. 2nd ed. New York: Noonday, 1990.

Brenner, Phillip, William M. LeoGrande, Donna Rich, and Daniel Siegel, eds. *The Cuba Reader: The Making of a Revolutionary Society*. New York: Grove Press, 1989.

Brugioni, Dino A. *Eyeball to Eyeball: The Inside Story of the Cuban Missile Crisis*. New York: Random House, 1991.

Castro, Fidel. *Etapes de la Révolution Cubaine*. Edited by Michel Merlier. Paris: François Maspero, 1964.

Clark, Ian. *Nuclear Diplomacy and the Special Relationship: Britain's Deterrent and America, 1957–1962*. Oxford: Clarendon Press, 1994.

Dean, Arthur. *Test Ban and Disarmament: The Path of Negotiations*. New York: Harper & Row, 1966.

Dobrynin, Anatoly. *In Confidence: Moscow's Ambassador to America's Six Cold War Presidents (1962–1986)*. New York: Random House, 1995.

Draper, Theodore. *Castroism: Theory and Practice*. New York: Praeger, 1965.

Escalante, Fabian. *The Secret War: CIA Covert Operations against Cuba, 1959–62*. Translated by Maxine Shaw, edited by Mirta Muniz. New York: Ocean Press, 1995.

Feklisov, Aleksandr. *Za okeanom i na ostrove: Zapiski razvedchika* [Overseas and on the island: The notes of an intelligence officer]. Moscow: DEM, 1994.

Franqui, Carlos. *Family Portrait with Fidel: A Memoir*. Translated by Alfred MacAdam. New York: Vintage, 1985.

Freedom of Communications: Final Report of the Committee on Commerce, U.S. Senate. Prepared by the Subcommittee of the Subcommittee on Communications. 87th Cong., 1st sess. Rept. 994, pt. 1, *The Speeches, Remarks, Press Conferences of Senator John F. Kennedy, August 1 through November 7, 1960*. [3 vols.: 1, Kennedy; 2, Nixon; 3, Kennedy and Nixon]. Washington, D.C.: U.S. Government Printing Office, 1961.

Garthoff, Raymond L. *Reflections on the Cuban Missile Crisis*. Rev. ed. Washington, D.C.: Brookings Institution, 1989.

Geyer, Georgie Anne. *Guerrilla Prince: The Untold Story of Fidel Castro*. Boston: Little, Brown, 1991.

Gironella, Jose M. *On China and Cuba*. Translated by John F. Byrne. Notre Dame: Fides Publishers, 1963.

Grose, Peter. *Gentleman Spy: The Life of Allen Dulles*, Boston: Houghton Mifflin Company, 1994.

Guevara, Che. *Che Guevara and the Cuban Revolution: Writings and Speeches of Ernesto Che Guevara*. Edited by David Deutschmann. Sydney: Pathfinder/Pacific Asia, 1987.

Guthman, Edwin O., and Jeffrey Shulman, eds. *Robert Kennedy: In His Own Words: The Unpublished Recollections of the Kennedy Years*. Toronto: Bantam Books, 1988.

Harrison, Hope M. "Ulbricht and the Concrete 'Rose': New Archival Evidence on the Dynamics of Soviet-East German Relations and the Berlin Crisis, 1958–1961." Working Paper no. 5, CWIHP. Washington, D.C., May 1993.

Haydon, Commander Peter T. *The 1962 Cuban Missile Crisis: Canadian Involvement Reconsidered.* Toronto: Canadian Institute of Strategic Studies, 1993.

Hilsman, Roger. *To Move a Nation: The Politics of Foreign Policy in the Administration of John F. Kennedy.* Garden City, N.Y.: Doubleday, 1967.

———. *The Cuban Missile Crisis: The Struggle over Policy.* Westport, Conn.: Praeger, 1996.

Hough, Jerry F., and Merle Fainsod. *How the Soviet Union Is Governed.* Cambridge: Harvard University Press, 1979.

Humble, Ronald D. *The Soviet Space Programme.* London: Routledge, 1988.

James, Daniel. *Cuba: The First Soviet Satellite in the Americas.* New York: Avon, 1961.

———. *Che Guevara.* New York: Stein and Day, 1969.

Johnson, Cecil. *Communist China and Latin America, 1959–1967.* New York: Columbia University Press, 1970.

Kardelj, Edvard. *Reminiscences: The Struggles for Recognition and Independence: The New Yugoslavia, 1944–1957,* (London: Blond & Briggs, 1982).

Keep, John L. H. *Last of the Empires: A History of the Soviet Union, 1945–1991.* New York: Oxford University Press, 1995.

Kennedy, Robert F. *Thirteen Days: A Memoir of the Cuban Missile Crisis.* New York: W. W. Norton, 1969.

Keith, Ronald C. *The Diplomacy of Zhou Enlai.* London: Macmillan, 1989.

Khrushchev, Nikita. *Khrushchev Remembers.* Translated and edited by Strobe Talbott, with notes by Edward Crankshaw. Boston: Little, Brown, 1970.

Khrushchev, Sergei. *Nikita Kruschev: Krizisi i Raketi* [Nikita Khrushchev: Crises and Missiles]. Moscow: Novosti, 1994.

Lebow, Richard Ned, and Janet Gross Stein. *We All Lost the Cold War.* Princeton: Princeton University Press, 1994.

Leonov, N. S. *Lixoletye.* Moscow: International Relations, 1994.

Levesque, Jacques. *The USSR and the Cuban Revolution: Soviet Ideological and Strategical Perspectives, 1959–77.* Translated by Deanna Drendel Leboeuf. New York: Praeger, 1979.

Levine, Alan J. *The Missile and Space Race.* Westport, Conn.: Praeger, 1994.

Mack Smith, Denis. *Mussolini.* New York: Alfred A. Knopf, 1982.

Murray, Charles, and Catherine Bly Cox. *Apollo: The Race to the Moon.* London: Secker & Warburg, 1989.

Nash, Philip. "The Other Missiles of October: Eisenhower, Kennedy, and the Jupiters in Europe, 1957-1963." Ph.D. diss., Ohio University, 1994.

Operation ZAPATA: The "Ultrasensitive" Report and Testimony of the Board of Inquiry on the Bay of Pigs. Frederick, Md.: University Publications of America, 1984.

Polmar, Norman. *Guide to the Soviet Navy.* 3rd ed. Annapolis: Naval Institute Press, 1983.

Pravda. *Viva Kuba!: Vizit Fidelya Castro Ruz v Sovestskii Soyuz.* Moscow, 1963.

Quirk, Robert E. *Fidel Castro,* New York: W. W. Norton, 1993.

Robinson, Thomas W., and David Shambaugh, eds. *Chinese Foreign Policy: Theory and Practice.* Oxford: Clarendon Press, 1994.

Salinger, Pierre. *With Kennedy.* Garden City, N.Y.: Doubleday, 1966.

Schlesinger, Arthur M., Jr. *A Thousand Days: John F. Kennedy in the White House.* New York: Fawcett Crest Book, 1965.

———. *Robert Kennedy and His Times.* Boston: Houghton Mifflin, 1978.

Schneider, Ronald M. *"Order and Progress"*: *A Political History of Brazil*. Boulder: Westview Press, 1991.

Sidey, Hugh. *John F. Kennedy, President*. New York: Atheneum, 1964.

Sorensen, Theodore C. *Kennedy*. New York: Harper & Row, 1965.

———. *The Kennedy Legacy*. New York: Macmillan, 1969.

Strober, Gerald S., and Deborah H. *"Let Us Begin Anew"*: *An Oral History of the Kennedy Presidency*. New York: HaperCollins, 1993.

Suyin, Han. *Eldest Son: Zhou Enlai and the Making of Modern China, 1898–1976*, New York: Hill and Wang, 1994.

Szulc, Tad. *Fidel: A Critical Portrait*. New York: William Morrow, 1986.

Vaisse, Maurice, ed. *L'Europe et la crise de Cuba*. Paris: Armand Colin, 1993.

Volkogonov, D. A. *Sem Vozhdei* [Seven leaders]. Moscow: Novosti, 1995.

Welch, Richard. *Response to Revolution: The United States and the Cuban Revolution, 1959–1961*. Chapel Hill: University of North Carolina Press, 1985.

White, Mark J. *The Cuban Missile Crisis*. London: Macmillan, 1996.

Wyden, Peter. *Bay of Pigs: The Untold Story*. New York: Simon & Schuster, 1979.

Yeltsin, Boris. *The Struggle for Russia*. Translated by Catherine A. Fitzpatrick. New York: Times Books, 1994.

Young, Major John M. *When the Russians Blinked: The U.S. Maritime Response to the Cuban Missile Crisis*. Washington, D.C.: History and Museums Division, Headquarters, U.S. Marine Corps, 1990.

Youngblood, Jack, and Robin Moore. *The Devil to Pay*. New York: Coward McCann, 1961.

Zagoria, Donald S. *The Sino-Soviet Conflict, 1956–1961*. Princeton: Princeton University Press, 1962.

Zubok, Vladislav, and Constantine Pleshakov. *Inside the Kremlin's Cold War: From Stalin to Khrushchev*. Cambridge: Harvard University Press, 1996.

Index

DATE DUE

APR 1 6